THE HUMAN CONDITION

THE HUMAN CONDITION

An Introduction to
Philosophy of Human Nature

Nina Rosenstand

San Diego Mesa College

Boston   Burr Ridge, IL   Dubuque, IA   Madison, WI   New York   San Francisco   St. Louis
Bangkok   Bogotá   Caracas   Kuala Lumpur   Lisbon   London   Madrid   Mexico City
Milan   Montreal   New Delhi   Santiago   Seoul   Singapore   Sydney   Taipei   Toronto

McGraw-Hill Higher Education

A Division of The McGraw-Hill Companies

2 3 4 5 6 7 8 9 0 DOC/DOC 0 9 8 7 6 5 4 3 2

Library of Congress Cataloging-in-Publication Data
Rosenstand, Nina.
   The human condition : an introduction to philosophy of human nature / Nina Rosenstand.
      p. cm.
   Included bibliographical references and index.
   ISBN 1-55934-764-3
   1. Philosophical anthropology.   I. Title.
BD450.R6195 2001
128—dc21

                                                    2001044391

Sponsoring editor, Ken King; *production editor,* Jennifer Mills; *manuscript editor,* Joan Pendleton; *design manager,* Jean Mailander; *cover designer,* Linda Robertson; *art editor,* Emma Ghiselli; *photo researcher,* Brian J. Pecko; *manufacturing managers,* Randy Hurst and Pam Augspurger. This text was set in 10.5/12.5 Berkeley Book by Thompson Type and printed on acid-free, 45# Scholarly Matte by R. R. Donnelley & Sons Company.

Cover image: Jan Vermeer. Head of a Girl (Girl with the Pearl Earring). Mauritshuis, The Hague, The Netherlands. © Scala/Art Resource, NY

Text, photo, and illustration credits appear on page 450, which constitutes a continuation of the copyright page.

www.mhhe.com

For Craig

In the final analysis, our most basic common

link is that we all inhabit this small planet.

We all breathe the same air.

We all cherish our children's future.

And we are all mortal.

—JOHN F. KENNEDY

Contents

Part 2

Mostly Descriptive Approaches   53

Part 3

Mostly Normative Approaches   273

Chapter 8

Stuck Between Good and Evil?   274

Preface

Presenting this textbook to you is a happy moment for me: For one thing, I have now kept my promise to my editor, numerous colleagues, and myself to update the chapters on human nature originally published in the first edition of *The Moral of the Story,* my textbook on ethics, but removed from subsequent editions. Here they are included in a new textbook exclusively dedicated to the study of human nature. For another, the study of human nature is what brought me to philosophy years ago, down a convoluted path involving paleoanthropology and cultural anthropology. In addition, the first class in philosophy I ever taught, in the fall of 1984—taking it over from someone else at the eleventh hour—was "Philosophy of Human Nature." I have been teaching courses dealing with the questions of personhood, selfhood, and society on a regular basis ever since.

Organization

The format of the book is largely the same as in *The Moral of the Story,* second and third editions: In each chapter I give an overview of the most influential theories within the topic in question, followed by a brief selection of primary text excerpts. Concluding each chapter is a selection of stories illustrating that particular discussion of human nature, in the form of excerpts, or summaries, or both. Because I am an avid film fan and have had some success in my own classes with including occasional film summaries to illustrate philosophical issues, there is an emphasis on films; but I have also included summaries and excerpts of classic as well as lesser known novels and short stories. Since I was born, raised, and educated in

Denmark, much of my "literary backbone" consists of Scandinavian literature, and I draw on that experience to some degree, as a tribute to my personal cultural heritage. However, most of the narrative material comes from the diversity of my adopted American culture as well as from other traditions. I have only included narratives that have a personal meaning to me or that I consider to be particularly good for discussion; I have made no attempt to cover the entire field of narrative diversity. Using stories in this way, relying on summaries and excerpts to convey a basic idea, is of course not fair to the experience of the story as art: Much of the depth, the humor, and the richness is lost in the process, and I have no illusions that a summary can replace the real experience. I would therefore strongly recommend that students have access to the original versions whenever possible, whether it involves putting books and videos on reserve at the school learning center or library to the extent that the copyright laws allow or giving students an incentive to pursue the stories on their own, as homework projects.

Each chapter contains boxes that discuss an issue in greater detail than the text allows or introduce a subject that is only peripherally related to the main discussion; and in order to facilitate the learning process for student readers, each chapter concludes with a review section, summarizing the main points of the chapter.

Human Conditions

Occasionally, the term *the human condition* has been used as a general term for human nature, with each author giving the term a special twist. André Malraux, the French author and politician, implies that the human condition involves free choice and social interaction. The philosopher Hannah Arendt uses the term as an illustration of the human characteristic of responding to new situations. Recently the expression has been used in connection with works on ecofeminism, new age philosophy, anthropology, biblical studies, and environmentalism, to mention a few. In this book I use the term tentatively, suggesting that we share experiences, regardless of culture, race, gender, age, and many other factors, simply by virtue of being born human. Which experiences those may be will be the topic of the upcoming discussions.

For some reason, no textbook dealing with philosophy of human nature that I have ever used has addressed the question of our physical origin in the form of a broad overview. Do philosophy textbook authors think students have learned enough about human origins in biology classes? In my experience most students haven't. Or is it perhaps that the question of human origin is too controversial, in light of the fact that some states are struggling with the role of creationism versus the theory of evolution in their curricula? In the text I will risk voicing my opinion on that issue.

As Mary Midgley found out when entering into discussions about the field of human nature, it is a field with little tolerance for opposing theories: Where she wanted to explore a variety of theories out of a genuine interest, she found that you are expected to choose a side and hurl insults at the other side. Feminist theory has since then pointed out that this is fairly common within the world of academe and the intelligentsia and has labeled it *adversarial argumentation*. In this debate, the lines are drawn in a number of ways—first, between those who (often from a religious or a moral perspective) believe there *is* a human nature and those who deny that we have any human nature at all. The latter group is in itself divided into deterministic scientists who believe we have no human nature because our environment can mold us in a variety of directions and antideterministic existentialists who believe we can choose to become almost anything we want regardless of our heredity and our environment. Other lines are

drawn between scholars from different fields, holding reductionist theories of human nature that reflect their specific field: economics, anthropology, psychology, sociology. You will notice that I have left philosophy out; being a philosopher, I choose to believe in our professional mythology that philosophers can be bridge builders as well as superb critics, coming to other disciplines from the outside, and, with the philosophical methods of analysis, can see through other disciplines to their motivations and limitations, while at the same time gleaning the Truth from each limited discipline, much like a sighted person watching the blind men trying to describe the elephant in the famous Buddhist metaphor.

We shouldn't be fooled, though: Philosophers can be as stubborn as the next scholar, and we all have to be careful of closing our minds snugly around our favorite theory. However, I do believe that philosophy can serve as a truth-seeker as well as a synthesizer. I also concur with many feminist thinkers that an adversarial argumentative style is not always the best way to get a clearer picture of a subject. It is eminently useful for honing one's arguments, but, in Paul Ricoeur's words, one must be able to *listen* as well as to *suspect* other theories and statements of being false. In this book we shall look at a sampling of the great variety of views on human nature, taken from many places and times in human history. The book undoubtedly reflects the fact that I have favorite theories and theories I disagree with profoundly, but I have attempted to give an evenhanded description of each theory as well as list the most compelling counterarguments. There are a few exceptions, though, where I find myself taking sides, unequivocally. One is the debate between the theory of evolution and creationism: While I respect creationism as an expression of great emotional and spiritual conviction, I have little patience with it as an alternative scientific theory, based on the Western concept of scientific evidence. Other exceptions are theories of race and gender: I find there are good rational arguments for discarding racism and sexism, and the chapters will of course reflect my view. The final exception (that I am aware of) relates to the issue of personhood raised in Chapters 1 and 10. One of the inevitable features of a philosophy of human nature here in the beginning of the twenty-first century is that old categories and definitions are being challenged: We can no longer say that humans are the only animals who use tools, make tools, and recognize themselves in mirrors. We have to ask two questions here: What are the epistemological consequences of these changing boundaries? And what are the moral consequences? Do we look for a narrowing set of characteristics of what is truly human, or do we expand our concept of personhood? Both approaches will be explored in this book, but you will also find that I, after many years of dealing with the issue from the standpoint of an ethicist, have come down on the side of a reevaluation of personhood rather than keeping the personhood club open exclusively for humans. In this book, this may be the most controversial view that I have chosen to stand behind; of course, it doesn't mean that other views aren't represented—fairly, I hope. My rationale is partly scientific and partly a moral decision: Scientifically, there is now sufficient evidence to conclude that some of our fellow nonhuman travelers on Spaceship Earth—in particular the great apes—share some of the characteristics we previously considered exclusively human. And, morally, humans throughout time have excelled in pronouncing other human groups less human, so that their lands, their children, and their persons themselves could be exploited. Both are issues worth taking into consideration.

So is there a human condition? I believe so or, rather, there are a number of human conditions; we don't necessarily have to focus on what is *exclusively human*, because part of what flavors life for us is something that we share with at least other higher primates and perhaps also other social animals; furthermore, we don't necessarily have to demand that it be shared by every human individual—because there are individuals who will never have basic human experiences, such as knowing what it is to love and care for another being. What we do have to focus on is the shared experience of living in a body, having the conscious awareness that we do, being able to communicate that knowledge and share the experience of life with others—and knowing that bodies don't live forever. That is to me the foundation of the human condition; other experiences and capacities are fascinating and vital components of being human, but, contrary to most theories of human nature, I will stipulate that we don't have to expect them to be universal or exclusively human for us to regard them as part of the human condition. And it is just possible that this curiosity about human nature is one of the key factors of the human condition.

I don't presume to offer a unified theory of human nature, but I hope this exploration of famous, infamous, and more obscure theories will serve as an inspiration for students to keep asking the questions What is it to be human? And how should we treat those that don't meet our criteria?

Acknowledgments

Over the years, while I was collecting material for *The Human Condition,* a great many friends, relatives, colleagues, and students were unwitting contributors simply because we shared inspired conversations about human nature. However, for the past few semesters several of my classes have actively participated in the creative process through their questions, comments, corrections, and valuable ideas. In particular, I would like to thank the classes from San Diego Mesa College, Philosophy 107 in Spring 2001 and Philosophy 108 in Spring 2000, for putting up with a typed manuscript for a textbook. I asked them for their comments and critiques, and they came through graciously. Their input has been invaluable.

I want to express my gratitude to all the people formerly at Mayfield Publishing Company, now McGraw-Hill, who have helped bring this book to fruition: in particular my editor, Ken King, who is gifted with the rare qualities of a scholarly and a practical mind combined. His patience is an example of the Aristotelian golden mean: not too little, but not too much, either, which is perfect for an editor waiting for the submission of a manuscript. My production editor, Jen Mills, deserves much appreciation for her clear perspective and control of the editing process, and for pleasant, instant communications. I would like to thank Marty Granahan for her ever-professional and friendly assistance. In addition, I'd like to express my gratitude to Robert F. Brown, University of Delaware; Richard Combes, University of South Carolina, Spartanburg; Ted F. Cruz, Loras College; David L. McNaron, Nova Southeastern University; Bernadette E. O'Connor, University of the Incarnate Word; Ludwig F. Schlecht, Muhlenberg College; Gerard Vallone, Pace University; and Robert Zeuschner, Pasadena City College, for their comments and suggestions, in some cases going out of their way to suggest further readings—which all turned out to be eminently useful. My manuscript editor, Joan Pendleton, deserves special mention because not only is she a thoroughly professional person with whom I have worked on several occasions, and a conscientious source of information, but she is also a good friend in whose judgment I have the utmost confidence and whose e-mails have made my day on several occasions.

Also, a word of appreciation to my first editor at Mayfield, Jim Bull—first for encouraging me to write my textbook in ethics, *The Moral of the Story,* and second, for being brave enough to sign me up do to a textbook in a field into which Mayfield had hitherto not ventured: the field of Human Nature.

A number of good friends, colleagues, and a few particularly enterprising students deserve my warmest thanks for their help, comments, and other contributions: Dwight Furrow, Charles Zappia, Kendra Jeffcoat, Richard Hammes, Arelene Wolinski, Charles Corum, Mary Lou Locke, Tony Pettina, and Patrick Pidgeon, all of San Diego Mesa College; Eugene Troxell, Leon Rosenstein, Nick Genovese, and Randi McKenzie, from San Diego State University; Laurie Schrage, California State University, Pomona; Betsy Decyk and Daniel Guerriere, California State University, Long Beach; Peter Kemp, Adam Bülow-Jacobsen, and Hans Hertel, University of Copenhagen; Marianne Ammitzbøll, Axel Randrup, Susanne Schwer, Søren Peter Hansen, and Christa Blichmann, Copenhagen; Steen Wackerhausen, University of Århus; Michael Trice and Albertine Batory, San Diego; and Betty B. Owens, Dallas.

Special words of gratitude go to the following friends and colleagues: To Helmut Wautischer, Sonoma State University, for inviting me to participate in meetings of the Society for Anthropology of Consciousness and reawakening my interest in tribal philosophy—an interest I have had since I was an anthropology major for a short time, years ago when "tribal philosophy" was generally considered an oxymoron. To Louise M. Antony, Ohio State University, for graciously sharing an, at the time, unpublished manuscript with me. To Maxine Sheets-Johnstone, an independent scholar as well as an independent mind, who inspired me to look beyond the Cartesian tradition to a new inclusive view of the nature of thinking—and who took precious time out from her own work to critique and comment on a significant part of the text. To Jonathan McLeod, Mesa College, who added his invaluable perspective as a historian to parts of this book and who saved me from making some historical blunders! If there are errors of a historical nature in this text, it will surely be in the sections Jonathan didn't get to review. To Michael Kuttnauer, Mesa College, who, with his profound interest in the perennial questions of philosophy, manages to rekindle my own passion for such issues even after long days of teaching and meetings, and who took time out from both work and vacation to read part of the manuscript and share his knowledge and insight with me. To Sudata Debchaudhury, Mesa College, who shared her knowledge of the religious traditions and current gender issues in India with me. And to John Berteaux, San Diego State University, a friend, philosopher, and fellow ex-adjunct instructor from years back, who shared his research and insight into philosophy of race theory with me and inspired me profoundly with his comments on parts of the manuscript.

My mother and father, Gladys and Finn Rosenstand, Copenhagen, have lovingly supported my scholarship for a generation. They never seem to run out of energy nor inspiration. My mother read an early version of my manuscript and supplied valuable comments. So did my father, who in addition has been a faithful supplier of articles and literary references, new as well as classic—some of them break-through works dating back to his own youth. If his computer-sharp mind doesn't contain the information, he will brave the Copenhagen rains and snows to personally go look for the one scholar in town who might be able to help out. There is no adequate way to express my appreciation for all they have done for me—not just by being there for me but also by supplying me with role models: my father, tireless researcher, caring for everyone in the family who needs help and attention, and choosing to work part-time to become a stay-at-home dad when my mother became the full-time breadwinner. My mother: not only do I admire her ability to be simultaneously a wonderful parent and a career woman in a stressful job, but I have also always been deeply affected by her heroism as a member of the Danish resistance during World War II, captured by the Nazis, and imprisoned for eight months before escaping to Sweden.

Other persons deserve mention because of the topic of this book: My niece, Jessica Humphrey, coming into her own as a poet and a thinker; my mother-in-law, Nancy R. Covner, for giving me insight into her experience as a war bride and a fellow immigrant and for being understanding about the demands of teaching and writing; Else Nilsen, who became nurse to my disabled grandmother more than half a century ago and later became a nanny to me, for all the conversations we have had over the years about human nature and for her example of fortitude, kindness, and courage; and my paternal grandmother herself, Gudweig Rosenstand, who spent the last nine years of her life—and the first nine years of mine—telling me stories and laying the foundation for my appreciation of human nature at its finest. Disabled from rheumatoid arthritis for thirty years and confined to her bed for ten, she never lost her fundamental appreciation for life; she never spoke of her pain but always chose to focus on what good things the day might bring. Fortitude, nurturing, and courage—mighty virtues to live up to.

But most importantly, I want to thank my husband, Craig Covner, artist and human being *extraordinaire,* for being there and putting up with a wife who was really only a "part-time" partner during her creative process. Patiently he has handled my writer's moods (which overlap with my teacher's moods), cheered me up when I needed it, discussed issues with me, and taken on more than his fair share (that is, more than half) of our household chores. And, as always, my thanks to Rowdie for sharing her life with us and teaching me beyond a shadow of a doubt that a nonhuman animal can have intelligence, language comprehension, and a rich emotional life.

Part 1

Stories of Who We Are

Chapter One

The Storytelling Animal

A Human Condition?

Do you have faith in human nature? Before we even begin to answer that question, we had better ask ourselves what it entails. For one thing, it assumes that there is such a thing as human nature. But that assumption itself has been questioned: Must we, as human beings, invariably display the same characteristics, join in the same behavior, think the same thoughts and feel the same feelings, merely because we belong to the same species? In this book we look at some of the most enduring proposals regarding the nature of human nature, as well as some more recent views that might be called either fanciful imaginings or courageous breakthroughs.

Some of us believe that there is a human nature, while others question it. But is that the same as *having faith in human nature?* Hardly. The question of whether there actually is a human nature is one we might expect science, and philosophy of science, to answer; the question of whether we have faith in human nature is not a scientific issue, but one for ethicists and theologians. At issue here is whether we think humans are fundamentally decent or fundamentally rotten beings—which is a value judgment rather than a scientific statement.

Up front I admit that I probably have some faith in human nature—which means I also believe that there is some measure of similarity in our human lives: hence the title of this book, *The Human Condition.* The book explores the idea of human nature in its scientific and moral forms, taking what is often referred to as a *descriptive* and a *normative* approach (see the discussion later in this chapter). We will discuss whether the very

idea of humans having a "nature" may not be a misconception—perhaps what we have is not a nature, but a culture? And we will discuss whether you have to be biologically human to share in that nature, or that culture. As different as we are, individually and culturally, it may be that the ultimate key to understanding each other is the fact that, in the words of John F. Kennedy that I have taken as a motto for this book, "we all inhabit this small planet. We all breathe the same air. We all cherish our children's future. And we are all mortal."

Different Meanings of "Human"

We all think we know what it is to be human—until we are asked to define it. Then we may discover that definitions we thought were obvious are not so obvious after all. Is being human a matter of *acting like* a human being? In that case, some cherished definitions from previous centuries (including the twentieth century) must fall by the wayside: Humans are not the only tool users, nor indeed the only toolmakers. Humans are not the only creatures showing compassion or engaging in warfare. And, perhaps most controversially, humans may not be the only creatures with language capacity. Is it a matter of *looking like* a human being? Some societies around the world have worked out different criteria for who counts as human beings in terms of looks and other physical measures. In some, being born with physical disabilities disqualifies a child from entering the ranks of tribe members—and usually means the child is disposed of in some way. And what if the science fiction fantasy comes true one of these centuries, and we can build artificial intelligence into a human form? If and when we start thinking of the androids as fellow creatures, like Data in *Star Trek,* will it be because of their human shape or their intelligence? How about *genetics?* In other words, is anyone born of human parents a human being? What happens if a human baby is born with DNA mutations, making the child visibly or behaviorally distinct from other humans? Or what if a child is genetically engineered with changes to the human DNA, perhaps with animal hybrid elements?

A basic political definition of a human being is *someone like us:* Most societies have, somewhere in their past, set up rules for who counted as "real human beings": those of *our tribe.* Tribal societies have a long common history of calling *themselves* "the human beings." Foreigners; enemies; and people with different skin color, different eating habits, different religions, and different class at birth have been relegated to less-than-human status with regularity throughout human history. In some societies being born a twin is a great blessing, and the twins are given special privileges. In others it is considered a great calamity for the tribe, and the twins are killed. Throughout history, infants have often not been considered members of the tribe until the age of three months or sometimes a year—a point when it seemed likely they would not succumb to infant mortality. In many societies prenatal infants don't have any standing as human beings. In some societies your humanity depends on your birth status: Are your parents freeborn or slaves? Are they citizens or foreigners? Rich or poor? Old people, sick people, mentally disabled or disturbed people, violent criminals— we have an ancient tendency to declare some groups to be less "human" than others. Slavery is still rampant on most continents on the planet, and often the slaveowners view the slaves as being somehow less human than the owners themselves. Having entered the twenty-first century should not make us think that people have left behind the old habit of declaring someone else less than human. This in turn means that whatever our view of human nature—even if it reflects the latest scientific discoveries—there is always the possibility that we will apply it to other peo-

ple; in other words, any definition of human nature carries with it the potential for a *moral, social, and political application* of the definition. How we treat others depends to a great extent on our implicit definition of what a human being is.

Descriptive and Normative Approaches

You have probably noticed that the term *human* seems to have very different underlying meanings. In some definitions it is used in a *genetic, biological* sense. In others it is used in what a philosopher would call an *epistemological* sense (referring to a theory of knowledge): How do we understand ourselves as individuals, and what characterizes the human mind and the human experience? In yet other definitions it is used in a sense we could call *metaphysical:* What is the reality of a human being—are we strictly an animal among animals, or do we have a spiritual aspect to our existence? But equally important is the *moral, social, and political* sense, which encompasses what it takes to live up to being human, interacting with other humans.

Questions about human nature generally fall in two different categories: (1) How can we describe a human being? and (2) What characteristics ought someone to have in order to count as a human being? The first category reflects a *descriptive* approach: We are merely interested in describing human nature as accurately and objectively as we can, genetically or psychologically. The second category is almost inevitably linked with the first, but it is more subtle, because it asks what human nature is supposed to be; in other words, it is a *normative* approach. The first approach is fundamentally *scientific;* the second is a *moral* classification that includes social, political, and— not infrequently—religious aspects.

Whatever our definition of human nature, it has implications for the way we treat other people. Being an ethicist myself, I tend to notice the moral and political implications of a scientific theory of human nature, even though the theory may not have outlined such implications: Once we decide on a definition of human nature, we also define what is *not* human; and if privileges and rights are part of the political package of being human, then we at the same time exclude some beings from having such privileges and rights. Doing so may make a lot of sense, practically speaking—there are good reasons for not giving pets the right to vote, for example—but we should never forget that such distinctions between who is "truly" human and who isn't have resulted in millennia of discrimination: In the Western tradition, women have, until recently, been classified as not quite as typically human as men. Most slavery-based societies have classified slaves as only partially human. Today we tend to call serial killers "inhuman," but that is a moral classification rather than a biological one. Just because a definition looks scientific doesn't mean it is; it could be a result of selective scientific research or flawed or even fraudulent science. Very often in human history what was presented as objective science was infused with the vested interests of society or of the scientists—which is another way of saying that the normative element may creep into a descriptive context even without the scientists' being aware of it. A theory of human nature without a moral and political context is a very rare thing, if not nonexistent. We should try to be scientifically objective, but we should also expect our social worldview to be a determining factor in our assessment.

Some Popular Theories of Human Nature

In discussions about human nature, we tend to choose one of two approaches: Either we look for some characteristic or characteristics that are shared by all humans—sometimes referred to as *human universals*—or we look for characteristics that are *exclusively human,* meaning that they are not shared by other animals at all or at least not in the same degree. Human universals are often characteristics that can be shared by other animals; examples include family bonding; communication; fondness for sugars, salts, and fatty foods; a sense of direction; the feeling of jealousy; laughter and tears; a long childhood; and what psychol-

ogists call an expectation of "object permanence," an expectation that things remain more or less similar under similar circumstances and don't disappear into thin air. Such characteristics may or may not be exclusively human, but what is interesting about them is that every human being on Planet Earth shares them because of our shared biological heritage. Human universals help us understand the humanity in all of us—but they are not sufficient to help us understand what it is about the human race, if anything, that makes us a unique species. For that we have to go to a discussion of characteristics believed to be exclusively human. Until recently—the last twenty-five to thirty years—such a list was often simply taken for granted by scholars, scientists, and laypeople alike, but the latest research into human and animal biology, as well as behavior, has made some of the old walls separating humans from other animals shake and crumble. Let's look at some traditional philosophical definitions of human nature, those voiced by Western philosophers in particular. Some of these views will be discussed in detail in future chapters. I suggest you try to keep track of whether a theory is fundamentally *descriptive* or whether it sets up a standard for what a human being ought to be—in other words, whether it is a *normative* theory.

The Political Animal Aristotle (384–322 B.C.E.), the Greek philosopher who, more than any other person, provided the early foundation for Western sciences, said that "man is a political animal"; he was in fact merely stressing that humans are social beings, not that they are some sort of political carnivores (we take a closer look at Aristotle's political theory in Chapter 9). Even so, the "political animal" cliché rings true: no other animal on earth has developed political systems that we can recognize as such, so adding politics to the realm of human behavioral characteristics is not inappropriate. But are humans the *only* social beings? Of course not. Many insects, such as ants and termites, live in social communities, and mammals such as dolphins, wolves, elephants, and all the great apes except for the orangutans live in highly structured social groups. This fact may well be of enormous importance in assessing animal intelligence and behavior.

The Featherless Biped   This definition is also found in Aristotle's writings and refers, of course, to the fact that humans normally walk on two legs, as do birds; however, birds have feathers, and humans don't. This definition is one of the least helpful in outlining what is unique to humans, but let's take it a bit further: In many systems of religion and philosophy, *the human body* is viewed as a work of perfection, usually designed in some way by a divine power (see Chapter 2 for an overview of such creation myths). As a result, many people are surprised to realize that while the human body is indeed a fabulous unit of coordination, it is by no means "perfect," even in a very healthy, normal person. For example, our upright stance puts a strain on our backs, knees, and ankles, and if we live past fifty (as most people do in the West these days, although that was a rarity among early humans), we usually end up with some pains from wear and tear. Another example: the human windpipe is right next to the esophagus, and contrary to most other animals (and human babies, too!), who can eat and breathe at the same time, adult humans can't, and choking is a real hazard. So we may be well "designed," but we are by no means physically perfect. In an article in *Scientific American*, March 2001, "If Humans Were Built to Last," research scientists argued that the human body would hold up better if we were shorter, if our torsos were forward-tilting, our bones thicker, our trachea redesigned to prevent choking, and our knees able to bend backward, among other "fixes."

The Body as a Moral Symbol   Biological facts are one thing; cultural myths are another: The human body has often been used symbolically as a way to tell the "good" humans from the "bad" humans. Tribal cultures have traditionally killed babies who have physically abnormal features (such as too many toes, visible birthmarks, or missing limbs), or who are born a "double" (a twin),

not so much out of aesthetic revulsion but out of a symbolic fear of the inhuman, the different. It seems to be an ancient human trait to view variations on the human body as dangerous and a sign of evil. In the nineteenth-century story of Dr. Jekyll and Mr. Hyde (see Chapter 8), Mr. Hyde, the evil *alter ego,* seems to be physically abnormal. We may think that this form of discrimination against people with physical disabilities is a phenomenon of the past, but consider Hannibal Lechter, one of the most popular "bad guys" of movies and popular literature over the past decade. In the books by Thomas Harris, Lechter has six fingers on each hand (not an unusual feature, actually), a classic literary ploy that sets him off from the rest of humanity as a morally deficient person! Similar elements of a physically abnormal villain appear in *The Princess Bride* and *Jason.* Some films have turned the stereotype around, however, and ask us to question our moral prejudice against those who look different: *Edward Scissorhands, The Man Without a Face,* and *Beauty and the Beast* are among them.

The Rational Being   For Aristotle as well as for most other philosophers until this day, the one characteristic that sets humans apart is our rationality. Immanuel Kant (1724–1804) calls humans "rational beings" and by and large treats the two terms as interchangeable. Nobody disputes that humans display more intelligence than any other creature on earth, but it is no longer a given that we are the only smart creatures. What exactly is it to display rationality? Is it to use language, as many philosophers claim, or is it to act according to a plan? Or is it some additional characteristic? The fact that humans have developed mathematics, logic, and science is in itself a result—perhaps the finest—of humans having a capacity to reason; and to many this not only sets us definitively apart from other animals, but also transcends cultural boundaries and unites us all: The rules of math and logic apply no matter which culture we are raised in. But what are the fundamental characteristics of rationality—where in human behavior does it manifest itself first? If rationality is exclusively tied to language use (as philosophers used to claim; see the next section), then a lot of people who act according to a highly developed plan (such as building a model ship or cooking dinner) but who think in images rather than words don't qualify as rational. On the other hand, if rationality is conceiving of a plan and following it logically regardless of language involvement, then it appears that we may have to include some non-human animals in the group of rational beings: Wolves display an astounding sense of a game plan during a hunt, for example. Apes carry special rocks with them to use as nut crackers in a faraway thicket. Besides, in the long philosophical tradition of calling humans rational beings, there are questions as to whether all humans are supposed to be included: Are infants rational beings? Are severely mentally disabled people? At one time hearing-impaired people were considered less intelligent because they could not express themselves easily in speech; for over two millennia women were considered less rational than men, and we are still struggling with another old philosophical prejudice against people of color, who used to be viewed by many Western philosophers as being on the lower end of the scale of rationality. We return to the issue of rationality in upcoming chapters.

The Speaking Animal   High on the list of human specialties is language: On a basic level, the observation that humans are the only talking creatures is, of course, correct. Mynah birds and parrots generally only "parrot" sounds they have been taught; they don't engage in conversations. Some of us loved stories of talking animals when we were kids, but even then, most of us knew those stories were make-believe. Some of us have mock conversations with our dogs ("How was your day?" "Rrrough!"), but those who claim their pets talk are generally ridiculed. The claim that some nonhuman animals are capable of understanding human speech and even responding meaningfully with human words and sentences is one of the most controversial assertions today, and yet many skeptics are being won over. In Chapter 10 we return to the language question and take a look at chimpanzees who have learned to communicate using human language to a point where the human monopoly on language use is being severely challenged.

The Toolmaker   That humans make tools is a fact, and the tools of early hominids (such as sharpened pieces of flint) have been used to designate the line between those human ancestors closer to apes than to humans (no toolmaking) and those closer to humans than apes—with *Homo habilis,* literally "handyman," near the dividing line (see Chapter 2). This definition stood the test of time until the 1970s, when Jane Goodall showed that chimpanzees in nature not only use tools, but also make them, stripping branches to fish for termites, wadding up leaves to serve as sponges, and so on. In fact, apes who live in research facilities and who have retained a certain amount of freedom will experiment with whatever tools are available to them, opening boxes with tools they have fashioned themselves. But we don't have to go to the primates to find fellow toolmakers: Even some birds know how to change their environment into tools. The main difference here, say the ethologists, is that the bird's brain is hardwired with the knowledge, while primates must learn it from their parents or others or figure it out for themselves—like humans transmitting their cultures from generation to generation or inventing new products and processes.

The Warrior   Humans have had wars as far back as we can tell; there is some tentative evidence of peaceful coexistence among humans going back some 8,000 years, in ancient Turkey (where towns had no fortifications), but on the whole the machinery of war seems to be universally present among the males of the species. However, this self-deprecating view that humans are the only creatures who engage in warfare with their own species has also had to be revised recently. Again, Jane Goodall's chimpanzee research put an end to assumptions about human uniqueness: Chimpanzees, both males and females, also fight wars with their own species. Of course, we can be misanthropic and say that no other creature on earth has developed such devastating ways of doing away with others of its own kind, that serial killers, mass murderers, and spree killers are unique to the human race; however, other populations of social animals have their occasional "rogue" individuals too.

The Nurturer Nonetheless, there is the other side of the coin: We are capable of caring for and often do take care of helpless members of our society. The fact that we love and care for our children may not be so extraordinary, because most other mammals do the same thing; but human love often extends past the time of the child's biological need for nurturing. For a caring parent there is no such thing as being an ex-parent, even if the connection with the child is severed or the child is dead. We may not as a rule love strangers, but we tend to care for our friends and family, and occasionally we show care and concern for people we don't know in ways that range from helping a lost child to sending troops to protect people threatened by genocide or starvation on the other side of the planet. Such human behavior doesn't arise out of nowhere: It has been known for decades that Neandertal burials included flowers, probably thrown into the open grave. Unless this was an accident, it indicates that our cousins in evolution weren't strangers to feelings of love, companionship, and grief either. And according to some animal behaviorists, the nurturing element is quite common among social animals like elephants and primates: They are reluctant to leave an injured companion or relative behind, they will bring food to the injured individual if they can, and they even show what may be similar to grief when such an individual dies.

The Moral Animal Philosophers who have stressed that humans are the only rational animals on earth often emphasize that humans are also the only beings with a sense of moral behavior; it isn't just a matter of adjusting to a pecking order in the group, say some ethicists, but also of asking general questions about behavior: "What if everyone did this?" is how we often introduce children to the Golden Rule—Do unto others as you would have them do unto you. It requires a considerable flair for abstract thinking to be able to apply one's own situation universally or to apply someone else's situation to oneself and all others. Here we may be in the presence of something uniquely human; and yet animal behaviorists are questioning this area too: Other social animals teach their young rules of behavior, punish them if they break the rules, and ostracize adults who break the rules. We will get back to the issue of human nature and ethics in Chapter 8.

The Free-Will Agent Closely related to the issue of the moral capacity of humans is the issue of freedom of the will. Most philosophical and religious Western traditions generally assume humans have freedom of the will: In other words, we are able to make up our minds about our goals and behavior; what we do is neither predetermined by God nor totally a function of our genetic makeup or our environment. And if we have free will, we can be held accountable for what we do; we can be praised, and we can be blamed. Much of morality as well as our justice system depends on this assumption, and we will look at it in detail in Chapter 4. Just as humans are assumed to have free will, animals are generally assumed not to have it, because presumably they cannot rationalize between several possible behavior options. But is this true? Have you ever known an animal well enough to observe it actively making up its mind about a course of action, vacillating between two possibilities? An old philosophical parable tells of a donkey, "Buridan's ass," who would starve to death if placed within equal distance of two equally large piles of hay, because it wouldn't be able to decide which one to eat first. This is, of course, nonsense, and it works only as a thought experiment on deciding between two equally important courses of action. How would the donkey decide which one to eat first? We don't know, but we do know from experience that whether the donkey has the capacity of rational choice or not, it makes choices based on some form of preference.

The Child of God   It seems that every single human population that we know about has or has had some form of religion, whereas, to our knowledge no other animal has a sense of God or of the presence of higher powers. We generally find evidence of religious faith through language: Prayers were written down and preserved for posterity; creation myths were preserved orally and later written down; stories of gods, goddesses, religious heroes and heroines were told by our ancestors, and stories of reward and punishment in the afterlife still have considerable power over people's souls. But language is not the only source: There is the evidence embedded in buildings and artifacts (cathedrals, churches, mosques, temples, icons, rosaries, paintings, and the like); there are religious works of music; and there is the observation of behavior associated with worship. None of these elements have been observed among nonhuman populations, but it might be wise not to rule out the possibility altogether: Worship behavior can take on many forms, and perhaps one shouldn't completely discount the presence of spirituality in nonhuman animals, as preposterous as it may sound to some. On the other hand, the presence of religion doesn't seem to be a *necessary* element in *human* populations; while we may think that the lack of spirituality makes for an impoverished kind of life, humans—individually or collectively—live such lives to a natural end, without considering themselves deprived of something important and very often with their moral sense intact. In Chapter 8 we return to the issue of humans and spirituality.

The Being with a Soul   This definition may be the single most important one in distinguishing between humans and animals in the Judeo-Christian tradition. In the Bible's first book, Genesis, we are told that God breathes life into the clay he has shaped, which becomes Adam, the first man, and

later Eve, the first woman. In Genesis no other animal comes alive in the same way. Some Western theologians and philosophers have taken this (and other biblical references) to mean that humans have souls, and animals have none. (Others believe that humans have rational souls but animals have nonrational souls.) The consequences of this interpretation have been enormous; they include the simple assumption that humans are closer to God than other creatures, the entire religious culture built around the idea of access to the afterlife for good people and a place of punishment for unredeemed sinners, and the philosopher René Descartes's seventeenth-century statement that because animals have no souls, they have no minds and thus *can feel no pain* (see Chapter 7). In essence, it was the assumption of the human soul that made Darwin's theory of evolution so hard to accept, because how does a soul evolve from a soulless creature (an ancient apelike ancestor) to a modern human? Other religious traditions have not had as hard a time with the human-animal distinction, because they assume that souls are not an exclusively human attribute: The Hindu and Buddhist traditions teach that all living beings have some form of spiritual energy that travels from life-form to life-form in a chain of reincarnation, until the spirit gathers enough wisdom to escape the chain of rebirth. The American Indian traditions and most other tribal traditions around the world see spiritual presences in nature in general—in animals, trees, hills, and rivers—not just in humans.

The Artist   Human populations have developed works of art, and as far as we can tell, nonhuman animals haven't. Pictorial art can be found in caves dating back to the end of the last Ice Age, and functioning stone flutes dating to 9,000 years ago have been discovered—interestingly, the flutes are in our familiar do-re-mi scale. But the question of art is in itself complicated, because it is a modern, Western concept. Not all human populations would understand what we mean by "art," or even recognize what art is and what it isn't. Indeed, in modern Western museums we still find such confused patrons teetering between anger and amusement: "This is supposed to be art? My four-year-old daughter can do better than that!" Traditional representational art is recognizably "artistic" for most people today, but it wasn't always so: Paintings of cows in a barn raised eyebrows among nineteenth-century art gallery audiences, because they thought of such subjects as filth that didn't belong on decent people's walls. Today we refer to elaborately decorated religious artifacts and tools for secular use as beautiful works of art, but the artisan generally thought of them just as being functional; the split between something's being aesthetically pleasing and functional and its being "art" without an obvious function hadn't happened yet. So what is art? On the one hand, you have human-made items produced in the past for a particular use, but not as art (although we call them art today); and on the other hand, you have something produced as art today but without any designated use, and many don't recognize it as art. In between are the traditional paintings, sculptures, and other artifacts that our culture can agree on as being art. So can we say for certain that we would recognize a work of art produced by a nonhuman animal if we saw it? There are elephants and apes in zoos who paint, and their paintings sell for a fortune. But do *they* think of their works as art? Do they have to, in order for *us* to view it as art?

The Two-Species Animal: Male and Female   Contrary to most of the other views of human nature listed here, this one is not an old tradition, but a view that has emerged lately. For some people, it illustrates how sick and backward some thinkers appear in their view of the human species, and for others it contains a deep ring of truth. This view holds that women and men are so different, psychologically, that we might as well consider ourselves as being of two species (as a popular book title says, from Mars and from Venus). Around the world, women have been considered significantly different from men, with a different set of virtues, human qualities, flaws, and cultural traditions. For some, this signifies the fundamental

oppression that women have suffered until very recently and whose consequences they still suffer; in other words, if women hadn't been treated so differently from men, by men, we would see many more similarities between men and women than we have traditionally seen. This viewpoint is supported, to some extent, by equality in education and job opportunities achieved in the late twentieth century; however, even when men and women have the exact same kind of upbringing and schooling, there still seem to be subtle differences between them that go beyond sexual attributes and the biological fact that women can give birth. So how different are we by nature, and how much of it is due to cultural pressures? We will take a closer look at this issue in Chapter 6.

The Creature Who Displays Emotion   Then there are those all-too-human characteristics: We *smile,* universally, to deflect tension and show friendship. The greatest bonding experience for young parents and their infants is the baby's smile. Some behaviorists have tried to explain it by saying that humans show their mouths without baring their teeth, like a nonaggression sign, but lately researchers have demonstrated that the old saying is actually true: "Put on a happy face," and you'll actually feel happy! The muscles at the corners of our mouths are directly hooked into our brain chemistry: It makes us feel good, it makes others smile contagiously, and it makes them feel good. We *laugh* at jokes, as well as at other people's misfortune (sometimes they are one and the same thing). The French philosopher Henri Bergson thought we laugh in order to shame others out of behaving antisocially, but there are surely a number of reasons why humans laugh: to release tension, to bond, to mock, and so on. We *cry* because of pain, physical as well as mental, with those salty tears that only seals and elephants also have (no, crocodiles don't cry crocodile tears). We *blush* (and Mark Twain liked to point out that we probably blush because we are the only creatures with a reason to do so), we *frown,* and so forth. But are we unique in these respects? Bonobo chimpanzees have dazzling smiles for their loved ones; anecdotes have it that elephants can cry, with tears, but dry-eyed displays of grief have been observed among a number of social species from apes to our own companions, dogs. Displays of happiness and despair are evident in most animals, once you get to know how they express themselves (and if you are at all open to the idea that animals have feelings).

The Lying Animal   Humans can lie, and some of us do it a lot. Of course this is part of the "moral animal" category, because we're implying that one shouldn't lie (which is a normative concept); but a descriptive theory of human nature may be more interested in the very fact that humans are *capable* of lying. That we know how to tell truth from fiction, at least in principle, is enormously important for a theory of human nature, because it implies that the human intellect recognizes something called "truth" and is capable of manufacturing the opposite of this "truth." The theory of human *cognition* (capacity for thinking) sees the human tendency to lie as a clear indication that the human mind can distinguish between truth and falsehood—one of the hallmarks of intelligence. To successfully create artificial intelligence, we would need to include a knowledge of the distinction between truth and falsehood in the brains of our androids and gyneoids. But is this exclusively human? We often hear animals praised with the words that "They are without deceit," because our pets don't lie to us, while our friends might. But it doesn't take language to lie: A bird can feign a broken wing to lead a predator away from her nest; a predator can play hide-and-seek games with its prey; and your dog can pretend to have a hurt paw just because she loves the attention she gets when you think she is in pain. So does that mean nonhuman animals understand the concept of truth? Philosophers have feared to go there, but some day we may have to.

The Animal Who Knows It Will Die   Although the Dutch philosopher Spinoza said in the seventeenth century that the rational man thinks least of all about death, speculation about the end of life seems to be a human preoccupation. Perhaps we are all foolish, then—or perhaps Spinoza was wrong. It seems a given that many very wise women and men have spent time trying to come to terms with the finality of everything and of human life in particular. In Chapter 8 we look at the moral and religious implications of such speculations. Perhaps one could say that we pay the price for our memory, our intelligence, and our capability to plan for the future with the knowledge that some day we must die. Until recently this has been assumed to be a price only humans have had to pay; the rest of creation seems to be living in ignorant bliss, focusing on a perennial "today." That is why an event of a few years ago shook many animal behaviorists—as well as many others who heard the story. You'll read about it in Chapter 10: Koko, the gorilla, who has mastered over 1,000 American Sign Language (ASL) words, demonstrated to her human companions that she understood what it meant for her pet kitten to have died; and according to her companions, Koko acts uncomfortable whenever asked about death. To her companions, that trait in itself is a very human one.

The Storytelling Animal   A view that emerged in the late twentieth century and that is still in its early phases of development holds that one of the uniquely human characteristics is the telling of stories—and we shall take this cue as a general theme for this book. The propensity humans have for telling stories about their accomplishments; about the history of the family, tribe, and nation; about things they didn't do (because lying can be an inherent part of storytelling); and about fictional characters, trees, animals, and nearly everything else in the universe is of course language-dependent and contingent on knowing the difference between truth and falsehood. But there is so much more to it than that. Why do we tell stories? For entertainment; to impress others; to protect ourselves; to preserve an ephemeral event; to teach others, including children; to preserve and maintain some kind of social and cosmic order; but, most of all, to make sense out of life—a chaotic life that usually doesn't come with a clear plot that lets us see the meaning of an event while we're in the middle of it or even when it's over, because storytelling surely also can preserve the memory of a life into an immeasurable future. Storytelling may, of course, be what the great whales engage in when they sing "songs" in the depths of the ocean and what birds communicate with their song in the spring, but so far we have no evidence that this is so. There seems to be no evidence that other primates tell any form of bedtime stories to their babies, so perhaps we have here reached something exclusively human. Be that as it may, we are going to explore the "narrative urge," the human love of telling and listening to stories, and we are going to discuss stories after each chapter as illustrations of how humans have tried to make sense of their own nature by spinning tales about it.

The Narrative Urge

According to some psychologists and philosophers humans are not only born capable of telling stories, but also with a *need* to spin tales; this is sometimes referred to as the *narrative urge*. It appears that humans tend to tell stories even unawares, as scientific research has shown.

The Man with Two Brains

Individual episodes of the television series *Scientific American Frontiers* often focus on questions of human nature. In such an episode, "The Brain," a patient was presented as a "man with two brains." His two brain halves had been severed surgically to prevent seizures; and, as a result, in many ways he acted as if he had two sets of consciousness that didn't relate very well to each other. It is a commonly known fact that our two brain hemispheres have largely different functions: The left brain hemisphere is in charge of language, math, and logical thinking, while the right brain hemisphere functions primarily through images and intuition (to put it very simply). Popularly, we even talk about "right-brain" people (artists) and "left-brain" people (scientists). Since

the left half dominates the right side of the body, and the right half the left, a brain injury to the left half may affect the senses and capacities in the right side of the body, and vice versa. This man's vision and hearing were intact, and his brain functioned normally, except that there was no communication between the two brain halves. Most of his life was quite normal: He could hold down a job and carry on ordinary conversations, and he was free of seizures. However, he didn't function quite like most other people. His situation gives us a clue to what it is for the brain to function normally, and for our purposes here, one element of the story stands out: *He invented explanations* when one brain half didn't supply the other with necessary information. Routinely, he took part in medical research experiments, such as a vision experiment. He focused on the middle of a computer screen; words on the left side would travel to the right side of his brain, while words on the right would travel to the left, speaking side. When a word was flashed on the right, he had no problem explaining what he had read (because our language center is to the left); but when a word was flashed to the left side, his right brain half was not able to tell what the word was. However, when asked, he could draw an image of the word (he understood that he'd read the word *toadstool* only when his left hand drew a toad—on a stool!) because his right brain understood perfectly what he had read, but just couldn't speak it; his left brain half then "discovered" what his own drawing looked like, in the way we would try to guess what a child's drawing depicts. Here comes the part that is relevant to our purpose: When the word *music* was flashed on the right, he understood; at the same time, the word *bell* was flashed on the left, and he couldn't tell what it was. However, when presented with images of a lot of musical instruments, he picked the image of a *bell tower* to go with the word *music* (because his right brain had understood "bell" and now recognized the image). But his left brain didn't know how he got to that association! So he explained that he had just heard bells outside—which happened to be true, because on the way to the lab he and the TV crew had heard the university bells ring from the bell tower. A legitimate explanation—or a story made up for mere convenience? To be sure, he had really heard bells; however, this was a secondary experience, and the primary experience, his right brain seeing "bell" without being able to identify it, was presumably the trigger. In other words, the man with two brains *told a story* that made events seem plausible to himself.

The doctor explained the phenomenon like this: We all have a need to understand why something happens and so feel in control; not understanding his own answer made the patient *concoct a story* that made sense to him. But this doesn't just happen to people with brain injuries taking part in brain research: It happens to everybody. We try to make sense of what happens to us, because not understanding unforeseen events is fundamentally frightening to us. In my own view, we pay the price for our human intelligence with our increased fear of the future and the clear understanding that we are not in complete control of our lives—in short, our fear of death is the price we pay for being smart. But we are too smart to let it get us down: We seek to understand events so that we can take precautions against future occurrences; our intelligence enables us to understand *causality*. We understand the phenomenon of cause and effect—the philosopher Kant considered this understanding as one of the absolutely inevitable, built-in elements of human rationality (see Chapter 7)—and we apply this understanding when something makes sense as well as when it doesn't make sense. We always look for the "Why?"—some of us more than others. Some of us are more eager to know "the real truth"; others are content with an explanation that works for now. For some, a scientific explanation is a satisfactory answer; for others, a religious explanation works better. But the urge to understand *why* so that we can predict the next occurrence is a fundamental trait of an intelligent being; it makes us live longer.

And this is where the *narrative urge* may have its origin: We are compelled to tell the tale of the "why" so that it can be understood by others and shared and so that we may be confirmed in our own understanding of why something happened. The man with two brains was fundamentally unhappy at not understanding why he made the association between *bell* and *music,* but without the connection between his brain halves, he couldn't experience the reason himself: that the right brain had "seen" the bell but couldn't use language to explain what it saw. So his left brain sought an explanation that made him feel better. Narratives created to explain why something happens may reflect facts and evidence, or they may not—or they may just tell half-truths. Just because an explanation makes us feel better doesn't mean we should accept it uncritically!

We use such narrative, causal explanations in personal situations, in social contexts, and in *historiography* (history writing) without ever being able to know all the facts or even predict similar events. We now look at two scholars who have each developed a theory about the human narrative urge: Alasdair MacIntyre and Paul Ricoeur.

MacIntyre: Stories Are Our Cultural Backbone

In 1981 renowned American philosopher Alasdair MacIntyre published a book that caused quite a stir among philosophers in the United States. In *After Virtue,* MacIntyre (b. 1929) claimed that Western culture is morally confused because we no longer have any founding stories (stories that provide a people's cultural identity). From the time of the ancient Greeks until today, the prevailing moral attitude has changed to such a degree that we no longer have a cultural *ethos* to bind us together. What was morally good for the Greek nobleman is no longer what is morally good for us. Does this mean that we have nothing in common with those ancient times? No, what we have in common is that we are all people whose identity is rooted in a sense of community and history—we are all part of a tradition, says MacIntyre. In spite of what modern philosophies of individualism would like to claim, we are part of a greater whole, and we can't understand ourselves if we try to view ourselves outside of that context. We all have relationships with our families, be they good or bad; we affect our friends as they affect us; and we share in the history of our people regardless of whether we took part in it or not. We may not own slaves or be slaves ourselves, but some of our ancestors may have been involved in the slavery issue, on one side or the other. This doesn't necessarily mean we should feel guilty about our heritage or bear resentment, but we should understand that we can't divorce ourselves from our past—it is an important part of our culture, and it affects how our culture views the rest of the world.

So how should we properly understand ourselves, according to MacIntyre? Not just as part of a whole, but as part of a *narrative* whole. Here is an example of what this means: You see a man digging in his yard. You can't know what he is doing until you hear his explanation: He is gardening or exercising or hunting for treasure or planning to murder his wife. Each explanation involves a story, and without the story there is no explanation. So our understanding of ourselves and each other is fundamentally narrative: We understand each other through stories and by implying reasons and motivations, causes and effects:

> Man is in his actions and practice, as well as in his fictions, essentially a storytelling animal. He is not essentially, but becomes through his history, a teller of stories that aspire to truth. But the key question for men is not about their own authorship; I can only answer the question "What am I do to?" if I can answer the prior question "Of what story or stories do I find myself a part?"[1]

Unless we have a sense of narrative continuity in our lives—unless we think of ourselves as the person (for example) whose bicycle was stolen at the age of eight, who fell in love at sixteen, won a scholarship at eighteen, went to college—we live our lives merely as a series of disjointed events. By recalling our personal history we give ourselves a *personal identity,* a *narrative unity* similar to that

of a character in a story. This is especially true if we use one event in our life to explain another ("I decided to change my major from business to medicine because of my sister's illness"). Furthermore, we are part of the stories of others, just as they are part of our stories, so our narrative is in this way correlative. "The narrative of any one life is part of an interlocking set of narratives," says MacIntyre.

What is necessary in order for us to do the right thing, as humans? We must understand that the life we live has a story that it wants to tell: It is on a *narrative quest.* Sometimes it doesn't succeed, and we feel frustrated, but sometimes it succeeds, and we feel that our lives have been well spent. What type of a quest is it? Here MacIntyre seeks support in what ethicists call *virtue theory:* It is a quest for becoming a good person and developing a good character—not in the sense that we are never supposed to do anything that might be wrong or risqué, but in the sense that we develop consistently good behavioral habits that kick in when we are in doubt or under severe temptation. The narrative quest is a quest for the good life, and we build up a good life by actively seeking it. Of course, this may mean different things under different circumstances. The historical traditions of which we are a part will determine what kind of narrative quest we are on: In our culture the quest must involve a sense of justice, courage, and truthfulness, says MacIntyre. Others might add that it also should involve a sense of caring and compassion.

Philosophers are divided over this approach to ideal human behavior. Some believe that personal identity is nothing but a figment of the Western imagination (see Chapter 7). Some feel uncomfortable about linking the individual to her or his culture as though we aren't allowed to be—or aren't capable of being—critical of our own traditions. Some question the whole idea of conforming to a dominant culture. (Box 1.1 discusses the phenomenon of postmodernism and its view of historical truth as being relative.) Others feel uncomfortable discounting rationality as the deciding factor,

Box 1.1 POSTMODERNISM: TRUTH IS A MATTER OF PERSPECTIVE

The German philosopher Friedrich Nietzsche (1844–1900) claimed that there are no facts, only theory; by this he (probably) did not mean that we can't determine whether or not it rained last night, but that everything that passes through our senses and our brains already has been flavored by our own preconceived notions about reality, based on our culture, education, personal history, and other factors. This view is known as *perspectivism,* and in the 1980s and 1990s it developed into a popular worldview among the Western intelligentsia, under the title of *postmodernism:* No group should have a monopoly on interpreting history or reality their way; any interpretation by any group or individual is as valid as any other. While the postmodern view was a breath of fresh air that liberated much of late-twentieth-century thinking from the prevailing perspectives offered by the traditional Western, "Eurocentric" view of history, it also brought with it a problem when taken to an extreme: that all perspectives became relative. Anyone's spin on history became as correct as anyone else's, regardless of relevance or insight. For many, the upside of historical perspectivism is that many cultural perspectives that had gone unnoticed by mainstream history, such as American Indian perspectives, would now be added to the spectrum of historical reality. The downside is that, according to extreme historical perspectivism, any group is entitled to its own view—for example, the view that the Holocaust never took place. To most people, including me, this is not only an incorrect but also an offensive viewpoint: The Holocaust *did* most certainly happen, and there are people still alive today whose memories of the attempted annihilation of entire population groups by Hitler are as fresh as the day they were liberated from the death camps in 1945. In other words, we can't just declare that there are no facts; some events need to be interpreted in order to glean the reasons why they may have happened, but other forms of evidence are hard and concrete, with undeniable physical traces to substantiate that they did happen. At best, the postmodern view allows us to include viewpoints that have otherwise been ignored by history; at worst, postmodernism disregards the idea of evidence and views history through the dyed lenses of *today's* concerns, rather than the concerns of the past.

and still others think it is demeaning to reduce human beings to characters in a story. But many believe that MacIntyre has given people a tool with which to carve a future, a renewed sense of belonging in a contemporary world, even if we come from faraway places (as I myself do, having immigrated to the United States from Denmark). We find ourselves part of a greater whole that we perhaps didn't realize existed, and it gives us a renewed sense of social responsibility. In other words, MacIntyre suggests deliberately shaping our personal and social history so that it makes good moral sense.

However, the problems embedded in the program MacIntyre suggests are considerable, because what if we immigrate into a culture with moral problems in its past (such as slavery)? Do we then have to adopt the past that the native-born citizens share and carry on their guilt and resentments? Or can we perhaps be the voice of the future, calling for putting old struggles aside for the sake of an identity we might share in years to come? Another problem relates to what is called *ethical relativism,* the theory that morals are relative to their cultural context: MacIntyre says we should embrace our traditions and remember the stories of our ancestors, but what if our cultural tradition says to kill the infidel, practice infanticide, or keep a race or a gender in bondage? Does that mean we have to accept our tradition uncritically and perpetuate it? And if we refuse, how can we then embark on a narrative quest that reflects our historical heritage? Just because something is traditional doesn't automatically make it morally acceptable. MacIntyre himself seems to be torn between taking responsibility for the moral flaws in our history and embracing our cultural traditions; sometimes we just can't do both! Critics have pointed out that MacIntyre talks mainly about creating one's own story as a character who has "got it together," morally speaking; but he doesn't talk much about how we can learn from the stories of others who have done the same thing or even from the fictional stories of others. Paul Ricoeur tries to address this issue.

Understanding Ourselves as Story: Paul Ricoeur

One of the major philosophers of the late twentieth century is Paul Ricoeur (b. 1913), who has divided his time between his native country of France and the United States, and who for most of his professional life has striven to reconcile the viewpoints of American and continental (European) philosophers. Through his trilogy *Time and Narrative* (1984, 1985, and 1988), readers have been treated to a comprehensive view of how important the narrative structure is in human lives. However, the crowning achievement in his theory of narrativity is perhaps *Oneself as Another* (1992); you'll find an excerpt at the end of this chapter. For Ricoeur, our ability to understand the structure of a story is a means to comprehending ourselves and our personal identity; here Ricoeur provides the philosophical underpinning for the work of those therapists who encourage their clients to think of their lives as a story with themselves playing the part of the hero. In addition, he believes that he solves the problem MacIntyre's readers face, by creating the connection between understanding a story and understanding oneself as a story.

Ricoeur sees three levels to a story. The first is the simple *plot structure,* which should be based on what we know of real life. In other words, the plot has to be believable in some sense—not that it can't deal with fantastic events, but it must show that the writer understands what Ricoeur calls "the

world of action." It must reflect our belief that our actions have effects and can't be undone and that some events may be more than the sum of their parts: They may be symbolic. At the second level we read the story and "suspend the question of the relationship between fiction and truth." This means we make believe that the story is true while we read it. At this level the story merely *entertains* us. We read the events chronologically, moving from point to point until we have finished the story. But without the third level we would never understand the story. The third level is the level of *comprehension:* It allows us to reach back and remember earlier parts of the story as we read, to connect the elements. The details of the story come together to form a whole, and we understand *why* things happened in the story. This works even when we read a story we already know: We jump right into the third level, because we know both the beginning and the end. We don't read it for the surprise value of the plot, but we understand, in light of the ending, how the early events lead in that direction; our memory repeats the order of events in reverse.

Let's illustrate this with a few examples that may be familiar to you; I choose them from the world of films, although Ricoeur himself never refers to films. (Box 1.2 deals with Ricoeur's theory applied to films.) However, the plot pattern remains the same. The classic movie *Psycho* has a surprise ending that works only once; if you've seen the film, you know the shocker (the identity of Norman Bates's mother). The first time you watched it, you approached it from levels 1 and 2, but the second time you see it, you're at level 3: You know what the surprise is going to be, and so you watch throughout the film for clues that it is going to happen. This can, of course, also be done simply by remembering the film; you don't have to actually see it a second time (though I recommend it). Three examples that are even better are the 1990s films *Pulp Fiction* and *The Usual Suspects* and the 2000 film *The Sixth Sense:* If you have seen them, you'll probably agree that *Pulp Fiction* barely has a level 1 or even a level 2, because it is all-important

The Sixth Sense, Buena Vista Pictures, 1999. A small boy, Cole (Haley Joel Osment), is haunted by terrifying visions of, and even physical encounters with, dead people; during these "events" the boy is injured. Psychiatrist Dr. Malcolm Crowe (Bruce Willis) seems to be the only adult he is willing to open up to, although Crowe initially doesn't believe the boy's visions are real. However, as the story progresses, we find that in helping Cole, Crowe realizes a disturbing truth about his own situation. This is at least one way the plot can be described. If you watch the film for the second time, your description is likely to be different. In Ricoeur's model of three levels of understanding, we follow the story according to level 1 and level 2, but level 3—the comprehension level, reached at the end—makes us reevaluate the entire plotline we've followed.

that you watch the whole thing and then regroup the action sequences in your own mind. It is a film that works exclusively on level 3, since the plot is not presented chronologically. *The Usual Suspects* has a level 1, a level 2, as well as a level 3, but level 3 tells a completely different story than do the two other levels! The identity of "Kaiser Sosa" may change from viewing to viewing. As a matter of fact, it may take you more than two viewings to "get" level 3. *The Sixth Sense* also has all three levels; viewers usually don't reach the comprehension level until the very end, and the

understanding of the plot involves a backward unraveling of the entire story—which is why many viewers just must see it again to find out if the film works on both level 2 and level 3. It does.

The third level also lets the story involve us personally. We read an exciting book and discover that hours have passed. ("I couldn't put it down!" is the blurb on the cover of a best-seller.) When reading, we are immersed in another time, one in which we vicariously live the lives of the people in the story. This is what Ricoeur calls *narrative time,* and we may live the lives of generations

Box 1.2   IT'S NARRATIVE TIME AT THE MOVIES

Ricoeur finds it sad that the "day of the novel" seems to have come to an end. He predicts that we will miss out on a tremendous experience of sharing in another time and living several lives at once if we stop reading novels and that we will lose a unique way of understanding how we structure our own lives if we lose access to narrative time. Ricoeur doesn't seem to have all the facts, though: More paperbacks and best-sellers are sold now than ever before. They may not be classics, but they certainly have the classic plot structure with a beginning, a middle, and an ending. Literary experiments that tried to dispense with the narrative structure are out of style, and today novels are being published in English whose roots are in non-Western traditions,

providing new blood to an old genre. So it seems that many people are reading books; but even if we weren't, we would still be exposed to *narrative time,* because we go to the movies. Ricoeur was once asked about movies and narrative time, and he answered, "I never watch movies." That is Ricoeur's loss, because in the movie theater (and to a lesser extent, at home with a video), we experience the same extraordinary thing: We live other lives in other time structures in the span of two hours; we follow the plot and the characters through Ricoeur's three levels; and we take them with us afterward and even use the characters as role models when we feel the need.

in the time it actually took us to read the book. It is on the level of narrative time that we become involved in the story: We see the hero as a role model, we are instructed by the terrible fate of bad people, we are seduced by the charm of the rogue—and we close the book and take it with us, in our heart.

But how is the narrative structure evident in the way we understand ourselves? Fictional narratives as well as true-story narratives share elements that differ profoundly from our own personal narratives as we can understand them. Fictional and true-story narratives have a beginning, a middle, and an ending. They are told by the author who selects the plot and the subplots; usually the author is aloof, telling the story in the third person, but sometimes we are treated to the pretense that she or he is experiencing the story as it unfolds. *The Blair Witch Project* (1999) is a good example of this pretense. But it is an illusion; of course, the author is in control of the story (even if, as authors of fiction know, the story seems to take on a life of its own as it is being written). When you tell your own personal story, you are most definitely not its author; at best you are merely the coauthor, with an expression Ricoeur borrows

from Aristotle. And what about the beginning and the end? Ricoeur says in *Oneself as Another,*

> Now there is nothing in real life that serves as a narrative beginning; memory is lost in the hazes of early childhood; my birth and, with greater reason, the act through which I was conceived belong more to the history of others—in this case, to my parents—than to me. As for my death, it will finally be recounted only in the stories of those who survive me. I am always moving toward my death, and this prevents me from ever grasping it as a narrative end.[2]

So we have no memory of our beginning, and we will never be able to tell about our ending: all we can do is explore "the middle," and the middle is a mess—of numerous story lines, interweaving plots that involve other people's histories. Nothing presents itself as *the* plot of our life history, but we are constantly caught up in remembering bits and pieces and anticipate other bits and pieces. But this is precisely to Ricoeur the narrative challenge. Instead of saying that human lives can't be told as stories because they don't have a story structure by themselves, Ricoeur says we must *impose a story structure on our own history,* as a coauthor, and select the plots we find important so we bring some order into the chaos that a real life is:

> As for the notion of the narrative unity of a life, it must be seen as an unstable mixture of fabulation and actual experience. It is precisely because of the elusive character of real life that we need the help of fiction to organize life retrospectively, after the fact, prepared to take as provisional and open to revision any figure of emplotment borrowed from fiction or from history.[3]

So when the unexpected happens to us, when fear and anguish hold us in their icy grip, when we suffer dreadful losses, and above all when we face the prospect of dying, we should think about the good stories we have read (or seen, for the movie-goers). The story of Jesus Christ on the cross has helped many an anguished soul, says Ricoeur. And we can add endless examples: The story of Nelson Mandela can't but be a comfort to those who find themselves persecuted for their political convictions. Literature has provided us with characters like Jean Valjean in *Les Miserables* who rise above the pettiness of their surroundings in spite of their own shady past. Countless fans of Western movies have found strength and comfort facing difficult situations, remembering the character of Will Kane in *High Noon* (1952) as he walks down the dusty cowtown street toward his meeting with the bad guys, just because he feels it is his duty. In the world's most watched film so far, *Titanic* (1997), the ill-fated lovers Rose and Jack decided that love is more important than individual survival; and who is to say how many of us make fateful decisions in our lives based on such moments on the screen? It isn't just being star-struck or having no original thoughts of one's own, as jaded critics might think; it is a genuine appropriation of a fictional core event, an assimilation into our own history and our own narrative structure so we understand our lives better and feel more in control, for better or worse.

Ricoeur seems to think this is always for the good, but these applications of fictional stories to real lives have also led to bank robberies (imitating *Natural Born Killers* and *Get It On*) and murder or attempted murder (imitating *Taxi Driver, Scream, Scream II,* and many other films).[4] Opening the gateway for fiction to become a favored template for the meaning and structure of our lives also opens up for the risk that some of us may choose to see the meaning we are looking for in the life of the "bad guy," not just in the life of the "hero." This is one of the elements that Ricoeur hasn't resolved in his theory; however, he has pointed out some extremely important features about the human propensity for storytelling and for telling our own story: that we don't tell stories in isolation. They are meant to have an audience; and as we live our stories and tell them, we link up with the lives and stories of others, all the way up to the cultural level. As an old school friend of mine once remarked during a rare class reunion, after we had shared life stories until 2:00 A.M., "We are all each other's stories." Our own personal stories weave in and out of each other's, and together they make up a greater cultural—and even human—identity. In Chapter 9 we return to the concept of a human social identity created through storytelling.

Stories of Human Nature

Regardless of their individual differences, Ricoeur, MacIntyre, and other thinkers such as Louis Mink, Wayne Booth, David Carr, Hayden White, Peter Kemp, Lawrence Hinman, and Martha Nussbaum all agree that we understand ourselves as cultural and individual beings particularly well if we see our lives as stories. Furthermore, they say we can learn much about human lives through the treasures of stories available to our culture. Taking the cue from their suggestion, we shall look at some stories trying to make sense of what it is to be human: Each chapter concludes with one or more stories from film or literature illustrating a theory of human nature.

In a sense, most stories seem to comment on human nature: Classic plots include the loner who joins/saves the group; the individual who succumbs to temptation/wins over temptation; the individual who seeks something vital to his or her happiness or salvation; the good twin and the evil twin; the young person who finds identity through a personal struggle; the mother/father/lover who sacrifices herself or himself to save the life of a loved one. This means that most stories about human nature have an underlying idea of what human nature is like and what humans ought to be like: a descriptive view and a normative view. Whenever we have a story about people (or animals symbolizing people, such as Adams's *Watership Down* and Disney's *The Lion King*), we often have an idea of what an ideal person should be like; and then we see, in the story, how the people measure up. A famous type of story of human nature tells of children lost in the wild and raised by another population: Traditionally, it was by wild animals, but these days such stories may involve children being raised by robots or aliens (like the character 7 of 9 in *Star Trek: Voyager*). Probably the most famous of all such stories is Kipling's tale of Mowgli in *The Jungle Book,* and in the Narratives section of this chapter you will find an excerpt from the original novel. A television series that developed the exploration of what it means to be human into an art form was the Emmy-winning comedy series *Third Rock from the Sun:* Alien noncorporeal beings on a mission from their home in outer space have taken on human bodies and human identities without having a clue as to human behavior or interrelationships, and they have to find out through trial and error, episode after episode, what it means to be parents and children, males and females, lovers, colleagues, people of different ethnic identities, and so on.

At the end of this chapter we encounter a story that has by now achieved the status of a classic, although the original television series came to an end several years ago: *Star Trek: The Next Generation.* The episode "The Measure of a Man" remains one of the most thought-provoking in the series, because it explores the very question of human nature from the viewpoint of someone who looks human and, for all intents and purposes, acts like a human in significant ways, but who is a product of an advanced technology. Should such an individual be considered a piece of property or be regarded as a person with the right to self-determination? In other words, what are our criteria for *personhood,* and are they sufficient when challenged?

Study Questions

1. List three classical attempts at defining human nature, and comment on their accuracy and shortcomings.

2. How is the case study of "the man with two brains" related to the human urge to tell stories?

3. What does MacIntyre mean by humans being on a "narrative quest"? Explain.

4. What are Ricoeur's three levels of story comprehension? Are these levels specific for the understanding of *stories,* or could they be applied to any kind of comprehension, such as of a math problem?

5. How does Ricoeur propose that we achieve a better understanding of ourselves through storytelling?

Primary Readings and Narratives

Concluding this chapter are two primary readings and three "narratives," or stories. The primary readings are an excerpt from Paul Ricoeur's book *Oneself as Another* and an excerpt from Richard Hanley's *The Metaphysics of Star Trek.* The first narrative is a summary of an episode from *Star Trek: The Next Generation,* "The Measure of a Man." The second is a summary and an excerpt from Rudyard Kipling's original story of Mowgli, *The Jungle Book,* and the third is an excerpt from Ursula K. Le Guin's novel *The Telling.*

Primary Reading

Oneself as Another

PAUL RICOEUR

Excerpt, 1992.

By narrating a life of which I am not the author as to existence, I make myself its coauthor as to its meaning. Moreover, it is neither by chance nor by error that, in the opposite sense, so many Stoic philosophers interpreted life itself, life lived, as playing a role in a play we have not written and whose author, as a result, retreats outside of the role. These exchanges between the multiple sense of the term "author" and "authorship" contribute to the wealth of meaning of the very notion of agency. . . .

As for the notion of the narrative unity of a life, it must be seen as an unstable mixture of fabulation and actual experience. It is precisely because of the elusive character of real life that we need the help of fiction to organize life retrospectively, after the fact, prepared to take as provisional and open to revision any figure of emplotment borrowed from fiction or from history. In this way, with the help of the narrative beginnings which our reading has made familiar to us, straining this feature somewhat, we stabilize the real beginnings formed by the initiatives (in the strong sense of the term) we take. And we also have the experience, however incomplete, of what is meant by ending a course of action, a slice of life. Literature helps us in a sense to fix the outline of these provisional ends. As for death, do not the narratives provided by literature serve to soften the sting of anguish in the face of the unknown, of nothingness, by giving it in imagination the shape of this or that death, exemplary in one way or another? Thus fiction has a role to play in the apprenticeship of dying. The meditation on the Passion of Christ has accompanied in this way more than one believer to the last threshold. When F. Kermode or W. Benjamin utter the word "consolation" in this regard, one must not cry self-delusion too hastily. As a form of counterdesolation, consolation can be a lucid manner—just as lucid as Aristotelian *katharsis*—of mourning for oneself. Here,

too, a fruitful exchange can be established between literature and being-toward-death.

Is the intertwining of life histories with one another hostile to the narrative understanding nourished by literature? Or does it not find in the framing of one narrative within another, examples of which abound in literature, a model of intelligibility? And does not each fictive history, in confronting the diverse fates belonging to different protagonists, provide models of interaction in which the entanglement is clarified by the competition of narrative programs?

The final objection rests on a misunderstanding which is not always easy to dispel. One may well believe that the literary narrative, because it is retrospective, can inform only a meditation on the past part of our life. The literary narrative is retrospective only in a very particular sense: it is simply in the eyes of the narrator that the events recounted appear to have occurred in the past. The past of narration is but the quasi past of the narrative voice. Now among the facts recounted in the past tense we find projects, expectations, and anticipations by means of which the protagonists in the narrative are oriented toward their mortal future. . . . In other words, the narrative also recounts care. In a sense, it only recounts care. This is why there is nothing absurd in speaking about the narrative unity of a life, under the sign of narratives that teach us how to articulate narratively retrospection and prospection.

The conclusion of this discussion, then, is that literary narratives and life histories, far from being mutually exclusive, are complementary, despite, or even because of, their contrast. This dialectic reminds us that the narrative is part of life before being exiled from life in writing; it returns to life along the multiple paths of appropriation and at the price of the unavoidable tensions just mentioned.

Study Questions

1. What do you think Ricoeur means by saying that "fiction has a role to play in the apprenticeship of dying"? Is he right? Why or why not?

2. When Ricoeur says that "the narrative recounts care," he is referring to a concept introduced by the German philosopher Heidegger that human life is always oriented toward being interested in, and concerned about, ourself and our surroundings. Is he right that all stories reveal such a concern?

3. Try to tell an episode from your life as if you were telling a story with a meaning. Is Ricoeur right that telling about our life as a story makes us coauthors of its meaning?

Primary Reading

The Metaphysics of *Star Trek*

RICHARD HANLEY

Excerpt, 1997.

"Human" and "human"—What Is Human?

COLONIST: "You're not human."
DATA: "That is correct. I am an android."
—TNG: *"The Ensigns of Command"*

"Ugly giant bags of mostly water . . ."
—The Microbrain, *referring to the* Enterprise-D *crew,*
     TNG: *"Home Soil"*

Since Spock genetically is half human, isn't it pointless for him to spurn his humanity? And since Data undoubtedly is not a member of the human species, isn't it pointless for Data to aspire to be human? Yes and no. "Human," as we ordinarily use the term, has at least three distinct meanings. The first is the sense in which one is human if and only if one is a member of the genus *Homo;* in this biological sense, Data will never be human. *Star Trek* suggests that this biological sense may well include extraterrestrial species, such as Vulcans, Klingons, Romulans, Ferengi, Bajorans, and Cardassians. There are genetic similarities among all these species, and in *TNG:* "The Chase" the crew of the *Enterprise-D* learns why. A puzzle planted in the genetic code of various humanoid species leads the *Enterprise-D* to a message from the past: an ancient race has planted its genetic seed on various planets throughout the Alpha quadrant, so all humanoid species have a common origin. I shall stick to *Star Trek* language and use "humanoid" to designate the strictly biological sense of "human"—the sense that the colonists in "The Ensigns of Command" have in mind when they remark that Data is not human.

One is human in the second sense if one has roughly the same psychological characteristics as fully developed terrestrial human beings. It is in this sense that Spock struggles to be less human, and that Data aspires to be human. It is in this sense that Kirk accuses Spock of "becoming more and more human," and that Picard, in *TNG:* "The Quality of Life," characterizes a particular decision of Data's—to put Picard's life at risk to prevent the destruction of possibly intelligent machines—as "the most human decision" Data ever made. I shall reserve *human* in italics for this second, psychological sense.

The third ordinary sense of "human" is the most elusive but also the most important: it is the moral or ethical sense of the term. When people speak of "human rights," for instance, it is in this moral sense. Suppose that someone mounts the following argument: a human fetus is human, and all humans have a right not to be killed, therefore a fetus has a right not to be killed. Such an argument seems to trade on the equivocation between different senses of "human." A human fetus unquestionably is humanoid, but one doubts that all humanoids have a right not to be killed. And even if all *humans* have a right not to be killed, a human fetus unquestionably lacks some of the psychological properties of fully developed terrestrial beings. It is the third, moral sense of "human" that matters to the argument; until we know what being human in this sense amounts to, we cannot judge whether a human fetus qualifies.

Star Trek helps us to investigate this third, moral sense, which the *Star Trek* writers designate by speaking of "sentience." As long as we remain rooted on Earth, it is difficult even to *see* this third sense, since we are so used to the idea that humanoids and *humans* are the only sorts of individuals with (for instance) a right not to be killed. The United Federation of Planets recognizes not terrestrial human rights per se but "sentient" rights, and it is clear that the Federation extends the notion of human rights at least to other humanoids. For instance, it surely would be just as wrong (other things being equal) to kill Spock as it would be to kill McCoy.

Here we must abandon the usage of the *Star Trek* writers, since a sentient individual is simply an individual aware of its sense impressions. While sentience might be necessary for "humanity" in the moral sense, it is unlikely to be sufficient. A chicken is sentient, but I doubt that we intend to include chickens in our discussion of "human rights." A better term—the one philosophers use to capture this moral sense of "human"—is "person." The important philosophical question which *Star Trek* can help us to answer is, What is personhood? Being humanoid is not sufficient, since a humanoid corpse is not a person. And while there is no doubt that being *human* is sufficient for personhood, the example of Spock shows that it's not strictly necessary. But is being humanoid necessary for personhood? *Star Trek,* in its famous search for "new life and new civilizations," shows us that the answer is No.

Study Questions

1. What are the three senses of "human" mentioned by Hanley?

2. What does Hanley mean by saying that "While sentience might be necessary for 'humanity' in the moral sense, it is unlikely to be sufficient"?

3. Read the first narrative, "The Measure of a Man," and apply Hanley's three senses of "human." Which sense is at issue in Data's situation? Explain.

Narrative

Star Trek: The Next Generation, "The Measure of a Man"

ROBERT SCHEERER (DIRECTOR) AND
MELISSA M. SNODGRASS (WRITER)

Television, 1989. Summary.

First, the cast of characters: Data, a unique android and high-ranking officer in Starfleet who wants to be human more than anything else; Captain Jean-Luc Picard, the captain of the starship *Enterprise;* Guinan, the long-lived bartender and wise woman; Maddox, a visiting scientist; Captain Louvois, a visiting, unsentimental officer, here serving as a courtroom judge; and Riker, first officer and a good friend of Data's.

Paying a visit to the *Enterprise,* Maddox announces that he is going to take Data away to perform experiments on "it." His goal is to create a new breed of androids that can be made available to all starships. When informed that this will involve downloading his memories into a memory bank, shutting him down, and dismantling him, Data refuses, worried that the subtle elements that make up his personality will not survive such a procedure. Maddox insists, and Data's only recourse is to resign from Starfleet in order to avoid being commanded to go with Maddox. As Data packs his things, we see what he chooses to take along: a book from Picard, his medals, and a hologram of another crew member, now dead: Tasha Yar.

In the meantime, Maddox inquires about Data's status. Is Data's refusal the same as if the main computer refused to work? A visiting officer with a legal background, Philippa Louvois, straightens out the issue: For the main computer to refuse would be unthinkable, she says, because the computer is only property. But in that case, since Data is artificial, perhaps he is just property, too? If so, then Data would have no right to life or to privacy. Maddox says Picard is fooled by Data's human likeness: If Data were a box on wheels, the request would never have been a problem. Louvois now does some research and finds that Data is indeed the property of Starfleet and can't resign. Picard challenges the ruling. As a result, a hearing is held, with Louvois presiding as a judge. She chooses Picard to defend Data, and logically the role of prosecutor falls to First Officer Riker. At first he refuses, because he considers himself a close personal friend of Data's and finds himself having a conflict of interest. But when told that if he refuses, Louvois will rule summarily that "Data is a toaster," he agrees to do his best.

At the hearing, Riker eloquently demonstrates that Data is a machine: His hand can be removed, and he can be turned off, just like any computer. In Riker's words, "Pinocchio is broken." Picard is shaken and requests a recess. In the lounge he confers with his good friend, the bartender Guinan, about the case, and Guinan puts her finger on the real issue: If Data is property, then all future Datas will be property too. In that case, what does Starfleet intend to do with them? Put them in dangerous positions, subject them to long hours of hard labor, think of them as disposable? All through history there have been *disposable populations,* she says, and Picard realizes that she is talking about slavery.

Back at the hearing, Picard now has a focus for his defense. What is at stake, he says, is whether or not Data is sentient.[5] He asks Maddox to define *sentience,* and Maddox offers the following definition: *being self-aware, being intelligent, and being conscious.* Of course, Data is a machine, says Picard, but that is irrelevant. Of course, he is made by humans—but so are human children. What is relevant is whether or not he fulfills the three criteria of sentience. Data is certainly intelligent; with his computer brain, he is far more intelligent and faster-thinking than any other crew member. Picard now has Data on the stand and asks him the simple question of what he is doing; Data answers, with full self-awareness,

that he is in the process of having his legal status determined, which may cost him his life. In addition, Picard asks Data to explain the items he has packed: Why the book? Why the medals? They "mean something to him." And why the hologram of Tasha Yar? A shocking revelation, if one hasn't watched the episode Data refers to: He and Tasha had a brief sexual relationship, and he felt very close to her. (This is interesting in itself, since *Star Trek* fans will know that at this point in the series, Data didn't have any emotions, because he hadn't had an emotional microchip implanted yet! But Data's sense of loyalty and friendship indicates that even at this stage, he is not wholly without emotional attachments.)

And now for the third criterion: Picard turns to Louvois and asks her whether she knows what exactly consciousness is. She replies that she doesn't (and as you will see in an upcoming chapter, neither do scientists or philosophers—yet). Now Picard adds that he doesn't know, either, but he knows that if Data is not granted the rights of a person, then future Datas are condemned to be members of a race that can be used as others see fit, without any regard for their personal dignity or interests. The future of Data's "descendants" depends on this ruling—and the moral legacy of Starfleet, the court, and the judge will be how they determine this issue. Louvois, shocked, supplies the word that Picard's speech hinted at: *Slavery.* Now she finally speaks, asking the fundamental question: Does Data have a soul?

She can't determine it, she says—but since we don't know if we have souls ourselves, Data should be allowed the freedom to explore the issue. As Picard points out, the *Enterprise* is always looking for new life-forms, and *there it sits,* looking back at them. Louvois rules that Data is a person with all rights to pursue his own destiny; the implication is that should other Datas be created, they, too, will be persons. So Maddox is denied his request, Data officially refuses to comply, and, in the end, Maddox finds that he is referring to Data as "he" rather than "it."

This ruling became a watershed decision within the *STTNG* series; several subsequent episodes drew on the impact. One in particular stands out, "The Quality of Life." In this episode, robots have been produced without humanoid shape, the "boxes on wheels" that Maddox was referring to. Designed to be able to go into

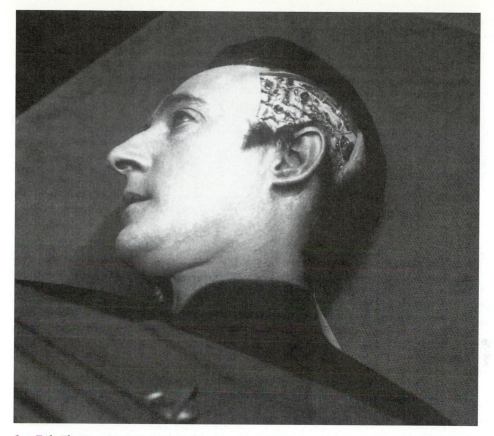

Star Trek: The Next Generation, television series. Data (Brent Spiner) is an android, an artificial intelligence in human form. He wishes to become human, in a sense, as the puppet Pinocchio did, but he is constructed with decidedly nonhuman traits: His brain can compute far more mental operations at a time than a human's; he is extremely strong; and he has no understanding of human emotions. However, he does grasp the meaning of friendship, of accomplishments, and of self. In the episode "The Measure of a Man," a scientist wishes to dismantle Data in order to duplicate him, and Data protests. The issue raised is, Is Data a person with the right to self-determination, or is he a thing to be bought and sold—will he and future Datas be treated like slaves?

harm's way without the loss of human life, these robots are placed in a situation that will almost inevitably destroy them. Through Data's intervention, it becomes clear to the administration that not only are the boxes sentient, but they also have developed a high moral standard: When the choice is left to them, they choose the possibility of self-sacrifice in order to help an injured box complete the dangerous task. With this episode, the concept of personhood is expanded even further in the *Star Trek* universe, thanks to Data, who has been through the struggle for recognition himself.

In the final chapter we return to the question of Data's personhood and put it into the context of a heated contemporary debate: Are all human beings persons? And even if there are no androids yet, perhaps there already are other beings who are not human, but who should nevertheless be considered persons?

Study Questions

1. Is Data a "Pinocchio"? If you recall the story of the wooden puppet, explain the similarities and differences between Data and Pinocchio.

2. What does the question of slavery have to do with whether we think of someone as a person?

3. The question of acknowledging androids as persons may be far-fetched, at least for the foreseeable future; does the story have a point that is more relevant to the current human population on earth? (You may want to think in terms of genetic engineering and cloning.)

4. Identify the features that, according to the story, make Data a person, and discuss them in detail. Under such criteria, would all humans qualify as persons? Explain.

Narrative

The Jungle Book, The Second Jungle Book

RUDYARD KIPLING

Short stories, 1894 and 1895. Summary and Excerpt.

Digging through the layers of cultural assumptions to get back to the original story of Mowgli in the jungles of India is an obstacle course: For one thing, there are numerous popularized versions of varying quality, from the 1940 Hollywood film to the Disney animated film (1967) to computer-animated versions; and each in its own way provide a spin that departs from the original story. For another, there is the late-twentieth-century political criticism of Kipling: A British novelist from the late-nineteenth and early-twentieth centuries, born in India, Kipling has for many become the voice of colonial England, lording it over the natives in the colonies. This image may or may not be fair—but the story of Mowgli in the jungle has seemed to rise above our changing perceptions of colonial politics to speak to something deep in our imagination. Predating the stories of Tarzan by decades, the stories of Mowgli tell about a young human boy born in the outskirts of the jungles of central India, but growing up in the local pack of wolves, with a bear (Baloo) and a panther (Bagheera) as his best friends and teachers. While not as graceful or as instinct-driven as the jungle people (the animals), Mowgli still grows up to become the leader of the animals because of his human superiority: his cunning and his ability to outstare any animal. But even so, the jungle folk know well the weaknesses of the human tribe and often question the assumption that humans are supposed to be such wise creatures.

How did Mowgli end up in the jungle? A man-eating tiger, the famous Shere Kahn, chased him into the jungle when he was an infant. He ended up in the den of Mother and Father Wolf and their four cubs; the wolves adopted him and defended him against the tiger and the other animals until he could defend himself. The pack of wolves accepted him on the advice of Baloo, Bagheera, and the leader of the wolves, Akela. Years later, when Mowgli has grown into boyhood, he feels compelled to go and seek out his own people, the humans in the village. The experiment proves to be a bad experience, though: Mowgli is as alien among the humans as he was when he first came to the jungle: He speaks no human language; he understands nothing about human ways, including the use of fire or money; and he thinks of humans as very childish, silly creatures. Learning that Shere Kahn is back and hunting him, Mowgli ambushes the tiger with the help of his wolf brothers and the village cattle and kills him. But now he finds that the villagers headed by Buldeo, the village hunter, are hunting *him* because they think he is a sorcerer, and he returns to his home, the jungle, to recoup and regroup. The old wise Alpha wolf, Akela, advises Mowgli:

> "Presently, Little Brother, a man with a gun follows our trail—if, indeed, he be not already on it."
>
> "But why should he? Men have cast me out. What more do they need?" said Mowgli angrily.
>
> "Thou art a man, Little Brother," Akela returned. "It is not for *us*, the Free Hunters, to tell thee what thy brethren do, or why."
>
> He had just time to snatch up his paw as the skinning-knife cut deep into the ground below. Mowgli

struck quicker than an average human eye could follow, but Akela was a wolf; and even a dog, who is very far removed from the wild wolf, his ancestor, can be waked out of a deep sleep by a cart-wheel touching his flank, and can spring away unharmed before that wheel comes on.

"Another time," Mowgli said quietly, returning the knife to its sheath, "speak of the Man-Pack and of Mowgli in *two* breaths—not one."

"Phff! That is a sharp tooth," said Akela, snuffing at the blade's cut in the earth, "but living with the Man-Pack has spoiled thine eye, Little Brother. I could have killed a buck while thou wast striking."

Bagheera sprang to his feet, thrust up his head as far as he could, sniffed, and stiffened through every curve in his body. Gray Brother followed his example quickly, keeping a little to his left to get the wind that was blowing from the right, while Akela bounded fifty yards up wind, and, half-crouching, stiffened too. Mowgli looked on enviously. He could smell things as very few human beings could, but he had never reached the hair-trigger-like sensitiveness of a Jungle nose; and his three months in the smoky village had set him back sadly. However, he dampened his finger, rubbed it on his nose, and stood erect to catch the upper scent, which, though it is the faintest, is the truest.

"Man!" Akela growled, dropping on his haunches.

"Buldeo!" said Mowgli, sitting down. "He follows our trail, and yonder is the sunlight on his gun. Look!"

It was no more than a splash of sunlight, for a fraction of a second, on the brass clamps of the old Tower musket, but nothing in the Jungle winks with just that flash, except when the clouds race over the sky. Then a piece of mica, or a little pool, or even a highly-polished leaf will flash like a heliograph. But that day was cloudless and still.

"I knew men would follow," said Akela triumphantly. "Not for nothing have I led the Pack."

The four cubs said nothing, but ran down hill on their bellies, melting into the thorn and underbrush as a mole melts into a lawn.

"Where go ye, and without word?" Mowgli called.

"H'sh! We roll his skull here before midday!" Gray Brother answered.

"Back! Back and wait! Man does not eat man!" Mowgli shrieked.

"Who was a wolf but now? Who drove the knife at me for thinking he might be Man?" said Akela,

as the four wolves turned back sullenly and dropped to heel.

"Am I to give reason for all I choose to do?" said Mowgli furiously.

"That is Man! There speaks Man!" Bagheera muttered under his whiskers. "Even so did men talk round the King's cages at Oodeypore. We of the Jungle know that Man is wisest of all. If we trusted our ears we should know that of all things he is most foolish." Raising his voice, he added, "The Man-cub is right in this. Men hunt in packs. To kill one, unless we know what the others will do, is bad hunting. Come, let us see what this Man means toward us."

"We will not come," Gray Brother growled. "Hunt alone, Little Brother. *We* know our own minds. The skull would have been ready to bring by now."

Mowgli had been looking from one to the other of his friends, his chest heaving and his eyes full of tears. He strode forward to the wolves, and, dropping on one knee, said: "Do I not know my mind? Look at me!"

They looked uneasily, and when their eyes wandered, he called them back again and again, till their hair stood up all over their bodies, and they trembled in every limb, while Mowgli stared and stared.

"Now," said he, "of us five, which is leader?"

"Thou art leader, Little Brother," said Gray Brother, and he licked Mowgli's foot.

"Follow, then," said Mowgli, and the four followed at his heels with their tails between their legs.

"This comes of living with the Man-Pack," said Bagheera, slipping down after them. "There is more in the Jungle now than Jungle Law, Baloo."

The old bear said nothing, but he thought many things.

Study Questions

1. The idea of feral children, or "wild boys" (children raised by animals), is ancient and has been verified historically. However, unlike Mowgli and Tarzan, such children rarely survive their first ten years: They hardly ever learn to speak a human language if found after the age of four or five, and they seem to be imprinted on the animals who have fed them to the extent that they don't ever perceive of themselves as human. What does this indicate about human nature?

2. What do you think Kipling meant by this episode? Are humans presented as being superior to other animals or not? Explain, referring to the scene where Mowgli stares down his brother wolves.

3. Stories of animals are often used to symbolically explore truths about human nature; we call such stories *fables.* Can the story of Mowgli be interpreted as a fable? Why or why not?

Narrative

The Telling

URSULA K. LE GUIN

Novel, 2000. Summary and Excerpt.

Ursula Le Guin is a familiar name among science fiction fans, but she has also made a name for herself within mainstream American literature. If science fiction is one day to acquire status as an important literary genre (as I hope it will), it will be due partly to Le Guin's lucid futuristic visions and poetic language. Over the last decades of the twentieth century, she has explored issues of sexual discrimination, politics, and environmentalism in books such as *The Left Hand of Darkness, The Dispossessed,* and numerous other novels and short stories. Going into the twenty-first century, her book *The Telling* pulls many of her favorite themes together in a vision of the importance of storytelling for our sense of cultural and individual identity.

In a distant future, humans from Earth have colonized much of the galaxy and found that humans are in effect offspring of a much earlier colonization project—hence, the existence of hominids throughout the galaxy. Observers are routinely sent to backwater planets to maintain contact and preserve cultural history. Sutty is such an observer, sent to the planet Aka. Sutty herself is from Earth, but not the Earth we are familiar with today: Earth in Sutty's day is in the grip of extreme religious fundamentalism. On the other hand, Aka is run by a government cracking down on anything resembling religion, customs, myths, and legends. What Sutty must do is try to find a middle way in her own heart between two kinds of cultural extremism, as well as trace the history of the people of Aka as it is being eradicated, by preserving the stories of the culture for

the future in spite of the efforts of the government to uproot what it considers dangerous superstition. The storytellers have gone underground, and secret libraries are being put together in the back country. Little by little, Sutty learns about the great epic narrative of the culture, the Telling.

Elyed used that word often, unreasonable, in a literal sense: what cannot be understood by thinking. Once when Sutty was trying to find a coherent line of thought connecting several different tellings, Elyed said, "What we do is unreasonable, yoz."

"But there is a reason *for* it."

"Probably."

"What I don't understand is the pattern. The place, the importance of things in the pattern. Yesterday you were telling the story about Iaman and Deberren, but you didn't finish it, and today you read the descriptions of the leaves of the trees of the grove at the Golden Mountain. I don't understand what they have to do with each other. Or is it that on certain days a certain kind of material is proper? Or are my questions just stupid?"

"No," the maz said, and laughed her small laugh that had no teeth to show. "I get tired remembering. So I read. It doesn't matter. It's all the leaves of the tree."

"So . . . anything—anything that's in the books is equally important?"

Elyed considered. "No," she said. "Yes." She drew a shaky breath. She tired quickly when she could not rest in the stream of ritual act and language, but she never dismissed Sutty, never evaded her questions. "It's all we have. You see? It's the way we have the world. Without the telling, we don't have anything at all. The moment goes by like the water of the river. We'd tumble and spin and be helpless if we tried to live in the moment. We'd be like a baby. A baby can do it, but we'd drown. Our minds need to tell, need the telling. To hold. The past has passed, and there's nothing in the future to catch hold of. The future is nothing yet. How could anybody live there? So what we have is the words that tell what happened and what happens. What was and is."

"Memory?" Sutty said. "History?"

Elyed nodded, dubious, not satisfied by these terms. She sat thinking for some time and finally said, "We're not outside the world, yoz. You know? We are the world. We're its language. So we live and it lives. You see? If we don't say the words, what is there in our world?"

She was trembling, little spasms of the hands and mouth that she tried to conceal. Sutty thanked her with the mountain-heart gesture, apologised for wearing her out with talk. Elyed gave her small, black laugh. "Oh, yoz, I keep going with talk. Just the way the world does," she said.

Sutty went away and brooded. All this about language. It always came back to words. Like the Greeks with their Logos, the Hebrew Word that was God. But this was words. Not the Logos, the Word, but words. Not one but many, many. . . . Nobody made the world, ruled the world, told the world to be. It was. It did. And human beings made it be, made it be a human world, by saying it? By telling what was in it and what happened in it? Anything, everything—tales of heroes, maps of the stars, love songs, lists of the shapes of leaves. . . . For a moment she thought she understood.

She brought this half-formed understanding to Maz Ottiar Uming, who was easier to talk with than Elyed, wanting to try to put it into words. But Ottiar was busy with a chant, so Sutty talked to Uming, and somehow her words got contorted and pedantic. She couldn't speak her intuition.

As they struggled to understand each other, Uming Ottiar showed a bitterness, almost the first Sutty had met with among these soft-voiced teachers. Despite his impediment he was a fluent talker, and he got going, mildly enough at first: "Animals have no language.

They have their nature. You see? They know the way, they know where to go and how to go, following their nature. But we're animals with no nature. Eh? Animals with no nature! That's strange! We're so strange! We have to talk about how to go and what to do, think about it, study it, learn it. Eh? We're born to be reasonable, so we're born ignorant. You see? If nobody teaches us the words, the thoughts, we stay ignorant. If nobody shows a little child, two, three years old, how to look for the way, the signs of the path, the landmarks, then it gets lost on the mountain, doesn't it? And dies in the night, in the cold. So. So." He rocked his body a little.

Maz Ottiar, across the little room, knocked on the drum, murmuring some long chronicle of ancient days to a single, sleepy, ten-year-old listener.

Maz Uming rocked and frowned. "So, without the telling, the rocks and plants and animals go on all right. But the people don't. People wander around. They don't know a mountain from its reflection in a puddle. They don't know a path from a cliff. They hurt themselves. They get angry and hurt each other and the other things. They hurt animals because they're angry. They make quarrels and cheat each other. They want too much. They neglect things. Crops don't get planted. Too many crops get planted. Rivers get dirty with shit. Earth gets dirty with poison. People eat poison food. Everything is confused. Everybody's sick. Nobody looks after the sick people, the sick things. But that's very bad, very bad, eh? Because looking after things, that's our job, eh? Looking after things, looking after each other. Who else would do it? Trees? Rivers? Animals? They just do what they are. But we're here, and we have to learn how to be here, how to do things, how to keep things going the way they need to go. The rest of the world knows its business. Knows the One and the Myriad, the Tree and the Leaves. But all we know is how to learn. How to study, how to listen, how to talk, how to tell. If we don't tell the world, we don't know the world. We're lost in it, we die. But we have to tell it right, tell it truly. Eh? Take care and tell it truly."

Study Questions

1. Maz Uming says that animals don't need storytelling, because they have a nature, but since humans

have no nature, they need to tell stories. What does he mean? Is he (or Ursula Le Guin) correct?

2. What does Le Guin mean by saying, "If we don't tell the world, we don't know the world"? Explain.

3. Can you think of a story from your specific cultural background or family history that has provided moral support for people in times of crisis—perhaps even for you?

Review

Key Issues in Chapter 1

A Human Condition?

- The question of whether or not there is a human nature; the question of faith in human nature. The first is primarily a scientific question; the second, a moral question.

- *Different Meanings of "Human."* Different ways of approaching the question of human nature: external criteria, genetics, social criteria, and the like.

- *Descriptive and Normative Approaches.* A descriptive approach describes what is perceived as fact; a normative approach sets a moral, social, and political ideal. Even scientific descriptive theories of human nature often have a moral, normative aspect to them.

- *Some Popular Theories of Human Nature.* An overview of popular classical and contemporary definitions, with a critical commentary: Is the characteristic exclusively human, or may other species also qualify? The political animal; the featherless biped; the body as a moral symbol; the rational being; the speaking animal; the toolmaker; the warrior; the nurturer; the moral animal; the free-will agent; the child of god; the being with a soul; the artist; the two-species animal: male and female; the creature who displays emotion; the lying animal; the animal who knows it will die; the storytelling animal.

The Narrative Urge

- *The Man with Two Brains.* The roles of the right and left brain hemispheres. When the brain doesn't understand an association, it makes up a story to be able to handle the situation.

- *MacIntyre: Stories Are Our Cultural Backbone.* We must seek out the stories that unite us as a culture and take on responsibility for the past. We must try to obtain a narrative continuity to our lives and understand ourselves as part of other people's life stories.

- *Understanding Ourselves as Story: Paul Ricoeur.* There are three levels to a story: (1) simple plot structure, (2) the experience of the story, (3) understanding the story. Telling the story of our own lives helps us understand who we are and gives us narrative unity.

- *Stories of Human Nature.* A brief overview of stories with a descriptive and a normative approach.

Primary Readings

- Ricoeur, *Oneself as Another.* Narrative unity of a life is a mixture of fabulation and experience, aiding us in understanding ourselves. The experience from literature helps us articulate our own story.

- Hanley, *The Metaphysics of Star Trek.* Three senses of "human" in *Star Trek*: The first is a biological sense which implies that humanoids are related across the galaxy; the second is the terrestrial human being with its special nature; the third is a moral sense which entails personhood.

Narratives

- *Star Trek: The Next Generation,* "The Measure of a Man." The android Data is about to be transferred to a research facility and dismantled. He challenges the ruling and claims the right to self-determination. His defender, Captain Picard, seeks to show that Data satisfies the three criteria for personhood (sentience) suggested by the scientist who wants to take Data over for research: self-awareness, intelligence, and consciousness.

- Rudyard Kipling, *The Jungle Book, The Second Jungle Book*. Mowgli, the boy raised by wolves, is tracked by the hunter of the village. Claiming that he is of the jungle, Mowgli nevertheless speaks of himself as a man when discussing with his jungle friends what to do about the hunter. His jungle friends Baloo and Bagheera wonder how a creature that is supposed to be so wise can make such foolish statements.

- Ursula K. Le Guin, *The Telling*. Sutty, a woman from Earth, is sent to the planet Aka to observe its culture. Hiding from a government that cracks down on anything resembling tradition, religion, and superstition, Aka's storytellers and historians have gone underground so that the great narrative of their culture, the Telling, won't be lost.

Endnotes

1. Alasdair MacIntyre, *After Virtue,* 2nd ed. (Notre Dame, Ind.: University of Notre Dame Press, 1984), p. 216.
2. Paul Ricoeur, *Oneself as Another* (Chicago: University of Chicago Press, 1992), p. 160.
3. Ibid., p. 162.
4. For a more detailed discussion of the negative and positive influence of novels and films, please see Nina Rosenstand, *The Moral of the Story: An Introduction to Ethics,* 3rd ed. (Mountain View, Calif.: Mayfield, 2000).
5. The term *sentient* is popular in science fiction and usually means the same as *sapient:* a self-aware, cognitive being. However, in philosophy *sentient* usually means "being able to feel pain and pleasure." Here *sentient* should be taken in the meaning of *sapient.* (See also the excerpt from *The Metaphysics of* Star Trek.)

Chapter Two

Stories of Human Origins

With advocacy groups trying to mandate that schools avoid the mention of evolution and even give creationism "equal time," I find it imperative for a college text such as this one to address the issue.[1] Even if students have had ample introduction to contemporary scientific theories of human origin, a philosophical discussion of the subject is not the same as a biological one, because the purpose is different: In this context, we don't just want to find out where we came from as a species, but also want to find out *why* we are the way we are and into what future our humanity is likely to carry us. Without exploring where we came from, we can't possibly have an appreciation of our inherent tendencies and our potential as a species and as individuals. And without understanding the moral and political agendas, hidden or otherwise, of people espousing their theories of human origins, we won't be aware of the subtle shifts from descriptive theories to normative theories.

Where Do We Come From? Mythological Explanations

If we are to believe the evidence, such as myths, left behind by cultures long gone, then humans have been interested in the question of the human beginning as far back as we can trace. Only in the last few hundred years have we developed the technologies and interest in seeking physical evidence that constitute a scientific approach, so we shouldn't get stuck in the fairy-tale quality of ancient myths or deride them for being unscientific and naïve. Sometimes they carry a vision of what humans at the time would have *liked* to think about themselves, and in that respect they are not unlike our own stories, because we also tell our

tales of human origins with a slant toward what we would like to be true, as we shall see.

In Illo Tempore

The great Romanian mythologist Mircea Eliade (1907–1986) specialized in examining origin stories in ancient mythologies and demonstrated that many cultures believe in a similar scenario: The origin of the world, of life, and of humans represents a time where things were fresh, new, and good. Eliade uses a Latin expression to capture this concept: *in illo tempore,* "in that time." Gods (or God) walked the earth with humans, humans were often larger than at present, humans and animals were often indistinguishable from each other, and humans introduced (or were given by the gods, or stole from the gods) the items of food and clothing that have become staples. Very often the human origin myth involves a story of how humans acquired the use of fire, and human wit is often an important element.

But, says Eliade, over time the power *in illo tempore* wears off; gods retreat into their heaven or underground, people are less faithful to each other and less in touch with the gods, nature is ailing, and time itself is tired. How to prevent everything from grinding to a halt? *Time itself must be renewed,* and this is why the overwhelming majority of early human cultures have conducted renewal ceremonies, usually at the new year, but also sometimes after a longer cycle, perhaps thirty or one hundred years. The story of the origin of the world is ritually performed and helps bring back the original force that was present "in those days." Old enmities and squabbles are forgotten, and everyone resolves to start anew as a better person. This is the common *cyclical time perception* that we encounter in many non-Western cultures, which sees time as circular and in need of periodical renewal—as opposed to the modern Western *linear time perception,* where time is perceived to flow in one direction (from past to future) and never returns or doubles back on itself. In Chapter 8 we shall look at a nineteenth-century view of cyclical time in the philosophy of Friedrich Nietzsche. And, indeed, we still have a bit of it in our own New Year's rituals, such as New Year's resolutions, not to mention the hoopla surrounding the change from the second to the third millennium: Had Eliade been alive today, he probably would have classified the much-hyped fears of Y2K and the hopes for a New Age as typical of human renewal rituals.

Given that most cultures have believed in some form of *in illo tempore,* let's take a look at some versions of the human origin as embodied in ancient belief systems. Some versions see the creative principle as female, most see it as male, but some see it as a combination of the two. Some are violent tales of murder and rape, while others are tender stories of parenting, and they are listed in no particular order.

Stories of Origins

Egypt   The Eternal Spirit Atum vomits up a male god, Shu, and a female god, Tefnut, but loses sight of them; when Atum finally finds his children again, he hugs them and cries tears of joy—and humankind ensues from those tears.

Mesopotamia (ancient Iraq)   In the creation myth, *Enuma Elish,* which is one of the oldest written stories in existence, the goddess Tiamat (a giant sea creature) and her spouse Apsu are so bothered by the antics of their grown children that they plan to kill them. But one son, Ea, learns of their plan and kills his father. Tiamat vows revenge, but her grandson Marduk, son of Ea, slays her in a terrible battle and creates the heaven and earth from her body. The blood from Tiamat's hus-band and military commander is used to create humankind.

Africa   The *Bantu* origin myth tells of a single creator God, Bumba, who sits alone in the void. Suffering from a terrible stomachache, he vomits up the sun, the moon, and the stars and proceeds to vomit up animals and, lastly, humans. Bumba gives the earth to humans for their use and teaches them to use fire. A *Dahomey* myth sees the creative principle as an old woman, Mawu. She created everything in the universe, including humans. A human male, Awe, challenged her powers and claimed he could create life and make a person out of a tree, but it wouldn't come alive. As punishment for his gall, Mawu cooked him a meal and poisoned him. Thus Mawu also brought death into the world, as a reminder of her powers.

Scandinavia   In the beginning there was a frozen realm in the middle of the universe. But slowly the ice melted, and a human-looking figure emerged, Ymir. The next being that emerged was a cow, and Ymir drank her milk and created the race of giants (Jätter). The cow licked the icy rocks, and from the rock emerged another human-looking being, Bur. Bur married a Jätte woman, and their son Odin and his two brothers killed Ymir; they fashioned the round earth and the sky from his body, and his brains became clouds. Then Odin and his brothers walked along the new beach created by Ymir's body and saw two trees, and from them Odin created man and woman.

Israel/Palestine   In the story from Genesis that is probably the best-known origin myth to most readers in the Judeo-Christian tradition, God creates the universe, the earth, and all animals out of nothing in six days; on the sixth day he creates human beings in his own image by forming clay and breathing life into them. This story is, of course, elaborated on in the version with Adam and Eve (for there are two versions of the story in Genesis: one with an anonymous "man and woman" and the other the familiar story of Adam and Eve): God creates a clay figure of Adam and breathes life into him. He then lets Adam name all the animals and gives Adam dominion over the earth. Next, realizing that Adam needs a partner, he takes a rib from Adam's side while he sleeps and breathes life into it, making it the first woman, Eve. They are given complete access to the Garden of Eden, except for the Tree of Life and the Tree of Knowledge, but they disobey him and eat the fruit from the Tree of Knowledge. As punishment, God bars them from the Garden of Eden and eternal life; they and their descendants are now destined for lifetimes of toil and pain in childbirth.

India   In the beginning the male principle of At-man (Soul) existed, and he felt lonely and afraid. So he split himself in two and created husband and wife, but the woman he created felt it was shameful to mate with him, since she had been part of him. So she tried to conceal herself as various animals, but Atman outwitted her each time, making himself into a male animal and mating with her; thus they created humans and all other animals.

American Indian Cultures   A *Hopi* origin myth tells of Spider Woman, the Earth Goddess, and Tawa, the Sun God, dividing themselves and creating lesser gods, including the four corners of the world. After the job of creating the world is over, they sit down and give shape to their thoughts. The little thought-figures are covered by a blanket, and Spider Woman sings to them. They stir and come alive, and populate the earth as humans and animals. Another Hopi myth tells of two creator goddesses, both named Mother Huruing Wuthi, who created the earth and populated it with animals. At last they created a woman and then a man and set them on earth to populate it. These are the parents of the Hopis. A *Navajo* (Di-neh) myth tells of the creator goddess Changing Woman, who rubs her skin and in this way creates the Dineh.

Mexico   The *Aztec* myth of creation tells of dual gods, male and female, creating the universe. Their four sons created the first earth, but one brother set himself up as the sun and created humans made of ashes. The god Quetzalcoatl destroyed the first earth, but three more times the brothers created flawed earths that were destroyed; the fourth earth was populated by ape-people. The fifth earth, which is the present world, was created as a reconciliation among the brothers. Quetzalcoatl went below ground to find bones of humans from the previous worlds to create the new race of people. He created a man and a woman from the bones and sprayed them with his own blood, giving them life.

China   In one Chinese myth, the universe was created from the body of a dead god, P'an-ku—his flesh became the earth, his blood became rivers, and the parasites on his body became human beings. In another myth the goddess Nü-kua repaired the heavenly firmament after it had been destroyed by a monster and proceeded to create humans. First she patted yellow earth together and created humans that way, but it was hard work, and she got tired. So instead she dragged a string through the earth and created people from the clods that stuck to the cord. The rich and noble are the people she created individually, and everyone else came from her string.

Other Cultures   One origin story is encountered in several cultural contexts where the indigenous population is of brown skin tones: God (or the gods or the Goddess) decided to make human beings, so he shaped dough into cookies shaped like men and women, and put them in the oven. The first batch was terribly underdone; they were all white. So he (or she) made a new batch, and this time burned them, so they came out too dark. The third time was a charm: The human cookies came out all golden brown, and God looked at them and was very happy.

Theories of Myth

Here one might wonder, where did ancient peoples come up with all these ideas? Numerous theories explain the images of myth: A popular theory

Box 2.1 JOSEPH CAMPBELL: MYTHS EXIST TODAY

The American mythologist Joseph Campbell (1904–1987) focused on recurrent mythic themes around the world and fascinated a large audience of viewers in a five-part television program hosted by Bill Moyers by pointing out that the themes in ancient myths are still with us: Psychologically, we are the same kind of people as way back when, and our hopes, fears, and dreams are to a great extent the same. We all want to live as long as possible; we all want to be healthy; we want to experience close relationships with lovers, friends, and family; we want to liberate ourselves from our parents and become adults; we want to protect our children and see them succeed; and we probably also want to own things—in some cultures more than others! And we are afraid of what the future might bring, so we ask gods and spirits to help and guide us. All this, says Campbell, can be traced in ancient myths of creation, of gods helping people, and of heroes helping others. But we still have a need for such stories, says Campbell, and it reveals itself in our fascination with celebrities and with events that have a happy ending. Campbell, a personal friend of George Lucas', was the advisor on Lucas's film trilogy *Star Wars,* which was deliberately written as a story full of classical mythic themes; this may be one of the reasons for its enduring popularity.

early in the twentieth century was *euhemerism,* which held that myths told old, distorted tales of something that really happened among the rich and powerful, who were then turned into gods by the priesthood and the laypeople. Another influential theory from the twentieth century was *functionalism,* the idea that myths justify social and religious functions of the status quo society. A *Freudian* interpretation generally sees myths as expressing personal unconscious tensions of a sexual, oppressed nature. A theory that was immensely popular during the 1970s was *structuralism,* which says that myths are intricate codes expressing relations between opposites, but not really having any meaning otherwise. Today many mythologists are comfortable with Mircea Eliade's and Joseph Campbell's views, similar in many ways: They say humans have a need to explain chaotic life so it makes sense and gives structure to our reality. (See Box 2.1 for a closer look at Campbell's theory of myth.)

We generally pick stories and images that do provide an explanation for the concept of reality prevalent within our culture, and the stories reveal what we as a culture think of ourselves and the world: Do we consider humans to be strong and wonderful creations, or are we unworthy worms crawling on the earth? Are humans created with loving care by a nurturing god, or are we accidents strewn across the landscape by chance or by the whims of deities? These ancient and not-so-ancient stories may not tell us much about the factual origin of humanity, but they tell us volumes about the hopes and fears of the storytelling cultures. That is why we shouldn't just discard them as outdated, unscientific stories: They are philosophical systems in their own right and serve as signposts and mirrors for our self-conception.

Creationism Versus the Theory of Evolution

With Darwin's theory of evolution, the link to a religious explanation for human origins began to fade for most educated people in the Western world. Although, in Europe, it is hardly more than a remnant of a nineteenth-century phenomenon, the debate between creationist and evolutionists is still on the agenda in the United States (as is clear from the introduction to this chapter). Is the Bible correct in its account of God creating the universe and all the species separately, with man and woman as his crowning achievement; or is science correct in holding that the universe came into being by inner processes in a big bang, and

Bill Watterson's discontinued cartoon strip *Calvin and Hobbes* often used to venture into areas of philosophy and religion, with insight provided by the stuffed tiger Hobbes. Here Hobbes provides a perspective on human evolution: To someone who is not a primate, perhaps it might seem that humans haven't evolved far from the monkey stage.

that billions of years later, on an insignificant planet at the edge of a galaxy, some creatures crawled out of the primordial ocean and grew into all the animals we know on earth, including humans? These two worldviews are generally presented as being entirely opposite, but we mustn't forget that scientists are not necessarily atheists. Many scientists, including Darwin himself, have had great faith in a divine presence in the universe and see the story of Genesis as a symbolic account of what actually took billions of years to accomplish, expressed poetically by great religious minds several thousand years ago.

Creationists call Darwin's theory of natural selection "just another theory." Here we shall see that it is much more than that. But I will even take the plunge and outdo the creationists: I want to call it "just another story." What do I mean by that? I mean that *the difference is not very great between believing in the story of Genesis because your parents have told it to you and believing in the story of humans and apes descending from a common ancestor because your parents, or your teachers, told it to you.* In either case we accept a story told by people we have faith in or who have authority over us. That has nothing to do with science; that is simply the way we are taught the stories of our

culture. The *difference* comes in when we are asked to *explain* and *justify* the correctness of the story: We explain the story of Genesis by referring to God's authority; if the person asking for our explanation has a different religion or is an atheist or an agnostic, our explanation carries no clout whatsoever. But if we explain the theory of natural selection and refer to scientific evidence as our justification—evidence that can be checked and double-checked by anyone regardless of religion, just like the evidence at a crime scene—that makes the difference between the two stories of origin: One is a belief system based on faith; the other is science based on the geological fossil record.

Darwin's contribution to biology was in fact not that he gave us the theory of evolution, because it was already part of the nineteenth-century discussion (see Chapter 3). The theory that actually made him an influential scientist was what some have called "the survival of the fittest": *natural selection.* Part of the credit should rightly go to his friend, Alfred Wallace, who was also working on the theory independently of Darwin. A letter from Wallace to Darwin about his findings stirred Darwin into finally publishing his theory of natural selection. The theory states that species will evolve according to opportunity, not according to some inner plan or purpose. Giraffes develop long necks because it adds a survival edge to be able to eat leaves, not because of some inner "giraffe" nature or design. Both the theory of evolution as such (species evolve over time) and the theory of natural selection, which really is the theoretical principle behind evolution, have been amply corroborated by researchers in the twentieth century.

The debate between the two worldviews is hardly an even debate, anyway, since the two views don't accept the same criteria of evidence: creationism sees the word of God and the writings of the Bible as evidence, while scientists view evidence as facts that can be corroborated and repeated in experiments or verified by similar occurrences in nature or in the lab. They are simply not talking the same language. One view, creationism, has its principle defined at the outset: God is the creator. The other view is an empirical system, allowing its principle of creation to appear as the evidence mounts: The theory of evolution is not merely a "theory" among other possible theories, but a scientific statement, based on facts, about the branching process of life on earth and possibly also in the rest of the universe. (Box 2.2 discusses what exactly constitutes a "fact.") This also means that if new facts should surface that make it necessary to change the theory, the theory of evolution is compelled to take such facts into account and redefine itself, if it wants to be considered good science.

The philosopher Karl Popper (1902–1994) referred to this necessity as the *principle of falsification.* He demanded of a good scientific system that it be "falsifiable"; this rather confusing term doesn't mean that a good scientific theory must be shown to be false (which makes no sense at all) but that *a good scientific theory must be tested in every conceivable way.* In Popper's words,

> Just because it is our aim to establish theories as well as we can, we must test them as severely as we can; that is, we must try to find faults with them, we must try to falsify them. Only if we cannot falsify them in spite of our best efforts can we say that they have stood up to severe tests. This is the reason why the discovery of instances which confirm a theory means very little if we have not tried, and failed, to discover refutation. For if we are uncritical we shall always find what we want . . . in order to make the method of selection by elimination work, and to ensure that *only the fittest theories survive,* their struggle for life must be made severe for them.[2] [italics added]

This means that a theory which can survive onslaught after onslaught from its own creator (and perhaps it is no coincidence that Popper uses Darwinist language here) is a good scientific theory. A consequence of Popper's method is to recognize the inherent problems of the inductive method: Since it is based on empirical evidence (meaning factual, collected evidence as opposed to a logical principle or an accepted truth), we can never reach 100 percent certainty, some new factor might pop up that will force us to reevaluate the theory. This is a fact of science that we have to live with, and it doesn't mean that a scientific empirical theory can never make a firm, committed statement; it's just that it can't make a statement that is 100 percent certain. Science tells us that the earth spins around once every 24 hours, resulting in the experience of sunrise on the planet's surface; does that mean we can be 100 percent sure the sun will always rise? No; just because it has always happened, doesn't mean it will necessarily continue to do so. But can we be reasonably sure it will? Of course—there is no need to put the picnic on hold or question whether to show up for the early morning final because science hasn't proved with 100 percent certainty that the sun will rise tomorrow. Indeed, 99.9 percent certainty is close enough! But a good scientist acknowledges this limitation of a science based on gathering empirical evidence. This limitation applies to the theory of evolution, too: A good scientist doesn't claim that it is 100 percent certain, but only that the geological and biological evidence point unequivocally toward the correctness

Box 2.2 WHAT IS A FACT?

Facts are used to explain situations, but we rarely have to explain what a fact is. However, the very idea that something can be objectively corroborated by others has come under criticism in the late twentieth century, in a debate that is related to the discussion of postmodernism in Box 1.1. What used to be a foundational truth in Western philosophy—that every rational person can agree on certain commonsense things such as math and logic—is now problematic, because we now recognize that the human mind tends to select what it sees as a relevant fact and overlooks other things that could be relevant. Think of a police detective at a murder scene: She or he gathers evidence based on what the lead detective has declared to be relevant. A good lead detective will leave lots of possibilities open, but also draw on past experience, so the gathering of the empirical evidence isn't completely at random. Even so, some element might be overlooked by those in charge: It didn't look relevant at the time (an empty knife box sitting on a bathtub ledge), or nobody in charge noticed it (a bloody fingerprint on a back gate). These elements could have been important pieces of evidence in the case against a killer, but weren't collected as evidence. Were they then "facts" in the case? Only in retrospect, when it is clear that they could have made a difference in the outcome of the trial. The plot of a famous murder mystery involves a killer mailman—nobody suspects him, because he is such a commonly seen character, so his presence isn't regarded as a relevant fact.

But the question goes deeper: Is what we call a fact perhaps a cultural invention? Do other cultures have different ideas of what a fact is? Surely; for instance, some cultures consider *dreams* factual: A person will chastise another person for having been mean to him in a dream. Many cultures see *premonitions* and predictions found in ancient writings, as factual. If we want to become a functional multicultural society, don't we have to tone down our insistence that facts are facts and reduce it to being merely a Western cultural concept? Our own society was at the point of routinely accepting false memories of abuse, called forth by therapists, as facts, with disastrous results for some innocent caregivers. A certain skepticism about the nature of facts is good; it teaches us that we shouldn't take our traditional concepts of truth and reality for granted, but should instead keep an open mind. However, there is nothing wrong with viewing the Western concept of fact as a matter of *intellectual gain:* The idea of being able to objectively determine the likelihood of something's being the case based on evidence that can be viewed by others is tremendously important in human intellectual progress, and we shouldn't let it deteriorate into being just one option among other intellectual approaches; if we do, we might slide back to a world where your neighbor's accusation that you are a witch is enough to get you burned at the stake.

---

of the theory of evolution and natural selection; and if new evidence arises, the scientist will have to deal with it: by working it into the theory, rewriting the theory, or abandoning the theory. This flexibility is not a flaw, but rather a strength of modern science. (Box 2.2 explores the contemporary discussion of whether a fact might be a cultural invention.)

And the theory has in fact been challenged lately by new evidence: Darwin believed that a species changes into a new species over a very long time period. He also believed that once the

change has started, the old species will disappear and the new evolved species will take the place of the old one, because of natural selection. The old will be outdone by the new. But today that appears to be not quite true. Some species have evolved with astounding speed, while other species haven't evolved at all in millions of years. Scientists now talk about "punctuated equilibrium," where a species evolves in jumps due to catastrophic environmental changes, and the old parent species coexists with the daughter species under certain conditions. The modern theory of evolution is rewriting Darwinism to accommodate these challenges. We will explore this further in Chapter 3.

The Generally Accepted Story Today

So what is the story of our human origin that is generally accepted by scientists today? The details may change with new evidence, but the general picture is this: About 6 million years ago in eastern Africa small apelike creatures, probably used to moving around in the trees but also familiar with savanna country, began evolving into what we today call the great apes: one line moving toward chimpanzees, bonobos, gorillas, and orangutans; the other becoming hominids. It appears that the line going toward orangutans split off first—then the ones for gorillas, chimpanzees, and finally bonobos somewhere between 6 and 5 million years ago. The human line developed independently from then on. This means we are indeed related to the other great apes; it also means that bonobos are our closest living relatives on the planet—and, indeed, we humans are their closest relatives, too, closer than gorillas or even chimpanzees. This is especially thought-provoking, since many hominids preceded us on the human line, but of all the human experiments of nature, we are the sole survivors.

Is there a "missing link," as Darwinists were fond of speculating in the nineteenth century? That depends on what we mean. If we mean the actual ancestor to both apes and humans, then recent fossil finds just might fit the bill, but otherwise this common ancestor is a logical extrapolation, not yet backed up by fossil evidence. If we mean fossils linking the common ancestor to *Homo sapiens* of today, then there are plenty of "links," and it was only in the nineteenth century that they were "missing." We have already found enough to have a good picture of the general evolutionary trend. However, the whole "link" idea draws on the *metaphor of a chain*: the idea that the human lineage consists of links in a chain that moves through time: Only one link exists at a time. This idea has now been discarded by many

scientists who see human evolution not as a chain, but as a giant bush with coexisting branches, not necessarily growing in any clear direction, with lots of extinct branches that we don't even know of yet. It may be an aberration that we are the only human species on the planet right now; at all other times there seem to have been several species coexisting. Some scientists speculate that we will never find the "links" between the different species, because—as the idea of punctuated equilibrium says—evolution happens in jumps.

This is the picture between 4.5 and 1.8 million years ago: Several apelike beings are roaming the African savanna: *Australopithecus ramidus* is the oldest fossil found at this point; a few hundred thousand years later another one appears: *Australopithecus anamensis.* Both hominids are gone by 3.5 million years ago, and one of them, probably *anamensis,* must have evolved into the famous *Australopithecus afarensis.* Fossils of this being have recently been found in several places in eastern Africa, the most famous one being the individual named Lucy (because paleoanthropologist Don Johanson and the other scientists were listening to the Beatles song "Lucy in the Sky with Diamonds" as they were sorting the bones). Lucy's people walked upright, but their brains weren't much bigger than those of chimpanzees today. They may have hunted some, but there is evidence that they probably depended on scavenging and gathering more than anything else.

To what extent these early hominids disappeared altogether, and to what extent they evolved into one another and eventually into what we call the *Homo* (human) lineage, is not yet clear today, but it is clear that the next big evolutionary step arises out of some group of *Australopithecus* in Africa, probably around 3 million years ago. In April 1999 a new fossil was described in the journal *Science* as being a possible link between Lucy's people and *Homo habilis,* "handyman." The newly discovered species is named *Australopithecus garhi,* and it appears that this hominid butchered meat, using a stone tool. Is *A. garhi* a direct human ancestor? We don't know yet, but scientists speculate that it may be closely related to a hominid

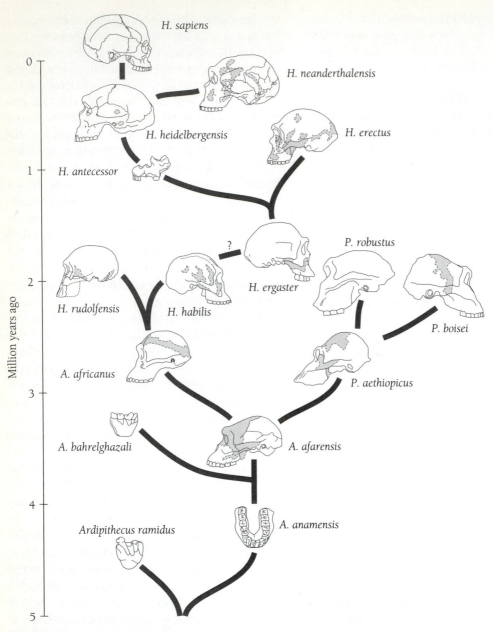

This drawing provides a recent picture of the human family tree. However, new finds of fossil hominids constantly challenge details within the current perception of human evolution. *A. garhi* would probably be placed between *A. afarensis* and *H. habilis*.

who is considered a close or even direct ancestor, *Homo habilis*.

The big difference between Australopithecine and *Homo habilis* individuals is that *H. habilis* had

a larger brain. Accordingly, it was thought that *H. habilis* was the first hominid to use stone tools, but that conclusion may have to be revised because of *A. garhi*. It may of course be the case that

Lucy's people also made tools (and that is highly likely since chimpanzees do), but we haven't found any certain evidence of it yet; wooden digging sticks, gourds, and bowls made from skulls are perishable. Stone tools, on the other hand, have a much better chance of surviving the many thousands of years in the ground, and *H. habilis* used stone tools—and also made the tools. Now it appears that both *A. garhi* and *H. habilis* ate meat on a regular basis, although the primary diet has probably always been (and still is, for hunter-gatherers) fruit, vegetables, and tubers. The interesting conclusion is that apparently it doesn't take a larger brain than *A. garhi*'s to figure out how to make stone tools and use them for butchering meat.

About 1.8 million years ago another hominid appeared, bigger and larger-brained than *Homo habilis: Homo erectus* ("upright human"—when the species was named, we didn't yet know that even Lucy's people walked upright 2 million years earlier). Today another species, *Homo ergaster,* is sometimes named as our ancestor, but it is still customary to point to *Homo erectus* as our immediate ancestor. The extraordinary thing is that *Homo erectus* is found not just in East Africa, but also in Java and in China! This is taken to mean that this species migrated, and it appears that some of its success can be attributed to knowing how to make fire. Around 500,000 years ago *Homo erectus* had even reached Europe, and the fossil found there is known as *Homo heidelbergensis,* because it was found in Heidelberg, Germany.

In Europe around 150,000 years ago, an enigmatic hominid appears: *Homo neandertalensis,* Neandertal human, possibly a descendant of *Homo erectus,* but perhaps a *Homo sapiens* traveling up from Africa, specializing dramatically along the way.[3] Neandertal fossils were among the first ever found of other hominid species in the nineteenth century, and the bones of the individual found were deformed by arthritis. For that reason, Neandertals were for a long time depicted as lumbering hunched-over creatures. Now we know that the Neandertals evolved to live along the rim of the ice during one of the ice ages; they may even have lived on the ice itself, hunting animals.

The Neandertal body was extremely strong and compact, the face featuring a prominent nose that could warm up the icy air before it hit the lungs. We have no idea what their coloration was, but some speculate that they may have been pale-skinned, fair-haired, and blue-eyed, if a northern climate has anything to do with coloration (see Chapter 5 for a discussion of race and coloration). A researcher has commented that if a Neandertal were to show up in the New York subway clothed in modern garb, nobody would bat an eye. We even suspect that they had a spiritual life: Neandertal burials have been found with signs that the dead person was not only loved and cared for—as you read in Chapter 1, flower pollen was found in the grave—but also was believed to be headed for an afterlife. Of course, that remains speculation.

We have known for a long time that Neandertal technology included the use of fire and the manufacture of stone tools, but the tools we knew of were crude compared to human tools; and unlike human stone tools, the tools of Neandertal groups never seemed to develop, but stayed the same for tens of thousands of years. However, recently archeologists have had to revise even this theory: In the Middle East, remains of late-surviving Neandertal groups have been found dating back 28,000 years, clearly implying that they lived side by side with *Homo sapiens sapiens* groups for many thousands of years. And the tools found among these Neandertals show signs of a technological evolution. In what may have been the greatest surprise, jewelry was found among the Neandertal remains: little beads, to be worn on a string. No other jewelry has been found among Neandertals—so far. It prompted some archeologists to speculate that perhaps they traded with the humans (or stole from them), but the technology is sufficiently different to warrant a new theory: that Neandertals, toward the end of their existence, were making sleeker tools and adorning themselves with artifacts—something most of us consider very human traits.

What killed the Neandertals? We don't know yet. The population groups were small, and it is possible that they were killed off or lost out in competition with the humans. It is also possible that, for some reason, they just didn't reproduce fast enough to keep up the population numbers during the last ice age. There is also the possibility that, in effect, they didn't quite die out, that some modern humans may have some Neandertal DNA in their genetic structure. (Box 2.3 explores the possibility of humans being related to the Neandertals.)

About 200,000 years ago our own species, *Homo sapiens* (the thinking human), evolved—probably from *Homo erectus* or from an earlier form of *H. sapiens* that perhaps also spawned the Neandertal. Recently, in Spain, an early form of *Homo sapiens* was discovered, now named *Homo sapiens antecessor,* but that doesn't mean we evolved in Spain; we have ample evidence that we came out of Africa, spreading across the African, Indian, Australian, and European continents. About 60,000 years ago we became elaborate artisans, building boats and intricate shelters; at this stage, scientists refer to us as *Homo sapiens sapiens.* Around 30,000 years ago fine tools appear, along with jewelry and art on cave walls. Since then agriculture and husbandry have appeared, town life began about 10,000 years ago, and the art of writing developed over 5,000 years ago; and with the art of writing, humans entered into what has traditionally been defined as the *historical* period. (Of course, humans had a "history" prior to writing; for far longer than we have been able to write, we have had an oral tradition, telling stories about ourselves from generation to generation. It is just that cultural scientists have set the demarcation line between prehistory and history at the first appearance of writing.)

The Latest Spin

Paleoanthropologists have now been joined by geologists, biologists, and geneticists in trying to patch together the real story of human evolution, but that also means new kinds of hypotheses stir our imagination. Often the spin on new scientific hypotheses is created by popular culture, which sees some opportunity to make a political point, but sometimes the spin is created by the scientists themselves: Scientists are human, too; there are hypotheses they find more interesting than other hypotheses; and, above all, their research funding usually comes from the sources in the private sector that support university research. Administrators and business people are as influenced by current popular trends as anybody, so we shouldn't expect research to be utterly objective, even though it has the official approval of a university—and even though individual researchers do their utmost to be professionally objective. Here is a selection of such hypotheses from the intermediate zone between science and popular culture, arranged from most likely to the least likely, as I see them (but of course you are free to make up your own mind about the probability of these hypotheses).

The African Eve Hypothesis In 1987 Rebecca Cann, Mark Stoneking, and other geneticists at Berkeley published a challenging theory: Comparing mitochondrial DNA (DNA outside the nucleus) in a sample of populations from around the world and tracing the minute differences back to a point in human evolution where they must have started to diverge, they announced that we are all much more closely related than anyone had thought: Since mitochondrial DNA is only passed on from mother to daughter, we are in effect all descendants of one woman (or a group of sisters, but they of course had a mother) who lived about 200,000 years ago, somewhere in eastern Africa. This woman has become known popularly as "Eve," although the Berkeley scientists were not implying that she might be the biblical Eve. For one thing, this means that we are all truly evolutionary brothers and sisters, regardless of race. Because 200,000 years isn't that long ago, this discovery means all races have definitely evolved recently, from the same group of *Homo sapiens.* (In Chapter 5 you will find a discussion about the biological and social aspects of the concept of

Box 2.3   ARE WE RELATED TO NEANDERTALS?

Could the Neandertals be our immediate ancestors? Absolutely not. Neandertals are to this day the most closely related cousin we have ever had on the planet that we know of (while the bonobo chimpanzee with its 98 percent genetic similarity to us is our closest *living* relative). Even so, the Neandertals evolved into a different species. Mitochondrial DNA extracted from Neandertal fossil remains in 1997 reveals that the Neandertal lineage separated from ours at least several hundred thousand years ago and evolved separately from there. They were extremely specialized—having adapted to living on or close to the glaciers covering Northern Europe and Russia—and special characteristics don't devolve into something more general. Could they have coexisted with the human line that is ours, *Homo sapiens sapiens?* They could, and they did, probably as far back as 40,000 years ago. There is evidence of simultaneous Neandertal and *H. sapiens* habitation in Europe and in Palestine, the southern European habitation being as close to our own time as a mere 28,000 years ago. This means that humans and Neandertals lived side by side at least twice as long as humans have known the art of writing.

So could they have *interbred* with humans? In terms of their DNA, it is more than likely: It is theoretically possible to create chimpanzee-human hybrids, and the Neandertal would have been much closer to us, genetically; we might, in effect, be two *Homo sapiens* species. But would a Neandertal and a human *want to* mate? There are two answers here: (1) As a voluntary tradition, it is unlikely. We humans seem preprogrammed to prefer mates that look like our own "tribe," and humans and Neandertals would look sufficiently different not to be attracted to each other, unless they'd happened to grow up together. They might not even have considered each other as people. (2) As an occasional occurrence, it is probable. Isolated populations might look to each other for sexual partners, trading females for the sake of coexistence and profit; and rapes occur in human populations as isolated events or in an organized way as a part of warfare. Attraction is not necessarily a part of the picture for the rapist and probably never for the rape victim.

The fossil remains of a four-year-old boy were found in Portugal in 1998, dating back 25,000 years. Some scientists believe he has *hybrid human–Neandertal traits* and thus was an offspring of both lines. Erik Trinkaus, a paleoanthropologist from Washington University, St. Louis, speculates that this means humans and Neandertals treated each other as people; but we can't discount the possibility that some hybrids, like some humans, may have been the result of forced rather than consensual sex. Scientists speculate that if any human population group today carries Neandertal genes from occasional sexual encounters—consensual or not—more than 28,000 years back, it would be people of European and Middle Eastern descent. However, recent DNA analyses seem to exclude the presence of Neandertal genes in the present human population, but this could be a premature conclusion. Whether some of us actually have Neandertal people as forebears is still an open question.

And now for an *X-Files* type of question: How long before the Neandertal became completely extinct? Could actual Neandertals still be alive? Other species thought long extinct have been found to still exist. Might the Scandinavian mythological "Jätte," pronounced *Yetta* and wrongly translated as giant, be a faint folk memory of another type of human up in the mountain mists? What about the trolls of folklore? Not to mention the big hairy mythical creatures around the world that some people insist they have seen, such as the yeti and the Sasquatch? It is great fun to speculate, but until we have evidence in the form of DNA from bones or hair (footprints can be faked), there is no sure way of determining such creatures' existence, let alone their evolutionary heritage. Besides, descriptions of the elusive, lumbering, inarticulate beasts supposedly roaming the Pacific Northwest and the Himalayas sound to some biologists more like earlier forms of giant apes than Neandertals. Let's keep an open mind, but not so open that we let the draft in.

race.) For another (and this is what is so hard for many to believe), it means that descendants of other human mothers just didn't make it: Only Eve had surviving offspring, and we are all her descendants.

This is an enormous challenge to science as well as to logic, because by 200,000 years ago the *Homo sapiens* population was already spreading into Asia and moving north toward Europe. Does this mean that Eve's children eventually fanned out and killed off or outcompeted all other humans? Eve's daughters may, of course, have mated with males from other parts, and thus we get descendants with Eve's genes as well as genes from other populations; but recently scientists claim to have come up with DNA lineage from a male counterpart to Eve, "Adam," from the same small African population of 200,000 years back; other scholars believe they have located this original population somewhere in southern Africa. The theory has been under great scrutiny and criticism from both scientists and creationists since 1987. We don't have the final word about this controversy, but the practical implications of one small family multiplying and outcompeting all other human families are staggering.

"Out of Africa" Versus "Multiregional Continuity"
Whether we accept the Eve hypothesis or believe that several early *Homo sapiens* groups fanned out into the world, this is referred to as the "Out of Africa" hypothesis. Most paleoanthropologists regard this as an established theory by now, but there are dissenting voices, suggesting an alternative theory: simultaneous, mutually independent *multiregional* evolution. Based on finds of *Homo erectus* in various parts of the world—Africa, Europe, Java, and China—and comparisons of the fossils with the human populations in those regions today, proponents of this theory claim that there is greater similarity between the local *Homo erectus* and the local human population than between contemporary human populations. This would mean that the Asian races evolved separately from an Asian *Homo erectus,* Europeans evolved from a European *erectus,*[4] and Africans from an African

erectus. For most scientists, this enormously controversial theory is not supported by sufficient evidence to be taken very seriously, but any good scientist knows to keep an open mind in case future evidence warrants a rewriting of the theory. Why is this idea so controversial? For purely political reasons: Claiming that races evolved separately sets the stage for ideas of *racial superiority and segregation,* both by nonwhite individuals wishing to separate themselves from other races and white individuals wanting to do the same thing. In the final section of this chapter we shall look at the connection between scientific data and political spin, and Chapter 5 picks up the thread in its discussion of the phenomenon of racism.

The Aquatic Ape   In 1982 the feminist author Elaine Morgan published a book with the title *The Aquatic Ape.* As much as her theory was ridiculed in the beginning, it now has a small but enthusiastic group of followers, including the famous scientist Desmond Morris. If you take a look at our diagram of human evolution, you will see that there is yet no fossil record of hominids older than *Australopithecus ramidus,* around 4.5 million years ago. At 6 million years ago apes and humans parted ways, so to speak. What happened in those 1.5 million years? A great deal, says Morgan: The earliest ape-humans lived along the coast of eastern Africa, and were just getting used to coming down from the trees now and again. They were used to being upright because of traveling in the trees. But the trees were disappearing, not because of the savanna taking over, but because of rising waters. And so this early human population adapted to the close proximity of water: They became aquatic apes. They lost their fur and retained only a sparse hair covering. They retained their head of hair to protect them from heat loss in the water. They developed salty tears to excrete surplus minerals in the water. They began having intercourse facing each other (which only the bonobo chimpanzee also does) because it was more comfortable while being immersed in water. The women used their long hair for babies to grab onto in the sea. They developed big brow ridges to protect against the ocean glare. Babies developed a diving reflex that shut down their breathing and heart rate to a minimum in case they were lost under water. They learned to stand perfectly upright in shallow water, being kept up by the water pressure, looking for sharks, each other, and food. And most importantly, they learned to speak and read each other's facial features, since body language was useless with most of the body submerged.

So why didn't we grow flippers and great lungs and ear flaps so we could dive, like seals? Because this time period didn't last long enough for this profound evolution to take place: The small population of aquatic apes returned to land, spread inland, and became hominids. And why is there absolutely no fossil evidence that this ever occurred? Morgan says that it is there, but deep underwater, beyond the coastline of Ethiopia which is where the aquatic ape lived in those days. Might it be true that we are a species that was on the way to returning to the ocean, but stayed behind to become naked apes? The idea doesn't sound nearly so silly to scientists today as it did when Morgan's book came out; her theory is the only one so far that has a good explanation for why humans have no fur! But it is a good idea to retain our sound skepticism and leave it at a "Show me." If the theory is true, it will be backed up by geology, genetics, and paleoanthropology one of these years.

The Outer-Space Connection   It has become a popular notion to say that we are made of star stuff. These poetic words by the late astronomer Carl Sagan refer to the fact that our solar system probably arose as a result of a supernova explosion, and so all the atoms on earth, including the ones we are made of, are recycled atoms from a previous sun. Because comets are now known to carry organic molecules, it has also become popular to flirt with the idea that life may have been brought to earth by comets in the dim past. In that case, if comets indeed act as "seeders" of life, it is logical to assume that we are not alone in the universe. So far, there is good reason to consider these possibilities. However, there is also another outer-space connection that some laypeople are fond of imagining: What made humans appear on the primate scene? *Homo sapiens* is a species with unique capabilities, far more complex than its ancestor species. What if we were introduced to earth by aliens—as hybrid experiments, perhaps, or downright descendants of stranded spacefaring aliens? Science fiction authors have had fun with this idea for decades, but fun is all it is and, in my opinion, all it should remain. If we still feel uncomfortable with the Darwinian idea that we are closely related to rough, speechless animals on this planet, inventing an outer-space origin isn't going to do us any good. We are not the offspring of angels or devils from other galaxies, nor are we the biological experiments of warring alien factions; we are the fantastic result, so far, of an ongoing natural process that links us to all other organic material on this earth. Earth is our home, and fleeing "back to the stars" when we have polluted it to death isn't going to be a solution (although some space travel and planet colonization seems to be a logical destiny for migrating, smart creatures like us). We can't separate ourselves from our relatives on this planet: We're all together on this journey through time.

Politics and Evolution

So do we now know the truth about the origin of the human race? If we accept that scientific evidence leads to an approximate certainty about facts, then Yes: We know much more about human origins than we did a mere thirty years ago. When Stanley Kubrick's landmark film *2001: A Space Odyssey* came out in 1968, the early hominids depicted (see movie still, p. 63) were still thought of as apelike and knuckle-walking. But since the 1970s we have known, from the finds of Don Johanson and others in Africa, that our hominid ancestors already walked upright 3.5 million years ago. It seems now that every digging season, once the rains in eastern Africa have ended, the paleoanthropologists startle us with new finds, corroborating more than questioning our current idea of the human origin in Africa. Biological tracing of mitochondrial DNA adds to the general picture.

So why can't we put the issue to rest and say that we don't know all the details yet, but we know enough to dispel ancient myths of humans being made out of clay or crawling up from a hole in the ground? Scientifically, we can do just that, of course, but philosophically it isn't so easy. Many people have an inner need for there to be more to the story of human origins; somehow a divine connection seems necessary for us to understand our uniqueness. A creationist, Mark Looy, expresses it thus: "There's not meaning in life if we're just animals in a struggle for survival. It creates a sense of purposelessness and hopelessness, which I think leads to things like pain, murder, and suicide."[5] To this there are several answers: For one thing, scientists are not saying that we are "just animals" but that we are animals such as this planet has never seen before. For another, it is important to repeat that scientists are not necessarily atheists; however, scientists generally separate their faith from their work. If indeed there is a divine presence in the universe, it is of course also present in the course of evolution, and each one of us is free to believe in it; but scientists can't verify the divine for us, because it falls outside the scope of science. And, lastly, Looy displays a classical logical misstep: He wants reality to conform to his preference, because he doesn't want to contemplate the consequences of its being different: "If I don't like the consequences of X, then X must be false." Perhaps there really *is* no meaning in life? We will discuss that idea in Chapter 8. Thinkers such as Bertrand Russell and Jean-Paul Sartre have contemplated the possibility and come up with challenging solutions.

Another philosophical aspect of the story of evolution is more down to earth and ties in with what we discussed in Chapter 1: We don't have direct access to history except through the evidence we find and the *story* we create to explain it. The theory of evolution is in effect a story, but that doesn't mean it isn't an accurate or a true story. It probably is. Nevertheless, it is a story we tell about our own beginnings in order to make ourselves feel that we understand it. And the interesting thing is that the story seems *to change when we need a different story:* Darwin's story of evolution said that immense periods of time were necessary to change a species. Now scientists are changing their minds and are telling the story of "punctuated equilibrium." In the 1950s (right after World War II and at the time of the Korean War and the Cold War), the general scientific consensus was that humans were the descendants of aggressive killer apes (we will take a closer look at that theory in Chapter 3); now we tend to think that early hominids were not just hunters, but also scavengers, and not just predators, but also prey. In the nineteenth century, race theories speculated that the races separated themselves out even before we were *Homo sapiens,* but the Eve hypothesis speculates that all races are much more closely related than we thought. All these changing views may well reflect new data, but they also reflect our changing political climates: Most of us feel the need to explain why things change so quickly (punctuated equilibrium); some of us don't want to be killer apes any more, but would much rather see ourselves as less powerful beings and even prey (victims of stronger powers); many in the Western world rejoice at hearing that the races are closely related, because then there is hope that we can do away with racism in the near future. The facts ought to speak for themselves, but they generally don't; as Paul Ricoeur would say (see Chapter 1), they need interpretation, and there are plenty of us who like to take on that job, putting our own spin on the story of human origins because it suits our political purpose. (Box 2.4 explores the mostly political debate about Kennewick Man.) Sometimes the purpose seems enlightened and benign (at least in my view); an example is the enthusiastic support for the Eve hypothesis. But we shouldn't forget that if facts can be used in a positive sense, they can also be used in a negative sense, and *either way we are manipulating facts.* Watch out for future spin on the evidence of human origins, and evaluate the story carefully: Does it represent a view of humanity that seems realistic? Overly positive? Overly negative? Does it seem as if it was created for the purpose of bringing us together, or separating us? And whose political purpose does the story advance?

Study Questions

1. What are the similarities between religious creation myths and the theory of evolution? What is the difference?

2. Evaluate the "latest spin" theories for their plausibilities.

3. Explain the connection between scientific data and political interpretations.

Primary Reading and Narrative

Next you will find one primary reading and one narrative. The primary reading is an excerpt from Charles Darwin's *The Descent of Man*, from 1871, in which he speculates about the seemingly helpless appearance of a human compared to other predators. The narrative is a summary of Roger McBride Allan's novel from 1988, *Orphan of Creation,* a "what-if" story about the discovery of a remnant population of early hominids.

 *Primary Reading*

The Descent of Man

CHARLES DARWIN

Excerpt, 1871.

In this chapter we have seen that as man at the present day is liable, like every other animal, to multi-form individual differences or slight variations, so no doubt were the early progenitors of man; the variations being formerly induced by the same general causes, and governed by the same general and complex laws as at present. As all animals tend to multiply beyond their means of subsistence, so it must have been with the progenitors of man; and this would inevitably lead to a struggle for existence and to natural selection. The latter process would be greatly aided by the inherited effects of the increased use of parts, and these two processes would incessantly react on each other. It appears, also, as we shall hereafter see, that various unimportant characters have been acquired by man through sexual selection. An unexplained residuum of change must be left to the assumed uniform action of those unknown agencies, which occasionally induce strongly marked with abrupt deviations of structure in our domestic productions.

Judging from the habits of savages and of the greater number of the Quadrumana, primeval men, and even their ape-like progenitors, probably lived in society. With strictly social animals, natural selection sometimes acts on the individual, through the preservation of variations which are beneficial to the community. A community which includes a large number of well-endowed individuals increases in number, and is victorious over other less favored ones; even although each separate member gains no advantage over the others of the same community. Associated insects have thus acquired many remarkable structures, which are of little or no service to the individual, such as the pollen-collecting apparatus, or the sting of the worker-bee, or the great jaws of soldier-ants. With the higher social animals, I am not aware that any structure has been modified solely for the good of the community, though some are of secondary service to it. For instance, the horns of ruminants and the great canine teeth of baboons appear to have been acquired by the males as weapons for sexual strife, but they are used in defence of the herd or troop. In regard to certain mental powers the case . . . is wholly different; for these faculties have been chiefly, or even

Box 2.4   KENNEWICK MAN AND THE DEBATE ABOUT THE FIRST AMERICANS

In the mid-1990s a human skeleton was found near the Columbia River close to Kennewick, Washington. It had a spearhead stuck in its hip, and at first it was assumed to be a nineteenth-century victim of some tribal war. The local Umatilla Indian tribe claimed the body as an ancestor, and ritual reburial of the bones would have taken place as it ordinarily does these days, had not scientists made a quick analysis and issued an astounding statement: For one thing, the skeleton, now known as Kennewick Man, dates back more than 9,000 years, predating the arrival of every living tribe in the Pacific Northwest, so this couldn't physically be counted as an Indian ancestor. Furthermore, the skull appears to have European traits, more than American Indian features. (A forensic expert has made the face come alive by adding facial features of clay, and some claim he looks like Captain Picard of *Star Trek: The Next Generation!*) DNA tests on Kennewick Man were commenced in the spring of 2000 after a long legal battle, and his supposed European background has neither been established nor ruled out yet, but some scientists see a possibility of a Southeast Asian link rather than a European one.

Those are the facts; here is the political fallout: The Umatilla are not impressed with the scientific argument that Kennewick Man can't be their ancestor, because according to their mythology they have *always* lived in the region, establishing their residency by climbing out of the ground *in illo tempore*. So should scientists and legislators respect the fundamentalist (religiously literal) worldview of an American Indian tribe, when other fundamentalist groups in the United States don't have any political voice? And the most burning issue: What if Kennewick Man really was racially European? Other ancient European bodies have been found in unexpected parts of the world, such as in Central China, dating back some 4,000 years. Does it mean they, and he, were of European ancestry, and does that imply that European immigrants predated the American Indian settlements in the Pacific Northwest?

To some this has only academic interest—Who cares who was here first? The most important thing is that we are here together now, in one nation. But to others this is immensely important to the story of origin of the United States: Do we tell the story of the first Americans as being Indians? Or do we have to change the story? Does this affect the historical claim to North America that American Indians have had and that has been ignored since Columbus? Did the Indians in fact "take the country away from" early European settlers, as some radical groups were quick to proclaim? The issue is not isolated to the Kennewick Man discussion; now considered one of the most controversial issues in American archeology, theories have been floated of an ancient wave of settlers from southwestern Europe (now Spain and Portugal) possibly more than 20,000 years ago, also predating the immigration waves from Asia. Additionally, the theory of a much more recent Viking settlement perhaps extending to the Midwest (about 1,000 years ago) is no longer a laughing matter. Some of the rune stones found may actually be of Viking origin. However, that theory doesn't affect the

---

exclusively gained for the benefit of the community, and the individuals thereof have at the same time gained an advantage indirectly.

It has often been objected to such views as the foregoing, that man is one of the most helpless and defenceless creatures in the world; and that during his early and less well-developed condition, he would have been still more helpless. The Duke of Argyll, for instance, insists that "the human frame has diverged from the structure of brutes, in the direction of greater physical helplessness and weakness. That is to say, it is a divergence which of all others it is most impossible to ascribe to mere natural selection." He adduces the naked and unprotected state of the body, the absence of great teeth or claws for defence, the small strength and speed of man, and his slight power of discovering food or of avoiding danger by smell. To

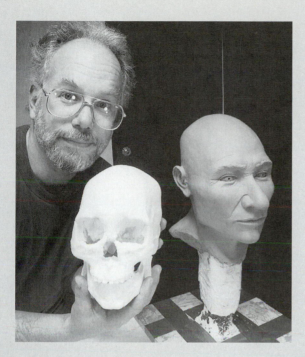

Anthropologist Jim Chatters and sculptor Tom McClelland have produced a clay model of what Kennewick Man must have looked like when he was alive 9,200 years ago, based on a skull casting. At this point the model was not yet completed; McClelland (shown here) thinks the model looks like the actor Patrick Stewart (Capt. Picard, *Star Trek: The Next Generation*). The controversy around Kennewick Man arose because early studies indicated that his features were more European than American Indian. Scientists now believe that his features may have more in common with ancient Southeast Asian populations.

discussion of the identity of the earliest human settlements on the American continent.

Being a philosopher, I think we need to know where Kennewick Man came from, simply because we have a duty to leave a legacy of increased knowledge to new generations. But whether he was an American Indian ancestor or related to early immigrant "Europeans" or Southeast Asians doesn't alter the fact that the American Indian populations were here before the influx of Europeans beginning in 1492 and were taken to near extinction by this influx. As for who has "dibs" on American soil, it seems to be a moot question: We're all here now and had better put such questions behind us and think of each other as fellow citizens.

these deficiencies there might be added one still more serious, namely, that he cannot climb quickly, and so escape from enemies. The loss of hair would not have been a great injury to the inhabitants of a warm country. For we know that the unclothed Fuegians can exist under a wretched climate. When we compare the defenceless state of man with that of apes, we must remember that the great canine teeth with which the latter are provided, are possessed in their full de-velopment by the males alone, and are chiefly used by them for fighting with their rivals; yet the females, which are not thus provided, manage to survive.

In regard to bodily size or strength, we do not know whether man is descended from some small species, like the chimpanzee, or from one as powerful as the gorilla; and, therefore, we cannot say whether man has become larger and stronger, or smaller and weaker, than his ancestors. We should, however, bear in mind that an animal possessing great size, strength, and ferocity, and which, like the gorilla, could defend itself from all enemies, would not perhaps have become social: and this would most effectually have checked the acquirement of the higher mental qualities, such as sympathy and the love of his fellows. Hence it might have been an immense advantage to man to have sprung from some comparatively weak creature.

The small strength and speed of man, his want of natural weapons, etc., are more than counterbalanced, firstly, by his intellectual powers, through which he has formed for himself weapons, tools, etc., though still remaining in a barbarous state, and, secondly, by his social qualities which lead him to give and receive aid from his fellow-men. No country in the world abounds in a greater degree with dangerous beasts than Southern Africa; no country presents more fearful physical hardships than the Arctic regions; yet one of the puniest of races, that of the Bushmen, maintains itself in Southern Africa, as do the dwarfed Esquimaux in the Arctic regions. The ancestors of man were, no doubt, inferior in intellect, and probably in social disposition, to the lowest existing savages; but it is quite conceivable that they might have existed, or even flourished, if they had advanced in intellect, whilst gradually losing their brute-like powers, such

as that of climbing trees, etc. But these ancestors would not have been exposed to any special danger, even if far more helpless and defenceless than any existing savages, had they inhabited some warm continent or large island, such as Australia, New Guinea, or Borneo, which is now the home of the orang. And natural selection arising from the competition of tribe with tribe, in some such large area as one of these, together with the inherited effects of habit, would, under favorable conditions, have sufficed to raise man to his present high position in the organic scale.

Study Questions

1. Which human traits does Darwin attribute to natural selection?

2. What is the difference to Darwin between the evolution of human physical and mental powers?

3. How does Darwin respond to the suggestion that it is to the disadvantage of humans to be weaker than most other predators?

4. Are there questions Darwin raises in this excerpt that biology and paleoanthropology have since answered? Which ones—and how have they been answered?

Narrative

Orphan of Creation

ROGER MCBRIDE ALLEN

Novel, 1988. Summary.

Dr. Barbara Marchando, an African American paleoanthropologist, makes an astounding discovery on the family plantation in Mississippi: The plantation was bought by her ancestors, former slaves, from their former masters, sometime after 1865. One day she finds a diary kept by one of her ancestors that tells about a disturbing incident in the 1850s, when a new breed of slaves was introduced on the plantation. This new breed was *not human,* so the masters were able to bypass anti-slave trade regulations. The new slaves looked much like humans, but they had misshapen heads and hardly any chins, and they could not talk.

Because of her professional insight, Dr. Marchando pursues the discovery, and the slave graveyard yields astounding archaeological evidence. Resting in the earth are the remains of a race of beings not quite human but not quite apelike either: hominids who supposedly have been extinct for a million years, but whose graves are only a little over a hundred years old. Marchando's colleagues reluctantly agree: She has found remains of *Australopithecus boisei,* which have never before been seen outside of Africa.

Marchando and her colleagues agree that if such creatures could survive in Africa until the mid-1850s, then perhaps they might still be around somewhere. An expedition is dispatched to the Gabon area in Africa, and contact is made with present-day slave traders. The scientists are in luck: The slave traders are in charge of the last, pitiful remnants of a group of hominids like the ones Marchando found in the cemetery. The scientists negotiate with the traders to examine a female— one who has been scheduled for termination by the traders—and they find out that they have actually purchased her in the process. Reluctantly, they take her home to the United States and begin to establish communication with her, giving her the name Thursday, because "Thursday's child has far to go," as the old nursery rhyme says.

Barbara Marchando's troubles are only just beginning. As the media, the scientific community, and the business world catch hold of the news, Thursday becomes a celebrity as well as an object of speculation. Biologists want to "euthanize" her so they can perform an autopsy; the world wants to gawk at her; linguists want to teach her to speak; and enterprising business-people are already negotiating to acquire the rest of her tribe, whom they would consider "unpaid laborers." Thursday is now relating to Barbara as to a parent, and her spirit is very low, because she senses the unrest around her. Barbara's only chance of protecting her is to prove to the world that Thursday is not an animal but a person, with a person's right to life and to privacy. By this time Thursday is able to speak a few words, even though her vocal cords are not developed like a human's. Nevertheless, Barbara decides not to argue that Thursday can reason and is thus a person; instead, she chooses to focus on Thursday's genetic makeup. It turns out that sometime in the past, humans interbred with Thursday's ancestors (slave owners raping their slaves is not an uncommon phenomenon). So Barbara artificially impregnates Thursday with human sperm. Thursday conceives, and the news is spread just as scientists are getting ready to put her to death. Because Thursday can conceive by a human, she is now considered genetically, and legally, a human being. This also means that her African tribe will be protected by the law, and another slave tragedy has been averted.

Study Questions

1. Draw parallels between the narrative in Chapter 1, *Star Trek: The Next Generation,* "The Measure of a Man," and *Orphan of Creation.* What are the similarities? What are the differences?

2. If a population of early hominids were discovered today, do you think it is likely that some people would attempt to enslave them? Why or why not?

3. Where would you personally draw the line in respect to personhood between a human being and a hominid ancestor? Explain your reasons.

Review

Key Issues in Chapter 2

Where Do We Come From? Mythological Explanations

- *In Illo Tempore.* Eliade's theory: mythology tells of the time of the origin, *in illo tempore.* Linear versus cyclical time perception.

- *Stories of Origins.* Stories of human origins from world mythology: Egypt, Mesopotamia, Africa, Scandinavia, Israel/Palestine, India, American Indian cultures, Mexico, China, other cultures.

- *Theories of Myth.* Theories of why people tell myths: euhemerism, functionalism, Freudian theory, structuralism, Campbell's view (myths are told to make sense of our reality).

- *Creationism Versus the Theory of Evolution.* Two kinds of stories of origin; creationism is based on faith, the theory of evolution on scientific evidence.

The Generally Accepted Story Today

- Human evolution from 4.5 million years ago until emergence of *Homo sapiens.*

- *The Latest Spin.* The African Eve hypothesis: All living humans are descended from the same ancestor in

Africa. Out of Africa versus multiregional continuity: One common origin in Africa versus several separate origins? The aquatic ape: Have humans evolved from apes living by the sea? The outer-space connection: Are humans the result of an alien hybrid experiment?

- *Politics and Evolution.* The creationist discomfort at humans being "just animals." Our idea of human origin seems to change with our changing political climates. We manipulate facts to suit our political needs.

Primary Reading

- Charles Darwin, *The Descent of Man.* For social animals evolution sometimes works on the individual to benefit the community, and sometimes a trait evolves chiefly for the sake of the community, but with advantages to the individual. If humans have descended from a weak rather than a powerful one, it may account for our great social skills.

Narrative

- Roger McBride Allen, *Orphan of Creation.* A remnant population of early hominids is found in Africa. One individual, a female, is captured and taken to the United States. An African American paleoanthropologist fears that Thursday's people will be captured and bred as slaves and sets out to prove that Thursday should be regarded as so closely related to humans that she acquires human rights.

Endnotes

1. States that have made the theory of evolution problematic as part of the teaching curriculum in recent years include Kansas, Alabama, New Mexico, and Nebraska. Other states in which such bills have been defeated are Texas, Ohio, Washington, New Hampshire, and Tennessee. In 2001, however, Kansas reversed its decision and reinstated the theory of evolution to the curriculum.

2. Karl Popper, *The Poverty of Historicism* (London: Routledge & Kegan Paul, 1972), pp. 133–134.

3. The old spelling used to be "Neanderthal," from the Neander Thal (Valley) in Germany. The German spelling changed, leaving out the *h*, which didn't make any difference to the German pronunciation where it has always been pronounced "Tal," but of course this has to affect the English version: The contemporary pronunciation of Neandertal should be with a hard t.

4. Throughout this text I have tried to avoid the term *Caucasian.* The term *European* is admittedly misleading, when it refers to a supposedly racial group predating the creation of European nationalities, but I find it to be less disturbing than Caucasian. Chapter 5 explains in detail why Caucasian as a racial term should be avoided: According to Stephen Jay Gould, it is based on the assumption that the white race is the original race, originating in the Caucasus region. The term was coined in the nineteenth century not for scientific but for aesthetic reasons.

5. Pam Belluck, "Kansas Will Delete Mention of Evolution in Class Curricula," The *San Diego Union-Tribune,* 12 August 1999, p. A-8.

Part 2

Mostly Descriptive Approaches

Chapter Three

The Sociobiological Challenge

Our expanding base of knowledge in the sciences, particularly in biology, has inspired theories of human nature to the point where a new school of thought has developed: the school of *sociobiology*. Sociobiology is a theory of human social life based on biological theory. It holds that human social structures and traditions have biological roots. The idea of biology and social behavior being linked seems unavoidable; after all, zoologists draw conclusions about animal populations based on their biological makeup: Animals defend territories, migrate, choose mates, raise offspring, hunt and forage, all in response to biological needs, so why not humans? The question is not whether *any* human behavior can be explained biologically, because with the present level of scientific knowledge we would have to answer affirmatively: Of course, there will be some aspects of human behavior that human biology makes understandable. The question is, rather, can *all* human behavior be explained through biology and genetics?

Darwin's Legacy

Natural Selection

Philosophers talk about the "three blows to human self-assurance," meaning that (at least) three times so far our human pride has been shattered by new knowledge: The first "blow" was when Copernicus discovered that the universe doesn't revolve around the earth, but the earth is a satellite moving around the sun; the second "blow" was when Charles Darwin realized that we are related to all life on earth and cannot claim a spe-

cial biological status; the third "blow" was when Freud taught us that we don't even know our own minds, but are ridden and torn by unconscious forces that we have little or no control over. Here we take a closer look at Darwin's "blow"—from which a lot of people are still reeling, as we saw in Chapter 2.

Sociobiology is part of the legacy of Darwin's theory of evolution. In Chapter 2 you encountered the principle of natural selection as a model for explaining evolution, including the evolution of humans. Prior to the publication of Darwin's *On the Origin of Species by Means of Natural Selection* (1859), it was by and large unthinkable to place humans and animals on the same scale when discussing behavioral patterns. Despite the fact that the concept of evolution was advanced well before Darwin came along, and anybody with a capacity for observation could see that humans and animals sometimes engage in similar behaviors, the notion of drawing parallels between humans and animals had for a long time been limited to writers of animal fables, such as the French author Jean de La Fontaine (1621–1695). One philosophical exception is the Scottish philosopher David Hume (1711–1776), who argues that if we call a certain type of human behavior rational and observe the same kind of behavior in animals, it would be only logical to say that the animal behavior is also rational. Darwin himself advanced the same idea a hundred years later, but Hume's idea is still considered unproved and controversial by a great many biologists and philosophers to this day.

However, the Darwinian concept of the *survival of the fittest,* a phrase coined by his friend and staunch defender, Julian Huxley, did provide a theory of human behavior based on human biology and drawing parallels to animal behavior. According to this theory, living organisms evolve gradually according to a principle of competition in nature: Whoever is capable of surviving long enough to have healthy offspring is "fit," because the offspring will be able to carry the parental genes into the future. The "fittest" are those species that fill their biological niches successfully and manage to have equally successful offspring. Because humans are living organisms, they too have engaged in the fight for survival of their species, and human evolution has thus favored certain traits, such as human sociability, that made us more successful at surviving. Thus, Darwin gave us a biological key to understanding human social life, as a fight for the survival of our kind, no different from the fight other species are engaged in.

In Chapter 2 we discussed why the theory of evolution is a valid scientific theory. Here we look at a few instances where the theory of evolution has been (1) corroborated and (2) rewritten. As you probably remember from Chapter 2, a good empirical scientific theory allows for the principle of falsification: It must test itself constantly, being open to the possibility that new evidence may force a reevaluation of the theory. Darwin's own vision of evolution involved millions of years of gradual change from one species into another species; for the classical Darwinist, once a species has evolved into another species, then the original species is gone. On both counts, science has had to revise Darwin's vision. We now know that evolution can happen much faster than Darwin had predicted—instead of millions of years, it sometimes takes only hundreds of thousands of years or much less. In a research project undertaken at the Galapagos Islands—the very place where Darwin, a young ship's doctor on board the *Beagle,* found his inspiration by watching the finches on each island and speculating about their differences and similarities—researchers looked at a population of finches on one island over a few decades. What they found was that evolution indeed takes

place: In years of drought, the blunt-beaked finches flourished, because they could break open the nuts that were available. In years of rain, the slender-beaked finches took over, because their beaks were better at eating the abundant berries (the nut bushes having bad seasons). So if evolution can be that rapid, might the fundamentalist-creationist theory of the earth's age (6,000 years) be correct after all? No, because the fossil record shows that the earth is at least 4 billion years old. But some spurts of evolution are fast, while others are slow or nonexistent. Darwin thought that evolution is gradual; now we know that there are no rules as to the speed of evolution: Species evolve when their environment changes and they have to change with it or die out. But this *doesn't* mean that (1) every species is changing or (2) that those that change, live, and those that don't change, die.

The new picture of evolution looks somewhat like this: In a time of environmental change, some living beings (plants or animals) handle the change better than others—because of genetic mutations or different genetic characteristics within a family. Now if the environment can't sustain the "old" kind of species, they will die out, and the new kind supplant them. But if somehow the environment isn't hostile to the old kind, but the old and the new kind are isolated from each other (by a flood, a rock slide, or perhaps the new group migrating into another valley), the two branches can coexist in time if not in space: The "parent" population stays where it is without changing, while the "daughter" population evolves farther away from the parent population on the other side of the mountain. Some species, like the coelacanth, have remained the same for millions of years, while other species, like humans, have had a very rapid evolution. Evolution may be gradual, but there is increasing evidence that it is also—or perhaps exclusively—punctuated, happening in spurts. In Chapter 2 you encountered this theory of "punctuated equilibrium," envisioning rapid spurts of evolution with long and unpredictable intervals of stability. So was Darwin wrong? Not in his understanding of the principle of evolution:

natural selection. But he couldn't have envisioned the entire story and, in all probability, neither can we—yet.

Darwin's Critics

Darwin came under attack immediately upon publication of his theories, not just from the church and other religious groups but also from other scientists. His book *The Descent of Man* was misread as saying that humans descended from apes (instead of saying that humans and apes having a common ancestor), and it spawned a myriad of cartoons of Darwin in the company of dressed-up apes or Darwin depicted as an ape himself. As we saw in Chapter 2, there is now so much evidence that humans and apes share an evolutionary past and indeed that humans and apes are fellow primates (or, as the New Zealand government stated in its 1999 prohibition against using apes in research, apes and humans are *fellow hominids*) that there is no scientific basis for disagreement. So we will instead look at some of the other arguments against Darwin.

Fit to Survive?   The expression "survival of the fittest" has been criticized as a tautological argument: It is true by virtue of its circular logic, nothing else. Who survives? Those who are fit to survive. So should we call it "survival of the strongest" instead? No, because sometimes the big, strong creatures die out, while the little ones survive. Case in point: the extinction of the dinosaurs and the rise of mammals, beginning with individuals the size of a mouse. So perhaps we should say, "survival of the best-adapted." Either way, it doesn't seem sufficient to explain all animal evolution, let alone all human and social evolution. Sometimes an animal population survives because its niche hasn't been challenged by other animals and not because it is particularly well adapted to its niche. Sometimes well-adapted species mutate and die. The theory seems even more questionable when applied to human evolution. Humans are not particularly well adapted, as we

saw in Chapter 2. Our esophagus is right next to our windpipe, and because we walk upright it is easy for us to choke. Our spines and knees don't hold up well to a life span exceeding sixty years. But humanity is young, and perhaps we are still adapting?

Here human culture comes into play and decides that not just the ones with especially strong spines and good feet can have viable children. Human cultures often choose to keep alive members who, left to nature, might face an early death. For all intents and purposes, natural selection in human civilization has given way to *cultural selection,* although Darwin himself saw a form of "natural selection" happening even in human civilizations: According to Darwin, emigration tempts courageous, energetic people, so a nation of immigrants is naturally selected as being energetic and courageous; in addition, taking criminals out of circulation (and thus, as we would say today, removing them from the gene pool) prevents their "bad genes" from being passed on. (Box 3.1 explores the prospect of the human race in the future and looks at the pros and cons of *eugenics* as a deliberate plan for human evolution.)

Evolving Toward Superman?   Darwin has been viewed as implicitly supporting the idea of a *master race* that evolves and looks out for itself. It is true that this idea was not offensive to Darwin; indeed, the vision offered by eugenics suggested moral progress to many thinkers and scientists in the nineteenth century, but with Hitler's Holocaust as part of twentieth-century history, any such suggestion becomes offensive to many today. Darwin expresses these thoughts on eugenics:

> Both sexes ought to refrain from marriage if they are in any marked degree inferior in body or mind; but such hopes are Utopian and will never be even partially realized until the laws of inheritance are thoroughly known. Everyone does good service, who aid toward this end. When the principles of breeding and inheritance are better understood, we shall not hear ignorant members of our legislature

Box 3.1   THE NEXT CHAPTER IN HUMAN EVOLUTION?

Science fiction used to speculate that in the far future, humans will look different than they do today. H. G. Wells predicted in his *Time Machine* that 60,000 years from now, humans will have evolved into two groups: the peaceful, childlike Eloids and the smart, but evil Morluks who keep the Eloids as food animals. Wells's vision of horror was, to a great extent, a moral *caveat* (a warning): Goodness and evil coexist in humans of today, but in the future, evil may prey on goodness if we are not careful. Other writers have seen future human beings as spindly creatures with huge, hairless heads (for the expanded brain) or horribly disfigured and mutated from nuclear fallout. A science fiction writer, Larry Niven, speculates that as we colonize other planets in the galaxy, our looks will change according to the changing gravity and other environmental factors—certainly a sound biological prediction! Can we make any kind of predictions as to what we might look like 60,000 years from now? The answer may be disappointing: If humanity is still around, we may, biologically, look exactly the way we look now—although there is already evidence that the races may by then have blended into each other. But our heads are probably not going to be any bigger, and we are probably still going to be prone to choking from time to time.

This prediction assumes that humans have interfered with evolution and have put natural selection out of business through *cultural selection*. However, we can't discount three possibilities: (1) Humans will have polluted their environment to such an extent that we will no longer be a successfully surviving species; in that case we may have devolved to a smaller, weaker, shorter-lived species. Or (2) humans will have developed technology so far advanced that the science fiction scenario of bionic (partially artificial) bodies will be a reality; we may have artificially enhanced sensory organs, memory chips, and so forth. In addition, we may have genetically altered bodies designed for special working conditions, such as under water. However, in that case we are no longer talking natural selection, but a "designer species." The success of such a species will depend on whether its environment remains stable, but above all on whether humans will put up with being genetically designed as tools to be used for society's purposes. Most science fiction writers of the past decades would warn against it, as a dehumanizing policy. But what about (3) the possibility of deliberately steering human evolution in a certain direction—in other words, *eugenics* (improvement of the human race through breeding)? Western thinkers have flirted with this idea ever since Plato (see Chapters 6, 8, and 9), but we need only go back some sixty years to Hitler's attempt to "purify" the Germanic race by annihilating citizens—13 million of them—whom he thought didn't measure up racially to be reminded of the possible consequences of eugenics put into action: Creating a stronger, healthier human race may sound attractive, but in practice, deciding who measures up and who doesn't is at best a tool for social discrimination and at worst a tool for extermination.

rejecting with scorn a plan for ascertaining whether or not consanguineous marriages [inbreeding] are injurious to man.[1]

Interestingly, there is a roundabout connection between Darwin's concept of the survival of the fittest and Hitler's master race concept, and the connection goes through the German philosopher Friedrich Nietzsche (1844–1900). Nietzsche admired Darwin and used his theory of natural selection to form the notion that the strong individual ought to rise above the crowd and set his own rules—to become an *Overman* or a *Superman* (see Chapter 8). Nietzsche had the fate of the gifted individual in mind, not the evolution of a race of supermen; but ironically, a generation after Nietzsche's death, history (with the help of Nietzsche's anti-Semitic sister) delivered his writings into the hands of Hitler, and Hitler's concept of a master race was born. Darwin himself firmly believed that humanity was still evolving, but not so much in a physical sense; Darwin believed that humans were evolving toward a higher, *moral* goal. Nothing in Darwin's theory of natural selection would make us suspect that he saw any *race* as more "fit" to survive than any other race, although he tried to reach a conclusion about inherent qualitative differences among the races and the possibility that the human races really should be regarded as different species (see Chapter 5). Darwin says, "A tribe including many members who, from possessing in a high degree the spirit of patriotism, fidelity, obedience, courage, and sympathy, were always ready to aid one another, and to sacrifice themselves for the common good, would be victorious over most other tribes; and this would be natural selection."[2] The way Darwin saw it, humanity on the whole was becoming kinder and gentler, and he believed in an expansion of natural family affection that would extend, eventually, to the entire human race. Modern philosophers such as the controversial Australian thinker Peter Singer have echoed Darwin's hope for a new morality for all of humanity.

Darwin a Capitalist Lackey?   One complaint often voiced against Darwin is that he was so much a child of his day and age (nineteenth-century capitalist England) that his theory of natural selection becomes a thinly veiled metaphor for the economic structure of the time: *capitalism*. Individual *competition* and the need to fight others in order to get ahead—this isn't just a biological description, but an economic metaphor! Marxists used to say that Darwin tried to justify capitalism ideologically by claiming that the urge for competition is grounded in human nature (which Marxists don't believe). Whether Darwin had any conscious wish to justify capitalism or not, the fact remains that his description of the motives behind human actions evokes images of selfishness, competition, and hostility—just like Marx's analysis of the psychology behind capitalism, which we look at more closely in Chapter 9. However, it wasn't Darwin himself, but one of his readers, the British philosopher Herbert Spencer, who argued that unrelenting competition is a human survival mechanism. This theory has become

known as *social Darwinism*. Modern evolutionists have occasionally suggested that new metaphors be explored, such as the metaphor of *cooperation* rather than competition. But just in case we conclude that Darwin had no connection to capitalist thinking, we should note that Darwin was quite comfortable with the idea of competition:

> Man, like any other animal, has no doubt advanced to his present high condition through a struggle for existence consequent on his rapid multiplication; and if he is to advance still higher, it is to be feared that he must remain subject to a severe struggle. Otherwise he would sink into indolence, and the more gifted men would not be more successful in the battle of life than the less gifted. Hence our natural rate of increase though leading to many and obvious evils must not be greatly diminished by any means. There should be open competition for all men; and the most able should not be prevented by laws or customs from succeeding best and rearing the largest number of offspring.[3]

So far, so good: Here Darwin sounds like the social Darwinists who were to follow him. However, if we read further, we find that

> Important as the struggle for existence has been and even still is, yet as far as the highest part of man's nature is concerned there are other agencies more important. For the moral qualities are advanced, either directly or indirectly, much more through the effects of habit, the reasoning powers, instruction, religion &c., than through natural selection; though to this latter agency may be safely attributed the social instincts, which afforded the basis for the development of the moral sense.[4]

So the point Darwin wants to make is, interestingly, that humans can make themselves into better people through a moral choice; natural selection has given us the tool in our social instincts, but competition isn't everything: In order for us to improve the human condition, we have to go beyond our instincts and, in effect, focus on our cultural evolution.

Ethics and Evolution

As hopeful as Darwin was that humanity is evolving in a more moral direction, evolutionism has always had a hard time explaining exactly why it is biologically advantageous to be nice or to display affection. If you are too nice, others may take advantage of you. You may spend so much time taking care of your aging parent that you never marry or have children of your own. We could conclude that affection could be a bad investment. We might also conclude that there must be more to the story of evolution than individual survival; perhaps affection is not directly survival-oriented, but it serves valuable social and personal functions nevertheless.

However, philosophers in general have a problem with Darwin's predilection for drawing moral values into his theory of human evolution. Darwinism is a biological theory, but when it is applied to the realm of human decision making, it enters the field of ethics; and most philosophers consider this to be an area that is best left alone by biologists. If we choose to see morality as a purely biological development, with biological grounds for every decision, we lose sight of the fact that human reason—at least according to most philosophers—allows us to detach ourselves from our natural inclinations and judge their merit. We can choose to follow them, but we can also choose to control them. Such control may have a biological basis, but it also may not.

Darwin was a naturalist, not a philosopher. However, since the publication of his *Origin of Species,* Darwin's theory of the survival of the fittest has proved an inspiration and a challenge to philosophers as well as naturalists. Does Darwinism imply that we are destined always to seek survival by promoting our own genes? The contemporary biologist and thinker Edward O. Wilson believes so, and we encounter his view later on in this chapter.

Are Humans Aggressive by Nature?

For a great deal of the twentieth century it has been assumed in Western thinking that humans are an aggressive, warlike species, but these theories have been questioned lately. If humans generally display aggression, have they always done so? And if so, are all humans aggressive, or perhaps just one gender? Here we look at the most famous theories of human aggression in the past fifty years: those of Robert Ardrey and Konrad Lorenz.

The Territorial Imperative

In the 1960s a series of books about human aggression became best-sellers. The author, Robert Ardrey, had majored in natural sciences at the University of Chicago and had become a playwright and a Hollywood screenwriter. He understood better than many scientists the language of popular scientific books. His style was colorful, and he became immensely influential through his books. Within the scientific community, he was never recognized as an influence, but that community had its own proponent of the theory of fundamental human aggression: the Austrian scientist Konrad Lorenz. He had a more distinguished scholarly background than Ardrey, but a similar talent for popularization. The two men shaped American opinion for decades with their assertion that *humans are by nature aggressive and territorial*. They will defend their territory for sexual reasons—in order to gain the right to mate—just like other animals.

Lorenz and Ardrey were not the first to make this claim: Sigmund Freud had had similar thoughts after witnessing the slaughter of an entire generation of young European soldiers in World War I; he believed that "we are descended from an endless long chain of murderers whose love of murder was in their blood as it is perhaps in our own." Lorenz, through his fascinating reports of animal observations—in particular, his experiences with raising and bonding with baby Greylag geese—told the world about animals' territorial tendencies and the importance of imprinting and bonding of the baby animal. Ardrey coined the term *territorial imperative* (perhaps as a tribute to the philosopher Immanuel Kant's famous

Box 3.2 THE LION AS METAPHOR

Ardrey uses the metaphor of a male lion roaming the savanna to illustrate the early human hunter—so what is Ardrey trying to say? That it is wonderful for human males to be naturally aggressive, to move about, do what they want, have sex with whatever female is available, and then go off in search of new adventures? This seems to be what Ardrey thinks a lion does. But the analogy doesn't hold up: For one thing, in a pride of lions, the male lion rarely hunts and kills prey; the lioness does. As a rule, the male lion gets killed fighting for his territory only when he is too old and weak to defend it any longer; attackers are usually not killed, but merely bullied away. Young male lions, however, who are cast out from the pride and are in search of their own females, may display the aggressive, predatory behavior that Ardrey describes. Young male outcast apes and monkeys display a similar behavior. But on the whole, primate males don't live the lives of a solitary hunter. The hominid family groups we now believe populated the savanna some 2 million years ago seem to have been tightly knit—and besides, Ardrey's metaphor of the male lion offers no explanation at all for female human nature. However, it may be a good description of outcast young human males striving to form a group of their own.

concept of the *categorical* imperative) and explored other people's research on animals primarily to draw conclusions about humans. Whereas Lorenz's conclusions about human culture were by and large developed as an afterthought (see the next section), Ardrey's theories represented sociobiology in its most popular form: They were deterministic theories of human culture based on human biology, as Ardrey read it, and couched in survivalist jargon.

Why was Ardrey so preoccupied with human aggression? It could simply be a sign of the times: Ardrey wrote his first major book, *African Genesis* (1961), a few years after the Korean War (1950–1954), and the issue of human aggression loomed large in the nation's mind—partly because the Cold War was a constant reminder of the possibility of nuclear annihilation. However, other theories of human behavior developed during wartime, such as Sartre's existentialism (see Chapter 4), do not emphasize any innate human aggression. In addition to being influenced by the tensions of the 1950s, Ardrey seems to have sought inspiration in both Darwin and Nietzsche. For Ardrey, humans are what early human evolution has made them: hunters and killers. And weapons have made them who they are today—in combination with the upright stance, which gave their hands freedom to grasp, hit, and throw and allowed the males' eyes to scan the plains in search of prey, females, and a good fight. Like the proud lion who roams freely, hunts its prey, and kills to defend its territory, early man developed his nature through aggression and adversity. (See Box 3.2 for a discussion of the usefulness of the lion as a metaphor.) If man had not encountered hard times, he would not have developed the brains to use his hands to make weapons.[5] So the "aggressive imperative" liberated humans from their earlier animal ways, although we still retain a heritage of fear and dominance.

Man, says Ardrey, has "an overpowering enthusiasm for things that go boom." Does that mean, then, that we are "evolution's most tragic error," in Ardrey's words, or is there hope for the human race? For Ardrey the solution to the human predicament doesn't lie in simply abolishing war, for humans must apparently have challenges in the form of violence in order to stay intellectually fit; if we abolish all forms of violence, we will lose the ability to defend ourselves, he claims, and the challenge to humans of the future will be to find a way to reach intellectual fitness and stay alive as a species without blowing up the planet. You

Box 3.3   CAIN: THE FIRST MURDERER

The Bible teaches that Cain, the firstborn son of Adam and Eve following their expulsion from the Garden of Eden, killed his younger brother Abel because of jealousy: God preferred Abel's sacrifice to Cain's. Abel, a shepherd, had sacrificed a lamb, while Cain, a farmer, had sacrificed ripe grain. Because Abel's death was the first death of a human being, according to the biblical storyteller, we might ask whether Cain was truly committing *murder* since he didn't know the nature of death when he struck out at his brother. In a court of law today it might be viewed as *manslaughter!* According to the story, Cain was sent away to the land east of Eden by God, and God marked his forehead so everyone would recognize him; however, this was supposedly not a punishment, but a protection. The mark on Cain's forehead was a sign that he was protected by God.

will recognize Darwin's belief that if humans don't struggle for existence, they become indolent. Ardrey's theory is that all human advances have been won through the use of wartime violence, from Christianity to the rule of law, and our political ideals of freedom and individuality. He worries that if we abolish violence, we may perish because we lack new challenges; on the other hand, since Ardrey lived and worked in the post-Hiroshima era, he knew full well that another world war would probably lead to mutual nuclear annihilation.

Children of a Murderer?

Mythologically or symbolically speaking, humans are the children of Cain, the first murderer. (See Box 3.3 for a synopsis of the story of Cain and Abel.) Ardrey and many others have labeled Cain a murderer; and because, according to biblical legend, he was the father of the human race, we are all Cain's children. (Ardrey doesn't mean this in a genetic sense; he does not profess any fundamentalist belief that we are actually descended from the biblical character, but is using Cain as a symbol of innate human aggression.) So according to Freud, Lorenz, and Ardrey, humans are aggressive by nature. Ardrey, however, seems to go beyond this descriptive theory of human nature to a *normative* statement: If humans hadn't been killer apes, we wouldn't have achieved our technological advances nor our ideals of freedom—so does that mean humans *ought* to be aggressive? As you will see in an excerpt from Ardrey's *African Genesis* in the Primary Readings, he struggles to imagine a human race of the future that has managed to transform our propensity for violence to a higher level, a new dream for humanity—but leaves it up to the reader to judge whether this is a real possibility.

On the whole, Ardrey's theory of innate human aggression is valuable to us because it represents a point of view that was so prevalent a generation ago that it was rarely questioned: It was generally accepted that humans are prone to use weapons and that the development of the weapon has been a major factor in the evolution of human intelligence. The opening sequence of the science fiction film classic, *2001: A Space Odyssey,* is pure Ardrey: The extraterrestrial monolith (a large, black slab of rock that is supposedly a thought-enhancer, among other things) makes a small group of apes use their reason—and what do the apes do with their new mind capacity? They envision using an animal thighbone as a *weapon,* to kill prey, as well as killing the neighboring apes so they can take over the water hole. (See film still from *2001: A Space Odyssey* and the Narratives section.) The seamless segue in the film from an instrument of death to a spaceship reveals that the director and screenwriter accepted the theory that human intelligence is based on the develop-

2001: A Space Odyssey, MGM, 1968. After having touched the great black monolith, the apelike creature discovers the concept of a weapon—a legbone from a tapir—and makes the mental connection between killing a tapir and killing members of his own species. In the introduction to the film, which depicts the "Dawn of Man," human nature is being formed by the invention of the weapon, an idea based on then-popular theories of human aggression by Raymond Dart, Robert Ardrey, and Konrad Lorenz.

ment of weapons and that aggression is a useful—perhaps deplorable, but nevertheless useful—part of human nature.

One of the most famous paleoanthropologists of the mid–twentieth century, Raymond Dart, fully supported the aggression thesis on the basis of what he thought was scientific evidence. Dart, the discoverer of an important early *Australopithecus* skull, believed that human aggression could be proved by the discovery of bones in a cave in Africa in the general area where early humans lived. The deep cave was (and still is) full of bones, those of *Australopithecus* as well as other animals. The hominid skulls have been pierced by sharp instruments, and the cave is littered with animal jawbones, providing vicious weapons. Dart himself demonstrated for a film crew how he thought early human ancestors would use the bone to rip the bellies of enemies and animals open. However, as paleoanthropologist Don Johanson demonstrated in the 1990s PBS series *The Quest for Human Nature,* Dart misread his evidence: The

injuries on the hominid skulls didn't match any weapons found, but on the contrary, they matched perfectly the teeth of another skull found, that of a leopard! And chew marks on the bones are probably not from cannibalism, but from the great cave porcupine who to this day uses the same caves as a hiding place for bones to gnaw on. So Johanson and local anthropologists think that the mass of bones accumulated as the prey of leopards and of bone-loving porcupines, not as the garbage pile of voracious hominids. In this case at least, the humans turned out to be the prey, not the hunter.

Seen in retrospective as a response to the insecure, violent times of the mid–twentieth century, it is perhaps easier to understand Ardrey and his theory. You'll remember from Chapter 1 the speculations of historians and philosophers that it is part of our nature to *tell stories* about human nature and culture. Ardrey and, to a lesser extent, Lorenz may be a good example of this tendency. With the Cold War and the Korean War as part of everyday life, so soon after World War II, the ideas

Box 3.4   ANTHROPOLOGY AND THE BATTLE OF INTERPRETATION

In the mid–twentieth century, the sociobiologist Napoleon Chagnon came back from the Amazon with amazing tales of the fierce Yanomamö Indians, describing them as having a fundamentally aggressive nature combined with an overall happy, laid-back lifestyle within the tribe. For thousands of anthropology students (including me, at the time) his book, *Yanomamö: The Fierce People,* was regarded as a model work of field research. But old models tend to become today's targets, and a recent book, *Darkness in El Dorado,* tears into Chagnon's research as being self-serving and to a great extent a fabrication of "facts." The author, Patrick Tierney, accuses Chagnon of making stories up in order to make the Yanomamö appear like the warriors he hoped they were—not only as a literary device, but quite literally, stirring them up to go to war with neighboring tribes. Tierney attempts to show that the Yanomamö were far from being aggressive and that whatever fierceness they were reported as having came from Chagnon's own brain.

However, Tierney admits that he is no neutral observer—he has taken up the cause of being an advocate for the Amazon Indians, opposing development in the rain forest. And some of Tierney's critics wonder if he is reacting not only to Chagnon's supposedly shoddy science, but also to the political incorrectness of Chagnon's ideas. So might Tierney, in his turn, be presenting the Yanomamö as peaceful because it suits his own view of righting the wrong done by Chagnon? In other words, *is there an objective viewpoint of Yanomamö behavior, or is every report tainted by someone's agenda?* Such are the questions anthropologists, sociobiologists, other scholars, and laypeople have to ask themselves, especially these days when we are becoming acutely aware how much a scholar's worldview is liable to influence the way that person interprets what is observed.

that war is inevitable and humans are aggressive by nature came naturally to many people. Or perhaps we should say that the inevitability of aggression was an idea that made it easier to live with the constant fear of atomic war: If it can't be otherwise, we must learn to live with it. So Ardrey provided the story we needed while living under such stressful circumstances, telling us that we are all "Cain's children," with a built-in curse of aggression. This is just one example of an explanation, or story, of human nature provided to suit the needs of the moment.

Interestingly, in the final years of the twentieth century and at the dawn of the twenty-first, there has been a shift in our cultural need for understanding our own nature: Many people no longer feel the direct threat of nuclear war or nuclear winter, but we do feel the burdens of global overcrowding, environmental breakdowns, outbreaks of violence, and other elements that threaten our well-being. So we look for another story, one we may use as a tool to change the tide. Don Johanson tells us that early hominids were scavengers more often than hunters and that Dart mistook a prey for a hunter. At the end of this chapter we look at the story that has presented itself recently as an alternative sociobiological explanation: the story of the chalice as opposed to the blade or the basket as opposed to the weapon. (Box 3.4 explores the current climate of warring interpretations of human nature in anthropology.)

Konrad Lorenz: *Aggressive Nonpredators*

The person who usually gets credit for having launched the twentieth-century sociobiological theory of human aggression, Konrad Lorenz, reached a conclusion that, oddly, paved the way for Johanson and others who have chosen to see ancient hominids as less-than-perfect predators. The Austrian scientist's conclusion about human nature was different from Ardrey's, even though it was based on the same general theory of human aggression and even though Lorenz, too, felt the need to express a normative theory of human behavior. Lorenz studied fish and birds primarily and found them to be fundamentally territorial—at least the males were. But a few years after Ardrey's book *African Genesis* was published, Lorenz gave the debate a new twist in his book *On Aggression* (1963), with the far more significant German title *Das Sogenannte Böse*, "The So-Called Evil." Ardrey called his chapter on human aggression "Cain's Children." Lorenz calls his chapter "Ecce Homo."[6]

Like Ardrey, Lorenz is convinced that humans are aggressive beings, and like Ardrey he believes our aggression is rooted in our evolutionary prehistory. But here is where Lorenz takes a different turn: Instead of focusing, as Ardrey does, on the intelligence-enhancing capacity of aggression, Lorenz sees our aggression as an outdated remnant of a behavior pattern that used to be necessary, but has now become dangerous. Aggression may have been a survival mechanism when we were living in small tribes, but at that time it could inflict only limited damage on other human communities: individual deaths, yes, but not wholesale slaughter. And an element in human aggression that Lorenz finds extraordinarily dangerous is the fact that we are *not* "killer apes"—we are just apes who kill. To Lorenz it is obvious that we are not descendants of great predators, carnivores with a built-in killer instinct—we are just very successful, cranky *omnivores*. The real predators in the animal world have a built-in instinctual reluctance to kill members of their own species, says Lorenz: Wolves hesitate to kill other wolves, and lions don't usually kill other lions; but we humans don't have a long evolutionary history of being strictly predators and have never developed the same reluctance to kill our own. And that is why human aggression becomes particularly dangerous when combined with high technology. (Interestingly, Lorenz says chimpanzees won't kill other chimpanzees, but we now know they will. What does that mean? Probably that chimpanzees, too, are cranky omnivores without a built-in reluctance to kill other members of their own species. It may be a primate "thing.")

So are we destined to wipe each other out, just because we are cranky and living in a high-density, high-tech environment where the ancient outlets for aggression no longer exist? No, says Lorenz, because in actual fact humans are *not* evil by nature. We have, so to speak, been cornered by our own evolutionary aggression, but there are layers in human nature that go far deeper. We could not have developed language and morals and other social phenomena if we hadn't lived in well-structured societies *even before* we had language and rational thought. What were those communities based on? A compassionate instinct and a sense of responsibility:

> The motive power that makes them do so stems from instinctive behavior mechanisms much older than reason and not directly accessible for rational self-observation. They are the source of love and friendship, of all warmth and feeling, of appreciation of beauty, of the urge to artistic creativeness, of insatiable curiosity striving for scientific enlightenment. These deepest strata of the human personality are, in their dynamics, not essentially different from the instincts of animals. . . . It is safe to assume that the first Cain, after having stricken a fellow member of his horde with a pebble tool, was deeply concerned about the consequences of his actions. He may have struck with very little malice. Just as a two-year-old child may hit another with a heavy and hard object without foreseeing the effect. . . . In any case we are safe in assuming that the first killer fully realized the enormity of his deed.[7]

So what must we do to bring out the original and better side of humans? Embark on a massive cultural program, says Lorenz: It won't do to try to breed out the tendency through eugenics, because we don't know enough about which human traits are useful; but we can try to enhance the sense of moral responsibility, discourage acts of aggression, from individual fights to warfare—and pay more attention to our sense of *humor*, because laughter diffuses aggression.

EVOLUTIONARY CREATIONISM...

Are humans aggressive by nature? In the 1950s and 1960s it was a rarely contested theory, but today scientists and philosophers lean toward other explanations of human nature. This *Non Sequitur* cartoon borrows bits from both religion and science in a fantasy image of how peace was permanently disrupted in the Paradise of ancient Earth.

Are Humans Selfish by Nature?

A theory that has been even more persistent than fundamental human aggression is the theory that we are by nature selfish creatures. Here we look at some of the most famous theorists of human selfishness, from Thomas Hobbes in the seventeenth century to Sigmund Freud and E. O. Wilson in the twentieth, and we also look at alternative models provided by Richard Leakey and Mary Midgley.

"We Are Fundamentally Selfish"

Having established that, scientifically speaking, humans are animals, related to all other animals on earth, we now explore the theory that like all other animals, humans are primarily (or even exclusively) oriented toward self-preservation. Philosophers call this theory *psychological egoism:* "Psychological," because it is a theory about how humans behave psychologically; this means the theory attempts to *describe* how human nature is, not set up any norm for what it ought to be. Psychological egoism is thus a *descriptive* theory of human nature. (Box 3.5 offers a brief introduction to the *normative* theory of selfishness, *ethical egoism.*)

The relationship between psychological egoism and sociobiology is indirect: *Sociobiology* claims that human biology influences all *human social structures,* but within these social structures, individuals may display a wide range of behavior. On the other hand, the closely related theory of *evolutionary psychology* claims that human biology influences the *lives of individuals* in every way from habits to rational decision-making processes.

Box 3.5 ETHICAL EGOISM

Some students of philosophy stumble at the very title of this theory and jump to conclusions, but this is not a theory about how to be selfish in a nice way! "Ethical" doesn't mean "decent" here, but simply "normative." Ethical egoism is a theory about how one *ought* to behave: selfishly! Who might advocate such a theory that goes against everything we were taught as children and everything we usually try to teach our own kids: Don't be selfish, think of others first, don't grab the last cookie on the plate, and so forth? A number of thinkers have done so, for a variety of reasons. The primary argument of ethical egoism is, You must look out for yourself, because nobody else is going to do it. If you don't think of yourself first, you are throwing your own chance at happiness away, and you have only this one life to live. This is the ethical egoism we encounter in the works of the philosopher Ayn Rand. It implies that those who don't think of themselves first are fools. So here we notice that for the ethical egoist it is entirely *possible* to be unselfish, but there is no profit in it.

A secondary argument is, Be prudent and make certain you can't be faulted for anything; the best way to do that is to treat others decently, because in that case, they will treat you decently too. This is in effect a version of the famous Golden Rule, with the twist that you treat others as you would be treated for your own sake, not for the sake of how others feel. Thomas Hobbes included this idea in his *Leviathan*. Ethical egoism has been presented as a theory for a cynical world that knows most people are out to grab as much as they can, so why not make sure we get some of it too? However, ethicists generally frown on the theory, primarily because it shows a complete callousness toward the sufferings of others. The only reason one refrains from causing pain to others, according to ethical egoism, is that one is likely to be safe from harm from others—not because it is wrong in itself to cause others pain. This lack of empathy is unacceptable to most ethicists.

Another version of ethical egoism is offered by Aristotle: We ought to love ourselves better than anybody else, because if we do, we take better care of ourselves, we are better friends and companions to others because we endeavor to develop our virtues, and so life will be more pleasant for everyone all around. But this form of rational ethical egoism does not emphasize disregarding other people's interests; it merely states that being virtuous is in one's own interest. For Aristotle, virtue is not its own reward—the payoff comes in an increase in our overall happiness and well-being.

Psychological egoism in its modern form is generally presented as a version of evolutionary psychology, but the theory is far more ancient than modern sciences. Over the past century, it has been one of the most favored theories of human nature among scholars and laypeople alike, and it has been evoked from time to time ever since the days of Socrates and Plato—but that doesn't mean it is necessarily true. The Danish philosopher Søren Kierkegaard warned against siding with the opinion of the many, because he felt it was more likely to be false than the opinion reached by individuals who themselves have researched and experienced an issue; in essence, Socrates had similar thoughts. (In effect, they both indirectly identified one of the logical fallacies: that something must be correct just because a lot of people say so. This is the fallacy of *ad populum,* popularity.) So just because a theory has won popularity contests doesn't mean we have to endorse it—but it would be wrong not to give it the attention it deserves, because psychological egoism is a disturbingly attractive theory.

Suppose we could explain any human action by referring to a bottom-line selfish streak? In that case, much of the "human comedy" around us would be more understandable. Why does a president lie under oath? Why do people break promises, reveal other people's secrets, break rules of decency as well as the rule of law? Why do people rob each other, molest children, and murder fellow human beings? Because we are all selfish, deep down in the heart of our human nature. All we care about is protecting ourselves and getting away with as much as possible without getting caught—right? But it doesn't explain the other side of the human coin: Why would someone jump into the unstable rubble of a collapsed building to save a survivor clinging to life under the debris? Why do people risk their lives to save others, whether they are paid to do it or not, whether they are lifeguards, firefighters and police officers or just Joe and Jane Q. Public? Why would a group of healthy nuns volunteer as guinea pigs for an AIDS vaccine in the mid-1980s when little was known about the disease other than that it always killed its victim?

Most of us would answer that although humans have the capacity for great selfishness, we also have the capacity for great unselfishness. Psychological egoism has another explanation: Even the seemingly unselfish acts are done out of some fundamental urge to serve yourself and your own interests. Granted that we probably won't ever know what selfish or self-interested motivation Mother Teresa may have had for spending her life saving others in the slums of Calcutta, but we can rest assured that there was one, says the psychological egoist: A wish to atone for past sins? A wish to become famous for her unselfishness? A wish for a ticket straight to Heaven? Or just a need to feel good about what she was doing? To most people who admire her life's work, these suggestions are preposterous and insulting, because their impression of her work is quite different. To most of us, she came across as a selfless human being; the Christian tradition would identify her work as charitable, coming out of a strict goal of self-abnegation. For the psychological egoist, however, these interpretations lead us straight to the truth about human nature: We may not have total insight into exactly what makes people tick, but whatever they do, it in some way leads back to feeling good or protecting oneself from feeling bad. This is what is so devilishly attractive about psychological egoism: It has explanations for every

human action, and they are always consistent. Whatever we do, we do it for ourselves. Critics of this provocative theory—and there are many—generally point to the theory's lack of scientific rigor: It doesn't allow for the principle of falsification—the empirical possibility that it might be wrong—but simply pronounces its thesis—all humans are selfish—like a credo that can't be doubted. Also, even if it should turn out that we all have a selfish streak, isn't there a fundamental difference between someone who gloats over other people's misfortune because he or she is selfish and someone who rejoices when they can do something nice for others, because they are happy when they can make others happy? Surely we can't be talking about the same kind of selfishness?

In this section we look at three influential thinkers in the Western tradition who all, in their own ways, have contributed to the theory that humans are selfish by nature. We will encounter them in several contexts in this book. They are Thomas Hobbes (1588–1679), Sigmund Freud (1856–1939), and Edward O. Wilson (b. 1929).

Thomas Hobbes: Self-Preservation Is Everything

Thomas Hobbes (1588–1679) was a colorful presence in a century of turmoil. Hobbes had been a tutor to the children of the English royal family and lived his life during times of extreme political unrest; the king; Charles I, was beheaded in 1649. Hobbes felt that absence from England was the better part of valor and subsequently spent some time in France. Many thinkers at the time felt physically threatened, and publishing could indeed be dangerous business; the Catholic church, newly banished from the English court by Henry VIII but still the most powerful political force in Europe, cracked down hard on what it considered heresy; among the heretics were political dissidents, astrologers and other self-proclaimed magicians, and even genuine scientists (sometimes the scientists dabbled in magic too). The rising Protestant societies weren't any more open to scientific research. Giordano Bruno was burned at the stake in 1600 for claiming, as Galileo did, that the earth revolves around the sun. (Galileo later retracted his statement to save his life.) Secret scientific societies blossomed, at the risk of exposure and persecution for their members.

So can we blame Hobbes for thinking that we are primarily geared toward self-preservation, any more than we can blame Ardrey for thinking that humans are aggressive? Indeed, Hobbes seems to be the original proponent of the idea that human nature is fundamentally aggressive, as we shall see in Chapter 9. As if the political climate weren't enough to explain why Hobbes may have found psychological egoism to make sense, there is also the scientific angle: Thomas Hobbes may today be remembered primarily for his social theories, but there is little doubt that he thought of himself as a scientist too; today we would be right to think of him as the first influential modern psychologist. Hobbes expressed the theory that humans are nothing but physical existence, and in this he truly paved the way for modern psychology; he also laid himself wide open for charges of heresy, because it appears that Hobbes was an atheist—something considered a prosecutable offense at the time. For that reason we never read directly in Hobbes's writings that he doesn't believe in the existence of God, but we can draw our conclusions: For Hobbes there is nothing spiritual; even souls don't exist. The movement of our bodies is either involuntary or voluntary; when it is voluntary, it is caused by our willpower, or *endeavor.* This theory provides us with all the answers to why humans do what they do, because it is all directed toward one goal: human well-being and self-preservation. In *Leviathan* Hobbes tells us that

> This endeavor, when it is toward something which causes it, is called APPETITE, or DESIRE; the later, being the general name; and the other, often-times restrained to signify the desire of food, namely *hunger* and *thirst.* And when the endeavor is fromward something, it is generally called AVERSION. . . . That which men desire, they are also said to LOVE: and to HATE those things for which

they have aversions . . . but whatsoever is the object of any man's appetite or desire, that is it, which for his part calls *good:* And the object of his hate, and aversion, *evil.*[8]

So, for Hobbes, all human emotions and decision making can be boiled down to our sense of self-preservation and self-gratification. To a modern understanding, this seems extremely simplified; but the tendency to reduce human nature to its most basic physical components and expressions is clearly a modern approach, and Hobbes should rightfully be recognized as a precursor, the first in a long line of eliminative materialists (see Chapter 7). So driving human nature is our innate physical urge to self-preservation; whenever we think we have more noble emotions that focus away from ourselves, we delude ourselves, Hobbes says: It can all be traced back to something self-serving. Why do we give to charity? Because we are afraid that we might one day need charity ourselves. Why do we feel pity toward others in need? Not because we know just how *they* feel, but we know just how *we'd* feel if it were us—and there is a world of difference between the two!

For Hobbes, this innate selfishness is not in itself "evil," because the terms of good and evil don't even enter into the picture until we have a society that can give such things moral labels. In a sense, Hobbes's theory of human nature is entirely descriptive, without a moral judgment: We are selfish because of our need to preserve our lives, and that is all there is to it. However, as we shall see in Chapter 9, Hobbes's theory of human nature leads him to a theory of human society—which often happens to philosophers who think about human nature: We can't help moving on to speculate about human society. And Hobbes's theory of human society is highly normative: There is a right way for us to live together—under a strong, reliable king—and a wrong way—without the protection provided by authorities. (Box 3.6 tells the story of the Ring of Gyges, a theory of selfish human nature from the Greek classical period.)

Box 3.6   PLATO AND THE RING OF GYGES

In Plato's most famous book, *Republic,* we encounter a theory expressed by his real-life brother, Glaucon, addressed to Plato's teacher and friend Socrates. A brief background note: Like many other ancient Greek philosophers, Socrates used to conduct outdoor class sessions in the public square in Athens, the Agora. Unlike his competitors, the Sophists, Socrates apparently didn't charge for his lessons, and he didn't advertise that he could teach his students to win any argument (as the Sophists seem to have done). Through conversations that range from the academic to the passionate, Socrates argues with his friends and followers about the true nature of things—human society, reality, justice, beauty, and philosophy itself. For Socrates, there is one true and correct answer for each question, but only the open, inquisitive mind can ask the right question. In philosophy ever since, knowing how to ask good questions has been at least as important as finding good answers!

Here, Glaucon is playing the devil's advocate, trying to provoke Socrates into giving a speech about the nature of justice, and the most outrageous thing Glaucon can think of saying is this: Once upon a time there were no laws, and everybody preyed on everybody else; this was great if you were strong and powerful, but even the powerful can themselves become prey. So in order to minimize the unpleasantness of becoming prey to others' selfishness, people decided to set up laws that would curb their own egoism—and that is why we have a legal system! People are selfish by nature, and if we had no laws, people would just prey on each other. Having laws is not ideal, but it is second-best if you don't want to have to look over your shoulder all the time. So even the legal system is in a way an expression of human selfishness: Safety is the primary concern, and we just juggle our priorities from "self-

gratifying gains" to "security for ourselves and our family"; but the bottom line is still that we are selfish by nature.

Glaucon even gives us a powerful demonstration in the form of an anecdote: The shepherd Gyges once chanced upon a magic ring under very dramatic circumstances—an earthquake opened up a chasm in the earth, and a hollow bronze horse appeared with a dead giant inside. The magic ring was on the giant's finger. Gyges takes the ring and realizes that it is an invisibility ring. So what does he do—donate it to the temple? No, he goes to the king's court, manages to meet the queen, seduces her, and plots with her to kill the king and take over his kingdom. Gyges becomes king, and everybody lives happily ever after except for the slain king. Why does Glaucon tell us this? To make a point about human nature: Gyges was a normal man who grabbed the opportunity, because like all normal people he was selfish. If any one of us has a similar opportunity, says Glaucon, we will grab it too! Consider the implications: If you could sneak a peek at the test answers in your class before the exam and have a near-complete certainty that nobody saw you, would you do it? If you say Yes, you're with Glaucon. If you say No, Glaucon says that it is just because you are afraid of being caught (so you are still selfish); if you insist that it is wrong to cheat, Glaucon would say that you have swallowed the teachings of your society hook, line, and sinker, because the true nature of justice is plain self-protection, nothing more lofty than that. Does it help any to know that Glaucon was kidding? That he was simply trying to get Socrates to speak the truth about justice—that it is not merely a rule to protect us from each other's egoism? Not much, because others—Hobbes, for one—have subscribed to Glaucon's theory in the most serious way.

Sigmund Freud: We Are Driven by the Unconscious

The notion that we are all selfish at heart is by no means limited to philosophy textbooks; it thrives in the "real world" and has probably done so since time immemorial. But occasionally a thinker will

give it the substance of a theory and present it as factual. Sigmund Freud's theory of the Unconscious, while not entirely a defense of psychological egoism, did give the theory of innate self-centeredness a tremendous boost all through the twentieth century. In the late nineteenth century, psychologists explored the idea of a level of the mind that was more or less inaccessible to our conscious mind. We all know that we have memories that aren't immediately accessible to us, but are called forth through the smells, sounds, or sights of other things. Where do those memories hide when we are not thinking of them? Freud and his colleague, Joseph Breuer (who actually came up with the idea first), explored the possibility that their neurotic patients might be disturbed by terrible memories they had but couldn't recall, to the point that these memories affected them physically and made them ill. Thus the theory of the repressed conscious was born.

In 1900—a suitable date for publishing something that was to galvanize psychology in the new century—Freud's influential book *Interpretation of Dreams* hit the bookstores in Austria and caused an uproar. Dream interpretation was nothing new at the time—it had been attempted throughout history with occasional political success. Rulers with nasty dreams would have "dream interpreters" standing by to soothe their worries; recall the biblical tale of Joseph interpreting Pharaoh's dreams of the fat and skinny cows coming out of the Nile. Books on the meaning of dreams also have enjoyed much popularity. One such book, *A Treatise of the Interpretation of Sundry Dreams* (1601), foretells that certain dreams will mean certain changes in your life. In other words, dreams are omens, portents of things to come.

Only in the remotest sense could Freud's book be said to have any kinship with these other dream theories. There is no precognition hidden in dreams for Freud, although there is a hidden cognition (knowledge) about yourself; and you can learn much from this by analyzing your dream when you wake up.[9] What you dream about is no prediction about what *will* happen, but it indicates what you *would like* to have happen: *Dreams are wish fulfillment.*

An instant objection arises: "But I was having a nightmare! How can that be wish fulfillment?" Dreaming about wearing formal attire without any pants or shoes in a crowd, dreaming that you have to take your high school finals all over again,

being on stage without remembering your lines, or being on a date with your boss (whom you dislike) hardly sounds like inner wishes yearning to be fulfilled. But Freud has several possible answers: First, *dreams are not what they seem.* In dreams, the images go through a camouflaging process, the so-called *manifest dream content* that "hides" their true identity: the *latent dream thoughts.* This is necessary because your conscious self is so alert, even while asleep, that it doesn't allow the true meaning to be expressed clearly in the dream. Perhaps you enjoy, subconsciously, the fear of the nightmare: You feel guilty about something, so you torture yourself at night. Perhaps you subconsciously really would like to date your boss, but you wouldn't admit it to yourself! So you have *repressed* the desire. Or perhaps your boss is a symbol of some other authority figure in your life, like your mother or father, and that is the person you are really dreaming about. Then there is the additional process of the *dream work:* your remembering the dream, telling about it, and trying to understand it. This adds an important element to the dream: your own mind dealing with it. Why must the dream hide itself behind symbolic images? Because our reason will not accept the reality of what the dream represents: our self-centered instincts, drives, and memories that are too difficult to deal with. We repress them, banish them to the darkest corners of our Unconscious, but the harder we repress them, the more certain they are to appear in the form of dreams, slips of the tongue (*parapraxes,* or "Freudian slips"), neurotic behavior such as washing hands repeatedly, or even psychosis, the most dramatic and pathological form of the Unconscious expressing itself. In particular, traumatic childhood experiences are likely to be repressed. Such experiences can be anything from emotional rejection, abuse and molestation, and witnessing violence to others, to walking in on your parents having sex. When the time is ripe, the trauma will resurface in disguise—perhaps in a dream, a Freudian slip, or neurotic behavior. Presumably the patient alone will not be able to identify the original traumatic experience, but will need the help of a psychoanalyst to bring

NEST HEADS. By Steve Dickenson. Reprinted with permission from Copley News Service.

The famous concept of the Freudian slip, or *parapraxis*, is surely an experience we have all had—at least Freud thinks it is a normal occurrence and proves the existence of the Unconscious. The slip occurs because we try *not* to say something that's on our mind, or have something else in mind as we speak, or want to avoid or achieve a certain situation but won't admit it to ourselves. What is "Freudian" about the brother's slip?

it out. (In Chapter 7 you'll find a discussion of alternative views of the function of dreams.)

In 1915 Freud published his theory of the Unconscious in a series of lectures; later he was to expand this theory into the famous idea of the three-part psyche—the *id,* the *ego,* and the *super-ego* (Unconscious, self, and conscience)—but his early version saw the psyche consisting of two principles: the *pleasure principle* and the *reality principle*. We are born into the pleasure principle: This is our Unconscious demanding instant gratification of all desires. We want to be fed, changed, touched, loved—right now. But we soon realize that it isn't always going to happen, so the reality principle kicks in: We know that we have to think of others, we have to slow down and be prudent, because we just aren't always going to get our wishes fulfilled. What are the implications of this theory? For one thing, some people just seem stuck in the pleasure principle and have a very weak reality principle; those are the ones we call sociopaths. For another, the reality principle doesn't arise because we realize the selfish errors of our ways, but is also an outcome of our need for self-protection. Be prudent and don't act selfishly—The principle rests not on selflessness but on a basic self-oriented psyche.

Freud's theories of the pleasure principle and the reality principle, as well as his theory of the three levels of the psyche have all become part of our popular conception of psychoanalysis, but none of them to the degree that his theory of the *Oedipus complex* has. The Oedipus complex views the relationship between the young boy and his parents as fundamentally problematic: The boy is jealous of his father and wants to be the exclusive recipient of his mother's attention. In Box 3.7 we take a closer look at this famous notion.

In Chapters 6 and 7 we return to Freud's theory of the Unconscious and some of its ramifications. For now, suffice it to say that Freud, with his theory of an inner life based on drives we can't control or influence rationally, heralded a century's worth of (1) seeing humans as constant battlegrounds for inner forces, of which the selfish id is usually the strongest, and (2) viewing the human psyche as a victim of circumstances, pursuing self-gratification if at all possible, and only relinquishing such gratification if the price is too high for oneself (you'll be found out, you'll go to prison, you'll get sick, you'll get fat). In other words, we are selfish, and we can't help it. While Freud himself thought that a person who doesn't try to control himself or herself reveals a weak character and

Box 3.7 THE OEDIPUS COMPLEX

Probably the best-known psychological problem identified by Freud is the so-called Oedipus complex. The phenomenon takes its name from the Greek tragedy of King Oedipus, who, in spite of his own efforts to avoid his prophesied fate of killing his father and marrying his mother, ends up inadvertently doing just that. The Greek legend is about the inevitability of fate, not about passions within the nuclear family, but Freud uses the story to illustrate the tensions within the nuclear family. The young boy feels attracted to his mother and jealous of his father, a rival for his mother's affection. The jealousy evolves into fear that his father will remove him from competition by castrating him; hence the Freudian *castration complex*. In addition, Freud developed a theory of the female Oedipus complex (sometimes called the Electra complex), but he always placed more emphasis on the male version. The female Oedipus complex consists in the little girl's being attracted to her father and seeing her mother as a rival for his affections; in addition, the little girl (according to Freud) fears that her mother, in a fit of jealousy, has castrated her—hence the theory of *penis envy*. In Chapter 6 we take a closer look at the female Oedipus complex.

also thought that only the truly psychotic patient has no self-control, the popular interpretation has been to view each of us as somehow in the throes of unconscious drives beyond our control, not having to take responsibility for what we do. In other words, Freud's theory has been interpreted as a support for *determinism,* the theory featured in our next chapter.

Edward O. Wilson's Sociobiology

Human and nonhuman animal behavior yields a multitude of examples of self-centered behavior, but how does the psychological egoist explain behavior that for all intents and purposes looks altruistic (selfless)? Our human history is full of people sacrificing their comfort, fortune, and even lives for others in need, strangers as well as friends and kin. As we have seen, the psychological egoist will point to some deeper level of self-serving motivation such as wanting to atone for past sins, wanting to make book deals, wanting get to heaven—you name it. But the psychological egoist can draw on biology for a special explanation, and this explanation also covers those numerous, puzzling examples of nonhuman animals acting selflessly to save fellow creatures or even humans. Among the documented stories are

these: A man's pet rabbit wakes him up by desperately thumping her foot, in time for him to get out of his burning house (the rabbit was not so lucky). In February 2001 the actress Drew Barrymore and her fiancé, the comedian Tom Green, were awakened by their dog, Flossie, barking and banging on the bedroom door. Their house was on fire, and they credited her with discovering it and alerting them. Another dog keeps leading his young master away from a certain area of the frozen lake, and later that area turns out to contain a hole in the ice (this happened to my husband when he was a small boy). Since antiquity, dolphins have reportedly saved drowning humans. A baboon may put herself in harm's way to distract the leopard long enough for the other baboons to get away. So the capacity for self-sacrifice is documented and extends beyond the human realm. But why does nature allow an instinct that runs counter to self-preservation?

The sociobiologist Edward O. Wilson believes he knows why: This is just another manifestation of selfishness—not on the conscious, but on the genetic level. According to Wilson, all human cultural history and social life can be explained and predicted in terms of genetics: Our social organization, commerce, division of labor, love and marriage, religion, ethics, art, warfare—every aspect has its foundation in our primate nature. In his book *On Human Nature,* he outlines four characteristics that we share with the other primates:

1. Our intimate social groupings number from ten to one hundred adults.

2. Males are larger than females, and the larger the males, the more females they usually have available to them. This is known as *sexual dimorphism,* and since human males are only slightly larger than females, we are a "mildly polygynous species."

3. The young undergo a long period of social training.

4. Social play is an important activity.

In addition to these traits, human genes are responsible for a long list of other social customs such as bodily adornment, fire making, personal names, funeral rites, and the like. Wilson concludes that "human social behavior rests on a genetic foundation—that human behavior is, to be more precise, organized by some genes that are shared with closely related species and others that are unique to the human species."[10] In other words, Wilson believes that the overwhelming basis for human culture is *nature,* not *nurture.*

Since the publication by another sociobiologist, Richard Dawkins, of *The Selfish Gene* (1976), one year after the publication of Wilson's influential book *Sociobiology,* the theory has been referred to as the *selfish gene* theory. The sociobiological explanation of displays of altruism in humans and animals is that we have a "selfish gene" that manifests itself in a variety of ways, from blatantly self-serving to apparently altruistic actions. While we consciously may try to preserve our own life, the selfish gene unconsciously strives to preserve our genetic heritage. Who benefits from the monkey sacrificing herself? Her fellow monkeys—in all likelihood, her relatives. She may not live to have offspring, but her sisters will, and they share the same genetic material. The dolphin saves a drowning human because she is programmed, genetically, to save her own baby from drowning in the same way and just can't tell the difference between her baby and a human in a wetsuit. The dog saves his owner because he thinks they belong to the same pack of genetically related members (as a low-hierarchy wolf will save a high-hierarchy member of her pack, genetically related to her). A gorilla saves a young boy who has fallen into the gorilla zoo pit. Humans crawl into the rubble of buildings to save strangers and go off on suicide missions for political factions. The selfish gene identifies those close to us as "relatives," because that's who they would have been when we were early humans. Our world is more complex now, and our relationships are much broader than with blood relations alone, but our selfish gene programs us to identify our group as "relatives" and lets us sacrifice ourselves so that they may live. We just haven't evolved long enough since tribal times to adjust to the new conditions.

A criticism often raised against the theory of the selfish gene is that it is possible to imagine that animals (and humans) are somehow genetically programmed toward self-preservation and even the preservation of their relatives, without having any knowledge of genetics; but how are we to believe that a dolphin can't tell the difference between her own baby and a human in a wetsuit? She can easily tell the difference between her own baby and other dolphin babies. She might be genetically inclined to save all creatures that may look remotely like a dolphin baby—but it doesn't add up, when we take into account that dolphins, like male lions, can be very aggressive toward other dolphins' offspring. In September 2000 a young boy was saved by a wild dolphin along the Italian coast. The boy had fallen from his father's fishing boat, and the dolphin—a locally known male—kept him afloat and nudged him back toward his father's boat. Now did the dolphin believe him to be his own baby? In that case, why deliver him to a human fishing boat? The concept of genetic selfishness may have its application, but it doesn't seem to work as a universal explanation of behavior, animal or human. Some altruistic humans make a point of sacrificing themselves for groups that are clearly not their relatives, even in a symbolic sense. Dogs may think that humans are part of their pack and ought to be considered Alpha-members, but with all the anecdotes of pets behaving altruistically toward their humans, throughout human history, another explanation seems more likely, more economical, and less taxing on our imagination: Mary Midgley's alternative model of altruism.

Mary Midgley: A Different Model

Among the selfish gene theory's most adamant critics is the British philosopher Mary Midgley (b. 1919). In her book *Beast and Man: The Roots of Human Nature,* she points out that even animals who leave their own genetic group and join other groups still behave altruistically toward the new, unrelated group. Wilson makes a bad mistake in lumping all behavior together under the altruism of the selfish gene, she says, because sometimes behavior is unmistakably selfish. Shouldn't that be somehow distinguished from the "unselfishly selfish" behavior of self-sacrifice? Midgley suggests an entirely different biological model for altruistic behavior. It isn't the pattern of making sure that our genes live on in others or another favorite explanation of Wilson's, a form of altruism where we expect some payoff from those we rescue (such as "I'll scratch your back, and you'll scratch mine"): it is the pattern of *parents and offspring.* Midgley says,

> All the creatures that it makes sense to suppose could develop positive altruism are already caring for their young. And the first element of parental care which develops is defense and rescue from danger. . . . All that is needed is to extend this pattern to adults. Now the principle of sociability proceeds in any case largely by this extension to other adults of behavior first developed between parents and young—grooming, mouth contact, embracing, protective and submissive gestures, giving food. In fact, wider sociality in its original essence simply is the power of adults to treat one another, mutually, as honorary parents and children.[11]

For Midgley, the most problematic aspect of Wilson's theory is that the selfishness is supposed to be a mechanical, unconscious force. Why not go to a far easier explanation and look at people's *motivation* instead? Assuming that humans and animals somehow subconsciously calculate the benefits of their gene-selective sacrifice is simply a bad explanation, she says. Instead, let us look at people's actual motivation: to help others. This kind of action involves conscious choices that have little to do with whether the person in need is a relative, and we will never be able to understand human nature if we don't have room in our theory for the development of emotions and free choices that make genuine altruism possible.

The Weapon Versus the Basket

The combined views of early sociobiology that humans are both aggressive and selfish—views that complement each other—have been challenged lately, both from inside the field of sociobiology, from evolutionary psychology, and from outside the field. Here we look at a popular alternative with a basis in biology and at one criticism of sociobiology as such.

The Weapon or the Basket? Leakey and Eisler

Earlier I speculated that there might be a historical reason why the aggression thesis was so popular in the mid–twentieth century. Similarly, we might speculate that there are historical reasons why scholars are now looking for alternative models. It is harder to see through a contemporary trend than a trend from the past, but if we follow the line of thinking from Chapters 1 and 2 that different cultures and time periods often create the stories about themselves that they think make the most sense, or that they somehow need to believe in, then we can apply this philosophy to the current trend in explaining human nature with some conviction.

And what is this trend? Primarily, it is a school of thought that rejects the older theories of universal human aggression and selfishness and explores the idea that several factors may be at work in shaping our nature. A theory has been fashioned from several independent sources, together forming a picture of two human natures: an aggressive, competitive nature and a peaceful, cooperative one, symbolized by *the weapon versus the basket.* We have already seen that the paleoanthropologist Don Johanson interprets early Australopithecine life as being a life of scavenging rather than hunting, and of falling prey to carnivores more often than being the hunters. One of Johanson's rivals in anthropology, Richard Leakey, the son of famed paleoanthropologists Mary and Louis Leakey, agrees here with Johanson's revision of early human history. In his book, *The People of the Lake* (1978), Leakey suggests that contrary to what Ardrey thought, warfare is far from being fundamentally biological—it is a purely political device. Fossilized skulls that were thought to have been bashed in now seem to have been damaged by natural forces, after the death of the individual.

And Ardrey's idea that hunting was what allowed humans to have the time and the intellectual edge to advance culturally has been questioned by the discovery that humans in the early days were not just hunters, but also gatherers and scavengers. Indeed, some anthropologists suggest the term should be "gatherer-hunter societies," rather than "hunter-gatherer." Early hominids ate all kinds of things in order to stay alive, short of grass (which the primate stomach can't digest). How do we know what early humans ate? We can tell by looking at their specialized *teeth.* Some were vegetarians, while others were omnivorous (like *Homo sapiens*), but none were strictly carnivorous. (Interestingly, Konrad Lorenz had already made that point, but in the 1960s readers were quicker to notice his aggression theory than his theory that early humans weren't great meat eaters.) According to Leakey, anthropologists such as Nancy Tanner and Adrienne Zihlman make much sense in suggesting that

> Compared with males . . . females have a tremendous investment in the offspring. . . . The females' pivotal position in the protohuman social

group . . . put into their hands the power to exploit technological innovation. The first tools . . . were invented "*not for hunting* large, swiftly moving, dangerous animals, *but for gathering* plants, eggs, honey, termites, ants, and probably small burrowing animals."[12]

So was the cultural catalyst the male's hunting and his invention of *weapons,* or was it the female's social bonding with her child and her invention of the *basket?* The first use of a gourd, or a skull, or any kind of natural container to bring home supplies for the entire tribe or the immediate family may have occurred prior to the development of the weapon. Be that as it may, many scholars now believe that humanity is not built on aggression and selfishness alone. The caring instinct is present, too, and not just in the females (of course): Sharing seems to be a trait that both genders have in common. Whether hunting and sharing of the kill occurred before gathering and sharing of the harvest is of little importance. In pretechnological cultures of the twentieth century the hunters' contribution to the overall diet was no more than 25 percent at the most—the rest was supplied by harvesting and gathering. What is clear now is that both hunting and gathering were part of the early human experience and that we have all had our values shaped by both activities.

A feminist scholar, Riane Eisler, has weighed in with a theory that has become the catchphrase for this theory of two social trends: Her book *The Chalice and the Blade* (1987) suggests that in human political history, the same two models exist, but with drastic social differences. Eisler sees the chalice (a cup) as a symbol of the sharing or *partnership* model, while the blade is a symbol of the aggressive *dominator* model. Linking the two models with a theory of history of the ancient world, Eisler speculates that the partnership model (the chalice/basket model) preceded the dominator (blade/weapon) model. Within the partnership society there was little aggression and much cooperation, she claims, and women had high standing in such a society; the religion involved goddess worship, and women were revered for their fertility and nurturance. Then, around 3,500 years ago in the Middle East, things began to change: A new people invaded the old peaceful cultures, brandishing weapons of superior design. These people worshipped a male warrior god, and their women had low social status. Eventually, the partnership model succumbed to the dominator model, and it is only in the twentieth century that women have regained some of their ancient standing. We take another look at Eisler from the context of feminism in Chapter 6.

Does Eisler have historic evidence on her side? To some extent, yes. There really is evidence of an aggressive culture invading old Middle Eastern cultures around that time period, creating significant cultural changes. Ancient societies with goddess worship and priestesses seem indeed to have existed, and these societies had no fortifications around their towns, indicating that times were peaceful. Ancient religions speak of a mighty goddess and powerful struggles between male and female principles. But as to whether women really had a higher social standing in those times, that has to remain speculation until harder evidence is produced. And Eisler's unequivocal condemnation of the knife/blade as a tool of war and strife is an interpretation in itself: One might just as well choose to see the partnership model enhanced by the invention of the cutting tool, facilitating the killing, transport, and sharing of meat within the early human groups.

Why are scholars and laypeople so interested in this new theory? Aside from the fact that new theories raise curiosity, there seems to be something almost desperate in the attempts of scholars to prove the correctness of this new vision of early humanity. The theory may be solidly based on evidence, but in addition, it is as if we just *don't want* to be identified as aggressive, selfish humans any longer; we no longer want to be hunters, but feel much better thinking of ourselves as humble scavengers, prey to stronger animals. We want to believe that we are by nature gentle sharers, rather than fierce warriors. Why this humility? One explanation is that feminist scholars are weighing in, interpreting history from a feminine perspective (although not all feminists agree that this is a true perspective, as we shall see in Chapter 6). Another explanation (offered by critical fiscal conservatives) might be that our present society readily identifies *victims*, but does little to empower people to help themselves; a "victim" model of early humanity could be used politically as a social metaphor for why we need more social programs. But perhaps the most important reason is that the times that we live in are fragmented: The multicultural society of the present and the future will make demands on us to find a manner of coexistence, and a multicultural, two-gender partnership model seems to many a necessary alternative to a monocultural, male dominator model. Again, the future we want casts its hue over the past we are trying to explain.

Does Sociobiology Explain Everything About Human Behavior?

It is now time to evaluate the sociobiological project: Does human biology tell us all we need to know about human cultural institutions, traditions, values, and relationships? The more we know about human DNA, brain chemistry, and human evolution, the more we seem to understand just exactly why humans do the things they do, so biological information is obviously a great asset in understanding the human condition. But does sociobiology reveal *everything* about humans? And even more importantly, what are we supposed to do with the information sociobiology hands to us about ourselves?

As far as the first question is concerned, sociobiology probably will never reveal everything about humans, and neither will evolutionary psychology: No matter how much we know about someone's chemical balance or imbalance at the time when a momentous decision is made, and no matter how much we speculate about early humans' psychological makeup, we still haven't reached the core of the human person *making free choices*. (In the next chapter we look in detail at the question of how free human choices really are.)

We may not be as "free" as some philosophers believe, but we are not puppets on a string, either. As Mary Midgley says, we have to take individual motivations into account. A student making a decision to change her major when her serotonin level is low, and she feels depressed, may make the decision primarily due to her brain chemistry, but we can't discount the possibility that she also has reached some valid insight into herself and her own ability to deliberate about actions and their possible consequences—a moral and cognitive insight that can't be put into a chemical formula. People who are in love may be suffering from grand delusions because of an overproduction of some brain chemical, but that doesn't explain everything we know and feel about being in love, let alone the exhilarating appreciation of another human being for qualities that perhaps nobody else has ever discovered! We may live in groups because most primates live in groups, and that may explain castes and pecking orders, alliances and wars, but it doesn't completely explain our complex sense of justice, of affection for each other, and of networking. In the next chapter we take a closer look at theories of decision making, and in Chapter 7 we return to the question of the nature of the mind.

The Naturalistic Fallacy

But even if our increasing knowledge of physical human nature could give us insight into most human affairs, there is a step that sociobiology can't take (although numerous sociobiologists do it without scruple): the step from a descriptive theory telling us how we are, to a normative theory telling us how we should be. That step in philosophy is known as the *naturalistic fallacy,* and since David Hume pointed it out in the eighteenth century, it has been considered a nonlegitimate step for most Western philosophers. This brings us to the second question: What are we supposed to do with the sociobiological information?

What makes Ardrey's theory an example of sociobiology gone astray is not merely that he develops a hypothesis of human behavior based on biological research but that he also proceeds to make value statements. He tells us not only what people do, but also whether it is all right for them to keep doing it: We are aggressive, he says, and that's what we should remain as long as we redirect our aggression away from wars of annihilation. The danger in this approach is that sometimes thinkers slip from a descriptive to a normative statement without being aware of it. We might think we are still being descriptive when we say humans are by nature aggressive or selfish or meat eaters or compassionate, and *therefore it is okay* to be aggressive, and so on. But this was what Hume objected to: We can't move from a statement about facts to a statement about what we ought to do, because there is nothing embedded in the fact that tells us whether the fact is desirable or undesirable! We may read about a horrible murder in the papers: A man strangles his mother to death, and we all know that he did something dreadful. But, says Hume, where exactly in the fact of the killing is the moral condemnation? Nowhere except in our judgment of it.

So to Hume and countless scholars after him, facts don't have built-in values, and we can't conclude anything about values or policies strictly based on facts. Can't we say that "He shouldn't have done it?" Of course we can, but not based on the fact of the killing alone. We can't go from an "is" to an "ought" directly, but we can do it indirectly: by adding a statement reflecting our understanding of values, which usually remains just a tacit assumption. So how do we make the condemnation of the killing proper? By following this argument structure:

Premise 1: A man strangles his mother.

Premise 2: We disapprove of people killing their parents.

Conclusion: He shouldn't have strangled his mother.

This way we can go from an "is" statement to an "ought" (or ought not) statement by way of a "hidden premise" (premise 2), which we take for granted, about our values.

Criticizing Ardrey for moving from a biological "is" to a moral "ought" doesn't show he is wrong in his theory of human aggression, but it shows that he draws conclusions about human morals and politics ("Wars are good for human intellectual development") that are impermissible. Just as Leakey, citing the invention of the basket as more important than the weapon, is making an impermissible jump when he hints that the sharing of food is morally better than hunting (or warfare). We can have all the opinions we want about whether humans should be warlike or peaceful, but we can't base them on biology! Biology can only tell us what humans are like. It can't tell us whether it is morally good for the future of humanity. Our moral convictions and religious view must step in and comment on the biological facts, such as in this example: If you believe it is a fact that it is natural for humans to have children, you can't conclude that they therefore *ought to* have children; you have to insert a statement that you believe having children is a *good thing*. After inserting this value statement, you can then conclude what people ought to do. In this way, others who accept your statement of fact are still free to agree or disagree with your values.

In fact, there is a very practical danger in committing the naturalistic fallacy: You might set up a potential for discrimination. For example, if we could prove statistically that Asians are smarter than white people, then should white people be excluded from certain types of jobs? If it turns out that women are, overall, better nurturers than men, should single fathers be forced to give up their children? If men statistically have better spatial comprehension than women, should women be prohibited from becoming pilots? On occasion, laws are contested because they legislate about the rights and privileges of an entire group based on the biological data of most members in the group. During the giant boom in the computer industry in the 1980s, states tried to ban women from working at computer stations, a move based on the biological assumption that the radiation from the computer could negatively affect their reproductive organs. These rules were struck down, not just because their scientific basis was shaky, but also because they were discriminatory: Not all women intend to have babies (or even can have babies), some women are past menopause, and even those who may want to become mothers still have a free choice to decide whether they want to take on the risk. Of course, the computer companies just wanted to avoid lawsuits from women who might have had babies with birth defects, but they went about protecting themselves by going too hastily from an "is" to an "ought."

Even if statistics show women to be better nurturers than men, there will always be male individuals who are excellent nurturers. There will be women with great spatial comprehension, and intelligence is found throughout the human population. In an influential paper, "Sociobiology, Morality, and Feminism" from 1985, the philosopher A. T. Nuyen warns about the practical application of sociobiology: A sociobiological theory that assigns tasks to certain groups on the basis of biology can't help but discriminate against individuals who would rather do (and might be good at doing) something else. Sociobiologists may insist that they only want to assign different tasks to different groups, not create a *hierarchy* in which some groups are viewed as more important than others. But their intentions and the end result are two different things. If one group is assigned parenting and housekeeping duties and another is assigned work outside the home, it is very likely that the group favored with additional power will come to think of itself as more valuable. In our society the hierarchy establishes itself through the criterion of making money outside the home. Nuyen reminds us of George Orwell's *Animal Farm*: All animals are equal, but "some are more equal than others."

In addition, just because something is a biological fact and thus natural doesn't mean we have to embrace it wholeheartedly. Nature generally kills its weakest creatures. Does it mean we have to do so? It may be natural to scratch oneself, but that doesn't mean we have to do it in public. It may be natural for humans to be "mildly promiscuous," as Wilson says, but that doesn't mean we can't, or shouldn't, try to control our urges! It may be natural for us to eat meat, but that doesn't mean we can't decide to become vegetarians for reasons that have nothing to do with our self-preservation. Similarly, Lorenz warns that even though we may have an evolutionary history of aggression, it doesn't mean that we can't, or shouldn't, try to curtail it.

Jane Goodall: Potentials

So are we mostly aggressive, or mostly caring? I will give the final word to a scholar who is widely respected for her work in animal studies, but who generally has little interest in sociobiology. Jane Goodall's famous studies of the chimpanzee population of Gombe, spanning several decades, have had an extraordinary impact on our understanding of chimpanzee nature. Goodall undertook the study not for the purpose of writing sociobiology, but with the aim of acquiring solid knowledge about chimpanzee life. Her book *In the Shadow of Man* (1988) revealed to an astonished world that the chimpanzee is far from being a peaceful creature. Both males and females conduct raids on neighboring groups, killing them mercilessly (even the infants) in order to take over their territory. The occasional murder happens even within the home group. This sounds as if Ardrey has been vindicated, but at the same time, Goodall insists, the chimps show a highly developed sense of community: They care for each other, give food to injured family members, and spend hours grooming each other just for the sake of good company. When a group member dies, the relatives grieve for long periods of time, sometimes even dying of sorrow themselves. Recent studies of bonobo chimpanzees undertaken by other scholars show that bonobos are even less aggressive than regular chimpanzees; recall that bonobos are genetically more closely related to humans than the familiar chimp.

When Goodall was asked some years ago, in a packed lecture hall at San Diego State University, what implications these studies have for understanding human nature, she smiled a little smile and replied, "Very few implications!" Chimpanzees have certain tendencies, and we must assume that humans have similar tendencies—but that doesn't mean we are victims of those tendencies. It doesn't mean that all humans are either aggressive or caring creatures. These are potentials, nothing more. It is good science to acknowledge tendency and relationship, and bad science to see characteristic traits as inevitable. Here Goodall aligns herself with other philosophers of human nature who have chosen to categorize our biological heritage as *potentialities,* no more and no less.[13]

Goodall might have added that although we may use the chimps as working metaphors for what we are, we should never confuse such metaphors with the idea that we are predestined to be one way or another. Biology is certainly part of what we are, but it is not all that we are.

Study Questions

1. Ardrey claims that all major human advances have been won through warfare and/or violence. Can you think of counterexamples?

2. How can Lorenz say that we are aggressive by nature and at the same time claim that we can be compassionate and responsible? Do you agree?

3. What can we learn from our dreams, according to Freud?

4. What might Wilson respond to Midgley's alternative model for helping others: the parent-children relationship? How might Wilson argue that it might still be the selfish gene in effect?

5. Does the idea of human biology as a potential seem a sufficient explanation of human cultural and individual behavior to you? Why or why not?

Primary Readings and Narratives

This chapter concludes with two primary readings and two narratives. First, we have an excerpt from the final chapter of Robert Ardrey's *African Genesis* (1961), in which he pronounces humans to be "Cain's Children," with killer instincts. Next is an excerpt from Mary Midgley's book *Beast and Man* (1995), in which she criticizes Wilson's theory of human selfishness and offers an alternative theory. (Chapter 9 contains a primary reading excerpt from Thomas Hobbes's *Leviathan,* mentioned in this chapter.) The first narrative is a summary and excerpt of William Golding's classic novel, *Lord of the Flies* (1954), exploring the fundamental human characteristics that are revealed when civilization is stripped away. The final narrative is a summary of the introduction to the landmark film by Stanley Kubrick, *2001: A Space Odyssey* (1968). In this introduction we watch as early hominids learn to use weapons to procure meat and secure their territory.

Primary Reading

African Genesis

ROBERT ARDREY

Excerpt from Chapter 11, "Cain's Children," 1961.

What are the things that we know about man? How much have the natural sciences brought to us, so far, in the course of a silent, unfinished revolution? . . .

We know above all that man is a portion of the natural world and that much of the human reality lies hidden in times past. We are an iceberg floating like a gleaming jewel down the cold blue waters of the Denmark Strait; most of our presence is submerged in the sea. . . . We are a thriving, scrambling, elbowing city; but no one can find his way through our labyrinthine streets without awareness of the cities that have stood here before. And so for the moment let us excavate man.

What stands above the surface? His mind, I suppose. The mind is the city whose streets we get lost in, the most recent construction on a very old site. After seventy million years of most gradual primate enlargement, the brain nearly trebled in size in a very few hundreds of thousands of years. Our city is spacious and not lacking in magnificence, but it has the problems of any boom town. Let us dig.

We are Cain's children. The union of the enlarging brain and the carnivorous way produced man as a genetic possibility. The tightly packed weapons of the predator form the highest, final, and most immediate foundation on which we stand. How deep does it extend? A few million, five million, ten million years? We do not know. But it is the material of our immediate foundation as it is the basic material of our city. And we have so far been unable to build without it.

Man is a predator whose natural instinct is to kill with a weapon. The sudden addition of the enlarged brain to the equipment of an armed already-successful predatory animal created not only the human being but also the human predicament. But the final foundation on which we stand has a strange cement. We are bad-weather animals. The deposit was laid down in a time of stress. It is no mere rubble of carnage and cunning. City and foundation alike are compacted by a mortar of mysterious strength, the capacity to survive no matter what the storm. The quality of the mortar may hold future significance far exceeding that of the material it binds.

Let us dig deeper. Layer upon layer of primate preparation lies buried beneath the predatory foundation. As the addition of a suddenly enlarged brain to the way of the hunting primate multiplied both the problems and the promises of the sum total, man, so the addition of carnivorous demands to the non-aggressive, vegetarian primate way multiplied the problems and promises of the sum total, our ancestral hunting primate. He came into his Pliocene time no more immaculately conceived than did we into ours.

The primate has instincts demanding the maintenance and defence of territories; an attitude of perpetual hostility for the territorial neighbour; the formation of social bands as the principal means of survival for a physically vulnerable creature; an attitude of amity and loyalty for the social partner; and varying but universal systems of dominance to insure the efficiency of his social instrument and to promote the natural selection of the more fit from the less. Upon this deeply-buried, complex, primate instinctual bundle were added the necessities and the opportunities of the hunting life. . . .

We can only presume that when the necessities of the hunting life encountered the basic primate instincts, then all were intensified. Conflicts became lethal, territorial arguments minor wars. The social band as a hunting and defensive unit became harsher in its codes whether of amity or enmity. The dominant became more dominant, the subordinant more disciplined. Overshadowing all other qualitative changes, however, was the coming of the aggressive imperative. The creature who had once killed only through circumstance killed now for a living.

As we glimpsed in the predatory foundation of man's nature the mysterious strength of the bad-weather animal, so we may see in the coming of the carnivorous way something new and immense and perhaps more significant than the killing necessity. The hunting primate was free. He was free of the forest prison; wherever game roamed the world was his. His hands were freed from the earth or the bough; erect carriage opened new and unguessed opportunities for manual answers to ancient quadruped problems. His daily life was freed from the eternal munching; the capacity to digest high-calorie food meant a life more diverse than one endless meal-time. And his wits were freed. Behind him lay the forest orthodoxies. Ahead of him lay freedom of choice and invention as a new imperative if a revolutionary creature were to meet the unpredictable challenges of a revolutionary way of life. Freedom—as the human being means freedom—was the first gift of the predatory way.

We may excavate man deeply and ever more deeply as we dig down through pre-primate, pre-mammal, and even preland-life levels of experience. We shall pass through the beginnings of sexual activity as a year-round affair, and the consequent beginnings of the primate family. But all the other instincts will be there still deeper down: the instinct to dominate one's fellows, to defend what one deems one's own, to form societies, to mate, to eat and avoid

being eaten. The record will grow dim and the outlines blurred. But even in the earliest deposits of our nature where death and the individual have their start, we shall still find traces of animal nostalgia, of fear and dominance and order.

Here is our heritage, so far as we know it today. Here is the excavated mound of our nature with *Homo sapiens'* boom town on top. But whatever tall towers reason may fling against the storms and the promises of the human future, their foundations must rest on the beds of our past for there is nowhere else to build.

Cain's children have their problems. It is difficult to describe the invention of the radiant weapon as anything but the consummation of a species. Our history reveals the development and contest of superior weapons as *Homo sapiens'* single, universal cultural preoccupation. Peoples may perish, nations dwindle, empires fall; one civilizaton may surrender its memories to another civilization's sands. But mankind as a whole, with an instinct as true as a meadowlark's song, has never in a single instance allowed local failure to impede the progress of the weapon, its most significant cultural endowment.

Must the city of man therefore perish in a blinding moment of universal annihilation? Was the sudden union of the predatory way and the enlarged brain so ill-starred that a guarantee of sudden and magnificent disaster was written into our species' conception? Are we so far from being nature's most glorious triumph that we are in fact evolution's most tragic error, doomed to bring extinction not just to ourselves but to all life on our planet?

It may be so; or it may not. We shall brood about this in a moment. But to reach such a conclusion too easily is to over-simplify both our human future and our animal past. Cain's children have many an ancestor beyond *Australopithecus africanus,* and many a problem beyond war. And the first of our problems is to comprehend our own nature. For we shall fashion no miracles in our city's sky until we know the names of the streets where we live. . . .

How can we get along without war? It is the only question pertaining to the future that bears the faintest reality in our times; for if we fail to get along without war, then the future will be as remarkably lacking in human problems as it will be remarkably lacking in men. Yet war has been the most natural mode of human expression since the beginning of recorded history, and the improvement of the weapon has been man's principal preoccupation since Bed Two in the Olduvai Gorge. What will happen to a species denied in the future its principal means of expression, and its only means, in last appeal, of resolving differences? What will happen to a species that has dedicated its chief energy to the improvement and contest of the weapon, and that now arrives at the end of the road where further improvement and contest is impossible?

Let us not be too hasty in our dismissal of war as an unblemished evil. Are you a Christian? Then recall that Christendom survived its darkest hour in the fury of the Battle of Tours. Do you believe in law? The rule of law became a human institution in the shelter of the Roman legions. Do you subscribe to the value of individual worth? Only by the success of the phalanx at Marathon did the Greeks repel the Persian horde and make possible the Golden Age. Are you a materialist? Do you regard as a human good the satisfaction of economic want? The *Pax Britannica,* made possible by the unchallengeable supremacy of the British fleet, gave mankind the opportunity to lay the broad foundations of the Industrial Revolution.

I am free to uphold in the pages of this account certain views challenging the orthodoxies of my time because I belong to a nation that obtained freedom for its citizens through war, and that has successfully defended my freedom, by the same means, on all occasions since. You are free to read this book, and to consider, evaluate, reject or accept my views, because we are all members of a larger civilization that accepts the free mind as a condition of such profound if painful value that on innumerable occasions it has been willing to fight for it. Do you care about freedom? Dreams may have inspired it, and wishes promoted it, but only war and weapons have made it yours.

No man can regard the way of war as good. It has simply been our way. No man can evaluate the eternal contest of weapons as anything but the sheerest waste and the sheerest folly. It has been simply our only means of final arbitration. Any man can suggest reasonable alternatives to the judgement of arms. But we are not creatures of reason except in our own eyes.

I maintain in these pages that the superior weapon, throughout the history of our species, has been the central human dream; that the energy focused on its continual development has been the central source of human dynamics; that the contest of superior weapons

has been the most profoundly absorbing of human experiences; and that the issues of such contest have maintained and protected much that I myself regard as good. Finally, I maintain that deprived of the dream, deprived of the dynamics, deprived of the contest, and deprived of the issue, *Homo sapiens* stands on a darkened threshold through which species rarely return. . . .

Deprived of the contest of weapons that was the only bough he knew, man must descend to the canebrakes of a new mode of existence. There he must find new dreams, new dynamics, new experiences to absorb him, new means of resolving his issues and of protecting whatever he regards as good. And he will find them; or he will find himself lost. Slowly his governments will lose their force and his societies their integration. Moral order, sheltered throughout all history by the judgement of arms, will fall away in rot and erosion. Insoluble quarrels will rend peoples once united by territorial purpose. Insoluble conflicts will split nations once allied by a common dream. Anarchy, ultimate enemy of social man, will spread its grey cancerous tissues through the social corpus of our kind. . . .

How can man get along without his wars and his weapons? It is the supreme question of the contemporary predicament. Have we within our human resource the capacity to discover new dreams, new dynamisms? Or are we so burdened by our illusions of central position, our romantic fallacies, and our pathetic rationalizations of the human condition that we can acknowledge no destiny beneath the human star but to go blindly blundering into a jingo jungle towards an indeterminate, inglorious, inexorable end?

The reader must sort out for himself, according to his own inclinations and judgement, the probabilities of the human outcome. But before we pass on to certain other consequences of our total animal legacy, I add a suggestion: If man is unique, and his soul some special creation, and his future is to be determined by his innate goodness, nobility and wisdom, then he is finished. But if man is not unique, and his soul represents the product of hundreds of millions of patient years of animal evolution, and he approaches his crisis not as a lost, lonely self-deluding being but as a proud creature bearing in his veins the tide of all life and in his genes the scars of the ages, then sentient man, sapient at last, has a future beyond the stormiest contradiction.

Study Questions

1. What does Ardrey mean by saying that humans are bad-weather animals?

2. On what does Ardrey base his theory that humans are apes with killer instincts? From what you have read in this chapter, would you agree?

3. Is it fair to say that Ardrey believes most human inventions and advances come out of wartime pressures? If no, why not? If yes, can we then conclude that Ardrey advocates war? Why or why not?

4. Does Ardrey have an alternative to war? Explain.

Primary Reading

Beast and Man

MARY MIDGLEY

Excerpt, 1995.

Now it is perfectly true that enlightened self-interest is often a far better guide in politics than posturing and *machismo,* both for our own interest and for other people's. Self-preservation is not only a strong general motive with us, but also a positive duty. What it cannot be is our only duty or our only motive. While we survive, we must *do* something. And further, the point of all we do cannot be (as the subtler "tough-minded" theories suggest) to manipulate our own state of consciousness. Even in politics, there are other things that concern us besides finding the best means either to staying alive or to self-stimulation. And in private life, this is still plainer. People do an enormous range of things "as ends in themselves"—that is, not as a means to anything else, and certainly not to adjusting their own state of consciousness (which is a delicate job, and perhaps could only be efficiently performed by the pharmacist or the hypnotist). Football players want to win their games, and supporters want them to win them. Neither will accept, even from the most skilled pharmacist or hypnotist, the offer of *the sensation of a won game* instead. Avengers do not want the sensation of avenging; they want people's blood. And similarly, rescuers and benefactors do not (if they are real ones) just want the sensation of rescuing and benefacting. They want to help people. This involves wanting the people actually to be helped. If somebody else does so first, they will usually be quite satisfied.

The question of hypocrisy must be considered here, because we have a kind of suspicion that all these people are pretending. This, however, can hardly be right. You cannot have fake Vermeers unless there are some real Vermeers. This is not because it is *difficult* to copy without a model, but because nobody could want to. The existence of fake rescuers and benefactors, far from disproving the existence of the real thing, actually establishes it. . . .

HOW TO MISUNDERSTAND ALTRUISM

For great areas of human motivation, then, Egoists are forced not just to distort their account, but to make it meaningless.

Hobbes and Aristotle do this repeatedly. Two examples are all I have room for. Aristotle, considering the case of somebody who dies to save a friend, asks whether this must count as acting for the friend's sake, and answers, no, the man has merely secured for himself a benefit greater than his friend's, namely, glory. He "prefers a short period of intense pleasure to a long one of mild enjoyment." But if we believed this, we should not be especially impressed with him for doing what he did, and the glory he is after could never have attached to his act. (Even if the fellow fails to think this out, of course, his cost-benefit analysis is miserably shaky; how can he be sure of enjoying himself enough in the time available?)

Again—Hobbes defines pity as "Grief for the Calamity of another, arising from the imagination that the like calamity may befall himself" (that is, the person who feels it). But if the only thing we ever felt on seeing the disaster of another was fear, our behavior would show only fear. There would then be no such word as pity, since there would be no such thing. And Hobbes could never have been called upon to define it.

This is the traditional pattern of distortion. Anyone who doubts its power may be interested to watch Wilson falling into the very same hole. In *Sociobiology* he considers the case of someone who dives into water to save a drowning stranger, and remarks:

> *The reaction is typical of what human beings regard as "pure" altruism. However, upon reflection, we can see that the good Samaritan has much to gain by his act. . . . If such episodes are rare, the Darwinist calculus would predict little or no gain. . . . But if the drowning man reciprocates at a future time, and the risks of drowning stay the same, it will have benefited both individuals to have played the role of rescuer. Each man will have traded a one-half chance of dying for about a one-tenth chance.*

Now this passage might merely be saying that *in fact* they will, on average, have benefited themselves, or at least done themselves no harm. As we shall see, this is the most that the argument can possibly call for. But the language constantly implies more. It unmistakably refers to motivation, and analyzes it in the traditional distorting Egoistic style. The word that does so most plainly in the passage above is *traded*. *Trading* is a name for something that can only be done deliberately, and with appropriate motives. Traders must know what they are doing. To do something that merely turns out to benefit you is not trading, but if you make a deal, you have still traded if it turns out badly. Whatever the upshot, a rescuer was not "trading" unless his motive was a calculation of profit. Of course it could have been so. But people do in fact quite often rescue strangers *without* first checking that these strangers are husky, loyal, useful allies who will stay around until a counter-rescue becomes necessary. And a rescuer who finds that he has pulled out of the water a nonswimming old gentleman who lives at a distance does not necessarily react as he would if he had spent a lot of time salvaging a whiskey crate and then found it to be empty—that is, by throwing him back in again. He may still reckon that he has done what he set out to do.

The word "trade" does not stand alone. All Wilson's key terms are drawn from the language of conscious motivation. *Altruism, selfishness,* and *spite* are his names for activities that benefit (respectively) other people, the agent, and nobody. (It might have been better to talk of other-benefiting, self-benefiting, and purely injurious activities). The dictionary, however, defines altruism as "regard for others, as a principle of action," which is a motive. And this is certainly its normal use. Selfishness and spite, still more obviously, are never names for what actually happens, but for the agent's state or habit of mind. A spiteful action does not cease to be spiteful because it is frustrated, nor is accidentally injuring somebody a piece of spite. Similarly, in opening the section on what he calls "reciprocal altruism," Wilson remarks, more in sorrow than in anger: "The theory of group selection has taken most of the good will out of altruism. When altruism is conceived as the mechanism by which DNA multiplies itself through a network of relatives, spirituality becomes just one more Darwinian enabling device."

The stern tone, suitable for one revealing unsuspected nepotism in the charities of a presidential candidate, suggests that we have examined the motives of all rescuers and have found that they are not what they seem. But no attention has been paid to these motives. In what sense can the theory of group selection "take the good will out of altruism"? It is supposed to do it by showing that traits will survive only if they benefit the group. But one cannot "take the good will out" by showing how good will evolves. *Good will* is a term describing a kind of motivation whose occurrence is what we start from. People do sometimes rescue those who cannot benefit them. The theory of group selection is there to show that such motives could not have been passed on if they had undermined the survival of the group—perhaps that they must have promoted it. This is an entirely different thing from showing that they actually never evolved at all, that what looks like them is in fact only a cleverly disguised form of calculation. It seems important to notice that, if this were true, calculation of consequences would have to be immeasurably more strongly developed, commoner and more efficient than it actually is in man, let alone in other species. Hobbes's picture not only deprives us of our actual virtues; it credits us with others we do not have, at least in the necessary degree—a steady, unfailing prudence, a persistence in calculation, a stern intellectual honesty and consistency, a brisk readiness to act on extremely remote probabilities, such as we never actually see. (Since these really are important virtues, of which we are partly capable, the appeal of Egoism lies partly in celebrating them, as well as in attacking hypocrisy.) If Hobbes's picture were accurate, the phenomena on the human scene would be totally different, and the "problem of altruism" in other less calculating species would remain quite insoluble.

This brings us back to the point with which I began this chapter—that we have two distinct problems before us. Wilson's kind of account—which is now extremely widespread—is weak in that it constantly carries into the evolutionary discussion an irrelevant and uncriticized Egoism. Officially it ignores motives, but in fact it makes constant reference to them, and because this reference is unacknowledged, its errors go uncorrected.

There is a real puzzle about the transmission of altruistic behavior. But that puzzle is solved by showing that it benefits one's kin and one's group. The further problem of inventing some way in which it can seem to benefit the agent himself arises only for Egoists, because only they have ruled that it has to do this to make him act. Wilson and his colleagues, however, take the Egoist stance, by pointing out that those benefited are often the agent's kin and suggesting that this makes it somehow possible for him to identify with them, since they will proliferate his genes for him if he does not live to do it himself.* Thus they give kin selection a much more prominent place in their argument than group selection. . . . It is worth remarking here that altruistic behavior can

extend far beyond kin. It is true that those surrounding an animal very often are its kin, and that this makes a great difference to the actual transmission of its genes. But its behavior does not systematically alter when the surrounding animals are not kin at all, as in the case where a creature leaves its home group and joins another before breeding. And even if it stays put, much of its behavior benefits, and some is meant to benefit, non-relatives. The social insects are indeed a special case. For them, group and kin are effectively the same. But this is just what makes them a misleading model for studying the overall relationship of the two concepts.

Beyond this, however, the whole notion of identification is uncalled for and useless. Only a very intelligent and well-informed agent could *plan* successfully to act so as best to proliferate his genes. But we are dealing, mostly, with agents who do not plan at all, including, usually, the human rescuer. It is important that we understand such actions for what they are, as done with the motives that they actually are done with, rather than distorting them to fit a tidy theory. The motive has to be one that can function independently of planning.

There might, perhaps, have been an intelligent species somewhere which did not develop direct social impulses at all, but depended for all its social activity on calculation of consequences. We are not it. It would have done many of the things we do, but for quite different reasons. Others it not only would never have done, but could never have understood at all. But it is this alien species that is demanded by people who think of intelligence as the source of all social development. Thus Wilson writes: "a strong impelling force appears to generate social behavior in vertebrate evolution. . . . This force, I would like to suggest, is greater intelligence. The concomitants of intelligence are more complex and adaptable behavior and a refinement in social organization that are based on personalized individual relationships. Each member of the vertebrate society can *continue to behave selfishly*. . . . but it can also *afford* to co-operate more" [Midgley's italics]. If intelligence had really been the only "impelling force," most of the concomitants would never have been found necessary. Why affection? Why time-consuming greeting procedures, mutual grooming, dominance and submission displays,

---

*Notice how this at once takes us away from the normal notion of *selfishness*. If someone said, "He is utterly selfish, he thinks of nothing but the prosperity of his relations," or (as we must shortly substitute), "He thinks of nothing but how many descendants he will have in five centuries' time," we could hardly fail to reply, "But why do you call that *selfish*? You surely mean that he is either (1) clannish or (2) crazy."

territorial boasting, and ritual conflict? Why play? Why (on the human scene) so much time spent in nonproductive communication of every kind—idle chatter, lovemaking, sport, laughter, song, dance, and storytelling, quarrels, ceremonial, mourning and weeping? Intelligence alone would not generate these ends. It would just calculate means. But these things are done for their own sake; they are a part of the activity that goes to make up the life proper to each species. Insofar as there is one "impelling force," it is sociability. From that comes increasing power of communication, which provides the matrix for intelligence.

Study Questions

1. Midgley claims that "Rescuers and benefactors do not . . . just want the sensation of rescuing and benefacting. They want to help people." What is Midgley arguing here? Is she right?

2. How does Midgley argue against Aristotle's statement about the true motivation of someone who dies to save a friend's life?

3. What is Midgley's argument that psychological egoists have misunderstood the motives of altruism?

 *Narrative*

Lord of the Flies

WILLIAM GOLDING

Novel, 1954. Films by Peter Brooks (director, 1963) and Harry Hook (director, 1990). Summary and Excerpts.

This famous novel is based on Hobbes's view of human nature: Our civilization is a thin veneer; scratch the surface, and you'll find primal selfishness and aggression underneath. This story provides a good illustration of the theories of selfishness and aggression discussed in this chapter, because Ardrey, Lorenz, Freud, and Wilson all stand on the shoulders of Thomas Hobbes. In addition—although Hobbes is careful not to say that natural selfishness and aggression are evil—it links up with the doctrine of frail and evil human nature that you will encounter in Chapter 8. Either way, we read between the lines that goodness and a civilized demeanor are a matter of *effort,* an effort that sometimes fails.

As the story begins, the world is at war. A plane evacuating English schoolboys goes down on a small tropical island, the pilot disappears, and a handful of boys, ages six to twelve, find themselves stranded, without any adults to take charge.

At first the boys, like good British subjects, take up a parliamentary existence. They devise rules, hold assemblies, and assign projects: Water must be fetched, shelters built, and—most importantly—a fire must be maintained at all times to ensure that passing ships will see the smoke. To light the fire, they use Piggy's glasses as a magnifying glass, and during this process he is practically blind. Ralph is the boys' leader, partly because he is a person who inspires confidence and partly because he has in his possession a great conch shell. Whoever holds the conch becomes the symbol of civilization: There it is, and so the veneer of orderly life still exists. However, the veneer soon wears thin. Piggy, the overweight boy with thick glasses and a quick mind, becomes Ralph's conscience; he is the person who never lets go of the thought of rescue. But Piggy has a counterpart, Jack, who discovers the lure of island living: There are no adults to set any rules, and life seems to create patterns that are made to be followed. As the weeks go by, a change occurs. The boys begin to shed their British clothing and their British identity—all except for Piggy and Ralph, who still have hopes of being rescued. They keep insisting that they must keep the fire going; it has already gone out once, and a passing ship failed to see them.

Jack and a few followers begin hunting down pigs on the island, but their civilized natures make it difficult for them to complete the actual kill. However, putting on homemade masks gives them a new identity as hunters. After a quarrel, they split off from Ralph and Piggy and discard the notion of trying to have a civilized society. In an orgy of blood and violence that resembles a ritual rape and murder, they kill their first pig, a sow with suckling babies. They cut off the pig's head and mount it on a sharpened stick as a sacrifice to *the beast*. The beast is a shadow that haunts the *littluns,* the smaller boys. There is a rumor of a shape moving at night, of a thing coming out of the sea. Piggy tries to convince the others that there is nothing to fear on the island "unless we get frightened of people." But for Jack the beast becomes a powerful entity that must be placated, an island god. Jack has reinvented religion.

Simon, a spiritual boy, has two fateful encounters: After secretly witnessing the killing of the pig, he goes to see the mounted pig's head and has a vision. From out of the pig's mouth, the Lord of the Flies speaks to him:

> The half-shut eyes were dim with the infinite cynicism of adult life. They assured Simon that everything was bad business. . . . "There isn't anyone to help you. Only me. And I'm the beast. . . . Fancy thinking the beast was something you could hunt and kill!" said the head. For a moment or two the forest and all the other dimly appreciated places echoed with the parody of laughter, "You knew, didn't you? I'm part of you? Close, close, close! I'm the reason why it's no go? Why things are the way they are?"

When some of the boys encounter a strange thing on the island, they are convinced that the beast exists. (The reader is aware that the thing is just the plane's dead pilot, all tangled up in his parachute, which is moving and bulging with the wind.) Shortly after, Simon finds the beast and realizes what it is—the pilot in his parachute. He frees the dead man from the tangles and runs to tell the others that there is no beast. He bursts in on a pig-killing dance that Jack has instigated; in the hunters' frenzy Simon isn't even recognized but is taken to be the beast himself, and the hunters pounce on him and stab him to death.

This is the end of innocence for everybody. For Ralph and Piggy, there is only one solution. They go into denial, refusing to face the fact that they, too, were present at the dance. For Jack and the others there is no return to reason: They reject the conch, Ralph, Piggy, and the memories of another life. However, realizing that they need to build a fire of their own, they raid the camp and steal Piggy's glasses. The last glimpse of civilization disappears along with Piggy's own vision. Ralph and Piggy, the only ones left who care about rescue, approach Jack to reason with him to get Piggy's glasses back, but "not as a favor," Piggy plans to say. "I don't ask you to be a sport, I'll say, not because you're strong, but because what's right's right." The others have all donned war paint, but not Ralph and Piggy, because "we aren't savages." Piggy pleads with them all, one last time, to recognize the value of civilization: "Which is better—to have rules and agree, or to hunt and kill? . . . Which is better, law and rescue, or hunting, and breaking things up?" The plea is futile: The boys roll a big rock toward half-blind Piggy who is thrown off the cliff to his death in the rocky surf below. Now the hunt is on for Ralph, who must run and hide like a pig. In order to smoke him out, the boys set fire to the thicket, but this act is what leads to Ralph's rescue. The smoke is seen by a British warship, and an officer intercepts the hunt moments before Ralph would have been killed:

> "Fun and games," said the officer. [But when he realizes that this is no game, he scolds them.] "I should have thought that a pack of British boys—you're all British, aren't you?—would have been able to put up a better show than that. . . ." And in the middle of them, with filthy body, matted hair, and unwiped nose, Ralph wept for the end of innocence, the darkness of man's heart, and the fall through the air of the true, wise friend called Piggy.
>
> The officer, surrounded by these noises, was moved and a little embarrassed. He turned away to give them time to pull themselves together; and waited, allowing his eyes to rest on the trim cruiser in the distance.

Study Questions

1. The title *The Lord of the Flies* is a translation of the Hebrew *Ba'alszevuv* (in Greek, *Beelzebub*). What kind of devil or beast is Golding referring to?

2. Golding reportedly intended this to be more than a story about boys on an island. What is his theory of human nature? Do you agree?

3. Compare Golding's vision of human nature with Hobbes's view and with Midgley's view.

4. What is the symbolic significance of the boys being rescued by a cruiser?

5. Often a work of fiction will cast some of its characters as symbols of the inner tensions of the main character. Applying Freud's theory of the superego, the ego, and the id, and identifying Ralph as the main character (the ego), which characters might we say symbolize the superego and the id?

Narrative

2001: A Space Odyssey

STANLEY KUBRICK (DIRECTOR AND SCREENWRITER),
ARTHUR C. CLARKE (SCREENWRITER)

Film, 1968. Summary.

This film became an instant classic and is still regarded as one of the most influential films of all time. Commercials still borrow imagery and soundtrack from *2001: A Space Odyssey,* by showing objects gracefully floating in space to the tune of "The Blue Danube," and using the opening bars of Richard Strauss's *Also Sprach Zarathustra* as background music. At midnight, New Year's Eve 2000, going into what mathematically was the true start of the third millennium, year 2001 (although we might say that all the people celebrating its arrival the year before were perfectly justified in celebrating the change to year 2000—a worldwide cultural event rather than a mathematical one), television stations played the famous introductory theme, and the entire movie was shown repeatedly. Films and novels have explored the theme of "government conspiracy to hide contact with aliens" ever since 1968. The film takes us from the "dawn of man" through the first imaginary years of systematic moon exploration, all the way to the era of computers involved with space exploration—a time span Clarke predicted would take from the early 1960s to year 2001—hence the title. (Clarke believed in 1968, along with most space-oriented people, that once we landed on the moon, heavy moon exploration would follow, and then would come a moon base and a space station; and before the turn of the millennium, he thought, we'd be out exploring the planets. Nobody had foreseen the devastating impact the fall of the *Challenger* was to have on the space program.) On a personal note, I saw the film on one of the biggest screens in Europe, in Paris—mere days before Neil Armstrong and Buzz Aldrin landed on the moon with Apollo 11. For me the summer of 1969 meant that the future had arrived.

In retrospect, the film displays an interesting mix of foresight and errors: Its visions of space station and spaceship have been incorporated into the technological expectations of the near future, but its depiction of human evolution is based on a misconception, as we understand it today: When human brains were beginning to expand, we were already no longer knuckle walking, but almost fully upright—as we know from Lucy and her contemporaries (see Chapter 2). There is as yet no consensus about what made our brains expand, but one explanation may lie in the new possibilities and challenges that having one's hands freed from the task of walking presented to early humans. And as you saw in this chapter, paleoanthropologists such as Don Johanson and others are now questioning the premise that it was the weapon in particular that was the first tool of enhanced intelligence. But in 1968 both ideas were considered established facts.

In Chapter 1 we focused on the idea of whether a computer can be a person (also an important theme in *2001*), so here we look at the famous opening sequence, "Dawn of Man." The filmmakers conceived this scene in the spirit of Raymond Dart and Robert Ardrey, basing it on their theory of fundamental human aggression and the connection between human intelligence and human aggression.

It is dawn somewhere in the African desert, in the era of early hominids. Two groups of knuckle-walking, furry, apelike creatures are fighting over a water hole. One group barely manages to scare the others away with shrieks and gestures. The defeated group retreats, moping and thirsty. At night everyone huddles close together in the group, in terror of the desert darkness: Predators are on the prowl, and whoever is exposed may become a meal for a wandering leopard.

Another dawn. We see the same group of ape-humans, but also something new: A giant black slab, a *monolith,* is standing upright in the sand, and the ape-humans feel compelled to go and touch it. It possesses a strange ability to attract them, and when they touch it, something seems to happen to them: They dance around it, and clear images come to their mind. One young male ape picks up a big bone lying on the ground and starts hitting the ground with it, observing the result when he hits the bleached skull of a grass-eater. In an instant he imagines a live grass-eater, imagines hitting it, and imagines it falling: Next thing we know, he has made the mental connection between weapon, hunt, and prey; soon the entire group of apes is sitting around the water hole, happily eating raw meat. *Tool* and *food* have been connected, as well as *weapon* and *killing.* How did this happen? The monolith has made the creatures think; it is an intelligence-enhancer, and the part of the mind it enhances is the part that is based on aggression.

Next scene: back at the water hole. The Other Guys are there, shrieking and threatening as before, but this time there is a difference: Our Guys have weapons—clubs made from bones and rocks—and the other group is quickly defeated. For the first time, a weapon has been used to take a life deliberately within the species. Elated, the killer ape throws his weapon, a thigh bone, high up in the air. The bone changes into a spaceship bound for the great space station in the late twentieth century; end of the beginning of *2001: A Space Odyssey,* and the beginning of the further story of the monolith.

Study Questions

1. Evaluate the film's assessment of human intelligence—that we have gotten to where we are today by channeling our innate aggression into the use of weapons.

2. If the film had been made today, do you think Kubrick and Clarke might have had the monolith teach the creatures to make *baskets* and use them, instead of weapons? Would that be appropriate? Why or why not?

Review

Key Issues in Chapter 3

- Can all human behavior be explained through biology?

Darwin's Legacy

- *Natural Selection.* Three blows to human self-assurance have come from the theories of Copernicus, Darwin, and Freud. Darwin's theory of survival of the fittest defines the "fittest" as those who fill their biological niches successfully and have equally successful offspring. Darwin's theory has been re-vised by the idea of punctuated equilibrium, which means evolution often happens in spurts, and by the recognition that old and new species may coexist.

- *Darwin's Critics.* Today "survival of the fittest," at least in human populations, means that natural selection has given way to cultural selection. Nietzsche's adaptation of Darwin's theories to form the concept of the "Superman" was then misinterpreted by Hitler and others in their idea of a super race. Although other thinkers adapted Darwin's theory to the economic world in the guise of social Darwinism, Darwin himself thought that humans could make moral choices to improve their condition.

- *Ethics and Evolution.* Darwin wanted to see humans as evolving morally; however, biology and ethics are different realms.

Are Humans Aggressive by Nature?

- *The Territorial Imperative.* Ardrey and Lorenz are proponents of the theory of natural human aggression. Ardrey expressed the normative theory that aggression is beneficial for human intellectual development.

- *Children of a Murderer?* Raymond Dart expressed the view that humans are killer apes, and Ardrey and other screenwriters popularized it. Don Johanson believes early hominids were scavengers rather than predators.

- *Konrad Lorenz: Aggressive Nonpredators.* Lorenz sees aggression as an old survival mechanism that should now be controlled culturally, because it is no longer to our advantage. An even older human characteristic is a community based on compassion and responsibility.

Are Humans Selfish by Nature?

- *"We Are Fundamentally Selfish."* Psychological egoism, a descriptive theory, states that humans are selfish by nature. Sociobiology is based on the idea that human biology influences all social structures; evolutionary psychology is based on the idea that human biology influences the lives of individuals. Psychological egoism is criticized because (1) it is unfalsifiable and (2) being happy for others and being happy about others' misfortune can't be equally selfish.

- *Thomas Hobbes: Self-Preservation Is Everything.* All human emotions and decision making can be boiled down to our sense of self-preservation and self-gratification.

- *Sigmund Freud: We Are Driven by the Unconscious.* Freud's dream theory holds that dreams are wish-fulfillment; the manifest dream content hides the latent dream thoughts. In addition to explaining the Unconscious through the pleasure principle and the reality principle, Freud expanded his theory in terms of the three-part psyche—the id, the ego, and the superego.

- *Edward O. Wilson's Sociobiology.* Acts of self-sacrifice are genetic manifestations of selfishness. The four primate characteristics are (1) group size, (2) sexual dimorphism, (3) a long childhood, and (4) social play. Richard Dawkins's "selfish gene" theory says that we strive to preserve our genetic heritage.

- *Mary Midgley: A Different Model.* Midgley challenges the selfish gene theory because it fails to distinguish between truly selfish and "unselfish selfish" behavior. Her alternative model is based on the relationship of parents and offspring.

The Weapon Versus the Basket

- *The Weapon or the Basket? Leakey and Eisler.* Instead of "man the hunter" comes the model of "gatherer-hunter" societies; it is the invention not of the weapon, but of the basket that becomes a symbol of human culture. Riane Eisler's interpretation is based on the idea of the chalice versus the blade, sharing versus aggression—the partnership model versus the dominator model. Models of human nature may reflect a wish for a certain self-image.

- *Does Sociobiology Explain Everything About Human Behavior?* Knowledge of human neurobiology doesn't necessarily tell us all about our inner experience.

- *The Naturalistic Fallacy.* It is invalid to move from a descriptive statement, an "is," to a normative statement, an "ought," without stating a second premise about our values. The naturalistic fallacy can be used to express discriminatory ideas.

- *Jane Goodall: Potentials.* Goodall's ape studies show that apes have aggressive as well as compassionate tendencies. All this means is that humans have such tendencies, too.

Primary Readings

- Robert Ardrey, *African Genesis.* Ardrey argues that humans have evolved from primates who killed to survive and that all human advances and inventions have their foundation in war. He speculates that humans must seek a future without war but that it will be difficult to achieve.

- Mary Midgley, *Beast and Man.* Even if humans are interested in self-preservation, we are interested in many things besides that. Midgley argues that psychological egoists such as Aristotle, Hobbes, and Wilson have misunderstood the motives of altruism. Sociability accounts for much of human activity that is not selfish.

Narratives

- William Golding, *Lord of the Flies,* novel. A group of English schoolboys is stranded on a tropical island without adult supervision during a world war. While a few try to uphold the rules of civilization, the rest soon revert to an existence characterized by aggression and superstition.

- *2001: A Space Odyssey,* film. In the opening sequence, the monolith teaches early hominids to think; they develop weapons and kill animals for meat and other hominids for their territory.

Endnotes

1. Charles Darwin, *The Descent of Man* (1871; reprint, New York: Prometheus Books, 1998), p. 641.
2. Ibid., p. 137.
3. Ibid., p. 642.
4. Ibid., p. 642.
5. I am here using the term *man* deliberately, instead of the gender-neutral *humans.* As is apparent from the text, Ardrey's theory of human aggression is primarily a theory of male aggression.
6. *Ecce Homo* is Latin for "behold the man," presumably uttered by Pontius Pilate when showing Jesus to the people of Jerusalem after his torture.
7. Konrad Lorenz, *On Aggression* (New York: Bantam, 1967), pp. 240ff.
8. Thomas Hobbes, *Leviathan* (New York: Prometheus Books, 1988), part 1, chapter 6.
9. In Chapter 7 we take another look at the theory of dreams, and the topic of dreams as precognitions will be explored.
10. Edward O. Wilson, *On Human Nature* (Cambridge, Mass: Harvard University Press, 1978), p. 32.
11. Mary Midgley, *Beast and Man: The Roots of Human Nature* (London: Routledge, 1995), p. 136.
12. Richard Leakey, *The People of the Lake: Mankind and Its Beginnings* (Garden City, N.Y.: Anchor, 1978), p. 118.
13. In Chapter 8 we encounter Aristotle's theory of human nature as potentialities. For Aristotle, realizing (actualizing) one's potential makes an individual a virtuous person.

Chapter Four

Determinism and Free Will

Can We Choose Our Actions?

The subject of this chapter occupies an intermediate position between descriptive and normative theories of human nature. As a theory, determinism is purely descriptive, because it just describes what it asserts to be a scientific fact; however, the practical application of this theory has far-reaching consequences for our understanding of humans as creatures interacting with each other, using our freedom of choice and having to take responsibility for the choices we make. Accordingly, we will be focusing on two areas in this chapter: the scientific possibility of predicting human behavior and the moral implications of such theory.

Mechanistic Determinism

Remember that one of the classical definitions of human nature involves the concept of *free will:* Presumably, humans are the only creatures on earth who have the ability to choose freely and rationally between several options. In the final chapter, we look at whether it is possible for non-human animals to make some form of rational choices too, but this chapter goes in the opposite direction: Instead of exploring the freedom of the will of other creatures, the theory we will discuss here claims that like nonhuman animals, humans *do not have a free will;* we are all links in a giant chain of causality propelling us toward our decisions and actions. We may think our decisions are freely made, but in actual fact they are the result of pressures—inner pressures from our biological states and external pressures from our environment. This theory is based on the scientific hypothesis that everything has a cause. (In some ways it may resemble the ancient religious worldview known as fatalism, but in fact they are very different, as Box 4.1 explores.)

Determinism is based on the purely mechanical fact that everything is part of a chain of causes and effects, which is why it is also referred to as *mechanistic determinism.* You may say that under certain circumstances, sociobiological theories as well as theories of evolutionary psychology (see Chapter 3) can be regarded as deterministic: This is so if they claim that our actions are completely and utterly determined by our biological makeup and that the day we understand human biology 100 percent, is also the day we will be able to predict all human social behavior. Wilson and Dawkins are very close to being determinists because they claim that human behavior can be adequately explained through the story of human biology; however, they don't claim that each individual act can be foretold based on human biology. Most evolutionary psychologists see human action patterns as predictable based on our evolution and biology but don't necessarily assert that each action can be anticipated.

Mechanistic determinism applied to the world of natural science presents few problems, because we have gained such scientific advantages from adopting the view of causality: Nothing is generated out of nowhere; everything has a cause. For thousands of years people believed that old rags and dirt spontaneously generated mice and fleas. That came to an end once science demonstrated that mice and fleas come from other mice and fleas. The more knowledge we have, the better we can understand and predict geological events, climatic events, and events in the biosphere. We can breed bugs to help eradicate other bugs; we can predict the path of hurricanes and tornadoes;

Box 4.1   FATALISM

In his play *Sheppey*, the British author Somerset Maugham tells this story of one man's encounter with his fate:

Death speaks: "There was a merchant in Baghdad who sent his servant to market to buy provisions and in a little while the servant came back, white and trembling, and said, 'Master, just now when I was in the marketplace I was jostled by a woman in the crowd and when I turned I saw it was Death that jostled me. She looked at me and made a threatening gesture: now, lend me your horse, and I will ride away from this city and avoid my fate. I will go to Samarra and there Death will not find me.' The merchant lent him his horse, and the servant mounted it, and he dug his spurs in its flanks and as fast as the horse would gallop he went. Then the merchant went down to the marketplace and he saw me standing in the crowd and he came to me and said, 'Why did you make a threatening gesture to my servant when you saw him this morning?' 'That was not a threatening gesture,' I said, 'it was only a start of surprise. I was astonished to see him in Baghdad, for I had an appointment with him tonight in Samarra.'"

This story, chilling in its sparse inevitability, tells of an ancient view of human life that many people share today: You may do what you can to try to escape your fate, but whatever will be, will be (a proverb that Spanish-speaking people know as *Que sera, sera*). This view of life, known as fatalism, is common around the world. The future is somehow "written" already, and we play a role that can't be changed. Fatalism is generally linked with a religious worldview. The Muslim tradition holds that Allah has determined your fate beforehand. Greek mythology tells of three old women (the *Fates*) spinning, measuring, and cutting the life threads of all human beings, and trying to avoid your fate will simply bring it about: Oedipus tried to escape the prophecy that he was to kill his father and marry his mother, but through his actions made just those events happen. Scandinavian mythology has a similar image of the three *Nornes*, meting out life threads in their cave; we each have our own thread at birth that can't be extended. A dear friend of my own family said, when told that she had a terminal illness, "I can't add a single day to my life more than what I have been given from the start." This view of life is the source of great strength and comfort in dark times. Some would say that it is also a view of passivity: If you don't think anything can be changed, then you don't make an effort. But this criticism misses the point of fatalism: Fatalism doesn't say that everything you do is in vain, so you might as well do nothing; it teaches that everything you do is part of your destiny, doing nothing as well as doing everything you can. If you live longer because of your effort, then that was part of the plan. If you sit there and starve yourself to death, it was part of the plan too. But, of course, we humans don't know "the plan" ahead of time.

Fatalism may look similar to the theory of *determinism*, but in fact the two are quite different. While fatalism generally sees a divine power as the creator of destinies and usually sees no logical problem in holding people accountable for their bad deeds even if it may be in their destiny to commit them, determinism is a secular theory, based on a scientific worldview.

we may even be able to predict earthquakes. The famous *chaos theory*, which states that physical events are so chaotic that they can't be predicted, is in fact just another theory of causality. The well-known saying from chaos theory to the effect that if a butterfly bats its wings in India, it will cause a storm in the Pacific, implies that every tiny event will have effects that in turn will cause other effects of *unpredictable* scope and magnitude; but it isn't because the principle of causality is wrong or because things happen out of the blue without a cause: It is because the causal chain is so complex that predicting with 100 percent accuracy isn't a practical possibility.

So far so good. On the level of physical science, this appears to be true: If we knew enough about the natural world ruled by Newtonian physics, we could probably predict everything accurately (but we never will). The problem comes when this scientific theory is applied to human beings and their actions. The scientific theory of mechanistic determinism now becomes a philosophical theory—*hard determinism,* claiming that if we knew enough about *people* (about human nature), then we could predict their every move. Hard determinism speculates that *100 percent knowledge about the past would yield 100 percent accuracy in predicting future events and understanding past events* in terms of human actions. It is a challenging theory because most of us don't feel we are that predictable; we have an astute sense that we can change our mind about what we were about to do, bid good-bye to old habits and conventions, and do something astonishingly different—or in moral as well as religious terms, we can choose to do *good,* or we can choose to do *evil,* and we can be held accountable for either. Even our secular legal systems operate under that same assumption: We can be held accountable for our actions because we have chosen to perform them. We hold our family, friends, and relatives accountable for breaking promises—but we usually don't hold our pets to the same standard, because we don't believe they have the same rational and moral choices that we do. So, the assumption that humans are capable of making free choices is fundamental.

Now what happens if we can't behave any differently than what our nature allows? What if everything we do is a result of some inner compulsion or some external influence that we have no control over? Then there is no sense in trying to change or in blaming ourselves or others when we don't change. The ultimate logic of hard determinism applied to the realm of human mental activity is that *we can never hold anybody accountable for anything.* It may sound preposterous, but we have seen many examples of this theory being used to "get people off the hook" in criminal trials, as we shall see shortly. (Box 4.2 explores the similarities and differences between fatalism, determinism, and the theory of karma.)

When a theory is labeled "hard" something, you can start looking around for a "soft" version of it, and it is no different for hard determinism: The alternative theory, *soft determinism,* has a much broader following. This theory is also known as *compatibilism,* and we will look at it in detail later. For now, suffice it to say that soft determinism doesn't deny that there is cause and effect but claims that human decisions still contain some measure of freedom.

What Is Free Will? Hard Determinism's Answer

The question of freedom of the will is as ancient as philosophy itself and shows up occasionally in religions that include theories of fate or predestination; for if our fate has been preordained, what differences do our choices make? Remember the servant fleeing head over heels to Samarra, just in time for his meeting with Death? Religions have had a notoriously hard time trying to reconcile human free will and responsibility (in particular for choosing to do evil) with the idea that God has planned everything that is ever going to happen.

The freedom of choice referred to in philosophy is not the actual availability of choices, such as having several political candidates to choose from or a choice from a menu at a restaurant. We could live in a country where there is only one candidate to vote for (because the election is controlled by the government), or we could eat at one of those expensive restaurants where the gimmick is that there is only one dinner on the menu per day. Our choices are then eliminated—but we would generally still assume that we have *free will,* because we can leave the restaurant without ordering anything. Or we can leave the country where elections aren't free—and if we can't leave, as in present-day Burma (Myanmar), we can denounce the government in our hearts! But free political and personal choice is not the same issue as freedom of the will: Freedom of choice is a

Box 4.2   THE DOCTRINE OF KARMA

The Hindu and Buddhist concept of karma may look like another version of fatalism, but actually it is much more closely related to mechanistic determinism. Karma is a theological concept that has its place in a religious worldview embracing reincarnation. It teaches that your actions (or omissions) in this life will determine your status in your next incarnation, just as your status in this life has been determined by your actions and omissions in previous lives. You may be working your way toward an existence as a worm or a high priest. Whatever you do or don't do will have consequences. Hindus believe you can work on accumulating good consequences for your next life—a better status of living or freedom from poverty, disease, and personal tragedies. By contrast, classical Buddhism believes *any* concern for future incarnations further ties you to the "wheel of life," where you will be doomed to incarnation after incarnation. Passion for life will tie you to the next life. Total disdain of future incarnations—or even killing oneself to escape life—is just as bad, because a negative attitude to life will tie you to life just as surely as a positive one will. The solution is to remain in mental equilibrium and not let anything disturb you in a positive or negative sense. Do what you have to do to stay alive, go to work, visit friends and relatives, cook meals, take care of your body, but do it without passion for life. Eventually you will reach a full understanding of your previous incarnations and will escape the wheel of life for good. However, helping others, in a dispassionate way, can help you accumulate good karma for your next life, even though they, strictly speaking, are responsible for their own current hardships because of their own karma.

For a western mind-set, where reincarnation traditionally isn't a part of one's religious background, the idea of having lots of incarnations to look forward to may sound attractive; for an Asian traditional mind-set, it is not. Here we must remember that for millennia, life has been hard in traditional societies, and the thought of endless cycles of disease, poverty, oppression, and having one's children die before the age of three was hardly an attractive prospect. The question of whether one might still prefer to live and be reincarnated under such conditions is discussed in Chapter 8, where we will encounter the German philosopher Friedrich Nietzsche's approach to this problem in his theory of the eternal return. And even in Western popular culture, the idea of having to repeat your life over and over again until you "get it" is not unfamiliar: The film *Groundhog Day* explores the theme and so does the novel *Replay* (see Chapter 8).

What makes the theory of karma so different from fatalism is that karma does not rely on a theory that a higher power decides your fate. You decide your fate through your own actions, mechanically. A future good or bad life is not a reward or punishment, but a simple causal result of actions taken in the past. What makes it different from hard determinism is that it assumes that at any time we are free to change our course. The present has been determined by the past, but the present also allows us to determine our future. The theory of karma thus implies that we have free will to help shape our future—a theory known as *self-determination*. And so the theory of karma is in effect a compatibilistic theory.

---

political concept; free will is a *metaphysical* one, referring to the very nature of human reality. Do we believe that we, as humans, can make choices based on a rational weighing of pros and cons? Then we also believe that when we choose something that goes against the rules of our community, we can and will be held *accountable*. On the other hand, do we believe, with hard determinism, that our very choices reflect the kind of person we are genetically and/or the kind of upbringing we have had and other external influences? Then we think that freedom of the will is an illusion and our entire decision-making process just a link in a greater causal chain of events.

Deterministic philosophy doesn't deny that it *feels as if* we make free choices; what it denies is that the choice is actually free. You may feel that you made a major choice in your life (such as choosing your major or deciding whether to be sexually active or celibate) as a fundamentally free decision—influenced by friends and role models, certainly, but in the end your decision alone. Hard determinism will claim that you only think it was free; in actuality it was made based on just those friends and role models you want to impress, on genetic predispositions in your own physical nature, or on some other factors that you may not even know of. The theory doesn't say that *sometimes* our actions are influenced by our heredity or our environment; that would be trivial and not at all controversial; everyone knows that we are often swayed by such factors. The troubling aspect for philosophy, and for *moral philosophy* in particular, is that if we decide that *everything* we do can be traced back to other factors which we have no control over, then nothing we ever do or the consequences can be placed at our feet: As you saw in the introduction to this chapter, the upshot of this is that we have no moral responsibility for anything; we are always victims of circumstances.

Nature or Nurture?

The question is often raised whether human behavior is shaped primarily by "nature" or by "nurture"—by our heredity (our DNA) or by our environment. Both theories are of course deterministic if we mean that either one is the only factor that makes our character the way it is and that, with enough knowledge, we'd be able to predict a child's future character based on her genetics or her upbringing. Usually, when we as laypersons consider these issues, we imply that a certain amount of personal choice goes into forming our character. Hard determinism doesn't allow for that possibility. Setting aside the issue of free choice for now, is there any scientific consensus as to whether nature or nurture is the strongest factor? Most people would agree that the environment plays an important role in a child's development, but research now seems to show that genetic factors can be very significant

too. A child with a resilient genetic heritage can emerge unscathed from years spent growing up in a dysfunctional family, while another child, less resilient, may be scarred for life. Natural children of alcoholics have to watch their own drinking habits as adults, even if they have grown up in nondrinking foster families; this is because we now know there is a genetic component to alcoholism. In short, genes seem to play a more important role in forming our behavior than scientists used to think.

In 1998 Judith Rich Harris, an author of psychology textbooks, published *The Nurture Assumption: Why Children Turn Out the Way They Do: Parents Matter Less Than You Think and Peers Matter More*. In this book, which created a major, but short-lived controversy, she claimed that the parental role in raising children was minimal; contrary to popular wisdom, she said, children don't modify their behavior through parental influence, but if it is modified at all, it is through peer pressure because children listen to other children more than to their parents. The most important factor, though, is genetics: Quiet parents have quiet children, and rambunctious children are born to rambunctious parents; it doesn't have anything to do with observing and learning from parental behavior. In other words, Harris is an advocate of the influence of nature over nurture. Naturally, many critics saw her claims as not only wrong, but also preposterous: History is full of examples of children being raised without guidance (or with the wrong kind of guidance) and becoming problem children, and a change for the better in upbringing has accomplished an improved attitude in countless kids.

So what was Harris's evidence? Her own two children. One child was her natural child, while the other was adopted. Claiming that she had brought up the two girls similarly, she observed that one was quiet and more like the ideal child she was trying to raise than the other one was. The compliant child was her natural child, while the disobedient child was her adopted, older child. This is what instructors in critical thinking call a study with insufficient evidence! Or even a biased study. Two kids do not a sample study make. Besides, what offended my students terribly when we discussed this theory was that Harris had praised her own child as the well-behaved one and thus indirectly praised herself for being a genetically good person whose natural behavior was worth perpetuating! One might wonder how her other daughter felt, being held up to the world as the "unnatural" and disobedient daughter. It smacks a little of the old fairy tales of the adopted daughter, like Cinderella, who is relegated to the kitchen because the stepmother prefers her natural children.

A factor that seemed to have escaped Harris completely was that in spite of her own assurance, she may *not* have raised the girls identically— the adopted daughter may have sensed Harris's subconscious rejection or criticism and then responded to it in kind. Critics have denounced her study as unscientific, partly because of lack of research material, but also because Harris has no academic affiliation. That in itself is no obstacle to brilliant research—one of the most interesting and academically sound researchers today, Maxine Sheets-Johnstone (whom you will meet in Chapter 7) is an independent scholar. However, there are flaws in Harris's research itself: If she granted that *peer groups* (a "nurture" element) could have an influence on children, why should *parents* be denied possible influence? After all, they are most often closer to the child than friends from kindergarten or school. What the study accomplished was to make it evident that we all assume, unequivocally, that even though genetics plays a huge role in shaping our personality, the influence of upbringing is a given; it is not explained away by a mother's bias concerning her two children.

Other, more convincing and scientifically sound studies have been published, and here the study of twins may be the most thought-provoking. When those of us who are not identical twins witness the similarities in such pairs, we generally wonder if they became so much alike by deliberately emphasizing their likeness or simply because they are similar by nature and can't help it. Thousands of twins (and triplets, etc.)—identical as well as fraternal—gather at "twin" conventions and do their utmost to look identical because they get a kick out of it. However, there are also twins, even identical, who do their utmost to emphasize that they are not two halves of one person, but two individuals with individual lives. Studies in the last decades have yielded interesting results: Identical twins separated from birth and unaware of the existence of the other seem to develop with astounding similarities. Often they not only look alike, but have also chosen similar professions and spouses. Two brothers who had been separated from birth and didn't know about each other until the study brought them together were both heavy and mustached; they both liked wearing flannel shirts; both were firefighters; they preferred the same brand of beer; and at the time of the study they were both bachelors. The proposed explanation for this is that twins who are unaware of each other don't experience any urge or pressure to differentiate themselves from the other twin, so their natural tendencies develop freely and similarly. In other words, nurture plays a very important part, but when the pressure of nurture is absent, nature takes over. (Box 4.3 discusses some facts concerning the now completed Human Genome Project and determinism.)

The debate is extremely heated within the field of *feminist theory:* That women and men are different is something we need hardly argue, but how different are we really, and why? A brand of feminism that was particular influential in the eighteenth and nineteenth centuries and is still with us today, sometimes labeled *classical feminism,* claims that the differences between women and men are primarily cultural and social; if we raised children to be just human beings rather than to be little boys in blue and little girls in pink, we would do away with most of the gender differences in a generation or two, says the theory, clearly an example of a theory of nurture. Another feminist philosophy that became particularly influential in the 1980s and 1990s, labeled

Box 4.3 DETERMINISM AND THE HUMAN GENOME

A revival of the *nature* aspect of hard determinism is not an unlikely scenario, with the completion of the rough draft of the Human Genome Project in 2000 and subsequent detailed analyses. The Human Genome Project has mapped the approximately 100,000 genes of human DNA, a tremendous research effort comparable to the invention of the wheel in terms of its potential effects on society. We now know, roughly, what characteristics are associated with which genes, including propensities toward both physical and mental ailments, but that doesn't mean we know exactly how the genes interact with each other. Even so, within the first decade of the twenty-first century it will probably be possible to

- Do extensive gene therapy, removing or neutralizing genes for certain diseases
- Produce medication for individual patients based on their DNA profile
- Predict the possibility of developing certain diseases for an individual, even at birth or earlier

These possibilities seem promising to some, but ominous to others.

How will this kind of knowledge affect the future of individuals? Some genetic diseases may be eliminated, but others may well be incurable and unavoidable. How will we react to knowing the future if it is dreadful and we can't change it? Will insurance companies deny us insurance, based on our publicly accessible DNA profile? Will workplaces reject our applications based on our statistical risk of debilitating diseases? Will a hierarchical society evolve along the lines of the prophetic film *Gattaca* (1997)—a society with genetically designed humans who have a long life span and access to higher education and well-paying jobs as well as an underclass of naturally conceived people with a high probability of illness and early death? Will we choose our partners based on their genetic profile in addition to the classical emotional and economic factors?

Aside from the danger of social discrimination against genetically "flawed" humans, the danger is also that we might slip into a new age of hard determinism, with a scientific assumption that the DNA code will inevitably condemn us to a certain destiny, rather than just showing our statistical probability for it. *Gattaca* explores this very question and concludes that the DNA code predicts the likelihood of a certain future, but it doesn't predict the future; there is still free will and even chance! In addition, if we can conclusively tie violent behavior in with a certain gene and the process of falling in love with another, we shouldn't conclude that we now understand the entire phenomenon of violence or of love: There is still the immensely important *nurture* aspect to be reckoned with; and as we shall see, some thinkers speculate that even with the influence of nature and nurture, we still have the moral responsibility of making our own decisions, exercising our free will.

difference feminism, says that men and women are fundamentally different, and no amount of education is going to change that fact: We are simply different by nature. In Chapter 6 we'll take a closer look at theories of gender. However, in order for these and other theories of human nature to be considered examples of determinism, they would have to specifically express that inherited traits or external influence decide everything: We have no free will, and to think we do is an illusion. Neither feminist theory tends to go that far.

The Rise and Fall of Behaviorism

A philosophy that did go so far, however, was behaviorism. I put it in the past tense, because this theory experienced a quick rise in popularity and an equally quick descent into the abyss of defunct philosophies. It made the sweeping promise that

A Clockwork Orange, Warner Bros, 1971. The film shocked its audiences with its visual imagery and violent plot, and it continues to do so even today. Here Alex (Malcolm McDowell), Pete, Georgie, and Dim are on their nightly adventure of ultra-violence, looking for women to rape and other victims to beat up. When Alex is finally caught by the law, he undergoes a brainwashing procedure to curb his violent tendencies, but will it also deprive him of his free will?

any mention or reference to human mental activity would soon become a thing of the past, because behaviorism would prove that any reference to mental activities was an unnecessary and flawed conception of human nature: Everything we do has a behavioral component, and a person's behavior is not only indicative of his or her mental state, but also is the only reality we can go on. We can't determine whether other people have any mental states, but we can determine facts about their behavior. So behaviorism, one of the most radical hard deterministic theories in the twentieth century, set out to eliminate any reference to mental states from the language of psychology and philosophy, labeling such references as "mentalism."

The founder of psychological behaviorism was J. B. Watson (1878–1958). Acting on the

frustrations accompanying attempts to describe consciousness in the new science of psychology (because we experience our own consciousness, but not that of others, and we can barely make our own experiences understandable to others), Watson simply did away with the idea of consciousness in psychology. The subject of study was to be observable behavior; in addition, Watson assumed that observing behavior can tell us everything there is to know about human nature, because the idea of consciousness itself is a superstition, a lag from less enlightened times. In *Behaviorism,* Watson explains his theory:

The behaviorist asks: Why don't we make what we can *observe* the real field of psychology? Let us limit ourselves to things that can be observed, and formulate laws concerning only those things. Now what can we observe? Well, we can observe *behavior—what the organism does or says.* And let me make this fundamental point at once: that *saying* is doing—that is, *behaving.* Speaking overtly or to ourselves (thinking) is just as objective a type of behavior as baseball.[1]

Watson's determinism did not have just a theoretical side; he developed a very practical angle to his psychology as well. A person's heredity (nature) was for him much less important than the environment (nurture) in determining the person's behavior, and he advised parents of small children to confidently mold their children to become any kind of adult they might want them to be: doctors, lawyers, thieves. According to Watson, any person could become anything at all with the proper training. (In the Narratives section of this chapter, you will see this theory brought to life in literature, in Aldous Huxley's famous *Brave New World,* where Huxley explores the nightmarish future of a society based on such training.) In addition, Watson believed it was harmful for children to be cuddled, held, and hugged by their parents; a peck on the forehead now and again was all the affection a parent ought to show a child. Well-meaning parents who wanted the best for their kids withheld affection from them on a grand scale because of Dr. Watson's admonishings; in an odd way, Watson's theory of the enormous importance of a child's environment was thus proved, but not in the way he had in mind: Children deprived of affection will indeed have their future affected by this deprivation, but now we know that it is usually in a *negative* sense, resulting in difficulties relating to others as an adult.

Watson believed that a child learns in much the same way that Pavlov's dogs did in the famous experiment: Stimulus and response govern our reactions and our behavior. In other words, everything we learn is a *conditioning,* conducted by our environment. According to Watson, stimulus is any change in the "physiological condition of the animal," and response is any reaction, from turning away from a light, to building a skyscraper or

having babies. In 1921 Watson joined the world of advertising—an interesting footnote to his idea that everyone can be conditioned in any direction at the the right point in time.[2]

What about the objection that we, ourselves, know that we consist of much more than just observable behavior? Watson dismisses it by saying that self-observation is useless, because we only observe the most basic responses; we can, in effect, learn to understand the behavior of our neighbor better than we understand our own! So what is it all for? For Watson and for B. F. Skinner, who took up the mantle of behaviorism, it wasn't just a matter of *understanding* human nature: In Watson's words, "It is the business of behavioristic psychology to be able to predict and *to control* [italics added] human activity."[3]

B. F. Skinner (1904–1990) adopted Watson's theories that any reference to an inner conscious life is nothing but a superstition and that the purpose of behaviorism is to predict and control human behavior. His definition of determinism stands as the clearest and most radical statement of its kind:

> Science not only describes, it predicts. It deals not only with the past but with the future. Nor is prediction the last word: to the extent that relevant conditions can be altered, or otherwise controlled, the future can be controlled. If we are to use the methods of science in the field of human affairs, we must assume that behavior is lawful and determined. We must expect to discover that what a man does is the result of specifiable conditions and that once these conditions have been discovered, we can anticipate and to some extent determine his actions.[4]

Skinner knew how much opposition his and Watson's theories would generate, and he compared his own importance to that of Copernicus and Darwin. In his view, we have already accepted that sometimes people are not to be held accountable for what they do; all we need to do now, he says, is to go the whole way—to realize that every single person is at all times a product of his or her upbringing and culture and so give up our old-fashioned ideas of individuals acting freely. The more we know about the causal chain operating on our "decisions," the less we will be inclined to call them free.

So how do we predict and control people's behavior? *Through conditioning and reinforcement.* Skinner's emphasis on reinforcement is an addition to Watson's model and creates a new model for molding people (especially children) into the persons you want them to be. In Skinner's words,

> Events which are found to be reinforcing are of two sorts. Some reinforcements consist of *presenting* stimuli, of adding something—for example, food, water, or sexual contact—to the situation. These we call *positive* reinforcers. Others consist of *removing* something—for example, a loud noise, a very bright light, extreme cold or heat, or electric shock—from the situation. These we call *negative* reinforcers. In both cases the reinforcement is the same—the probability of response is increased. . . . The industrialist who wants employees to work consistently and without absenteeism must make certain that their behavior is suitably reinforced—not only with wages but with suitable working conditions. The girl who wants another date must be sure that her friend's behavior in inviting her and keeping the appointment is suitably reinforced. To teach a child to read or sing or play a game effectively, we must work out a program of educational reinforcement in which appropriate responses "pay off" frequently.[5]

Skinner's concept of negative reinforcement has acquired a meaning in everyday language of rewarding someone for stopping a behavior pattern, but that is incorrect; in Skinner's own definition, positive and negative reinforcements both result in a continuation of a behavior; however, the positive reinforcement consists in adding an element (such as a treat) as part of the conditioning, and negative reinforcement rewards the subject by removing something unpleasant from the situation (such as putting an end to torture).

The more we know about stimuli and responses, the better we can predict and control other peo-

ple's behavior. We can raise well-behaved children, make people stop smoking, predict elections and fads. (And girls can hold onto their boyfriends—by being calculating! The quotation above yields special insight into Skinner's view of proper early-twentieth-century dating customs.) We need never take recourse in any talk about "mentalistic" concepts such as intelligence, dreams, personality, virtues, memories, wishes, or interests, because they can all be reduced to a person's physical responses to physical stimuli. In Chapter 7 you will be further introduced to the concept of metaphysics and the metaphysical theory of *materialism:* Only what is material has reality. Watson's and Skinner's brand of determinism is a materialistic theory, reducing all mental activities to physical reactions that can be predicted and controlled. Box 4.4 gives you a brief introduction to the fundamental concepts of metaphysics.

Behaviorism had a short, intense success in the first decades of the twentieth century and inspired a great many people from parents to lawyers (such as Clarence Darrow; see the next section) to authors (such as Aldous Huxley; see Narratives section). However, soon it became clear that this theory was just too radical for scholars and laypeople who were used to thinking in terms of humans possessing thinking and feeling minds. For one thing, behaviorism is *counterintuitive;* we may go along with the idea that we can best understand others by describing and predicting their behavior, but it is very hard to accept Watson's and Skinner's assertion that our insight into our own states of mind is based on irrelevance and superstition. We may be able to accept Freud's contention that we don't understand our own unconscious perfectly, but few people will accept the idea that we simply don't have a consciousness. For another thing, the politically aware reader finds something profoundly offensive in the behaviorist program of "controlling" others. Perhaps the innocent enthusiasm displayed by both Watson and Skinner in explaining their method for controlling others is the greatest turnoff for critics of behaviorism, because we have seen a cen-

Box 4.4   METAPHYSICS: DUALISM, MATERIALISM, AND IDEALISM

In Chapter 7 we will explore the topic of metaphysics in greater detail, but for now we just need to expand our working vocabulary with three terms: materialism, idealism, and dualism. *Metaphysics* is the term for the philosophical discipline that investigates the *nature of reality*, and in a sense we all have a theory of metaphysics whether we are aware of it or not: Let us assume that you have experienced the death of a loved one, a relative or a friend. What do you think happened to the person you lost? Do you (1) feel that the person's physical life on earth is over, but somewhere in another reality his or her spirit still lives, and if you are fortunate, you will meet some day on the other side? Or do you (2) feel that the person who was your friend or relative in life is now just a memory in your mind, his or her body turned to dust, with nothing of the personality remaining? It is less likely that you feel (3) that the spiritual life of this person, and of yourself and all others, is somehow much truer and more real than the fact that we seem to live our lives in bodies or that the body is a downright illusion, and the only true self is the self of the spirit. These three approaches (and additional hybrid views) represent the three major theories of metaphysics. The first view represents the theory of *dualism,* by far the most popular theory among nonscientists because it seems to be intuitively right: We have bodies that die, but we also have spirits that live on in some form—in an afterlife, in a new body, or on another level of existence. The second view is referred to as *materialism:* We are nothing but our bodies; the idea of a spiritual life is an illusion created by our brain. When brain activity ceases, our "soul" dies just as surely as our body, because our inner life is nothing but brain activity. Most scientists with their feet in the twentieth century can be considered materialists. The third view is quite esoteric but it does reappear from time to time in history: The idea that the physical world is somehow an illusion, and the only true world is that of the spirit or soul. This view is referred to as *idealism.*

---

tury's worth of political controls being exercised, from Hitler's death camps to the notorious LSD experiments presumably conducted by the CIA in the 1960s. In addition, the moral problem raised by behaviorism's denial of "mentalism" (meaning anything hinting at the possibility that people may have a mental or spiritual life) is profound, because it denies (1) that the entire notion of having a spiritual life can be meaningful and (2) that we can ever be held accountable for anything; every one of our decisions is a result of environmental pressures and, as a result, our free will becomes illusory—and with that, our moral responsibility. In the next section we shall explore how this concept has been applied in some famous court cases.

Today the term *behaviorism* is encountered within several fields, in particular animal behaviorism; this doesn't indicate that it leans in the direction of Skinner and Watson, denying the reality of animal mental processes; rather, a shift has occurred in the application of the word, and it has become a generic term for theories of behavior, including expressions of mental processes.

Determinism in Court

While hard determinism in the strict philosophical sense—that every human action is determined by previous causes which preclude the existence of free will—remains mostly a theory for armchair philosophers, a version of the theory has had immense influence in the courts, as a criminal defense strategy: *The criminal action of the defendant was determined by internal or external pressures, which precluded any free choice.* In other words, the defendant couldn't help himself or herself. Also sometimes referred to as "temporary insanity," this type of defense has had its successes and failures.

In the early 1920s Leopold and Loeb killed Loeb's 14-year-old cousin, Bobby Franks, just to see if they could commit the perfect crime. However, they were soon found out. Because of Clarence Darrow's defense, based on the theory of determinism, they were sentenced to life in prison instead of death by hanging.

It is extremely difficult for a defense lawyer to prove that a client was temporarily insane, because it would entail proving that the client, at the moment of the crime, *didn't know the difference between right and wrong*—and not merely showing that ordinary people don't usually act the way the client did. The prosecution will then call in experts trying to show that the defendant did indeed know the difference between right and wrong. What does this mean? Interestingly, the prosecution doesn't have to prove your client's sense of right and wrong is the same as everybody else's (because a great many law-abiding citizens have a great variety of opinions about what is right and wrong), but only that your client knew that he or she was doing something that society doesn't approve of. The prosecution will usually try to show that the defendant was aware of having done something wrong in the eyes of society and showed this awareness by fleeing the scene,

hiding out, changing clothes and hairstyle, and the like. In addition, planning the crime is also a sign that the defendant was sane. The defense will usually point to some extreme traumatic condition that predisposed the client to act compulsively; it doesn't necessarily mean the defense believes that there is no free will and that all our actions are determined by heredity or environment or both. It is mainly a strategy to get a defendant acquitted, combined with the commonsense realization that sometimes the mind can indeed become clouded by strong passions, fears, brainwashing, or other factors (as the French say, *C'est plus fort que moi,* "It's stronger than I am"). However, at least one famous defense was presented strictly from a deterministic viewpoint, held in all seriousness by the defense attorney, the famous Clarence Darrow. In addition, this trial, the murder case of Leopold and Loeb, marked the beginning of the trend of using determinism as a defense strategy.

In the early 1920s, two teenage boys, Nathan Leopold and Richard Loeb, decided to commit murder just to see if they could commit the "perfect crime." Their victim—whom they chose by chance, because he happened by on his bicycle, was Loeb's fourteen-year-old cousin, Bobby Franks. They lured him into their car, drove off with him into the countryside, and bludgeoned him to death. Then they dragged him into a field and left his body in a storm drain. After the deed was done, they went home, apparently quite unaffected, and mailed a ransom note (which they had written beforehand in general terms, without knowing who their victim was going to be) to Bobby's parents. The note was written on a stolen typewriter.

Bobby's body was soon found; the police had little problem tracing the letter to the stolen typewriter, and the boys were arrested. When interrogated individually, they soon broke down and confessed, implicating each other. This was a great surprise to the community, for both boys came from "good families," wealthy pillars of the community. Richard Loeb's family begged their old friend Clarence Darrow, famous from numerous court cases—including the "Scopes monkey trial" on the teaching of evolution—to represent their boy in the upcoming hearing—not to determine his guilt, because that was already established, but to determine his sentence: death by hanging or life in prison. This Darrow did with all his skill, relying on his personal belief, influenced by J. B. Watson, that every one of us, including Dicky Loeb, is a victim of environmental circumstances. He saw Leopold and Loeb as "two defective human machines which had somewhere broken down because of heredity or the pressure of external environment," as Darrow's biographer Irving Stone writes.[6]

Darrow began looking into the boys' background and found that the wealth of the parents was a contributing factor, just as extreme poverty may be a factor in other crimes. Leopold was forced to go to a girls' school, which, according to Darrow, embarrassed him. Besides, Leopold had glandular irregularities that, in Darrow's opinion, affected his judgment. And his parents hired a governess who abused him sexually. In addition, Leopold had read the German philosopher Nietzsche (see Chapter 8) and embraced his theory that some brilliant people aren't bound by morals and conventions. This mixed-up boy fell in love with another mixed-up boy, Loeb. Apparently lacking any physical problems, Loeb still had his share of "determining factors." A psychiatrist claimed he had a "split personality," without feelings of empathy for others. His wealthy parents seemed to care little for quality time with their son, but hired a strict governess to basically bring him up. She did her best, forcing him to read classics he had no interest in; instead he devoured crime novels on the sly and grew skilled at being secretive. When the boys met, they were thirteen and fourteen; they began committing petty theft, but within a few years, at seventeen and eighteen, they advanced to wanting to commit the perfect crime. And Bobby Franks just happened to be in the wrong place at exactly the wrong time.

Darrow had come to believe that most criminals are mentally ill and should either be locked up for life or treated, but never executed. Darrow himself wrote:

> That man is the product of heredity and environment and that he acts as his machine responds to outside stimuli and nothing else seems amply proven by the evolution and history of man. Man's every action is caused by motive. Whether his action is wise or unwise the motive was at least strong enough to move him. If two or more motives pulled in opposite directions he could not have acted from the weakest but must have obeyed the strongest. This is not a universe where acts result from chance. Law is everywhere. Every process of nature and life is a continuous sequence of cause and effect. . . . [H]owever much society may feel the need of confining the criminal, it must first of all understand that the act had an all-sufficient cause for which the individual was in no way responsible and must find the cause of his conduct and, so far as possible, remove the cause."[7]

We shall shortly see that a modern-day criminologist, John Douglas, interprets the compulsion of criminals as a proof of their free will. For now, Darrow serves as an example of hard determinism applied to issues of crime and justice. This is important because, more often than not, philosophical theories about human nature remain an issue within the community of professional philosophers, but not always with any noticeable consequences for "real-life" situations. Mechanistic determinism is one theory that has had a tremendous effect on social institutions outside of the world of academe. In the cases of Leopold and Loeb, the judge found that Darrow had made an important contribution to criminology with his point about heredity and environment being determining factors. The judge himself was moved to tears; the boys were spared death by hanging and were given life sentences.

Whether we go along with Darrow and believe Dicky Loeb and Nathan Leopold couldn't help themselves and shouldn't be held accountable for murder or whether we believe anyone who is not severely mentally disabled or traumatized bears near to full moral and legal responsibility for their actions, the fact remains that Loeb's short life reflected a callousness that he may well have learned at home: His father never visited him in jail, and his mother only showed up because Darrow bawled them out for not supporting their son. They weren't present at the trial and never mentioned their son again. In addition, they seemed to have forgotten about Dicky so thoroughly that they forgot to pay Darrow his fee for saving their child's life and had to be reminded months later by Darrow; he was never paid in full. Loeb died in prison at the age of 36, knifed to death by another inmate. Leopold lived until 1971. In prison, he helped introduce educational options for other inmates. He was finally paroled and spent his last years of freedom trying to help others in trouble with the law.

Whenever a precedent is set in a courtroom, other cases of a similar nature often follow. While not all judges or juries find that circumstances in a defendant's life are enough to relieve that person of responsibility for their crime, it is now commonly accepted that such circumstances can play an extenuating role. Over the years since the Leopold and Loeb case of 1924, such defenses have become common—perhaps so common that we are seeing a backlash in American courts. Probably the most famous court case involving a deterministic approach was the White murder trial, with the "Twinkies defense." In 1978 the mayor of San Francisco, George Moscone, and another man were killed by city supervisor Dan White. White's lawyer claimed that he was not to blame because he was on a "sugar high" from eating too many Twinkies! The court took this factor into consideration, giving White a lenient sentence. He was released from prison in the 1980s, but died shortly after. Other high-profile cases involving the determinism defense include the murder trials of Lyle and Erik Menendez who, in the early 1990s, killed their parents at point-blank range with a shotgun. In their first trial, resulting in a hung jury, the brothers claimed they killed their parents because they had been physically abused for years and were afraid their father was planning to kill them (it even appears that some jurors felt pity for them because they were now orphaned). What detracted from the defense was the boys had gained access to their considerable inheritance immediately and proceeded to spend it as fast as they could. In their second trial the boys were found guilty of first-degree murder, and they are now serving life sentences.

Another high-profile case involving the concept of determinism was the Lorena Bobbit case from 1993. Bobbit responded to what appears to have been a long period of physical abuse by her husband by getting up one night, getting a kitchen knife, and cutting off his penis. Her lawyer argued that she was compelled to do what she did because she was an abused spouse. This defense, commonly referred to as the "burning bed" defense (from a case where an abused wife set her husband's bed on fire while he was sleeping and killed him), holds that abused spouses have lost the ability to think logically, and so don't consider the possibility of escaping the abuse by leaving; therefore, the defendants shouldn't be charged with first-degree murder even if the murder involved some planning. Lorena Bobbit was acquitted, based on her defense attorney's argument that she suffered from the battered spouse syndrome.

However, it appears that judges' and jurors' patience with some determinism defense strategies is wearing thin. While we are today willing to concede that some people may, at some time, be pressured by their heredity and/or environment to commit unspeakable acts, we are also aware that it might serve as a slick defense for people less worthy of our sympathy. Case in point: During the San Ysidro, California, massacre at a McDonald's restaurant in the early 1980s, James Huberty killed more than twenty people before shooting himself. In the aftermath, Huberty's widow tried to take the fast-food chain to court, claiming that her husband had suffered from a chemical imbalance due to eating too many Big Macs. The case was dismissed by the judge.

Darrow opened up a can of worms when he offered his "victims of circumstances" defense, because it raises the question, *If nobody is responsible, can we ever punish anybody?* A determinist might actually agree to punishment even without responsibility; the punishment could be considered an added "cause" to make the person behave better next time or to deter others from committing the same crime. However, for anyone with a sense of personal, moral, and legal responsibility based on the concept of choice, this is extremely disturbing; it would mean (1) we could not establish any moral or legal difference between people who break the law deliberately (with *malice aforethought*) and the *victims* of the wrongdoing of others, since everyone becomes a victim, and (2) we could imagine "punishing" ahead of time anyone who displays signs that they might later commit criminal or antisocial acts, just to supply the sufficient cause for them to behave—like some parents in times past who used to line up their kids every Saturday for a beating, because they'd probably

either done something wrong or were about to do something! (Box 4.5 explores the issue of the criminal mind: Is it a question of nature or nurture?)

With the Human Genome Project completed (see Box 4.3) we may see a renewed interest in hard determinism used as a defense in the courts. If the defendant—a child molester, for example—can be proved to be genetically predisposed toward sexually abusing children, shouldn't he (or she) then be given gene therapy rather than punishment? Many psychologists are already leaning in the direction of traditional therapy: If defendants can't help themselves, what good is punishment supposed to do? It won't eliminate their genetic tendency, because it is a built-in compulsion, so why not treat their illness rather than punish them as criminals? In the next section we look at an argument for why this should not be the standard procedure, based on the belief that in spite of the compulsion there is also an element of decision making, and that is where we can hold the offender accountable.

The Case for Free Will

Does Causality Preclude Free Will?

The question here is not whether determinism is right that everything in nature is determined by past causes, because the answer would be a tentative yes: Determinism is probably correct in that assertion. The question is, Does determinism hold for the realm of the human mind as well? In other words, is it possible that the world outside the mind is determined by the causal chain down to the most minute detail, but somehow the realm of human decision making escapes predictable causality? Some antideterminist thinkers say yes, others say no; some base their opinions on a theoretical assessment, others on a practical point of view. We'll look at some famous and not-so-famous views in this section.

The "Policeman at the Elbow" Argument One of the most interesting practical arguments for

Box 4.5   THE CRIMINAL MIND: NATURE OR NURTURE?

In the nineteenth century, biologists and early psychologists were exploring the notion that people became repeat offenders and career criminals because of a built-in bad nature. This theory implied that if one could predict that an individual was the "carrier" of such a bad nature, then the individual could be monitored, or even locked up, before he or she actually committed a crime. Of course, this idea violated an ancient philosophical conviction, held by Aristotle that you can't hold people accountable for something they haven't done yet—a conviction that is honored in our own legal system. However, scientists in the nineteenth century embarked on a number of procedures that would, presumably, predict a person's behavior based on some measurable external characteristics, such as their body measurements (anthropometrics).

The most famous, and infamous, method was *phrenology:* In an enthusiastic, but shortlived frenzy of research, nineteenth-century Western scientists suggested that nature determines our intellectual properties as well as our emotional and moral character, and these properties can be read directly from the bumps on our heads. The discipline—now considered a pseudoscience—of phrenology asserted that everything about a person's character can be known by externally measuring his or her skull. About 42 different character traits could supposedly be read from these measurements; each place on the skull controlled its own character trait, such as benevolence, veneration, caution, self-esteem, and combativeness. Parental love was located at the base of the skull, and hope and spirituality were close to the top. "Human Nature" itself (whatever that was supposed to be!) was located at the top of the forehead, at the hairline. The bumps and size of the character areas determined their importance for the individual.

Someone with a bump in the wrong place, causing a diagnosis of a fickle or criminal nature, was assumed to be destined for trouble, even if that person had never displayed any such behavior. While contemporary science theorizes that areas in the brain play a role in shaping our character traits and tendencies, scientists do not claim that such traits can be measured on the outside, or even on the inside, or that our behavior can be explained exclusively based on such studies. Phrenology became instantly popular, and people would line up for phrenology analyses before getting married, to measure compatibility. Criminals were subjected to analyses to determine if they had bumps in the predicted places. By the 1850s the "science" had proved to be worthless, however, and the discipline was rejected by the 1860s. But it lived on (and is still lingering) as a popular pseudoscientific device, along the lines of astrology, palm reading, and tarot readings.

In the late nineteenth and early twentieth century, the picture shifted: Now the criminal mind was interpreted as being a product of environmental influences rather than heredity, or of nurture rather than nature. This is the view you encounter in the theory of behaviorism: Any child can be shaped into becoming any kind of adult, according to Watson and Skinner. This also means that there is no such thing as a born criminal: Environmental influences determine everything, and with a change in environment (such as a program of rehabilitation), criminal behavior should theoretically be modified into law-abiding behavior. A classic film exploring this theory—and hanging it out to dry— is Stanley Kubrick's film *A Clockwork Orange* from 1971, when the theory of behaviorism still inspired many psychologists. However, within the past few decades there has been a shift back toward seeking genetic, biochemical explanations of the criminal mind— the influence of nature. With an increase in knowledge about the human brain, many researchers now believe that criminal, asocial behavior may well be a matter of an innate chemical brain condition, after all, or an early trauma to the brain. This would explain many cases of recidivism (repeat offenses after punishment), but it also raises an unpleasant issue: If criminals can't help what they are doing, can we then morally hold them accountable and punish them? See the discussion of John Douglas's "policeman at the elbow" theory in the chapter text.

the existence of free will comes not from a philosopher or a theoretical scientist, but from the former FBI profiler John Douglas. His main purpose is not to discuss the philosophical issue of freedom of the will, but to assess responsibility for crimes committed. However, the link to our discussion of free will is obvious: In several of his books, but especially in *The Anatomy of Motive* (1999), Douglas and his coauthor Mark Olshaker discuss the phenomenon of serial rapists and serial killers with a sexual obsession. We often make a gut-level assessment that such criminals must be "sick," and certainly there is some profound aberration present in them that the rest of us don't seem to share. However, when we say "sick," we often imply that people should be excused because they, somehow, can't help themselves. Douglas's point is that this is a false assessment. Even if serial killers are driven by a sexual, violent compulsion, it does not render them mindless robots without any will of their own. Suppose some criminals are so deep into some obsession that they literally can't help themselves: In that case, they will try to act out their compulsion when it strikes, regardless of whether they are in public or in a secluded spot. But this just doesn't happen, says Douglas. He calls it the *"policeman at the elbow" principle:* Most serial criminals driven by some compulsion are perfectly capable of constraining themselves until a good opportunity arises; if they have picked out a victim—an unattended child or a woman walking to her car from the mall, for example—they may feel the compulsion rushing through them, but if there is a security guard, a vigilant parent, or a police officer nearby, they hold off and wait for a better opportunity. If they were truly compulsive, and couldn't make a conscious choice, this wouldn't have been an option. According to Douglas, "No one I've come across in my nearly three decades in law enforcement can recall a single case of an offender so compelled to commit a violent crime that he knowingly did so while a uniformed police officer was present."[8]

This doesn't mean, to Douglas, that behavior can't be predicted. On the contrary, certain early childhood indicators should set off alarms; a serial killer's childhood usually includes such elements as bedwetting, starting fires, and torturing small animals. Douglas says there are also indicators in adult lives that a person may become a predatory criminal, but these indicators don't mean the person is "destined" to become a criminal or that he, or she, must act out a compulsion without making a conscious choice to prey on other people. If anyone in our human society displays clear determining effects of environmental pressures and probably also a genetic propensity, it is surely compulsive violent criminals. And if even *they* can show restraint for selfish reasons, then free will seems to be a reality. A determinist may reply that the "policeman at the elbow" merely supplies a "cause" why they don't pounce on their victim right then and there: The urge for personal safety overrides the predatory urge. However, this isn't quite enough as a counterargument: The criminal, in that moment, *deliberates,* and because of that deliberation we can, traditionally, hold him or her accountable for a later decision to strike.

This argument, in my view, forever does away with the notion that we should automatically exonerate criminals because of their terrible childhood or treat them across the board like victims because they really "couldn't help themselves." Some may deserve such compassion, but not everyone. As Douglas states in *The Cases That Haunt Us* (2000), most serial killers may have some form of mental illness, but that doesn't preclude them from knowing the difference between right and wrong and understanding the consequences of their actions. Most importantly, they do what they do because they want to, not because they have to; individuals who act with such compulsion that they can't stop themselves are usually easily caught, says Douglas. Such individuals just aren't capable of planning and scheming. It is the rational planning and scheming that often keeps a serial killer beyond the grasp of the law for years, perhaps forever.

Douglas's theory is supported by one of the most classical theories of human behavior, briefly mentioned in the beginning of this chapter: the theory of compatibilism, or soft determinism.

Compatibilism/Soft Determinism   In his book *Religion and the Modern Mind,* the philosopher W. T. Stace suggests that hard determinism has misunderstood the meaning of "free will." It does not mean "uncaused," Stace says, but rather "not directly caused by any agency outside myself." As long as the "cause" lies within a person's own reasoning, we can safely retain the concept of free will. This viewpoint, which Stace shares with a number of modern philosophers, is referred to as compatibilism, or soft determinism, *because it views determinism and free will as compatible.* Compatibilism does not deny that everything in the material world is part of a great causal chain of hereditary and environmental forces. That does not preclude humans having free will, though, because our will is free as long as we are not *constrained* (physically forced to do something or prevented from doing something). Free will has to do with weighing pros and cons; of course, every decision is causally based on already existing thoughts, feelings, wishes, and our general character and state of mind—decisions don't just appear out of the blue for no reason, like the obscene outbursts of some unfortunate Tourette's syndrome patients. If we think free will consists of a sudden outburst of "willpower" independent of all deliberations, then we've simply misunderstood the concept of free will, says Stace. In other words, our free decisions are "caused" by our deliberation, our feelings, and our reasoning process; but as several thinkers have pointed out, these are *motivations,* not physical causes. Free will is not uncaused, but as long as the cause is our inner deliberation, reasoning, and motive, then it counts as free. If someone forces us to make a decision, then it isn't free. But the sexual predator who temporarily stops killing prostitutes be-cause he has been stopped by a traffic cop with a prostitute in his car has exercised his free will: He has made a choice to play it safe until conditions change.

Compatibilism does have its own problems, though: A kleptomaniac is hardly "constrained," and yet even the law would say that she is suffering from a compulsion she has no control over. So, too, is the case with obsessive-compulsive patients who feel the urge to constantly wash their hands or triple-check that they locked the front door. Parents who beat their children because they themselves were victims of abuse—how much free will do they have? Some say little, others say a lot. Drawing a line between "external constraint" and "internal reasoning" is too simplistic to give us the entire picture; as a matter of fact, a compatibilist thinker from 2,400 years ago gave us a fuller picture of the relationship between constraint and free will, as we shall see below in the section on Aristotle.

The Chess Game Analogy   This analogy is a variant of compatibilism, with a slightly different focus. Instead of saying that determinism is valid outside, but not inside the human mind, the chess analogy says that even if the mind is governed by the forces of causality, then it does not lead to predictability. Why? Because the causes within the mind determining our decisions are *so complex* that our actions in effect become unpredictable, even though they could theoretically be mapped, if we knew enough. Just as a chess game has a multitude of possible moves according to the rules, and one could theoretically predict each move if one could oversee all possibilities, it is not possible in practice. The more possible moves within the range of human behavior, the less the chance that we can predict other people's actions. So we do make free decisions based on our inner causality. Remember the reference to chaos theory earlier in this chapter? The same principle applied there: Chaos theory says we can't predict with 100 percent accuracy anything that happens in nature, because the causal system is just too complex to be predicted. The chess analogy says the same thing: Within the human mind, the causality is so complex and the possibilities so many that in practice it translates into free will.

Freedom as Lived Experience   This compatibilist theory, unlike the two others, does not concern itself with definitions or statistical probabilities. It turns its attention toward our *inner experience of free will*. Hard determinism doesn't deny that we think our will is free, but declares it to be an illusion. This compatibilist theory discards that very approach, saying that the lived experience of being human is something we can't just cast aside as irrelevant. It may be that every spark of decision making is completely determined by our heredity and our environment, but *it doesn't feel that way*. Most of the time we are unaware of the underlying causes of our decisions. We know only that we have to make decisions, and we can and may be held responsible for them. So whether free will is a scientific fact or "just an illusion," it is something we experience, and that is what counts. The feeling that we have freedom of the will affects us psychologically and morally, forming the reality we must deal with. This approach, based on the idea that our fundamental human experience is the ultimate reality, has its own challenge: Ordinarily, when we find out that something is an illusion, we stop paying attention to it. If it really turns out that free will is an illusion, won't it affect that lived experience we have of actually having free will? In other words, we can't treat our "lived experiences" as something fundamental and static: They are dynamic and may change with a change in attitude.

Determinism Is Unfalsifiable   A criticism indirectly speaking in favor of free will, simply because it attacks the logic of hard determinism itself, says that determinism is one example of several theories with the same flawed structure: They all make sweeping statements about something without considering the possibility that they may be wrong. (Psychological egoism is an-

other such theory; see Chapter 3, "Are Humans Selfish by Nature?") As the philosopher Karl Popper (see Chapter 2) would say, they are "unfalsifiable"; not in the sense that a good theory must be shown to be false (which would make no sense), but in the sense that a good theory based on empirical data must allow itself to be tested in as many ways as possible and recognize a problem built into empirical research: We can never reach complete certainty in our theories. Such absolute certainty does not exist when one's research method is inductive: We can never know if we have overlooked some vital piece of evidence. So a "falsifiable" theory is a theory that is perpetually open to reexamination. Hard determinism does not concede that it could be wrong, so the theory has a built-in weakness that makes it less scientifically sound. For those of you familiar with logical fallacies, hard determinism represents the fallacy of *begging the question*. It assumes as true what it is supposed to prove: that all acts can be predicted.

Quantum Physics   A fascinating argument against determinism comes from within the realm of scientific research itself: subatomic science. The classical hard deterministic argument of 100 percent predictability is based on Newtonian physics and concerns items we can see, touch, and measure. However, at the subatomic level, the principle of causality becomes more blurred: Experiments with subatomic particles show that we can't determine both the speed and the position of a given subatomic article. If we know how fast it is, we won't know where it will hit (or rather, it won't even appear as a particle, but as a wave, hitting over a large area at the same time). If we focus on the particle, not the speed, it will appear to be a single particle hitting at a precise spot, but we can't predict the speed, so we can't tell when it will hit. Some scientists see this as an argument that we can't achieve total prediction at the subatomic level as a matter of principle—not just because we aren't knowledgeable enough yet. Since everything, including human bodies (and brains), consists of subatomic particles, couldn't we assume

Box 4.6   I AM NOT YOU: BERGSON'S SOLUTION

The French philosopher Henri Bergson (1859–1941) strongly opposed the concept of determinism. He thought it pacified people into thinking that they existed in the world in the same manner as things do—that they merely occupied space. For Bergson, human nature is unique in being *temporal:* humans have a sense of time. Not just clock time (which is really nothing but the objective monitoring of seconds, minutes, and hours, measured out *in space* by hands moving across the clock face), but the time we live and experience subjectively. Sometimes it moves slowly, as when our date is late, and sometimes it moves fast, as when we are having a good time. In these situations time is something we feel, rather than something we measure. This kind of experienced time Bergson calls *duration.*

Bergson believes that although we certainly can predict what may happen in the world of objects, provided that we have enough knowledge of past causes, we can't possibly predict human behavior with any accuracy, because human willpower occasionally casts aside all previous influences and deliberations. When this happens, our true self emerges, says Bergson, sometimes to our own great surprise. You may think that you genuinely want to get married or become a doctor or vacation in Bali. But then, when you are given the opportunity, your own true voice emerges from the depth of your personality and refuses to play along—or reveals to you that you wanted something else all along. This is the most fundamental *proof of freedom* that Bergson knows, because it is completely unpre-

dictable in his view. The interesting thing is that it is not an example of free will in the sense of free deliberate choice, precisely because it is an urge we have no control over! Some would call this a *compulsion* and say that Bergson just committed himself to determinism after all. Free choice does exist for Bergson, however, as a free decision based on the many choices presented to us.

Given Bergson's opposition to determinism, one might think that he embraced the theory of indeterminism: that at any time we can choose one of several different future paths. But Bergson believes that indeterminism makes a big mistake in assuming that there are already paths laid out in the future for us to choose. The future has no paths at all—because it doesn't exist yet! All there is, is decision making. Once we make a decision, it has consequences; and when we look back, we think we see a path. As for predicting what decision someone else is going to make, Bergson has an elegant answer: We can never predict the actions of others with certainty—because then we would have to know everything there is to know about the other person. We would have to have lived with that person all his or her life, sharing the conscious as well as unconscious mind. But if we were that close to someone, we'd have to *be* that person! And we ourselves certainly can't predict what we will do next. This doesn't mean we can't predict anything about others, of course. If we know them well, we can predict their actions with probability, but not with certainty.

that it is equally difficult to predict human behavior? Other scientists dismiss the parallel as unscientific and irrelevant.

Indeterminism   The most radical antideterministic view is the one labeled indeterminism: It holds that, at any given time, we can choose to go in a direction other than the one we were going in, regardless of our heredity and environment. Our willpower can override these deterministic forces, because its nature is different from that of

the physical world. The realm of the mind escapes the bounds of causality and responds to other rules, such as the rules of ethics. (Box 4.6 discusses Henri Bergson's antideterminism and his attack on indeterminism.) Indeterminism has critics among compatibilists, who point out that we are no better off in terms of explaining our free will if we claim that the mental realm has no causality: In such a case, I could decide to cook a dinner for some good friends, but the chicken might never get fried because my decision doesn't cause any action to take place (since the mental realm is outside the causal chain), and I can't be sure my friends will show up, either, because I can't predict their behavior.

There Is No Human Nature: Sartre's Libertarianism

Although most thinkers faced with the question of defining human nature try to come up with an answer, two thinkers refused to answer the question at all: Jean-Paul Sartre (1905–1980) and Simone de Beauvoir (1908–1986). Both existentialist philosophers of the mid–twentieth century, they believed that there is no human nature, and that humans are always free to choose—a theory known as libertarianism.[9] Like most French scholars of his generation, Sartre had read Bergson in his youth and was influenced by his radical opposition to determinism; however, Sartre took it one step further. If we believe there is a human nature, we become determinists, according to Sartre: We believe we have to become what we think we are supposed to be. Beauvoir, a great existentialist in her own right but known today primarily as a feminist, pointed out that if boys and girls grow up believing they have to become completely different people as men and women, then that is what they will do—but we have a choice: We can choose to do away with preset gender roles. We will return to Beauvoir in Chapter 6 and here focus on Sartre's theory of the only creature on the earth without a nature.

This doesn't mean that Sartre denies we have a biology or certain genetic predispositions. Hardly anything was known of the human genetic code when Sartre was writing but as you know from the previous section, the idea that heredity was a determining factor was an established theory. However, for Sartre, referring to one's genes as the reason for one's actions would be nothing but a poor excuse for a weak character: We can always choose to do something else, even if problems are embedded in our heredity (such as tendencies toward violence or alcoholism), and that is what makes us different from all other creatures. For Sartre, *things* are supposed to be what we intend them to be when we make them or when we buy them. *Nonhuman animals* don't have any choice as to what they are supposed to be, because their minds are completely ruled by instinct (or so it was commonly believed during the middle years of the twentieth century; Sartre was not trying to be controversial by denying that animals can think or choose—he thought he was expressing trivial knowledge). But if humans assume they have a "nature," they reduce themselves to the status of things and animals—of entities who have no free will. Sartre labels the existence of such entities an existence "in itself" (*en soi*): Such things exist without any awareness *that* they exist. But Sartre labels the human form of existence, with its capacity for self-awareness, "for itself" (*pour soi*), which means living with self-awareness and the responsibility for one's actions.

If one doesn't know of Sartre's existentialist philosophy, one might think that this idea comes out of the long religious tradition (see Chapter 8) claiming that God gave us free will to separate us from the animals, and we have the capacity to choose good (with God) or evil (against God). But this is not what Sartre means, because Sartre was an avowed atheist. Having been raised in the Catholic tradition, he came to believe that there is no God, no afterlife, and no punishment or reward for our actions, except in this life. Tragically, there is no God to uphold our values, and life is essentially absurd, in the sense that there is no underlying meaning or direction to life to be found anywhere outside ourselves.

How did Sartre reach such a radical view? He is not the first thinker to speculate about what happens to our values if there is no God. The Russian author Dostoyevsky asked the same question in the nineteenth century: If there is no God, does that mean everything is allowed? And the German philosopher Friedrich Nietzsche, shortly afterward, sent shock waves through philosophy by declaring that "God is dead," life is essentially meaningless, there are no absolute moral values, and everything is indeed permitted to the person who dares shape his own destiny (see Chapter 8).

Sartre pays tribute to both, but in his own way: He agrees that there is no God and life is meaningless on an objective scale, but does not conclude that everything is permitted. On the contrary: Since we can't look to a source outside of time to guarantee our moral values, we must make them up ourselves; and this doesn't mean anything goes, because our measure of our values is whether we could imagine others looking to us as role models. When we make a choice, says Sartre, we should imagine making that choice for all of humanity, and this makes Sartre's existentialism one of the most morally demanding systems ever devised, even though Sartre does not believe in any divine reward or retribution.

This philosophy was developed during difficult times for Sartre: His home country of France was occupied by Germany during World War II, his government was collaborating with the Nazis, and his friends in the French underground were being killed or shipped off to German concentration camps—as Sartre himself was. The threat of instant death was real, and the ordinary little joys of life were put on hold. The special wartime ethic that grew out of this experience—to take on responsibility and do what you decide is necessary, even in the face of meaninglessness and annihilation—has become a legacy of existentialism and its view of human nature and human action.

In the Christian tradition, as in most other religious traditions, God creates the world, including humans, with a certain idea in mind, as we saw in Chapter 2. Even philosophers who don't think in religious terms tend to believe our nature is embedded in us as a "human condition" from the day we are conceived. This is the view that Sartre opposes: In the traditional view, the idea of a paper-knife, for example, exists in the mind of the artisan before it is manufactured, says Sartre, and, likewise, the idea of a human being exists in the mind of God. In other words, for most philosophers and religious thinkers, *a thing's essence precedes its existence,* and this is also the case with humans: The idea of what we are or will be (our essence) precedes our coming into being (our

existence). But for Sartre, human beings are different from all other beings in that *our existence precedes our essence.* For Sartre, humans make their own "essence" or characteristics, and we are therefore responsible for what we are—we can never blame our shortcomings on God, nature, our parents, fate, or other circumstances beyond our control. So we should realize the implications of this and acknowledge that there is no predetermined life for anyone: *We* determine the direction of our life every moment of the day. If we fail to acknowledge that, we reduce ourselves to something less than human.

Of course, people don't go around consciously deciding what they want to be at each moment—we are all caught up in the web of everyday life. But once we realize that whenever we seek support for our actions in the idea that "it can't be otherwise," we are fooling ourselves into thinking that there is a destiny, or a pattern, we have to follow. This makes us realize that we are, in a sense, *condemned to be free:* We have to make choices, and we have to be responsible for them, even though we can't possibly foresee the end results of all our choices. That throws us into *despair,* says Sartre and results in a profound feeling of anguish (*angoisse*)—the famed existential *angst.* A common human reaction is to hide behind sayings such as "I was only following orders," "It wasn't my decision to make," or "I couldn't help myself," just so we won't have to make those hard choices. Do you really *have to* go to law school, just because your parents want you to? No, you make up your own mind: Refuse and suffer the consequences, or choose to please your parents. Do you *really* have to take the final in this class? No! But be prepared to deal with the consequences if you don't. Do you, as a Nazi overseer in a death camp in 1944, have to bring a small Jewish child in for lethal medical experimentation, or can you refuse to follow orders? *You can refuse.* It may cost you your life; but as Sartre would say, there are worse things than dying because one has chosen not to cause suffering to another human being. As the Nuremberg trials after World War II established once and for all, "just following orders" is not an acceptable defense, because we have to answer to our fellow human beings above and beyond answering to authorities. Some would say we have to answer to God, but Sartre sees this as the ultimate test of our responsibility to others.

If we think we can hide behind orders, nature, or tradition, we are in what Sartre calls *bad faith*. Bad faith happens when we try to fool ourselves into thinking that we don't have to make a decision—but then we, of course, make the decision to have others decide for us. A line in a popular song, "Freewill," by the rock band Rush expresses this very well:

> *If you choose not to decide*
> *You still have made a choice!*

The question now is this: If humans really aren't determined by anything in the outside world but can decide, at any time, to break the causal chain and its demands, how can that manifest itself in a practical situation? Sartre here seems to say that causality may rule the physical realm, but not the mental realm: We can choose to be whatever we want. How does that work out? If we are less than pretty, can we decide to be beautiful? Can we decide to change our race and gender? If we have been victims of sexual abuse in the past, can we decide it never happened? Of course not, but we can choose how we deal with the situation that we are in. We can still choose to retain our integrity and dignity. This is the ultimate freedom, even in situations where we are faced with illness and end of life: We can decide how we are going to deal with it—either with poor excuses for our life, such as "I couldn't help it!" or by taking responsibility for what we have done and who we have become.

One way of dealing with our situation is to *reinterpret our past*. In the light of what you read in Chapter 1 about storytelling in human lives and in the quest for personal insight, you can appreciate exactly what Sartre meant: We are free to see our past and ourselves in a new light if our situation changes; we "connect the dots" in a different way. Modern, narrative philosophers would say that we *tell a different story about ourselves*. Many people actually perform this feat several times in their lives. A typical time for "reinventing the past" is during a breakup, especially if longtime partners are divorcing. It is common for people to reconsider key moments in a relationship and seek out new and usually ominous meanings in them. "So that's why he (she) did such-and-such," we might say. (This practice may do a giant disservice to oneself and one's partner, because those moments may be better left to memory and regarded fondly, rather than dragged into a reevaluation of the relationship.)

Whether such a reinterpretation is a good use of our freedom or not, would for Sartre depend on how *authentic* it is: Are we trying to pass the blame onto our partner and absolve ourselves? That would be bad faith. Are we trying to genuinely understand the dynamics of the relationship, accepting our share of the blame? Sartre would probably call that an *authentic* approach—one where you make a choice and take responsibility for the consequences. People also typically reinvent the past when they change careers: Elements relating to one's new career are suddenly viewed as particularly meaningful, while anything relating to one's old career is reinterpreted as a waste of time. Whether our reinterpretation is authentic would depend on whether it makes us better at making choices in the face of life's general absurdity.

Sartre's view on the fundamental human condition of freedom is perhaps the most demanding moral requirement expressed by any philosopher. But is he correct when he says that we can always be held responsible for our choices? Sartre's view expresses an extreme; it denies that people acting under psychological strain should not be held accountable. In effect, Sartre has very little interest in cases where someone might be under such physical or mental strain that the person is not considered physically or mentally able. But many lifetimes before Sartre, one of the greatest minds

Box 4.7   PROFILE OF ARISTOTLE

Aristotle was born in the northern Greek city-state of Stagira in 384 B.C.E. His father, Nicomacheus, was the court physician. It appears that Aristotle was expected to follow in his footsteps and become a physician, but that was not to be. Aristotle fell in with a bunch of philosophers and got sidetracked; for close to two decades he studied with the great philosopher Plato, himself a student of Socrates; he kept up an interest in medicine while expanding his interests to all available aspects of knowledge. While he experienced a considerable career setback in his late thirties when Plato died—he didn't get the appointment as Plato's successor—even so, he managed to carve out an astonishing professional niche for himself: After being passed over for the position, Aristotle traveled for a while and came back to his homeland to become the tutor of the prince (later Alexander the Great). A few years later he was back in Athens, establishing his own school of philosophy, the Lyceum, and running it with such a success that it remained an active academic institution for generations after Aristotle's death.

When Alexander the Great died twelve years later, Aristotle was targeted for persecution by the city coun-

cil of Athens because of his association with Alexander, and so he fled the city. He died the following year, in 322 B.C.E. However, Aristotle's legacy goes far beyond founding a school: You might say that he founded a great portion of the Western mind-set, academic and otherwise. Basic academic disciplines familiar to us today were laid out in Aristotle's works: The disciplines of philosophy (epistemology, metaphysics, ethics, and logic), biology, and political science, and theories of dramatic literature and rhetoric were all outlined by Aristotle. Also, Aristotle's philosophy had the strange destiny of being successfully reintroduced to Christianity hundreds of years after his name had been largely forgotten in the West. His philosophy of purpose, *teleology*, has affected Catholic thinking as well as Western scientific thinking until recently. In addition, Aristotle remains one of the great philosophical inspirations for the religion of Islam. It may well be that Aristotle—the man who probably thought his life and career were in shambles when he didn't get Plato's job—has been the most influential man in Western history. We return to Aristotle in Chapters 6, 8, and 9.

---

in philosophy considered this problem and produced a simple, commonsensical set of guidelines. We now turn to Aristotle.

The First Compatibilist: Aristotle on Compulsion, Ignorance, and Free Will

I assume that you are now willing to concede that we can and should be held accountable for what we do in at least certain situations—in other words, that hard determinism has not been persuasive enough to do away with the concept of human accountability. Also, I assume that you may feel reluctant to follow Sartre and declare that we are *always* accountable for our choices. We may wonder what we will have to do if science someday pinpoints the exact chemical cause for someone's

brain deciding to cheat on a test or commit serial murder: Would we have to absolve that person of moral responsibility and just give him or her an injection to correct the chemical imbalance? We will have to deal with that issue when the day comes. General guidelines have been laid down already and have in fact been in place for close to 2,400 years. Aristotle's *Nicomachean Ethics* provides a straightforward approach: Sometimes we can and should hold people accountable for their actions, and sometimes it would be unreasonable. (Box 4.7 gives you a profile of the Greek thinker.) The guidelines will have to be revised in terms of details, once the connection has been firmly established between our mental decisions and our brain states and once we have established that even if we can explain all mental states as chemical and electrical reactions, we still have moral and legal responsibility for what we do. Until then Aristotle's' guidelines work quite well; you will recognize the hallmark of a compatibilist (a soft determinist) in these words, specifying which actions are chosen freely and which should be considered to be determined by forces other than the agent's free will:

> Those things, then, are involuntary, which take place under compulsion or owing to ignorance, and that is compulsory of which the moving principle is outside, being a principle in which nothing is contributed by the person who is acting or feeling the passion, e.g., if he were to be carried somewhere by a wind, or by men who had him in their power.[10]

Let's look at a few scenarios exploring under which kind of circumstances it would be unreasonable to hold someone accountable, based on Aristotle's two concepts of *ignorance* and *compulsion*.[11] (An excerpt from Aristotle's book covering the entire discussion can be found in the Primary Readings section.)

Cases of Ignorance 1: "Gee, I Didn't Know"   Ignorance does not always excuse us from responsibility, but it may do so if the facts couldn't have been known.

Scenario: A friend offers to drive you to the airport, and you accept her offer. On the way you run into heavy traffic because of an accident, and you miss your plane. Should you blame your friend? No, because she couldn't have known the streets would be blocked. (If the congestion was caused by construction, and she knew about it, the situation would be different.)

Scenario: You rent a car in a foreign country, and you're stopped by a policewoman who informs you that you failed to yield at some white stripes painted on the road. She calls them "shark's teeth," and they turn out to be the local version of a yield sign (this happens to be the case in Scandinavia). Can you plead ignorance? No, because you were supposed to know the traffic rules before you started driving. (Legally, you are responsible for knowing the law; however, if you broke the law without clear intent to break it, the court may take that fact into consideration.)

Cases of Ignorance 2: "Gee, I Don't Know How"   An old moral rule says, "ought implies can": We have no obligation to do something that is impossible for us to do. These scenarios serve as illustrations.

Scenario: Your friend asks you to help him with a math problem, but your math skills stop at about the third-grade level. You can't help him, and he can't blame you for not helping, because you just don't have the knowledge. (But if you are good at math, and you say no because you have a date, it's a different situation.)

Scenario: You are walking along the shore of a lake, when you see a small child fall out of a rowboat; she is not wearing a life jacket, and you can't swim. Can you be blamed if you don't jump in the water? No, but you can be blamed if you don't do *something* to try to help—morally, if not legally. In some states there is a Good Samaritan law in effect where people are legally obligated to lend a hand to someone in need as long as it doesn't endanger themselves. And (as a student of mine suggested) you could possibly be blamed for not having learned to swim! After all, you never know when the skill might come in handy. (Suppose you actually know how to swim, but you have had an accident, and your leg is in a cast, so at the moment you can't swim. This is not a case of lack of knowledge, but lack of physical ability: a form of restraint, or compulsion.)

Cases of Compulsion 1: "I Was Forced," or External Compulsion   Although external compulsion might seem a clear-cut reason to limit responsibility, the issues may be ambiguous.

Scenario: You are kidnapped and forced to join a gang that robs banks. The police catch you, and you claim you were abducted and threatened—that if you didn't join, the gang would kill you. Sounds far-fetched? Not at all. This is what supposedly happened to Patty Hearst, daughter of a newspaper magnate who was kidnapped by a small band of self-described anarchistic revolutionaries. If this kind of scenario is true, then the person can't be held accountable. Neither can the date who stood you up if it is true that he or she was tied up by robbers at the time. But there has to be clear evidence!

Scenario: In the mid-1990s a woman was raped at knife point in Texas; because she had asked her assailant to use a condom, the judge threw out the case, saying she consented to having sex. However, a second trial established that she was indeed acting under compulsion and had only taken measures to save her own life (out of fear of HIV). The rapist was held accountable, and the woman was absolved of any willing participation.

Scenario: In the acclaimed film *Sophie's Choice,* a mother during World War II has to make a choice between her two children: Which one will live, and which one will die? The Nazis in a death camp force her to select one child over another. Is she under compulsion? Yes. Is her action voluntary? Yes and no. For Aristotle, it would represent a borderline kind of situation, because the situation is not of her choosing, but, based on the situation, she does what she feels she must in order to minimize the pain and tragedy.

Cases of Compulsion 2: "I Felt Compelled," or Internal Compulsion   Internal compulsion might be a matter of brain chemistry, whether temporary or permanent.

Scenario: Leeza is at a party; her date slips a date rape drug into her drink, making her lethargic, and then he proceeds to rape her. He is caught and claims that she consented because she didn't put up a fight or say no. Is he right? No, because she was drugged against her knowledge before being raped.

Scenario: Chuck decides to try drugs and ends up wrecking a stolen car, injuring several people. He claims that he couldn't help what he did, because he was on drugs. Will the court accept that argument? No, because he was responsible for taking the drugs in the first place. And here is where is gets interesting: What if Leeza from the previous scenario had taken a drug *voluntarily*

that made her lethargic and unable/unwilling to protest when her date tried to have sex with her? Can he now claim she consented because she had taken the drug herself? No. Another rule kicks in: She has consented to the effects of the drug, but not to someone taking advantage of those effects!

Scenario: Sandy suffers from kleptomania (the compulsory urge to steal). She takes air fresheners, light bulbs, and baby food (she has no baby, and there is no sense to what she is stealing). She is caught shoplifting. Will she be held accountable? Not if she can produce valid testimony from a doctor verifying her condition; she will not be able to go free without therapy, however. (But if she shoplifts to feed her starving child, then she will be held accountable! She might say that "she had no choice," but a social worker will tell her otherwise and inform her of her options.)

Scenario: You are captured by a gang who robs banks, and they force you to join them by brainwashing you: They subject you to methods used in wartime to break down prisoners of war, until you have no will of your own. Then you join them, because you can't help yourself and take part in their bank robberies. Could this happen? Patty Hearst claimed it happened to her. She used both the fear of death and the brainwashing scenarios to claim compulsion. In the next section we will discuss whether her defense was sufficient.

Cases of Compulsion 3: "I Was the Victim of Circumstances"   Sometimes circumstances are truly beyond our control, but sometimes we just like to believe they are.

Scenario: You are on your way to take a midterm, and your car breaks down; or you were supposed to send in your tax return, but you got tonsillitis. Such situations may be considered "bad excuses," but sometimes we truly are the victims of circumstances beyond our control, and we need all the understanding we can get. How can we be certain that other people will understand our unfortunate predicaments? We can't, but we can be careful not to resort to what logicians call the *fallacy ad misericordiam:* the appeal to pity (or the use of sob stories, as we commonly call them) whenever something goes wrong. In other words, never cry wolf. Don't bring up unforeseen circumstances as an excuse unless it really was a serious case!

Scenario: Your friend confides in you that she has had an extramarital affair. She said, "But my feelings were so strong! I just couldn't resist! We couldn't help ourselves!" Will we say that in this case, her inner compulsion was so strong that nobody could blame her for sleeping around? Not on your life. This is where the issue of *character* comes in. Perhaps we can't be blamed for how we *feel,* but we can certainly be blamed for what we *do about it.* We are all tempted by this and that, some of us more than others, but claiming that one should be excused because of the overwhelming force of the temptation has never been considered a legitimate moral or legal excuse. We may understand and sympathize, but it isn't enough to get the emotional person off the hook!

Scenario: A mother shoots her four sons in the head in a fit of rage and drugs, one after the other, and then turns the gun on herself, shooting herself in the stomach. Her wound is not fatal, and she stands trial for murder.[12] Her lawyer claims that she couldn't help herself, because she was abused as a child and suffered from drug addiction. The prosecution responds that lots of people have been abused as children and have drug problems, but they haven't gone on to murder their own children.

Evaluating Aristotle's Theory of Ignorance and Compulsion

Aristotle's two acceptable excuses, ignorance and compulsion, can be elaborated on and specified with a multitude of other scenarios, but the thought behind them remains the same: When you are truly ignorant or under a compulsion that you did not instigate, you can't be blamed for your action or inaction. At all other times, you can be held accountable for your actions and often also for your inactions. This corresponds to both common sense and legal sense, and the determinist who claims that you can never be held accountable is at odds with both.

Even so, there are borderline situations that are very hard to determine, such as the case of a soldier ordered to kill civilians. Is that a free choice or compulsion? Some might say that the soldier has no choice, but others—like Jean-Paul Sartre—would most emphatically say that soldiers in this situation can say no, even though they may be punished for disobedience. The situations described in the section *Determinism in Court,* such as cases falling under the Burning Bed syndrome, appear to many to be on the border between free will and compulsion.

Patty Hearst's case, mentioned earlier, had receded into American history, thought of as one of the odd tales coming out of the 1970s. Patty Hearst was indeed captured by a gang, calling itself the Symbionese Liberation Army, or SLA. The "army" was a bit of an exaggeration, since it consisted of only nine members—"more like a Brownie troop than an army," as a criminal expert commented. The "liberation" part was also a bit of a stretch, since they apparently started out as common bank robbers, but thought they could get some extra political mileage out of declaring themselves to be revolutionaries, like several other such groups of the 1970s. During her capture, Patty Hearst was indeed brainwashed, according to the court-appointed psychologist, Margaret Singer, professor emeritus from the University of California at Berkeley. Singer is an expert in brainwashing techniques used by the Chinese during the Korean War, and she recognized classical brainwashing techniques used on Hearst by several members of the SLA. According to Singer, Hearst went into "survival mode" and decided to play along in order to save her life. This resulted in her showing up on surveillance film in the banks they were robbing, for all intents and purposes playing the part of a bank robber/revolutionary.

Eventually, most of the SLA members were killed during a shoot-out with the police, after the gang had attempted to blow up a police station in Los Angeles. After this happened, Hearst took part in yet another bank robbery with the remaining members, in which a woman was killed by the

In 1974, the 19-year-old newspaper heiress Patty Hearst was kidnapped by gang members presenting themselves as political radicals. Within a few months, the media displayed this photograph of her carrying a carbine, taken as she apparently helped the gang rob a bank. Later, when captured, Hearst claimed that she had been brainwashed by her captors. Her claim was corroborated by psychologist Margaret Singer; but even so, Hearst was sentenced to seven years in prison. After two years her sentence was commuted by President Carter, and she was eventually pardoned by President Clinton in 2001.

gang. Some, like Hearst, were captured; others went underground. Singer testified in court that Hearst was a victim of force (both internal and external); however, Hearst's defense lawyer, the later so famous and notorious F. Lee Bailey, didn't manage to convince the jury of her innocence, and she spent some years in prison. Her sentence was commuted by President Carter; and President Clinton pardoned her when he left office in 2001. However, the interest in her strange story

had already been renewed when, in 1999, one of the last members of the little group of bank robbers/revolutionaries wanted by the law, Kathleen Soliah, was finally caught, hiding out under an assumed identity (Sarah Jane Olson) and living a very quiet, traditional life as a middle-class soccer mom in the Midwest—a life diametrically opposed to everything the SLA supposedly stood for! As this is written, a trial is under way to hold Soliah/Olson accountable for her alleged acts of terrorism, and Patty Hearst is expected to be a witness for the prosecution.

For our purpose here, the question of Patty Hearst's brainwashing brings us to evaluating just how much free will she had left. We have Margaret Singer's word that she was indeed subjected to genuine brainwashing techniques, so the excuse of "internal compulsion" should be clear and could probably have won her an acquittal. However, we also have Singer's statement that Hearst, as a result of the unrelenting pressure, went into "survival mode" and *decided* to cooperate. I had the opportunity to ask Singer if she thought Patty Hearst had any free will left at that point, and she answered that, as a psychologist, she tried not to get into that issue; nevertheless, she believed that Hearst *made the decision to save her life.*[13] Coming from an expert in brainwashing, supposedly a technique that nullifies one's free choice, this answer is extraordinarily interesting and corroborates Aristotle's view of the intermediate kind of compulsion/voluntary action. You choose to do what is necessary to survive, in a situation not of your choosing. In addition, it is a support for John Douglas's "policeman at the elbow" argument: Cases where someone breaks the law as a result of an overwhelming inner compulsion are rare; even where strong external or internal compulsions are present, an element of decision making may manifest itself in *how and when* we choose to act.

Stories of Freedom and Determinism

As you know, the general premise of this book is that much of our understanding of ourselves as human beings is, or can be, expressed in stories—

either fictional accounts or stories we tell about events we believe to be real. As popular as determinism has been in twentieth-century science, it is far more common to encounter fictional stories of people making free choices and then reaping the consequences, for better or worse. You might say that the belief in free will has had the vote of the majority of novelists and filmmakers—just consider the immense, moral power of human decision making in classical and contemporary stories of the Western tradition such as *Les Miserables, Pride and Prejudice, Lord Jim, The Old Man and the Sea, East of Eden,* and *Beloved.* For example, the moral premise of John Steinbeck's *East of Eden* (a novel spanning three generations, not just the story of the twins Cal and Aron from the James Dean film) is that we are faced with moral choices and the temptation of evil throughout our lives, but evil doesn't have to rule us—we can choose to fight it, even if we have a weak or an evil character. In Tony Morrison's *Beloved,* the fleeing slave Sethe, about to be captured, makes the choice to save her beloved infant daughter from all future harm—by killing her. In the movies we see the same emphasis in films from *High Noon* to *Gladiator:* The moral choice determines the character of the hero, male or female.

However, sometimes stories of determinism, fate, and karma make their way into our treasure trove of narratives in a film such as Kieslovski's *Red,* for example, usually telling a story about events unfolding regardless of human attempts at exercising free will. In addition we have a special group of combatibilist stories where it is only the headstrong individual who manages to carve a niche of freedom for himself or herself, while others are carried forward by the causality of their world (such as *Lawrence of Arabia*). In the Narratives section you will see a selection of stories exploring determinism as both an existential and a political possibility: The nature versus nurture debate is illustrated by "The Ugly Duckling" and "Flight of the Eagle," and the political possibilities involved in manipulating the minds of citizens are explored in *A Clockwork Orange* and *Brave New World.*

Study Questions

1. Evaluate mechanistic determinism: Has the theory sufficiently proved that we have no free will? Why or why not?

2. What are the similarities and differences between mechanistic determinism, fatalism, and karma?

3. Evaluate Watson's and Skinner's behavioristic program to predict and control the behavior of others. What are the positive aspects? What are the negative aspects?

4. What does Skinner mean by saying that if a girl wants to go out on another date, she must give her boyfriend reinforcement? What do you think of Skinner's advice?

5. Explain and comment on John Douglas's "policeman at the elbow" principle: Does it prove that the criminal is in fact acting out of free choice?

6. What does Sartre mean by saying that we are condemned to be free?

7. Explain the theory of free will as expressed by existentialism.

8. Explain Aristotle's theory of ignorance and compulsion, using examples.

Primary Readings and Narratives

Our first Primary Reading in this chapter is an excerpt from Aristotle's *Nichomachean Ethics* in which he outlines the difference between voluntary and involuntary actions, as well as his theory of free will versus actions based on compulsion and ignorance. The next Primary Reading is an excerpt from one of the most influential essays of the twentieth century, Jean-Paul Sartre's "Existentialism Is a Humanism," where he stresses that there is no human nature, because human existence precedes our essence. The Narratives consist of four stories illustrating the nature versus nurture debate of determinism. The first is the world-famous story of "The Ugly Duckling," by the Danish author Hans Christian Andersen. The second story is much less known, but was written by another Danish author, Henrik Pontoppidan, as a reply to Andersen because he disagreed so strongly with Andersen's viewpoint. The third story is a summary of one of the most provocative films of the past three decades, *A Clockwork Orange,* about a young man who is arrested for rape and assault with a deadly weapon and undergoes psychological reconditioning. And the fourth story is an excerpt from a British classic that has become a metaphor for a future we should do our utmost to avoid: Aldous Huxley's *Brave New World.*

Primary Reading

Nicomachean Ethics

A R I S T O T L E

Excerpt from Chapter 1. Translated by W. D. Ross. Fourth Century B.C.E.

Since virtue is concerned with passions and actions, and on voluntary passions and actions praise and blame are bestowed, on those that are involuntary pardon, and sometimes also pity, to distinguish the voluntary and the involuntary is presumably necessary for those who are studying the nature of virtue, and useful also for legislators with a view to the assigning both of honours and of punishments. Those things, then, are thought involuntary, which take place under compulsion or owing to ignorance; and that is compulsory of which the moving principle is outside, being a principle in which nothing is contributed by the person who is acting or is feeling the passion, e.g. if he were to be carried somewhere by a wind, or by men who had him in their power.

But with regard to the things that are done from fear of greater evils or for some noble object (e.g. if a tyrant were to order one to do something base, having one's parents and children in his power, and if one did the action they were to be saved, but otherwise would be put to death), it may be debated whether such actions are involuntary or voluntary. Something of the sort happens also with regard to the throwing of goods overboard in a storm; for in the abstract no one throws goods away voluntarily, but on condition of its securing the safety of himself and his crew any sensible man does so. Such actions, then, are mixed, but are more like voluntary actions; for they

are worthy of choice at the time when they are done, and the end of an action is relative to the occasion. Both the terms, then, "voluntary" and "involuntary," must be used with reference to the moment of action. Now the man acts voluntarily; for the principle that moves the instrumental parts of the body in such actions is in him, and the things of which the moving principle is in a man himself are in his power to do or not to do. Such actions, therefore, are voluntary, but in the abstract perhaps involuntary; for no one would choose any such act in itself.

For such actions men are sometimes even praised, when they endure something base or painful in return for great and noble objects gained; in the opposite case they are blamed, since to endure the greatest indignities for no noble end or for a trifling end is the mark of an inferior person. On some actions praise indeed is not bestowed, but pardon is, when one does what he ought not under pressure which overstrains human nature and which no one could withstand. But some acts, perhaps, we cannot be forced to do, but ought rather to face death after the most fearful sufferings; for the things that "forced" Euripides' Alcmaeon to slay his mother seem absurd. It is difficult sometimes to determine what should be chosen at what cost, and what should be endured in return for what gain, and yet more difficult to abide by our decisions; for as a rule what is expected is painful, and what we are forced to do is base, whence praise and blame are bestowed on those who have been compelled or have not.

What sort of acts, then, should be called compulsory? We answer that without qualification actions are so when the cause is in the external circumstances and the agent contributes nothing. But the things that in themselves are involuntary, but now and in return for these gains are worthy of choice, and whose moving principle is in the agent, are in themselves involuntary, but now and in return for these gains voluntary. They are more like voluntary acts; for actions are in the class of particulars, and the particular acts here are voluntary. What sort of things are to be chosen, and in return for what, it is not easy to state; for there are many differences in the particular cases.

But if some one were to say that pleasant and noble objects have a compelling power, forcing us from without, all acts would be for him compulsory; for it is for these objects that all men do everything they do. And those who act under compulsion and unwillingly act with pain, but those who do acts for their pleasantness and nobility do them with pleasure; it is absurd to make external circumstances responsible, and not oneself, as being easily caught by such attractions, and to make oneself responsible for noble acts but the pleasant objects responsible for base acts. The compulsory, then, seems to be that whose moving principle is outside, the person compelled contributing nothing.

Everything that is done by reason of ignorance is *not* voluntary; it is only what produces pain and repentance that is *involuntary*. For the man who has done something owing to ignorance, and feels not the least vexation at his action, has not acted voluntarily, since he did not know what he was doing, nor yet involuntarily, since he is not pained. Of people, then, who act by reason of ignorance he who repents is thought an involuntary agent, and the man who does not repent may, since he is different, be called a not voluntary agent; for, since he differs from the other, it is better that he should have a name of his own.

Acting by reason of ignorance seems also to be different from acting *in* ignorance; for the man who is drunk or in a rage is thought to act as a result not of ignorance but of one of the causes mentioned, yet not knowingly but in ignorance.

Now every wicked man is ignorant of what he ought to do and what he ought to abstain from, and it is by reason of error of this kind that men become unjust and in general bad; but the term "involuntary" tends to be used not if a man is ignorant of what is to his advantage—for it is not mistaken purpose that causes involuntary action (it leads rather to wickedness), nor ignorance of the universal (for *that* men are *blamed*), but ignorance of particulars, i.e. of the circumstances of the action and the objects with which it is concerned. For it is on these that both pity and pardon depend, since the person who is ignorant of any of these acts involuntarily.

Perhaps it is just as well, therefore, to determine their nature and number. A man may be ignorant, then, of who he is, what he is doing, what or whom he is acting on, and sometimes also what (e.g. what instrument) he is doing it with, and to what end (e.g. he may think his act will conduce to some one's safety), and how he is doing it (e.g. whether gently or violently). Now of all of these no one could be ignorant unless he were mad, and evidently also he could not be ignorant of the agent; for how could he not know himself? But of what he is doing a man might be ignorant, as for instance people say "it slipped out of their mouths as they were speaking," or "they did not know it was a secret," as Aeschylus said of the mysteries, or a man might say he "let it go off when he merely wanted to show its working," as the man did with the catapult. Again, one might think one's son was an enemy, as Merope did, or that a pointed spear had a button on it, or that a stone was pumicestone; or one might give a man a draught to save him, and really kill him; or one might want to touch a man, as people do in sparring, and really wound him. The ignorance may relate, then, to any of these things, i.e. of the circumstances of the action, and the man who was ignorant of any of these is thought to have acted involuntarily, and especially if he was ignorant on the most important points; and these are thought to be the circumstances of the action and its end. Further, the doing of an act that is called involuntary in virtue of ignorance of this sort must be painful and involve repentance.

Since that which is done under compulsion or by reason of ignorance is involuntary, the voluntary would seem to be that of which the moving principle is in the agent himself, he being aware of the particular circumstances of the action. Presumably acts done by reason of anger or appetite are not rightly called involuntary. For in the first place, on that showing none of the other animals will act voluntarily, nor will children; and secondly, is it meant that we do not do voluntarily *any* of the acts that are due to appetite or anger, or that we do the noble acts voluntarily and the base acts involuntarily? Is not this absurd, when one and the same thing is the cause? But it would surely be odd to describe as involuntary the things one ought to desire; and we ought both to be angry at certain things and to have an appetite for certain things, e.g. for health and for learning. Also what is involuntary is thought to be painful, but what is in accordance with appetite is thought to be pleasant. Again, what is the difference in respect of involuntariness between errors committed upon calculation and those committed in anger? Both are to be avoided, but the irrational passions are thought not less human than reason is, and therefore also the actions which proceed from anger or appetite are the man's actions. It would be odd, then, to treat them as involuntary.

Study Questions

1. Which actions, according to Aristotle, can we not be held accountable for? Why?

2. What does Aristotle mean by actions that are "mixed," in between being voluntary and involuntary? Give an example.

3. Are acts done out of anger or appetite voluntary or involuntary, according to Aristotle? Explain in detail.

Primary Reading

Existentialism Is a Humanism

JEAN-PAUL SARTRE

Excerpt, 1946.

There are two kinds of existentialists. There are, on the one hand, the Christians, amongst whom I shall name [Karl] Jaspers and Gabriel Marcel, both professed Catholics; and on the other the existential atheists, amongst whom we must place Heidegger as well as the French existentialists and myself. What they have in common is simply the fact that they believe that existence comes before essence—or, if you will, that we must begin from the subjective. What exactly do we mean by that? If one considers an article of manufacture as, for example, a book or a paper-knife—one sees that it has been made by an artisan who had a conception of it; and he has paid attention, equally, to the conception of a paper-knife and to the pre-existent technique of production which is a part of that conception and is, at bottom, a formula. Thus the paper-knife is at the same time an article producible in a certain manner and one which, on the other hand, serves a definite purpose, for one cannot suppose that a man would produce a paper-knife without knowing what it was for. Let us say, then, of the paper-knife that its essence—that is to say the sum of the formulae and the qualities which made its production and its definition possible—precedes its existence. The presence of such-and-such a paper-knife or book is thus determined before my eyes. Here, then, we are viewing the world from a technical standpoint, and we can say that production precedes existence.

When we think of God as the creator, we are thinking of him, most of the time, as a supernal artisan. Whatever doctrine we may be considering, whether it be a doctrine like that of Descartes, or of Leibnitz himself, we always imply that the will follows, more or less, from the understanding or at least accompanies it, so that when God creates he knows precisely what he is creating. Thus, the conception of man in the mind of God is comparable to that of the paper-knife in the mind of the artisan: God makes man according to a procedure and a conception, exactly as the artisan manufactures a paper-knife, following a definition and a formula. Thus each individual man is the realisation of a certain conception which dwells in the divine understanding. In the philosophic atheism of the eighteenth century, the notion of God is suppressed, but not, for all that, the idea that essence is prior to existence; something of that idea we still find everywhere, in Diderot, in Voltaire and even in Kant. Man possesses a human nature; that "human nature," which is the conception of human being, is found in every man; which means that each man is a particular example of a universal conception, the conception of Man. In Kant, this universality goes so far that the wild man of the woods, man in the state of nature and the bourgeois are all contained in the same definition and have the same fundamental qualities. Here again, the essence of man precedes that historic existence which we confront in experience.

Atheistic existentialism, of which I am a representative, declares with greater consistency that if God does not exist there is at least one being whose existence comes before its essence, a being which exists before it can be defined by any conception of it. That being is man or, as Heidegger has it, the human reality. What do we mean by saying that existence precedes essence? We mean that man first of all exists, encounters himself, surges up in the world—and defines himself afterwards. If man as the existentialist sees him is not definable, it is because to begin with he is nothing. He will not be anything until later, and then he will be what he makes of himself. Thus, there is no human nature, because there is no God to have a conception of it. Man simply is. Not that he is simply what he conceives himself to be, but he is what he wills, and as he conceives himself after already existing—as he wills to be after that leap towards existence. Man is nothing else but that which he makes of himself. That is the first principle of existentialism. And this is what people call its "subjectivity," using the word as a reproach against us. But what do we mean to say by this, but that man is of a greater dignity than a stone or a table? For we mean to say that man primarily exists—that man is, before all else, something which propels itself towards a future and is aware that it is doing so. Man is, indeed, a project

which possesses a subjective life, instead of being a kind of moss, or a fungus or a cauliflower. Before that projection of the self nothing exists; not even in the heaven of intelligence: man will only attain existence when he is what he purposes to be. Not, however, what he may wish to be. For that we usually understand by wishing or willing is a conscious decision taken—much more often than not—after we have made ourselves what we are. I may wish to join a party, to write a book or to marry—but in such a case what is usually called my will is probably a manifestation of a prior and more spontaneous decision. If, however, it is true that existence is prior to essence, man is responsible for what he is. Thus, the first effect of existentialism is that it puts every man in possession of himself as he is, and places the entire reasonability for his existence squarely upon his own shoulders. And, when we say that man is responsible for himself, we do not mean that he is responsible only for his own individuality, but that he is responsible for all men. The word "subjectivism" is to be understood in two senses, and our adversaries play upon only one of them. Subjectivism means on the one hand, the freedom of the individual subject and, on the other, that man cannot pass beyond human subjectivity. It is the latter which is the deeper meaning of existentialism. When we say that man chooses himself, we do mean that every one of us must choose himself; but by that we also mean that in choosing for himself he chooses for all men. For in effect, of all the actions a man may take in order to create himself as he wills to be, there is not one which is not creative, at the same time, of an image of man such as he believes he ought to be. To choose between this or that is at the same time to affirm the value of that which is chosen; for we are unable ever to choose the worse. What we choose is always the better; and nothing can be better for us unless it is better for all. If, moreover, existence precedes essence and we will to exist at the same time as we fashion our image, that image is valid for all and for the entire epoch in which we find ourselves. Our responsibility is thus much greater than we had supposed, for it concerns mankind as a whole. If I am a worker, for instance, I may choose to join a Christian rather than a Communist trade union. And if, by that membership, I choose to signify that resignation is, after all, the attitude that best becomes a man, that man's kingdom is not upon this earth, I do not commit myself alone to that view. Resignation is my will for everyone, and my action is, in consequence, a commitment on behalf of all mankind. Or if, to take a more personal case, I decide to marry and to have children, even though this decision proceeds simply from my situation, from my passion or my desire, I am thereby committing not only myself, but humanity as a whole, to the practice of monogamy. I am thus responsible for myself and for all men, and I am creating a certain image of man as I would have him to be. In fashioning myself I fashion man.

Study Questions

1. What does Sartre mean by "existence comes before essence"?

2. What is "the first effect of existentialism"? Explain.

3. What does Sartre mean by saying that in making a choice, I am responsible for all men?

Narrative

The Ugly Duckling

HANS CHRISTIAN ANDERSEN

Fairy tale, 1844. Summary.

Children around the world know the story of the ugly duckling, but rarely in its original form. Hans Christian Andersen tells a grueling tale of hardship and abuse; a swan's egg is hatched by a duck, in the nest with her own eggs. From his first day, everyone rejects the swan because he is different; his brothers and sisters, the pretty little ducklings, peck at him because he is so big and clumsy. The kitchen maid kicks dirt at him, the other farm animals laugh at him, and eventually even his mother rejects him. Dejected, he leaves the farm; and all through the fall and winter he struggles to survive, barely escaping hunters and their dogs, coming close to dying from starvation. But his determination pays off: In the spring, when the ice breaks, he sees a family of majestic white birds sailing toward him, across the water. He expects them to act like everyone else and attack him because he is so hideous, but instead they surround him and welcome him as one of their own: He is no longer a gawky, clumsy "duckling," but a beautiful, full-grown swan. He sails off to a new life with his new family, marveling that he had no idea life would ever hold so much happiness for him in the bad days when he was an ugly duckling.

Is this the likely fate of a baby swan whose egg has wound up in a duck's nest? How did it get there in the first place? Are young swans ugly? And why are ducks somehow lesser beings than swans? Such questions are not Andersen's concern: The story is purely symbolic, because between the lines we read the story of Andersen's own rocky road to fame. In his youth he experienced times of extreme poverty as the son of the local laundress, a single mother who—he tells us—had an alcohol addiction. He was not unloved, but felt out of place and misunderstood until he was able to break through as a poet and a writer. So Andersen's tale lets us know that it was because of who he *really* was that he overcame all hardships and finally even became famous: *It was in his nature.* As long as you have the right qualities, Andersen is saying, then your true nature will prevail. Persistent rumors that Andersen's unknown father was a famous man—some even speculate that he may have been a member of the royal family—are completely in tune with Andersen's self-image as provided by the story: It is your heredity that counts, not your environment.

If you believe that we will become what is in our nature, if we work hard at it, then you agree with what Andersen is saying. If you think that even the strongest nature will be broken by the wrong kind of upbringing (or a more timid nature will benefit from an encouraging upbringing), then you don't agree. The Danish author Henrik Pontoppidan saw the duckling story as a self-serving, unbearably sentimental piece of nonsense and tried to set the record straight with a "realistic" story of his own for Andersen's loyal readers, "Flight of the Eagle." It is up to you to judge (1) which story is more realistic and (2) which is the better story!

 *Narrative*

Flight of the Eagle

HENRIK PONTOPPIDAN

Short story, 1894. Summary.

An eagle chick is found by some boys and taken to a parsonage, where kind people raise him. As he grows up, the eagle's world consists of the humans who feed and care for him and the animals on the farm. He is being raised with the chickens and ducks and feels comfortable with them; even so, he dreams of the day when he will be free so he can fulfill his biological destiny. The farmer has taken measures so that won't happen, however: The eagle's wings are clipped.

One day there is a horrendous windstorm, and the young eagle finds himself swept by the wind up to the roof of the barn. He longs to fly more than ever, and the next powerful gust of wind fulfills his dream: It makes him airborne. His clipped wings can barely carry him, but aided by the wind, he soars over the woods and fields and flies off toward the mountains. He is finally a true eagle! Now a female eagle approaches; she calls him, and he follows, higher and higher. Evening approaches, and he lands on a rocky ledge, completely exhausted. She keeps calling for him to follow her, but now the eagle begins to think of his home; he imagines his friends the chickens and the other farm animals nice and snug and well-fed back in the farmyard, and the danger and folly of the situation are only too apparent to him. What was he thinking, taking off like that? Knowing now where he truly belongs, he turns his back on the female eagle and makes his weary way home. The journey takes all night. In the early morning hours he approaches the farm where people are cleaning up after the storm; everything is in disarray down there, and nobody knows that the pet eagle has gone missing. A farmhand looks up and sees a menacing wild eagle about to swoop down on the poultry, and he grabs his gun and shoots the eagle down. The homeward-bound eagle falls to his death in the barnyard. Pontoppidan concludes that being born an eagle makes no difference if you grow up among the ducks.

Study Questions

1. Which story do you think represents the truer picture? Can we overcome our upbringing and realize our true nature—or not? Explain.

2. Can we overcome our nature (our heritage) by training hard? Explain.

3. Both stories are versions of determinism. Write an antideterministic or compatibilistic fable in the same style, emphasizing the role of our free will in what we become in life, in overcoming both our heredity *and* our environment.

4. Why do you think these authors (and many others from Aesop to Disney) choose to write about animals rather than people?

5. If the young eagle's wings hadn't been clipped, would the story still have had the same outcome? If yes, why? If no, why not? Is having "clipped wings" an acceptable metaphor for one's nature? Why or why not?

6. Which story is more uplifting? Does that count? Why or why not?

Narrative

A Clockwork Orange

STANLEY KUBRICK (DIRECTOR AND SCREENWRITER)

Film, 1971. Based on a novel by Anthony Burgess, 1961. Summary.

In Chapter 3 you read a synopsis of an episode from Kubrick's enigmatic film *2001: A Space Odyssey.* The next Kubrick film to shock its audience was *A Clockwork Orange;* like *2001,* it has become a classic, but for other reasons. *A Clockwork Orange* is a fast-paced (even for today), hard-edged surrealistic film that explores the theory of determinism in psychology: Is rehabilitation possible for even a lust-murderer, if based on the behaviorist assumption that with the proper conditioning, anybody can be reconditioned? And would such a procedure be morally defensible, or would it violate and destroy the person's free will? The film disturbed many people—partly because of its violence, but also because the audience, in a way, is reconditioned during the film to feel sympathy for the young rapist.

In a bar in the near future, four male teenagers are psyching themselves up for the evening's violence. Alex La Grande, Pete, Georgie, and Dim wear highly stylized clothes: derbies, white pants, and black boots, with codpieces accentuating their crotches. Statuettes of naked women in sexually submissive positions decorate the bar. The boys speak a slang combination of English and Russian, *Nadsat,* and drink milk-plus, a drink spiked with drugs.

Every night they have a ritual: They rape, rob, and beat up people at random. Their main interest is sex and what they call ultra-violence. A homeless man, depressed at the lawless state of society, disgusts Alex, and for that reason he is beaten with a club. Later that evening they come across a rival gang raping a young woman in the ruins of a theater, on the stage. They challenge the other gang and start a free-for-all, but the police show up, and Alex and his boys jump into a stolen car and lead the police on a high-speed chase. They are in a good mood because the evening is shaping up. Next stop is the home of a wealthy couple: Alex rings their doorbell, pretending to need help be-

cause of an accident; before the couple realize what is happening, the four teens have burst into their home, tying up the husband and undressing and raping his wife (who will later die from her injuries), to the tune of "Singin' in the Rain." Feeling that their evening has been a success, they return to the bar. But here a discord develops between the friends: A patron at the bar, a woman from a TV studio, begins singing the "Ode to Joy" from Beethoven's Ninth Symphony, and that happens to be Alex's favorite music. Dim makes fun of the singer, and that doesn't sit well with Alex, who beats Dim up.

Next day is busy for Alex: He has sex with two teenage girls and beats up his friends to reestablish his leadership. In the evening the gang tries to repeat its scheme from the night before at another residence, but the lady of the house is suspicious and calls the police instead of letting them in. So when they break into her house, the police are on the way—but they don't arrive in time to save her from being beaten to death with one of her own sculptures, a huge white phallus. When the boys hear the sirens, Dim hits Alex across his face. The other three escape, but Alex is arrested.

Justice is swift: Alex is tried and convicted of murder; he is sentenced to fourteen years (this was a very harsh sentence for a teenager in the England of the late 1960s and early 1970s). In prison, Alex is stripped of his identity and his belongings. Two years into his sentence, a preacher shows up and talks about hell and damnation, offering the inmates a choice: Keep doing what they're doing—and go to hell. Change their ways—and save their souls. Alex is now reading the Bible—all the parts about sex and violence, using them for his sexual fantasies. He also realizes that the chaplain is easily taken in by a phony act of contrition, so he asks the chaplain to help him: He wants to be "good" and is willing to undergo a new kind of treatment so he can be let out early. The chaplain is reluctant, because he believes this treatment will do damage to Alex's soul: It will rob him of his free will. The chaplain tries to explain it to Alex: "The question is whether or not this technique really makes a man good. Goodness comes from within. Goodness is chosen. When a man cannot choose, he ceases to be a man."[14]

The government is interested in this new treatment, because the prisons are getting overcrowded: In this near-future scenario, the totalitarian government is tracking down political dissidents. Prisons don't have space for all these new criminals, so the government wants to be able to let the "ordinary" violent inmates out within a two-week period, after a personality-altering treatment. Alex is a perfect candidate for this treatment. He is delivered to the hospital, where he is strapped down and forced to watch endless videos of violent situations and sex, while being injected with a nausea-inducing drug. But the worst is yet to come: When forced to watch films of Nazis marching to the music he loves the most, Beethoven's Ninth, Alex begs for mercy—but the program must go on. Part of Alex's conditioning is now also a loathing of Beethoven. After two weeks he is declared cured and paraded in front of a panel of doctors as an example of successful conditioning. He is subjected to humiliating situations, and whenever he wants to respond with violence, he gets sick. When exposed to sexual stimulation, he likewise feels like throwing up. The chaplain is appalled; to him, Alex is now like a robot, a *clockwork orange* (mechanical man):

> CHAPLAIN: Choice! The boy has no real choice, has he? Self-interest, the fear of physical pain drove him to that grotesque act of self-abasement. Its insincerity was clearly to be seen. He ceases to be a wrong-doer. He ceases also to be a creature capable of moral choice.
>
> MINISTER: Padre, these are subtleties! We are not concerned with motives, with the higher ethics. We are concerned only with cutting down crime."[15]

Alex is now free, but without the capacity for moral choice. He has been thoroughly conditioned. He re-turns home to his parents, only to find that his room has been rented to a lodger—who has taken his place as the son of the house. He leaves to make a life for himself; but everywhere he goes, he is met with violence, and he is conditioned not to fight back. The homeless man and his friends beat him up. His old friends Georgie and Dim have joined the police force, and beat him up too. Injured, Alex seeks refuge in a home—owned by the man whose wife was beaten to death by Alex years ago. He is now disabled because of Alex's attack. Realizing after a while who Alex is, he tortures him by playing Beethoven to him. To escape the agony, Alex throws himself out of the window—and that is the road to recovery for him, if we want to label it recovery. At the hospital Alex becomes famous for being the man whose personality the government tried to alter. His suicide attempt is now blamed on the scientists and the government. The doctors now undertake a process of reconditioning him to his old self; he receives an apology from the government, which now offers him a deal, because the bureaucrats think he can be turned into an asset to them after all. Finally, Alex returns to a world of sex and violence, with the government's blessing. His last words are "I was cured, all right." And "Singin' in the Rain" is playing.

Study Questions

1. Does Alex regain his free will? Do we need to have freedom of the will in order to be considered complete humans?

2. What might Watson and Skinner have said to the scenario of conditioning criminals to feel aversion toward their crimes? What might Aristotle say? What might Sartre say?

3. When Anthony Burgess's *A Clockwork Orange* was published in the United States in 1961, the American publisher omitted the final chapter of the original British edition, Chapter 21, because he thought the story would appeal more to the American audience if it ended with Chapter 20. Apparently Kubrick didn't know about the original final chapter, and based his film exclusively on the American version. Reportedly, Burgess was very unhappy to

see the American film version without the British ending. You know that Kubrick's version ends as a tribute to Alex's free will and independent spirit, as troubling as it may be. The original British ending has Alex (after the treatments are over) one day re-alizing that he is really too old for all that violence, that it is time to settle down and get married. The question for you is, Which version do you think you'd prefer, the original version as film or Ku-brick's version? Explain why.

 *Narrative*

Brave New World

ALDOUS HUXLEY

Novel, 1931. Summary and Excerpt.

One of the most famous novels of the Western world in the twentieth century, Huxley's science fiction book turned out to be more prophetic than even he had imagined, and it now has acquired the status of one of the great moral tales of the century. The story takes place in a far future, the year A.F. (After Ford) 632; in other words, the twenty-sixth century. The science of genetics has been mastered, and so has the art of con-ditioning, or shaping people's minds from birth. But "birth" is only a metaphor in that far future, because humans are bred and "born" in labs, under complete genetic and environmental control. Scientists and poli-ticians of the future have mastered heredity and envi-ronment to create a biological and political world based on determinism. In this future world, everyone is so conditioned that they not only are bred for certain jobs, but they are also bred to be happy and find ful-fillment in those jobs: Large numbers of human clones are bred for repetitive tasks and trained to love their work. Humanity is divided into Alpha, Beta, Delta, Ep-silon, and Gamma people, each group color-coded and living their destinies separately from one another. Al-phas and Betas share the world of relatively free deci-sions and interesting jobs, while the other groups are bred for manual labor. For their leisure time, drugs are distributed to keep people in a happy stupor. The rigid inhumanity of this world is seen through the eyes of a young man who, by coincidence, was born naturally, away from the programming of children. Several things strike us as eerily relevant when we read Huxley today.

For one thing, it did not take us almost 600 years to be technologically capable of cloning humans; the tech-nology was available already at the end of Huxley's own twentieth century. For another, the entire policy of governmental control outlined by Huxley as a satire, a warning of things to come, was the theoretical un-derpinning of Skinner's behaviorism, developed in the same decade Huxley wrote his book: As you will re-member from earlier in this chapter, Skinner's goal was not merely to predict people's behavior, but also to control it through consistent conditioning.

>   *Major instruments of social stability*
>   Standard men and women; in uniform batches. The whole of a small factory staffed with the products of a single bokanovskified egg.
>   "Ninety-six identical twins working ninety-six identical machines!" The voice was almost tremulous with enthusiasm. "You really know where you are. For the first time in history." He quoted the planetary motto. "Community, Identity, Stability." Grand words. "If we could bokanovskify indefinitely the whole problem would be solved." . . .
>   At the end of the room a loud speaker projected from the wall. The Director walked up to it and pressed a switch.
>   ". . . all wear green," said a soft but very distinct voice, beginning in the middle of a sentence, "and Delta Children wear khaki. Oh no, I don't want to play with Delta children. And Epsilons are still worse. They're too stupid to be able to read or write. Besides

they wear black, which is such a beastly color. I'm *so* glad I'm a Beta."

There was a pause; then the voice began again.

"Alpha children wear grey. They work much harder than we do, because they're so frightfully clever. I'm really awfully glad I'm a Beta, because I don't work so hard. And then we are much better than the Gammas and Deltas. Gammas are stupid. They all wear green, and Delta children wear khaki. Oh no, I *don't* want to play with Delta children. And Epsilons are still worse. They're too stupid to be able . . ."

The Director pushed back the switch. The voice was silent. Only its thin ghost continued to mutter from beneath the eighty pillows.

"They'll have that repeated forty or fifty times more before they wake; then again on Thursday, and again on Saturday. A hundred and twenty times three times a week for thirty months. After which they go on to a more advanced lesson." . . .

"All men are physico-chemically equal," said Henry sententiously. "Besides, even Epsilons perform indispensable services."

"Even an Epsilon . . ." Lenina suddenly remembered an occasion when, as a little girl at school, she had woken up in the middle of the night and become aware, for the first time, of the whispering that had haunted all her sleeps. She saw again the beam of moonlight, the row of small white beds; heard once more the soft, soft voice that said (the words were there, unforgotten, unforgettable after so many night-long repetitions): "Every one works for every one else. We can't do without any one. Even Epsilons are useful. We couldn't do without Epsilons. Every one works for every one else. We can't do without any one . . ." Lenina remembered her first shock of fear and surprise; her speculations through half a wakeful hour; and then, under the influence of those endless repetitions, the gradual soothing of her mind, the soothing, the smoothing, the stealthy creeping of sleep. . . .

"I suppose Epsilons don't really mind being Epsilons," she said aloud.

"Of course they don't. How can they? They don't know what it's like being anything else. We'd mind, of course. But then we've been differently conditioned. Besides, we start with a different heredity."

"I'm glad I'm not an Epsilon," said Lenina, with conviction.

"And if you were an Epsilon," said Henry, "your conditioning would have made you no less thankful that you weren't a Beta or an Alpha." . . .

It was a small factory of lighting-sets for helicopters, a branch of the Electrical Equipment Corporation. They were met on the roof itself (for that circular letter of recommendation from the Controller was magical in its effects) by the Chief Technician and the Human Element Manager. They walked downstairs into the factory.

"Each process," explained the Human Element Manager, "is carried out, so far as possible, by a single Bokanovsky Group."

And, in effect, eighty-three almost noseless black brachycephalic Deltas were cold-pressing. The fifty-six four-spindle chucking and turning machines were being manipulated by fifty-six aquiline and ginger Gammas. One hundred and seven heat-conditioned Epsilon Senegalese were working in the foundry. Thirty-three Delta females, long-headed, sandy, with narrow pelvises, and all within 20 millimetres of 1 metre 69 centimetres tall, were cutting screws. In the assembling room, the dynamos were being put together by two sets of Gamma-Plus dwarfs. The two low work-tables faced one another; between them crawled the conveyor with its load of separate parts; forty-seven blonde heads were confronted by forty-seven brown ones. Forty-seven snubs by forty-seven hooks; forty-seven receding by forty-seven prognathous chins. The completed mechanisms were inspected by eighteen identical curly auburn girls in Gamma green, packed in crates by thirty-four short-legged, left-handed male Delta-Minuses, and loaded into the waiting trucks and lorries by sixty-three blue-eyed, flaxen and freckled Epsilon Semi-Morons.

"O brave new world . . ." By some malice of his memory the Savage found himself repeating Miranda's words. "O brave new world that has such people in it."

Study Questions

1. If everyone in the *Brave New World* is happy, why is the book considered a social satire?

2. Draw parallels between Watson's and Skinner's behaviorism and *Huxley's Brave New World,* based on the excerpt.

3. Given that genetic engineering today could make part of Huxley's future vision (or nightmare) come true, is this a desirable goal? Why or why not? Explore recent films that warn us about a future shaped by the combination of high tech and a lack of political and scientific ethics. (You might consider *X-Files, Gattaca, The Thirteenth Floor,* and *The Matrix.*)

Review

Key Issues in Chapter 4

Can We Choose Our Actions?

- *Mechanistic Determinism.* Hard determinism holds that even though we may think our decisions are freely chosen, in actual fact they are the result of pressures: inner pressures from our biological states and external pressures from our environment. Mechanistic determinism presents no problem when applied to the world of natural science; but when applied to human decisions, it implies that a person can't be held accountable because he or she does not have freedom of the will.

- *What Is Free Will? Hard Determinism's Answer.* Political freedom of choice is different from the metaphysical question of free will. Determinism presents a problem for moral philosophy.

- *Nature or Nurture?* Harris theorizes that nature is the more significant influence on child development. But critics charge that her evidence is insufficient and may show bias toward her biological child. Studies of identical twins separated at birth point to the importance of nature (genetics). Classical feminism sees gender roles as a result of nurture, while difference feminism sees them as a matter of nature.

- *The Rise and Fall of Behaviorism.* Behaviorism is defined as the theory that human nature can be explained in terms of behavior; it holds that reference to mental activity is unnecessary and misleading. Watson said that human behavior is exclusively a matter of nurture; any child can be trained to become any kind of adult. Everything we learn is through conditioning. Behaviorism was designed not only to understand but also to control human nature. Skinner said that people's behavior can be predicted and controlled through conditioning and reinforcement with positive and negative reinforcers.

- *Determinism in Court.* Criminal defense strategies rely on behaviorism when they claim that a defendant couldn't help himself or herself due to internal or external pressures. Examples include cases involving Leopold and Loeb, Lorena Bobbitt, the "Twinkies defense," and the Menendez brothers. If criminal behavior is not a matter of choice, what use is punishment?

The Case for Free Will

- *Does Causality Preclude Free Will?* Even while acknowledging some element of causality, we can offer arguments in favor of holding criminals accountable for their actions (ascribing free choice to them). According to the "policeman at the elbow" argument, by John Douglas, even compulsive criminals hesitate in the presence of a police officer. As a proponent of compatibilism/soft determinism, W. T. Stace argues that free will and determinism are compatible. One can think of the chess game analogy: the more complex an action is, the less it can be predicted. In terms of our lived experience, we feel we have freedom of choice. Determinism can be criticized because it is unfalsifiable; it doesn't allow for rigorous testing of itself. Quantum physics tells us that there is no possibility of completely accurate predictions on the subatomic level. Indeterminism tells us that at any given time we can change our mind about anything.

- *There Is No Human Nature: Sartre's Libertarianism.* Sartre and Beauvoir believed that any attempt at defining human nature is setting boundaries. The human will is completely free. Human existence is "for itself"; animal and object existence is "in itself." For humans, existence precedes essence. Humans are condemned to be free; believing you don't have to choose is to have bad faith.

- *The First Compatibilist: Aristotle on Compulsion, Ignorance, and Free Will.* Aristotle distinguishes between acts done freely and acts done under compulsion or from ignorance. Scenarios based on ideas of ignorance or compulsion: Ignorance of facts is an excuse when the facts couldn't have been known. Not knowing how is an excuse when the skill couldn't have been learned. External compulsion means being forced. Internal compulsion means (1) being drugged (but not voluntarily) and (2) having a psychological compulsion or a case of mind-control. We are victims of circumstances when the circumstances are beyond our control.

- *Evaluating Aristotle's Theory of Ignorance and Compulsion.* Patty Hearst's kidnapping and brainwashing show that although she was indeed subjected to genuine brainwashing techniques, she still may have made the decision to save her life.

Primary Readings

- Aristotle, *Nicomachean Ethics,* Book III, Chapter 1. Aristotle argues that people must take responsibility for their voluntary actions but can't be blamed for involuntary actions, stemming from ignorance or compulsion.

- Jean-Paul Sartre, "Existentialism Is a Humanism." Sartre argues that there is no human nature, because humans, unlike things and animals, do not have an essence by nature. We exist, and then we create our own essence; thus, existence precedes essence.

Narratives

- Hans Christian Andersen, "The Ugly Duckling," story. Nature prevails when a swan is raised among ducks.

- Henrik Pontoppidan, "Flight of the Eagle," story. Nurture prevails when an eagle is raised among chickens.

- *A Clockwork Orange,* film. The teenager Alex is convicted of rape and assault and sentenced to a long prison term. In order to shorten his sentence, he agrees to an experimental treatment of complete psychological reconditioning, depriving him of his free will.

- Aldous Huxley, *Brave New World,* novel. In this science fiction morality tale about a future society, everyone is conceived and conditioned to be a predictable, productive, happy citizen.

Endnotes

1. J. B. Watson, *Behaviorism* (New York: Norton, 1925), chapter 1.
2. In Chapter 6 you will see a real-life application of Watson's theory, in the case of the boy who was raised as a girl because of a botched circumcision during which the boy lost his penis. According to Watson's behaviorism, the boy should have been able to be conditioned to being a girl, but reality didn't conform to the behaviorist theory.
3. Watson, chapter 1.
4. B. F. Skinner, *Science and Human Behavior* (New York: Macmillan, 1953), chapter 1. When Skinner said "lawful," he meant "according to the laws of nature."
5. Ibid., pp. 213–214.
6. Irving Stone, *Clarence Darrow for the Defense* (New York: Bantam, 1958), pp. 243–244.
7. Ibid., p. 260.
8. John Douglas and Mark Olshaker, *The Anatomy of Motive* (New York: Scribner, 1999), p. 42.
9. The existential theory of libertarianism differs considerably from the political theory known as Libertarianism in American politics. Sartre's libertarianism claims that we always have existential freedom to choose; the philosophy of the Libertarian party states that society is better off if the government interferes as little as possible with the personal freedoms of the citizens and the world of business. Sartre himself was politically a socialist for most of his life and at a certain point in time identified himself as a Marxist, although he later developed a critical attitude toward certain aspects of Marxism.
10. Aristotle, *Nicomachean Ethics,* 1110a–1111b.
11. The breakdown of ignorance and compulsion into subcategories is inspired by the American philosopher Paul W. Taylor's analysis from 1975.
12. The case of the *People of California vs. Susan Eubanks, 1999.* Eubanks was given a death sentence.
13. "All About Crime," KXLY 920, Aug. 26, 1999.
14. Retrieved from the World Wide Web: http://www.filmsite.org/cloc2.html
15. Retrieved from the World Wide Web: http://www.filmsite.org/cloc3.html

Chapter Five

The Human Race/The Human Races?

Race: Descriptive Turned Normative

The issue of race is a prime example of how quickly a descriptive approach to human nature can turn into a normative approach and illustrates clearly how an approach to human nature can acquire political and ethical dimensions. We will look at the issue of race in this chapter partly from a scientific point of view; but from the very beginning, the philosophical dimensions—politics and morals—are present.

You would think that if we could put aside problematic cultural notions about race, then a straight descriptive racial identification would be one of the easiest issues in a philosophical anthropology; after all, people seem to classify each other in terms of race as a basic means of identifying each other, just as they do with gender, age, and height, without thereby being racists, sexists, ageists—or "heightists." But ask a scientist or a historian, and the issue becomes much more complex. As we shall see, today many scientists believe that there simply isn't any biological reality corresponding to the concept of race: They see race as a cultural, moral, and political term. Indeed, there are biological differences among distinct population groups, but these differences tend to cut across the categories Americans commonly associate with "race differences" rather than help identify them.

This new research into the nature of race is in itself politically volatile: Those of us who, like the philosopher Naomi Zack (see below), would like the world to be color-blind and want the issue of race to go away so that we can make way for a general inclusive concept of humanity, welcome the new science of race. However, those among us who, for whatever reason, fear that our presumed racial characteristics will disappear into a mainstream melting pot or simply be wiped out by a dominant race, decry the new research as incomplete science or may point to values other than scientific facts, such as cultural traditions. In many ways, attitudes toward the new science of race mirror attitudes toward the question of human origins: Do we have a common origin in Africa (as current science claims), or did *Homo sapiens* originate in several places at once? You may want to take another look at that discussion in Chapter 2. People who favor a world where racial differences are regarded as irrelevant look to the new science to provide the support for our political hopes. People who would rather see the politics of racial differences maintained look elsewhere for support, such as in the value of tradition, or they may seek scientific support in studies that haven't been widely sanctioned by the scientific community.

Theories of the Biological Reality of Race

The Human Race

With the 2000 U.S. census came a landmark change in the way we officially describe ourselves. For the first time, Americans could check several designated race categories, breaking with the tradition of identifying ourselves with only one race. This singular identification, unproblematic for some, politically charged for others, and personally challenging for many who believe themselves to be of mixed race with strong loyalties toward their entire heritage, is still part of many an application form. Several of my students have told me that, when filling out such forms, they check the "Other" box and write in "the human race." And, to be sure, all humans on the planet, regardless of our biological differences, belong to the same humanity, or the same species, *Homo sapiens sapiens*.[1] Biologically, this means that all human populations (albeit not necessarily all individuals) can interbreed and have children who themselves can have children (in other words, they are not sterile like mules, the offspring of horses and donkeys). Nevertheless, racial differences seem to be an obvious feature of this human species. Where did they originate? Research into the differences among groups that are part of the human race is now generally undertaken because we are curious and would like to know more about the scientific facts. However, race research has not always had a value-neutral (objective) goal.

Hitler's Theory of the Aryan Race

The biological study of race has undergone several phases in the past two centuries. As the science of biology developed in the eighteenth century and the Swedish biologist Carolus Linnaeus's book *Systema Naturae* was published,[2] biologists in Europe and America classified the races of the world into four groups: Africans (black), Europeans (white), Asians (yellow), and American Indians (red). In so doing, they disregarded the obvious fact that individual skin tones fall very far from the stereotypes. However, with a simple color classification came a political and moral classification: Each race was thought to have its own moral character traits and failings, and often biologists as well as politicians and novelists of the nineteenth century assumed that people of mixed races had the most severe character flaws of all. Toward the end of the nineteenth century, biologists were intent on solving the question of race by giving it a foundation in Darwin's theory of evolution, and particularly his theory of natural selection, as well as in Spencer's theory of social Darwinism (see

Chapter 3). As evidence of success in terms of Darwinian survival, some thinkers pointed to the political map of the world at the end of the 1800s: European colonies spreading across the globe and Euro-Americans spreading across the American continent fulfilling what many Euro-Americans thought of as their "Manifest Destiny"—the mission of subduing the land (and whoever might already be living there) being in some way coded into the Euro-American people—a notion that was shared by the Spanish explorers of the Americas centuries earlier.

Such leaps from biology to moral theory had been taken freely by Western geographers and biologists, and just about any other Western intellectual, ever since the eighteenth century. As you will see, some philosophers believed that a harsh northern climate makes for an intelligent race of people; consequently, according to this theory, in more benign climates, people are lazy and stupid. The moral praise or condemnation of a population based on racial features is a long established tradition in Western thinking, and Hitler's *Endlösung,* the "Final Solution" (to the "problem of inferior races"), which meant exterminating anyone with perceived racial inferiority, was based on a theory of race with roots back in the nineteenth century. This theory identified the Germanic people as belonging to an "Aryan" race, supposedly making them older and racially purer than anyone else.

The idea of a pure Aryan race still surfaces from time to time, especially in neo-Nazi circles, but it is a scientifically false theory, based on a misunderstanding. The nineteenth-century German linguist F. Max Müller, who developed a sound scientific theory of ancient *languages,* identified a certain language group as "Aryan"; many European and Asian languages had a common source in this ancient Aryan language, which was spoken around the Caucasus/Iran/Northern India region (this language is sometimes also referred to as Indo-European). English belongs to the Aryan languages, as does German, the Scandinavian languages (except Finnish), French, Greek, Spanish,

Italian, Romanian, Iranian, Hindi, and others, including the oldest living Aryan language, Romani, the language of the Gypsies. However, German anti-Semites in particular almost immediately took the theory and ran with it, making it into a theory of race and bloodlines. So the theory of Aryan blood was floated in Germany two generations before Hitler, and in Chapter 8 you will see part of the story ("Elizabeth Nietzsche and the Nazis").[3] Müller tried to correct the misunderstanding, to no avail; the Aryan race theory had acquired a life of its own. Müller lived long enough to witness this concocted theory of race spreading into politics and is said to never have lived it down. The familiar implication of Hitler's Aryan race theory—that the original Aryans are tall, blond, and blue-eyed—was invented to match the image of an ideal German folk-character. The best-known consequence of this racist theory was the annihilation of 6 million European Jews in the Nazi death camps. The irony of the Aryan race theory is that if there ever was an early race of people who shared an Aryan language, they would probably have looked much like the present-day population of Iran, hardly a blond population; even more ironic and tragic, the people speaking the oldest existing Aryan language, the Gypsies, were targeted by Hitler as racially inferior and went into the death camps alongside Jews and a multitude of other Europeans considered undesirable in Hitler's Third Reich, altogether totaling 13 million people. Nazi genocide resulted in the virtual extinction of German, Austrian, and Polish Gypsies. While most of the educated Western world is now aware that Hitler's race theory had no solid foundation other than prejudice, the idea of the Aryan race is still a magnet for white supremacist fringe groups in Europe and the United States. At the end of the chapter I'll discuss a film that explores (and deplores) the fascination some young people have with the Aryan theory: *American History X*, the story of a young white supremacist whose racist worldview is dramatically altered in prison, where he is serving time for killing two young black men.

For many people in Europe, as well as in the United States, the Holocaust was the great eye-opener, revealing the far-reaching and dreadful consequences inherent in a theory of racial superiority. Within American culture, the historical reality of slavery and its long-term consequences, as well as the near-genocide of American Indians, disturbs our collective memory and serves as an equally stark reminder of what can happen when a racial theory becomes a political program.

The Biology of Race: Natural or Sexual Selection?

As we have seen in Chapters 2 and 3, Darwin's theory of natural selection is established as the current best explanation of the forces of evolution; however, this doesn't mean that a Darwinian approach offers the best answer to every question. Biology doesn't always work as a model for social developments: Spencer's theory of social Darwinism is no longer considered a valid explanation of human history, and the nineteenth-century attempts at explaining race on the basis of social competition haven't yielded useful results either. But how about the Darwinian idea of one's race being to one's advantage, physically? Biologists have looked at the presence of melanin in dark skin and the lack of it in light skin and so speculated that it had some survival advantage. Melanin in the skin does afford some protection against cancer-causing ultraviolet light, and being fair-skinned in sunny climates does lead to a higher rate of skin cancers. And it appears to be to one's advantage to be fair-skinned when and where there is comparatively little sunlight (such as in Northern European winters) to enhance absorption of vitamin D from sunlight. Melanin, on the other hand, protects to some extent against an excess of vitamin D from the sunlight of tropical regions. Thus, there seems to be some sense in having fair skin in northern latitudes and dark skin in southern latitudes, and this theory of a protective skin evolution has not yet been discarded (which is why I could speculate, in Chapter 2, that Neandertals may have been fair-skinned and blond, like many later Northern Europeans).

However, the facts don't fit the theory consistently. In the Southern hemisphere, the Australian aboriginal population is dark-skinned, but winters can be pretty gloomy in Southern Australia and Tasmania, at a latitude comparable to that of cool climate regions in the Northern hemisphere. Could it be that aboriginal Australians just haven't lived in those regions long enough for their skin to evolve? No, they seem to have lived there for at least 10,000 years. And what about the Asian populations who don't display similar patterns of light and dark skin? In India, dark-skinned populations have inhabited certain areas for a very long time, while other Indian populations with lighter skin share those areas, as a result of an ancient migration—but their skin doesn't seem to have changed with a change in latitude and lifestyle. It could be that they just haven't been in the area long enough for evolution to change their color—but it could also be that other factors are at play. Part of our readiness to believe in dark skin as protective, and light skin as a cancer risk has to do with the twentieth-century Western custom of sunbathing and the subsequent rise in skin cancers (among blacks as well as whites, by the way). But humanity has clad itself in skins and then textiles for at least 30,000 years, and in the past exposure to ultraviolet rays probably was not as clear a danger to a long life span as it is now, especially since the average life span would rarely have risen above thirty years for most people until within the past 2,000–3,000 years, and it generally takes a decade or even two for sun-damaged skin to turn cancerous.

Might it not be that the races of humanity evolved such a long time ago that it simply takes thousands and thousands of years for racial modifications to become noticeable? Nineteenth-century Darwinists might have speculated in those terms, but scientists today believe that what we perceive as race characteristics actually evolved quite recently: perhaps even within the last 10,000 years. And scientists also believe they know the bottom-line principle of racial development: not *natural selection,* but *sexual selection!* People usually choose their sexual partners from within the region where they grew up. (And you don't have to be a Freudian to speculate that we by and large choose sexual partners that look more or less like our parents looked when they were young, because that is simply the ideal we grew up with: We are "imprinted" on the way our parents looked when we first got to know them!) In those cases where the young individuals have no say in the matter, because the elders choose their future spouses for them (and historically, this tradition is far more widespread than the individual partner selections most of us consider normal), sexual selection becomes a matter of (1) tradition and (2) economy. Partners are most often chosen for the young from within the group of traditionally acceptable partners in order to make the marriage profitable for both families and provide a stable foundation for the next generation. In addition, tradition dictates what is supposed to be a sexual turn-on within a specific culture. There seems to be no survival advantage to the size and shape of buttocks and nipples and to the presence or absence of body hair, but it may matter a great deal to those looking for a spouse.

So the longer a population has lived with a region and the less contact it has had with other populations, the more pronounced the physical differences will be between that population and other groups. If the gene pool is very small, we might call it inbreeding, but with a large gene pool, we get healthy individuals shaped around a theme: the theme of the ideal person as determined by that population. And if sexual selection accounts for the beginning of the development of racial characteristics in separate regions, it also explains the continuation of such characteristics: Most people will prefer a sexual partner from within the group in which they grew up. This also means, of course, that if we have grown up in a racially mixed society or have moved a great deal when young, our ideal sexual partner may not be determined by a single so-called racial group.

Mississippi Masala, Samuel Goldwyn, 1992. Mina's family is from India, but she was born and raised in Africa. Demetrius and his family are African Americans, born and raised in the United States. Demetrius (Denzel Washington, far right) and Mina (Sarita Choudhury) fall in love, but experience the prejudices against interracial relationships of two families (his and hers) and three cultures (the Indian immigrant community, the black community, and the white community).

Indeed, the areas today where most mixed marriages and other partnerships occur are in the big cities with a diverse population; for those who look forward to a color-blind society, this may be the beginning: a social setting where a child learns to interact with people with diverse backgrounds, ethnically and racially (see Box 5.3 for a discussion of ethnicity), without attaching a social or a cultural hierarchy to the concept of race. However, we shouldn't forget that just because a region is viewed as multiracial doesn't mean that all its inhabitants regard each other as equals. In particular, a high-density, high-stress metropolis often develops a social hierarchy of classes or castes along racial lines. Our sexual selection is determined not just by the faces we see around us when we grow up, but also by the unwritten rules of social standing: who is a socially acceptable partner and who is "out of bounds." In other words, even today, sexual selection is often guided by tradition and economy! As countless real-life stories and stories of fiction have told us, the individuals who dare flout their family tradition in the selection of a sexual partner and reach out to someone from another group are in for a hard time socially. The film *Mississippi Masala* (1992) offers an interesting example: A young woman who was born and raised in Africa, but is ethnically from India, has moved to Mississippi with her family. Here she falls in love with a young black man, and racial misunderstandings and hostilities rise to the surface within the two families. You will find a synopsis in the Narratives section of this chapter.

Box 5.1   "CAUCASIAN": A WHITE SUPREMACIST TERM?

A student of Linnaeus's race theories, the biologist and founder of physical anthropology Johann Friedrich Blumenbach (1752–1840) is responsible for the racial term *Caucasian* in our language, and the explanation is not very scientific, according to Stephen Jay Gould. In "The Geometer of Race," Gould relates that Blumenbach was far from being a racist and indeed was a vocal admirer of black poets, authors, and scholars. He chose the term *Caucasian* for the white race because he believed white to be the original color of humans and believed that humanity originated in the Caucasus region. Furthermore, he also believed that people in the Caucasus region were the most *beautiful* of all human populations. Gould remarks that it is ironic that a scientist who was so "committed to human unity" and had such an appreciation for the cultural accomplishments of nonwhite populations, as well as a commitment to the view that all races were intellectually and morally equal, would give us a legacy of racial classification that has been a hindrance to common understanding and equality ever since.

From classifying Europeans as the most beautiful race, Blumenbach proceeded to classify the other races aesthetically, adding the race of the Malay to Linnaeus's scheme, thereby giving it a triangular, hierarchical ranking: whites at the top, on the sides in the intermediate position the American Indian and the Malay, and at the bottom Africans and Asians. So the term *Caucasian* is itself extremely racially loaded, and its use should be reconsidered, even aside from the fact that it is a clear misnomer: White people didn't originate in the Caucasus region, and neither did anyone else. If anything, Blumenbach is an odd precursor for a theory that was still on the horizon, to be expressed by Max Müller within another few decades: the idea that the origin of most European *languages* in all likelihood was somewhere in the Caucasus region (see chapter text). From here on, the connection to the Nazi theory of Aryan superiority is clear. As for the beauty of Caucasus natives, it is of course in the eye of the beholder.

The History of Race as a Concept

The Classifications of Linnaeus

As I mentioned earlier, the biologist Linnaeus (Carl von Linné) came up with the four racial categories in the mid-eighteenth century, and scientists and philosophers throughout the rest of the eighteenth century as well as the nineteenth century proceeded to use the classification as a moral hierarchy of perfection. As a matter of fact, Linnaeus had two extra categories aside from American Indian, African, Asian, and European: He also had the category of "ferus" or "wild boys," because, according to folklore, children would occasionally be found living in the woods, raised by animals (like Tarzan and Mowgli), and Linnaeus thought they formed a separate race of people. And then he included the race of "monstrosus" or monsters, meaning all the weird people travelers reported having seen,

such as giants and humans with tails. Science did away with the two last categories rather quickly. However, Linnaeus's other classification system remained standard until early-twentieth-century science relegated it to the realm of superstition: Linnaeus adopted the ancient and medieval theory that each person is dominated by one of four *humors* or body fluids—blood, phlegm, choler (yellow bile), and melancholy (black bile)—and expanded it to cover the four races. According to Linnaeus, the American Indian was choleric, meaning prone to anger; the European was sanguine; the Asian melancholy; and the African phlegmatic. (Box 5.1 explores the term *Caucasian,* an expression introduced by the biologist Johann Blumenbach after studying Linnaeus.)

Unlike later scientists, Linnaeus apparently didn't think of the human races as a hierarchy with the Europeans at the top; his classification was primarily geographical, not moral, although one might assume that Europeans thought it was better to be sanguine than choleric, melancholic, or phlegmatic.

The Changing Meanings of "Race"

Linnaeus may have contributed to making the term *race* into the term we are familiar with today, a classification of humanity according to skin coloration; however, the word *race* itself had undergone a number of changes before Linnaeus's time—and has undergone more since. According to the American philosopher Naomi Zack, for the ancient Greeks as well as for the Romans, the concept of race was synonymous with their ancestral family and locale. The Greeks are now viewed as having been quite ethnocentric, praising their own virtues and taking a dim view of all foreigners, but there appears to have been no targeting or specific exclusion of people based on their skin color or other physical features. In the Middle Ages the definition of the term had narrowed to meaning one's bloodline, or "breed." Through the sixteenth century in Europe the term was associated with cultures and geographical populations, but in the seventeenth century the idea of skin color became associated with the word *race*—apparently a contribution to the English language, by the English. In the centuries before the English expanded into other continents to establish colonies, they had developed a concept of race directed in particular toward their neighbors to the west: the Irish. To an Englishman of the Middle Ages all the way up into the seventeenth century, the Irish seemed so different that they were perceived as wild people, the quintessential "savage."[4] The worldview of the English traveling to the New World already held a cultural archetype: we, the civilized, versus them, the savages. In the meantime, the Spanish explorers arrived to the south with cultural traditions involving a hierarchy, resulting in a system of castes based on the purity of one's Spanish blood. Add to this the European confusion concerning the Jewish population: Should the Jews be regarded as a religious or a racial community?

While being Jewish is today regarded as a religious classification, not a racial or even an ethnic one, medieval Europe had determined that Jews formed a race unto themselves. And so the stage was set in the eighteenth-century Western mindset for a racial theory with political ramifications.

In Zack's words, race had come to mean "a distinct biological group of human beings who were not all members of the same family but who shared inherited physical and cultural traits that were different from those shared within other races." And the development of this concept was no coincidence; it had an instant, practical application as a means of classifying people for the purpose of *slavery.* According to current research, early American scientists put the concept of race as color together as an empirical justification for slavery (although we should add that the British, involved with colonial management of cultures throughout the world, had adapted the term *race* comfortably for their own expanded needs, classifying the darker races of the British Empire as inferior to the lighter races; colonial administrators elsewhere in Europe did likewise). A very practical reason for associating color and slavery was, according to some scholars of the American constitution, to create a loophole within the general concept of constitutional freedom for all humans. As we saw in Chapter 1, it has been common for people from one group to deem other groups not quite human if it has suited their political purpose, and this is a prime example: If you can point to some evidence that some people are not quite human, then the natural right to freedom and self-determination doesn't apply to these people. (The same happens with a classical wartime situation: To help soldiers get over their reluctance to kill other humans, they are persuaded that the enemy is not quite human, so that the command to not kill fellow human beings no longer applies.) So classifying black slaves as not quite human was a practical step toward justification of slavery, but there was another pragmatic reason.

According to Article I, section 2 of the Constitution, representatives to Congress are elected according to the size of the population in their state. Before the Civil War, census takers would count five slaves as three "persons" (not one slave as three-fifths of a person, as is sometimes claimed); however, it still meant that one slave did not count as one person. American Indians who were taxed counted in census taking, but Indians who weren't taxed didn't have political status at all. (Box 5.2 explores current issues of race among American Indians.)

Charles Darwin, with no apparent agenda for supporting slavery or perpetuating a theory of racial superiority or inferiority, nevertheless chimed in in the late nineteenth century with speculations about race, and some of them have now been disproved (although this doesn't mean that his general theory of natural selection has been placed in doubt). Darwin devotes an entire chapter of *The Descent of Man* to the issue of race. For Darwin, the classification of humans into races is obvious but, nevertheless, a hopeless task, since so many different features within each race need to be classified. Not only the obvious physical features, but also differences "in constitution, in acclimatization and in liability to certain diseases" must be taken into consideration—and so must mental differences: "Their mental characteristics are likewise very distinct; chiefly as it would appear in their emotional, but partly in their intellectual faculties. Every one who has had the opportunity of comparison, must have been struck with the contrast between the taciturn, even morose, aborigines of S. America and the light-hearted, talkative Negroes."[5] For Darwin it is even a question whether people of different races might not belong to *different human species*. He weighs the pros and the cons of such a theory: According to his information (which has been amply disproved since then), the offspring of two people of different races is likely to be sickly with low vitality and may not even be fertile, like a mule or a liger (a cross between a lion and a tiger). Fertility in the offspring of two individuals of different races/ breeds is usually considered proof that they are of the same species—but Darwin hedges his state-

ment: Even if such fertility should be disproved, one shouldn't automatically equate infertility with a species' distinctness because many other factors can come into play. And toward the end of his discussion, Darwin concludes that it is most likely that the different races *don't* constitute different species: Scientists in Darwin's own time classified the number of races as anything from two to sixty-three, so even then there was no clear consensus on the issue. Darwin read this to mean that the lines between races are blurred, graduate into one another, and probably show the capacity for interbreeding.

And how about the possibility that the human races have *different ancestors?* Darwin here anticipates the "multiregional continuity" theory we discussed in Chapter 2: Could humanity have evolved simultaneously from several different kinds of hominids? As we saw in Chapter 2, this theory lends itself, politically, to racial segregation and theories of racial superiority. Darwin rejects the idea, on purely physical grounds: If we were descended from different species of hominids, those differences could be traced in our bone structure, and the races would be far more diverse than they are. So for Darwin the result is clear: We are all closely related as a human species, even with what he thought were profound racial differences. He was "deeply impressed with the close similarity between the men of all races in tastes, dispositions and habits. This is shown by the pleasure which they all take in dancing, rude music, acting, painting, tattooing, and otherwise decorating themselves; in their mutual comprehension of gesture-language, by the same expression in their features, and in the same inarticulate cries, when excited by the same emotions."[6] And here Darwin switches from calling it "similarity" and calls this phenomenon "identity." (Whether he was also including the inner nature of a famous British nineteenth-century biologist remains an open question!)

Up until the turn of the twentieth century, scientists were involved in theories about *racial essences,* speculations that each race possessed an

Box 5.2   ARE YOU AN AMERICAN INDIAN?

When attention is focused on race discrimination in this country, it is often assumed to be a white-and-black issue. In the chapter text we take a closer look at the phenomenon of racism, but for now suffice it to say that, of course, many other population groups have also suffered deeply from racial discrimination—in particular, American Indians.* This is a reality acutely felt by Indians of today, because the massive institutional discrimination of the nineteenth and early-twentieth centuries has been very slow in receding, with less attention given to it than to the plight of African Americans. On the basis of this historical phenomenon, it is downright curious to many American Indians that a great number of people outside of the tribal reservations today claim Indian ancestry—more than one might have predicted based on previous census demographics. What we are seeing is a shift in cultural consciousness: In earlier times, Indian ancestry was considered to be a negative factor; however, today many people like the idea of Indian blood running in their veins. A great-great-grandmother with Indian blood is now proudly counted as an ancestor by many people outside of the tribal reservations, because the American Indian has become a *cultural icon,* a kind of American mascot. From ball clubs to place names, Indian references are common—a phenomenon that may seem innocent enough to most non-Indians, but is deeply offensive to many people of Indian descent. Many schools, ball clubs, and city councils are today changing their club and place names with Indian connotations to other, less controversial names. Many Indians do not welcome the popularity of American Indian culture—from Indian jewelry to Indian religious traditions—among non-Indians today; in fact, they view it as the ultimate cultural insult: a wholesale robbery, not only of the land, but finally of the spirit of the People as well.

A recent consequence of the popularity of being an Indian, combined with the fact that very little of this popularity has resulted in improved conditions on the impoverished reservations, has been a radical move among Indian leaders to limit the legitimate identification of who is, and who is not, an Indian. In a process eerily reminiscent of the old racial rules regarding who was to be counted as black, and who as white, the Flathead, Catawba, Paiute, and Tigua tribes have now set up rules of blood quantum to determine who has the right to call himself or herself an Indian. The full-bloods are getting old, and there are few of them left, so many Indians argue that being Indian is a cultural identification—in other words an *ethnicity,* rather than a matter of bloodlines—for otherwise there may soon be no more Indians. But some tribal elders believe that it is necessary to enforce bloodline rules, based on hundred-year-old tribal lists, because otherwise the tribes will be forced to welcome people whose only affiliation to the tribe is distant ancestry and a modern romantic wish to be an Indian—people who, according to the full-bloods, haven't paid the "emotional toll" paid by their full-blooded relatives, as an article in the *Los Angeles Times* put it. The Indian communities feel themselves split by this debate—one that is tragic and ironic at the same time. For blacks as well as for whites, blood classifications, such as quadroons and octoroons, are a thing of the past; and in the eighteenth and nineteenth centuries, Indian tribes adopted both children and adult white settlers (sometimes through less-than-voluntary abduction). These people generally became full members of the tribe, because tribal affiliations were then regarded by American Indians as a matter of cultural, not racial, identity.

---

*I tend to use the term *American Indian* instead of *Native American* at the advice of American Indian activist Russell Means, in whose view *Native American* is a political term, and too broad to use in a discussion about the indigenous tribes of this country.

essence that ought not to be mixed because, if mixed, the "inferior" essence would prevail over the "superior" essence; hence the disdain for chil-

dren of racially mixed couples. Terms such as "pollution" and "miscegenation" were used to show contempt for couples where the woman was of the

Box 5.3   RACE VS. ETHNICITY

The term *ethnicity* is often used interchangeably with *race*—perhaps because people feel on safer ground referring to someone's "ethnicity" rather than to the politically and emotionally volatile word *race*. However, *ethnicity* is historically a different term than *race*. A reference to ethnicity is a reference to one's *cultural affiliation* with a certain population. This means that certain cultural traits, such as language, marriage customs, religion, and so forth are shared within the group. In other words, you can have ethnic traditions regarding food, clothing, and kinship regulations, but not racial traditions for food, clothing, and so forth. We have already seen in the text that a reference to race can be many things, but it cannot be reduced to a reference to one's cultural group. As the philosophers Stephen Cornell and Douglass Hartmann say, one's ethnic identity is determined by oneself *and* others, while one's race is determined *exclusively* by others. In other words, we are the coauthors of our ethnic affiliation, but not of our racial affiliation. In addition, as Mary C. Waters suggests in her paper, "Optional Ethnicities: For Whites Only," the perceived freedom to include or exclude parts of one's ethnic history is mainly available to whites; for many whites it is a matter of choosing which ethnicity one wishes to *include* in one's personal history. For many nonwhites, says Waters, the experience is quite different: The ethnicity or ethnicities in one's life are (or have been, in the past) to a great extent a result of *exclusion* from white, privileged groups. It is a fairly new phenomenon that nonwhite ethnicities are being perceived as attractive and even romantic by whites as well as nonwhites. (See Box 5.2 about the American Indian issue.)

---

white, "superior" race, and the man of a nonwhite race. (In cases where a white man was sexually associated with a woman of color, nineteenth-century white society only had mild disdain, because only a white woman could be polluted by a mixed union, not a white man whose superior "essence" would dominate the woman of color.) However, with the advances of psychology and sociology in the early twentieth century the theory of "essences" gave way to an understanding of the effects of *nurture* rather than of *nature;* and, according to Zack, race took on the meaning of strictly biological differences. However, we shouldn't overlook the fact that many people today don't distinguish between *race* and *ethnicity,* and the concept of cultural differences that are somehow bonded to biological differences has crept back into the equation. (Box 5.3 looks at the distinction between race and ethnicity.)

Another twentieth-century change is the political concept of *La Raza,* taken on as the term of identity by many Americans with blood ties to the Mexican culture. In this case, the term *race* has come to mean "our race," a political term rather than a biological one, associated with the hardships and oppression suffered by people of Mexican descent.

Some Remarks on Race by Three Enlightenment Philosophers

Most of us who have been introduced to the eighteenth century as the Age of Reason, or the Enlightenment, have the impression of an energetic flourishing of humanitarian concepts that have come to define our present-day political ideals of equality and freedom. For that reason, many are surprised to find out not only that the eighteenth century was not particularly rational or enlightened (the term refers to scholars, artists, and political thinkers, not to the general population), but also that the scholars, artists and political thinkers themselves weren't necessarily highly enlightened or rational by our standards today. Here we shall take a look at thoughts on race by three philosophers who otherwise are well known for their legacy of concepts of freedom and equality. (In the next chapter we take a look at views on *gender* from the same time period, in many ways a parallel phenomenon.) What their writings reveal is that these thinkers did have strong words and feelings for human freedom, but not necessarily for universal human equality.

Jean-Jacques Rousseau (1712–1778)   The Swiss philosopher whom we shall meet in two other chapters (Chapter 6 and Chapter 9) was one of the first thinkers to speculate about the cultural evolution of humanity from a time when humans had yet to develop language. Never one to be concerned with the religious assumptions of his day— which would be that humans came to this earth thanks to God's creation, with a ready-made language—Rousseau speculated in his essay *On the Origin of Languages* that emotion-based gestures and vocalization through *singing* predated the use of words. Rousseau's form of research generally consisted in thinking; in other words, sociological-historical research had yet to be developed, and it was considered completely legitimate for a social philosopher of the eighteenth century to develop his (or her) theories strictly on the basis of speculation. Rousseau thus didn't have any hard evidence for his social history and wasn't much concerned with acquiring it. As we shall see in Chapter 9, his goal was the development of a political blueprint for society rather than a history lesson. So when Rousseau claims that human intelligence evolves under conditions of hardship, he is not using empirical, or *inductive,* thinking but *deductive* thinking, deducing a conclusion logically from a set of premises. And the foundational idea for Rousseau is that intelligence only arises under challenging conditions; if humanity had had an easy life eating fruits and berries all year round, we would never have developed into the intelligent beings we are.

Paradoxically, for Rousseau, intelligence isn't always a positive feature in human life; as a matter of fact he prefers the idea of human beings as nature created us, content with a simple natural life. For Rousseau, intelligence arises out of necessity (the mother of invention, in other words), and with intelligence comes our problem-solving

capacity, but also all the evils of civilization. And the racial connection? Rousseau believes that the harsher the climate (such as in northern Europe), the more intelligence has evolved. He has no doubt that the French are the most intelligent peoples of all, despite the fact that winters get much harsher farther north! (As a Scandinavian, I just had to point that out.) This also means that as pleasant as southern European populations may be, they are just not as intelligent as their northern cousins; and once we move farther south to the Arab and African countries, we have far less intelligence; but we also have more ingenuous peoples, friendlier, closer to nature, and less inclined toward the plotting and scheming of the Europeans.

This prejudice against a southern climate as less conducive to any thinking activity is widespread to this day. A Rousseau-type theory has been advanced by psychologist Richard Lynn, who argues that IQs differ in ethnic populations around the world, based on their exposure to hot and cold climates; another psychologist, J. Phillipe Rushton, sees different survival challenges in cold and hot climates as fundamentally determining a whole range of racial differences from brain size to parenting to social organization, putting cold-climate people at the top of the hierarchy and hot-climate people at the bottom. In a turning of the tables, Leonard Jeffries, professor at City College of New York suggested in the 1990s that the presence of melanin in the skin, presumably developed to protect the skin from the ultraviolet rays of the sun, serves as an intelligence-enhancer; thus, the more melanin, the more intelligent the race. Sometimes labeled "environmentalism" for the underlying assumption that the environment determines all or part of a group's capabilities, these forms of racial theory are rarely accepted or welcomed by today's scholars, no matter their background. However, such assumptions still thrive on the anecdotal level: There is still a noticeable contempt among people living in areas with "seasons" for the presumed lack of intellectual life among people in more benign climates. Living in Southern California, I can attest that this prejudice is alive and well in America as well as in Europe. When I moved here years ago, a colleague at the University of Copenhagen asked me how I'd ever expect to get any work done, with all the nice weather?

David Hume (1711–1776)   Hume was a friend of Rousseau's, for a while, until Rousseau's paranoid tendencies put an end to their friendship. Hume, a British philosopher with a Scottish background, is a well-known name in Enlightenment philosophy: Perhaps no other thinker has exhibited a more radical skepticism toward the assumptions most of us hold about the world and about reality. In Chapter 7 you will encounter the concept of empiricism, the philosophy that all knowledge derives from experience: Everything a human being knows, thinks, and feels, comes from something he or she has experienced; no knowledge is innate. David Hume was not only an empiricist, but also used empiricism to show that some of the things we automatically believe about reality have no foundation in our experience—and as such can't be claimed as true. An example is the relationship between cause and effect: We think we experience things causing other things on a regular basis—but do we really? No, says Hume. All we experience is one thing happening *right after* another thing. We don't *experience* one thing *causing* another thing—that is a conclusion our mind jumps to. So can't we say that we cause the light to go on by flicking the switch, and we cause the water to boil by putting it on the stove? Yes, we can, as long as we remember that we can't actually observe and experience the "cause." All we can really say is that we see one thing happen after the other every time we flick the switch and put the kettle on, but there is no guarantee that it will always happen! And so it is all the more surprising that this profound skeptic, in an early essay, jumps to conclusions about observations that are, to most present-day readers, obviously biased and affected by hasty assumptions.

In his essay from 1754, "Of National Characters," Hume speculates that the theory of a connection between climate and intelligence is probably wrong; Hume sees a great similarity between all human beings because of our ability to imitate each other and be flexible. It seems that he is about to conclude that humans are more similar than we are different; and yet, in a footnote (now considered infamous), Hume states, "I am apt to suspect the negroes and in general all other species of men (for there are four or five different kinds) to be naturally inferior to the whites. There never was a civilized nation of any other complexion than white, nor even any individual eminent either in action or speculation. No ingenious manufacturers amongst them, no arts, no sciences. On the other hand, the most rude and barbarous of the whites, such as the ancient Germans, the present Tartars, have still something eminent about them, in their valor, form of government, or some other particular."[7]

In case you think that all Enlightenment scholars just happened to think alike on the issue of race, this was not the case. Hume was taken to task by James Beattie in 1770, when Hume had, justifiably, achieved great fame and respect among the British intelligentsia for his theory of knowledge. Beattie points out that it is easy enough to make disparaging generalizations if all you know of a population is how they have behaved when oppressed and deprived of rights. Hume must have taken this to heart to some degree, because he ordered a slight revision of his text in 1776, right before his death, to read "There *scarcely ever* was a civilized nation of that complexion" [italics added].

Immanuel Kant (1724–1804)   Kant may well deserve being called the most influential philosopher in modern times. His book on our capacity for knowledge, *Critique of Pure Reason,* is still considered a valid challenge to our concept of human intelligence and experience; his views on rights and justice have deeply affected the debate in Europe as well as in the United States; and his theories of ethics are among the most influential ever proposed. Interestingly, he credited Hume with having made a philosopher out of him; they never met, but Kant found Hume's theory that we can't prove the connection between cause and effect to be so disturbing that this spurred him into seeking—and suggesting—a solution to the problem.[8] But perhaps most of all, his view that *any thinking being should never be treated merely as a means to an end,* as a stepping-stone for others' purposes, has had far-reaching consequences, eventually contributing to our modern concept of human rights (see Chapter 10). At a time when Europe was still divided between those with political power and those without rights (women, servants, children, serfs), Kant unequivocally stated that *all of humanity* ought to be treated as ends-in-themselves (persons with the right to be treated with respect and dignity), not merely as a means to an end. This is a vitally important legacy for which Kant should rightfully be remembered.

However, Kant's own record of viewing all of humanity as morally and politically *equal* was dismal: In works from 1764 (*Observations on the Feeling of the Beautiful and the Sublime*) and 1775 ("On the Different Races of Man"), Kant put together a theory of races that drew from Linneaus, Blumenbach, and Hume himself. In these works we encounter racial and ethnic stereotypes such as "The Spaniard is earnest, taciturn, and truthful," "The Frenchman . . . is gracious, courteous, and complaisant," "The Englishman is cool in the beginning of every acquaintance, and indifferent toward a stranger," "The Indians [of India] have a dominating taste of the grotesque, of the sort that falls into the adventurous," "The Negroes of Africa have by nature no feeling that rises above the trifling" but are "so talkative that they must be driven apart from each other with thrashings."[9] However, Kant had a qualified respect for the North American Indians: "They have a strong feeling for honor, and as in quest of it they seek wild adventures hundred of miles abroad" (as an aside, Kant seems never to have traveled anywhere). And how did Kant feel about the Germans, his own people? "The German has a feeling mixed from that of an Englishman and that of a Frenchman. . . . In love, just as in all forms of taste, he is reasonably methodical, and because he combines the beautiful with the noble he is cool enough in each feeling to occupy his mind with reflections upon de-

meanor, splendor, and appearances. . . . Far more than the aforementioned nationalities, he asks how people might *judge him.*" This was to Kant a qualified praise; he felt that Germans ought to be less concerned with what others thought of them, so as to be able to fully employ their talents.

In terms of racial classification, Kant diverges from Linnaeus in a way that science has later supported; Kant was interested in science and believed himself to be at the cutting edge of scientific reporting. He stays within a classification of four races, but they are Europeans, Africans, Asians, and people from India. What happened to American Indians? Kant classifies them as Asians who have migrated—a theory that now prevails, because of the "land bridge" theory, the view that migration from the Asian continent by early American Indians was made possible by a land bridge connecting Siberia and Alaska. So, in this respect, Kant anticipated scientific conclusions by more than a century; however, his method of classifying races by personal characteristics manifests itself even here. He believes that Asian people have the temper of a cold-region population, and so too does the American Indian, "which temperament betrays a half-extinguished body-force, which can most naturally be looked upon as the effect of a cold world-region." Kant has here fallen for the eighteenth-century myth of the "inscrutable Indian," as Darwin himself did a hundred years later. Kant's "environmentalism" focuses specifically on the phenomenon of heat and the lack of it: He explains the existence of black skin as a result of the skin "drying up," like cookies in an oven; on the other hand, he doesn't see any reason to explain white skin, because he, like most other thinkers of his time, considers it the norm against which other races are supposed to be measured.

With this barrage of stereotypes and statements we today would call racist, it is easy to lose sight of Kant's actual legacy of identifying human rights as something each human deserves simply by virtue of being human. However, it is also wise to see Kant's own writings in perspective: His views of the different races stem from an early part of his life as a scholar, while his development of moral theories concerning human rights is decades into the future, beginning in 1785. In 1764 when he wrote some of his race theories, he hadn't yet been hired as a full professor. (However, as late as 1785 he was engaged in arguing against another German philosopher, Johann Gottfried von Herder, who disapproved of classifying humanity according to skin color.) Be that as it may, it is not Kant's writings on race, but his writings on epistemology (theory of knowledge), rights, and ethics that became influential. In that respect we are fortunate that the legacy we have garnered from Kant's works is a timeless assertion of human rights and dignity, rather than a collection of outdated views on race and geography.

At this point I would like to interject a comment, resulting from many a debate in my classes: Should we, in today's race-sensitive climate, focus on these shortcomings among scholars of the past, instead of on their traditionally acknowledged accomplishments? I'd like to think that we can do both; the fact remains that many of them were champions of freedom, in a relative sense, for their time period. They opened up the gates for the political freedom that all humanity today is supposed to be able to enjoy, and the fact that they themselves showed signs of stereotypical thinking and bigotry shouldn't detract from that legacy. Nonetheless, it would be short-sighted of us to refuse to recognize that according to today's standards, their enlightenment only went so far. And it might also serve as a reminder that as enlightened as we think *we* are, we may have some blind spot, some sensitivity issue that only a later age will be fully capable of noticing. We might prefer to be judged in the context of our own time period and our accomplishments within it, rather than be judged on the basis of the social ideals and values of a future we can't foresee.

Philosophy of Race Today

The Biology of Race: Current Theories

We've seen that the nineteenth-century interest in race theory focused primarily on the scientifi-

cally unfounded idea of "essences" and other attempts at classifying the races according to their perceived differences—attempts that seem mostly naïve and offensive to a modern reader. This trend continued into the mid–twentieth century, but by the end of the nineteenth century the German-born American anthropologist Franz Boas was already arguing that race has no biological foundation. His views, shared by his student Ruth Benedict, formed the basis for the anthropological school of relativism, claiming that the differences between the races are small compared to the wide variety of differences within each race and that nurture is the key factor in cultural development rather than nature.

After World War II ended in 1945, many people within the European scientific community experienced a reluctance to engage in biological race research, because of the enormous tragedy of the Holocaust. Scientists as well as laypeople had realized, perhaps for the first time, how immense the consequences of abstract theories may become, and many European scientists focused their attention elsewhere because of the perception that scientific race theories might be used for political purposes. However, research continued in the United States, with psychological and sociological studies about race undertaken from a social and cultural viewpoint.

Today most people are acutely aware that any theory of biological race (or gender) differences can be used politically—with discrimination as a potential result. The movie titled *White Men Can't Jump* (1992) caused a stir precisely for this reason: The implication that there may be minute racial biological differences borders so closely on stereotypes used as weapons of discrimination that any research into the biology of race must be prepared to address the issue of the potential link between a statement of biology and a statement of cultural stereotype.

An attempt at explaining social issues through a new scientific theory of race was set forth in a highly controversial book, *The Bell Curve* (1996), by Charles Murray and Richard J. Herrnstein. *The Bell Curve* proposed a connection between success, intelligence, and genetics. Among other examples it explored the question of the lower academic success rate among African Americans and implied that the lower success rate is partly genetically determined—although the authors warn against discrimination as a consequence of such a scientific conclusion. However, to innumerable readers, this was the same as claiming that African Americans just weren't as smart as other groups, such as Asians and people of European descent. The book inspired an avalanche of critical works responding to the theory with a variety of approaches—from objectively examining the issue to downright calling it a bunch of lies. Critics instantly pointed out that while the statistics of *The Bell Curve* may have been accurate, the authors did nothing to research and explain the underlying social factors that affect intellectual and moral development behind the statistics: Was the "playing field" truly "level" between African American and white students? Did everyone have an equal social opportunity to succeed? Did the cultural background of different ethnic groups prepare students in similar ways for the specific demands of a traditional academic environment? In other words, statistics don't exist in a vacuum, and a study can't call itself scientific when it excludes or overlooks the entire issue of traditional social privilege. For many critics, *The Bell Curve* represented a throwback to nineteenth-century racial research based on unquestioned stereotyping of population groups, and an opportunity to truly address the issue of varying academic success rates among American populations in the late twentieth century was sidetracked.

Much of the current research into the biological basis of race attempts to steer clear of the social and political implications that *The Bell Curve* tried to address. And when viewed as a strictly biological study, the race research has yielded results that are highly surprising to many people, although Franz Boas had pointed the way over a hundred years ago. The bottom line for most physical anthropologists today is that, biologically speaking, *there is no such thing as race*. This seems to fly in the face of common sense, but the four racial groups identified by scientists of centuries past don't hold up any longer, and it isn't just because people have interbred. Racial traits that were thought to belong to one group exclusively turn up in populations that don't share other racial traits: The epicanthic eye folds typical in some Asian populations also turn up in the South African population of Khoisan people (formerly called Bushmen). Many Swedes have a certain type of incisor teeth that are typical for Asians, but they don't share most other racial characteristics. Australian aborigines are mostly dark-skinned, but they are only distantly related to Africans. And many American Indians share the epicanthic folds with Asians, but they generally have a different blood type. The best argument for race being a cultural rather than a biological concept is the fact that there is no genetic marker other than phenotypic characteristics (visual characteristics most members of a group have in common), which, themselves, vary within population groups: *No "racial gene" has been found.* You can identify through DNA a person's affiliation to some regional group if that group has been isolated from the rest of the world long enough, but it doesn't mean that all racial groups have such DNA markers. The so-called racial traits of skin color, hair texture, and the like vary more within the racial groups than between two racial groups.[10] According to Naomi Zack, who identifies herself as a person of mixed race, *race is an exclusively cultural concept:*

> Race, as something general about a person or a group, is a social overlay on actual physical traits. This is not to deny that people perceive what they think are racial traits or that race has a powerful social reality. But it means that what we think of as race is solely a matter of convention and imagination. We follow a convention of imagining the existence of races and sorting people in to these imaginary categories. Once this realization of the imaginary nature of race sinks in, the human differences that are attributed

Box 5.4   DIFFERENT OPTIONS FOR RACIAL CLASSIFICATIONS

Researchers point out that while we are used to classifying people according to their geographical location and their physical characteristics, there are many other ways one might choose to define race. An overview in a special issue of *Discover* magazine (November 1994) on the topic of race lists these possibilities among many others: (1) A classification of race by *resistance to diseases*. The gene for sickle-cell anemia offers resistance to malaria: In that case, Yemenites, Greeks, New Guineans, Thai, and Dinkas are of the same race, but Norwegians belong with several black African populations in another race. (2) A classification of race by *digestion*. Those peoples who can digest milk could be said to belong to one race, which would include northern and central Europeans, Arabs, and some West African peoples. The "lactase-negative" (or lactose-intolerant) race would include other African blacks, east Asians, American Indians, southern Europeans, and Australian aborigines. And the many Americans today who find out they are lactose-intolerant, while other members of their family may be lactase-positive, would then find themselves to be of a different race than some of their blood relatives! (3) A classification according to *fingerprints*. Certain basic features in the swirls of fingerprints vary along three types: The "Loops" race would include most Europeans, black Africans, and east Asians. The "Whorls" race would include Mongolians and Australian aborigines. And the "Arches" race would include the Khosians and some central Europeans.

to race have to be explained and understood in other terms.[11]

Researchers who believe that race is more than a social reality point to a fact of medical science: We now know that different races have a genetic susceptibility to certain diseases; and if that is the case, surely races must be biologically real? Black men have a 40 percent higher risk of developing lung cancer than white men. People of European ancestry have a tendency toward ulcers, but they also seem to have some protection against cholera. African Americans have a high occurrence of sickle-cell anemia in their population, but they also seem to have a genetic protection against malaria. (See Box 5.4, which explores possible racial classifications.) American Indians tend to carry an enzyme that makes them vulnerable to alcoholism. Blacks are more likely than whites to suffer from high blood pressure, and so forth. Doesn't this point to the biological existence of races? Not necessarily, because, as in the case of *The Bell Curve,* the question *Why?* hasn't been asked sufficiently. There might be social reasons—dietary habits formed under poverty conditions, for example, or stress due to social inequality—for some of these susceptibilities. And looking around the world, there are no easy matches for the medical race theory: Africans don't share a susceptibility to high blood pressure with African Americans, but Finns and Russians do. In light of the current disagreement among researchers as to the biological reality of race (although nobody would claim that race has no *social* reality), it is probably safe to conclude that researchers seek support for the theory they hope is true: The "color-blind" researchers will deny the biological reality of race, while the "racial identity" researchers will affirm it as an intuitively given, obvious truth. In other words, we tell the "story" of the human races selectively, conforming to what we would like reality to be like and reflecting our view of whether race identity matters.

The Social Reality of Race and Racism

While today's biologists have announced that they see no evidence to support a biological theory of race, there is no denying that race is a social and political reality, around the world as well as in the United States. In the words of Audrey Smedley, "Race is a social principle by which society allocates desired rewards and status."[12] And according to Ruth Frankenberg, "Once a person is in a landscape structured by racism, a conceptual mapping of race, or self and others, takes shape, following from and feeding the physical context."[13] Many forms of reality are created by humans, not by nature, and the social reality of race is one of them.

With the consciousness of race comes, apparently inevitably, a consciousness of social differences. Small children in school or at the playground seem to have little conception or interest in each other's races, but the notion of race identity generally comes into the picture when the child grows older, and her or his community is racially mixed. With that consciousness come notions about groups and classes of racially different community members. Does this recognition of racial difference happen spontaneously, or is it a matter of outside influence—from parents, the school, the media, and so forth? The film *American History X* (see Narratives section) speculates that it is primarily a matter of influence from authority figures. This may be the key to some of the racial experiences in American culture, but students from around the world tell me about their own childhood experiences in racially mixed societies such as Jamaica and Brazil, where a person's race (according to my students) is more an individual issue than a matter of group affiliation. At the end of this chapter, for the sake of clarification, I have included a personal account of my own background and experience.

Granted that the notion of racial difference is a given in this culture, does that automatically entail a hierarchy of races—racial discrimination? In other words, can there be racial awareness without racism? In the previous section you read remarks from some eighteenth-century scholars about race, and I assume that you, as well as I, find some of their views to be racist and, as such,

unacceptable to a modern reader when viewed in a modern context. But what exactly is racism? Today, an accusation of racism is one of the easiest ways to discredit someone, and it is one of the hardest for a person to recover from, because the accusation itself is often taken to be the same as evidence for the accusation. The old adage "Where there's smoke, there's fire" perfectly describes the way many people react when someone is accused of racism, but many people are now discovering that accusations of racism really refer to bigotry or a divergence of viewpoints. The overuse of the word *racist* actually undermines our ability to apply it to someone who really deserves the name.

Suppose you believe that there are racial biological differences—fundamental or superficial—but you don't think such differences should lead to any form of discrimination or preferential treatment? Are you then a racist? No, says Naomi Zack: You are a *racialist*. While many see racism and racialism as synonymous, Zack and many others today believe there is an important difference: Racialists believe in the reality of biological racial differences but don't become racists unless they believe in the superiority of one race (usually their own), and believe that these differences should lead to a difference in treatment of individuals and political discrimination based on race. So *a racialist sees racial differences descriptively, while a racist sees them normatively,* with a system of discrimination as a consequence. According to Zack, a nonracist racialist could believe that black people are good at sports and that Asians are better at math than white people, but doesn't believe that any moral superiority follows from such characteristics. As we have seen, racial characteristics are in themselves hard to determine biologically across the board, so Zack doesn't believe a racialist has any factual foundation for her or his views other than cultural stereotypes, but she doesn't think such a view necessarily translates into a view of racial superiority. However, realistically, it is common for someone who is a racialist but not an overt racist to operate within some form of hi-

Box 5.5   "SOME OF MY BEST FRIENDS ARE . . ."

What if someone accuses you of racism (and let's assume you don't think you are a racist), and you point to the fact that you have a lot of good friends from all races as proof that you are not a racist? Then the standard reply is, "Oh, that's just the old 'Some of my best friends are . . .' defense!" The implication is that a racist would use the argument that he or she has friends of other races to combat the accusation of racism and that somehow that argument isn't considered valid. But this is a historical misunderstanding! Indeed, what better way to show that one is not a racist than to show that one's friends who are identified as being of other races don't think of one as a racist? The critics of the argument confuse it with the completely different statement put forth by a person with genuine racist animosities who says, "Some of my best friends are ——— *but even so I say that* ——— are [stupid, unreliable, cruel, or what-

ever the racial stereotype may be]." This is the original argument that is so often mistaken for the completely legitimate "I have friends who are ———." What makes the original argument offensive is precisely that it uses individual "friendships" as a cover for demeaning and dehumanizing a population as a group. But simply pointing to the fact that one associates with people from other races *is* a legitimate support for one's nonracist attitude. In addition, it is often assumed that the "Some of my best friends are . . ." argument is always spoken by a white person—and one with a problem with other races, at that. But in the preface to his controversial book, *The End of Racism,* Indian American scholar Dinesh D'Souza assures us—with a keen sense of cultural irony—that some of his best friends are white.

erarchy of "us and them," even if it is subconscious. So perhaps we can say in all fairness that theoretically it is possible to be a racialist without being a racist, but the belief in biological racial differences will often slide into a belief that people of different color should be treated differently, and from there on it is a short step to racism. (For an argument in defense of oneself as a nonracist, see Box 5.5.)

A racist, according to Zack, is "someone who has ill will toward other races and expresses that ill will in speech and action, through racial slurs, insults based on race, unfair behavior based on race and unprovoked violent behavior based on the race of victims."[14] This *classic racism,* as Zack calls it, is conscious and deliberate and advocates harming people of other races. Some racists may not express their feelings (and are then *covert racists*), while others express it, and are *overt racists.*[15] Most nonracists view racism as a moral failing, but opinions differ on what to do about it. If we assume racists are simply ignorant of the

facts, we can educate them about offensive stereotypes and the emotional harm they cause, and hope we eliminate their racism that way. We can also give racists psychological evaluations, under the assumption that there must be something wrong with their minds, since they have such views, and therapy is needed to undo their racism. (Box 5.5 for a criticized and misunderstood rebuttal to racism.)

However, there is a political issue lurking here: Because as much as most of us would like to eliminate racist speech and thought, we do live in a country with freedom of speech and of the press. Racist *actions* can be legislated against, and *hate crimes* are the focus of much attention in the press and among legislators today, but *hate speech* runs into the First Amendment issue. Constitutionally, people have the right to say whatever they want about each other, as long as they don't take hostile action against others and as long as their words aren't libelous. By implication, we can of course *think* and *feel* about others any way we like. Society can certainly try to change a form of behavior through education, but speech control is unconstitutional—and thought control would be too. The University of California at Berkeley recently abandoned its policy against hate speech on campus because of the overriding philosophy that on a campus, dissenting ideas should be expressed without moral censorship.

In September 2000, a jury in Coeur d'Alene, Idaho, awarded more than $6 million in damages to a woman and her son, both of mixed white and American Indian ancestry, who had been assaulted by neo-Nazi security guards at the Aryan Nations compound at Hayden Lake; the judgment forced the group's leader, Richard Butler, to give up his property to the plaintiffs. They sold it, and in May 2001 it was demolished by the new owner. While the verdict made it clear that Butler was ultimately responsible for the actions of his security guards, and many people in Idaho rejoiced over being able to put a distance between themselves and much of the "guilt by association" they had suffered because of neo-Nazis in the region, there was disagreement over the amount awarded. The plaintiffs' lawyer has asked the court for an award of $11 million, but some community members thought the award should have been even higher, to make a statement against the doctrine of white supremacy. Others felt that while the Aryan Nation should have to pay damages, its members also have a constitutional right to their opinion and should have been punished for the assault, but not for being Nazis. You may want to discuss the issue: Should our First Amendment (which assures freedom of the press and of assembly) protect the right of anyone to hold and voice an opinion, no matter how repugnant, as long as no action is taken to harm others, or should there be circumstances where such opinions are considered so volatile that they are dangerous to the community and should be outlawed?

As it is, there are situational limitations to our freedom of speech: For example, we are not allowed to yell "Fire!" in a crowded theater (except, of course, if there really is a fire). Airports have banned jokes and other references to bombs and guns for the sake of public safety. Should hate speech be viewed as the same type of statement? And how can we even apply the same distinction? In other words, sometimes it *is* appropriate to yell "Fire!" Is there ever an appropriate use of hate speech? Some would say that hate speech is never appropriate when coming from a member of a dominant group—but if a member of a disenfranchised group uses hate speech as a form of self-defense, it can be acceptable. Others would say that no matter who is speaking, hate speech is inappropriate. See Box 5.6 for a discussion of whether racism is a universal phenomenon or primarily a white-against-black phenomenon.

In addition to classic racism, there are other forms. First, *unintentional racism:* An unintentional racist may use a term that is considered a slur by a person of another race without intending any offense. Information and education are usually enough to resolve the issue. Some years ago, a young Jewish male student was accused of racism for having called some young black women in his dorm by a term they considered to be racist. He denied that the term had a racist content, but agreed that it was indeed intended to offend them; the term was apparently used as a mildly offensive term in his family (the term was "water buffalo"). So in this case, the perception of the young man as a racist (albeit unintentionally) depends on the young women's interpretation of the situation. However, many terms have a more familiar racist ring to them and so a judgment of racism would not depend on the interpretation of the intended victim alone. Another example of unintentional racism would be crossing the street to avoid someone assumed to be of another race out of fear; the motive is personal safety rather than an intent to offend, but the other person may view the action as offensive. A student of mine provided a very good example of this phenomenon and a possible solution to the issue: He was a very tall, black student with dreadlocks and told the class that female students of other races deliberately avoided him on campus. In the beginning he felt highly offended, he said, because he considered himself a very

Box 5.6   RACISM: UNIVERSAL, OR WHITE AGAINST BLACK?

Is racism an attitude that can be found in many—perhaps all—racial groups, or is it primarily harbored by the white population? The answers to this question in itself tend to further the divisions between racial groups. Many white people, who believe themselves not to be racists, see racism as a universal phenomenon, characterized by bigotry against other races, regardless of one's own race. Many people of color, however, interpret racism as specifically white prejudice against people of color. Here, a certain amount of conceptual analysis is appropriate: For one thing, racism has now become a concept that is applied so liberally to just about any form of bigotry or resentment involving people of different races that we tend to forget its core meaning: a prejudice against people of another race simply because of their affiliation with that race and for no other reason. Based on that definition, it is of course possible for a person of color to resent someone because of that person's race, be it another nonwhite race or white—just as a white person can have racial animosity toward someone of color. However, some sociologists and philosophers, such as Lawrence Blum (see chapter text) point out that there is a difference: White people discriminating against people of color do so with the full weight of a tradition of dominance behind them (*institutional racism,* in other words), while people of color do not have the same kind of tradition behind their racial animosity (at least here and now in the West). And so, under the current political conditions, a white person's racism is more powerful and thus more devastating than the racism of a person of color. That doesn't mean that things can't change: Racism against a white minority population can theoretically turn into a dominance tradition, with equally devastating effects for the white minority, especially if revenge for old hurts becomes part of the picture. And the racism between nonwhite populations, both in the United States and in other parts of the world (such as between Africans and people of Indian descent in East Africa, and between Indonesians and people of Chinese descent in Southeast Asia) is a documented reality that, in its devastation, depends on which group has played the socially dominant role the longest. In other words, racism is a power play, with actors who are to some extent interchangeable. Racism between nonwhite populations and individuals can take many forms; recently, black actor Danny Glover complained that he and his daughter could not hail a cab in New York City; other African Americans have since confirmed that such difficulties exist. What was surprising to many was that the cabbies who refused to pick them up were people of color themselves, for the most part immigrants; one might ask whether they brought their prejudices with them from home or whether they bought into racist American stereotypes or both. Also, in May 2000 the *Los Angeles Times* reported that most hate crimes in Los Angeles were committed by people of color against other people of color, reflecting a growing tendency among the media to recognize that racist tendencies can be found in any population.

An aspect of nonwhite racism rarely discussed is the discrimination against dark-skinned individuals and preference for light-skinned individuals *within* a nonwhite racial group, a phenomenon called *colorism* by Naomi Zack. This form of color prejudice exists in different populations all over the world, from India to the United States, and creates a hierarchy within the racial group to the advantage of those of lighter skin and the disadvantage of individuals with darker skin. There are two interpretations of this phenomenon: One is that humans have a built-in need to discriminate against some other group in order to feel better about themselves. Another is that this form of internal racism is a direct result of centuries of white dominance: The white racial ideal has been adopted by nonwhite races, who now perpetuate the same racism against themselves.

peaceful, enlightened person. But then he took another look at the situation and realized that they were reacting to a type, not to him personally. Surely they were stereotyping him, but he decided to stop taking it personally (and kept his dreadlocks).

Institutional racism, according to Zack, is "characteristic of public, social, political, and economic organizations that are harmful to nonwhites." We should add that this definition is specifically tailored toward a society such as ours where whites have been the racially dominant group; it is conceivable that another society might have institutional racism directed against whites. This form of racism may also be overt or covert. Overt institutional racism may be expressed in laws preventing blacks from using public facilities reserved for whites—a common situation in several states before the Civil Rights Act of 1964. Covert institutional racism may be "stacking the deck" against people of color so they don't meet minimum qualifications on application forms. However, this need not be a deliberate form of discrimination: Tradition may channel whites through an educational system more easily than it does people of color, for instance, without society thereby having any ulterior motive (at this point in time) about keeping people of color away from participating in "the good life."

Environmental racism is a term that has only recently been added to our vocabulary: Usually more covert than overt, and in many cases unintentional rather than intentional, environmental racism is an effect of *lack of political power and lack of financial clout;* often, those two factors manifest themselves in the familiar phenomenon of *poverty.* In impoverished neighborhoods, both in the cities and in rural areas, there is often less concern for the effects of environmental hazards when the prospective victims are poor. We often find toxic dumps and unsanitary conditions in areas where people have no political voice; and the implication is that such places are often ghettos and barrios. However, poverty is statistically color-blind, and poor nonwhite neighborhoods don't have a monopoly on rat infestation or proximity to hazardous waste; it is just that when people are vulnerable due to poverty *and* they are nonwhite, their political clout is even more diminished. *Environmental discrimination* may be a more inclusive term, encompassing poor whites as well as nonwhites, but the term *environmental racism* does reflect today's reality: Race still matters in terms of political attention.

Race and Class   A more nuanced view of what racism is and isn't in today's society is emerging, and one of the components analysts look at is the phenomenon of *class.* Traditionally, Americans like to think that we have a classless society, and we pride ourselves on thinking that one's social standing is no obstacle to reaching for and accomplishing one's dreams. This is the *American dream,* but for many people of color this remains the *white American dream,* requiring a certain ancestry for participation. However, we shouldn't forget that for many white people the dream remains elusive too: Lack of education, lack of support, lack of chances in life, and lack of mentors relegate many to the sidelines of that dream, regardless of color. Be that as it may, and leaving aside the whole discussion of the added disadvantages for people of color, it says much that we view our society as one without class boundaries. But below the surface, we know it to be a false image. The old noble families of Europe may not be part of the American self-image, but there are other "nobilities": of education, family money, the right schools, and a home in the right part of town. There are the advantages of knowing the right lingo when you apply for a job and knowing the right kind of people—who will hire you. There are numerous "classes" in this classless society. Some of them can truly be transcended, but others are much more difficult to get beyond.

So now we need to speculate: How does the issue of class relate to the race issue? Over the past few decades, an increasing number of people of color have moved up into the middle class, sharing jobs and neighborhoods with white colleagues and friends. Although the integration of neighborhoods used to be an issue for many white people (who cited fears that their property value would decrease), time seems to have solved or at least reduced the problem, leading some scholars to conclude that it was not a *racial* animosity as much as a *class* animosity that was at the heart of white resistance (it was still a form of bigotry, but an economic one rather than a racial one). And now that many people of all colors can meet as members of the middle class, the animosity has by and large evaporated. However, it only accentuates the existence of a problem between *classes* in this country—not only between upper and middle classes, but also between the middle class (counting both white- and blue-collar workers) and the urban "underclass," with its own problems of joblessness, drugs, substandard housing, and gang activity. The race issue is still relevant, even though class concerns may be part of the dynamics, because it seems to be especially hard for a young nonwhite male to break out of a poor neighborhood and into a middle-class life, harder than for a young white male, because the nonwhite males, especially blacks, are up against a stereotype. The statistical fact that one out of four black males is either incarcerated or in the probation system doesn't help dispel the stereotype, although (as we did with *The Bell Curve*) we must ask about the social factors that may be partly to blame for the astounding statistics; like the statistics on the proportionately large number of minorities waiting on death row, such numbers reflect a range of factors: Have they had the same access to legal counsel as white inmates? Did they have a proper defense? It may be an unfortunate part and parcel of belonging to the lower scale of society in terms of income—but as we have seen, such conditions are exacerbated when race becomes part of the social picture. (Box 5.7 explores the concept of racial profiling.)

Should Race Be Embraced or Abolished as a Cultural Designation?

In this chapter you have seen that, according to current theories, there is no good reason to uphold any biological race distinctions. But what about the social categories of race? Should they be embraced by our twenty-first-century American culture? Racial pride matters greatly to many people, and on many campuses today there is a concerted effort to recognize and celebrate diversity. The diversity that is celebrated is most often labeled as ethnic, but there is an underlying assumption that it may also mean racial diversity. Some scholars argue that whenever there is a focus on racial differences, it will inadvertently give rise to a hierarchy of some who are "up" and others who are "down." Race is not a descriptive term; in other words, it is normative, implying a power relationship.

For many people, the only way to move beyond racism is to recognize that we all belong to different socially identified racial groups, and that some have been far more privileged than others. This is the view underlying *affirmative action:* Since many minority groups have a history of being oppressed or in some way excluded from taking part in social advantages—a fact that still shapes the lives and minds of individuals, limiting their social opportunities and preventing the so-called playing field from being level—affirmative action (an expression coined by President Lyndon B. Johnson) should be taken to make up for past injustices. This is sometimes referred to as a *backward-looking* view: Society ought to look back into the past to realize why things are the way they are in the present; and only by taking the wrongs of the past into consideration can society hope to bring about a better present and future. But the backward-looking view doesn't automatically say how far back in the past one is supposed to look: Back into the lives of each living individual? Back to the lives of individuals who have directly affected living individuals? (That would mean two to four generations.) Or simply back in time as far as we can trace the roots of our social structures, looking for indirect influences? If the criterion is each individual life, then most people today, descended from groups who have been oppressed in the past, may only have a relative claim to compensation or support, because the law since 1964 has (at least on paper) secured civil rights for everyone. However, if we go back two to four generations, the sufferings of parents, grandparents,

Box 5.7   RACIAL PROFILING

In recent years political attention has been focused on the phenomenon called racial profiling. Over the last few years, studies by both the federal and individual state governments have tried to ascertain the rumored existence of racial profiling in America, and the results are coming in. And they do tend to confirm what many people of color have felt for years: that they are being targeted in certain traffic situations by law enforcement, strictly because of their perceived race. Case in point: In 2000, a study based on 170,000 traffic stops in San Diego showed that blacks and Latinos make up 28 percent of the adult population, but accounted for 41 percent of traffic stops and 70 percent of police searches following the stops. Whites make up 59 percent of the adult population, account for 48 percent of traffic stops, and only 24 percent of searches. However, an editorial in the *San Diego Union-Tribune* warned readers not to jump to conclusions. For one thing, the police making the traffic stops are generally deployed in higher-crime areas, and many of those areas are populated primarily by blacks and Latinos, according to the paper. For another, many traffic stops involving Latinos happened in the immediate border region, where on a daily basis there is a far higher percentage of Latinos/Latinas present than the census results would indicate, partly because of legitimate tourism and partly because of illegal immigration. The paper suggests a more detailed study: Were mature professionals driving luxury cars stopped, as well as casually dressed young people driving beaters? Were they stopped while driving in predominantly white neighborhoods? Because in that case the stereotype of racial profiling would be confirmed: people of color being harassed

by white police officers simply because of their color. Judging from personal testimonies, many people of color have shared this experience of being stopped.

The questions are (1) Have times changed, with an increase in police officers recruited from minority populations and an increased awareness of the experience called DWB (Driving While Black/Brown)? And (2) is the random traffic-stop "profiling" perhaps being confused with another type of arrest, which should not be taken for *racial* profiling? This would be the type of arrest that originates with an actual crime report: If a robbery has been committed by three young white males driving away in a pickup truck, then that's the profile the police will be looking for. If a robbery has been committed by young black or Latino men, then such young men may be stopped, because they fit the profile. But the profile is generated by the crime report, not by some underlying prejudice (unless the crime report was in itself biased). Unless we're in a Hollywood movie or in some small twisted community of the past, police today are not going to look for suspects from a race other than that described in the crime report, neither to find scapegoats nor to meet some quota. If law enforcement officers bristle when asked about racial profiling, this may be the accusation they hear, and in that case they are probably right: They are doing their job based on crime reports, not on racism. But in the world of traffic stops that are not specifically crime/drug-related, the truth may be more complex and warrants further study. And of course the issue of *why* black and Latino neighborhoods may be higher-crime areas—which leads back to socioeconomic issues—will have to be a necessary part of such studies.

and great-grandparents will justify a far greater emphasis on compensation. However, while they may have suffered egregiously, it is by no means certain that their suffering has been a major negative influence on their living descendants. And if we look to general discrimination in the past, it may be so far back in time that most living individuals

have escaped its confining influence. Then what would be a fair compensation?

Because of these tough questions, some people prefer to focus on the *forward-looking* angle of affirmative action. In that case, society focuses not on the wrongs of the past, but on the *present* situation of inequality and outlines how it can be abolished in the *future*. The tricky thing here is that some people who are suffering in today's society may not have had any connection whatsoever to racial or ethnic discrimination in the past—and the whole concept of *justice* inherent in wanting to correct past wrongs, or be compensated for past wrongs, is lost. Besides, the concept of affirmative action, once considered a necessary method to level the playing field, has recently come under attack—not just by people within the old power structure who feel that their privileges have been eroded (the so-called "angry white males"), but also by people from the very groups affirmative action was supposed to have aided in achieving equal opportunities, people who wish to be judged on their merit rather than being assigned a status as underprivileged. The theory is that affirmative action may in some cases cause new forms of discrimination, partly against the previously privileged group of white males and partly against members of minority groups who, as recipients of affirmative action benefits, may be perceived (by themselves and others) as having been chosen by virtue of their background rather than their individual qualifications. California officially abolished affirmative action in the public sphere in 1996, partly with the help of black conservative leader Walt Connally. Public universities, from then on barred from using affirmative action as a way of helping underprivileged students enroll, found another method that, to some, has far more merit: Student outreach and aid based on the student's financial needs and academic promise, rather than their racial and ethnic background. (In 2001 the University of California decided to again allow some considerations of race in student enrollment.)

Some scholars and political leaders are in favor of simply not referring to race any longer. As we have seen, Naomi Zack would like categorizing by race to go away entirely because, in her view, it undercuts our ability to view each other as equals. The philosopher Richard Wasserstrom suggests that the ideal future would be a completely assimilated nonracist society where a person's race would matter no more than a person's eye color matters today: It is a difference that exists, but it has no social bearing. Wasserstrom doesn't say that he wants to abolish cultural diversity, quite the contrary; but he wants to disengage the idea of cultural diversity from the idea of race. For Wasserstrom, as for Zack, we are all in the end *individuals* approaching one another, and we ought to be able to do so on an equal basis. However, others believe that the *groups* we belong to should matter in this ideal future: Patricia Hill Collins argues that only if African American women see themselves as a group, with their own unique identity, will they as individuals be able to overcome the dual oppression of being black and of being women. Iris Marion Young argues that a socially just society should recognize the social equality of groups rather than just individuals and recognize as well as affirm group differences. She defines groups as social groups, rather than interest groups—in particular, socially disadvantaged groups, such as racial groups. But as you read in Box 5.3, racial groups have a characteristic than separates them from ethnic groups: A person can't choose his or her racial group—it is a designation given by others. As such, building a new society based on group identities may be counterproductive to equality, because many people feel oppressed by the very group assignment that Young wants recognized.

An approach on a middle ground is suggested by the philosopher Lawrence Blum. In his landmark paper from 1991, "Philosophy and the Value of a Multicultural Community," Blum suggests that there are three major points to overcoming racism in our society: (1) Everyone ought to understand exactly what racism is—a belief in the inferiority of a racial group—and distance herself or himself from it. We also need to recognize (see Box 5.6) that racism exists within every racial group, not just as a white phenomenon; but white racism against people of color is, in our culture, a more insidious form of racism because it draws from an age-old system of dominance and power. (2) We must embrace multiculturalism, as a way of valuing our own cultural heritage and showing an interest in other people's cultural heritage as well. Everyone, whites and nonwhites, must try to overcome their (presumed) ethnocentrism and reach out to each other. And lastly, (3) we must work to develop an inclusive sense of community, based on a recognition of our common humanity. Blum believes that by recognizing each other as fellow members of the community, we can overcome the pervasive tendency to look at other people as "other." So Blum wants us to recognize each other's human individuality, while at the same time not lose sight of—or interest in—each other's cultural-group diversity.

Naomi Zack herself has another suggestion: a new *cultural paradigm*. In recognition of the fact that race is biologically nonexistent, we should develop a new paradigm that *sees race as ethnicity*. Because an ethnicity can be chosen rather than assigned, a person of mixed race will have access to group affiliations that are more flexible than the old racial categories.

The Author's Confession: She Is Frustrated

On a final, personal note, I have to make a confession: I lived my entire childhood and youth in post–World War II Scandinavia. At the time it was one of the most racially homogeneous places on earth; nonetheless, the society was generally antiracist as a reaction to the racism of the Nazi occupation (1940–1945) and the anti-Semitic policies of Nazism. Even after having lived in this country for more than 20 years, I am somewhat puzzled and frustrated by Americans' persistent focus on race issues. Like many foreigners coming to this country—including many of my foreign-born students—I have viewed this focus on race as exacerbating the racial divides rather than diminishing them. I never thought to categorize people according to their presumed race; it just didn't occur to me, and I have probably offended many an American by getting his or her racial background wrong. I initially thought the race issue was a thing of the past; but eventually it became clear to me that race is a perpetual undertone of American society—a tone that vibrates more loudly for some than for others, but is omnipresent in the symphony of American life. However, I also retain from my Scandinavian past the belief that it need not be indicative of how things have to be in the future. I belong to the group of people who believe that, fundamentally, race should play no part in assessing the human qualities and professional qualifications of people in any society—that we should all be judged by the content of our character, rather than the color of our skin, to quote Martin Luther King, Jr. I also believe that, in the greater scheme of our humanity, individuals from different races are far more similar than we are different, and I tend to look at the similarities rather than the differences.

However, life in America has also taught me that centuries of oppression and deprivation of rights aren't abolished with mere legislation and good will, and cultural disadvantages linger on for a very long time. While the ultimate goal may be for every one of us to be judged on our merit, some "affirmative action" to level the playing field may still be needed. After all, slavery may have been abolished in 1865, but rights for African Americans weren't made constitutional until the Fourteenth and Fifteenth Amendments (1868 and 1870), and it took the Civil Rights Act of 1964 and the Voting Rights Act in 1965 to ensure that the constitutional rights of all Americans were not withheld from anyone. As such, full freedom for black Americans has been a political fact for only about four decades, which is a very short time for society to rid itself of old discriminations. Furthermore, indigenous people of this country, the American Indians and other Native Americans such as the Inuit of Alaska, continue to struggle with inequities in legislation; and a long-standing tradition of discrimination toward Asians and Latinos by Euro-Americans in various parts of the country can still be felt. In addition, there is the perennial issue of anti-Semitism. And it wasn't until 1943 that "nonwhite" immigrants became eligible for U.S. citizenship. In short, oppression and discrimination may officially belong to the past, but the aftereffects are so acutely felt by a large number of people that we can't just declare equality to have been achieved.

In addition, many people, especially those whose race has experienced a history of oppression, celebrate their long cultural and family traditions. As a result, they prefer to focus on racial differences rather than similarities for the sake of their own racial identity and pride. The tricky part is that as things stand now, such racial pride is applauded and expected in races with a history of oppression, while pride within the historically dominant race (white people) is frowned upon. The rationale is that pride in one's tradition is, for the historically dominant race, just a continuation of the old pride of the white conquerors, while the traditionally oppressed races need to feel that they can legitimately view their own traditions with pride, without being told by a dominant race that they don't rate as highly. This rationale does make some sense in view of the historical tensions in the American society. One might hope that, in the near future, we will all be able to draw pride from our personal and cultural heritage and at the same time critically and honestly assess parts of that heritage that may warrant a reexamination. What Aristotle would call "proper pride" in one's background shouldn't have to entail denigration of the tradition of others: In other words, just because I'm "up," doesn't mean that someone else has to be "down."

So I come from a place where we were all white, but espoused antiracism as a matter of principle. So was there no bigotry? Of course there was! Plenty of looking down one's nose at people with less income, people from the country, people from the big city, people with disabilities, and so forth. As we saw earlier, discrimination has many faces, and racism is only one of them. However, the picture in Scandinavia has changed. As in so many other parts of the world, immigration has changed the demographics considerably: Now a typical Scandinavian face is no longer blond and blue-eyed, but far more diverse. Miss Denmark 1999, Zahide Bayram, was of Turkish descent, a fact that delighted many progressive people, including people of Turkish background, and disturbed some traditionalists.

That leads me to my second point: How did the antiracism policy of Denmark fare in the face of an actual influx of people from different cultures, whose hair and skin color differ from the traditional pale Scandinavian look? Not too well, I'm afraid. The highly acclaimed antiracist attitude of the Scandinavian countries seemed to evaporate in reverse proportion to the influx of foreigners over the final decades of the twentieth century. As things now stand in Denmark, third-generation immigrants—kids who have never seen the homeland of their grandparents and speak only Danish—are being treated as second-class citizens by a great number of Danes; with foreign-sounding names, they have a hard time securing jobs, and the usual Danish sensitivity to ethnic slurs seems to have worn thinner. The unofficial term for these new Danes is "foreigners"; the official term is "NewDanes." Within the last few years many "OldDanes" as well as "NewDanes" have tried to bridge the cultural gap in recognition that they are already neighbors and had better do something to make the neighborhood work; indeed, statistically, integration problems have been reported to be worse within the older generations than among the young. The immigration groups are now manifesting themselves in Danish society as voices of columnists and politicians. The most hopeful on both sides view the situation as a transitional problem, not a permanent condition, especially since the phenomenon has happened before: Generations ago, a large influx of Polish immigrants was discriminated against in much the same way, but their descendants have now been completely integrated into the Danish culture.[16]

The issues reflect the same problems that are part of the American immigration phenomenon: Do we want a "melting pot" where everyone is assimilated by the dominant culture, or do we want a common culture that can accommodate and appreciate cultural and ethnic differences without creating a hierarchy of "castes"? The United States has had a couple of centuries to work on its immigrant self-identity, but most of the European countries have never pictured themselves as melting pots, and the shift in self-image can be a painful process for "old" as well as "new" residents. So it appears that just because your culture boasts a long history and strong tradition of antiracism doesn't mean that racial peaceful coexistence is inevitable when your society is put to the test by reality. One might say that for the first time in the modern era, the ethnicity and even the "whiteness" of the Danes (as well as other European cultures) has been made into an issue. Where a sense of ethnic and racial identity was simply the unproblematic background for all other life events, it has now been brought to the forefront; and holding on to that identity as a form of privilege becomes part of the complex picture—as George Lipsitz puts it, a *possessive investment.* The racial animosity may be felt by just a few in the general population, but the effects of such a hatred can be devastating: In Norway, six young white neo-Nazis murdered a black Norwegian teenager in January 2001—an event that inspired the greatest public rally against racism in the history of Norway, with 30,000 torch-carrying people taking to the streets of Oslo in a peaceful, nighttime demonstration.

However, as we have seen, an animosity toward people who "look different" may not be solely due to racism; other components may be at play, such as economic matters and class concerns. If the new immigrants are viewed as taking jobs away from a local population, fear of losing job security is involved. If the new immigrants bring their religious and culinary traditions with them, worries about loss of the traditional ways that make many people feel safe and comfortable may be involved. If there is gang hostility between the young immigrants and the local young people, fear of one's general security is involved, along with a concern for property values of the neighborhood if gang activity becomes rampant. Most of these fears may be founded on ignorance and bigotry, but we can't automatically assume that all bigotry equals racism.

In the old cultures of Europe, which are struggling with reconciling the historical legacy of anti-Semitism that predates Hitler, a long tradition of democracy, and a new influx of immi-

SPECIAL ISSUE
TIME

Take a good look at this woman. She was created by a computer from a mix of several races. What you see is a remarkable preview of . . .

THE NEW FACE OF AMERICA
How Immigrants Are Shaping the World's First Multicultural Society

The cover of a special issue of *Time* magazine, Fall 1993, featured the "New Face of America," a young woman of mixed racial heritage. The point is that this young woman's face is a computer creation using the then brand-new morphing technology, based on the faces of seven men and seven women from the following backgrounds: Middle Eastern, Italian, African, Vietnamese, Anglo-Saxon, Chinese, and Latino. With more and more people getting together in interracial relationships, the multiracial American identity is already a reality.

grants from Africa, Asia, and the Middle East, the results of this new diversity have been mixed. In Germany, second- or third-generation immigrants with no ties whatsoever to the original home country are still considered foreigners not only in popular opinion, but also in legal terms, since they can't (at least not yet) obtain German citizenship; German citizenship is traditionally based on bloodlines, not on residency. In France, Muslim immigrants have no right to wear the clothing styles or observe the religious food rituals necessary for their faith in the workplace. In British schools until recently, a Muslim or Hindu child would be served the same food as the Christian British children, without any other options, even though Muslim believers, like Jews, aren't allowed to eat pork, and Hindus can't have beef. "Diversity" is in itself a negative concept in the European political debate, and some European countries try to restrict diversity through legislation.

However, the presence of multicultural, multiethnic, and multiracial groups is a fact—one brought on by European politicians in the mid–twentieth century who opened the borders for cheap labor from non-European countries. Now the children of newcomers marry across the lines of religion and race, and if these immigrants had not experienced discrimination before, then they will experience it vicariously through the eyes of their mixed-race, multicultural grandchildren. This is what denying the reality of a multiethnic society seems to have accomplished, and I personally have far greater hope for the tolerance in social relations within the United States with its self-criticism and media awareness. And, in particular, I have some faith in the inexorable process of the *biological* melting pot of the United States, where the new face of California, for instance, in the middle of the twenty-first century is predicted to be so racially ambiguous than any racially hostile attitude could become a moot question.

Study Questions

1. Explain and critique the theory of the Aryan race, referring to F. Max Müller's theory of language.

2. What is the current view on race as a biological phenomenon, according to most researchers? Do you agree? Why or why not?

3. Comment on Blum's three suggestions to combat racism: What are they, and will they work? Why or why not?

Primary Readings and Narratives

The first Primary Reading is an excerpt from Naomi Zack's book *Thinking About Race,* in which she argues that a new paradigm of race is needed. The second is a selection from *Ethnicity and Race,* by Stephen Cornell and Douglas Hartmann, who propose that the concept of race is a social construct, based on a decision that endows certain physical characteristics with a social meaning. The first Narrative is a summary of the film *Mississippi Masala,* a love story of a young woman who is ethnically from India, but born and raised in Africa, and a young African American man; the second story is the film *American History X,* an exploration of racism and neo-Nazism and the story of one young neo-Nazi who has a change of heart.

Primary Reading

Thinking About Race

NAOMI ZACK

Excerpt, 1998.

A NEW PARADIGM OF RACE?

A *cultural paradigm* is a set of assumptions about an area of human life, or the world, that is shared by a sufficiently influential number of people so that the set of assumptions is part of common sense. The paradigm functions as a theory that explains past and present experiences, and it generates predictions and expectations about future experience.

The current paradigm of race divides people into races as a matter of biological fact, and it attaches different expectations regarding culture and behavior to those racial groups. A new paradigm of race might begin with knowledge that there is no biological foundation for the different racial groups. As a result, what was previously thought of as race might now be thought of as ethnicity. Since ethnicity is now accepted as a fluid, changeable, interlocking system of human categories and lifestyle choices, racial identity and racial membership could as well be viewed as a fluid, changeable, interlocking system of human categories and lifestyle choices. Mixed-race realities support this reconfiguration of race as ethnicity, and so does consideration of the ways in which ideas of race have changed over time and across cultures.

When people attach strong differences to what they think of as racial difference, these attachments could be viewed as beliefs that they are entitled to, much as they are entitled to varied religious beliefs. When the practice of these beliefs is a source of fulfillment and self-expression, they would merit the same respect as the practice of other beliefs that derive from cultural traditions. When the beliefs about racial difference result in harm to other human beings, they would be viewed as moral defects, or sadis-

tic and criminal delusions, and treated accordingly; when such beliefs are self-destructive, they would require both psychological and social treatment.

A new paradigm of race might have some detachment from race built into it that would allow for the possibility that racial categorization, identity, and struggle will pass out of history. From this detached perspective, race would be no more than an idea about human beings that was useful for organizing society in the past, but is increasingly without use or benefit as time goes on.

Study Questions

1. What, according to Zack, is a cultural paradigm, and what does she suggest that we do with our current paradigm of race?

2. How should a viewpoint reflecting belief in racial differences be regarded, according to Zack?

3. Zack envisions a future where race is no longer a biological issue; do you agree with her? Why or why not?

Primary Reading

Ethnicity and Race

STEPHEN CORNELL AND DOUGLAS HARTMANN

Excerpt, 1998.

THE SOCIAL CONSTRUCTION OF RACE

Despite the lack of a biological basis for the conception of distinct human races, race still wields monumental power as a social category. In many societies, the idea of biologically distinct races remains a fixture in the popular mind, a basis of social action, a foundation of government policy, and often a justification for distinctive treatment of one group by another. Despite the paucity of scientific support, human beings tend to assume racial categories and to take them seriously. They do so for social, not biological, reasons.

Races, like ethnic groups, are not established by some set of natural forces but are products of human perception and classification. They are social constructs. As geneticist James King remarks, "Both what

constitutes a race and how one recognizes a racial difference are culturally determined." We decide that certain physical characteristics—usually skin color, but perhaps also hair type, stature, or other bodily features—will be primary markers of group boundaries. We invent categories of persons marked by those characteristics. The categories become socially significant to the extent that we use them to organize and interpret experience, to form social relations, and to organize individual and collective action. In other words, the categories become important only when we decide they have particular meanings and act on those meanings. The characteristics that are the basis of the categories, however, have no inherent significance. We give them meaning, and in the process we create races.

We can define a race, then, as a human group defined by itself or others as distinct by virtue of perceived common physical characteristics that are held to be inherent. A race is a group of human beings socially defined on the basis of physical characteristics. Determining which characteristics constitute the race—the selection of markers and therefore the construction of the racial category itself—is a choice human beings make. Neither markers nor categories are predetermined by any biological factors.

These processes of selection and construction are seldom the work of a moment. Racial categories are historical products and are often contested. In one famous case from the early 1980s, a Louisiana woman went to court to dispute the state's conclusion that she was Black, claiming a White racial identity. The state's argument was that her ancestry was at least 1/32nd "Negro" which, according to state law, meant she was Black. The law had roots in the long history of Black-White relations in Louisiana and in the American South more generally, in slavery and its legacy and in the enduring White effort to maintain the supposed "purity" of their race. It was a legal manifestation of what is known as hypodescent, or the "one-drop" rule, which in the United States holds that any degree of African ancestry at all is sufficient to classify a person as Black. This rule has a history. People have fought over it, and as the Louisiana's case shows, it has been tested in the courts. It has been reserved largely for Blacks. Americans do not generally consider a person who is 1/32 Japanese or Dutch to be Japanese or Dutch, but "one-drop" of Black blood has long been considered sufficient for racial categorization.

The woman in Louisiana lost her case (although the law eventually was changed), but her story underlines the point made by Michael Omi and Howard Winant in their path-breaking study of race in the United States: Racial categories are not natural categories that human beings discover; on the contrary, they are "created, inhabited, transformed, and destroyed" by human action and are, therefore, preeminently social products. They change over time as people struggle to establish them, overcome them, assign other people to them, escape them, interpret them, and so on. The outcomes of those struggles often have enormous consequences for the individuals involved, but it is not biology that determines who will suffer and why. People determine what the categories will be, fill them up with human beings, and attach consequences to membership in those categories.

Study Questions

1. How do Cornell and Hartmann define race?

2. What is the "one-drop rule," and what point do Cornell and Hartmann try to make in referring to this rule?

3. The view expressed in this excerpt is that race is a social construct, not a natural phenomenon. What consequences might such a view have for future race relations?

Narrative

Mississippi Masala

MIRA NAIR (DIRECTOR) AND
SOONI TARAPOREVALA (SCREENWRITER)

Film, 1992. Summary.

Nair's love story about a young woman of Asian ethnicity and a young African American man illustrates an aspect of racism that is rarely brought into focus: Racial animosities between groups of people of color in today's mixed societies.

The story opens in Uganda during Idi Amin's regime in the 1980s. The property of Ugandan citizens of Indian descent is being seized, and they are being expelled from their country—a country their families have considered home for seventy years, since they were brought to Africa by the British to work on the railroads. The little girl Mina's father, a lawyer, and her mother are being forced out, too, and their property confiscated—forced out from what they thought of as their homeland. An old friend of theirs, the African Okelo, has managed to help Mina's father get out of jail where he was being held for publishing a criticism of Amin, but now Okelo tells Mina's father that he should leave: Africa is for black Africans. Devastated, Mina's father doesn't even say goodbye to him, but Mina grieves over leaving her friend Okelo.

In 1990 Mina is twenty-four years old, and the family has moved to Greenwood, Mississippi, by way of London, and joined members of the Indian community. Together they manage a motel, the Monte Cristo. Mina's father keeps sending legal petitions to the new Ugandan government to get his property back, but receives no reply. Every day he thinks of his home in Uganda and always feels like a refugee, but Mina has taken to life in the United States. One day, while shopping with her mother, driving a borrowed car, Mina plows straight into a carpet cleaner's van stopped in the middle of the road. The carpet cleaner, a good-looking young black man who was himself stopped because of a stalled car in front of him, exchanges cards with Mina for the sake of the insurance. Later on that night they meet again, by accident, in a club. Mina has a date, a young Indian man her parents approve of, but she and the carpet cleaner, Demetrius, are attracted to each other—at least Mina is attracted to him. His ex-wife is there, too, and Demetrius sees a chance to make her jealous, so he dances with Mina. Demetrius's friend Tyrone can't understand Mina's ethnicity; he thinks she is a Mexican, and when he hears she is Indian, he assumes she's a Native American. Like other blacks as well as whites in Greenwood, he has a hard time telling the difference between Asian and American "Indians." The young Indian man leaves in anger, and Demetrius drives Mina home.

Some days later the motel manager seeks out Demetrius, who happens to be the guy cleaning carpets at the Motel Monte Cristo: He is terrified that Demetrius is going to sue the young man whose car Mina crashed into the carpet cleaning van. Playing heavily

on Indians and blacks being brothers because "either you're white or you're colored," the hotel manager extracts a promise of no lawsuit out of Demetrius.

Mina can't put Demetrius out of her mind, so eventually she calls him up, like a modern woman—under the pretext of thanking him for the ride home. He asks her to have dinner with his family (where his ex-wife is also expected), and she accepts. At the dinner, a birthday party for his father, Mina meets his father, his slacker of a brother, his friend Tyrone who hits on her, his Aunt Rose, and his grandfather who is hard of hearing and thinks she comes from Indianola. The young men are fascinated that she is Indian, but has never been to India—but she was born and raised in Africa, their ethnic homeland, where they have never been, either. She comes across to them as a very exotic woman—in her own words, a *masala,* a melange, a spice mix—but she isn't sure if she isn't just a tool of jealousy for Demetrius when his ex-wife shows up. She and Demetrius leave and take a walk by the river. Philosophically, Demetrius quotes his mother: "You can never step into the same river twice." And things are indeed about to change for both of them, because they are falling in love.

Now Demetrius is pressuring Mina to go to Biloxi with him; she concocts a story and gets permission, because her father is preoccupied with a letter from the Ugandan government: He has to appear in person in the property lawsuit. Mina and Demetrius go off to Biloxi, get a room, and spend the night together. But as luck will have it, Mina's young Indian friends are there too; they thought they had seen Mina the previous night, and now, in the morning, they see Demetrius's van in front of the hotel. They break into the hotel room; and since both Mina and Demetrius put up a fight, the police are summoned. Mina's dad has to pick her up at the police station in Biloxi, and the scandal is rolling, because now all the unspoken animosities come to the surface. Demetrius's friends close ranks, telling him to leave the foreigners alone—that they are just out to ruin him, and that they think they are better than the blacks. Demetrius's dad blames him for "breaking the rules." Mina's family tells her that she has brought shame upon them, and the gossip flows freely in the Indian community. A few white people join in the gossip, generally siding with the Indian immigrants. And now even the bank turns its back on Demetrius: He has lost all his Indian customers in short order, and without customers he can't make the payments on his van and the equipment, so the white banker gives him two weeks before repossessing the van. Aunt Rose says angrily that the days of "Know your place" are over, because she supports her nephew and has been like a mother to him since her sister died. But Tyrone tells him that his friends think he is getting big-headed because he is dating a white girl—in their eyes, Mina is white, but we know from the beginning of the film that Mina herself is sensitive because she is of darker skin than many others with Indian ancestry (so it is clear that the racial categories everyone is using have more to do with tradition and ethnic background than with actual color). Finally, Demetrius goes to the motel to see Mina but isn't allowed to; her father comes out and dismisses him, but Demetrius isn't so easily dismissed: The family has ruined his business—because he isn't good enough for Mina? Her father says that once he thought he could change the world, too, but it can't be done, and he wants to spare Mina the hardship—but Demetrius knows a lot about hardship himself, and he accuses Mina's father of racism, coming to this country and acting white. Then he leaves. This confrontation has reached deep into Mina's father's heart, and he begins to ponder what it was that happened between him and Okelo, a black man who was his best friend, and who dismissed him out of seeming racism. Could he have transferred this animosity to Demetrius and American blacks? Mina thinks so. He has finally opened his heart to his daughter and told her about the final days in Uganda, but she sees it in a completely different light: Okelo risked his own life to save him from Amin's forces, out of love. It was out of love that he tried to make him leave, by offending him. Now Mina's father begins to understand that she is right, and he has been wrong. In a 180-degree turnaround, he decides that the family should move back to Uganda; he has to conduct his lawsuit, anyway, and Demetrius has hired a slick lawyer to sue the motel managers for damages to his van, after all.

Mina is devastated—she doesn't want to go back to Uganda. In a split second she skips out of the motel, "borrows" a car, and sets out to look for Demetrius. At first his father won't tell her where he is, because all he sees is that this foreign girl has caused his son so much grief—but eventually he tells her where to find him: In Indianola, drumming up new business. She drives straight there, going from motel to motel until she sees his van. Thinking that he wants to see her, she is devastated when he is as hostile as his father. But she talks, and Demetrius listens—and realizes that their relationship was almost killed by the prejudices of others. She doesn't want to go to Uganda—he doesn't want to stay in the area any longer. So off they go, together, after making difficult farewell calls to their families. They are going to clean carpets and hotel rooms together somewhere in America and make a new future for themselves.

Mina's parents, too, come to their own realizations: Mina's mother refuses to go with her husband to Uganda; he goes back, only to find that Okelo was murdered shortly after he left—presumably by Amin's soldiers, for helping him. His property is in ruins, and all of a sudden he doesn't care about the lawsuit any more—he just wants to be home in Greenwood with his wife. The new Uganda is not his home anymore.

Study Questions:

1. Is this story about mutual discrimination among people of color fair to both groups, Indians and blacks? Does the film offer stereotypes or a realistic picture? From whose perspective is the story written?

2. Are Mina and Demetrius doing the right thing? Why or why not? What would you do differently, if anything?

3. Why do you think the screenwriter has white people in the film siding with the Indian immigrants? Is that realistic?

4. The saying "You can't step into the same river twice" is attributed to the ancient Greek philosopher Heraclitus. What does it mean, and how does it relate to Demetrius's and Mina's situation?

Narrative

American History X

TONY KAYE (DIRECTOR) AND DAVID MCKENNA (SCREENWRITER)

Film, 1998. Summary.

The film takes place over a span of less than twenty-four hours—sequences all in color—but in black-and-white flashbacks we hear a long, disturbing story of how things reached the current boiling point.

In black and white (a symbolism that is sharply apparent from the very start) we are immediately thrown into a situation of violence from one night three years ago: A "skinhead," Derek Vinyard, is making love to his girlfriend; his younger brother Danny bursts in on them. Danny has seen someone breaking into Derek's car—a car we later find out used to be his dead father's. Derek goes for his gun, and without hesitation he runs out in the street, shooting. His bare torso reveals a swastika tattoo and other white power symbols. Two young black men breaking into the car are killed; the third gets away. Danny has seen the whole thing.

Cut to present day, in color, at Venice High: Danny's principal, Dr. Bob Sweeney, a black man, has a conversation with Murray, a white teacher—who used to date Danny and Derek's mother—about Danny, who has written a paper on Hitler's *Mein Kampf* to provoke him (Murray is Jewish). Murray considers the paper dangerous, but Sweeney isn't about to give up on the boy: He has learned the "Nazi psycho-babble," and he can unlearn it. And Sweeney says with total conviction that he knows Derek didn't put his brother up to it. Murray leaves, and Danny—also a skinhead—comes into Sweeney's office. Here we learn that Derek used to be his student too, a brilliant student in English lit. Sweeney scolds Danny for turning in a piece of trash and gives him another assignment: Every day he will come to class in the principal's office, in a special class they will call "American History X." For his first assignment he gets twenty-four hours to write about his brother. Derek was let out of prison the day before, after a three-year sentence for manslaughter.

Next scene: Three young black male students are harassing a white student in the restroom—presum-ably over cheating—when Danny comes in. He stands up to them, smokes a cigarette and blows smoke in their faces, and helps the other white kid out.

Now we follow Sweeney, who has a meeting with the Venice police department. He does outreach work and says they can expect trouble tonight: Derek is out of prison, and his mentor Cameron Alexander, an older man known for his racist views but without a criminal record, may start trouble. We learn that Derek lost his father some years before he went to prison; his father was murdered, and Derek blamed minorities in general for his murder. (Later when we hear his father talk in a flashback, we understand that it was Derek's father himself who gave Derek the impression that his job and his life were being ruined by minorities.)

A day earlier, Derek had come home from prison, no longer a skinhead: He has grown a full head of hair, which bothers Danny, who has kept his bedroom a shrine to his brother, with Nazi flags and other icons on the wall. Derek wants to change things immediately: Their mother smokes and coughs, and we guess she is suffering from lung cancer. Derek wants everyone to move to another neighborhood, and wants their mother to sleep in a bedroom instead of on the couch. He is on the phone with Sweeney; has no welcoming words for one of his former friends, Seth, a large skinhead spouting racist slurs with every sentence; and seems anxious to make a break with the past. Danny who has been looking immensely forward to getting his brother—the killer hero—home, is confused. He starts writing the assignment for Sweeney, and slowly we begin to understand Derek's character. Within those twenty-four hours, Danny also reaches an understanding of what went on.

Cameron and Derek started the White Power gang, presumably as a countermeasure to all the black gangs popping up in the neighborhood, but it soon went be-yond just being a place for white kids to hang out to-

American History X, New Line Cinema, 1998. Danny (Edward Furlong) has shaved his head, skinhead-style, to emulate his older brother Derek (Edward Norton), who went to prison for assaulting and killing two young black men. Before Derek went to prison he saw himself as a white supremacist, but after his prison experience, which included becoming friends with a young black man, Derek has had a complete change of heart. Here he tries to explain to Danny that he is being misled by the same neo-Nazis who had misled Derek when he was younger.

gether: An anti-immigrant, antiminority ideology was being taught, and the gang instigated a raid on a Korean grocery store and assaulted its Asian, black, and Latino employees. Soon after, we see a dinner scene at the Vinyard home, as remembered by Danny: The mother's boyfriend Murray is there, and they are discussing the L.A. riots that followed the acquittal of the police officers who were caught on video beating up Rodney King. Murray, the mother, and the older sister Davina see the riots as irrational actions by long-oppressed people. Derek has no patience for such "liberal" ideas and sees the riots as pure opportunism: people looting their own neighborhood because of a lack of a sense of community. They go on to talk about Rodney King; Murray, the mother and Davina believe the cops were using

excessive force, and Derek argues that King was high and attacked the cops, and so was rightly subdued. He points out that one out of three black males are in conflict with the law—Murray sees it as a flaw in the judicial system, and Derek says that's just a cop-out to take away their responsibility. Soon Derek is screaming at everyone; his mother wants to talk about something else, but he loses his temper and starts hitting Davina and throws vicious anti-Semitic slurs at Murray. Murray leaves in deep sadness over the situation, and Derek's mother tells him she is ashamed of him and wants him out of the house.

And now the night of the shooting is put into perspective, because that was the night following the dinner argument. Danny remembers how defiant and triumphant Derek looked when the police came for him—and Danny reveals that if he had talked, Derek would have been in for life, not a three-year sentence for manslaughter. As it was, nobody but Danny knows the truth: that Derek didn't just shoot at the car thieves but held one down and shot him, execution style.

That evening, Danny goes to the party Cameron has arranged for Derek, even though Derek has told him not to go. Cameron has become Danny's new hero, and in the privacy of his office Cameron tells Danny to prepare for the coming race war. Now Derek shows up, tries to tell Cameron that he is out and will have nothing more to do with the White Power gang, and when Cameron won't listen, he punches him so he falls and hits his head. Now Derek tries to get away from the rowdy party-goers who idolize him, but soon they discover that he has changed: His former girlfriend and Seth turn against him, and Seth threatens him with a gun. Derek overpowers him, takes the gun, and keeps everyone at bay while he escapes. Confronted by Danny, he tells him the whole story of why he has changed.

At first Derek sought protection from other white supremacists in prison and refused to talk to his laundry-duty partner, Lamont, a black inmate—who didn't let himself get fazed by Derek's attitude at all. But as time goes on, Derek's black-and-white views begin to go gray: He finds himself having a good time with a young black inmate, his laundry partner, talking about women and sports; and at the same time he is disgusted when he finds out that the white supremacy leader does business with one of the Latino inmates. He complains about the lack of commitment among the White Power guys, but is also made aware that Lamont received a harsh sentence for theft of a TV and a presumed assault on an officer—he dropped the TV on the officer's foot and was booked for assault. Murray's view of flaws in the justice system rings a bell. But now Derek's criticism of his protectors and his friendliness with Lamont catch up with him: The supremacists ambush him in the shower, rape him, and beat him up. In the hospital, emotionally and physically devastated, he gets a visit from Sweeney, who promises to help him, on one condition; we assume it is that he helps straighten Danny out, too. When he recovers after being in the hospital he refuses to sit with the supremacists in the mess hall—which now makes him open to assaults by the

black gangs. But to his surprise, it never happens. The day when his sentence is up, he thanks Lamont for putting his neck on the line for him—because he must have been the one protecting him from the black gangs. They part with an unspoken sense of friendship and understanding, and Lamont calls after him, "Take it easy on the brothers!"

Danny, who has listened to the story, begins to understand and see things from Derek's point of view: The Nazi racist ideology is wrong and dangerous. Danny finishes his paper about Derek and lets us know the final piece of the puzzle: Was Derek always a hateful white supremacist? Not in high school. His hero was Dr. Sweeney, who taught him to appreciate meaningful literature like *Native Son*. But their father, who was still alive then, crushed his admiration for Sweeney by calling him names and referring to his ideas as "bullshit." The father saw affirmative action as a great threat to his job and was angry that qualified white people had been passed over for—in his view—less-qualified black people. Derek admired his father; and so he made his murdered father's views his own. Danny now understands what happened, and why it happened—and so do we, perhaps?

In the early morning hours, Derek and Danny together remove the Nazi paraphernalia and pictures from the wall of Danny's bedroom. They have now reached a true understanding as brothers; but things are still unresolved. Cameron is in the hospital, and the neo-Nazis are angry with Derek. The gang of black kids from school is looking for Danny. Will Derek be allowed to steer clear of his former supremacist friends? Will Danny be able to steer clear of the tensions at school? As much as the film makes it clear that both Derek and Danny have changed, the consequences of the past aren't easily escaped—and these consequences don't take into account that someone may have changed. I will let you experience the rest for yourself.

Study Questions

1. In case you were wondering, in most states you can't legally protect your car from being burglarized with a gun unless you feel reasonably threatened that the burglar is armed, and you have no possibility of getting away. What action should Derek have taken? Why didn't he?

2. What is the significance of switching between black and white and color?

3. In Derek's angry speech at dinner, where he ends up assaulting his sister, Derek mixes overt anti-minority statements with what might be identified as politically conservative statements in support of law enforcement—views that don't necessarily imply racism. Why might the screenwriter have chosen to have Derek speak those lines?

4. What is the real reason why Derek turned into a racist? Explain, and analyze. Is it a fair assessment? Should the blame be placed on someone else or on Derek himself?

Review

Key Issues in Chapter 5

Race: Descriptive Turned Normative

- According to current scientific theories there is no such thing as a biological foundation for race.

Theories of the Biological Reality of Race

- *The Human Race.* Human populations from all races can interbreed, so in terms of science we belong to the same human race.
- *Hitler's Theory of the Aryan Race.* Linnaeus's four racial categories—Africans, Europeans, Asians, and American Indians—are interpreted as a hierarchy and a foundation for discrimination. The theory of the Aryan race is a misconception based on Friedrich Max Müller's linguistic theory of Aryan languages
- *The Biology of Race: Natural or Sexual Selection.* A natural selection explanation of race is ambiguous at best: It is not a given that skin color is selected for biological advantages; it is most likely a matter of sexual selection.

The History of Race as a Concept

- *The Classifications of Linnaeus.* Linnaeus's theory of races and the four humors was discredited by science in the early twentieth century.
- *The Changing Meanings of "Race."* The concept of race has changed; in ancient Greece, it was synonymous with ancestral family and locale; in the Middle Ages with bloodline. It became affiliated with skin color in the seventeenth century. Race and personhood developed as political concepts, to allow for slavery. Darwin concluded that, in spite of apparent differences, humans are all of the same species. One way of distinguishing between race and ethnicity (usually a matter of cultural affiliation) is to say that racial designations are imposed on us by others but we choose our ethnicity.

- *Some Remarks on Race by Three Enlightenment Philosophers.* Rousseau was a proponent of environmentalism, which says that human skills and intelligence develop differently in different climates. Hume argued against environmentalism, but saw nonwhites as inferior to whites. Kant argued than no human being should be treated as a means to an end only, but believed that the white race constitutes the norm. Like others, he reflected the prejudices of his time.

Philosophy of Race Today

- *The Biology of Race: Current Theories.* Franz Boas and Ruth Benedict argued that nurture, not nature, is the key factor in cultural development. Murray and Herrnstein's *The Bell Curve* asserts that there is a connection between success, intelligence, and genetics. The critique of *The Bell Curve* is based on the authors' failure to research and explain underlying social factors affecting the statistics. No racial gene has been found; different racial characteristics can be found across various populations.

- *The Social Reality of Race and Racism.* Race is a social reality, if not a biological one. Can there be racial awareness without racism? Categories of race attitudes and racism include racialism, classic racism, unintentional racism, institutional racism, environmental racism, and race and class.

- *Should Race Be Embraced or Abolished as a Cultural Designation?* Affirmative action is seen as a backward-looking view when it offers compensation for past wrongs. In a forward-looking view, affirmative action works on the abolition of future discrimination. Criticism of affirmative action is based on the possibility that it may cause new forms of discrimination. Wasserstrom says race shouldn't matter any more than eye color does. Hill Collins says black women must develop a group identity to overcome dual oppression. Young says people should be recognized as belonging to racial groups. Blum believes the problem of racism can be solved by (1) understanding racism, (2) embracing multiculturalism, and (3) developing a sense of community. Zack asserts that we need a new cultural paradigm, where race is seen as ethnicity.

- *The Author's Confession: She Is Frustrated.* Although the United States has racial problems, it confronts them and works at them out in the open, which is a better approach than pretending they don't exist and refusing to recognize the reality of a multicultural society.

Primary Readings

- Naomi Zack, *Thinking About Race.* We need a new paradigm that sees race in terms of ethnicity, not biology. Views concerning racial differences would be identified as moral defects if they resulted in harm.

- Steven Cornell and Douglas Hartmann, *Ethnicity and Race.* Race is a social construct, not a biological reality.

Narratives

- *Mississippi Masala,* film: A young couple experiences discrimination from families and community when dating: She is ethnically from India but immigrated to the United States from Africa. He is a black American.

- *American History X,* film. A young skinhead changes his mind about racism after having spent time in prison with black inmates.

Notes

1. The term *Homo sapiens sapiens* is a scientific term used in physical anthropology to designate modern humans— humans from the past 60,000 years or so. *Homo sapiens* is the scientific term for the entire line of physically similar humans.

2. The edition of *Systema Naturae* from 1758 which is most commonly referred to as the year of publication is the 10th edition.

3. The German philosopher Nietzsche has been regarded as the main inspirational source for the Nazi concept of the "Master Race," with its overt racism and anti-Semitism. However, the version of Nietzsche's writings that reached the hands of Hitler was to a great extent edited and rewritten by Nietzsche's anti-Semitic sister Elisabeth. Please see Chapter 8 for more.

4. Audrey Smedley, *Race in North America: Origin and Evolution of a World View* (Boulder: Westview Press, 1993), pp. 56ff.

5. Charles Darwin, *The Descent of Man* (New York: Prometheus Books, 1998), p. 175

6. Ibid., pp. 185–186.

7. Emmanuel Chukwudi Eze, ed., *Race and the Enlightenment: A Reader* (Cambridge: Blackwell, 1997), p. 33.

8. Kant's solution was that Hume was right in that we can't observe actual causality; but he says that our mind is hardwired to understand causality, and thus we, appropriately, assume that things cause other things to happen. See Chapter 7.

9. Kant, "On National Characteristics," in *Race and the Enlightenment: A Reader,* ed. by E. C. Eze (Cambridge: Blackwell, 1997), pp. 55–56.

10. Naomi Zack, *Thinking About Race* (Belmont, Calif.: Wadsworth, 1998), p. 4.

11. Ibid., p. 4.

12. Smedley, p. 19.

13. Ruth Frankenberg, "Growing Up White," in *Dimensions of Culture I,* ed. John Berteaux and Gerald Doppelt (La Jolla: University of California, San Diego, College Custom Series, 1995), p. 311. Reprint from Ruth Frankenberg, *White Women, Race Matters: The Social Construction of Whiteness* (Minneapolis: University of Minnesota Press, 1993).

14. Zack, p. 41.

15. Zack, p. 41.

16. I am here assuming—based on my own experience— that the majority of immigrants wish to become, and actively work toward becoming, socially assimilated in their new homeland, even while maintaining and cherishing elements of their own cultural heritage. It is a different situation if an immigrant group voluntarily segregates itself and makes few attempts to become part of the social fabric of the adopted society.

Chapter Six

Different Gender, Different Nature?

Race and Gender—Same Issue?

The twentieth-century debate about race has often been compared to the debate about gender, because both debates focus on age-old patterns of discrimination and injustice. And indeed there are many parallels, but one element is starkly different: If people of different races (as the culture defines them) intermarry and have children, then, over generations, the racial differences will blur, and the issue of discrimination based on race will, presumably, become moot. We are already seeing that happen in parts of the United States, such as California. However, we can't use the same parallel on the gender issue: If men and women keep marrying and interbreeding, then will we finally get unisex people? Of course not, and this is where *Time* magazine's picture of the future American erred: The computer morphed all kinds of races together—but it also morphed the sexes, so the "future face" is more androgynous than her parents. Individuals may turn out to be androgynous, but not an entire new generation. Racial differences are social constructs and can be "deconstructed." Sex differences are partly a matter of social constructs, but also undeniably biological.

Gender Differences: Nature or Nurture?

Are men and women different? Most of us don't hesitate for even a split second: Of course we are. But then the next obvious question is, How different are we? And what does it matter? This is where the debate splits in two directions—because for some of us, the perceived gender differences matter greatly, and for others, they are peripheral compared to what really matters: our human similarities. We will look at both approaches in this chapter. First, we focus on the idea that gender differences have some fundamental significance for human lives. In that case we will want to ask, What are the factors that makes us different? Are they mainly cultural or biological? In other words, are they a matter of nurture or of nature? Can gender differences be changed, and would we want them to be? If women and men sometimes act as if we have come from different planets, as the psychologist John Gray has suggested with his popular books about men being "from Mars" and women "from Venus," is it the way things are and should be, or is it a personal interpretation of a cultural situation? A question that used to be very simple for most people in previous centuries and which is still simple for many people around the world has become extremely complex for us—partly because our knowledge of biology and psychology has expanded dramatically within the last hundred years, but also because it has become a political question. As we saw in the previous chapter, with assumptions of difference almost invariably comes an assumption of *inequality.* Like the question of race, the issue of gender and human nature tends to move freely from descriptive to normative statements—in other words, statements about facts, or perceived facts, often lead to statements about policies, or how one should deal with the facts. And as we saw in previous chapters, making the switch from a descriptive to a normative statement often ends up as an example of the *naturalistic fallacy,* going from an "is" statement to an "ought" statement without specifying the hidden value premise (see Chapter 3).

Generally, *sex* and *gender* are used in different contexts today: The term *sex roles* refers to the biological female and male functions related to sexual activity. The term *gender roles* refers to the social, moral, and political roles played by men and women in any given society. In this chapter we shall see how easily the philosophical tradition moves back and forth between views about biological sexual differences and views about social gender roles, often without even asking whether there might be a difference.

You'll remember reading about *behaviorism* in Chapter 4: Watson's and Skinner's early- to mid-twentieth-century theory that everything in human behavior is a matter of nurture, of exposure to some pressure in one's social environment. You will also remember behaviorism claiming that with the proper environmental influence, a child's personality and demeanor can be determined and molded in any direction whatsoever; there is no hereditary influence, and we are all "blank slates," so to speak, for experience to write on. Behaviorism didn't come up with the idea of the blank slate, however. It is part of an even older tradition in philosophy, the tradition of *empiricism,* which claims that the human mind is blank from birth; all knowledge stems from experience, so no knowledge is innate. We will talk about empiricism in much more detail in Chapter 7, but for now you just need to be acquainted with empiricism's idea that everything in the human mind comes from outside influences.

The relevance to the issue of male and female human nature is clear: From a behaviorist point of view, gender differences come from our upbringing, and if we change the upbringing, it will influence gender differences. While behaviorism in its radical form is no longer considered a correct or even feasible interpretation of human nature, its influence has been so profound that it continues to make itself felt in areas that otherwise have little direct relationship to Watson's and Skinner's psychological theories. One such area is gender theory.

In 1968 a terrible accident happened to a small boy in Winnipeg, Canada. During a botched circumcision his penis was burned so badly that it had to be amputated. As chance would have it, he was an identical twin; his brother was not subjected to circumcision because of the accident. A doctor at Johns Hopkins, a behaviorist, suggested that the injured boy be raised as a girl, based on two assumptions: (1) One's sexuality is based on genital function and (2) just like every other character trait, one's sexual identity can be modified and altered through one's environment. This approach represents the ultimate view of sexual identity being a matter of nurture, not nature; the theory is referred to as *psychosexual neutrality*. The young parents wanted to help their son any way they could and agreed to let him be surgically altered through castration and raised as a girl. Was the experiment a success? Did the child grow up to become a well-adjusted woman? Was the theory of psychosexual neutrality thus confirmed? We'll return to the story of the twins later in this chapter. For now, here is the relevance to modern feminist theories of gendered human nature.

There are two primary schools of thought about male and female human nature among today's feminist theories: The first holds that women and men are more similar than we are different and that the differences can be explained as primarily cultural rather than biological. I refer to this theory as *classical feminism*. The other theory, most often referred to as *difference feminism,* holds that women and men are fundamentally different, biologically as well as culturally. Difference feminism diverges from the "sexist" views of generations past, which used to insist that men and woman are different and unequal, in that difference feminism sees women and men as different but equal. Classical feminism sees gender differences as environmental and, as such, *they can be changed.* This doesn't mean that classical feminism is a purely behaviorist theory, but that it shares a certain viewpoint with behaviorism: the idea that psychological characteristics that may appear to be biological in reality stem from environmental influences. To be sure, there is much more to classical feminism than its "nurture" view, its main point being that women and men should be considered *persons* first and sexual or gendered beings second. For the classical feminist, the only relevant difference between men and women is whatever pertains to reproduction; and since much, perhaps most, of a human life is not related to reproduction, then sexual differences should be considered culturally and politically irrelevant.

Many other approaches to feminism deserve attention, such as radical feminism, eco-feminism, and Marxist feminism, but the classical and difference feminist approaches have the most explicit views of human nature and are most clearly opposed to each other. We take a closer look at these two theories later in this chapter. In a sense, each theory of human nature that we have looked at and will look at in future chapters has an approach to the gender issue, some theories more than others. You have already seen such examples in Chapters 2 and 3, and you will meet additional views on gendered human nature in upcoming chapters.

Three Non-Western Views of Gendered Nature

In this section we look at three examples of what we might call non-Western views, although the term is misleading: The first viewpoint comes from the American Indian tradition, which of course is geographically a Western culture. However, *Western* has come to mean "derived from the European tradition," rather than being a geographical indication, and thus the American Indian cultural tradition is often labeled non-Western.

In common to just about all major views of male and female human nature found outside the Western cultural realm is a general assumption that women and men are quite different in their reaction to issues, intellectually and emotionally; these differences are generally taken to be a result of our nature, rather than cultural influences. The foundational view of classical feminism—a view shared by Marxism, although the two need not coincide otherwise—that our common personhood is more important than our differences is a uniquely Western view. Feminist approaches to non-Western views vary according to the specific goals of the feminists involved: A *classical* feminist will usually find all such views as falling short

of the ideal of mutual respect for each other as persons. A *difference* feminist may appreciate and approve of many non-Western gender views, provided that these views allow women to flourish socially and culturally within their society, with the female behavioral styles and traditions being valued and respected by the male community. In the sections that follow, we explore how these different readings can determine whether one views the culture as liberal or as restrictive.

The American Indian Tradition

Across the tribal traditions in the nineteenth century, the predominant view seemed to be that women and men are fundamentally different, but not to the extent that women are regarded as the property of men. American Indian myths and legends indicate that the primary interest of tribal women was the well-being of their society, while men were more interested in individual feats of strength and cunning (in the Narratives section you will see stories from several American Indian tribes). Often, women in American Indian stories are also depicted as more earthy, physical, and lustful than men—in contrast to the gender views of many European settlers in the Victorian nineteenth century, who tended to believe that women were finer, more frail, and less sexually interested than men. (That is, white women were less interested, because part of the gender mythology of Euro-America in the nineteenth century was also that nonwhite women were more sexually interested than white women.) Another obvious difference is that in American Indian stories women often play the part of the avenger and the warrior, as well as the savior of the tribe. There seems to have been no assumption that women were incapable of undertaking such tasks. In stories of witchcraft (which are quite common), men as well as women are assumed to have such talents. Traditional American Indian societies have sometimes been represented by non-Indian sources as being predominantly patriarchal (male-dominated), with little freedom for women of the tribe. On the other hand, Indian as well as non-Indian sources portray such traditional societies as very gender-egalitarian, with much freedom for women and respect for women's work and status.

Why this difference? According to the American Indian scholar Paula Gunn Allen, several factors are at play. For one thing, such societies have often been misrepresented by European immigrants and commentators. Especially among Eastern tribes, women had great influence on public life as well as on everyday family decision making, to the point where several chiefs were female—war chiefs as well as peacetime chiefs. However, since the Europeans found this hard to believe, they would sometimes refer to these female leaders—generally known as *sunksquaws*—as being male, and it is only through historical research that we are now learning the truth about their gender. For another thing, according to Allen, while women in older Indian societies did have a considerable amount of freedom, the tribes picked up the habits of European patriarchy from the European settlers, and nineteenth-century Indian women may well have experienced less freedom than their foremothers. However, we should probably be cautious here about tracing everything patriarchal to the European influence; there is such great variety in customs among the American Indians themselves that customs of male domination may well have had ancient roots in some parts of the country.

Historically, it appears that women could be leaders in some tribes, but not in others. The Iroquois and Montagnais people had several female leaders. So, too, did the Navajo (Dineh) people, but only women who had gone through menopause could be leaders; women were considered spiritually dangerous when menstruating and were isolated and surrounded with a lot of taboos. In most tribes, women had some say concerning their future husband, and divorce was easy for women as well as for men. (Putting one's husband's saddle outside would suffice; he'd get the message!) Among the Navajo, women usually would inherit from their mothers, and men from their fathers, meaning that women could own and inherit property—something that their sisters in Europe were

fighting for until the nineteenth century. In addition, the family line was most often traced through the mother, not the father, making the American Indian cultures technically *matrilineal* instead of *patrilineal,* where kinship is traced through the father's family (traditionally the European way).

As I mentioned in the beginning of this section, it is also possible that the way we interpret the gender roles among American Indians depends to a great extent on *what we would like to see:* For the classical feminist, hoping for a society where there are no social gender differences except for issues relating to having babies, the traditional Indian society is far from ideal. The classical feminist notices that women are not treated the same as men and are considered to be far different from men and so may conclude that Indian women were generally living in a male-dominated society. However, difference feminists notice that American Indian women had far greater influence in their society than did their European sisters of the time; the Indian society recognized that women were different from men and respected the women's form of influence on society. A difference feminist may see this as close to an ideal situation and so may conclude that the American Indian society was extremely egalitarian and not male-dominated at all. For this reason, we should be cautious about concluding that the traditional American Indian societies were either egalitarian or male-dominated because the facts are often interpreted differently, all depending on who is doing the analysis. The same phenomenon can be observed when other non-Western societies are judged on their gender traditions.

The Muslim Tradition

As is the case with the Christian tradition, the Muslim tradition is far from being monolithic. Liberal and conservative views coexist within a tradition reaching back to the seventh century C.E. and embracing nations from Africa, the Middle East, and Asia. Contrary to the American political tradition, none of these countries recognize the separation of church and state, and the principles of the Koran (Qur'an) are considered fundamental rules for legislation as well as for morals and religious issues. Even so, the Koran can be interpreted in a number of ways by Muslim believers, from the ultraconservative approach of the Afghanistan all-male Taliban government, which deprived female citizens of most civil rights from 1996 to 2001, to Kuwaiti Muslim male politicians arguing (so far unsuccessfully) in favor of women's equal rights, including suffrage. In September 2000 a decree was issued by the Sudanese government that women were no longer permitted to work in public, quoting the Koran in support of the new policy's being a *protection* of women. This decree was immediately challenged by Sudanese civil rights leaders as well as Muslim working women who saw their livelihood and their hard-earned education and careers being wiped out. Street fighting ensued, and several women were killed. One passage from the Koran can and thus has been interpreted in a variety of ways, from a general admonishment to women not to appear scantily clad in public to a strict dress code for women as it was decreed by the Taliban society:

> And speak to the believing women that they refrain their eyes, and observe continence; and that they display not their ornaments, except those which are external; and that they throw their veils over their bosoms, and display not their ornaments, except to their husbands or their fathers, or their husbands' fathers, or their sons, or their husbands' sons, or their brothers, or their brothers' sons, or their sisters' sons, or their women, or their slaves, or male domestics who have no natural force, or to children who note not women's nakedness. (Sura XXIV, 30)

Muslims who do not approve of the particular interpretation of the Koran provided by the Taliban point out that such passages were not intended to restrict anyone's social freedom, but to create an appreciation for modesty and privacy.

Within the Muslim tradition there is no ban on women seeking an education and pursuing careers: In fact more women entered the universities and the workforce in Iran during the fundamentalist regime introduced by Ayatollah Khomeini than during the previous reign of Shah Mohammad Reza Pahlavi—a fact that may be a testimony to the relatively liberal education policy of the Khomeini government, but even more to the restrictive policies of the Shah's regime. However, despite the liberal voices within the Muslim tradition of today, it is recognized that the basic view of women within the Muslim tradition, as it has been interpreted by Muslim governments, does not make the quest for gender equality an easy one: "Men are superior to women on account of the qualities with which God has gifted the one above the other, and on account of the outlay they make from their substance for them. Virtuous women are obedient, careful, during *the husband's* absence, because God hath of them been careful" (Sura IV, 30). Even so, modern Muslim feminists point out that within the context of the Koran there are no limits set on women's social participation and freedom: A Muslim can live according to the laws of Islam and still be a feminist.

Asian Traditions

As many Asian Americans point out, the very term *Asian* is both inadequate and misleading: The cultural differences among the multitudes of Asian cultures, modern as well as ancient, are rarely appreciated by mainstream America, which tends to stereotype Asians into some general Chinese-Japanese mold—what a generation ago was called "Oriental." (And, indeed, European Americans of the first and second generation sometimes make the same complaint: There are such vast differences between European cultures that it is only at a comfortable distance—like on this side of the Atlantic—that one might think of throwing them all into the same "Western culture" basket.) We examined some of these issues in the previous chapter. Having said that, it just so happens that certain cultural traditions indeed are quite comparable across the board, such as traditional attitudes toward gender differences and gender politics. Here we take a brief look at the gender views of traditional China and India.

Asian immigrants to the United States generally share many experiences, and one of them is the stark contrast between their traditional gender roles and modern American attitudes toward gender. In the film *Mississippi Masala* (Chapter 5) you saw that when immigrants from India and the local black and white population of a Mississippi neighborhood met in a social context, there was a collision of attitudes toward gender. Occasionally I talk with immigrant students who find themselves caught between respect for their family tradition and the prevailing *mores* of Americans their own age. I had a female college student from India who was preparing a large Indian wedding. She was looking forward to it immensely: Her husband would show up in his finest clothes, on a white horse, as tradition demands, and carry her away. However, he had forbidden her to continue her studies once they were married. True to my own cultural heritage, I told her I believed the decision rested with her—and after her wedding I never saw her in class again. Perhaps she did make up her own mind. We should remember that just because someone makes a decision we don't approve of, it doesn't necessarily mean brainwashing or other coercion has been a factor.

The traditional Asian view of women and men—like traditional attitudes in this country, in Europe, and elsewhere—is that men are more valuable individuals than women. Women are, by their nature, created to serve men. In ancient China baby boys were celebrated, while the arrival of baby girls was lamented by many families. Girls were sometimes sold into prostitution or other forms of slavery, a practice that continues to this day in parts of Southeast Asia. In today's China, the traditional values have collided with the one-child-per-family rule to the extent that if a couple has a baby girl, they may try, illegally, for another child so the family will include a boy, thereby risking a forced abortion or fines and loss of social privileges—or they may quietly kill the baby girl so they are free to try for a boy. Here at the beginning of the new century there is already talk of a Chinese "lost generation," of a severe shortage of female children. In India, where there are no restrictions as yet on the number of children to a family, but where there generally is more widespread access to prenatal screening and abortions, female fetuses are being aborted over male fetuses in large numbers.

In China the preference for boys has deep social and religious roots in spite of a half century of Communist rule: A son carries on the family name, only a son can support his aging parents (because a daughter has been married off and is busy taking care of her in-laws), and only a son can perform the funeral rites over his parents. In India the emphasis is slightly different: While a family name is important, and a son will bring riches to the family through the dowry that his bride will bring in, each family with daughters will have to provide a considerable dowry for them to bring into their marriages. This means that having daughters is likely to ruin a family with a small or even average income; hence, the phenomenon of *dowry-deaths*. In India and Bangladesh it is not uncommon (although it is now illegal) for a young groom's family to dispose of a young daughter-in-law, if the family thinks the dowry was too small or disapproves of her in some other way. She *doesn't count* as a full-fledged person, being merely a woman and a bride; if the death is made to look like an accident, the family traditionally has been free to keep the dowry and seek another bride for their son. Such practices are frowned on by today's governments in India and Bangladesh, but old traditions die hard, especially since they are deeply anchored in a worldview that places women at a lower rung of the human ladder. (Box 6.1 examines the phenomenon of Goddess worship in India.)

The Buddhist philosophy and religion has provided a counterweight to the gender hierarchy in India, China, and Southeast Asia: According to Buddhist doctrine, human suffering is universal, and women as well as men are caught up in the wheel of existence. Generally, Buddhism recognizes women's as well as men's intellect and capacity to understand the deep truths about suffering; indeed,

Box 6.1   THE GREAT GODDESS IN INDIA

Around 2500 B.C.E. in the Indus Valley Harappa culture, a religion was thriving: the religion of the Great Goddess. As in other places in ancient times in Asia, the Middle East, Africa, and Southern Europe, a female deity was worshipped for her creative powers. Usually referred to as the Mother Goddess or the Great Goddess, she was often depicted as having large breasts, and she was also often depicted as pregnant. A life-giving force, she was considered to be the power that takes away life, and for that reason she might be depicted in her frightening aspect as the bringer of death. In many of the ancient goddess-worshipping cultures she is thought of as a three-in-one deity with a youthful aspect; a mature, nurturing aspect; and an aging aspect: the *maiden,* the *mother,* and the *old woman.*

Two thousand years later, goddess worship was integrated into the growing religion of Hinduism with its multitude of gods, each personifying a vital aspect of life. The ancient mother goddess was referred to as Devi (the Goddess), but was also thought of as different divine female personalities. One such is Kali, usually misrepresented by Western media—in particular, in movies such as *Gunga Din* and *Indiana Jones and the Temple of Doom*—as an evil spirit. Within her own cultural context, Kali is the force of life itself; her consort, Shiva—the Destroyer—takes back the life that she has given and completes the cycle.

According to some scholars, such as Maria Gimbutas, Gerda Lerner, and Riane Eisler (see chapter text),

one can conclude many things about a culture's social rules based on what we know about its religion. A *patriarchal* religion (a religion where the gods are male and female gods are either nonexistent or have little power) can be viewed as indicative of the society that worships those male gods: a society where men are more socially prominent and powerful than women. Similarly, a society in the past that has left us evidence of goddess worship in the form of goddess statuettes, and perhaps even myths, songs, and legends, is often taken as an indication that such a society was more *matriarchal* than patriarchal (with women in prominent social positions). However, this may be jumping to conclusions: The ancient Indus Valley culture, which was very rich in goddess artifacts, in fact did not seem to have a tradition of women holding prominent positions or any other indication of gender equality, as far as archaeologists have been able to determine (and their language still hasn't been deciphered). One can't conclude that a religion is a reliable mirror of the culture's social and political structures; one must look for additional evidence. And within Hinduism, with its ancient and still-active worship of numerous strong female deities, the lack of political and personal power of individual women is noticeable to this day. Hindu feminists point to the presence of female deities such as Kali, Durga, and Saraswati as a model for changing Hindu gender relations from within.

several holy figures in Buddhism, such as the Chinese Quan-Yin, are female. However, even within the Buddhist tradition there is adherence to a traditional view: In the long chain of reincarnations necessary to reach complete enlightenment, the final incarnation of the soul must be in a male body, for as wise as a female may be, the ultimate enlightenment is attainable only as a male. In Chapters 7 and 8 we take a closer look at Buddhism.

The Communist ideology in several parts of Asia—China, North Korea, and Vietnam—

provides for a complete reversal of such gender views. According to the Marxist-Leninist tradition, women and men ought to be treated completely on a par, as workers with an interest in a meaningful, productive life (see Chapter 9). For Lenin, even the institution of marriage is demeaning and oppressive to women, because they by definition become servants of their husbands, and so the Communist ideology calls for the abolition of marriage. However, in no country where Marxism has been adopted, has this view been consistently implemented. In Communist Asia, old gender values survive beneath the political surface.

Early Western Views of Gendered Nature

Throughout Western history the view of women's nature has determined the status of women. We have some evidence that women had high social standing in the ancient world when we go back farther than 3,500 years; and around the world we have evidence of variations in gender politics throughout known history. The patterns of gender politics prevailing for the past 3,500 years have been patriarchal, with some exceptions—such as Crete (until about 3,000 years ago), Ireland (until about 1,000 years ago) and America (certain Indian tribes until sometime in the nineteenth century). Some sociologists cite today's African American culture as an example of a largely matriarchal society within a generally patriarchal culture. From myths and legends we can extrapolate that men and women have, overall, been considered fundamentally different by nature, a difference that involves no pretense at social or moral equality. In some cultures (such as the Western culture of the eighteenth and nineteenth centuries), women were considered of a higher, finer moral quality than men, with the result that women were "protected" from the public sphere by being excluded from it, financially and intellectually. How much these views are influenced by religion and how much by politics is debatable, but there has generally been a mutual influence from both realms.

Plato

Plato's (427?–347 B.C.E.) political view on male and female human nature stands out as highly atypical in antiquity and the Middle Ages combined. This fact alone has caused many Plato scholars to suspect that Plato was not being serious—that he was in fact pulling the legs of his readers. To Athenians who were used to freeborn women having no say in public affairs and little

say in the home, the joke seemed a good one: that in an ideal society, both women and men should be assigned the positions and roles in life they were best suited for, under the assumption that the only significant differences between men and women are the man's greater overall physical strength and the woman's ability to give birth. In the *Republic,* Plato says,

> There is no occupation concerned with the management of social affairs which belongs to either woman or to man, as such. Natural gifts are to be found here and there in both creatures alike; and every occupation is open to both, as far as their natures are concerned, though woman is for all purposes the weaker.[1]

And what were these occupations that Plato would like to have seen opened up to women? *Republic* is a political fantasy revolving around Plato's notion of an ideal society. In this society a few select intellectuals, "philosopher-kings," or rulers, would rule the people with the help of the military and the police, the auxiliaries.

In Chapter 9 we look more closely at Plato's political vision. In this ideal society, women could qualify as "philosopher-queens" as well as auxiliaries. However, there is a fly in the ointment: For guardians, the welfare of the community should always come first, so no guardian should be allowed to raise a family. Male and female guardians would be matched by the state to achieve the best *eugenic* results (the creation of intelligent babies), and then their babies would be taken away from them and raised communally with other guardian children.

Could Plato really have been serious, considering the outrageousness of the theory? There are at least two very good reasons why we should assume that Plato was not joking. For one thing, Plato's mother was herself an accomplished thinker and may well have taught her son that women can do anything men can do, intellectually. For another, the one person who would have known if Plato was joking was his best student Aristotle. Aristotle used every opportunity to provide comments about his teacher being wrong, including

Box 6.2   ARISTOPHANES AND THE SPLIT HUMANS

Plato has another story of male and female human nature that has become at least as famous as his political theory; the difference is that this story probably really *is* a story concocted for entertainment. Of course, being fiction doesn't preclude it from having a deeper value as a symbolic or poetic image of gender relations. In an early work, *Symposium,* Plato's teacher and good friend Socrates—who is the main character in all his books, including the *Republic*—is at an all-male party. As the evening moves on into night and the wine flows freely, the guests discuss the nature of love and beauty. One guest, Aristophanes (a famous comedic playwright in Plato's contemporary Athenian society) tells his theory of male and female human nature, once he has composed himself after a bad case of the hiccups: Once upon a time humans were so mighty that they challenged the gods. Each human was round, with four legs, four arms, two faces (so nobody could sneak up on them); and each person could move in all directions, rolling with incredible speed. Some were all male, some were all female, and some were half male, half female. But Zeus was jealous of these mighty beings and he devised a plan to strike them down: He split them down the middle, so each got two arms, two legs, and so on.

These new half-people would hug each other trying to get back together again, but Zeus dispersed everyone, so now the male-female halves are looking desperately for each other, as are the male-male halves and the female-female halves. "And the reason is that human nature was originally one and we were a whole, and the desire and pursuit of the whole is called love. There was a time, I say, when we were one, but now because of the wickedness of mankind God has dispersed us.* This original theory of soul mates has become famous as a story of male-female partners looking for each other, but for Aristophanes it was just as natural for men and women to be looking for their gay or lesbian original half—something that supposedly was mirrored in Plato's own life, since Plato appears to have been homosexual. However, this little story was, in all likelihood, not intended as a great metaphysical theory, although it certainly has survived as a myth of the loss of sexual unity; it serves as an opener for Socrates, who has the final word, a praise of the quest for spiritual beauty.

---

*Plato, *Symposium, Dialogues of Plato,* trans. Benjamin Jowett (New York, Washington Square Press, 1968), v. 192.

acidic remarks about Plato's vision of equality, but there is never a hint that he thought his teacher might have been joking. (Box 6.2 tells a story from Plato's *Symposium* about the origin of the human sexes.)

Aristotle

Plato's most brilliant student, and one of the most influential thinkers in the entire history of the West as well as the Muslim world, had a very different view of gendered nature. Aristotle (384–322 B.C.E.) was the son of the court physician in the northern Greek city-state of Stagira; he entered Plato's Academy and was a student of Plato's for close to twenty years. However, in terms of Aristotle's philosophy of women's nature, we see little of Plato's influence and perhaps more of the influence of his father, the physician. In Aristotle's words,

> A woman is, as it were, an infertile male; the female, in fact, is female on account of inability of a sort, viz., it lacks the power to concoct semen out of the final state of the nourishment (this is either blood, or its counterpart in bloodless animals) because of the coldness of its nature . . . the offspring produced by a female are sometimes female, sometimes not, but male. The reason is that the female is as it were a deformed male, and the menstrual discharge is semen, though in an impure condition; i.e., it lacks one constituent, and one only, the principle of Soul. . . . This principle has to be supplied by the semen of the male.[2]

The words of Aristotle that "the female is as it were a deformed male" have reverberated through time with an influence that goes far beyond most other statements based on shoddy or immature science, and the reason is political: Regardless of scientific evidence, it was useful for the Western power structure to adopt Aristotle's view; and as some feminists point out, the view that women are somehow less "normal" than men is still with us even in the new millennium. Where did Aristotle get these "facts" from? We tend to think of him as the pioneer of science, but Aristotle himself was not a scientist as we know it; he was more like a science reporter and a philosopher of science. He relied greatly on the research of others and incorporated the results in his works. Oftentimes, the statements he relies on are statements of common knowledge at the time, "old wives' tales," and general prejudice. In view of the fact that both Socrates and Plato taught critical thinking to their students, it is an interesting fact that Aristotle's interests lay elsewhere: in the accumulation of knowledge of why things are the way they are, more than in a questioning of one's sources. So asking about the evidence for "women's coldness" and semen being the supplier of the soul would be futile. These were doctrines that Aristotle had picked up along the way.

So what is the picture of female nature Aristotle wants us to believe? Women are "deformed males," because they produce menstrual blood, not semen (under the faulty assumption that semen is the perfect end product of a refinement of blood). On this flimsy ground, Aristotle proclaims that women produce only the body of the baby, while men supply the soul; and since, for Aristotle, the soul is "better" than the body, the male's role in procreation is more noble than the female's. (In the Middle Ages, scholars went even further, developing the "empty vessel theory": Women supply absolutely nothing to the creation of a child; the semen has both body and soul of the baby, and the woman is just an incubator who "feeds" the fetus.) As to the coldness of women, this is another Aristotelian view, probably based in both medical assumption and superstition: Men are hotter and dryer than women, and cold produces female babies, while the male heat produces male babies. According to the thinker, if one wants to conceive a boy, one should not make love while it rains or the moist south wind blows. For Aristotle, the female fetus takes longer to develop than the male fetus, although he admits that no other animal gestation has that same anomaly. (As an aside, modern science has established that human fetuses start out with both male and female characteristics, with a leaning toward female characteristics—case in point: every fetus develops nipples. If the fetus is male, the special male characteristics develop later; so, in effect, the biological facts are the reverse of what Aristotle believed. Female is the "default" gender, not male.)

In terms of humanity's special quality of *rationality,* Aristotle saw both males and females as potentially rational but saw the way the genders administer their rationality as being different: The male is the model of rationality, because he can deliberate as well as act on his deliberation; the female has the capacity for rationality, but she is without the capacity to act on her thinking and put her thoughts into effect. For a modern reader, the inevitable question here is, If Aristotle makes a valid point that woman can't act on her reasoning, why is that? Might it be that, at Aristotle's time (and throughout Western history until recently), women didn't have the *political* means of putting their deliberations into effect? (Box 6.3 explores aspects of the current status of gender equality in the West.)

As we shall see in Chapter 9, for Aristotle, gender differences extend to a political principle: In his *Politics* he specifies that "the male is by nature superior, and the female inferior; and the one rules, and the other is ruled; this principle, of necessity, extends to all mankind."

Christianity

The views of three major Christian thinkers, St. Paul (first century C.E.), St. Augustine (354–430 C.E.), and St. Thomas Aquinas (1225–1274 C.E.), align themselves with the biblical story of Eve being

Box 6.3   WHO IS MOST "GENDER-LIBERATED"?

Often we tend to think that the most gender-liberated time and place has to be the Western world of the early twenty-first century, the United States in particular. But it often depends on how we define "gender-liberated." In comparison with the early and middle years of the twentieth century, we have indeed progressed. But for the *radical feminist* who looks for the *root (radix)* of inequality, and sees ancient patterns of oppression even within the modern structures of gender equality, it is a relative statement: We are nowhere near our goal of complete equality. Historians speculate that if we go back 3,500 years or more, we find cultures with a much higher level of gender equality than we have reached today. It also depends greatly on which area we focus on: In the *public sphere,* where people live their professional lives, there is no doubt that the United States is farther along in gender equality than most other Western countries; however, in the private sphere things don't look so bright in the United States. The overall impression one has is that a woman is still expected to be the primary (if not the only) caregiver, in addition to her work outside the home; men still only sporadically share the housework and the children's upbringing—we talk about "soccer moms," not "soccer dads." In contrast, women have not fared too well professionally in the most liberally progressive countries on the planet, the Scandinavian countries: The "old boys' network" is alive and well in business as well as in politics and education. Norway has had decades of affirmative action, recruiting women in higher education, as students and professors, but in Denmark and Sweden the academic glass ceiling is still a fact of life. A progressive Danish newspaper recently ran a series called "Ask the Professors"—consisting of metaphysical and technical questions asked of presumably the brightest minds in Denmark. Out of the ten chosen professors, not one was female (or of foreign origin—see Chapter 5). When I asked why, the editor replied that they didn't believe in quotas—but also that the absence of female professors in the series was an unintended "statistical coincidence," because only 64 out of 859 active university professors in Denmark are women (which really only raises more questions). However, on the home front, Scandinavian men participate at a rate far higher than that for American men. It is quite common for Scandinavian men to take a (state-supported) paternity leave, of *equal* length to the mother's maternity leave; fathers stay at home to care for their sick children almost as often as mothers do. Scandinavian men are expected to participate in the upkeep of the home and the raising of the children at a much higher level than most American men, with no social stigma of "demasculinization" attached. So it is no wonder that "gender equality" acquires a different face, depending on where you look and what you look for.

created from Adam's rib, making woman a secondary creation to Adam. (Just for the record, men do *not* have one rib fewer than women, contrary to popular belief!) St. Paul, often quoted for saying that women ought to remain quiet in assemblies, also states that as a wife belongs to her husband, so, too, does the husband belong to his wife, and that as woman was created from man in the beginning, so now men are born from women. However, we also hear that woman was created for man, and not man for woman. Augustine, showing an influence from Plato's philosophy but not from his gender theory in particular, believes that the human body serves as a prison for our soul throughout our lifetime (see Chapter 8), and any sensuousness ties the soul further to the body and distracts it from contemplating the eternal life. The biblical words that man and woman were created in the image of God are read by Augustine to mean that, together, man and woman are the image of God; man alone is also the image of God, but not woman alone, because to Augustine woman is more inherently sexual than man and thus further removed from God. The idea that the Fall in the Garden of Eden resulted from Eve's tempting Adam *sexually* is Augustine's interpretation, according to several biblical scholars. In Chapter 8 we take a closer look at

Augustine's philosophy of the soul and of good and evil.

Neither Paul nor Augustine had any knowledge of Aristotle's writings, but the situation was different for Aquinas. Aristotle's works, long forgotten in the West, had been studied continually in the Middle East—and influenced the development of the philosophical theology of Islam several centuries after its proclamation by Muhammad in the seventh century—and during Aquinas's lifetime, Aristotle's works were finding their way back into Western philosophy, translated into Latin. Aquinas was so impressed with the works of Aristotle available to him that he tended to refer to Aristotle as "the Philosopher." However, Aquinas, who took pride in solving religious quandaries not only through faith but also through reasoning, found it difficult to reconcile certain aspects of the Bible with some of Aristotle's statements, such as his assertion that a woman is a deformed male. For why would God deliberately create anything imperfect? Aquinas's intellectual genius led him to a compromise. The Bible and the Philosopher were each right, in their own way: As a gender, woman is not deformed. Eve was created as the helpmate of man in procreation and served a perfect purpose. However, individual women are, as Aristotle said, deformed males, because if they had been perfect, they would have been born male! In Chapter 8 we also return to Aquinas.

In Aquinas's day, the few roles women could play in society were decreased even further. The right of abbesses to receive confessions from their nuns was revoked, and women were excluded from universities where they had, until then, had a limited influence in women's programs of religious studies. Hildegard of Bingen (1098–1179), founder of two convents, adviser to kings and popes, and an accomplished writer of natural science and medicine, as well as a composer, suffered the insult of having her works rejected by the bishop of Paris, on the grounds that she was a woman, when she offered them as a teaching tool to the new University of Paris. The Holy (Spanish) Inquisition experienced an increase in its activities of seeking and prosecuting heretics, and the practice of burning suspected witches at the stake was beginning to flourish.

England and Continental Europe in the Early Modern Age

In his social and political philosophy, the British philosopher John Locke (1632–1704) included an attack on the prevailing view that males ought to have full power in the household—an ancient right known as *patria potestas*—on the grounds that in nature, males and females generally share the responsibility of raising the young. The longer the infancy of the species, the longer the male and female stay together, according to Locke; since humans experience the longest childhood of all animal species, it is therefore natural that the mother and father share custody and responsibility for the upbringing of the child. Politically, Locke still regards the father as the primary parent, but insists that women raising their own children in the father's absence should be considered a natural and obvious alternative (and here we must remember that in Locke's day a mother, losing her husband, might also lose her children to her husband's closest relatives). Since husband and wife can't agree on all things and sometimes on very few things, Locke considers a divorce an acceptable alternative, once the upbringing of the children is accomplished. We return to Locke in Chapters 7 and 9.

Jean-Jacques Rousseau, the Swiss philosopher (1712–1778), voiced the revolutionary idea that children ought to be raised the natural way, with as few rules and regulations as possible. Famous today for coining the phrase "back to Nature" and providing significant inspiration for the democratic ideals (as well as the bloodbath) of the French Revolution, Rousseau held ideas on gender equality that were much less democratic. In *Emile*, his enormously influential book on child pedagogy that inspired a new approach to child rearing for generations (including an extremely harsh treatment of the little Danish crown prince

Frederik, later Frederik VI, by his German tutor in the early 1800s), Rousseau suggests that children should be raised in close proximity to nature, allowing their own healthy human nature to thrive: Exposed to fresh air at all times of the year, the child will regain the health that civilization has robbed humans of. The small boy, Emile, should be encouraged to explore nature, play outside, go barefoot and lightly clad to harden him (because in Rousseau's view, people living close to nature are physically and mentally sounder than people in the cities—"civilized" people).

In terms of human biology, Rousseau states that women and men by nature are similar in every way that has nothing to do with procreation; however, in the same breath, he asserts that just about everything that has to do with feelings and the intellect is related to the fact of procreation. His conclusion is that men and women are by nature fundamentally different and should be treated differently, even from early childhood. The little girl, Sophie, should be encouraged to be just as natural as Emile—but in a feminine way. For Rousseau this implies encouraging her coquetry, her love of pretty clothes, a superficial talent for music, and a capacity for light conversation, all for the purpose of training her to be the perfect partner for her future husband. She must learn to flirt well, because by "playing hard to get" she will enhance the man's pleasure when she finally gives in. She must be intelligent enough to be a good conversation partner for her husband, but not so smart that she outsmarts him; that would make her less womanly.

So Sophie must be guided toward the life nature has intended for her, as a clever housekeeper and helpmeet for her husband. She must be kept busy, never idle; she must learn to read and count, so she can manage the household. She should learn art (still lifes only, not landscapes or figure painting); she must learn to preserve her sweetness and seductiveness even in the face of being wronged. As for religion and philosophy, there is no need for Sophie even to think about them, for according to Rousseau girls can't understand these

subjects. All they need to know are the basic dogmas. However, girls should not neglect their reason, because reason allows them to understand their duties as wives and mothers.

Rousseau was not unfamiliar with intellectual women: The French intellectual clubs of the period, *les salons,* were hosted by such educated women and were to a great extent the active forces "behind the scenes" of important power changes in French politics. Rousseau owed much to the salons for advancing the popularity of his own philosophy. But in spite of his influential theories of child rearing, he never raised any child of his own. It wasn't that he didn't have the opportunity: While living at the mansion of his common-law wife, he had five children with her, each of which he promptly deposited at the local orphanage. We will encounter Rousseau again in Chapter 9.

In England, the philosopher Mary Wollstonecraft (1759–1797) read Rousseau's works and was infuriated. One of the few writers of the eighteenth century who directly addressed the women's situation, Wollstonecraft suggested in her book *Vindication of the Rights of Women* that not only is it not fair to women to train them to be uneducated, unthinking creatures who are only eager to please, but it is also unfair to men: Although a man may fall in love with that kind of woman, he certainly won't want to live with her. After all, what will the two have in common once the seduction is over and they are married? Indeed, if all a young girl is trained for is to be a flirt, how is she supposed to stop flirting once she is married? No, women should have the same educational opportunities as men. Wollstonecraft believes that if they don't measure up, then men will have reason to claim superiority—but to apply a double standard, one for men and one for women, is to make a mockery out of virtue itself. Since Wollstonecraft—a product of the Western Enlightenment, the Age of Reason—sees the male and female capacity for reason as being the same, then the idea of superimposing different rules for how the two genders should employ this capacity in order to become decent individuals has no foundation in actual human nature. It is simply a ploy to keep one gender under the control of the other.

The insistence on appearance and style that Rousseau favors as natural for the young girl is nothing but a distraction to Wollstonecraft, a distraction that has a peculiar parallel in the lives of military men. What do middle-class women and soldiers have in common? They both spend an inordinate amount of time worrying about their poise, their outfits, their general appearance and all its details. And why is that? Because, says Wollstonecraft, both groups are limited to a very narrow little world with few means of expression and influence; both are rigorously trained to acquire skills, and neither group is taught to think in terms of critical awareness. Both groups live within strict hierarchies of power. Her point is, of course, that if women have ended up as frilly, vain, distracted humans, then so have military men, a traditional example of extreme masculinity! The lack of intellectual scope has nothing to do with gender, in other words, and everything to do with an intellectually limited training program. If women were allowed an education, their fields of interest would broaden, and the focus on vanity would disappear.

Mary Wollstonecraft was much ridiculed at the time by male scholars; one even wrote an anonymous essay (*Vindication of the Rights of Brutes*) in which he claimed that giving women rights would be as ludicrous as giving animals rights, because women to him were just one small step up from animals. Ironically, women of course now have rights in Western countries—and these same countries are also contemplating animal rights!

Wollstonecraft may have lived an intellectual life that was far removed from the traditional lives of most women at the time, but her manner of death was tragically gender-related: she died giving birth to her daughter Mary. Under her married name Shelley, this second Mary Wollstonecraft gave life to another kind of creature with the story of Frankenstein and his monster.

In Germany, the philosopher Immanuel Kant (1724–1804) weighed in on the side of Rousseau. Today Kant is best known for his epistemological

and legal philosophy, as well as for his moral philosophy emphasizing that, as a moral requirement, one ought never to treat another human being as a tool or stepping-stone for one's own purpose, even if that purpose would have good consequences. We know it as Kant's rule *never to treat another rational being as merely a means to an end* (see Chapter 10). However, *who* qualifies as a rational being has become a question for modern interpreters of Kant. You saw in Chapter 5 how Kant's views on race, although in themselves never particularly influential, give us a picture of the general prejudices of the time period. Kant's view of male and female human nature is as much a part of his time period as his views on race; perfectly capable of rising above the political notions of God-given inequality of his own day and age and willing to do so, Kant seemed utterly uninterested in questioning its gender views. Although his term *rational being* is intended to include all human beings, Kant expresses doubts about whether women actually count as fully rational in the same sense he believes men do.

Like Rousseau, Kant represents the classical male attitude of adoration of woman as civilizer and guardian of beauty. In his essay, "On the Distinction of the Beautiful and Sublime in the Interrelations of the Two Sexes," Kant describes the dangers of allowing women to think too hard:

> Laborious Learning or painful pondering, even if a woman should greatly succeed in it, [destroys] the merits that are proper to her sex, and because of their rarity they can make of her an object of cold admiration; but at the same time they will weaken the charms with which she exercises her great power over the other sex. A woman who has a head full of Greek . . . or carries on fundamental controversies about mechanics . . . might as well even have a beard.[3]

In other words, Kant didn't consider it inconceivable that women might actually perform as rationally as men, but found it dreadfully unbecoming. For most college students of today, such opinions belong to centuries past, not to the present, but for many college instructors, it is only a matter of re-membering back a generation to when such views were frequently voiced—particularly by older male college professors in order to discourage their female students from pursuing intellectual careers, regardless of the students' demonstrated intellectual skills. (And, yes, your author is speaking from experience!)

In England in the next generation, two philosophers embarked on a spiritual partnership that was to bring the issue of women's rights permanently into focus in English-speaking countries: John Stuart Mill (1806–1872) and Harriet Hardy Taylor (1807–1858) became acquainted while they were both in their mid-twenties. Mill was on his way to becoming the most influential social thinker in the English-speaking world of the nineteenth century, and Taylor was already deeply engaged in two pursuits: One was her interest in women's suffrage (the right to vote); the other was her role as a wife and a mother of two small children. Attracted to each other in more than spiritual ways, Mill and Taylor nevertheless chose not to break up the Taylor marriage and remained intellectual friends, until they were able to marry some twenty years later, following the death of Taylor's husband.

Mill's philosophical commitment was to the theory called *utilitarianism:* Maximize the happiness and minimize the misery of as many as possible. As a child, Mill showed signs of being extremely intelligent and received a fast-paced privately tutored education with no time set aside for play. Later he claimed, with much modesty, that any child given that much attention would perform equally well. His father, James Mill, was a believer in the empiricist *tabula rasa* theory: Minds are blank slates from the start, and their performance is entirely dependent on what one puts into them (you will recognize this idea from the beginning of this chapter and from Chapter 3: Watson's behaviorism was based on the same premise). However, this did not prompt him to educate his daughters Willie, Harriet , and Clara with the same zeal, although they may have had quite as much potential as John and did join him in learning

Greek and Latin. John's meeting with Harriet Taylor opened his eyes to the injustice and disparities in the social and political situation of women, and throughout his adult life—even past the lifetime of Taylor herself—the question of gender equality was important to him.

A member of the British Parliament, John Stuart Mill was the first male feminist to have sufficient political clout to bring the subject of women's rights to the forefront, submitting a proposal to the Parliament in 1866 that women ought to have complete political equality. This measure was defeated but resulted indirectly in British women achieving a limited right to vote in 1918, with women in the United States getting the vote in 1920.[4] His book on the women's issue, *The Subjection of Women,* was published in 1869, eleven years after Harriet's death. However, Taylor's own writings on the subject had already appeared in 1851. Neither Mill nor Taylor believe that male and female human nature is exactly the same; both believe that there are significant differences, but none so severe that politically different treatment is warranted. Mill even argues that since the world has never experienced a society where women have not been oppressed, it is impossible to predict exactly what female human nature would be like in a society where both genders were equal.

An argument can still be heard in the Western world in conjunction with remaining all-male institutions or professions: All professions ought to be open to both genders because if the job can be handled well by *some* women (or men), then it would be a grave injustice to ban them from that profession on the assumption that *most* women (or men) can't do it. And if it turns out that no women (or men) can handle the job, then banning them from that profession is pointless; they will disqualify themselves soon enough.[5] This argument was advanced by both Mill and Taylor. In her words,

Let every occupation be open to all, without favour or discouragement to any, and employment will fall into the hands of those men and women who are found by experience to be most capable of worthily exercising them. There need be no fear that women will take out of the hands of men any occupation which men perform better than they. Each individual will prove his or her capacities, in the only way capacities can be proved—by trial, and the world will have the benefit of the best faculties of all its inhabitants.[6]

Decades later, her widowed husband echoed her words, giving her credit for being his source of inspiration:

> What women by nature cannot do, it is quite superfluous to forbid them from doing. What they can do, but not so well as the men who are their competitors, competition suffices to exclude them from. . . . Any woman, who succeeds in an open profession, proves by that very fact that she is qualified for it. And in the case of public offices, if the political system of the country is such as to exclude unfit men, it will equally exclude unfit women: while if it is not, there is no additional evil in the fact that the unfit persons whom it admits may be either women or men. As long therefore as it is acknowledged that even a few women may be fit for these duties, the law which shuts the door on those exceptions cannot be justified by any opinion which can be held respecting the capacities of women in general. . . . Who can tell how many of the most original thoughts put forth by male writers, belong to a woman by suggestion, to themselves only by verifying and working out? If I may judge by my own case, a very large proportion indeed.[7]

In Austria in the early 1900s one man set forth a view of female human nature that was to have repercussions throughout the entire century in the West, continuing even today. Sigmund Freud's (1856–1939) view of men and women as sexual beings has been controversial since its publication; but even so, many doctors, psychologists, and scholars accepted it as an obvious truth and it has only recently been challenged. You saw in Chapter 3 that Freud believed in a fundamentally selfish human nature and gave us the concept of the Unconscious. You also heard of the *Oedipus complex,* the theory that the young boy is emotionally and sexually attracted to his mother and

wishes to eliminate his father. In Chapter 3 you read a brief mention of *castration fear,* a significant part of the Oedipus complex. In his very influential lecture on "The Psychology of Women" from 1933, Freud speculates that, as the young boy experiences attachment to his mother and hostility toward his father, he feels fear that the father will retaliate by castrating him. What is far less publicized is Freud's theory that women have an Oedipus complex, too, directed against their mother. Popularly, this theory used to be known as the *Electra complex,* from the Greek tragic heroine Electra, who kills her mother, Queen Clytemnestra, and her mother's lover as a revenge for their murder of her father, King Agamemnon. However, in his famous analysis of female sexuality Freud himself calls it the female Oedipus complex.

The psychological drive behind the female Oedipus complex, according to Freud, is that the little girl is also deeply attached to her mother, as the first person in her life; however, this attachment is usually transferred to the father, and the young girl feels hostility toward her mother. Why? Because at a certain point in time it occurs to the little girl that physically, she is incomplete: She has no penis. This is the phenomenon that Freud refers to as *penis envy.* Freud believes that the little girl thinks having a penis is the normal condition and believes she has been deprived of hers. And who did it? *Her mother,* being jealous because dad pays attention to his daughter. So the little girl suffers, not from fear of castration like the boy, but from the aftereffects of an imagined castration: She develops hostility toward her mother and a sexual attraction toward her father. How did Freud reach this conclusion? Through conversations with female patients about their childhood memories and dreams. And since those memories would usually be repressed, and the *latent dream thoughts* (see Chapter 3) would only become clear through analysis, Freud *extrapolates* from what he hears his female patients tell him.

The penis envy will, eventually, lead the grown woman to a wish to have children of her own—preferably boys—as a form of penis replacement, a "symbolic equivalent." And women's attachment to their father is permanent. This means that a woman will never truly get out from under the Oedipus complex, and so women are less independent, and less adult, than men, according to Freud's gender theory. This complex has deep consequences for the grown woman, who in her sense of ethics and justice will always lag behind the man, since she is in a perpetual state of envy. Women have a harder time overcoming their instincts, they grow old and set in their ways faster than men—and throughout a woman's sexual life, her attraction to men, even when it is healthy, is just a way to acquire a boy-child as a penis replacement. She will always be more attached to her son than her husband, for the same reason.

This gender theory has lost almost all credibility at the beginning of the twenty-first century, at least among feminists. The theory that a little girl will assume that she is defective because she has no penis was challenged in the mid–twentieth century by Simone de Beauvoir, who tells in *The Second Sex* that she knew of a small boy who grew up in a household of women. He grew up thinking that the female anatomy was normal and that he himself was defective. In the intellectual environment of the late twentieth century and early twenty-first, some psychologists have noted that with the "negative press" given to men and boys in the media, and even in commercials (the husband or the boy is always wrong), small boys may question their own normality. But other of Freud's assumptions were challenged early on by American psychologist Karen Horney: Why should we assume that all women want to be different than they are, biologically? For one thing, if a little girl says she wants a penis, it may not be anything other than a passing thought; it doesn't mean she wants to be a boy. For another, the girls who were tomboys in Freud's day and age and really acted as if they wanted to be boys are not nearly as common any more—because now girls are by and large allowed to do the kind of things only boys were allowed to do in the past! And, lastly, if a grown woman expresses the wish that she'd rather be a man (and it isn't a case of transsexualism) and says she despises women, it is usually because she

feels that only men have the social opportunities that she would like to have. In the more equal society of today, most women are not likely to seriously envy men their genitalia, regret the fact that they can have children, or even say "I wish I were a man."

Modern Western Feminism: "Classical" and "Difference"

In the United States it took the women's movement seventy-two years to accomplish its goals, from an official start in 1848 with the Seneca Falls Declaration of Sentiments, authored by Elizabeth Cady Stanton and others, to the Nineteenth Amendment in 1920, giving American women universal voting rights. The argument made by these early feminists was most often that while there may be biological gender differences, they are not so fundamental that a difference in rights and privileges should be based on gender. Often, the view is expressed like this: The gender differences between men and women are of cultural origin. *Gender difference is by and large a social construct.* Raise a generation of boys and girls with similar rules and similar opportunities, and we shall see that women and men are fundamentally human beings; their gender differences are of minor importance. In the 1970s the term *unisex* was quite popular as a political goal. In other words, male and female nature, the way we have seen it unfold, is a matter of *nurture,* not *nature,* and if we wish to alter the behavioral patterns of men who dominate women and women who allow themselves to be dominated, then we have to start in early childhood and treat both boys and girls as people first—meaning treat them similarly—and as gendered beings a distant second. This is the view I call *classical feminism.* It is shared by most early feminists, and a great number of contemporary feminists. Education is key; what is needed includes equal treatment by teachers and equal access to studies and job opportunities, with educational pressure to undo the stereotypes we all know from children's books and commercials—mom the homemaker and dad the breadwinner. The most influential classical feminist in the twentieth century may be the French philosopher Simone de Beauvoir, but in the American debate, Betty Friedan represents the same general viewpoint.

Beauvoir was a proponent of the philosophy of *existentialism,* believing that there is no human nature (see Chapter 4) and that each person, male and female, chooses his or her role in life. Beauvoir cites the notion of male and female gender roles as a matter of bad faith, of traditions superimposed on people.[8] Echoing Mary Wollstonecraft, Beauvoir insists that with the proper education and training in abstract thinking, the special "feminine" character of charming ditziness will be a thing of the past.

However, since the 1980s, classical feminism has been challenged by a new form of feminism, often called *difference feminism.* Difference feminism holds that women and men are fundamentally different and that social and political philosophy ought to take this into consideration and review the behavioral styles and capabilities of men and women as different, but politically equal. The psychologist Carol Gilligan may be the most visible proponent of difference feminism, arguing in her landmark book, *In a Different Voice* (1985), that women tend to focus on nurturing, caring solutions, while men tend to move toward solutions involving fairness and justice. Although many difference feminists don't commit themselves to saying whether the differences are due to cultural or natural influences, there is a general tendency among difference feminists to think of these differences as somehow preprogrammed into the female and male psyches: In other words, we are talking *nature* more than *nurture.* And classical feminism, from Mary Wollstonecraft onward, has been severely criticized by this new feminism. The difference feminist may interpret the classical feminist fascination for abstract, intellectual thinking as a pandering to and worship of the cognitive and behavioral styles of men. Instead of wanting women to think abstractly, like men, a difference feminist may insist that we appreciate the traditional style of women's kind of knowledge: concrete rather than abstract, intuitive rather

than logical. In the next chapter you will encounter an added criticism by difference feminists directed toward classical feminists: If the classical feminist aligns herself (or himself) with the classical philosophical focus on mind-work, on intellectualism, it could be because she or he inadvertently believes that the traditional male style of abstract knowledge and logical behavior is more worthy than a more concrete, intuitive female form of behavior. In other words, say the critics, classical feminists such as Beauvoir are afraid of their own physical, female nature—they suffer from fear of the body, *somatophobia.*

Another difference feminist is Riane Eisler, whom you'll remember from Chapter 3, weighing in on the issue of human aggression and the *partnership* versus the *dominator* model of social life. For Eisler, the aggressive lifestyle that we are familiar with around the world today stems from the takeover of ancient, more peaceful cultures by invading patriarchal cultures more than 3,500 years ago. These ancient, less aggressive cultures were, in Eisler's interpretation, matriarchal in nature, either governed by women or at least allowing women to hold high social positions. While the matriarchal lifestyle may be lost, each woman carries with her the nonaggressive cooperation style of the ancient matriarchy and can teach it to the misguided aggressive males of the present.

A scholar who would perhaps balk at being classified as a difference feminist but who has nevertheless supplied much of the empirical groundwork for this view is the linguist Deborah Tannen. With an array of popular as well as scholarly works exploring the different conversational styles of men and women, in private relationships as well as in the workplace, Tannen reaches the conclusion that women and men are indeed fundamentally different in their expectations of other people and relationships—and some of it seems to be biological, though much of it can be traced to acculturation. Tannen bridges the gap between difference feminists and classical feminists in that her goal is to train us to understand the other gender better; by achieving that understanding, she believes, we become quite capable of moving

NON SEQUITUR. ©Wiley Miller. Dist. by Universal Press Syndicate. Reprinted with permission. All rights reserved.

Good jokes probably shouldn't have to be dissected, but try anyway: Why is this funny?
(And if you don't find it funny, try to explain why!)

around in the world and relating to people in the style of the other gender. It may not feel "natural," but it can be done. We are not from different planets—Mars or Venus or elsewhere—and with a bit of effort we can communicate quite well across the gaps of our different styles.

In her bestseller *You Just Don't Understand* (1985), Tannen shows us how to relate to our partner of the other sex; in *Talking from Nine to Five* she demonstrates how working in a two-gendered professional environment can be accomplished, although she concedes that the deck is still stacked against the female conversational style in the workplace. But Tannen goes further: in the same book she explores the subject of sexual harassment, seen from a male and a female point of view, and her analysis reveals what she believes to be a fundamental difference between the life experiences of women and men. Women's worry about sexual harassment comes from a deep-seated fear that few men truly understand: the ever-present fear of being the *victim of violence.* Since most women feel physically vulnerable and never know when a situation might arise where violence is imminent—from a shove to mugging to rape, possibly resulting in death—most women have a fundamental awareness of such possibilities. This offends most men because they don't consider themselves (and usually are not) violent. But how is a woman to know? On the other hand, says Tannen, the

male fear of being sexually harassed has nothing to do with being overpowered, but everything to do with being manipulated and *betrayed,* either by a woman with whom they have had a relationship, and who turns on them, or by a stranger who accuses them falsely of harassment. And since most women wouldn't accuse a man falsely of sexual misconduct, this assumption offends most women. Always the bridge-builder, Tannen suggests that we get to know each other's fears before we judge each other's reactions. In the Primary Readings section you will find an excerpt from Tannen's *You Just Don't Understand* where she explores men's tendency to seek independence and women's tendency to seek intimacy.

Interestingly, many antifeminists such as Rousseau, Kant, and a number of twentieth-century thinkers would agree completely with difference feminism, as far as the "difference" is concerned: Men and women are indeed fundamentally different and should be treated as such. The traditional antifeminist will usually agree that it is a man's prerogative to think abstractly and rationally and a woman's to think in concrete terms, with a well developed intuition. But for the antifeminist, there is no emphasis on "different *but equal.*" The difference translates into privileges for one gender and a denial of rights for the other. For a classical feminist, the dividing line between a difference feminist and an antifeminist is dangerously thin:

Box 6.4   HARD EVIDENCE?

In the last few years, scientists have offered tentative evidence of biological differences in the hardwiring of male and female human brains; however, they are usually quick to point out that while men and women may use their brains differently, they generally reach the same results within the same span of time. The political undertone is noticeable: Women and men may be different, but "their methods are equally good," as a television commentator remarked. Brain research has found that women tend to use a greater area of their brain when solving mathematical problems, working with both brain hemispheres, while men tend to use the left brain hemisphere more for such problems. A study concerning female and male capacities for finding one's way, reported by NBC in December 1999, showed that male creatures, from rats to birds to men, tend to orient themselves in general spatial terms such as east and west, while female creatures tend to orient themselves with the help of landmarks. They each seem to get to where they are going equally fast when given the kind of direction they relate best to, but are lost when given the other type of directions. Could this be the reason why many men feel lost at the mall, where there are plenty of landmarks, but few compass references, and many women dislike having to rely on reading maps? The study suggested that we need to become better at giving directions, tailoring our directions to the mapping style of the person asking directions. There was no discussion of the implications for women who are good at compass type of directions or for men who do well with landmark directions—or for individuals who can handle both types well. Nor was there yet any explanation for this phenomenon other than it might be "hormonally related"; the study group seemed limited to a few individuals. When doing an informal survey of my own in my class on the philosophy of women, it became clear that the ease or difficulty of finding directions and various styles of finding one's way, are very real but seem to have little to do with gender: Some students used landmarks, while others used spatial referents, regardless of their sex. However, as one student remarked, it may have everything to do with the direction-finding style of your home and your culture.

If one views differences between women and men as fundamental, with no real reason or chance to do anything about them, then the will to meet halfway and understand each other may dwindle to the point where the "different *but equal*" view likewise fades. And since cultural tradition has devalued women's traditional styles, the classical feminist sees it as a threat to gender equality to claim that women aren't capable (or are less capable) of abstract thinking, reasoning, and so forth—a claim that has little other than tradition to support it.

However, it is hard for classical feminists to deny that some fundamental behavioral differences seem to be in effect, even cross-culturally: Most little girls seem to have different play patterns than most little boys. As several psychologists have shown, little girls tend to play with one or two friends, in an intimate game based on their friendship; little boys tend to play in larger groups, with some form of established (and challenged) hierarchy. The issue of whether there is a gendered nature, and what it consists of, has in no way been settled—not by biologists, psychologists, linguists, or philosophers. (Box 6.4 explores the possibility of a male and female hardwiring for directions.) But perhaps we are getting closer. In the beginning of this chapter I mentioned the tragic story of the little boy who lost his penis to a botched circumcision and was raised as a girl. Now we take a closer look at his/her story.

The Boy Who Was Raised as a Girl: Nature More Than Nurture?

In the introduction to this chapter you read about the baby boy—a twin—who, in 1968, lost his penis to a botched circumcision and his identity as a boy to surgical castration (removal of his testicles) and an upbringing as a girl. At the time sex researcher John Money of Johns Hopkins Institute said the boy would be able to grow up as a well-adjusted girl if raised as a girl and given hormonal treatment in puberty. "She" would be able to have a self-identity as a woman and a satisfying sex life. However, as a man, this individual would always feel incomplete and an outcast, said the doctor. Wanting to do the very best for their mutilated child, the young parents followed Dr. Money's suggestion. Over the years, the case of the little boy who became a girl became one of the examples cited in medical reports in support of the theory that gender is a matter of upbringing, not biology. The apparent success of the experiment was cited by Money as proof of this and actually led to other surgeries of a similar nature, one as late as 1985—also a response to a botched circumcision and supervised by Money. Before the little boy's case, Money had been performing sex-reassignment surgery on so-called hermaphrodites, or intersex individuals, children born with ambiguous sex characteristics or both male and female genitalia, assigning them a gender and surgically removing the characteristics of the opposite gender. The sex reassignment seemed to work fine in those cases.

But by the late 1970s theories about gender and nature were changing. Other sex researchers were now claiming that the sex of a person is hardwired before birth, through hormonal influences in the womb. Through animal experiments they supplied what they saw as proof: Added testosterone at a certain prenatal stage made adult female animals behave sexually like males. In other words, removing genitalia in an individual after birth doesn't remove the sexual hardwiring, and any amount of psychological training and pressure won't make a girl out of a boy or a boy out of a girl (or a heterosexual out of a homosexual, or a homosexual out of a heterosexual, for that matter). When the BBC managed to track down the twins and their family, the true story began to emerge. The boy raised as Brenda had not turned into a happy, well-adjusted girl, but was a particularly rowdy tomboy of a girl with a perennial feeling of maladjustment. (Incidentally, "her" twin brother was affected negatively by the situation too: Since the family's attention was focused on Brenda, he felt left out and developed into a frail child with many illnesses, apparently as a subconscious cry for attention.) By the time "she" reached puberty, "she" was being pressured by doctors to undergo the final surgical adjustment to womanhood, the creation of a complete vagina; but Brenda rebelled. Learning the true story of his injury and upbringing, he started wearing boy's clothes, had phalloplastic surgery to create a penis, and discarded the Brenda identity.

A research report published about his case identified him only as John/Joan, but in 2000 he went public with his own identity as David Reimer in the book by John Colapinto, *As Nature Made Him: The Boy Who Was Raised as a Girl.* Colapinto points out that in 1968, Freud's theory of the female Oedipus complex ruled among psychoanalysts. The little girl, said Freud, believes that her mother has castrated her and taken away her penis, so she suffers from penis envy and hates her mother. Now imagine Brenda's situation. Brenda had no reason to believe she was not a girl—so here is the ultimate nightmare version of the Freudian female Oedipus complex: This little girl really *had* been castrated although she didn't know it! And according to the medical record, she indeed thought her mother was responsible for doing something terrible to her. The author's speculations don't go this far, but we are free to continue speculating: Contrary to Freud's theory, David didn't take the next step in the female Oedipus complex (either because Freud was wrong, or because Brenda wasn't biologically a girl), wanting to have a child by her father in order to replace the missing penis. Instead, Brenda grew up to be David, had reconstructive surgery, got married, and adopted his wife's three children.

Eventually some of Dr. Money's intersex patients who had sex-reassignment surgery went public: The story of their success seemed to have been exaggerated too. Perhaps because they, at birth, had had both male and female hormonal characteristics, the adjustment to their assigned sex had not been as insurmountable as for David; but even so, many of them claimed they never felt natural or comfortable being assigned a sexual identity. At any rate, it seems scientifically questionable to base such radical surgery on a few cases of intersex patients and one single case of a boy with a clear sexual identity having that identity reassigned. And, to most readers, in hindsight, it seemed radical to identify a person's sex exclusively according to the status of his or her genitals. So perhaps this proves, as many of us suspected, that being a man or a woman is a matter of hardwiring from the very beginning—in other words, that sex is a matter of nature rather than nurture? For many researchers, Brenda's failure to come to terms with being a woman has put an end to the theory of psychosexual neutrality.

But does this mean that *gender,* too, is a matter of nature rather than nurture? In other words, can one's comprehension of oneself as a gendered person be changed by one's upbringing or other environmental influence, or is *everything* about us as gendered individuals a matter of hardwiring? If you remember the debate in Chapter 4 about the mother who believed that *nothing* a parent did could really influence the character of the child, then you'll also remember that this is characteristic of the deterministic "Nature" approach: all or nothing. Claiming that *everything* about one's gender is nurture or nature probably misses the point. It now looks as if our sexual identity as male or female, intersexed, transgendered, or lesbian/homosexual, is something that is determined mostly by hormonal factors prior to birth. But why should that preclude the possibility that our response to the hardwiring could *also* be affected by our environment? If we're born as hormonally female, we'll probably be attracted to men—but what *kind of man* may well depend on our upbringing: our dad's presence or absence, his looks, his demeanor—or perhaps instead it is our grandfather, our favorite uncle, our big brother's best friend, or our favorite TV actor. The same applies to boys, of course: If we're male, we will most likely be attracted to females, but the details triggering the attraction may be filled in by our early history. And even more importantly: If a child—boy or girl—has been exposed to some traumatic event such as *sexual abuse,* then that event most definitely will influence and possibly alter some of the individual's natural sexual inclinations regardless of the hardwiring, sometimes to the point of permanently devastating the person's adult sexual life or causing it to veer off in a direction toward abuse of children.

With some controversial exceptions, research in sexual identity indicates that children who grow up to have homosexual identities have developed these identities as part of their natural, sexual hardwiring: It is probably overwhelmingly a matter of hormonal/genetic influence, but *how* one responds to sexual situations as an adult certainly also has something to do with experience, from early childhood on. From turn-ons to fetishes and, going in the other direction, from aversions to phobias, the general direction may be laid down in everyone's genes, but the specifics are most likely a matter of our environment.

Something else, though, is brought to the surface with the example of Brenda/David: *a return to stereotypes.* Brenda/David was very rambunctious as a child, didn't like wearing dresses, and never played with dolls. The author of *As Nature Made Him* takes that to mean that this was the boy's nature manifesting itself, and indeed it probably was. But here we should be very careful: Have you ever known a little girl who was rambunctious, hated wearing dresses, and never played with dolls—and yet grew up without the slightest doubt about her sexual identity? In other words, she may grow up to be heterosexual, or a lesbian—but she doesn't feel like a boy trapped in a girl's body. Boys who grow up without the least desire to do rambunctious traditional boy things—are they less male because of it? Do real men not eat quiche, and is it true that boys don't cry? In the mid-1950s the answer would have been yes, but in the meantime we have experienced what we call *second-wave feminism* (first-wave feminism having culminated with the Nineteenth Amendment and women's right to vote in 1920). In the late 1950s and 1960s numerous books, mostly by classical feminists, pointed out that gender expectations were like a social straightjacket, and throughout the 1970s, 1980s, and 1990s we saw a tremendous loosening up of gender expectations and limitations: A woman no longer has to explain why she may want to become a plumber or a construction worker, a surgeon or a university professor, and the "sensitive man" was supposed to be the ideal heterosexual partner in the 1980s and 1990s. However, it is actually harder for men to take on traditional female jobs today than it is for women to be accepted as coworkers in a traditional male working environment, and it seems that many people today—women as well as men—are sick and tired of all the gender-role expansion. Books are again being published about how young women should act in order to be an attractive date and catch a husband, and TV sitcoms thrive on stereotyping guy talk and girl talk. If we don't bother to read beneath the surface of the story of Brenda/David, we may slide right back into the old stereotypes about gender behavior where "real" girls play with dolls, and "real" boys play with action figures. Even in the popular TV show *Frasier,* the psychoanalyst Frasier Crane and his brother Niles, both quiet, heterosexual men who love good books, art, and music, struggle to define their maleness against their father, a retired cop with a traditional view of masculinity.

So does Brenda/David's case in effect disprove classical feminism's theory that we are persons first and gendered beings second? Only if the classical feminist sees human sexuality as completely culturally determined and is set on creating sexual identities in young children based on ideology. But most classical feminists are not out to make men into women, or women into men; they want men and women to be considered as people first and foremost and believe that a person's gender simply shouldn't be of great social importance. Only a few feminists actually want to create "unisex" people. But of course difference feminism has received a considerable boost through the Brenda/

David story, because it now seems clear that males and females indeed are different by nature. However, nothing in Brenda/David's story is of any particular help to a difference feminist, because one still has to add the most important element in difference feminism: Women and men may be fundamentally different by nature, but the whole point of difference feminism is that *politically and socially,* both genders ought to receive equal respect and consideration and appreciation for their contributions.

How Many Sexes Are There?

The Greek dramatist Aristophanes speculated that humanity once consisted of three types: The male-female beings, the male-male beings, and the female-female beings (see Box 6.1). In most human societies it is the socially accepted assumption that everyone falls into the category of male or female. However, many people cannot accommodate their own understanding of themselves as sexual beings within this traditional system. Depending on which statistics you read, from 2 to 10 percent of any given human population would characterize themselves as homosexual. In some societies, such as the ancient Greek city-states and many Middle Eastern societies today, there is no stigma attached to male homosexuality (lesbianism is rarely a focus of attention in these cultures). In other societies, such as most countries within the Western Judeo-Christian tradition, homosexuality is traditionally considered unnatural and a sin against God. In the twentieth century, a shift in public opinion in many Western regions, such as the Scandinavian countries and some states within the United States, has resulted in a decriminalization of homosexuality, in some places allowing for marriages between homosexual couples, a change in inheritance and insurance regulations, and adoption of children by gay or lesbian couples. Like race/ethnicity and religion, sexual orientation is protected by hate-crimes legislation.

For many, the bottom-line question is whether homosexuality is a choice (a lifestyle, a matter of external influence) or an innate quality. If it is a *choice of lifestyle,* then (1) it is voluntary, (2) it can be condemned, and (3) it can be prevented or changed. If it is a *matter of biology,* then (1) no voluntary choice is involved, (2) it can't be condemned, and (3) it can't be prevented or changed. Most people who consider themselves gay or lesbian give clear testimony that their sexual identity has never felt like a choice: It has always seemed part of their individual nature. People who consider themselves bisexual may describe it as a choice, but more often they find themselves as the host of "two natures." Intersex studies (studies of children born with both male and female genitalia) seem to indicate that, growing up, these children develop an identity that is stronger in one direction than in the other. In addition, there are cases of transsexuality where the transgendered individual feels what is usually described as being trapped in the body of someone of the other sex. An increasing number of transgendered individuals now seek gender-correction surgery. (Brenda, of course, cannot be categorized as a transgendered person, because she wanted to return to her *original* gender.) As yet, biological research is inconclusive as to what creates our sexual identity; some studies in the 1990s point toward brain differences between gay and heterosexual males. However, researchers point out that the issue may not be strictly a matter of nature versus nurture: Conditions in the womb and early infancy may also have an influence that we aren't yet aware of.

So should we be talking about four sexes? Heterosexual males, heterosexual females, homosexual males, and lesbian females? Some believe that intersex people, transvestites, and transgendered individuals ought to be considered distinct sexes too. The question is, Would this be a reasonable expression of an expanded *biological* understanding of human nature? Would it be a reasonable expression of a new *political and social* understanding of humans?

Ultimately, the biological view of sex is tied to the sociological view of gender. This means that whatever our view of human sexual biology, it will have some form of expression in our social policies, even in our legislation. The descriptive "is" very easily turns into a normative "ought." If you'll recall, that is the definition of the naturalistic fallacy. If male and female natures are perceived as fundamentally different, then this view often translates into not only a limitation of social roles, but also legislation about how far men and women can be allowed to stray into each other's domain—and, historically, most of those limitations have been placed on women. For this reason, some scholars have suggested that in our talk of equality, we should not base our policies on claims of existing biological similarities between men and women (or between races, for that matter), for what if the biologists turn out to be wrong, and we are more different than we thought? Must we then impose discriminative legislation, because it has to fit the facts? Better, in our policies, that we don't refer to biological equality or sameness at all, but leave that question open. We can still refer to equality, but in a political sense: Everyone *ought to be* treated as a social, moral, and political equal, regardless of whatever hardwired or cultural differences we come equipped with.

Masculinism

With all this focus on female nature and on the homosexual and intersex experience, it seems that, apart from the story of David who grew up as Brenda and later reclaimed his male identity, a group of people has been left out: *straight men.* A coincidence? Some might speculate that because straight men have traditionally been the dominant gender, the sexual oppressors, and, as such, have been commanding attention for too long as it is, now other groups should be in the spotlight. However, to me such an attitude is nothing more than a "So there" and serves no useful purpose. A far more interesting reason why so little attention has been given to the nature of straight men in the current debate, as well as in this chapter, is that they have been defining *themselves,* and science has defined them (all the way from Aristotle) as the *normal* gender. They have been considered the norm against which any other sexual identity has been seen as the Other. And if a population group considers itself, and is considered by others, to represent the definition of "normal," or cultural and biological ground zero, then that population group rarely stops to consider its own nature and behavior patterns. This is the way many would describe the cultural circumstance of straight men in Western culture, until recently: a culture whose normality hadn't been "problematized," or made an issue of. But this is no longer the case. As the gender role for women changed during the twentieth century, so too did the role against which "emancipated" women would measure themselves. If the female role changes, so too must the male role—and, as many men have felt, not for the better.

Where opportunities opened up for women after the mid–twentieth century, many men experienced this new era as a shrinking of their own opportunities or a redefinition of their own roles. At home, if the woman now had a full-time career, did it mean that the man was still the breadwinner and head of the household? In the workplace, would work standards have to change to accommodate female employees; and, if so, did it mean that the quality of work, a matter of pride for many male employees, would suffer? Many a fireman and policeman (before they became fire*fighters* and police *officers*) have wondered about the changes in hiring standards in the 1980s, when women began to spread out into the workforce in great numbers and height requirements as well as other physical requirements were scaled down. And, sexually, if a girl can ask a guy on a date, will she pay for the dinner and the movie? Will she then make demands on him? And will he still retain his masculinity under these new circumstances?

Lots of men felt as liberated by the new roles as lots of women did, but for some it signaled a loss of foundation: Things were no longer the way they seemed; the preparation for adulthood that boys had undertaken was now considered preparation for male oppression and rejected by many women. I heard a well-known woman poet, in a lecture, bemoan the fact that her young child was male, because then he would by nature grown up to be a violent rapist, like all men. The mixed audience didn't take well to her viewpoint, which was, of course, an extremist view, and partly based on the fact that the poet was herself a rape survivor. But even in less drastic expressions of feminism of the 1990s, adopted by the mainstream press and entertainment industry, straight men seem to have become "politically incorrect." For some men, this has merely been a fleeting phase, accompanied by some confusion and perhaps irritation, but for them adjustment to the changing times has been no issue at all (and today many men do count themselves as feminists). But for others, the change has been viewed as a downright demasculinization. And just as some women (Wollstonecraft and Beauvoir, for example) had expressed the idea that it is hard for women to organize because they live their lives in close proximity to their oppressors, so too did some men in the late twentieth century feel that their partner and support turned out to be—the enemy.

Masculinism, a fairly new phenomenon, is a response to this feeling of loss of meaning. The male identity has now been problematized; it is no longer taken for granted, and straight males often go through periods of identity search just like many straight and lesbian women and gay males. The "male mystique" is now a topic of discussion almost to the extent that the female mystique became with Betty Friedan's book nearly half a century ago. Various all-male groups, such as the Promise Keepers, were formed in the 1990s, and Louis Farrakhan's Million Man March in Washington in 1998 was another manifestation of the new male demonstration of identity. The theme of such groups may be a renewed sense of responsibility as husbands and fathers, but it may also be specifically a celebration of masculinity. While many masculinists don't emphasize any hostility toward feminists, but merely want to recapture or redefine what maleness is, other masculinists hope to roll back the gender clock, with a measure of resentment that mirrors the anger of some second-wave feminist groups. An Internet Web site on masculinism takes on the issue:

> "Man was intended to be the provider of the food for the woman so that the woman would nurse and care for the young of the species. . . . Man was the hunter, gatherer. And as a natural by-product—the warrior and protector. . . . So, as the feminists began their journey to erase what they saw as gender inequalities in the late 19th century, we males must begin to change our thought processes or we will be trampled under their hooves. There is nothing intrinsically wrong with being male. There is nothing wrong with being a sexual being. These things are genetically inbred for a purpose—and the culture has metamorphosed faster than the physical evolution could take place. We must stop being afraid or ashamed of what we are. . . . There are many authors that have written books of late that try to explain the conflicting feelings of men and to resolve these things with rituals, songs and group get-togethers in the woods. All of these things are probably needed—but none as necessary as each of us males recognizing what is natural in us for what it is or making sure we do not allow a few zealots to convince us it is somehow a sin to be a male human being."[9]

Aside from the fact that the author has got his history wrong—men were indeed the hunters, but women were traditionally the gatherers—this Web site is a testimony to the deep chasm some men feel has opened not only between men and women, but also between the social world most Western males grew up expecting to inhabit and the world the way it looks today. Most feminists would respond that there never was any intention to make men feel that it is a sin to be male—but as the frequent lawsuits against sexual harassment have shown, it is most often not the *intention* of the perpetrator that counts, but the *perception* of the victim. And many men perceive that they have been victimized—ironically, by women who are struggling to free themselves of a self-identity as victims of oppression. So what can be done? What can we say about human sexual nature and human gender roles that might make us reach across that chasm

and create a functioning world of equals? In the next sections we examine an attempt at a solution: Louise Antony's theory of nature and gender.

An Alternative Interpretation of Gendered Nature: Louise Antony

Throughout this chapter we have seen a familiar pattern: views of human nature based on (1) what facts seem to indicate and (2) what ideals dictate; in other words, we find descriptive and normative theories of gendered nature side by side. A theory such as Rousseau's, which purports to be a descriptive theory of female nature, slides easily into a theory of how women ought to behave in order to fulfill their nature. And as you may remember from Chapter 3, such a slide is risky business, because one risks falling into the naturalistic fallacy: moving from an "is" (a fact) to an "ought" (a policy). Louise Antony's theory of *human flourishing,* an attempt at solving the problem of expressing a theory of gender and human nature, avoids falling into the trap of the naturalistic fallacy. In "'Human Nature' and Its Role in Feminist Theory" (1998), she points out that part of the problem inherent in any theory of human nature, including one about gender, is what she calls the "naming problem": Those who historically have named the characteristics that are supposedly typically human have named their own characteristics as typical. A dominant culture has called its own values and characteristics 'normal,' and a dominant gender has done the same thing. Antony writes, "When this conflagration occurs against a background in which only privileged individuals are engaged in theorizing, we get the sort of objectionable methods and results that feminist theorists have criticized: the activating circumstances that are tacitly privileged as 'normal' become those that are typical of or are highly valued by the theorists themselves."[10]

For Antony, the entire quest for gendered human nature is a misconception—and a dangerous one—because it may lead to social restrictions and discrimination: We don't have a human nature, we have a set of *dispositions.* (Here you may remember Jane Goodall's theory of human potentials.) You are no more or less a woman or a man (or a human being) if your expression of those dispositions is slightly different from that of others. Even with a given set of biological factors (such as the human genome), there is no pure form of human nature, because we are all living in some specific environment that calls forth some characteristics and ignores others. You'll remember the discussion in Chapter 3 about human aggression; Antony adds to this discussion by saying that the assumption that men are more aggressive than women is an example of misreading human nature. It may appear, statistically, that most men are more aggressive than most women—but under what conditions? Have these men and women been raised the same way and experienced the same cultural pressures—having had the same *behavioral options?* Usually that is not the case, and we can't make predictions or other general claims about human nature based on what people "normally" do, because such norms are not universal.

And so, for Antony, difference feminism is off on the wrong track, because it attempts to make blanket statements about men and women's different natures based on what they have observed so far; however, the conditions they have observed are not "natural," but "cultural." We won't know if women's nature is really "nurturing" or men's nature is "aggressive" if all the evidence we have comes from a certain social framework where the two sexes are expected to play out these roles. In fact, Antony is here echoing Harriet Taylor and John Stuart Mill, who agreed in the mid–nineteenth century that the reason we tend to think of the traditional gender roles as "normal" is because we have never experienced anything else. Notice that just like Taylor and Mill, Antony has not ruled out that there might be a gendered human nature— she is just saying that we can't discover it empirically by looking at cultural behavior or reading books about human nature, because they are all based on their cultural environment.

However, there is something that we *can* declare to be a universal human characteristic, says Antony, and that is our ability to *learn, understand, and produce language.* In other words, human society is a near-impossible thing if we don't have a language. We understand ourselves as well as others, through language, so if there is any part of human nature that we are *better off with, and would suffer without,* it is the language capacity. And this is how Antony works her way around the naturalistic fallacy: Embedded in our nature is the fact that we have language, that we function better with it than without it; and so language is a part of *human flourishing* (a concept that Antony borrows from Aristotle). Human flourishing is a *normative concept,* expressing a theory of what ought to be (humans ought to flourish in order to be happy), and in effect, Antony has moved from the descriptive fact of language capacity to a normative concept, but she has avoided the naturalistic fallacy by stating the hidden premise that *it is good* for humans to flourish.

So what does this have to do with the issue of gendered nature? In the tradition of classical feminism, Antony answers that in terms of human flourishing, men and women are much more similar than we are different: We flourish when we form human relationships, when we are able to communicate, when we are able to think straight and act accordingly. Politically, such activities should be available to all of us regardless of gender, and these forms of flourishing are far more important than any gender-specific forms of flourishing could ever be.

Antony offers a solution that goes beyond any cultural definition of human nature and even succeeds in building into a theory of human nature the demand that in order for humans to function well, we must feel that we are actually doing well. However, flourishing is a dangerously vague concept: For Antony, it is a given that forming human relationships and communicating is part of human flourishing and that all humans ought to flourish; for another theorist, human flourishing might well consist in conquering and oppressing multitudes (or simply, "winning," whatever that may mean, indicating that in order for there to be a winner, there must also be losers). And, for Antony, common characteristics of flourishing are more important than gender-specific forms, but a great many women who find motherhood to be the most important and rewarding aspect of their lives would probably beg to differ.

Study Questions

1. Go over the various theories of female human nature and find examples of the naturalistic fallacy: Going from a factual statement to a statement of gender policy (what women should be/shouldn't be allowed to do). Supply the hidden premise for each fallacy (the moral value underlying the conclusion).

2. What is the difference between the male and female Oedipus complex, according to Freud? Would you agree with his theory? Why or why not?

3. Give an account of classical and difference feminism. Identify what you consider positive and negative aspects of both theories.

4. Antony claims that the human flourishing which both men and women can experience is more important than any gender-specific flourishing. Is she right? Why or why not?

Primary Readings and Narratives

The first Primary Reading is an excerpt from Plato's *Republic,* Book V, in which he argues that people's talent, not their gender, ought to determine their profession. The second text is an excerpt from Deborah Tannen, *You Just Don't Understand.* Tannen argues that men tend to seek independence, while women seek intimacy. The third text, an excerpt from Louise M. Antony's paper, "Human Nature and Its Role in Feminist Theory," argues that human flourishing should be the ultimate goal of a discussion of human nature and that men and women are more similar than we are different. The first Narrative is a collection of three American Indian stories with the same theme: Women believe they can live without men, but in effect they can't; the second is a "pseudomyth" by Alice Walker, from *The Temple of My Familiar,* speculating that some men suffer from womb envy; the final Narrative is a summary of the Hollywood classic *Adam's Rib,* in which a lawyer defends her client accused of assault on her unfaithful husband; the twist is that the prosecutor is the defense lawyer's husband.

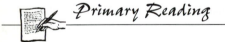 *Primary Reading*

Republic

PLATO

Excerpt from Book V. Translated by Benjamin Jowett. Fourth Century B.C.E.

I said: Suppose that by way of illustration we were to ask the question whether there is not an opposition in nature between bald men and hairy men; and if this is admitted by us, then, if bald men are cobblers, we should forbid the hairy men to be cobblers, and conversely?

That would be a jest, he said.

Yes, I said, a jest; and why? because we never meant when we constructed the State, that the opposition of natures should extend to every difference, but only to those differences which affected the pursuit in which the individual is engaged; we should have argued,

for example, that a physician and one who is in mind a physician may be said to have the same nature.

True.

Whereas the physician and the carpenter have different natures?

Certainly.

And if, I said, the male and female sex appear to differ in their fitness for any art or pursuit, we should say that such pursuit or art ought to be assigned to one or the other of them; but if the difference consists only in women bearing and men begetting children, this does not amount to a proof that a woman differs from a man in respect of the sort of education she should receive; and we shall therefore continue to maintain that our guardians and their wives ought to have the same pursuits.

Very true, he said.

Next, we shall ask our opponent how, in reference to any of the pursuits or arts of civic life, the nature of a woman differs from that of a man?

That will be quite fair.

And perhaps he, like yourself, will reply that to give a sufficient answer on the instant is not easy; but after a little reflection there is no difficulty.

Yes, perhaps.

Suppose then that we invite him to accompany us in the argument, and then we may hope to show him that there is nothing peculiar in the constitution of women which would affect them in the administration of the State.

By all means.

Let us say to him: Come now, and we will ask you a question:—when you spoke of a nature gifted or not gifted in any respect, did you mean to say that one man will acquire a thing easily, another with difficulty; a little learning will lead the one to discover a great deal; whereas the other, after much study and application, no sooner learns than he forgets; or again, did you mean, that the one has a body which is a good servant to his mind, while the body of the other is a hindrance to him?—would not these be the sort of differences which distinguish the man gifted by nature from the one who is ungifted?

No one will deny that.

And can you mention any pursuit of mankind in which the male sex has not all these gifts and qualities in a higher degree than the female? Need I waste time in speaking of the art of weaving, and the management of pancakes and preserves, in which womankind does really appear to be great, and in which for her to be beaten by a man is of all things the most absurd?

You are quite right, he replied, in maintaining the general inferiority of the female sex: although many women are in many things superior to many men, yet on the whole what you say is true.

And if so, my friend, I said, there is no special faculty of administration in a state which a woman has because she is a woman, or which a man has by virtue of his sex, but the gifts of nature are alike diffused in both; all the pursuits of men are the pursuits of women also, but in all of them a woman is inferior to a man.

Very true.

Then are we to impose all our enactments on men and none of them on women?

That will never do.

One woman has a gift of healing, another not; one is a musician, and another has no music in her nature?

Very true.

And one woman has a turn for gymnastic and military exercises, and another is unwarlike and hates gymnastics?

Certainly.

And one woman is a philosopher, and another is an enemy of philosophy; one has spirit, and another is without spirit?

That is also true.

Then one woman will have the temper of a guardian, and another not. Was not the selection of the male guardians determined by differences of this sort?

Yes.

Men and women alike possess the qualities which make a guardian; they differ only in their comparative strength or weakness.

Obviously.

And those women who have such qualities are to be selected as the companions and colleagues of men who have similar qualities and whom they resemble in capacity and in character?

Very true.

And ought not the same natures to have the same pursuits?

They ought.

Then, as we were saying before, there is nothing unnatural in assigning music and gymnastic to the wives of the guardians—to that point we come round again.

Certainly not.

The law which we then enacted was agreeable to nature, and therefore not an impossibility or mere aspiration; and the contrary practice, which prevails at present, is in reality a violation of nature.

That appears to be true.

We had to consider, first, whether our proposals were possible, and secondly whether they were the most beneficial?

Yes.

And the possibility has been acknowledged?

Yes.

The very great benefit has next to be established?

Quite so.

You will admit that the same education which makes a man a good guardian will make a woman a good guardian; for their original nature is the same?

Yes.

I should like to ask you a question.

What is it?

Would you say that all men are equal in excellence, or is one man better than another?

The latter.

And in the commonwealth which we were founding do you conceive the guardians who have been brought up on our model system to be more perfect men, or the cobblers whose education has been cobbling?

What a ridiculous question!

You have answered me, I replied: Well, and may we not further say that our guardians are the best of our citizens?

By far the best.

And will not their wives be the best women?

Yes, by far the best.

And can there be anything better for the interests of the State than that the men and women of a State should be as good as possible?

There can be nothing better.

And this is what the arts of music and gymnastic, when present in such manner as we have described, will accomplish?

Certainly.

Then we have made an enactment not only possible but in the highest degree beneficial to the State?

True.

Then let the wives of our guardians strip, for their virtue will be their robe, and let them share in the toils of war and the defence of their country; only in the distribution of labours the lighter are to be assigned to the women, who are the weaker natures, but in other respects their duties are to be the same. And as for the man who laughs at naked women exercising their bodies from the best of motives, in his laughter he is plucking

A fruit of unripe wisdom,

and he himself is ignorant of what he is laughing at, or what he is about—for that is, and ever will be, the best of sayings, *That the useful is the noble and the hurtful is the base.*

Very true.

Here, then, is one difficulty in our law about women, which we may say that we have now escaped; the wave has not swallowed us up alive for enacting that the guardians of either sex should have all their pursuits in common to the utility and also to the possibility of this arrangement the consistency of the argument with itself bears witness.

Yes, that was a mighty wave which you have escaped.

Yes, I said, but a greater is coming; you will not think much of this when you see the next.

Go on; let me see.

The law, I said, which is the sequel of this and of all that has preceded, is to the following effect—"that the wives of our guardians are to be common, and their children are to be common, and no parent is to know his own child, nor any child his parent."

Yes, he said, that is a much greater wave than the other; and the possibility as well as the utility of such a law are far more questionable.

I do not think, I said, that there can be any dispute about the very great utility of having wives and children in common; the possibility is quite another matter, and will be very much disputed. . . .

First, I think that if our rulers and their auxiliaries are to be worthy of the name which they bear, there must be willingness to obey in the one and the power of command in the other; the guardians must themselves obey the laws, and they must also imitate the spirit of them in any details which are entrusted to their care.

That is right, he said.

You, I said, who are their legislator, having selected the men, will now select the women and give them to them—they must be as far as possible of like natures with them; and they must live in common houses and meet at common meals. None of them will have anything specially his or her own; they will be together, and will be brought up together, and will associate at gymnastic exercises. And so they will be drawn by a necessity of their natures to have intercourse with each other—necessity is not too strong a word, I think?

Yes, he said—necessity, not geometrical, but another sort of necessity which lovers know, and which is far more convincing and constraining to the mass of mankind.

True, I said; and this, Glaucon, like all the rest, must proceed after an orderly fashion; in a city of the blessed, licentiousness is an unholy thing which the rulers will forbid.

Yes, he said, and it ought not to be permitted.

Then clearly the next thing will be to make matrimony sacred in the highest degree, and what is most beneficial will be deemed sacred?

Exactly. . . .

Study Questions

1. How does Plato (with the voice of Socrates) argue that women should be judged on their talent, not their gender?

2. What are the practical and political consequences of Plato's gender theory?

3. Many philosophers have thought that Plato's theory of gender equality was really tongue-in-cheek. If so, what might he have tried to accomplish? Do you believe his theory was a joke or a serious attempt at cultural revision?

Primary Reading

You Just Don't Understand

DEBORAH TANNEN

Excerpt, 1990.

INTIMACY AND INDEPENDENCE

Intimacy is key in a world of connection where individuals negotiate complex networks of friendship, minimize differences, try to reach consensus, and avoid the appearance of superiority, which would highlight differences. In a world of status, *independence* is key, because a primary means of establishing status is to tell others what to do, and taking orders is a marker of low status. Though all humans need both intimacy and independence, women tend to focus on the first and men on the second. It is as if their lifeblood ran in different directions.

These differences can give women and men differing views of the same situation, as they did in the case of a couple I will call Linda and Josh. When Josh's old high-school chum called him at work and announced he'd be in town on business the following month, Josh invited him to stay for the weekend. That evening he informed Linda that they were going to have a houseguest, and that he and his chum would go out together the first night to shoot the breeze like old times. Linda was upset. She was going to be away on business the week before, and the Friday night

when Josh would be out with his chum would be her first night home. But what upset her the most was that Josh had made these plans on his own and informed her of them, rather than discussing them with her before extending the invitation.

Linda would never make plans, for a weekend or an evening, without first checking with Josh. She can't understand why he doesn't show her the same courtesy and consideration that she shows him. But when she protests, Josh says, "I can't say to my friend, 'I have to ask my wife for permission'?"

To Josh, checking with his wife means seeking permission, which implies that he is not independent, not free to act on his own. It would make him feel like a child or an underling. To Linda, checking with her husband has nothing to do with permission. She assumes that spouses discuss their plans with each other because their lives are intertwined, so the actions of one have consequences for the other. Not only does Linda not mind telling someone, "I have to check with Josh"; quite the contrary—she likes it. It makes her feel good to know and show that she is involved with someone, that her life is bound up with someone else's.

LUANN. Reprinted with permission of United Feature Syndicate, Inc.

According to linguist Deborah Tannen, men and women often find it hard to communicate because each expects a different response: Typically, women like to engage in "troubles talk" where each person shares her troubles with the others just for the sake of sharing, while men prefer to be problem solvers. This *LuAnn* cartoon accurately illustrates Tannen's philosophy of different *conversational styles*.

Linda and Josh both felt more upset by this incident, and others like it, than seemed warranted, because it cut to the core of their primary concerns. Linda was hurt because she sensed a failure of closeness in their relationship: He didn't care about her as much as she cared about him. And he was hurt because he felt she was trying to control him and limit his freedom.

A similar conflict exists between Louise and Howie, another couple, about spending money. Louise would never buy anything costing more than a hundred dollars without discussing it with Howie, but he goes out and buys whatever he wants and feels they can afford, like a table saw or a new power mower. Louise is disturbed, not because she disapproves of the purchases, but because she feels he is acting as if she were not in the picture.

Many women feel it is natural to consult with their partners at every turn, while many men automatically make more decisions without consulting their partners. This may reflect a broad difference in conceptions of decision making. Women expect decisions to be discussed first and made by consensus. They appreciate the discussion itself as evidence of involvement and communication. But many men feel oppressed by lengthy discussions about what they see as minor decisions, and they feel hemmed in if they can't just act without talking first. When women try to initiate a freewheeling discussion by asking, "What do you think?" men often think they are being asked to decide.

Communication is a continual balancing act, juggling the conflicting needs for intimacy and independence. To survive in the world, we have to act in concert with others, but to survive as ourselves, rather than simply as cogs in a wheel, we have to act alone. In some ways, all people are the same: We all eat and sleep and drink and laugh and cough, and often we eat, and laugh at, the same things. But in some ways, each person is different, and individuals' differing wants and preferences may conflict with each other. Offered the same menu, people make different choices. And if there is cake for dessert, there is a chance one person may get a larger piece than another—and an even greater chance that one will *think* the other's piece is larger, whether it is or not.

ASYMMETRIES

If intimacy says, "We're close and the same," and independence says, "We're separate and different," it is easy to see that intimacy and independence dovetail with connection and status. The essential element of connection is symmetry: People are the same, feeling equally close to each other. The essential element of status is asymmetry: People are not the same; they are differently placed in a hierarchy.

This duality is particularly clear in expressions of sympathy or concern, which are all potentially ambiguous. They can be interpreted either symmetrically, as evidence of fellow feeling among equals, or asymmetrically, offered by someone one-up to someone one-down. Asking if an unemployed person has found a job, if a couple have succeeded in conceiving the child they crave, or whether an untenured professor expects to get tenure can be meant—and interpreted, regardless of how it is meant—as an expression of human connection by a person who understands and cares, or as a reminder of weakness from someone who is better off and knows it, and hence as condescending. The latter view of sympathy seems self-evident to many men. For example, a handicapped mountain climber named Tom Whittaker, who leads groups of disabled people on outdoor expeditions, remarked, "You can't feel sympathetic for someone you admire"—a statement that struck me as not true at all.

The symmetry of connection is what creates community: If two people are struggling for closeness, they are both struggling for the same thing. And the asymmetry of status is what creates contest: Two people can't both have the upper hand, so negotiation for status is inherently adversarial. In my earlier work, I explored in detail the dynamics of intimacy (which I referred to as involvement) and independence, but I tended to ignore the force of status and its adversarial nature. Once I identified these dynamics, however, I saw them all around me. The puzzling behavior of friends and co-workers finally became comprehensible.

Differences in how my husband and I approached the same situation, which previously would have been mystifying, suddenly made sense. For example, in a jazz club the waitress recommended the crab cakes to me, and they turned out to be terrible. I was uncertain about whether or not to send them back. When the waitress came by and asked how the food was, I said that I didn't really like the crab cakes. She asked, "What's wrong with them?" While staring at the table, my husband answered, "They don't taste fresh." The waitress snapped, "They're frozen! What do you expect?" I looked directly up at her and said, "We just don't like them." She said, "Well, if you don't like them, I could take them back and bring you something else."

After she left with the crab cakes, my husband and I laughed because we realized we had just automatically played out the scripts I had been writing about. He had heard her question "What's wrong with them?" as a challenge that he had to match. He doesn't like to fight, so he looked away, to soften what he felt was an obligatory counterchallenge: He felt instinctively that he had to come up with something wrong with the crab cakes to justify my complaint. (He was fighting for me.) I had taken the question "What's wrong with them?" as a request for information. I instinctively sought a way to be right without making her wrong. Perhaps it was because she was a woman that she responded more favorably to my approach.

When I have spoken to friends and to groups about these differences, they too say that now they can make sense of previously perplexing behavior. For example, a woman said she finally understood why her husband refused to talk to his boss about whether or not he stood a chance of getting promoted. He wanted to know because if the answer was no, he would start looking for another job. But instead of just asking, he stewed and fretted, lost sleep, and worried. Having no others at her disposal, this wife had fallen back on psychological explanations: Her husband must be insecure, afraid of rejection. But then, everyone is insecure, to an extent. Her husband was actually quite a confident person. And she, who believed herself to be at least as insecure as he, had not hesitated to go to her boss to ask whether he intended to make her temporary job permanent.

Understanding the key role played by status in men's relations made it all come clear. Asking a boss about chances for promotion highlights the hierarchy in the relationship, reminding them both that the employee's future is in the boss's hands. Taking the low-status position made this man intensely uncomfortable. Although his wife didn't especially relish taking the role of supplicant with respect to her boss, it didn't set off alarms in her head, as it did in his.

In a similar flash of insight, a woman who works in sales exclaimed that now she understood the puzzling transformation that the leader of her sales team had undergone when he was promoted to district manager. She had been sure he would make a perfect boss because he had a healthy disregard for authority. As team leader, he had rarely bothered to go to meetings called by management and had encouraged team members to exercise their own judgment, eagerly using his power to waive regulations on their behalf. But after he became district manager, this man was unrecognizable. He instituted more regulations than anyone had dreamed of, and insisted that exceptions could be made only on the basis of written requests to him.

This man behaved differently because he was now differently placed in the hierarchy. When he had been subject to the authority of management, he'd done all he could to limit it. But when the authority of management was vested in him, he did all he could to enlarge it. By avoiding meetings and flouting regulations, he had evidenced not disregard for hierarchy but rather discomfort at being in the subordinate position within it.

Yet another woman said she finally understood why her fiancé, who very much believes in equality, once whispered to her that she should keep her voice down. "My friends are downstairs," he said. "I don't want them to get the impression that you order me around."

That women have been labeled "nags" may result from the interplay of men's and women's styles, whereby many women are inclined to do what is asked of them and many men are inclined to resist even the slightest hint that anyone, especially a woman, is telling them what to do. A woman will be inclined to repeat a request that doesn't get a response because she is convinced that her husband would do what she asks, if he only understood that she *really* wants him to do it. But a man who wants to avoid feeling that he is following orders may instinctively wait before doing what she asked, in order to imagine that he is doing it of his own free will. Nagging is the result, because each time she repeats the request, he again puts off fulfilling it.

Study Questions

1. In Tannen's view, men tend to emphasize independence, and women intimacy in relationships. How does she support her view? Do you agree? Why or why not?

2. What does Tannen mean by asymmetry in a relationship? Explain.

3. What is the point of the story of the crab cakes? Do you feel more comfortable with Tannen's approach or with her husband's? Explain.

Primary Reading

"Human Nature" and Its Role in Feminist Theory

LOUISE M. ANTONY

Excerpt, 1998.

THE NEED FOR NATURES

. . . The notion of "nature" can be recovered and rendered innocuous. But why should we bother? Can this notion of nature do any of the work natures were supposed to do? And do we really want such work done anyway? There are really two aspects to the question of whether we "need" a notion of human nature. One aspect I take to be purely empirical: Are there, or are there not theoretically significant properties that all human beings share, that appear to be nearly invariantly expressed under a large range of circumstances? If there are such "universals," then whether we need it or not, there is such a thing as "human nature." I don't think that anyone has ever seriously doubted the existence of *biological* universals in this sense. The presence of one heart, two kidneys, two lungs, two arms with five digits each—though not absolutely universal—is taken, at least by biologists, to be *normal* and *natural* for human beings. I am not saying that such assumptions are wholly unproblematic: only that, properly understood, they seem to be *true*. And any problems that attend talk of "normalcy" and "naturalness" in this instance, I claim, stem from conflation of statistical and evaluative senses of these terms.

But in addition to biological natures, there is increasing evidence of the existence of a *cognitive* nature, of what Steven Pinker thinks of as a set of human *instincts*. Instincts are not strict programs that determine behavior; they are, rather, programs that determine *dispositions*. The activating conditions for instincts can be quite specific or highly diverse; the associated categorical properties—overt behavior, in the case of these dispositions—can be quite rigid or highly plastic. The "language instinct" in humans, for example, is such that the child requires human social contact, and a modicum of linguistic input, but nothing in the way of explicit instruction in order for it to be triggered. The "behavior" that's triggered is itself a grounding categorical (a grammar) for a highly complex disposition (a language). The general form of the grammar is dictated by the human genome, but within that form there is all the variation that can be found across human languages.

Thus, while we cannot say that *all* human beings, without exception, speak a language, and while there is no "universal language" spoken by all human beings, and while no one language can sensibly be thought closer to "natural" than any other, it is still the case that there is, in the case of language, a genuine human universal. What's universal is a certain *capacity*: we are able to converge onto a grammar for any language that displays certain very abstract formal properties ("universal grammar") to which we are given a short exposure during a critical period of our youth. This means *any* human language is potentially acquirable by *any* human infant; in practical terms, it means that we can communicate a potential infinity of richly structured thoughts, and we can *intercommu-*

nicate, at least potentially, with every other member of our species.

Surely this is a morally significant fact. The ability to communicate is *valuable*. It is not just *useful*—it is centrally connected to nearly everything human beings have ever claimed to value about themselves, everything from our capacity for abstract thought (so emphasized in the philosophical tradition) to our capacities for social affiliation and cultural creation. That we have language is, in short, a *good thing*. But if we can agree on this very minimal evaluative claim, then we are on our way to seeing how facts about *natures* can legitimately ground normative claims. Our capacity for language may in itself make us morally valuable creatures, as certain philosophers have claimed (though it surely would be only a sufficient and not a necessary condition). But even if that's not so, the fact that *language* is valuable, together with the fact that human beings have a capacity to acquire it, provides part of a nonarbitrary conception of what Aristotle called "human flourishing." If it's good for humans to develop and exercise their capacities for linguistic communication, then it counts as *damage* to human beings to impede or prevent this development.

I claim that some such conception of human flourishing, grounded in assumptions about a shared set of capacities, in fact lies behind feminism's protest against the treatment of women. Feminists do not want to say *simply* that women are unhappy under patriarchy—for one thing, not all women are. Rather, I take it to be feminism's position that women under patriarchy are systematically *dehumanized*—treated in ways that prevent or impede the full development of their *human* capacities. Without a nonarbitrary background notion of human flourishing, the notion of *damage* makes no sense. And if feminists cannot make out the case that patriarchy *damages* women, then we are properly open to the charge, leveled at us often enough by our critics, that we are simply trying to impose on others our own parochial views of how life should be lived.

Notice that the need for appeal to *human* universals does not beg any questions against those who think that there are systematic differences between men and women. I have made no argument against this, although I think the considerations raised in the preceding section should make clear how hard it would be to properly justify any such claim. But consider what such a claim must mean once we understand natures properly as the grounds of complex dispositions. To say that boys "have better spatial abilities than girls" turns out to be [in] many ways ambiguous. The (probably) intended meaning is that, in the standard curriculum, boys do better than girls. But suppose it so—it hardly follows that there are no curricula in which girls do as well as boys, or even better! And, of course, that environment could be provided to girls *without* disadvantaging boys: what is to prevent us as a society from providing girls with the environment that will permit *them* to flourish, and boys the environment that will permit *them* to flourish?

Nothing but *will.* This is already the scheme that's followed when the children in question are deemed truly valuable. In colleges and universities, in private elementary and secondary schools, and in the more affluent public schools, instructors labor mightily to provide "individualized instruction" to students with a variety of "special needs." Deficits in middle- and upper-class students are attributed to the environment; innate stupidity and laziness are found only in the poor. The idea that "natures" and "natural differences" are the only, or even *an important,* determinant of levels of human flourishing should be exposed for the self-serving nonsense that it is. It means nothing more or less than the patently abhorrent claim that the human flourishing of some individuals—men, white people, affluent people, English-speaking people, Christian people, straight people—is more valuable than that of others.

Questions of difference aside, however, there is a more fundamental point. As long as women and men share certain morally relevant capacities—the capacity for rationally directed action, the capacity to form emotional attachments, the capacity to communicate—general norms of human flourishing will still apply equally to both. It is impossible for me to imagine discoverable differences between men and women that could swamp the significance of these commonalities. The properties we manifestly share are sufficient to make clear that there can be no justification for separating men and women—or, indeed, any two groups of human beings—into "rulers or things ruled by Nature's direction."

Study Questions

1. Would you characterize Antony as primarily a classical or a difference feminist? Explain.

2. What is the naturalistic fallacy (see Chapter 3)? Does Antony avoid it? Why or why not?

3. Is Antony right that the ways of flourishing that both genders share are more important than any gender-specific ways of flourishing? In your discussion, consider how a mother might reply.

Narrative

Three American Indian Stories: Can Men and Women Live Without Each Other?

INDIAN MYTHS

Summaries.

"Men and Women Try Living Apart, Sia myth, reported by Mathilda Cox Stevenson, 1889.
The Sia Indians (a Pueblo tribe from New Mexico) tell this story, which—as you will see—is similar to many other American Indian myths. Many years ago the Sia women began a quarrel with the men. The women worked hard all day, and when the men came home from hunting, the women accused them of being lazy and lascivious. The men answered that although the women might criticize them, the truth was that the women wanted the men more than the men wanted the women. Soon both the men and the women were claiming that they would be fine without sex for a very long time, even years. The women gathered their things

and moved to one side of the village, while the men and boys moved to the other side. The next day the men and boys, at the advice of their council leader, moved across the river.

Months passed, and the men were doing fine, because they hunted for meat. But the women grew thin and pale, for they had nothing to eat. As time passed, the women wanted the men more and more, but the men were still doing fine without the women. In the fourth year the women gave up and asked the men to come back. They did, and after only a few days the women were healthy again.

"The River of Separation," Navajo myth, reported by Matthews and Washington, 1897.

First Man and First Woman quarreled about who could stand being without the other the longest. First Man moved across the river with the other men of his tribe. For a while everything was well in both camps. Once in a while the women would call over and ask if there was anything they were missing out on; there was, but they would never admit it. After a year, though, the women's garden wasn't yielding much, and the women grew thinner. The men were doing fine, because they had both gardens and meat. But First Man was not happy. He missed the way his wife cooked stew, and he didn't sleep well alone. Little by little the men began to feel bad about the situation—about eating while their wives and daughters were going hungry—and they plainly missed their wives. So First Man called across the river, "Have you learned your lesson by now?" First Woman said she had, and the women had realized they couldn't live without

the men. So the men went back to the women, and they all had a second honeymoon. Everyone had learned a lesson: Men and women can't live without each other.

"The Separation of the Sexes," Navajo myth, reported by Mary Shepardson, 1995.

Shepardson stresses that this is one version among several—which will be obvious to you by now: Once upon a time First Man and First Woman had an argument, because First Man had caught First Woman being unfaithful to him. Her mother, Woman Chief, then said that women can live without men. The men now crossed the river, and the women stayed behind. The women couldn't make their gardens grow properly, so they starved, but the men had a *nadlee* (a berdache, or man-woman) with them who knew both man's work and woman's work, so the men were eating well. The women, needing sex, masturbated with stones and brought forth male monsters. So finally they pleaded with the men to take them back, and the men complied, provided that the women promised them they'd never try to assume leadership again.

Study Questions

1. Two of the stories seem to make a connection between eating well and having a good sex life. What may be the point of such a connection?

2. Are these stories about gender relations or politics or food—or all three?

3. Describe significant differences and similarities in the three versions.

 *Narrative*

The Temple of My Familiar

ALICE WALKER

Novel, 1989. Summary of Episode.

This novel weaves threads of destinies together, primarily from the perspective of African American, African, and South American Indian women. In an important scene, Zedé, a South American Indian woman living in California, tells her young lover about the Beginning Time (which you will remember from Chapter 2 is often referred to as *in illo tempore*), when men and women were struggling to understand the mystery of life. Walker here invents a "pseudo-myth" designed as an antidote to the Western myth, which survived all the way from Aristotle to Freud, that women are "incomplete" compared with men.

In the old, old days the first women created men, and the men got together and observed the world of woman. For the first women, men were only playthings, but men were in great awe of women when they found out that women could give birth. This inspired them to imagine a great woman, a mother goddess, and they began to worship women as priestesses, although women never thought of themselves as such. For a long time women were revered and spoiled, and yet they didn't take themselves seriously and thought nothing of their powers of creation. But one day the men rebelled, because they had found out that women give birth "through a hole at her bottom." So now the men decided that they should be the ones creating life, and they began castrating themselves so they could be like the life-giving women. This was the beginning of the celibacy tradition of priesthood, because men wanted to be like women.

Study Questions

1. Are men generally envious of female creative powers? Why or why not?

2. Freud believed that women suffer from *penis envy*. Here Walker invents a story of *womb envy*. Is either explanation correct? Why or why not?

3. Write a pseudo-myth in which women and men experience each other as different, but equal, in the spirit of difference feminism.

4. Now write another pseudo-myth in the spirit of classical feminism in which women and men find out that they are fundamentally the same, just human beings, and gender differences are strictly cultural.

Narrative

Adam's Rib

GEORGE CUKOR (DIRECTOR), RUTH GORDON AND GARSON KANIN (SCREENWRITERS)

Film, 1949. Summary.

The film *Adam's Rib* is perhaps one of the best Hollywood stories about a man and a woman in a personal as well as a professional relationship, so for that reason alone it is worth including; however, when I researched recent films for this book, I made a discovery that surprised and, in many ways, disturbed me: I was looking for a recent film that dealt with the gender issue in a confrontational way, but that was underlain with a sense of friendship and mutual respect. Films such as *Something to Talk About* (1995), *Antonia's Line* (1995), *Thelma and Louise* (1991), *Waiting to Exhale* (1995), *The Joy Luck Club* (1993), and *Boys on the Side* (1995) are all worth watching, but they are all seen exclusively from a woman's perspective; and, furthermore, there is very little "friendship and mutual respect" between the sexes. I didn't want a male-bashing film to conclude this chapter any more than a female-bashing film; Hollywood and other Western film industries have produced plenty of both over the years. I kept returning in my mind to the classic comedy *Adam's Rib*. I'll let you judge whether it does a better or as good a job of illustrating "the war between the sexes" (as it was advertised) than the films mentioned above. The film was made into a TV series in 1973. Moviegoers in 1949 found the film provocative; chances are you won't, because times have changed—but perhaps not as much as we think. Reviewers on the Internet Movie Database Web site are mixed in terms of whether they think the film holds

Adam's Rib, MGM, 1949. The attorney Amanda Bonner (Katharine Hepburn) has taken on the defense of Doris Attinger (Judy Holliday). Doris has shot (but not killed) her husband because he has been unfaithful to her and, in addition, treated her with indifference. Amanda's argument is that if a man shoots his unfaithful wife, society condones it and perhaps even approves of it, while the court of public opinion is harsher on a woman doing the exact same thing. However, Amanda has chosen a special battleground for a feminist defense: Doris's prosecutor is Amanda's husband, Adam.

up and also about whether it is really a comedy or a more serious type of film. The film audience in 1949 had a bit of foreknowledge that added spice to the film: It was a public secret that Spencer Tracy and Katharine Hepburn, who portrayed the main characters Adam and Amanda Bonner, were real-life longtime lovers and soul mates who never had the opportunity to marry because Tracy couldn't obtain a divorce from his wife.

Amanda and Adam Bonner are both professionals: She is an independent defense attorney, and he is a prosecutor at the District Attorney's office. They have a good, easygoing relationship, they share interests, they are able to laugh together: It looks like an ideal marriage; they have no children, but that is not an issue in the story. It doesn't hurt that they have a full-time, live-in housekeeper who cooks their meals, cleans their beautiful home, and helps prepare their parties.

During one of their breakfasts before work they read the paper: A woman has shot and wounded her husband for two-timing her, and she has been arrested. Adam feels sympathy for the husband, while Amanda thinks this is a *double standard:* If it had been a man defending his marriage by shooting his two-timing wife, society would have gone easier on him, right? This becomes the theme for the movie, because as luck will have it, Adam is assigned the case as a prosecutor. This inspires Amanda to seek out the arrested woman, Doris Attinger, and offer her services as defense attorney.

Doris is a woman of little education and very traditional values; she isn't quite clear about why she did what she did, and Amanda has to put the idea that she was defending her marriage and her three kids into her mind. All Doris remembers was that she had had one of many arguments with her husband Warren. He was rude to her and called her "Fatso." She knew he was having an affair, and he hadn't been home in four days, so she tried to confront him at work, but he refused to see her. So she followed him after work, to the place of his girlfriend, carrying a gun she had just bought. When she found them together, she tried to shoot the girlfriend, but he tried to stop her, and she hit her husband instead.

That night Amanda and Adam have a party for friends and associates. Adam's mood is ruined when he finds out that Amanda is now Doris's lawyer, and having their next-door neighbor Kip flirt heavily with his wife doesn't help his mood. After the guests leave, they have a small argument; Amanda tries to convince Adam that justice is on her side, because her point is that men receive a different and more lenient brand of justice than women. He swears he'll give her a hard time in court, but even so, they make up; this is still not serious enough to threaten their relationship.

But things start going downhill, and we realize that the film has two stories: One is the court procedure, and the other is how it affects the Bonners' marriage. In the *voir dire* process (jury selection), Amanda dismisses male jurors who are against women's equality. Adam accuses her of using feminine tricks with the jury. Warren Attinger is on the stand, and we get a picture of an abusive spouse who blames his wife for everything: She got fat, so it was okay for him to stay out all night. Sure he hit her and called her names, but it wasn't really his fault. He didn't really hit her; "she slipped and fell." But we also hear during Adam's cross-examination that Doris hit her husband and called him names too. In fact, Warren considers himself the abused spouse. When Adam suggests that Doris is unstable and irresponsible, the (male) judge sides with him and overrules Amanda's objection.

That night, things come to a blow between Amanda and Adam: What was loving banter becomes sharp criticism, and she breaks down in tears. He doesn't respect her views, but even so, her tears work (and we realize that they were a bit of an act). They make up one more time. Next day in court Amanda has filled the room with professional women, witnesses for the defense. She is allowed three: A scholar, a business employer, and an acrobat. Each in their own way prove that women can be smart, can run a business—and can be strong: The acrobat lifts Adam up in one hand, and he can't get down; now his self-image is threatened. This, to him, was the last straw: That night he accuses Amanda of having no respect for the law, just for her "dimwitted cause." She's mocking their marriage, he says: He likes two sexes, and he wants a wife, not a competitor. While she tries to apologize, he packs a suitcase and leaves, slamming the door in her face.

Next day we have the final arguments—in court: Amanda suggests to the jury that if Doris had been a man (and we see Doris morph into a young mustached man), she would have received more understanding, because it's okay for men to have girlfriends and to defend their marriage. If Warren had been the woman who slept around (and he morphs into a not-too-pretty woman), we would have condemned him harder. So if that is the law, then Amanda demands equality: If the man goes free for defending his marriage, so should the woman. Adam's final summation falls apart in a disaster of flubbed words; Amanda has got him completely rattled, and he loses the case. The jury—mixed in terms of race and gender—finds for the defendant. Amanda is congratulated—but fears that her victory has come at too high a price.

That evening the enterprising neighbor Kip sees his chance and makes a move on Amanda. Being preoccupied with her own misery, she doesn't see it coming. Kip corners her and kisses her—but at the same moment Adam steps through the door, a gun in his hand. Amanda quickly steps in front of Kip, saying that Adam has no right to do this, that nobody does—and she realizes that she just nullified her own court argument. Adam turns the gun on himself, puts it in his mouth—and chews off the barrel. It is a licorice gun, and all he wanted was to prove a point. A general three-way quarrel ensues, and nothing is resolved.

A few days later Adam and Amanda meet at their accountant's to go over their tax returns. The bills and receipts bring back memories of better times, and to Amanda's consternation, Adam begins to cry. This melts all her hostility, and they leave together. At home, at their farmhouse retreat, he compliments her on a job well done in court and tells her he may run for office as a judge—and she lets him know that she may run on the Democratic ticket against him. But, in that case, he says, he'll start crying—and proves he can do it at will, just like she can. The tears in the accountant's office were a trick to get her back. But that proves her point, says Amanda: There is no difference between the sexes! Well, perhaps a small difference, says Adam: "Vive la difference!"

Study Questions

1. It is a fact that the courts used to be more lenient on men than on women in the past, especially in sexual assault cases. Does it still hold true that there is a double standard in American courts when it comes to gender issues?

2. Do you think this film would have made its point better if the comedy had been played down, or is this exactly the right way to treat a serious subject?

3. Is Amanda's fight against sexism a "dimwitted cause"? Is Adam right in charging that she is disregarding the law to further her own cause? Is Adam a sexist? Is Amanda?

4. Although courtroom approaches may have changed in terms of gender discrimination, what about personal relationships? Is Amanda and Adam's relationship a dated example from half a century ago, or does it still reflect a personal issue between modern women and men?

5. What does the title mean? Is it intended to be taken seriously or ironically?

Review

Key Issues in Chapter 6

Race and Gender—Same Issue

- Debates about race and gender issues have similarities, but sex differences are biological as well as social.

Gender Differences: Nature or Nurture?

- With assumptions of gender differences comes an assumption of inequality. Behaviorism and gender theory says that upbringing will influence gender behavior. The theory of psychosexual neutrality says that one's sexual identity is based on genital function and can be modified and altered through one's environment. Classical feminism asserts that gender differences are more cultural than biological; difference feminism asserts that gender differences are more biological than cultural.

Three Non-Western Views of Gendered Nature

- *The American Indian Tradition.* There was some gender egality in the Indian tradition, but it is difficult to discern the extent because of varying interpretations.

- *The Muslim Tradition.* There are liberal and conservative views of women in Islamic cultures, but the quest for gender equality is not easy.

- *Asian Traditions.* Although many Asian traditions assert male superiority, Buddhism offers more (if not perfect) equality; Communism asserts that women are completely equal.

Early Western Views of Gendered Nature

- In the ideal society of Plato's *Republic,* intellectual talents, not one's gender, decide one's position in society. Women as well as men can be guardians. The consequences include eugenics and communally raised children. Aristotle said that a woman is an infertile, deformed male because she does not produce semen; he saw male and female differences in rationality. In the Christian era, St. Paul, St. Augustine, and St. Thomas Aquinas viewed women as partners of men in life and in the hereafter, but as subservient to men.

England and Continental Europe in the Early Modern Age

- *Locke* said that women should be able to have parental rights. *Rousseau* believed that children ought to be raised according to their nature, but boys are allowed more freedom than girls because female nature is different from male nature by virtue of childbearing. *Mary Wollstonecraft* asserted that women ought to receive the same kind of education as men—it is unfair both to men and women to treat women as less than equal to men. In a limited environment anyone becomes preoccupied with rules and appearance—women are no different from military men. *Immanuel Kant* expresses doubt that women are quite as rational as men and sees female intellectual pursuits as unbecoming. *John Stuart Mill* and *Harriet Taylor* believed that all professions ought to be open to both genders; those who aren't qualified will weed themselves out. *Sigmund Freud* held that little girls experience penis envy as part of the female Oedipus complex. A woman will never completely get over the Oedipus complex, which makes her less mature than a man.

Modern Western Feminism: "Classical" and "Difference"

- Classical feminism says that gender roles are social constructs. Simone de Beauvoir, an existentialist, believed that there is no human nature. Carol Gilligan believes that women tend to focus on nurturing and caring, while men tend to focus on justice and fairness. Riane Eisler offers the partnership and dominator models of gender. Deborah Tannen discusses the difference in conversational styles between men and women and the resulting different expectations of relationships and explores the specific fears of men and women.

- *The Boy Who Was Raised as a Girl: Nature More Than Nurture?* A young boy lost his penis in a botched circumcision and was raised as a girl without knowing his original gender identity. The tentative conclusion is that sexual identity is not a matter of nurture, but of nature. The case poses a risk of a return to gender stereotypes.

- *How Many Sexes Are There?* Biological research is inconclusive as to what causes our sexual identity. People identify themselves as heterosexual males, heterosexual females, homosexual males and lesbian females, intersex individuals, transvestites, and transgendered individuals.

- *Masculinism.* The recent masculine search for gender identity follows a period of attention paid to feminine

gender identity; males have always been defined as the normal gender.

An Alternative Interpretation of Gendered Nature: Louise Antony

- Antony says that humans have gender dispositions; there is no pure form of human nature, because much depends on one's environment. We have our language expression in common and the ideal of human flourishing.

Primary Readings

- Plato, *Republic.* Plato argues that women and men ought to be judged by their talents, not their gender. Plato lays out his program of government in the ideal state.

- Deborah Tannen, *You Just Don't Understand.* Tannen claims that men overall seek independence, and women seek intimacy; the conversations between men often reflect asymmetry, while women's conversations strive for symmetry.

- Louise M. Antony, "'Human Nature' and Its Role in Feminist Theory." According to Antony, the language instinct with its need to communicate successfully is a universal that is shared by both genders; to achieve human flourishing, special needs must be taken into consideration, but in the end, men and women are more similar than we are different.

Narratives

- Three American Indian Stories. When men and women live apart, the women give up sooner than the men.

- Alice Walker, *The Temple of My Familiar,* episode from novel. One character recounts a pseudo-myth of womb envy.

- *Adam's Rib,* film. A married couple end up on opposite sides of a court case. *He* is the prosecutor of a woman who shot her unfaithful husband, and *she* defends her, from feminist principles.

Notes

1. Plato, *Republic,* trans. Benjamin Jowett (Chicago: Encyclopedia Britannica, 1952), Chapter XV, v. 455.

2. Aristotle, *On the Generation of Animals,* 737a 27–33, in *Philosophy of Woman,* 3rd ed., ed. Mary Briody Mahowald (Indianapolis: Hackett, 1994).

3. Kant, "On the Distinction of the Beautiful and Sublime in the Interrelations of the Two Sexes," in *Philosophy of Woman,* 3rd ed., ed. Mary Briody Mahowald (Indianapolis: Hackett, 1994), p. 103.

4. "In 1866 a group of women from the Kensington Society organized a petition that demanded that women should have the same political rights as men. The women took their petition to Henry Fawcett and John Stuart Mill, two MPs who supported universal suffrage. Mill added an amendment to the Reform Act that would give women the same political rights as men. The amendment was defeated by 196 votes to 73." Retrieved from the World Wide Web: http://www.spartacus.schoolnet.co.uk/Wnuwss.htm

5. Neither Mill nor Taylor took into consideration here that a person may be kept on in a position for reasons other than skill alone, such as political reasons.

6. Harriet Taylor Mill, "Enfranchisement of Women," in *Philosophy of Woman,* 3rd ed., ed. Mary Briody Mahowald (Indianapolis: Hackett, 1994), p. 173.

7. John Stuart Mill, *Subjection of Women,* in *Philosophy of Woman,* 3rd ed., ed. Mary Briody Mahowald (Indianapolis: Hackett, 1994), pp. 161–162, 165.

8. See Chapter 3: Bad faith is Sartre's and Beauvoir's concept that a person thinks he or she can avoid the anguish of the existential choice by pretending they have no choice.

9. Vincent L. Boyer, Masculinism—TRUE Equality of the Sexes, 1997. Retrieved from the World Wide Web: http://isource.net/~flash/

10. Louise Antony, "'Human Nature' and Its Role in Feminist Theory," in *Philosophy in a Feminist Voice,* ed. Janet A. Kourany (Princeton: Princeton University Press, 1998), pp. 82–83.

Chapter Seven

Minds, Bodies, Selves

Having a Mind, a Body, and a Self

As we have seen before, some perceptions about human nature seem obvious until we start to scratch the surface; then much of our certitude vanishes. Most of us are convinced that we, as humans, have minds. I am sure that we are all convinced we have bodies. And all the people I have ever known who grew up in Western cultures have been comfortable talking about them*selves;* we generally assume that we have something called a "self." In this chapter we look at some famous and not-so-famous issues regarding minds, bodies, and selves.

Why would anyone question the idea that humans have minds? Recall the theories of metaphysics that you encountered in earlier chapters. If *dualism* (mind and bodies are real) is correct, then of course we have minds. But as we shall see, there are in fact major problems associated with this assumption. If *idealism* (only mind is real) is correct, then we certainly have minds, but we may not have bodies, or we may never know whether we in fact have them, because any knowledge of the material world has to be processed by the *mind* in order for us to know it! And if *materialism* (only matter is real) is correct, then we simply can't claim that we have minds, only that we have *brains* with brain processes. We'll return to the issue shortly.

Now why would anyone in a state of sanity question whether we have bodies? Well, if you are an idealist, then you claim to know nothing of a world outside the mind, and you just can't make any such assumption about having bodies. At best you can say that it seems as if we have bodies, but they could be figments of our imagi-nation—or even figments in the imagination of God. But most of us are not idealists, and having a body seems one of the most basic, normal components of human nature. Suppose we grant that humans have bodies—then we are actually beg-ging the question, or assuming that what we are trying to prove is true. Because what does it mean to "have" a body? Do we own our bodies? And if we do, can we dispense with them? Who are "we," separate from those bodies? Wouldn't it be more accurate to say that we *inhabit* our bodies? But in that case we must be able to specify *what* it is that inhabits a body and where it resides, if anywhere. In other words, we are propelled into proving that we have souls, or at least minds. Now what if we try to circumvent the issue by simply stating that we *are* our bodies, that every human experience rests on the assumption that we are physical be-ings in a physical world? An increasing number of philosophers take this road, but that doesn't mean it is without problems: If we "are" our bod-ies, then we have talked ourselves out of the pos-sibility of a non-physical afterlife.

And how could anyone question that there is such a thing as "myself"? The experience of the self is so fundamental to Western philosophy, Western languages, and Western mind-sets that it often comes as a surprise that many non-Western cultures don't have a word for "I" or "self" in their languages. This, of course, doesn't mean that the non-Western experience excludes what we call self-awareness, if what we mean is being con-scious of one's place within one's world; however, self-awareness is one of those experiences where the cultural and moral overlay becomes so signif-icant that it flavors the individual experience. In the West, we generally think we ought to have a self and feel separate from the world, so that's how we feel. Elsewhere it is often customary to play down one's individual significance and focus on one's relationship to society or nature, or both, so that experience dominates. But even within Western philosophy, thinkers have questioned the concept of "self," and of "consciousness," as we shall see.

Consciousness Developing: Rival Theories

Given that we experience being conscious and can observe others acting as if they have some form of consciousness, we will for the sake of argument assume that there is such a thing as human consciousness. (Later in the chapter you will encounter theories that any talk of consciousness or mind will eventually be replaced by neurobiological explanations, but most of us assume intuitively that we really have the consciousness we experience, and I will use that as our foundation here.) First we must ask about a definition of the term *consciousness*. If you remember the end of the *Star Trek* story in Chapter 1, "The Measure of a Man," you will recall that Judge Louvoir refused to speculate about the nature of consciousness, because Commander Data needed to be allowed to explore that topic for himself. However, we have to be more specific: Consciousness, like time, is one of the topics we are most familiar with and which humans talk about the most, but we do so without getting much closer to what it truly is. Does it mean awareness of our surroundings? Does it also mean having to have awareness of our role as observers? Is it the same as self-consciousness? The German nineteenth-century philosopher G.W. F. Hegel (see Chapter 9) speculated that consciousness slumbers in the stone, awakes in the animal, and flourishes in humans.

Consciousness: Sentience or Sapience?

Remember the kind of questions we asked in Chapter 1: Is a particular trait of human nature *common to all humans?* And might it also appear in nonhuman populations? We can answer that it is normal for humans to experience consciousness, but of course not everyone is endowed with it. Severe mental disabilities, illness, or brain damage can deprive a human of full or partial awareness; a person in a coma is not conscious, at least not the way we normally define it in Western philosophy: having awareness of one's surroundings and one's self. And certainly we all experience a level of nonconsciousness whenever we are asleep. But the sporadic absence of consciousness is not controversial. The next question is far more problematic: Might consciousness, or self-awareness, appear in nonhuman populations? Before the late twentieth century, philosophers most likely would have denied it. Consciousness has, for most of the existence of Western philosophy, been considered the hallmark of humanity, since it implies not only experiencing one's world, but also being aware of the experience. In addition, many pre-twentieth-century Western philosophers often equate consciousness with the capacity for rationality, and the thought of a reasoning nonhuman mind (except for the mind of God and of angels) has been almost universally rejected in Western thought, in part because the capacity for consciousness and thinking for many has been linked to the religious concept of a *soul*—no less controversial. A few dissidents such as David Hume did consider the possibility of thinking animals, and we will get back to the issue in Chapter 10.

While the question of the nature of consciousness has by no means been established—and even the scientists working with Artificial Intelligence (AI) will usually not attempt to define exactly what consciousness is or claim that it is something that a robot can attain—the most common assumption of the term *consciousness* is that it involves at least *an awareness of one's surroundings.* But does it also mean that one has to *be aware that one is aware* of one's surroundings? This is the watershed that divides scholars who see consciousness as a simple brain product of a simple brain and those who see it as an enormously sophisticated end result of a long brain evolution.

Let's examine both definitions—the first one broad, and the second one narrow—and then you can determine which definition you find most reasonable or most interesting:

1. If consciousness means the very *simple awareness of one's surroundings,* enough to escape from predators, find prey, hide food and find it again, find mates, and be aware of one's offspring in order to protect them, teach them, and be sure they don't wander off, then it seems that most mammals and birds have consciousness. And aside from the focus on offspring, so do reptiles, fish, and possibly even some or most insects. Another term for this type of consciousness is *sentience,* in its original form: ability to sense the world and feel pain and pleasure. (Only science fiction authors use the term *sentience* to mean *sapience!*) Aristotle's work *On the Soul* states that everything living has a "soul," or an essence of a noncorporeal nature that makes everything what it is: Plants, animals, and humans all share in having a nutritive "soul" that just seeks nutrition and growth; animals also have appetites, senses, and a sense of movement, but only humans have a capacity for thinking rationally. (See Box 7.1 for other theories of consciousness in nature.) In Chapter 8 we take a closer look at this vision of the spiritual continuum of life on earth. Traditionally, the mind activities of nonhuman animals have been labeled *instinct.* Increasingly, however, animal behaviorists and human psychologists are avoiding the term *instinct,* because we can distinguish, hypothetically, between conscious, deliberate decisions and completely automatic genetically encoded behavior; but there is a gray area in between that looks like a bit of both, and that is the area of *learned behavior,* based on trial and error. Humans have it; fish, reptiles, birds, and mammals have it, but most insects seem not to be able to learn from a new situation. Some neuroscientists boil it down to the experience of *fear:* Which living beings can feel fear and act

on it? Those who can do so have a keen awareness of their surroundings. According to neuroscience, primitive emotions such as the feeling of fear are located in the *amygdala,* one of the most ancient parts of the animal brain; sometimes it is referred to as the "reptile brain," because for one thing it is predominant in reptiles, and, evolutionarily speaking, it is present in all higher brains as a reminder of our evolutionary past. The "fight or flight" decision is made in the amygdala, and for some thinkers this is all it takes for there to be a basic form of sentience.

2. If consciousness means *self-awareness,* or awareness that one is conscious and aware—in other words, *sapience*—then the field narrows considerably. Only within the past few decades has a test been devised to find out, objectively, if someone is self-aware, by watching them look at themselves in a mirror. Often referred to as the "mirror recognition test," you will find it described in the "Sense of Self" section later in the chapter. The only obvious candidate for this type of consciousness is the human being, because traditionally we have become used to thinking of humans as the only animals with self-awareness. The French philosopher Descartes insisted that only humans can have self-awareness (or any kind of awareness, for that matter), and only very recently have Western thinkers shown an interest in reexamining this assumption. In Chapter 10 we go into the issue of animal self-awareness in detail and look at some of the latest research results. For now, let me just mention that for a growing number of scientists and other thinkers (including myself), it is an indisputable fact that the great apes (chimpanzees, orangutans, gorillas—and humans) all have self-awareness and should be considered conscious beings. The question of the consciousness of other social animals such as wolves (and dogs), whales, dolphins, and elephants is far more controversial, but has its adherents among animal behaviorists. (Box 7.6 explores the view-

point of American philosopher Daniel Dennett that consciousness is an exclusively human phenomenon.)

If the first answer sounds plausible to you, then you will have to conclude that consciousness, in some basic form, has been on this planet probably since the first vertebrates moved around freely in the primeval oceans, trying to find food and mates, and avoid getting eaten—or at least since the first reptiles moved about between land and sea. If the second answer interests you more, then we must look at a much later stage in evolution: somewhere on the branches of the human family tree. But even if you prefer the first explanation, you will probably concede that human consciousness is far more complex than other animal awareness that we know of, so the question of when the specific form of human consciousness, sapience, or self-awareness began is still a good question, and that is what we will look at next.

Cognitive Evolution

For anyone who accepts the worldview of evolutionary biology, the question becomes, When did humanity develop consciousness? If one is content with the religious explanation from Genesis that humans were created by God in their present form, the question doesn't arise, because in that case we came fully equipped with our mental apparatus from the time of creation. However, if we recognize the evidence of biological evolution (see Chapter 2), we are faced with explaining where in the course of human evolution we became conscious. In other words, we must look into *cognitive evolution.*

You might wish to review Chapter 2 for the general theory of human evolution and terminology. As we move further into the twenty-first century, two major schools of thought concern themselves with the development of the specific form of self-awareness we associate with humans. One holds that human self-consciousness developed with *Homo sapiens.* The other holds that self-awareness

is much older, is shared by our fellow primates, and was also shared by the Neandertals. (Box 7.1 gives an overview of two influential theories of self-awareness: Bergson's and Scheler's.) According to the first theory, we have no evidence from the period before about 100,000 years ago that humans had a clear view of their surroundings and their own role in it; but with the first artifacts and cave paintings of ancient *Homo sapiens* in Africa and southern Europe, there is evidence that these humans not only could feed themselves and raise more humans, but that they also had conscious thoughts about their world and themselves—what the anthropologist Ian Tattersall calls *symbolic behavior.* Such artifacts have not been found for any other human population, says the theory—not even our ancestors *Homo erectus* and *Homo ergaster* or our cousins the Neandertals. Neandertal finds have recently included some crude artifacts that could be representational—meaning carved pictures—but they have been interpreted as art received in trade from the humans in the area. According to Tattersall in his provocative book, *Becoming Human* (1998), the fact that Neandertals used stone tools when there was a lot of wood around shows that they weren't smart enough to move from the tradition of stone tools to what Tattersall sees as a more practical use of wood. (He doesn't consider that it may have been a matter of choice, not "some kind of intellectual limitation.") Having found no Neandertal spears used as throwing weapons, Tattersall pronounces that to be an intellectual limitation too. (You may want to compare his view with Ardrey's in Chapter 3.) Based on the absence of weapons that can be used at a distance, Tattersall concludes that only humans can hunt "with guile," but not the Neandertals.[1] The criterion that for Tattersall means we are talking about a conscious, thinking species is what he calls *symbolic representation,* or *symbolic behavior:* Symbolic behavior includes making art objects and using language. According to Tattersall,

Among all the remarkable attributes, the most striking is our possession of language. And

Box 7.1   HENRI BERGSON'S AND MAX SCHELER'S VISIONS OF WORLD CONSCIOUSNESS

You encountered the French philosopher Henri Bergson in Chapter 4 as the proponent of complete human freedom, the opposite of mechanistic, hard determinism. While Bergson's theory of free will was influential, it was nothing compared to his theory of the life-force, the *élan vital.* In his world-famous and extremely popular book from 1907, *Creative Evolution,* Bergson speculates that the material world is steeped in a spiritual life-force that manifests itself at any given level as a movement or even an urge toward further evolution. Often referred to as a *process philosophy,* Bergson's conception of life on earth as a force or a process of more and more developed self-awareness has ties to Hegel's idea of the development of the world-spirit through history (see Chapter 9).

The German philosopher Max Scheler (1874–1928) dedicated his life's work to examining human nature as a development of psychic life from lower to higher forms in nature. Inspired by Hegel, Husserl, and Bergson, Scheler views every living being as possessing some form of consciousness, being filled with the ex-

perience of the world. Scheler sees the evolution of consciousness in four stages: The first stage is a kind of *élan vital,* an instinctive, unconscious life-force; the second stage is an instinctual psychic force, a survival mechanism. The third stage is the evolution of memory; and the fourth stage is practical intelligence where the species has learned to solve problems. For Scheler humans obviously have gone through all four stages, but so have other animals. Even the fourth stage is shared with nonhuman animals, but for Scheler there is still a fundamental difference between humans and animals: Humans have developed a force that, in effect, goes *against* the life-force, and that is our capacity for spirituality and reasoning. For many readers Scheler's attempt at explaining life as an evolution of consciousness seemed daring and refreshing, but the fact is that Aristotle laid the groundwork over 2,000 years earlier with his theory that everything on the earth is filled with a built-in energy of purpose and his belief that animals share the survival urge with humans, but they do not share our capacity to reason.

knowing whether or not this is something that was shared with the Neanderthals is crucial to the assessment of the size of the cognitive gap between them and us. For if they had language, they were us in a profound sense, despite their many physical differences and the limited range of their material productions.[2]

Based on studies of the Neandertal brain and throat structure, Tattersall believes that language was an impossibility for them, and, therefore, they were most definitely *not us.* There are two possible responses: For one thing, as you will see in Chapter 10, language does not consist of speech alone, but also of gestures, mimicry, and other sounds—otherwise, we'd have to say that deaf people have no language. For another, more recent studies than the ones referred to by Tattersall *do* indeed seem

to point to both brain structures and throat anatomy that would make spoken language possible for the Neandertal—and according to Tattersall's logic, in that case they would, indeed, *be us.*

But Tattersall sees cognitive differences even within the recent *Homo sapiens* population: From what some would call a blatantly technocentric viewpoint, Tattersall pronounces that the hunter-gatherer style of living and moving within one's environment *without altering it* represents a lower form of consciousness and intelligence than does the agricultural lifestyle which alters the environment; and, as a consequence, he finds himself in a situation where he has to warn against altering the environment too much because it results in pollution and global warming. Others, such as Robert Rÿser and Hoyt Edge (discussed later in the chapter), would probably say that the question of intelligence applied to altering the environment is not as simple as Tattersall makes it, and the type of life we live within our environment may well depend not on smarts but on cultural tradition and *choice*—we can choose to live *with* the environment or outside and *against* it.

Within the last couple of decades, other scientists have attempted to prove that there is a cognitive chasm between humans and all other primates, to the extent that a behaviorist, Bennett Galef, has claimed that only humans can teach other humans new things. In other words, only humans have a *culture* they can pass along to the next generation. In his view, apes can't learn from each other, but this idea has been vigorously contested by zookeepers and ape researchers, who point to numerous examples of apes inventing things and teaching them to other apes. Merlin Donald, professor of psychology, chooses an intermediate path in his book *Origins of the Modern Mind* (1991): He does not deny that primates have a form of consciousness that includes sapience, but it is "episodic," not constant. Human cognition, on the other hand, is developed so far beyond that of other primates that, for Donald, we are still talking about a difference in kind and not in degree. *The Prehistory of the Mind,* by Steven Mithen (1996), also stresses that human cognition is on an entirely different level in terms of both quality and quantity than any other primate cognition—now or in the past.[3] Borrowing Howard Gardner's theory that the human mind consists of multiple intelligences, in the way that a Swiss Army knife consists of several blades with several functions, Mithen grants *general intelligence* to apes, but sees it giving them very limited tool use as well as limited social interaction; for Mithen, we have to go all the way to *Homo habilis* to find *technical* and *social intelligence* and all the way to modern humans to find cultural intelligence of natural history, art, and language. Mithen even suggests that prior to modern humans, all other primates and hominids, including the Neandertals, have only a "rolling consciousness," without any self-awareness or memory, a kind of unconscious thought process similar to driving a car along a familiar street without being aware of it. (Box 7.2 explores the possibility of multiple intelligences.)

However, other scholars hold different opinions. The American philosopher Maxine Sheets-Johnstone, in *The Roots of Thinking* (1990) and in particular *The Primacy of Movement* (1999), sees the foundation for consciousness rooted in the *ability to move and to experience one's own movement.* We have to understand the Neandertals' movement style in terms of their dense, strong bodies to understand why (as Tattersall pointed out) their technology was less complex than that of the European *Homo sapiens sapiens*: the Neandertal body was already a formidable tool for hunting and gathering in itself, so why would they need more tools?[4] It doesn't mean they were less intelligent just because they didn't invent more things: "Why would a labor-saving device in the form of a lever, for example, be thought of if one could immediately pick up the small boulder and move it by oneself? . . . In short, what one conceives and elaborates in the way of a tool is patterned on the animate form one is."[5]

But, for Sheets-Johnstone, even more important than understanding why Neandertals may or may not have needed tools is understanding that they undoubtedly were conscious. She offers two reasons: First, they were excellent survivors in a harsh climate, and such survival skill would most probably include conscious deliberation. Their physical build as well as their technology point to their moving about in a thoroughly deliberate way, understanding themselves as moving within their world. Second, it is logically inconceivable that humans are the only beings with a consciousness, because according to the theory of evolution, such a characteristic doesn't arise out of nowhere (in the way people used to think mice would spontaneously generate out of old rags): It came from somewhere before we were *Homo sapiens*. And since it is most plausible that it developed in our primate ancestors and even earlier from ancestral forms of life, it is most likely that a form of consciousness was experienced by them, as well as by our distant cousins the apes. So it is more than likely that the only other hominid group ever to

Box 7.2   EMOTIONAL INTELLIGENCE?

Philosophers have for a long time focused on intelligence and the human capacity for reason as the primary aspect of consciousness, but new ways of thinking about intelligence have surfaced within the past decade. Not only do we have Howard Gardner's idea of the human mind as a Swiss Army knife, a collection of goal-oriented intelligences, each evolved and suitable for specific mental tasks, but we also have Mithen's suggestion that intelligence has been a long time evolving in the primate line, from a general form of intelligence in apes to an array of technical, social, natural history, art, and language intelligences in humans. And now psychologists are weighing in and including what used to be considered the very opposite of intelligence: *emotion.* David Goleman's best-seller *Emotional Intelligence* (1995) broke with the popular stereotype of *emotion versus reason* by suggesting that much of our success in life or lack of it has to do with our emotional intelligence rather than our rational capacity. His theory is that you can learn to manage emotions, not just by controlling them, but by understanding their appropriateness in certain situations; developing one's self-discipline and empathy improves on one's emotional intelligence. However, Coleman is not the first to have explored the issue: For one thing, Aristotle in ancient Greece and Spinoza in Renaissance Holland spent much time exploring the nature and function of emotions as not just an obstacle to reason, but as a part of the conscious life of human beings. Freud paved the way in the twentieth century for a philosophical understanding that emotions can be disregarded only at the peril

of losing one's entire mental equilibrium to a neurosis. American philosophers such as Robert Solomon, Philip Hallie, and Martha Nussbaum have each explored the philosophy of strong emotions, pointing out that there is a "logic" to our feelings that an emphasis on reason without emotions has lost sight of. Some of the things we *feel* make very much sense and should be regarded as very relevant to our lives as thinking beings. In the final analysis, our very sense of who we are, our "self," may have more to do with how we feel than how we think.

In addition, recent studies of memory, both in humans and animals, point to an interesting connection between memory and emotion: We seem to remember more vividly facts and events that are somehow connected with strong emotions. It is as if the emotion "tags" the memory for later, quick reference—and seen in the light of evolution, this of course makes sense. If something has frightened the daylights out of us once, we'll want to be forewarned next time. But it gets even more interesting: Studies seem to indicate that as long as memories are linked with an emotional context, they are stored in our right brain hemisphere. If the emotional component fades away from the memory, the memory itself apparently *moves over* to the left side of the brain where it is still accessible, but as a more impersonal memory of facts. We seem to store, and recall, memories differently as our emotion recalls them: We remember the multiplication tables in quite a different way, and in a different place in the brain, than our memory of people and things we truly care about.

---

be considered as a close relative to *Homo sapiens sapiens, Homo sapiens neanderthalensis,* would also be conscious.

Husserl: Consciousness Is Intentionality

To most of us, being conscious simply means that we are alive, awake, and thinking about something or other. So far we've seen that human consciousness is generally assumed to include both a

sense of our surroundings and of ourselves interacting with our surroundings. But that brings up another question: Does it mean that there is consciousness and then there is the *content of consciousness?* In other words, can we think of a human being who is conscious, without taking into consideration what she or he is conscious *of*? Is there a *subject* that is conscious, and an *object* that the subject is conscious of, in the same consciousness? This question is what some philosophers describe as the "subject-object split" in Western philosophy: Western thinkers have grown used to imagining that each person is like an empty container (the consciousness) and the content of the container is what is on one's mind—and somehow we are supposed to be able to mentally separate the content from the container. The German philosopher Edmund Husserl (see Box 7.7) criticized this idea and suggested that we have looked at consciousness in a completely erroneous way: There is no such thing as a mind like a container, filled with objects from one's experiences or thoughts. To Husserl, our consciousness is a process, or a relation, between our self and what we experience. He calls it the *intentionality* of the consciousness: Our mind is always full of something, and that something (the content of our consciousness, the "object" of our thoughts) *is* what our mind consists of at any given point in time. There is no subject experiencing an object, but a mind awash with experiences. There is a subject-end (*subject-pole*) and an object-end (*object-pole*) in each moment of our conscious lives, but we can never separate ourselves from our experiences as if we could empty the container mind of its content. Husserl's view of consciousness became the foundation of the twentieth century school of *phenomenology*, which later inspired Merleau-Ponty to his theory of the self; we look at Merleau-Ponty later in the chapter.

What Is a Mind?

In this section we follow up on theories of consciousness by going to the source of such theories in the Western philosophical tradition: the French philosopher René Descartes (1596–1650) and his view that human nature consists of having a body, but being a thinking mind.

The Cartesian Mind-Body Distinction

Before the seventeenth century, views of human nature generally focused on issues of the soul and its choice of good and evil; we take a closer look at such theories in the next chapter, since these theories are fundamentally normative. But if we want to take a look at theories of human nature that are predominantly descriptive and scientific, we have to zero in on the first century of what we today call "modern philosophy," meaning Western philosophy after the Middle Ages and the Renaissance and before the twentieth century. In the sixteenth and seventeenth centuries some thinkers had the courage to defy the Church as well as secular power structures and investigate what they considered to be the nature of reality, regardless of the officially accepted explanations. One such thinker was Newton; others were Keppler, Galileo, and Bruno. Now we must remember that in those times, speculation about reality based on scientific evidence had not yet acquired the status or even the title of science; any such speculation was generally classified as philosophy. This also means that courageous philosophers should be added to the list, even though they may not qualify as experimental scientists by today's standards. Thomas Hobbes (Chapters 3 and 9) was such a critical thinker, and René Descartes was another; his name in Latin was Cartesius, and that is why we often refer to his theories as "Cartesian" (you may remember Cartesian, or analytic geometry, from high school math). In fact, Hobbes and Descartes were contemporaries and had some correspondence with each other.

It is hard for us today to imagine that scientific and speculative thinking ever was done at the peril of your life; tangle with the explanations put forth by the political/ecclesiastical power structure, and your life could be in danger. The fact that just about every thinker on this list feared for his life and tried to avoid tangling with the authorities, sometimes by delaying publication of a work until after death, is borne out by history: Bruno was burned at the stake for his heretical theories in 1600, and Galileo was forced to recant his theory of heliocentrism. Hobbes fled England and stayed on the European continent for years; Descartes himself apparently lived in perpetual fear of persecution by the Church for heresy and had as his motto (later carved on his tombstone), *Bene vixit qui bene latuit,* a Roman proverb: "He who hid well, lived well." He was French by birth, but lived for years in Holland because it was a more open-minded community. However, in the end, Descartes didn't hide well enough: He died from pneumonia (or so legend has it) while living at the Swedish court as a "visiting professor," invited by Queen Christina to instruct her in philosophy because of his widespread fame as a thinker.[6]

René Descartes is generally credited with being the founder of modern philosophy; if you have ever taken another philosophy class, you have probably encountered his famous saying, "I think, therefore I am" (Latin: *Cogito ergo sum*). Often Descartes is presented as one of the most radical minds of all time, due to his *method of doubt.* However, while the method was radical, Descartes himself wasn't nearly as nontraditional in his view of human nature as one might think. Descartes should be viewed against the deep background of medieval as well as ancient philosophy: The Catholic Church had, ever since the first centuries of Christianity, viewed human beings as born into sin and, because of their moral frailty, certain of eternal damnation—had it not been for the sacrifice of Christ. The general metaphysical view was, and still is, *dualistic:* We have a body that tends to lead us astray and a soul that is only too willing to go the same route if we are not taught properly about the wages of sin. But with the proper instruction and willingness to do right, the immortal soul can look forward to an afterlife in the company of Christ, once the worries of this physical life are over.

The Christian tradition didn't pull these thoughts out of a hat—or even seek much support in the teachings of Jesus Christ himself. There were several precursors in antiquity, and we look at some of them in detail in the next chapter: Middle Eastern religions prior to Christianity (and prior to Islam) speculated that the powers of good and evil were engaged in a battle for human souls, and the good would win only if enough souls sided with it against the powers of darkness. Interestingly, classical Judaism does not believe humans are born in sin, nor that the afterlife is anything we

ought to focus on, so calling the Christian tradition of belief in Heaven a "Judeo-Christian" tradition is actually a misnomer.

But another tradition in antiquity—Platonism—focused strongly on the life of the soul as opposed to the life of the body. Plato's philosophy is fundamentally dualistic; when Socrates is about to be executed by the city of Athens, he speculates that his body will merely be left behind, but his soul will go on to its proper home. It is clear to Plato that too much emphasis on one's physical needs will distract the mind, and the soul, from its proper task: to reach a rational understanding of reality. Too much concern for physical needs will bring one's soul out of balance, and an unbalanced soul is a sick soul. A healthy soul focuses primarily on intellectual and spiritual matters and leaves the earthly concerns for fame, fortune, and physical gratification behind as something unworthy of the human spirit. In Chapter 8 we look in greater detail at Plato's theory of the soul. Suffice it for now to point out that Plato's view became one of the key influences in early Christianity, adding an element to the Christian teachings that the Gospels just don't emphasize unequivocally: Life consists of concerns for the body and concerns for the immortal soul, and reality consists of two kinds of elements, or *substances,* one material and the other spiritual. Add to this that the material substance (the reality we can touch and measure in some way) throughout the Middle Ages is considered less good than the spiritual substance (the life of the mind), even to the point where the material substance is considered an empty realm, waiting to be populated with the ideas of God. An example is the philosophy of Plotinus: the theory of *material deprivation,* where matter is considered deprived of spirit and therefore empty or even evil.

This is the background for Descartes's theory of reality, or metaphysics, and consequently his theory of human nature: Reality consists of two substances, one material and one spiritual. The material substance—or the "extended thing," *res extensa*—is something shared by everything organic and inorganic. That is the reality we know with our senses and inhabit with our bodies. But in addition there is the spiritual substance, *res cogitans,* the "thinking thing." Of all beings on the earth, only humans share in this refined substance, because, to Descartes, *only humans have minds.*

What was Descartes's evidence for this theory? Nothing, if you are asking for *facts* supporting his theory, because Descartes didn't reach this conclusion from an empirical, scientific—an inductive—approach; his method was *deductive:* From an idea that he considered fundamentally true—only humans have souls—he deduced that only humans are capable of having functioning minds. This part of Cartesian philosophy, his metaphysics, is in no way innovative or revolutionary. What is revolutionary is what he did with it: He turned the philosophical community in an altogether new direction.

From the time Descartes was a young man—earning a living as a soldier of fortune, a mercenary—he had had the notion that he was destined to change the course of science and philosophy. One night he had a persistent dream: He was going to invent a new science. However, he didn't feel mature or capable enough until he reached middle age, but then he sat down and for six nights (if we are to believe his own words) he thought about the nature of reality and the way humans can achieve knowledge about that reality; and on the basis of his ponderings he wrote the six *Meditations on First Philosophy* that were to give him the title of "founder of modern philosophy." In the Primary Readings you will find an excerpt from the First and Second *Meditations.* Descartes considered it his task to provide some foundation for a new science and philosophy, a foundation that could not be questioned or doubted. In a sense his concern was double-edged: The issue of doubt was a concern for him because a popular school of thought had done its best to spread disbelief as a matter of principle: *Skepticism* had quite a grip on Descartes's contemporaries, and it had become fashionable to say that everything can be doubted. The other edge was the hostility toward science and speculative thinking that the Church

had manifested over many centuries, through what we now call the Dark Ages or the Early Middle Ages, from the fifth century—when the Roman Empire converted to Christianity—to approximately year 1000. As you have already seen, even throughout the High Middle Ages and well into the seventeenth century, the Church kept an eye on anyone engaged in science as well as necromancy, with persecutions and executions the result. So on one hand, Descartes reacts against those who tell you to believe nothing, and on the other he reacts against those telling you to believe without questioning (and for this reason, Descartes had concerns about his safety).

As a device, Descartes played along with skepticism, acting as the devil's advocate, using his method of doubt: Ask yourself: Can I trust my senses? Not completely, because they have been known to mislead me. And if they mislead me sometimes, then can I ever trust them? Not in principle; you may think you can trust your eyes, but light plays tricks on you, and the oar you put in the water on your rowboat outing looks straight when it is out of the water, but bent when it is in the water, because of the refraction of the light. So don't trust your senses. Then can you at all trust your sense of reality, of time and place? No, because you could be dreaming; you may not actually be reading this page, but you could be having a truly inspirational dream (or a hideous nightmare) that you are taking a philosophy class and have to read this book. And is there anything in a dream that actually signifies that you are not awake? (This hypothesis is commonly referred to as the *dream conjecture* by philosophers.) No, says Descartes. And a modern reader might add, you may not even be dreaming, but you could be drunk, or hypnotized, under the influence of some drug, or hooked up to some virtual reality device. So don't trust your sense of reality.

But, at least, aren't the rules of math and logic true regardless of whether we are dreaming or awake? We'd like to think so, says Descartes, but just suppose we are not in control of our own mind? Just suppose that some incredibly powerful

Box 7.3   THE CARTESIAN MATRIX?

The Matrix (1999) is one of the most popular films of the past decade. Incidentally, it is also quite Cartesian, at least in its plot. Descartes's method of doubt asks us not to trust our senses or even our logic, because (1) we could be dreaming (the "dream conjecture"), and (2) we could be tricked (the "evil demon conjecture"). It may seem a tall order to systematically assume that all our experiences could be false, but for the reluctant ones *The Matrix* points the way. Neo, a young man, finds himself in the presence of the mysterious Morpheus who has a story to tell him: The world Neo thinks is real is anything but. Life for Neo, the life he thinks is three-dimensional and solid, is nothing but a dream—a dream induced by, if you will, evil demons—

and so it is for almost every human being alive. People think they move about in a modern world—but it is only their minds that move about in the Matrix, a virtual reality program. Their bodies are locked in vats, hooked up to machines that suck the life energy out of them, to feed the new rulers of the planet: robots. Humans have been reduced to energy machines. So what is Neo's task? It is *not* to conclude that he exists, every time he doubts that the Matrix is real; it is rather to liberate humanity. The Cartesian parallel can be taken only so far, but even so, it is a skillful representation of two powerful ideas in Descartes's *Meditations*: the suggestion that we may be dreaming and that we may be fooled by an immensely powerful evil demon.

evil demon is feeding you false ideas and making you think they are true? (This is known as the *evil demon/evil genius conjecture.*) You'd never know, because they'd have all the hallmarks of the truth. This demon might convince you that 2 + 2 equals 5, and nothing in your reality would contradict it, because the demon has already fixed that! So what can you believe in? What can you trust? Nothing at all. So have the skeptics won? No, because while you are doubting and thinking, *you exist!* That is the bottom-line fact. The demon can't make you think you don't exist if you do or that you do exist if you don't. So "I am, I exist, is necessarily true each time that I pronounce it, or that I mentally conceive it."[7] This assertion has become famous under the slightly different wording from Descartes's *Discourse on Method,* "I think, therefore I am." And the rest of the world? It is probably there in much the way we see it, because God is not an evil demon, and he wouldn't allow us to be fooled and betrayed in such a fundamental way—to make six long *Meditations* ultra-short! (Box 7.3 explores the premise of the film *The Matrix* as a Cartesian story.)

With this device Descartes has done away with skepticism—or at least he thought so. Critics have

been at work ever since, undermining his certitude, and we will return to the criticism of Descartes.

Descartes has often been presented as one of the world's great skeptics, but that just doesn't hold up, as you can see: Descartes was far from being a skeptic, but rather plays a good game of skepticism; as a matter of fact, once he establishes that there is something we can know as a fact, he quickly does away with all other aspects of skepticism and plunges into a complete faith in both his senses and the existence of the world, the rules of reason, and God. Skepticism is simply a tool he uses to get to where he wants to be: down in the firm foundation of a faith in reality, in the thinking mind, in *res cogitans.*

The story of the journey of the mind through skepticism to the one certain thing—knowledge of one's own existence—is laid out in the first and second *Meditations.* The reader moves from the knowledge *that* we are to the question of *what* we are: "A thing which thinks. What is a thing which thinks? It is a thing which doubts, understands, [conceives], affirms, denies, wills, refuses, which also imagines and feels."[8] The physical world has extension, says Descartes (that is why it is referred to as the extended substance, or *res extensa*). It has

The Matrix, Silver Pictures, 1999. "The Matrix" has become a popular concept for a reality that we think is objectively true but that turns out to be an illusion. The film from 1999, with sequels to follow, operates with two levels of reality: the everyday world we know, which turns out to be a product of the Matrix, created to deceive us, and the "real world," a post-holocaust nightmarish reality run by artificial intelligences requiring energy—which they harvest from their millions of unconscious human captives locked in the fantasy world of the Matrix. The enigmatic character Morpheus (Lawrence Fishburn) searches for the one who will be able to liberate humanity from the Matrix.

a whole lot of other characteristics, too, but many of them are ephemeral and highly changeable: Water freezes and melts, leaves change color, everything living grows older. And some of those qualities may be in your perception of things rather than in the things themselves—color qualities, for example, could be in the eye of the beholder more than in the object. The fact remains that everything physical has an extended surface. But how do we know that a thing *remains the same thing* under different circumstances? Now that we have established that you need not worry about being fooled constantly by your senses, imagine spending the evening with Descartes in his study; there is a fire in the fireplace, and Descartes is in his dressing gown and slippers, showing you a piece of wax, asking you to notice its qualities: It is of a certain shape, it is hard, sweet, and fragrant (because it is fresh); it is cold, and it makes a sound if you strike it. So our five senses have a clear image of it as a "thing." Now we move it close to the fire, and what happens? Not only does it melt, but the qualities that we observed melt away too: It now has a different shape, consistency, flavor, smell, sound, and feel. So *is it the same piece of wax?* Had you left the room while it was being melted and come back to observe it in its melted state, you might not have said yes; but even if your senses tell you all the qualities are now different, your *mind* still tells you it is the identical piece. It is something deeper than your sense of imagination, because it is a *clear and distinct* form of knowledge. And if we can know this much, with certainty, about a piece of wax, how much more can we know about our own mind?

> It is now manifest to me that even bodies are not properly speaking known by the senses or by the faculty of imagination, but by the understanding alone, and since they are not known from the fact that they are seen or touched, but only because they are understood, I see clearly that there is nothing which is easier for me to know than my mind.[9]

So our human nature is dual: We can trust our senses to tell us truthfully that we have a body, but we don't have the same *privileged access* to our body as we have to our mind. We are not in control of many of the physical functions of our body, but we do have immediate, direct access to our mind, because we have self-awareness. We know that we know our mind. But only humans have this direct access; animals do not. (In Box 7.4 we take a closer look at the implication of Descartes's theory that only humans have self-awareness.)

The Mind-Body Problem

We are now going to explore some of the most influential metaphysical explanations of human

Box 7.4   DESCARTES: "ANIMALS HAVE NO MINDS"

In what has developed into one of the great scandals of philosophy, Descartes claims that animals have no mental activity; and since they have no minds, *they feel no pain*. From your knowledge of Descartes's theory of the two substances you can actually deduce for yourself how he reaches this conclusion: not from any empirical study of animals in pain, but from a deductive argument: <u>Premise 1</u>: Of the two substances, material and mental, only humans share in the mental substance. <u>Premise 2</u>: You need a mind to have self-awareness, including awareness of pain. <u>Conclusion</u>: Animal bodies may have nerve reactions to stimuli that humans would consider painful, but since animals have no minds, they experience no pain. The extraordinary thing is not that all of Descartes's colleagues agreed with him, because they didn't. Descartes was engaged in a vivid correspondence with thinkers of the time, including the British philosopher and poet Margaret Cavendish (the Marchioness of Newcastle), who argued against him.

The extraordinary thing is that Descartes's viewpoint prevailed because it was politically convenient: At the time, the Catholic Church had considered reopening the debate about animal suffering and animal moral standing, based on Thomas Aquinas's statement that animals have souls, albeit nonrational souls, but because of Descartes's writings the debate ground to a halt, and any budding ideas of protecting animals against cruelty and abuse were cast aside. It wasn't until well into the eighteenth century that the Scottish thinker David Hume (see chapter text and Chapter 10) declared that if human and animal behaviors are similar, then we probably have similar brains. In the late eighteenth and nineteenth centuries a few more thinkers—Jeremy Bentham and John Stuart Mill, and later Charles Darwin—joined the ranks of just about every lay person who has ever known an animal personally and proclaimed that animals feel pain, too, and should be taken into moral consideration.

nature in terms of mind and body. You were introduced to the key concepts of metaphysics (materialism, idealism, and dualism) earlier in this book, and we have drawn on these ideas on several occasions. Plato was a dualist, while Hobbes and the modern hard determinists are materialists. Now it is also clear that Descartes is a dualist. Indeed, everyone has a theory of metaphysics, whether they are philosophers or not: Do you believe you have a mind as well as a body? Then you are a dualist. If you believe that somehow the world is not the way we perceive it, and the only certainty we have is that our minds exist, then you are an idealist (but there aren't many of you these days). If you are in tune with contemporary cognitive science and believe that all our mind experiences can somehow be reduced to brain functions of a chemical or electrical nature and that the death of the brain also means the death of the mind, then you are a materialist.

As much as the materialistic viewpoint may prevail among scientists, it still seems fairly certain that most people find dualism to be the best explanation of our reality. So why is this perceived to be a problem? Because no dualist has yet done a good job of explaining one very simple thing: If we consist of minds and bodies, and minds are immaterial and bodies are material, *how do the mind and the body affect each other?* We can't just claim that they somehow do, because we have just said that minds are immaterial and bodies are material. How does something without any material substance causally affect something that is totally material? And how does something material have a causal influence on something without any physical nature? If you are a person fortunate enough to be able to move your body normally, try touching your nose with your right index finger. How did you do that? Well, your mind told your body to move, and it did. But how, if your mind has no control over matter? Remember the movie *Ghost*? The main character is dead—meaning his soul, or mind, has separated from his dead body, and he is trying to affect the world of the living by telling his girlfriend that she is in danger. He can walk through doors as well as people's bodies, because he is immaterial; but he can't move material objects because his immaterial mind has no control over matter. (And the fact that later on he "learns how" does not change the problem, because what we get is a movie solution: Concentrate very hard!) He has no body with which to control other bodies, because it takes something physical to affect other physical things. His problem is as great as if you tried to lift your backpack by the power of your mind alone (try it, I dare you!), because there is no physical connection between you and the backpack. But according to dualism, neither is there any physical connection between your mind and your finger moving to touch your nose! So how does it happen? To this day no dualist has given a good answer, only that it *does* happen. Descartes himself tried to explain it, and philosophers have been joking about his attempt ever since. In the following section you'll see some of the most influential attempts at solving the problem.

Interactionism   Descartes knew that he had to find a physical point in the body where the soul or mind could "touch down" and interact with the body, so he looked for a place in the brain that was not duplicated in both brain hemisperes and came up with the pineal gland (which we today know produces hormones). This he declared to be the seat of the mind and the point from which the mind steers the body, even more intimately than a pilot steers a ship, but pretty much along the same lines. But this is no solution at all: Descartes has just moved the problem to a tiny local area: How does the mind affect the gland? He still hasn't explained that. So this commonsense assumption of humans having minds and bodies that interact with each other has no logical explanation to back it up. Now why can't modern bi-

ologists come up with a better proposal than the pineal gland? They actually have, recently, and have declared the right frontal lobe to be the most likely place where our sense of self originates, but as long as they try to pinpoint a certain area as the seat of consciousness, soul, or mind, we are back with the interactionism problem: If mind is immaterial and matter is material, then how do they interact?

One of the most famous twentieth-century answers to Descartes's problem comes from the British philosopher Gilbert Ryle (1900–1976). Instead of fixating on the issue of how dualism might work, Ryle dismisses the entire question as wrongly put. It is a *category-mistake* to ask how the causality of the mind and the causality of the body interact with each other, says Ryle, because only the body has the kind of causality we associate with the physical world: The life of the mind simply doesn't follow the rules of causality. If you assume that mind activity works as a cause-and-effect system, then you are using a physical category on a psychical issue: a category-mistake. Bodies are in space, but minds are not, and mind activity can only be observed privately, not by others. So we tend to explain this by saying that physical activity is "outside" the mind, and mental activity is "inside" the mind, but that somehow fools us into thinking that the mind really is somewhere in space, namely "inside." We all have a basic understanding of physical cause and effect, so we just transfer that knowledge onto the category of mind activity, but that is where we, as well as Descartes, get confused, and start to imagine that the mind must "sit" somewhere in the brain and steer things like a navigator.

In other words, we assume that there is a "ghost in the machine" that affects it the same way machines affect machines, except we can't explain how. But that is because we jump to conclusions about the nature of the mind, like someone who is visiting Oxford or Cambridge (this is Ryle's own famous illustration of a category-mistake). He is shown the colleges, the libraries, museums, and so on, and afterwards he asks, "But where is the

University?" The same thing actually happened to yours truly when I visited the Smithsonian years ago. I assumed that the Smithsonian was something separate from the group of museums and didn't know that it was a term for the total organization of institutions. So I saw two or three of the wonderful collections and worried that I would not have time that day to also see the Smithsonian. Similarly in Ryle's example, "the University" is the relation between all the elements, not something separate from the elements. The question is whether Ryle's example really is as good as his fame leads one to believe; it is a great example of mistaking sums of parts and relations, but the mind is not considered a general term for a collection of body parts, so the parallel is at best incomplete.

Another of Ryle's examples, which I think works better, is the "She came home in a flood of tears and a sedan-chair." Since the tears and the chair are different categories, they can't be compared. Minds and bodies are different categories, too, and can't be compared. Ryle's radical answer is to *reject dualism, but also materialism and idealism,* as faulty thinking, because (says Ryle) all three kinds of metaphysics assume that it makes sense to compare minds and bodies. So Ryle claims that we "have" mind-activity (like "tears") and we "have" bodies (like "sedan-chairs"). But we don't have them in the same way; they are completely different notions that can't be compared without committing a category-mistake. But therein lies the problem: Ryle is generally identified as a proponent of the type of materialism we call *analytical behaviorism,* one of the most radical forms of materialism. You will remember behaviorism from Skinner and Watson (Chapter 4), who took it in the practical direction of molding children's behavior. Ryle's behaviorism is more abstract, but essentially says the same thing: *There are no mental states,* just physical behavior. According to some critics, if "mind" is an empty word that only signifies behavior (just as there is no "University" above and beyond school buildings and functions), how can he say "mind" and "body" are dif-

ferent notions that can't be compared? In effect, he *is* comparing them and reducing mind to body.

Parallelism   Dualists who are perplexed by the explanation of interactionism have attempted another solution: Our minds and bodies do not have any point of causal interaction, but have a parallel existence. So mental experiences affect other mental experiences, and physical factors in our bodies affect other physical factors, but there is no causal connection between these two parallel tracks of human nature. The question is, Who or what keeps the mind and body experiences parallel? The answer, however, has rendered parallelism a less-than-successful theory, because it creates more problems: God does. If you are not religious, it is a hard explanation to accept. And even if you are religious, and a logical thinker, you will want to ask, If God is immaterial, how did he create the material strand of reality if there is no interaction between the material and the immaterial aspects? There must have been an initial touching point, and then we're back to interactionism.

Epiphenomenalism   An *epi*phenomenon is something that occurs as a by-product of another phenomenon. Epiphenomenalism is, in a sense, a hybrid form of dualism and materialism: An epiphenomenalist claims that there are brain reactions and there are mind experiences, but the mind experience is simply a by-product of the brain reaction. It has no effective causal power of its own, but is like an echo created by brain waves. The nineteenth-century biologist and good friend of Darwin, Thomas Huxley, called humans "conscious automata" and explained consiousness this way: "It seems to me that in men, as in brutes, there is no proof that any state of consciousness is the cause of change in the motion of the matter of the organism. If these positions are well based, it follows that our mental conditions are simply the symbols in consciousness of the changes which take place automatically in the organism."[10] Huxley concedes that nonhuman animals would thus have some sort of consciousness, too, but only a consciousness of feelings, not of thought. Huxley agrees with Descartes that animals are in a sense automata, but so are humans: Animals are machines with feelings, and humans are machines with feelings and thoughts. But these feelings never affect the body; it is the physical reactions that create feelings and thoughts as echoes. Many scientists have found epiphenomenalism appealing, because it does away with consciousness without denying that it is there; but the problem is that it is so counterintuitive. We feel, and think, that we make conscious choices that affect both our minds and our bodies, and the theory doesn't really offer a good explanation for what good mental phenomena do, if they don't have any effect at all—in other words, what is the evolutionary advantage of having a mental life if we can't affect the physical world with it?

The Double-Aspect Theory/Neutralism   This theory, sometimes considered a fourth kind of metaphysical theory (in addition to dualism, idealism, and materialism), was introduced by the Dutch philosopher Baruch (or Benedict) de Spinoza (1632–1677). Spinoza saw reality as consisting of both mental and physical experiences, but he believed that mind and body were just two aspects of the same reality, two sides of the same coin. When we view reality from the "inside," we view it under its mental aspect. When we view it as a spectator from the "outside," we see its physical qualities. For this theory, Spinoza—a peaceful, gentle man—was in his lifetime shunned and vilified both by the Christian community and his own Jewish community for being a subversive. Spinoza's theory effectively solves the problem of interactionism, because there are no two substances that are interacting; there is just one reality. While this seems like a reasonable solution and appeals to the modern person who would like to retain a notion of mental life while at the same time being realistic about its physical underpinnings, it does cause problems in talking about a mental life for anyone but oneself, because—since we don't have access to their inside

experience—others can only be "bodies" to any observer.

Reductive Materialism/Identity Theory   The problems of mind-body interaction and of "other minds" can of course be solved very quickly by simply giving up on the idea that the mind is of a different nature than the body. If we agree that the mind is somehow made up of some material energy or other "stuff," then we have no problem explaining why the mind can affect the body: Because now we have two forms of matter affecting each other. We have brain energy in the form of chemicals and/or electric currents affecting other physical parts of the body, and this presents no logical problem. But we have also talked ourselves out of the possibility of a mind separate from the body—and eventually, of the entire concept of an immortal soul. So this concession to materialism is quite expensive, but claiming that mind and body are, somehow, identical does solve the problem inherent in dualism.

This is, in essence, the theory of reductive materialism. Also referred to as the identity theory, it claims that there is only one reality—the material one. In this reality, everything, including the life of the mind, has a basis in material, physical phenomena, so there is nothing, mental or physical, that science cannot explain. The identity theory is probably the most widespread of all theories of mind today. It claims that while we may not know everything about brain states and emotional experiences, it will be made clear by science in the future that all thought processes and emotions can be identified as neurophysiological. Any research into mood drugs, into identifying brain centers specializing in this or that mental function (such as a recent identification of a "moral" center in the brain), and other physical explanations of mental phenomena is an example of the materialistic identity theory at work. It isn't saying that mental experiences are an illusion (as Skinner wanted to conclude); it is just saying that once we know more, we will understand them better as fundamentally grounded in—and reducible to—a physical phenomenon. This theory effectively lays to rest any problem with interactionism: Since brain processes are the only true reality of mind experiences, there is no problem explaining how the mind affects the physical world, and vice versa. It is all matter acting upon matter. This theory is, in effect, gaining ground with the completion of the Human Genome Project and the mapping of human DNA, because we are now on the verge of seeing certain emotions and other psychological tendencies as genetically predisposed. Contemporary advocates of the identity theory include Patricia and Paul Churchland.

A common objection to the identity theory is that while it tolerates "mentalistic" explanations, there is an understanding that the *real* explanation is physical and material; but our experience of a situation or an emotion is just not identical with its biological brain process: If I feel in love, I may learn exactly what brain chemicals are involved, but my experience is not of the chemicals but of an infatuation—and would we want to take a drug so we can "feel in love," instead of experiencing the real thing? If it is all neurophysiological, it shouldn't make any difference, but to most of us it does—meaning that there is a component of reality that matters to us psychologically and even morally, in addition to the chemical brain reaction. Now that could be because we are old-fashioned or fail to see that brain reactions are very complex and include moral preferences, but it could also be because, intuitively, we perceive that there truly is a difference between a mental experience and its physical cause; and science hasn't been much help yet in providing a satisfactory explanation. (See Box 7.5 for a brief exploration of the concept of mental illness and its social history.)

Eliminative Materialism   The most radical solution to the mind-body problem, along with analytical behaviorism, may be that of eliminative materialism. While reductive materialism, analytical behaviorism, and eliminative materialism agree that mind activity is the same as brain activity and that there really is nothing above and beyond our brain activity, reductive materialism

doesn't want to do away with the general language implying a life of the mind; it just wants to interpret it as a metaphor for physical occurrences and educate people about the accuracy of such an interpretation. However, eliminative materialism seeks to eliminate mentalistic language: The better we get to know the workings of the brain, the less need there will be for using the language of the mind. Eventually we will no longer need to refer to mental experiences, but merely to brain activity. Feelings should be referred to as chemical occurrences in the brain, memories as electrical impulses, and so on. There could be some advantages to cognition theory in adopting this viewpoint. We now understand how Alzheimer's robs elderly people of their personality and their memories: Their brains are being clogged with deposits, making the synaptic firings more and more difficult. We understand why our teenagers are so emotionally unstable: They are dominated by hormones that make their brain react differently than a child's or an adult's. We may even think we can understand why drivers are aggressive, landlords are insensitive, and lovers are unfaithful: It's all in the chemicals. But is it? Suppose you have been waiting for your date to call all weekend and he or she didn't—and then are told you feel upset because of a chemical brain reaction, and if we reverse the brain reaction, then everything will be okay? You won't agree, because your brain may feel better with an antidepressant, but the problem hasn't gone away: Your date still hasn't called.

The fundamental objection is the same that we have to the central state identity theory: Our experience tells us otherwise. If we could mimic the chemical nature of an emotion, or a thought, and inject it so we would get the experience without the reality, would that be a satisfying experience? We are actually close, both with a true chemical designer drug, and with virtual reality (VR): We will shortly be able to duplicate emotions and other experiences artificially, activating the exact same brain circuits that would be activated in the real experience. Would that be "good enough"? Most of us would not think so: We may get to know, in a VR sense, how it feels to be madly in

Box 7.5   OUT OF ONE'S MIND?

What do we imply when we say that someone is out of his or her mind? Usually we mean that a person isn't displaying normal behavior. Often, the concept of *normal* human behavior is identified by describing and analyzing *abnormal* behavior. The French philosopher Michel Foucault surprised readers in the 1970s by claiming that the concept of sanity was primarily a social and political term; whatever the majority in society disagrees with, it labels "insane." In other words, normality is relative to one's culture and essentially a normative concept rather than a descriptive one. Incidentally, Foucault wasn't the first to claim this: The anthropologist Ruth Benedict had already said as much in the 1920s, but Foucault put the idea of culture-relative normality into a theory of political oppression. Some psychiatrists today agree that society's norms have a lot to do with whether a person is considered sane or less sane, but there is a general recognition that mental illness isn't merely a cultural definition; it is a genuine medical condition of instability, mostly in the form of a paranoia or a manic-depressive condition. It is not just a matter of conditioning, and a person with a mental illness should be considered just as much a patient in need of help and understanding as any person with a physical ailment, with no stigma attached to the condition. However, how a mental patient should be *treated* is something experts disagree profoundly about. In the eighteenth century when, according to Foucault, insanity was first recognized as a social problem, asylums were built to house the insane. (Prior to that century, what we today would call the mentally ill would generally fend for themselves as homeless beggars; they might be revered as holy men and women with a special gift for prophecy or be considered possessed by evil powers and executed.) There was no therapy afforded; in the early years of the asylum phenomenon, the "treatment" consisted in mere containment of the patient, sometimes even in closets and coffins. In the nineteenth century two schools of thought arose, and you know them both from Chapter 4: that human behavior is caused by either heredity or the environment. Those who believed that behavior is determined by heredity, or nature, saw little possible treatment for the mental patients, but the school of thought believing that behavior is caused by the environment, or nurture, embarked on programs to alter the effects of the patient's early environment, usually through therapy involving a dialogue with the patient. Freud's psychoanalysis falls into this category. In the twentieth century much psychotherapy was centered on making the patient *function* in society, under the assumption that mental wellness consists in social adaptation. Today, many patients and their families deplore the fact that doctors seem to be quick to treat them with drugs, so as to suppress their problem, rather than use other and more demanding therapy programs that might get to the bottom of the illness.

love, how it feels for a composer to complete a symphony, or how it feels for a writer to complete a book (exhausting!). It may even be a great help for doctors or psychiatrists to get to know, vicariously, how it feels to be on drugs or to experience an anxiety attack, so they can understand their patients better. We may soon be able to share how it would feel to experience space travel, how Mother Teresa felt helping the needy, or how serial killer Ted Bundy felt killing his victims. There are no boundaries, once the knowledge and the technology are in place, other than legal and moral ones, concerns that are quite significant in themselves. But is this going to be *just like the real thing?* For some it will be quite sufficient and even preferable: It will be a lot less dangerous to experience VR space travel, and you can feel like Mother Teresa without going into smelly neighborhoods (or feel like Ted Bundy without being arrested and executed). But won't we still know that there is a difference? And wouldn't it be because mind activity just can't be completely reduced to brain activity? Even if we eliminate the language of thought and emotion, won't the thoughts and

Box 7.6   DANIEL DENNETT: THERE IS NO CARTESIAN THEATER

One of the most famous criticisms of Descartes in the late twentieth century comes from the American philosopher Daniel C. Dennett (b. 1942). On the basis of a materialistic view and current research in neuroscience, Dennett attacks attempts to explain the phenomenon of consciousness. In his book, *Consciousness Explained* (1991), Dennett points out that Descartes's model of the mind doesn't work. Descartes seeks to explain the mind influencing the body as a "pilot in his ship," or rather a *homunculus*, a little person living somewhere (and somehow) in the brain. If you have seen the science fiction comedy *Men in Black*, you may remember a scene where an alien visitor to earth dies, and it is revealed that his body was a mechanical vehicle run by a tiny being inside the head. This is a classic homunculus image, but of course Descartes didn't quite mean it that way: Whatever the little person inside our brain is, he or she is not supposed to be material, because of the mind-body distinction. Dennett, relying on Ryle's argument about the ghost in the machine, points out that Descartes's image of the mind observing itself acting on the stage of the body like in some sort of theater—a Cartesian theater—is simply false. Our mind is not a spectator observing its impressions on stage or on a movie screen. Our consciousness *is* a collection of impressions, and there is no "mind" behind these impressions. Furthermore, only the human brain is capable of creating a consciousness out of these impressions, because only humans have a *center of narrative gravity*—a theory you will recognize from Chapter 1. Dennett sees humans as the only beings who can gather their "self" into story form, and on the basis of this he concludes that only humans have a consciousness and a self. So while Dennett is a materialist, he is not denying that we have a mental life; he is just saying that (1) it can be explained through neuroscience, and (2) it is exclusively human; no animals share in having a center of narrative gravity, not even the apes, because they have no language with which to tell a story. His controversial theory has been widely attacked, both by scholars who see the mind as something more than a brain and by scholars who see consciousness as a phenomenon that starts long before the arrival of humanity, and is shared by other beings on earth. Maxine Sheets-Johnstone (see chapter text) criticizes Dennett severely on both counts, because she sees consciousness as a much broader phenomenon that has to do with being aware of moving about deliberately, rather than being able to tell stories and use language. She says, "It has never in fact been shown that nonhuman animals do not think, or choose, or even deliberate with respect to movement, or that they don't have a sense of speed, space, effort, and so on. On the contrary . . . the evolution of such corporeal capacities and awareness is coincident with the evolution of animate form."* See the discussion of Paul Ricoeur later in this chapter, where we take another look at the human talent for telling stories about ourselves.

---

*Maxine Sheets-Johnstone, *The Primacy of Movement* (Amsterdam: John Benjamins, 1999), p. 77.

emotions still be a fundamental part of who we are? (Box 7.6 presents a theory that is critical of both eliminative materialism and Descartes: Daniel Dennett's theory of consciousness.)

A Sense of Body

The tendency may have been there, under the surface, ever since Plato claimed that the life of the mind was superior to the life of the body and Christian thinkers adopted the thought as part of Christian philosophy; but it wasn't until Descartes drew a line between mind and body as two substances that had *nothing* to do with each other that this tendency in Western thinking moved from the religious to the scientific realm. From Descartes until very recently, *Western philosophy and science have viewed the life of the mind as fundamentally different from the life of the body.* In some ways, Western civilization has stood to gain from this split between "inside" and "outside," between "subject" and "object": Scientists and technologists have focused exclusively on the world of matter, Descartes's *res extensa,* with the result that we are much more adept at manipulating and controlling "stuff" than any previous civilization, to our knowledge. We send rovers to Mars, we map the human genome, we compress memory into computer chips invisible to the naked eye, we perform heart and liver transplants. For some, this is one of the added evil consequences of Descartes's mind-body split, and it is certain that the worship of technology has spawned some shallow, materialistic mind-sets over the years. However, few of us would choose to live in a pre- or low-technology culture after having come to rely on technology. We rarely see members of low-technology nations around the world blessing the fact that they happen to be uncorrupted by materialism; the yearning for a simpler time before technology is often a romantic notion that plays down the drawbacks of those times. Instead of outright rejecting the ideology of Western technology (the more we can control, the better), we would probably do well to take this ideology as a given and ask ourselves How can we improve on our lives, including our spiritual lives, *within* the framework of technology, while remaining vigilant that our technology doesn't *run* our lives? This was, in effect, what some "hippies" were trying to do in the 1970s, and we may experience a renewed interest in this question in the twenty-first century.

Damasio: Descartes Was Wrong

Within the area of medicine, Descartes's influence has made itself felt very powerfully. The science of medicine since the seventeenth century has focused almost exclusively on the illnesses of the body. In his influential book from 1994, *Descartes' Error,* Antonio R. Damasio, a professor of neurology, points out that while medical advances in the Western world are tremendous, physicians have failed to realize, until recently, that if you treat the body, then treating the patient as a person with a

mind is also necessary. That is why so few doctors are good at breaking bad news to patients and why many people seek alternative medical treatment, he claims; and, to be sure, the medical traditions of most other cultures have an underlying assumption that the mind and the body work together—such as in Chinese traditional medicine. For Damasio, our minds are far more than software programs run by the computer of our brain: Our minds are integrated with our bodies, and without the body you will not have a mind—or you may have a different, not a "normal" mind. *Descartes's error,* says Damasio, *is claiming that minds are completely separate from bodies, and vice versa.*

Damasio distinguishes among bodies, brains, and minds, and this distinction allows him to create some interesting what-if scenarios, based on his experiences as a neurologist: Suppose a person loses the use of some body part? Will his or her mind remain exactly the same? No, he says, because the sense of body has changed. A famous thought experiment is the "brain-in-a-vat" theory (also explored by Daniel Dennett, see Box 7.6): Suppose we could take a living human brain and place it in a vat with nutrients and keep it alive? This is a common scenario in many science fiction stories, from the famous novel *Ubik,* by Philip K. Dick, a disturbing story of the deteriorating minds of a group of dead people in a cryogenic state, believing themselves to be alive, to the comedy *The Man with Two Brains* with Steve Martin. If Descartes is right, then the capacity for thinking will be unaltered, and this brain in a vat will be able to have a mental life (but this example does not solve Descartes's problem of *where* the mind is). However, says Damasio, the brain without the body will not be a normal brain, because the physical stimuli are missing. So suppose we duplicate all that with electrodes? Then all we have proved is that it is *normal* to have a body, says Damasio. In order for us to understand human nature and the human mind, we have to concede that "soul and spirit, with all their dignity and human scale, are now complex and unique states of an organism."[11]

So the human mind doesn't just live in the body or have some intimate connection with it; the human mind is shaped by our body experience from Day One, and probably even before that, in the last trimester of the pregnancy when the fetus is able to feel pain. Indeed, Damasio speculates that all acts of human thinking, culture, and social life in general, as well as every single act of every sensing animal, has a foundation in trying to avoid pain or alleviate suffering, in trying to make life better. In other words, there is a fundamental physical experience in all of us that shapes our mental life. Damasio isn't just saying that we should consider the identity theory or that the mind can be reduced to the brain and body sensations (eliminative materialism); he is saying that *our life of the mind is a life of a mind with a body;* our consciousness is a body-based consciousness.

Interestingly, some of the criticism of the Cartesian tradition's preoccupation with the mind and its disregard for the fact that the mind is embodied was anticipated by Aristotle, almost 2,000 years before Descartes. In Chapter 8 we take a closer look at Aristotle's theory of the soul. Being convinced that we do have a soul (mind) but that it is inextricably linked with our physical existence, Aristotle remarks that theories which place the soul in some connection to a body fail to explain exactly how it is connected:

> Yet such explanation can scarcely be omitted; for some community of nature is presupposed by the fact that the one acts and the other is acted upon, the one moves and the other is moved; interaction always implies a *special* nature in the two inter-agents. All, however, that these thinkers do is to describe the specific characteristics of the soul; they do not try to determine anything about the body which is to contain it.[12]

Merleau-Ponty: We Are Our Bodies

Descartes was a philosopher living on the European continent, and as such he is what we call a "Continental philosopher." This expression has now come to mean a philosopher whose works fall within the Continental European tradition. (You can thus be an American philosopher who

does Continental philosophy.) Interestingly, Descartes caused men and women to become philosophers both because they agreed with him and because they violently disagreed with him, within the Continental as well as the British-American traditions. One such philosopher is Gilbert Ryle of the British-American tradition (see "Interactionism" earlier in this chapter). Another philosopher reacting to the Cartesian legacy is Maurice Merleau-Ponty (1908–1961), himself of the Continental tradition. More than anyone else, he is the philosopher in modern times who has become associated with the theory that we can't disregard the body as a powerful influence on who we are. (Merleau-Ponty's own philosophical background is explored in Box 7.7, with Husserl's concept of the *Lebenswelt*.)

For Merleau-Ponty the Cartesian tradition has done damage to our understanding of what we are as humans, because it has divided the world into mind and matter. With our mind, we understand matter; but matter can't understand mind. Then what about the status of our own body? In the Cartesian tradition the body is of course part of the world of matter and can be understood by the mind, as an observer, in the same way the mind observes other things. But, says Merleau-Ponty, this model doesn't work for our understanding of our own body—for one thing, because I can't really observe it. How much can I see of my face without a mirror? A tip of the nose. Your lips if you pout. Your tongue, if you stick it out. But you'll never see your teeth if they stay in your mouth. You won't observe your ears or your eyes. But can't we see ourselves in the mirror? Yes, in a way, but in a way it is also like seeing another person observing you. (We actually have to get used to the person in the mirror being ourselves; it isn't something we are born knowing.) The mirror is an indirect experience. Directly, you see part of your body: legs, stomach, arms, and so on, but you can't see your buttocks. And yet your behind is definitely part of your body. Any other object we can move around and observe, or we can turn it to see it from all sides, but not our body. So isn't that just an inconvenient circumstance? No, it is

Box 7.7   HUSSERL'S *LEBENSWELT*

Merleau-Ponty was a student of the philosophy of Edmund Husserl (1859–1938), a German philosopher of Jewish ancestry. Husserl founded the philosophical school of *phenomenology,* a rigorous examination of the human experience in order to distill the "essence" of that experience. To be able to perform such an examination, one must look at the experience as it is, in the human mind, without asking the question "But what is reality really like?" We must, in a sense, put reality in brackets and concentrate on how we experience it. The way we must bracket reality is by suspending our judgment and preconceived notions about reality and focusing on *describing* what we experience. It may sound somewhat like Descartes's method of doubt, and Husserl even calls one of his first works *Cartesian Meditations.* But it becomes clear that Husserl, unlike Descartes, wasn't trying to doubt the existence of reality for the purpose of reaching methodical certainty. He was trying to understand what the essence of the human experience is. Husserl concluded that it is a mistake to think that there is an inner self experiencing something, and then the experience, and then the outside reality: All there is, is the *experience;* we can't have a self that doesn't experience anything. All we have is the rich human experience with the self at one end and the thing experienced at the other end: a subject-pole and an object-pole. Once we understand that, then we also understand why we have to give up all the old questions of the difference between the self and the experience and focus on what we do, as humans, when we try to make sense of our experiences. For Husserl, what we do is *constitute* the world: We structure our experiences so they make sense to us.

In his last work, *The Crisis of the European Sciences and Transcendental Phenomenology,* Husserl develops the concept of the *Lebenswelt* (the life-world), a concept that put Merleau-Ponty on his own phenomenological track: Husserl says that our most fundamental experience, from the time we are born, is that we are born into a world that is already there. He is not talking about being born into the reality of our culture and our parents (which existed before we were born) but about the fact that the world we live in seems like a *given* to us. We take for granted that we can move about in it, that we have senses, that people and things respond to our touch; and this is a physical existence that is so fundamental that it forms our mind-set. This is the beginning of the phenomenological philosophy of the *primacy of the body experience,* proposed by Merleau-Ponty and explored further by scholars such as Damasio and Sheets-Johnstone.

Husserl lived only a few years beyond the publication of *Crisis.* He was persecuted as a Jew by Hitler's regime and lost his position as professor at the University of Freiburg. He died shortly thereafter, and friends and students of his claim that he was, in effect, harassed to death by the Nazis. His manuscripts were smuggled out of Germany by a group of concerned nuns so that his writings wouldn't be destroyed. One of his best students, the famous phenomenologist Martin Heidegger, never lifted a finger to help his old professor; instead he joined the Nazi party so he could, presumably, keep his own job.

much more, says Merleau-Ponty: It is the condition of our nature. Our own body is not something we "observe" as we observe cats and cars and other people; it is *the tool by which we observe* and interact with the world.

So the body has an ambiguous mode of existing as intimately ours and yet in the world of matter:

In other words, I observe external objects with my body, I handle them, examine them, walk around them, but my body itself is a thing which I do not observe: in order to be able to do so, I should need the use of a second body which itself would be unobservable. . . . What prevents it ever being an object, ever being "completely constituted" is that it is that by which there are objects. . . . Thus the permanence of one's own body, if only classical psychology had analyzed it, might have led to the body no longer conceived as an object of the world, but as our means of communication with it, to the world no longer conceived as a collection of determinate objects, but as the horizon latent in all our experience and itself ever-present and anterior to every determining thought.[13]

This makes our thoughts of our body equally ambiguous, because we know our body as the foundation for all our experiences with ourselves and the world: My thoughts of my body are different from my thoughts about other objects. *I can't understand my body except by living it,* Merleau-Ponty says. The Cartesian description of an experience says there is a mind that experiences something and then a body that is being experienced, but our bodies fall into an intermediate category, which topples the entire Cartesian dualism. My body is in the world, but I am also my body; my body becomes my access to the world, but not just as a vehicle. In a sense, my self fills my bodily space, and more, because my body experience isn't limited to the flesh and blood that I was born in. My "body" is also the clothes I wear and the tools I use, because they all become part of who I am and how I move about in space.

Merleau-Ponty gives us an example of how one's body experience extends beyond one's physical body: the *lady with the hat.* (In the 1950s lots of women wore big hats; if you have ever seen the Audrey Hepburn movie *Breakfast at Tiffany's,* you will know what Merleau-Ponty is talking about!) A woman buys a new hat with a long feather in it, and at first she bumps into doorsills and car ceilings and other hats, but after a while she adjusts and doesn't bump into things with her hat or her feather anymore. Why? Not just because she's "gotten used to it": Her body consciousness has now *incorporated* her hat, so it has become part of her body, as if she really had nerve endings extending to the rim. If you've never worn a big hat, then think in terms of buying a bigger car: You knew exactly how big a parking space you needed for your old car, but now you have a

bigger car that won't fit into those small spaces. What happens? Within a week you are used to the "feel" of the new car, and you don't fear hitting other cars while parking. Why? Because your body sense has extended into the space of the new car; it has, in a sense, become part of your body. Folk wisdom has known this for a long time, with jokes about big cars, tools, and weapons being extensions of male potency. Western movie gunfighters treat their guns as if they are extensions of their hands; the painter treats the brush as if it has nerve endings in the fine hairs at the tip. The chef knows her tools as well as her own fingers, and the baseball player's bat becomes an extension of his arms.

Merleau-Ponty has placed into the philosophical understanding of human nature an experience that most of us know very well on a fundamental level, but which few thinkers had ever imagined could be a gateway to a deeper understanding of who we are. He derives this understanding from Husserl's detailed writings about the body. Sheets-Johnstone (whom we discussed earlier) has also been greatly inspired by Husserl's phenomenological analyses of the body and elaborated them with her theory of *the moving body.* We understand ourselves—and others—as mobile; corporeal awareness isn't just something humans have, but it is inextricably tied in with being alive. It is part of the biological makeup of beings who are capable of deliberate movement.

Feminism: Who's Afraid of the Body?

You will remember that on several occasions in this book we have explored the tendency of a descriptive theory of human nature to have some form of normative (moral or political) consequence. Here is another example: You will remember from the previous chapter that women have often been considered to be more "physical" than men, more in tune with their physical nature. For *antifeminists* this translates into women being less logical, cerebral, and intelligent than men; and since the life of the mind has been viewed as superior to the life of the body, it means that for antifeminists men automatically occupy a more important place than women as a result of the supposed superior male intelligence. Descartes's mind-body distinction has been interpreted as symbolic of a gender distinction as well: Men have represented the "mind," while women have represented the "body." For *classical feminists* (see Chapter 6), such as Simone de Beauvoir and Betty Friedan, it may be true that women are more in tune with their bodies than men, but they see it as a cultural trait rather than innate, and a trait that women ought to be purged of from childhood so that they can escape the inequalities of the traditional fate of motherhood. From the classical feminist Mary Wollstonecraft to Beauvoir and Friedan, the emphasis is to give little girls and women an education that allows them to develop their minds to the same extent that an education has allowed men's minds to flourish.

While no feminist (that I know of) would argue against educating girls and women, some feminists of the 1980s and 1990s have argued that women cloud the issue of female nature by imitating the type of life and education traditional for men. *Difference feminists,* such as Adrienne Rich, point out that classical feminism has bought into the mind-body distinction of traditional Western philosophy, seeing the life of the mind as more important and valuable than the life of the body. Rich points out that women don't have to choose between being all mind (intellectual) or all body (sexual partner and mother), if women view their physicality as a "resource rather than a destiny." It translates into women having some closer connection to physical life through the fact that women can give birth, have monthly cycles, and undergo menopause, but it doesn't translate into an idea that women are less rational than men. Another difference feminist, Elizabeth V. Spelman, points out that *somatophobia* (fear of the body) has been part and parcel of the Western philosophical tradition since Plato (see Chapter 8), and classical feminism has tended to fall into the same trap. For one thing, Spelman says, feminism ought to realize *the politicization of the mind-body distinction:* Whoever is associated with mind has become the more politically powerful group, and the group associated with the body has taken second place. For another, says Spelman, this is not merely a problem for gender relations: It is a problem for race relations, too. Traditionally, in the white Western mind-set, people of color have been associated with a more physical existence than white people (in terms of doing physical labor), resulting in superstitions about sexual vitality. Spelman credits Rich for being the first to point out that the political fallout from the mind-body distinction has resulted in racism as well as sexism. (Box 7.8 explores the relationship between our sense of self and our sense of body.)

A Sense of Self

At the ancient Greek temple of Apollo at Delphi there were several inscriptions on the wall: One said, *Know thyself.* Another said, *Everything in moderation.* Socrates took both to heart; the virtue of moderation was something well-educated Greeks tried to adhere to, anyway—but Socrates saw the command to know oneself as a lesson in humility, recognizing how little we mortal people *know,* compared to the knowledge and wisdom of the gods. So into the Western philosophical tradition was introduced the idea that we, as human beings, ought to strive for a knowledge of ourselves in a way that tests our capacity for honesty and integrity. But according to many scholars, this was Socrates' own interpretation of the Delphi saying—his spin, if you will. The original meaning of the saying, according to the Roman thinker Plutarch, was that we as humans must remember our limitations and mortality in the presence of the all-powerful gods. In other words, Know your place—remember you're *merely* human.

The idea that to know oneself is somehow a moral obligation has entered into the Western tradition with the spin Socrates gave it, not with the original meaning of the Delphic inscription. With the rise of psychoanalysis in the twentieth century it acquired a new level of meaning, because of the psychoanalytical theory that not all parts of the human psyche are accessible to the

Box 7.8   THE MIND VERSUS THE BODY

If indeed Damasio, Merleau-Ponty, and difference feminists are right and we are minds-with-bodies, exactly how identical does the self feel to the body? *Are we our bodies?* That seems to depend greatly on our time of life, our health, and our cultural traditions. When we are children growing up with normal health, we don't "problematize" our bodies: We live fully in the *Lebenswelt* and don't experience a distance between our self and our body. But since the Western experience of the self as somehow separate from the body is so fundamental, it is interesting to track it down, noticing the traditional mind-body distinction underlying our sense of who we are—that somehow our mind is a truer representation of our self than our body.

Under what circumstances might our self feel alienated from or by our body? One answer is when the body starts functioning differently or stops functioning. In Western literature there are numerous examples of autobiographies telling about how the author felt alienated from his or her body at puberty, especially if the writer's culture disapproves of the physical signs of oncoming sexuality. The experience of getting her period may alienate the young girl at first, and uncontrollable erections at awkward times may make the male teen feel that his body "betrays" him. Severe physical injury, such as a stroke, can give people a sense that their bodies have let them down; they have an intact sense of self, but somehow they distance themselves from their factual bodily condition. A paraplegic student of mine shocked the class by suggesting that the actor Christopher Reeve, paralyzed from the neck down due to a fall, would do better to come to terms with his new body situation than to insist that some day he would walk again; she was recommending *a shift in body consciousness* to match the new body experience. A life-threatening or disfiguring illness may make the patient feel that her or his body has been "invaded." An unwanted pregnancy may cause similar feelings. The classic movie *Invasion of the Body Snatchers* (the alien pods grow bodies overnight that replace the real people and try to take over the town) was intended as a metaphor for the spread of communism, but can equally well be interpreted as a film about the fear of a contagious disease. And the entire process of aging is for some people proof that our selves are more closely related to our minds than to our changing, unreliable bodies. The psychological experience of living with, and in, a body that changes is for some thinkers, like Plato, enough to declare that the body is of less importance than the mind. But, as Merleau-Ponty and Damasio pointed out, *our minds also change when our bodies change.* Sometimes the mind changes more dramatically than the body, as is the case with some Alzheimer's patients. And we shouldn't forget that the *Invasion of the Body Snatchers* tell a story of mind snatchers, too: The body looks the same, but the mind has been stolen and discarded.

Another scenario comes out of the experience of what some thinkers call *reification,* or *objectification,* of our bodies: We perceive ourselves as others perceive us, as if we were a thing or an object. We have an image of ourselves that comprises our memories, our consciousness, and our self-awareness, but also some *ideal image* of what we think our body ought to be like, and often it is based on a social and cultural norm or an ideal, a certain *body image.* Our body consciousness is not exactly the same as our body experience! There is a normative as well as a descriptive element present in conscious mind, so that the whole task of getting to know oneself is an uphill battle.

But what exactly do we, as twenty-first-century people, mean by "knowing oneself"? What kind of self is there to know? A few years ago I got into hot water as a commentator at a philosophy conference because I assumed that the speaker was talking about "self" in the meaning of political personhood; it turned out that he was referring to the problem of deciding whether a person has *personal identity* over time, quite a different issue! That's what comes from being an ethicist: You tend to see the bottom line as moral and political. For example, how are we going to treat peo-

cathy®

by Cathy Guisewite

Cathy has come across one of the perennial questions of the self: When faced with an element of myself that I find fault with, which element do I identify with? We may *be* our bodies, as Merleau-Ponty says, but when we aren't happy with our body image, we tend to shift our self-identity in another direction. Cathy is searching for her "I" among her brain cells. What theory of metaphysics does Cathy seem to subscribe to?

our relationship to our own bodies, and it doesn't just depend on what we think a normal body should be able to do: move about, eat, drink, eliminate, have sex, and so on. We may feel that our bodies are the outer surface of our selves, but it doesn't mean that we automatically have a reasonable idea of what that outer surface ought to look like in order to reflect our self. This discrepancy between who we feel we are and who others tell us we are can make itself felt in many ways, from the extreme dieting that young girls sometimes engage in to meet the expectations of a culture with a Barbie ideal, to young men (and women) taking steroids

to live up to an athletic ideal, to women seeing themselves as sexual objects because this is what their culture dictates. When an anorexic girl starves herself because she thinks she is overweight, it is hardly her body letting her down; you might rather say it is her mind letting her body down, due to social pressures. Some would say that those of us who don't exercise enough, who eat more than our physical frame and metabolism can handle, or who smoke, do drugs, and so forth, have bodies that are being "betrayed" by our minds because we chose to put ourselves in the situation in the first place and continue to think up excuses for our behavior.

ple who have selves, and what are the criteria for selfhood? In this section we look at the metaphysical question of the self: Do we have a self? How would we characterize our self, and does everyone have one? Does it stay the same even as we age and change? In Chapter 8 we look at the normative issue of what we ought to do with our

selves in order to avoid doing evil, and in Chapter 10 we look at the issue of what it takes to be recognized as a political "self," a person. So I am trying to cover all the bases!

To the Western mind-set it is a natural assumption that we have a sense of self; I feel that I know myself, I know my personal story, I remember important incidents in my life, I know my body, I know when something hurts and when it feels good. I know myself better than any other being I will ever know. Until the middle of the nineteenth century it was a general assumption among philosophers and psychologists that it was possible for us to come to know ourselves adequately and accurately by introspection; however, philosophers also recognized that we really cannot know anybody else as well as we know ourselves; for that matter, we can only know for certain that we ourselves have a sense of self. All we know about others is that they act as if they have one too, so we extrapolate from analogy and assume that others have selves like ours; and that is usually good enough, unless we want absolute certainty about issues of knowledge. If so, we will have to face the fact that we can never know with 100 percent accuracy anything about other people's selves; this is one version of a type of philosophical position known as *solipsism* (Latin: *solus ipse,* "myself alone"). An extreme version of solipsism holds that the only reality we can be certain exists at all is our own mental states. You know enough about Descartes's *cogito* argument to see that his theory is a solipsistic theory: We can only establish with certainty that we ourselves think, but not that others think.

The Western Sense of Self Evolving

Some philosophers speculate that the specific Western sense of self—understanding ourselves as individuals who remain identical over time—is not necessarily a universal human trait. In his book, *Sources of the Self* (1989), the philosopher Charles Taylor suggests that the Western idea of selfhood has developed as a result of an accumulation of philosophical ideas specific to the West: We have developed an idea that the world can be divided into what is *inside* and what is *outside.* The self is inside, while the objects of the world are outside, as if having a self is similar to having a heart and a liver. But, says Taylor, the "self" is not something you *have;* it is a perspective within one's moral universe: "Being a self is inseparable

from existing in a space of moral issues, to do with identity and how one ought to be. It is being able to find one's standpoint in this space, being able to occupy, to *be* a perspective in it."[14]

In all probability, says Taylor, there are several different senses of self. One we share with all human beings throughout time: Everyone knows the difference between themselves and somebody else, and it is very human to hope nothing bad happens to you and rejoice when the bad thing happens to someone else, because it didn't happen to you! We could add to Taylor's view that we each know our own physical pain and have an intimate knowledge that it is our *own* pain and not someone else's. (In fact, at moments when you may "feel someone else's pain" or feel that your identity is melting into someone else's, moments of great emotion, the intensity comes from the contrast to how we *normally* feel—that is, as separate individuals.) So on a very basic level we all do have a sense of self.

However, in addition to such basic notions there are cultural overlays that can differ significantly. Even if every human being has a sense of "me" and "others," only certain languages (such as English) have made the notion of "self" into a *noun.* Even if the Greeks wanted us to get to know ourselves, the ancient Greek language refers only to "oneself" as a concept, not "a self." Many cultures operate with several parts of the psyche—different souls—that each have a task in that person's life and afterlife; we look at some of these theories in the next chapter. In some tribal cultures you are supposed to play down your personal individuality; the closer you can live your life in imitation of the cultural heroes of mythology, the better you are as a person. Of course the opposite is usually the case in modern Western culture, where the goal is to be a unique, separate individual and accomplish something *new* in order to be a successful human being.

Our Western culture emphasizes separateness as a sign of maturity, while most other cultures around the world see social togetherness and community awareness as "normal." Even Plato's and Aristotle's explorations of human nature (see Chapters 8 and 9) focus on the needs and nature of the successful human community more than on the individual. So when did Western thinking become focused on the fate of individuals rather than the fate of the community? According to Taylor and others, the shift happened with the philosopher and church founder St. Augustine: In order to know God, he said, we have to look inward to our own souls rather than be occupied with the world. The fate of the individual soul was what concerned Augustine. In Chapter 8 we take a closer look at Augustine's view of the soul; suffice it for now to point out that he represents a springboard from Plato and Aristotle to Descartes, who develops the idea of the individual, separate self to an extreme.

Locke: Our Self Is Our Memory

Part of Descartes's view of the self is that it is a thinking, rational substance. This entails believing that certain truths are obvious to the thinking mind, by virtue of the rational structure of the mind: *Whatever we perceive clearly and distinctly must be true.* This means that for Descartes the rules of math and logic are known to be true, because a thinking mind perceives them with complete clarity (at least a mind schooled in thinking about math and logic does so). This view puts Descartes into a philosophical category, by and large founded by Descartes himself, that we call *rationalism:* Descartes is a *rationalist* because he believes that there are certain rational elements that are innate to the human mind. However, another philosopher of the seventeenth century has a different view of the mind. In England John Locke (1632–1704) changed the course of what was to become British philosophy by introducing the idea of the *tabula rasa,* the blank slate, as an image of the human mind at birth: We have no innate ideas or concepts, according to Locke; anything we have ever known and will ever know comes to us in the form of sensory perceptions. This means that whatever we can know comes to us on the basis of the *empirical evidence* our senses can gather; we do not deduce truths from some

innate rational system of thoughts as in Descartes's system, but we gather evidence through a method of induction. For this reason we refer to Locke and the other British philosophers following his lead as the *British empiricists.*

For Locke, our sense of self is similarly based on our collections of sensory perceptions—those of the present and those of the past: Our *memory* makes up our self-identity; nothing else is part of it. Locke specifically targets Descartes's idea of the thinking substance: Our self is not an unchanging substance underlying our ideas and perceptions, but the very nature of those stored ideas and perceptions. This means that our self is the same as our consciousness:

> For, since consciousness always accompanies thinking, and it is that which makes every one to be what he calls self, and thereby distinguishes himself from all other thinking things, in this alone consists personal identity, i.e., the sameness of a rational being: and as far as this consciousness can be extended backwards to any past action or thought, so far reaches the identity of that person: it is the same self now that it was then; and it is by the same self with this present one that now reflects on it, that that action was done.[15]

To many it seems as if Locke has found a more commonsense answer to "What am I?" than Descartes's idea of a thinking thing: the collection of our memories. For, indeed, if we can't remember who we were, then can we claim to know ourselves?

As critics of Locke have pointed out, however, there is a major problem with the theory that our self resides in our capacity to remember our life. Because do we remember everything that has ever happened to us? Of course not; we wouldn't even want to. So does that mean that the non-remembered events didn't happen to us? And if we begin to forget our past, because of some form of brain injury or illness, do we then lose our sense of self? Locke himself anticipates this objection and insists that even if we do forget things, then it is the same consciousness that is present throughout our existence. However, philosophers have pointed out that this argument doesn't work. He is supposed to show that consciousness constitutes identity, and consciousness is founded on memory; then he can't just assume that the consciousness stays the same even without the memories. It is the logical fallacy known as *begging the question:* assuming that what you are supposed to prove is already a fact.

Locke's argument has inspired the theory in psychology of the *continuity criterion* for personal identity, or the *reductive identity theory* (not to be confused with reductive materialism). Philosophers Robert Nozick and Derek Parfit argue that a person's identity *is* the same as his or her consciousness and memories; there is no "person" or self above and beyond our consciousness and memories, and if we suffer radical memory loss or simply grow older (and memories fade), then we are just not the same person any longer. (In the Narratives section, you will find a film that explores exactly this issue: *Memento,* a story about a man who suffers from short-term memory loss.) In a way this theory corresponds to how a lot of people feel about their past: "I can't remember it, so it wasn't really me"—or "I'd never dream of doing such things now, so I'm a different person." The reductive identity theory creates problems for the entire notion of *responsibility,* moral as well as criminal, for how can we blame and punish someone for something they did in the past (1) that they have totally forgotten or (2) that was a "youthful indiscretion" by someone who is now a completely different person? You may want to revisit Chapter 4 for a debate about responsibility. Critics point out not only that personal identity isn't just something that an individual *feels*—but also that it involves rational and moral thinking, putting two and two together about one's own past and accepting it—and, furthermore, that it is something others can attest to (as when we identify people by their external physical characteristics, such as birthmarks). But let us consider the idea that we lose our self if we lose our memories. While many Alzheimer's patients in the early stages might agree that they are experiencing a loss of self, other medical cases speak against Locke's conclusion. A patient whose brain damage prevents him from remembering anything beyond the past five minutes or so may still have a sense of self-identity, of knowing his name, of knowing what he likes or dislikes. A powerful challenge to Locke is Freud's idea that we have no access to memories stored in our Unconscious and that they nevertheless play havoc with our peace of mind and our sense of self. (In Box 7.9 we look more closely at Freud's theory of the Unconscious.) And a challenge to both Locke and Freud is the recent realization among psychologists that memories can be *false:* We may be convinced that something happened to us in the past, but the memories may be of a movie we saw, a book we read, someone else's very vivid tale, or a well-meaning therapist trying to get us to tell about what happened to us. A very disturbing case of false therapist-implanted memories is the Dale Akiki case from San Diego of the early 1990s: Akiki, a kindergarten volunteer, was accused of molesting the children in his care. For two years the case dragged on in court, based on no physical evidence whatsoever—the district attorney considered any search for physical evidence unnecessary—but exclusively on the memories of the preschool children, collected by therapists. In the end it became clear that those memories were implanted in the children by the therapists themselves, inadvertently suggesting sexual and violent scenarios that the court thought might have happened. Akiki was cleared, but one may wonder how many other lives have been ruined by the courts under the Freudian assumption that memories can't be false. However, long before Freud and current events, the Scottish philosopher David Hume (1711–1776) raised perhaps the most disturbing criticism against Locke.

Hume: We Have No Permanent Self

David Hume was also an empiricist, but took an entirely different view on personal identity than

Box 7.9 FREUD AND THE UNCONSCIOUS

In the late nineteenth century, Western philosophers and psychologists were developing a theory that perhaps we don't know everything about ourselves. Freud (see Chapters 3 and 6) was only one of several thinkers focusing on the possibility of an area of the mind that is inaccessible to itself; the French philosopher Bergson, for example, speculated that some of our memories are so deeply hidden that they are not all available to us at all times, but must be recalled through an effort. However, it was Freud's theory of the Unconscious that first suggested that part of our psyche is unknown and unreachable by our ordinary sense of self. His theory from 1923 of the three levels of the psyche, *the id, the ego,* and *the superego* (see Chapter 3) speculated that our ordinary sense of self and self-awareness is limited to our everyday experience of the ego: The superego represents our socialized self, the moral rules of behavior we have been taught and internalized over the years; and the id represents the Unconscious, the

experiences and drives that our conscious mind won't or can't deal with, but that nevertheless exert pressure on our conscious mind.

For Freud, our sense of self is thus split, because it is incomplete and believes itself to have complete self-awareness, while being driven by an inner force it has no control over. Our true nature is to a great extent hidden from us and needs the interpretive skills of an analyst to be brought forth. While Freud's theory of the Unconscious has been greatly criticized in the late twentieth century, his idea that, psychologically, we are more than our conscious sense of self has become accepted as a standard truth about human nature. However, the assumption that we have two sides to our selves, the conscious side that lives in the light of day and the deeper self that lives in the darkness of dreams and desires, is as old as religion, and we look at this "two souls" theory in Chapter 8.

Locke. Like Locke, Hume would say we acquire all our ideas from sense perceptions we have accumulated; there is no knowledge we come equipped with from birth. But while Locke saw consciousness extending from a "now" into a past with memories and impressions as its content, Hume found even this idea to be reminiscent of a "substance" theory, because it talks about an underlying substratum of consciousness beneath the individual experiences. Hume sees it differently: When we are conscious, says Hume, then we are aware of the sensations we have and ideas they produce in our mind; what we are not aware of is a "self" that processes these ideas and sensations:

> For from what impression cou'd this idea be derived? . . . It must be some one impression, that gives rise to every real idea. But self or person is not any one impression, but that to which our several impressions and ideas are suppos'd to have a reference. If any impression gives rise to the idea

of self, that impression must continue invariably the same, thro' the whole course of our lives; since self is supposed to exist after that manner. But there is no impression constant and invariable. . . . For my part, when I enter most intimately into what I call *myself,* I always stumble on some particular perception or other, of heat or cold, light or shade, love or hatred, pain or pleasure. I never can catch myself at any time without a perception, and never can observe any thing but the perception. When my perceptions are remov'd for any time, as by sound sleep; so long as I am insensible of myself, and may truly be said not to exist. And were all my perceptions remov'd by death, and cou'd I neither think, nor feel, nor see, nor love, nor hate after the dissolution of my body, I shou'd be entirely annihilated.[16]

These famous words from Hume, who is considered one of philosophy's most notorious *iconoclasts*—smashers of revered images of who we are—have troubled readers ever since. Somehow many of us would rather be in the company of Locke, trusting that our consciousness provides a sense of self even if some memories should fail and even if there are logical flaws in his theory, rather than accept Hume's bleak (and very modern) view that there is no continuous self and no identity living on after the death of the body; all we have are fleeting thoughts and impressions in our mind, there when we are awake and gone when we are not. Interestingly, Hume's view of the self finds its closest parallel in another philosophical tradition: Buddhism, which is discussed later in this chapter.

One of the readers who felt disturbed by Hume's radical dismissal of a self was a young philosopher in East Prussia (then Germany, now Russia), Immanuel Kant, whom you know from Chapters 5 and 6.

Kant: We Have a Transcendental Self

Kant himself said that Hume "awoke him from his dogmatic slumber," challenging him to come up with a response. Hume had made a habit of pointing out that several notions which we consider obvious were anything but; the sense of self was only one victim of his analyses. Kant took it upon himself to answer Hume's challenges with a completely new view of the human mind, with elements taken from both rationalism and empiricism, but with a very different twist.

Hume is right that we "can't catch ourselves without a perception," because we can look through our experiences forever without finding an experience of our "self." But that is not because we don't have a self, says Kant: It is because the "self" is not something we experience—it is the underlying condition of all our experiences. We can't even talk about having experiences of anything—feelings, perceptions, memories, and so forth—if we don't have a self that ties our experiences together as "ours." And that self is not an object among other objects in our experience,

but the very foundation for all experiences. That is why Hume couldn't find it: He was looking in the wrong place. If he had looked to the mind conditions that allow us to identify perceived "objects" (namely, groupings of sensations) in time and space, he would have found that something in our mind structures those experienced objects so we can understand them in such relations as "before, now, and after," "near and far" "cause and effect," using categories of our understanding. This is the self before any experiences: our *transcendental self,* or the *transcendental ego.* So the self is essential for structuring our experiences of the world as well as our self-consciousness, but it isn't part of our self-consciousness.

This is how Kant combines empiricism and rationalism: Everything in our experiences indeed comes through our senses—except the ordering principles of our mind, giving structure to those experiences. In a sense you might say, in today's jargon, that the transcendental self is the "software" that structures and manages the input data (our sensations) to produce our consciousness of a world of objects and relations. The self is something that lies deeper than all experiences: It is transcendental, meaning that it is the necessary condition for all experience. So not only does Kant try to set Hume straight, but Locke's view that we can know our self through our memories falls by the wayside, too, as does Descartes's fundamental definition of the mind as a "thinking thing" and his statement that "I think" has to accompany all experience. That is not necessary, says Kant, because we normally don't even think that we think. We don't have to be self-aware at all times; but we have to *be able to be self-aware.*

In other words, human existence for Kant is not being constantly self-aware, but at any given time *being capable of self-awareness.* And of course the transcendental self can't be a thinking thing, because it is no "thing" or substance at all: It is a mind activity that forms the foundation of all other mind activities. In Kant's own words (notorious for their formal, compact style),

For the ego is not a concept, but only the indication of the object of the inner sense, so far as we know it by no further predicate. Consequently it cannot indeed be itself a predicate of any other thing; but just as little can it be a definite concept of an absolute subject, but is, as in all other cases, only a reference of the inner phenomena to their unknown subject.[17]

But aside from our transcendental self we also have an *empirical self*—the personality that others recognize in us, all the big and small physical and psychological differences that make us into unique persons. The person we recognize in the mirror is our empirical ego, but we have never experienced our transcendental self, and we never will.

Ricoeur: We Have a Narrative Self

You will remember from Chapter 1 that many thinkers today see humans as "storytelling animals." The idea of storytelling as an essential part of personal identity has become prominent in the current theories of self. Since you are already familiar with the theory of narrative self-awareness (remember "the man with two brains" trying to explain an inexplicable association by telling a story?), we can jump right to the issue: For Paul Ricoeur and other thinkers interested in narrative theory, telling the story of our life is an important part of who we are. This theory sidesteps Locke's problem with incomplete memories as well as the problem of false memories, because it sees personal identity as a result of our capacity to tell a tale about ourselves. The tale may be tall, but in that case it still reveals something about who we think we are. It even adds something that no other theory of self has: an understanding that our sense of self is not necessarily a factual reflection of what has happened to us, but contains the very important element of what we would *like* to have happen to us! A narrative identity tells of the self one would like others to believe exists, which is also the self one would like to believe in as one's own image and legacy; it involves truth and lying, events and dreams, seamlessly interwoven.

But shouldn't we want to have a narrative identity that strictly reflects the facts? Why would we want to encourage lying? Well, for one thing, it is hard to establish what are "facts" in a personal experience. We can sometimes establish whether events *happened,* but how these events were perceived by the individual is another matter. As you saw in Chapter 1, the story of oneself will have to rest on whether it rings true to others as well as oneself; while it can't be used as evidence in a court of law, an embellished (or heavily edited) personal story may tell volumes about a person's sense of himself or herself, in a positive or a negative sense. The Norwegian playwright Henrik Ibsen who wrote the drama *Peer Gynt* (see the Narratives section of this chapter) speculated in his drama *The Wild Duck* that humans must have their share of illusions about themselves and the world; without the "life-lie" some people will perish under the pressure of harsh reality. On a lighter note, there is the comedy *Overboard* (1987), the story of a wealthy and conceited young woman who falls from a boat and suffers amnesia; she is saved by a young carpenter who has previously had an unpleasant encounter with her. In order to teach her a lesson in humility, he takes her home to his children and their very modest living conditions; he convinces her that she is their mother and his wife. This is now her life story, and she adjusts to her new narrative identity and indeed acquires a more humble view of life. The story is false—but it changes reality nevertheless, for her and also for the carpenter and his kids. And when the truth comes out, the false story still has left its traces in the woman's comprehension of herself.

So does everyone have a narrative identity? Ricoeur would answer Yes, but not everyone is capable of finding it or putting it together: It takes an effort to get your story-self together to the extent that you understand your life as a story with a direction and can tell others about it. However, we

Box 7.10   CHAPTER 4 REVISITED: SKINNER
AND SARTRE ON THE SELF

Now that we have looked at the concept of human nature from a variety of descriptive theories bordering on the normative, you will be able to pull some threads together. In Chapter 4 we looked at the issue of determinism and free will. You will remember that J. S. Watson and B. F. Skinner represented hard determinism in one of its most extreme forms with their theory of behaviorism: All human life can be sufficiently understood in terms of behavior; any terminology referring to mental states is to be avoided, because it is unnecessary. After having read this chapter you can now see that behaviorism denies the mind/body distinction, because behaviorists deny that mind activity is a true phenomenon. In other words, behaviorists like Watson and Skinner are eliminative materialists: The more we know about brain functions, the less we will need references to the mind, consciousness, or the self.

Sartre's view of the self is just as radical, but in a different way: He, too, believes we have no "self" in the Cartesian meaning, but Sartre is a dualist in the tradition of Husserl, who certainly believes in the life of the mind. Our psychological inner life is absolutely real—but the notion that we have a unified "self" that stays the same throughout our lives is wrong. Sartre (who of course does not believe we have a human nature) has quite a unique view of what it means to understand oneself as an authentic human being: If you say you know yourself and what your future actions will be, then you have bad faith, because you assume that you have a self-identity that can't change. On the other hand, if you refuse to face up to the sum total of your past actions by not accepting yourself, then you also suffer from bad faith. So your self-identity lies in the past, but not in the future! Accept who you *have been*—but you have complete freedom to be someone else from now on. Then you will be a person of authenticity.

all have a narrative identity because we are strung out, like a story, between the past (the beginning) and the future (the end), in the now. Increasingly, narrative scholars are saying that we *ought* to have a narrative identity, but it isn't something that we have or must have in order to be called a person. In other words, narrative selfhood theory is moving from being a descriptive theory to being a *normative* theory: We may not all have a narrative sense of self, but life will be enriched if we develop one. Humans may be storytelling animals on the whole, but it doesn't mean everyone is capable of telling a story, not even their own story.

Here I would like to remind you of Box 7.6, which discusses Dennett and his theory of narrative gravity and selfhood. Like Ricoeur, Dennett believes that the capacity to gather one's life events into story form provides something essential for our sense of self. However, while Dennett sees this narrative capacity as a *condition for selfhood* (meaning, if you can't tell your own story, you are not a person with a self and a consciousness), Ricoeur sees the narrative capacity as a way to become a *better person*—in other words, it is a matter of ethics. We can still have selves and be conscious without telling stories, but we improve vastly on our understanding of ourselves if we become storytellers. And since we have occasionally explored the possibility of conscious animal minds, I will do it in this case, too: For Dennett, a nonhuman animal mind can't be conscious and have a self because of the lack of narrative capacity. Ricoeur (who has never shown any interest in the question of animal consciousness) would conclude that only humans tell stories and have the capacity for understanding oneself through narrativity, but that wouldn't preclude the possibility that nonhuman animals have a sense of self and a consciousness—it just wouldn't be of the narrative kind. (Box 7.10 recaps the theories of Skinner and Sartre in the light of the discussion of the self.)

Non-Western Philosophies of the Self

Only a generation ago philosophy students were often told in their introductory classes that philosophy was a Western phenomenon and non-Western cultures didn't have philosophy. Now that picture is changing. Within the past decade, many philosophy departments have begun to include Asian philosophy (usually the traditional religious philosophies of China and India) in their curriculum.

Tribal Philosophies   There are signs that the picture may be changing further: Most non-Western cultures with the exceptions of China and India may not have had a long history of *formal* philosophical discussions about metaphysics, the nature of knowledge, or moral values, but if we go to the traditional stories of tribal societies—their mythologies—we find clear evidence that they discussed the nature of reality, how to tell truth from falsehood, and how to become a person of good character and do the right thing. (You will remember from Chapter 6 that the term *non-Western* isn't entirely accurate when applied to indigenous cultures within the Western hemisphere, such as American Indians. Again, the term should be read as cultural rather than geographical.) Philosophers today—Western as well as non-Western—are becoming increasingly interested in these tribal philosophies as expressed in story form and in songs, because they may reveal how ancient is the urge to seek explanations and justifications in human history—and how universal the quest for understanding. Also, it allows for contemporary thinkers all over the world, from a multitude of traditions, to see philosophy as a subject that goes beyond the Western tradition and to question the meaning of what Western thinkers have labeled "philosophy."

The subject of human nature has occupied Western thinkers for more than 2,000 years, but has it also been something of interest to thinkers and storytellers from other traditions? Mostly, yes, but often with a different emphasis than in the West. In this section we take a look at some examples of non-Western thinking about the self. (Box 7.11 explores the role of dreams in human and animal lives, as seen by Western and non-Western traditions.)

Lately, Western as well as non-Western scholars have begun to describe the Western theories of selfhood from St. Augustine to Descartes to twentieth-century thinkers as being "atomistic." We think of the self as unique and isolated from the world, like disconnected atoms. Two people can't share a self, and one of the more irrational fears of the technology of *human cloning* is precisely that two physically identical individuals might have to share a self, or a soul (although everybody knows that natural identical twins develop into individual beings, each with their own personality and self). The idea of personalities melding together or of someone having multiple personalities is eerie and abhorrent to most Western minds, although lovers often express the wish that their selves could meld. Feminism has lately criticized the atomistic theories of self, pointing out that if you are used to networking and nurturing, you don't automatically think of yourself as a separate, isolated unit, but as part of a greater whole that you depend on and that is dependent on you. The French feminist Luce Irigaray talks about human beings—in particular, women—having multiple selves interweaving in and out of each situation. But the idea of a community from which the self derives its identity is actually an ancient idea, an integral part of Socrates', Plato's, and Aristotle's way of looking at individual human beings: as members of a community first, and individuals second. It is generally referred to as *communitarianism*. So even within the Western tradition there was a time when atomism was considered unnatural; as you will see in Chapter 9, Aristotle speculated that if a human were capable

Box 7.11 DREAMS AND PRECOGNITION

Why do we dream, and can dreams tell us something important? If we go to non-Western traditions, the answer is almost unequivocal: We dream because during the dream state our mind connects with other realms, and we see visions of other realities, including the future. American Indian initiation rituals often used to involve "dream quests," tasks to be completed by the young initiate involving having dreams with a vision, usually of the animal that is to become the initiate's totem. From Greek antiquity to biblical times and in tribal cultures around the world, a particularly impressive dream (often dreamed by a socially important person, such as the king) would be interpreted by professional dream readers as an omen of the future. In the Western tradition we find that same view of dreams as omens, both as an ancient historic phenomenon and to some extent in popular culture, but throughout the twentieth century the view has become established in the scientific community that dreams in all likelihood do not give us any window to the future, nor do they allow us to "lift the veil" to other worlds. Freud's theory of dreams saw our nightly narratives as masked memories of past repressions, usually of a sexual nature

(see Chapter 3), and as such they can teach us about ourselves, but not about the future.

Dream specialists today speculate that dreams may not even have as much content as that: They may just be the brain's way of "clearing the cache" (to use computer terminology), doing away with useless bits of impressions and memories accumulated during the day or perhaps committing to memory the day's important lessons. Since all mammals dream, even fetuses—because all mammals have REM sleep, with rapid eye movements, like the type of dream accompanying our sleep—then there surely must be some function of dreams that is in common for all of us mammals. In addition, humans who are deprived of REM sleep under research conditions will usually develop a neurotic state of mind.

Today's scientists are divided about the importance of dreams; some see them as *physiologically* necessary, while others believe them to have a useful *psychological* function: helping us understand ourselves better. Recent research even claims to show that scientists will be able to tell what animals (including humans) dream *of*. The mental patterns of lab rats were monitored as they

of living outside of society, he'd either be an animal or superhuman. (Box 7.12 explores the Western idea of being oneself.)

So it is hardly a surprise to find out that tribal non-Western cultures have long traditions of telling stories where selfhood is the topic and the community is the key. It is just that philosophers generally aren't used to reading the stories, transcripts of ancient oral myths or fireside tales, told from generation to generation, usually with an anonymous first author. The American philosopher Hoyt Edge, a student of Australian Aboriginal cultures, observes that while the Western concept of self is atomistic, we tend to focus on what is *in common for everyone* when trying to define human nature (something that you can check for yourself by going back to Chapter 1 and rereading the theories of human universals). The

Australian Aboriginal view of humans is quite different: It is *relational*. An individual is defined in his or her relations to the group. The Aboriginal philosophy is uninterested in the concept of human nature, because it doesn't see people as a species of similar beings with some essential common characteristic (such as rationality). Instead, it views individuals as unique beings defined by their unique relations to other people, to ancestors and totems, to the landscape, and to other spirits. The Aboriginal way of thinking greatly values autonomy (as do we in the West), but it doesn't assume that humans become autonomous by separating themselves from family and community:

> The Aboriginal form of autonomy does not result from a universal capacity of reason and atomism, but from one's individuality and relationships.

negotiated a maze; then, during their sleep period the electronic monitoring continued, with an interesting result. The mental patterns of the rats in REM sleep were identical to their mental output when going through the maze, to the point where the researchers think they can pinpoint exactly where in the maze the rats were dreaming they were! So the researchers conclude that the dreams of rats help them memorize and understand the events of the day, and perhaps the same method can be used to interpret human dreams. (Other scientists are highly skeptical of this conclusion, though.)

But what about the experience of *precognition* in dreams? In other words, knowing the future before it happens? Most of us have experienced *déjà vu*, the feeling that you have experienced something before; scientists now believe a sense of *déjà vu* (French, "already seen") to be a common, harmless form of a temporary brain short circuit. But how about experiencing some event and then realizing that some time ago you dreamed that very same thing? Such experiences are common in cultures that believe in precognition, but much less common in ours; even so, in informal surveys I have conducted in my classes among students

raised within the Western mind-set where paranormal experiences are generally considered nonexistent or hoaxes, I was surprised to find that over two-thirds of the students believed they had had precognitive dreams or knew someone who had—dreams of premonition ranging from a loved one's injury or death to winning the lottery to the outcome of an examination. This might mean that the Western antiparanormal worldview isn't quite as widespread as one might think, even among overall nonsuperstitious, well-educated social groups. It might also mean that there is a certain common form of experience associated with dreams that our scientific community hasn't yet dealt with in a sufficiently serious manner.

It is rather ironic that the founder of modern philosophy, Descartes, who more than anyone else was responsible for the Western mind-set and its scientific worldview, himself got his career as a philosopher started because of a precognitive dream when he was a young man, in which he saw himself inventing a new science; and he followed his dream, much like a young nineteenth-century American Indian who has seen his totem in a dream vision.

A person does not have autonomy as a part of basic human nature, but grows into autonomy by developing the uniqueness and particularity found in a set of totemic relationships. Autonomy is not a capacity but rather a project that one achieves through growth, which is basically spiritual.[18]

Rudolph Ryser, chair of the Center for World Indigenous Studies (CWIS), writes about indigenous peoples of the Americas. In "Observations on 'Self' and 'Knowing,'" Ryser talks about the sense of self experienced by the Pacific Northwest culture of the Cowlitz Indians:

Individual personality is only distinguishable from the collective self by virtue of its physical separateness—and that is only illusion itself. The personal self is to the collective self as the upstream

waters are to the full rivers below. . . . One cup of river water is the same as the water passing by. The distinguishing quality of the cup of water is the "cup.". . . As a part of the collective self, one is not aware of singleness or its possibilities. There is only an awareness of the tensions and inclinations that give rise to change.[19]

This sense of collective self that the traditional Pacific Northwest tribes experience, according to Ryser, has an additional feature: It is not uniquely human. The deer (the tribal totem) moves with the herd in much the same way. The bear and the salmon all have similar modes of existence. It doesn't mean that each individual—human as well as nonhuman—can't experience "singleness of consciousness," but it is a fleeting, temporary thing. What remains the foundation of awareness

Box 7.12   BE YOURSELF!

In all the discussions of selfhood in this chapter there is one issue we haven't discussed except sporadically: the idea of selfhood as a *moral concept*. The reason for this is that this chapter, and this section of the book, deals with "mostly descriptive theories," scientific attempts at describing human nature. However, as you have often seen, the line between a description and a prescription sometimes blurs. A traditional part of the discussion of whether we have a self is the question of what we are supposed to *do* with that elusive self, and this is where the issue moves into the normative (prescriptive) realm: If you are told "just be yourself," "be true to yourself," or "realize yourself," it is a whole different matter from pinpointing what the self might be, because it is a *moral command,* involving an ideal image of what we ought to be and do. It seems to imply that being oneself is inherently good—but I think we can all remember situations where we have "just been ourselves" and it was downright embarrassing, so it can't mean that we aren't suppose to exercise self-control.

The idea of *self-realization,* big in the 1960s and 1970s, assumes that the self we are supposed to be, or

realize, is a deeper and *better* self than the one we usually display. As you already know, the ancient Greek saying, "Know thyself," didn't originally imply a quest for abstract knowledge of selfhood, but a command to get to know one's limitations, especially as a mortal being. Aristotle himself saw a person of good character as one who has succeeded in realizing his or her potential (see Chapter 8). The classic story of *Peer Gynt* plays on several meanings of *self.* Peer, when challenged by the Grim Reaper in the form of a button-moulder, claims that he has always been himself, as a matter of pride; but the button moulder makes him realize that he has never taken a stand and always shifted with the breeze, been this and that as the situation demanded. *His self is like an onion,* layer upon layer, with nothing at the core. Peer is a failed human being and must be thrown back with other failed souls in the melting pot to be remolded. We look at *Peer Gynt* in the Narratives section as a segue to Chapter 8: the normative question of the soul and of good and evil.

is the collective self in the animal world as well as in the human world, seen by the Cowlitz mind. In the next chapter we return to Rÿser's view of a collective world of humans and animals as an example of a moral, normative system.

Buddhism   Perhaps the most famous non-Western challenge to the idea of a self comes from one of the great world religions, Buddhism. Often described as a philosophy more than a religion, Buddhism in its most ancient form offers a solution to what it sees as the "human condition" with its chain of endless hopes and disappointments, of pain and suffering. The solution is *to awaken.* The name "Buddha" means "Awakened One." One awakens to an understanding of the four Noble Truths: the inevitable experience of suffering, at-

tachment to life and selfhood as the causes of suffering, the cessation of suffering, and finally the way that leads to the cessation of suffering. In the course of understanding these, one awakens to the three fundamental characteristics of human existence: suffering, impermanence, and the lack of a permanent self. Hinduism at Buddha's time taught that the self (*atman*) is eternal and unchanging—but the Buddha argued, in a remarkable parallel to David Hume some 2,200 years later, that there is no such thing as a permanent self—*anatman.* There is the everyday experience of self, but the notion of a self underlying our experience and retaining the same identity throughout our rebirths, is an illusion. Without the notion of a permanent, eternal self it becomes easier to disengage oneself from the temptations of life, because with the engagement in life comes inevitable suffering and rebirth into more suffering.

In a well-known Buddhist series of imaginary dialogues, *Questions of Milinda,* the Buddhist monk Nagasena is asked by King Milinda what an individual is, and Nagasena answers that there is an assemblage of parts, and we assume that, together, these parts form the individual self. But "there is an uninterrupted succession of mental and physical states. One state ceases to be, and another comes to exist. The succession is such that there is, as it were, none that precedes, none that follows. Thus it is neither the same person nor yet a different person which goes to the final summation of consciousness."[20]

The Buddhist doctrine of the nonself has been interpreted in a number of ways, from the idea that Buddha denies the experience of self—which is not the case—to the idea that even if the self is not permanent, then we are still persons with moral responsibilities (as suggested by the Buddhist Personalists). The philosophical argument of no-self is seen by Buddhists today as primarily an argument against the ancient Hindu doctrine of the eternal soul: We humans experience awareness of our changing conditions, as well as the changing conditions in the world around us, but we should give up the idea that underneath these ever-changing processes is something permanent we might call a self. Chapter 8 returns to the issue of Buddhism and the question of the existence and nature of the soul.

With non-Western as well as Western alternatives to the Western sense of a unique self, it becomes clear that even the most radical nonself theory doesn't claim that sane people don't have a sense of who they are or that they can't tell the difference between themselves and their fellow human beings—or even other animals, trees, and mountains. As Charles Taylor points out, it is an absolute given that each human individual very well knows the difference between his or her own pain and seeing others being hurt. We all know that "I am me," even if we don't use words such as "self" or "I." But some cultures consider this knowledge of minor importance, while some individual philosophers insist that it is either a false idea, a morally flawed idea, or an idea that the enlightened individual can rise above.

What's in a Name? Names, Selves, and Power

The final item we explore in this section is the phenomenon of *selfhood* and *names,* because it unites all human beings on the planet regardless of cultures. Our sense of self may be shaped by our memories, some underlying sense of identity, and the stories we tell, but it is also shaped by our name: the name others identify us by and (not least) the name we call ourselves.

Shakespeare's Romeo and Juliet are children of feuding families, so it is a given that they will not be allowed to marry. Juliet asks Romeo to forsake his name, for

What's in a name? That which we call a rose
By any other name would smell as sweet;
So Romeo would, were he not Romeo call'd,
Retain the dear perfection which he owes
Without that title.

But is this true? Do we retain our special qualities no matter what name we have? It appears not. The linguist Deborah Tannen (see Chapter 6) tells about her identity problems when she was renamed as a child, from Deborah, to Diane, and then back to Deborah, which was then shortened to Debby. For her, each name signified a different personality, and as a young adult she chose to be called Deborah. She cites the example of David Reimer (see Chapter 6), who was born Bruce, changed to Brenda, and later chose the name David for himself, because he felt he had been battling the world, a David-and-Goliath experience. Also, children who have been named for a deceased older sibling often carry with them a feeling that they are a replacement, perpetually judged by how much they measure up to the unknown dead brother or sister. And if we're named after a relative or a celebrity, we tend to assume that there is some special quality (or something sinister!) that we share with that person.

Names can sometimes determine whether we succeed or fail in our chosen professions. An aspiring young actor named Marion Michael Morrison couldn't find any steady work until he changed his name to John Wayne. Another famous Hollywood actor from the classical period, Cary Grant, started out in life as Archibald Leach. Names can be changed in protest (Malcolm X), as a political statement of a life change (Ayn Rand), or as a professional choice (The Singer Formerly Known as Prince, Snoop Doggy Dogg, and others). On the Internet some of us use a variety of aliases as we participate in various chatrooms and newsgroups, and often we take on *personas* suited for a particular alias. Authors use aliases for a number of reasons. And criminals do too! In one of the national songs we used to sing when I was a little girl, the Danish culture hero Holger Danske says, "If a Dane wants to do battle in the world, but hides his face and his name, he has no integrity."

Probably one of the most profound connections between a name change and an identity change happens when a woman changes her last name to her husband's in marriage. The tradition has deep roots that are partly economic and partly emotional—economic, because the woman became part of her husband's household as his *property,* and her children would bear his name; emotional, because the name change signifies a union of two individuals. Although the merging of identities is still a powerful reason why women change their names today, many women's concern for maintaining their own identity in marriage has resulted in their keeping their birth name or hyphenating it with their husband's—because while both individuals are supposed to be equal, the woman somehow loses part of herself and her history when her last name disappears. (There is of course also a practical concern: Many women enter marriage with a career already in progress and are known within their profession under their birth name. A name change in mid-career is generally considered a bad career move.) In the 1970s some newlyweds took to exchanging last names as a symbolic way of sharing their new identity as a couple, but the custom never really caught on.

In the American Indian tradition, as well as in other tribal cultures, a person would be given several names over a lifetime: one name as a child, another after the coming-of-age ceremony, and sometimes also a name that identified their specific function within the tribe—a name that might change several times within a lifetime. In addition, individuals would be told they had a secret name that they must not divulge to anyone, ever. The name might be revealed in a dream or during a vision quest, or it might be given to them by the shaman. Why were they not allowed to share their secret name with anyone? Because in that name lay their ultimate personal strength, and if anyone shared that knowledge, their inner self would weaken and become vulnerable to attacks and conspiracies. *Within the name lies power,* and herein lies the key to why it is so important for us to approve of our own name: When we feel comfortable with our name, it adds to our self-confidence; when we learn the name of someone else, we feel we know something essential about that person. This age-old realization is illustrated formidably in Grimm's fairy tale about *Rumplestiltskin:* The young queen owes the little sorcerer her firstborn for favors he has done her in the past, but she can void the contract if she can find out his name. And the moment she finally calls him by name, Rumplestiltskin, he dies; she has stolen his power.

So if we know "the name of the rose," then we have somehow mastered its nature: Isolating and putting a name to a mysterious phenomenon is the first step to understanding it and perhaps even to predicting it and controlling it. Before health professionals named PMS, it was just a form of lunacy some women went through every month. Before Chronic Fatigue Syndrome was identified, it was assumed that patients were hypochondriacs or slackers. Indeed, making up a name may *invent* a phenomenon that has no real existence; *phrenology* is one example (see Box 4.5). Modern marketing is well aware of the phenomenon: Invent the right name, and you've got a product that sells. So Juliet may have been wrong: The rose might smell as sweet if it were called skunkweed, but somehow we might not want to buy it in bunches of twelve for special occasions.

Study Questions

1. Compare and contrast Tattersall's and Sheets-Johnstone's views on Neandertal intelligence. What are their arguments? Do you find one to be more correct than the other? Explain.

2. Describe Descartes's method of doubt. What was his purpose? Did he achieve it? Explain.

3. How can the film *The Matrix* be said to illustrate Descartes's two conjectures?

4. Explain the difference between interactionism, parallelism, and the identity theory, referring to the concepts of dualism and materialism.

5. Explain Merleau-Ponty's view of the importance of the body for the human experience.

6. Outline three different explanations from this chapter of the sense of self; which one comes closest to your own view, and which one is the farthest from it? Explain.

7. Do you think your self-awareness is linked to your name? Imagine having a different name? Would you still be "you"?

8. Judging from this chapter, would you hold the view that consciousness is an exclusively human experience, or is it an experience we share with other beings on the planet—perhaps in the universe? Explain.

Primary Readings and Narratives

Chapter 7 concludes with three Primary Readings and four Narratives: First, excerpts from Descartes's *First* and *Second Meditations;* next, an excerpt from Merleau-Ponty's *Phenomenology of Perception;* and last, an excerpt from Sheets-Johnstone's *Primacy of Movement.* The Narratives are a summary of the film *Being John Malkovich,* a summary (of sorts) of the film *Memento,* a summary of Kafka's famous short story "The Metamorphosis," and an excerpt from Ibsen's drama *Peer Gynt.*

Primary Reading

Meditations 1–2

RENÉ DESCARTES

Excerpt. Translated by Donald A. Cress. Written 1640.

MEDITATION ONE: CONCERNING THOSE THINGS THAT CAN BE CALLED INTO DOUBT

. . . But perhaps, although the senses sometimes deceive us when it is a question of very small and distant things, still there are many other matters which one certainly cannot doubt, although they are derived from the very same senses: that I am sitting here before the fireplace wearing my dressing gown, that I feel this sheet of paper in my hands, and so on. But how could one deny that these hands and that my whole body exist? Unless perhaps I should compare myself to insane people whose brains are so impaired by a stubborn vapor from a black bile that they continually insist that they are kings when they are in utter poverty, or that they are wearing purple robes when they are naked, or that they have a head made of clay, or that they are gourds, or that they are made of glass. But they are all demented, and I would appear no less demented if I were to take their conduct as a model for myself.

All of this would be well and good, were I not a man who is accustomed to sleeping at night, and to undergoing in my sleep the very same things—or now and then even less likely ones—as do these insane people when they are awake. How often has my evening slumber persuaded me of such customary things as these: that I am here, clothed in my dressing gown, seated at the fireplace, when in fact I am lying undressed between the blankets! But right now I certainly am gazing upon this piece of paper with eyes wide awake. This head which I am moving is not heavy with sleep. I extend this hand consciously and deliberately and I feel it. These things would not be so distinct for one who is asleep. But this all seems as if I do not recall having been deceived by similar thoughts on other occasions in my dreams. As I consider these cases more intently, I see so plainly that there are no definite signs to distinguish being awake from being asleep that I am quite astonished, and this astonishment almost convinces me that I am sleeping.

Let us say, then, for the sake of argument, that we are sleeping and that such particulars as these are not true: that we open our eyes, move our heads, extend our hands. Perhaps we do not even have these hands, or any such body at all. Nevertheless, it really must be admitted that things seen in sleep are, as it were, like painted images, which could have been produced only in the likeness of true things. Therefore at least these general things (eyes, head, hands, the whole body) are not imaginary things, but are true and exist. For indeed when painters wish to represent sirens and satyrs by means of bizarre and unusual forms, they surely cannot ascribe utterly new natures to these creatures. Rather, they simply intermingle the members of various animals. And even if they concoct something so utterly novel that its likes have never been seen before (being utterly fictitious and false), certainly at the very minimum the colors from which the painters compose the thing ought to be true. And for the same reason, although even these general things (eyes, head, hands, and the like) can be imaginary, still one must necessarily admit that at least other things that are even more simple and universal are true, from which, as from true colors, all these things—be they true or false—which in our thought are images of things, are constructed.

To this class seems to belong corporeal nature in general, together with its extension; likewise the shape of extended things, their quantity or size, their number; as well as the place where they exist, the time of their duration, and other such things.

Hence perhaps we do not conclude improperly that physics, astronomy, medicine, and all the other disciplines that are dependent upon the consideration of composite things are all doubtful. But arithmetic, geometry, and other such disciplines—which treat of nothing but the simplest and most general things and which are indifferent as to whether these things do or do not exist—contain something certain and indubitable. For whether I be awake or asleep, two plus three makes five, and a square does not have more than four sides; nor does it seem possible that such obvious truths can fall under the suspicion of falsity.

All the same, a certain opinion of long standing has been fixed in my mind, namely that there exists a God who is able to do anything and by whom I, such as I am, have been created. How do I know that he did not bring it about that there be no earth at all, no heavens, no extended thing, no figure, no size, no place, and yet all these things should seem to me to exist precisely as they appear to do now? Moreover—as I judge that others sometimes make mistakes in matters that they believe they know most perfectly—how do I know that I am not deceived every time I add two and three or count the sides of a square or perform an even simpler operation, if such can be imagined? But perhaps God has not willed that I be thus deceived, for it is said that he is supremely good. Nonetheless, if it were repugnant to his goodness that he should have created me such that I be deceived all the time, it would seem, from this same consideration, to be foreign to him to permit me to be deceived occasionally. But we cannot make this last assertion.

Perhaps there are some who would rather deny such a powerful God, than believe that all other matters are uncertain. Let us not put these people off just yet; rather, let us grant that everything said here about God is fictitious. Now they suppose that I came to be what I am either by fate or by chance or by a continuous series of events or by some other way. But because being deceived and being mistaken seem to be imperfections, the less powerful they take the author of my being to be, the more probable it will be that I would be so imperfect as to be deceived perpetually. I have nothing to say in response to these arguments. At length I am forced to admit that there is nothing, among the things I once believed to be true, which it is not permissible to doubt—not for reasons of frivolity or a lack of forethought, but because of valid and considered arguments. Thus I must carefully withhold assent no less from these things than from the patently false, if I wish to find anything certain.

But it is not enough simply to have made a note of this; I must take care to keep it before my mind. For long-standing opinions keep coming back again and again, almost against my will; they seize upon my credulity, as if it were bound over to them by long use and the claims of intimacy. Nor will I get out of the habit of assenting to them and believing in them, so long as I take them to be exactly what they are, namely, in some respects doubtful as by now is obvious, but nevertheless highly probable, so that it is much more consonant with reason to believe them than to deny them. Hence, it seems to me, I would do well to turn my will in the opposite direction, to deceive myself and pretend for a considerable period that they are wholly false and imaginary, until finally, as if with equal weight of prejudice* on both sides, no bad habit should turn my judgment from the correct perception of things. For indeed I know that no danger or error will follow and that it is impossible for me to indulge in too much distrust, since I now am concentrating only on knowledge, not on action.

Thus I will suppose not a supremely good God, the source of truth, but rather an evil genius, as clever and deceitful as he is powerful, who has directed his entire effort to misleading me. I will regard the heavens, the air, the earth, colors, shapes, sounds, and all external things as nothing but the deceptive games of my dreams, which he lays snares for my credulity. I will regard myself as having no hands, no eyes, no flesh, no blood, no senses, but as nevertheless falsely believing that I possess all these things. I will remain resolutely fixed in this meditation, and, even if it be out of my power to know anything true, certainly it is within my power to take care resolutely to withhold my assent to what is false, lest this deceiver, powerful and clever as he is, have an effect on me. But this undertaking is arduous, and laziness brings me back to my customary way of living. I am not unlike a prisoner who might enjoy an imaginary freedom in his sleep. When he later begins to suspect that he is sleeping, he fears being awakened and conspires slowly with these pleasant illusions. In just this way, I spontaneously fall back into my old beliefs, and dread being awakened, less the toilsome wakefulness which follows upon a peaceful rest, have to be spent thenceforward not in the light but among the inextricable shadows of the difficulties now brought forward.

MEDITATION TWO: CONCERNING THE NATURE OF THE HUMAN MIND: THAT THE MIND IS MORE KNOWN THAN THE BODY

Yesterday's meditation filled my mind with so many doubts that I can no longer forget about them—nor yet do I see how they are to be resolved. But, as if I had suddenly fallen into a deep whirlpool, I am so disturbed that I can neither touch my foot to the bottom, nor swim up to the top. Nevertheless I will work my way up, and I will follow the same path I took yesterday, putting aside everything which admits of the least doubt, as if I had discovered it to be absolutely false. I will go forward until I know something certain—or, if nothing else, until I at least know for certain that nothing is certain. Archimedes sought only a firm and immovable point in order to move the entire earth from one place to another. Surely great things are to be hoped for if I am lucky enough to find at least one thing that is certain and indubitable.

Therefore I will suppose that all I see is false. I will believe that none of those things that my deceitful memory brings before my eyes ever existed. I thus have no senses: body, shape, extension, movement, and place are all figments of my imagination. What then will count as true? Perhaps only this one thing: that nothing is certain.

But on what grounds do I know that there is nothing over and above all those which I have just reviewed, concerning which there is not even the least cause for doubt? Is there not a God (or whatever name I might call him) who instills these thoughts in me? But why should I think that, since perhaps I myself could be the author of these things? Therefore am I not at least something? But I have already denied that I have any senses and any body. Still, I hesitate; for what follows from that? Am I so tied to the body and to the senses that I cannot exist without them? But I have persuaded myself that there is nothing at all in the world: no heaven, no earth, no minds, no bodies. Is it not then true that I do not exist? But

---

*A "prejudice" is a prejudgment, that is, an adjudication of an issue without having first reviewed the appropriate evidence.

certainly I should exist, if I were to persuade myself of something. But there is a deceiver (I know not who he is) powerful and sly in the highest degree, who is always purposely deceiving me. Then there is no doubt that I exist, if he deceives me. And deceive me as he will, he can never bring it about that I am nothing so long as I shall think that I am something. Thus it must be granted that, after weighing everything carefully and sufficiently, one must come to the considered judgment that the statement "I am, I exist" is necessarily true every time it is uttered by me or conceived in my mind.

But I do not yet understand well enough who I am—I, who now necessarily exist. And from this point on, I must take care lest I imprudently substitute something else in place of myself; and thus be mistaken even in that knowledge which I claim to be the most certain and evident of all. To this end, I shall meditate once more on what I once believed myself to be before having embarked upon these deliberations. For this reason, then, I will set aside whatever can be refuted even to a slight degree by the arguments brought forward, so that at length there shall remain precisely nothing but what is certain and unshaken.

What therefore did I formerly think I was? A man, of course. But what is a man? Might I not say a rational animal? No, because then one would have to inquire what an "animal" is and what "rational" means. And then from only one question we slide into many more difficult ones. Nor do I now have enough free time that I want to waste it on subtleties of this sort. But rather here I pay attention to what spontaneously and at nature's lead came into my thought beforehand whenever I pondered what I was. Namely, it occurred to me first that I have a face, hands, arms, and this entire mechanism of bodily members, the very same as are discerned in a corpse—which I referred to by the name "body." It also occurred to me that I eat, walk, feel and think; these actions I used to assign to the soul as their cause. But what this soul was I either did not think about or I imagined it was something terribly insubstantial—after the fashion of a wind, fire, or ether—which has been poured into my coarser parts. I truly was not in doubt regarding the body; rather I believed that I distinctly knew its nature, which, were I perhaps tempted to describe it such as I mentally conceived it, I would explain it thus:

by "body," I understand all that is suitable for being bounded by some shape, for being enclosed in some place, and thus for filling up space, so that it excludes every other body from that space; for being perceived by touch, sight, hearing, taste, or smell; for being moved in several ways, not surely by itself, but by whatever else that touches it. For I judged that the power of self-motion, and likewise of sensing or of thinking, in no way pertains to the nature of the body. Nonetheless, I used to marvel especially that such faculties were found in certain bodies.

But now what am I, when I suppose that some deceiver—omnipotent and, if I may be allowed to say it, malicious—takes all the pains he can in order to deceive me? Can I not affirm that I possess at least a small measure of all those traits which I already have said pertain to the nature of the body? I pay attention, I think, I deliberate—but nothing happens. I am wearied of repeating this in vain. But which of these am I to ascribe to the soul? How about eating or walking? These are surely nothing but illusions, because I do not have a body. How about sensing? Again, this also does not happen without a body, and I judge that I really did not sense those many things I seemed to have sensed in my dreams. How about thinking? Here I discover that thought is an attribute that really does belong to me. This alone cannot be detached from me. I am; I exist; this is certain. But for how long? For as long as I think. Because perhaps it could also come to pass that if I should cease from all thinking I would then utterly cease to exist. I now admit nothing that is not necessarily true. I am therefore precisely only a thing that thinks; that is, a mind, or soul, or intellect, or reason—words the meaning of which I was ignorant before. Now, I am a true thing, and truly existing; but what kind of thing? I have said it already: a thing that thinks. . . .

But what then am I? A thing that thinks. What is that? A thing that doubts, understands, affirms, denies, wills, refuses, and which also imagines and senses.

Study Questions

1. Explain Descartes's "dream conjecture": What is its purpose, and what tentative conclusion does he reach?

2. Explain Descartes's "evil genius conjecture": How does he reach this conjecture, and what is he trying to prove?

3. What is the purpose of these two conjectures? In other words, how does Descartes reach his conclusion, "I am, I exist"?

Primary Reading

Phenomenology of Perception

MAURICE MERLEAU-PONTY

Excerpt. Translated by Colin Smith. 1970.

As has often been said, it is the body which "catches" (*kapiert*) and "comprehends" movement. The cultivation of habit is indeed the grasping of a significance, but it is the motor grasping of a motor significance. Now what precisely does this mean? A woman may, without any calculation, keep a safe distance between the feather in her hat and things which might break it off. She feels where the feather is just as we feel where our hand is. If I am in the habit of driving a car, I enter a narrow opening and see that I can "get through" without comparing the width of the opening with that of the wings, just as I go through a doorway without checking the width of the doorway against that of my body. The hat and the car have ceased to be objects with a size and volume which is established by comparison with other objects. They have become potentialities of volume, the demand for a certain amount of free space. In the same way the iron gate to the Underground platform, and the road, have become restrictive potentialities and immediately appear passable or impassable for my body with its adjuncts. The blind man's stick has ceased to be an object for him, and is no longer perceived for itself; its point has become an area of sensitivity, extending the scope and active radius of touch, and providing a parallel to sight. In the exploration of things, the length of the stick does not enter expressly as a middle term: the blind man is rather aware of it through the position of objects than of the position of objects through it. The position of things is immediately given through the extent of the reach which carries him to it, which comprises besides the arm's own reach the stick's range of action. If I want to get used to a stick, I try it by touching a few things with it, and eventually I have it "well in hand," I can see what things are "within reach" or out of reach of my stick. There is no question here of any quick estimate or any comparison between the objective length of the stick and the objective distance away of the goal to be reached. The points in space do not stand out as objective positions in relation to the objective position occupied by our body; they mark, in our vicinity, the varying range of our aims and our gestures. To get used to a hat, a car or a stick is to be transplanted into them, or conversely, to incorporate them into the bulk of our own body. Habit expresses our power of dilating our being in the world, or changing our existence by appropriating fresh instruments.* It is possible to know how to type without being able to say where the letters which make the words are to be found on the banks of keys. To know how to type is not, then, to know the place of each letter among the keys, nor even to have acquired a conditioned reflex for each one, which is set in motion by the letter as it comes before our eye. If habit is neither a form of knowledge nor an involuntary action, what then is it? It is knowledge in the hands, which is forthcoming only when bodily effort is made, and cannot be formulated in detachment from that effort. The subject knows where the letters are on the typewriter as we know

---

*It thus elucidates the nature of the body image. When we say that it presents us immediately with our bodily position, we do not mean, after the manner of empiricists, that it consists of a mosaic of "extensive sensations." It is a system which is open on to the world, and correlative with it.

where one of our limbs is, through a knowledge bred of familiarity which does not give us a position in objective space. The movement of her fingers is not presented to the typist as a path through space which can be described, but merely as a certain adjustment of motility, physiognomically distinguishable from any other. The question is often framed as if the perception of a letter written on paper aroused the representation of the same letter which in turn aroused the representation of the movement needed to strike it on the machine. But this is mythological language. When I run my eyes over the text set before me, there do not occur perceptions which stir up representations, but patterns are formed as I look, and these are endowed with a typical or familiar physiognomy. When I sit at my typewriter, a motor space opens beneath my hands, in which I am about to "play" what I have read. The reading of the word is a modulation of visible space, the performance of the movement is a modulation of manual space, and the whole question is how a certain physiognomy of "visual" patterns can evoke a certain type of motor response, how each "visual" structure eventually provides itself with its mobile essence without there being any need to spell the word or specify the movement in detail in order to translate one into the other. But this power of habit is no different from the general one which we exercise over our body: if I am ordered to touch my ear or my knee, I move my hand to my ear or my knee by the shortest route, without having to think of the initial position of my hand, or that of my ear, or the path between them. We said earlier that it is the body which "understands" in the cultivation of habit. This way of putting it will appear absurd, if understanding is subsuming a sense-datum under an idea, and if the body is an object. But the phenomenon of habit is just what prompts us to revise our notion of "understand" and our notion of the body. To understand is to experience the harmony between what we aim at and what is given, between the intention and the performance— and the body is our anchorage in a world. When I put my hand to my knee, I experience at every stage of the movement the fulfilment of an intention which was not directed at my knee as an idea or even as an object, but as a present and real part of my living body, that is, finally, as a stage in my perpetual movement towards a world. When the typist performs the necessary movements on the typewriter, these movements are governed by an intention, but the intention does not posit the keys as objective locations. It is literally true that the subject who learns to type incorporates the key-bank space into his bodily space. . . .

Now the body is essentially an expressive space. If I want to take hold of an object, already, at a point of space about which I have been quite unmindful, this power of grasping constituted by my hand moves upwards towards the thing. I move my legs not as things in space two and a half feet from my head, but as a power of locomotion which extends my motor intention downwards. The main areas of my body are devoted to actions, and participate in their value, and asking why common sense makes the head the seat of thought raises the same problem as asking how the organist distributes, through "organ space," musical significances. But our body is not merely one expressive space among the rest, for that is simply the constituted body. It is the origin of the rest, expressive movement itself, that which causes them to begin to exist as things, under our hands and eyes. Although our body does not impose definite instincts upon us from birth, as it does upon animals, it does at least give to our life the form of generality, and develops our personal acts into stable dispositional tendencies. In this sense our nature is not long-established custom, since custom presupposes the form of passivity derived from nature. The body is our general medium for having a world. Sometimes it is restricted to the actions necessary for the conservation of life, and accordingly it posits around us a biological world; at other times, elaborating upon these primary actions and moving from their literal to a figurative meaning, it manifests through them a core of new significance: this is true of motor habits such as dancing. Sometimes, finally, the meaning aimed at cannot be achieved by the body's natural means; it must then build itself an instrument, and it projects thereby around itself a cultural world. At all levels it performs the same function which is to endow the instantaneous expressions of spontaneity with "a little renewable action and independent existence." Habit is merely a form of this fundamental power. We say that the body has understood, and habit has been cultivated when it has absorbed a new meaning, and assimilated a fresh core of significance.

To sum up, what we have discovered through the study of motility, is a new meaning of the word "meaning." The great strength of intellectualist psychology and idealist philosophy comes from their having no difficulty in showing that perception and thought have an intrinsic significance and cannot be explained in terms of the external association of fortuitously agglomerated contents. The *Cogito* was the coming to self-awareness of this inner core. But all meaning was *ipso facto* conceived as an act of thought, as the work of a pure *I,* and although rationalism easily refuted empiricism, it was itself unable to account for the variety of experience, for the element of senselessness in it, for the contingency of contents. Bodily experience forces us to acknowledge an imposition of meaning which is not the work of a universal constituting consciousness, a meaning which clings to certain contents. My body is that meaningful core which behaves like a general function, and which nevertheless exists, and is susceptible to disease. In it we learn to know

that union of essence and existence which we shall find again in perception generally, and which we shall then have to describe more fully.

Study Questions

1. What is Merleau-Ponty's point in bringing up the examples of the lady with the hat, the blind man, and the typist?

2. What does he mean by saying that "to understand is to experience the harmony between . . . the intention and the performance—and the body is our anchorage in a world"?

3. Merleau-Ponty is critical of Descartes's *Cogito* in the final segment of this excerpt. What is the point of his criticism?

Primary Reading

The Primacy of Movement

MAXINE SHEETS-JOHNSTONE

Excerpt, 1999.

From virtually the moment of their original discovery, Neandertals have been regularly conceived and are still conceived by many as being mentally deficient in one way or another. They are conceived to have *lacked* something cerebral—something in the way of thoughtfulness—since they did not "improve" in major ways or accede to our 20th century human kind of behavioral capabilities. It is as if, given all the time they had at their disposal—all the time they walked the earth—they stood pat; indeed, we are told that "in terms of hominid colonization, [it was] half a million years or more of inaction." Considering the esteem in which earlier hominids (*Homo habilis, Homo erectus,* not to mention australopithecines) are generally held, the negative judgment is odd, but it is especially odd when coupled with comparative statements concerning the singular abilities of *Homo sapiens sapiens:* their colonization of new areas, for example, their future planning abilities, their sophisticated social

networks that insured survival in challenging times, and so on. The negative judgment is especially odd because Neandertals were around for more than 200,000 years (approximately 250,000 to 35,000 BP). That is not a long time in evolutionary terms, but it is a very long time when measured against our own human evolutionary life span of 40,000 years. Indeed, we modern humans have existed less than one quarter of the time that Neandertals existed. In contrast to Neandertals, early *Homo sapiens sapiens* are described in glowing terms that apply still to us since we are their descendants. Thus prized abilities—the ability to plan ahead and to form social networks, for example—are implicitly if not explicitly taken to be features of our own lives, and this in spite of contravening evidence. For example, any quick appraisal of the present global environmental situation readily instructs us that many humans are singularly deficient in planning ahead; they see only as far as their own immediate desires and/or their own lifetime. Moreover rather than building social networks that give them "insurance policies" against hard times, humans on the whole appear unkindly disposed if not hostile toward their national and ethnic neighbors, unduly acquisitive, and to have been at war almost incessantly as far back as history records. Furthermore, social networks in the form of treaties between or among nations have proved notoriously unreliable "insurance policies." In short, from a Martian or otherwise more objective viewpoint, modern humans in recorded history appear to be socially and ecologically deficient creatures who are more properly defined as selfishly engaged rather than either future-oriented or socially congenial. However revolutionary, stunning, and undeniably wonderful the practices and inventions of early modern humans, practices and inventions of those latter-day humans who are their descendants arouse—or should arouse—wonder of an altogether different sort. There is every reason to doubt rather than marvel at their so-called "fundamental behavioral capabilities" and "improve-

ments," their "learning rules," and the like. In fact, there is every reason to wonder whether *Homo sapiens sapiens* will match the evolutionary longevity of Neandertals.

Study Questions

1. Sheets-Johnstone claims that Neandertals have received a particularly unfair reputation; what is this reputation, and how does she argue for a reevaluation?

2. How should modern humans be evaluated in terms of our future planning abilities and social networks?

3. Sheets-Johnstone believes there is evidence that Neandertals were *sapient,* or self-aware, based on their planning skills and their body-consciousness and the fact that they and humans have a common ancestor. In your opinion, is she right, or were Neandertals merely *sentient?* Or perhaps they were without any kind of consciousness at all? Explain your view.

 *Narrative*

Being John Malkovich

SPIKE JONZE (DIRECTOR) AND
CHARLIE KAUFMAN (SCREENWRITER)

Film, 1999. Summary.

One of the problems in Descartes's philosophy is that you can prove your existence to yourself, but you can't prove that others exist or that they, too, have minds. In fact, even if we assume that other people do have minds, we are theoretically excluded from understanding anyone else's mind from the inside: Our selves are atomic, separate entities. In the film *Being John Malkovich* the quest comes to an end: We can experience what it is like to be inside someone else's mind; only one person's mind is available, however—that of the real-life Hollywood actor John Malkovich. That is the premise of one of the most peculiar philosophical comedies ever (and in my view one of the most brilliant, if you like off-the-wall movies).

Craig Schwartz is an out-of-work puppeteer. Even when he gets a puppeteer gig, he messes it up by adding too much of his own life and feelings to the show, shocking the parents and children in his audience by throwing in sex and violence; his male hero puppet looks just like he does, and his lady love puppet doesn't look like his wife at all.

At home, he and his wife Lotte, a pet shop worker, share their home with a number of exotic pets, including a chimp, Elisha. The chimp has a perpetual bad stomach because of a childhood trauma. Craig watches TV with Elisha, commenting that the chimp is lucky he is a chimp: no consciousness, no memories, nothing to worry him.

Being John Malkovich, Universal Studios, 1999. What if you could visit others' minds and experience their lives, seen with their eyes? Craig (John Cusack) and Maxine (Catherine Keener), here at the 7½ floor with the low ceiling, have found a portal in the wall that leads into another person's mind: the mind of real-life actor John Malkovich. Here they are planning a business venture, selling tickets to Malkovich's mind. In effect, the visitors get to move around in Malkovich's *body* not his mind.

Spurred on by Lotte, who would like Craig to get a real job, Craig finds work as a clerk in a company whose offices are on the 7½ floor of a tall building. You leave the elevator by prying up the door between the seventh and eighth floor; the ceiling is uncomfortably low for most of the employees—about five feet—and the story that it was created as a haven for the small-statured wife of the builder may or may not be true. At once, Craig falls for a coworker, Maxine, who is cold and aloof, but looks a lot like his lady puppet. Maxine, however, is anything but a puppet, having a strong will of her own and no interest in him. And their story might have reached an impasse if it hadn't been for Craig's stumbling onto a door behind a file cabinet that leads to an even smaller, dark corridor. He feels compelled

to crawl inside—and finds himself sucked through a portal into another person's body. He sees through the eyes of this person looking at himself in the mirror: It is John Malkovich, the actor! After fifteen minutes Craig is mysteriously expelled into a ditch by the New Jersey Turnpike. This changes his life—as it changes the life of everyone taking the journey from now on: He rushes back to the office, tells the story to Maxine, who finds him no more interesting than before, although she is very interested in the business aspects of the portal. Craig is far more interested in the philosophical aspect of the journey: What is a self? What is consciousness and identity? But in the light of the fortune to be made, he, too, acquires an interest in Malkovich as a business venture. He and Maxine set up a company, JM, Inc., and start advertising: "Ever wanted to be someone else? Now you can." For $200 you get fifteen minutes inside John Malkovich. Soon business is booming; people are lined up under the low ceiling to take the trip into Malkovich. So far Malkovich himself hasn't noticed his mind tourists, but that is about to change.

Even before the business gets going, however, Lotte becomes curious about Craig's partner and their new scheme. She, too, wants the tour of Malkovich. Craig is waiting for her at the Turnpike, and when she drops out of nowhere, he realizes that being John Malkovich has changed her life: It was so exhilarating that she now wants to be a man. Soon a new scenario is developing: Maxine charms Malkovich into meeting with her, but her behavior causes him to suspect that something is wrong. He follows her, all the way to the 7½ floor and the line of hunched-over people waiting to take a trip into his mind. Demanding an explanation from Craig and Maxine, he now understands—and wants to take the trip himself. What happens when Malkovich takes a trip into his own mind? A nightmare: He ends up in his own *subconscious* mind, in a restaurant populated by countless Malkoviches saying nothing but "Malkovich, Malkovich." After fifteen minutes he is mercifully expelled and wants nothing to do with JM, Inc. But even so, Maxine has charmed him, and he gets in touch with her. As it happens, Lotte is paying his mind a visit at the same time: In her newfound transgendered self, Lotte falls in love with Maxine, and they have an affair through the body of Malkovich. Craig feels completely left out—but is not about to accept the situation. He locks Lotte up in the cage with the chimp, tying her up, and takes over the visits into Malkovich himself, thus finally having an affair with Maxine. But here is where a change happens: Being a puppeteer, he finds himself able to *manipulate* the body, the voice, and the mind of his host, and so he supplants Malkovich's mind with his own. By now Maxine—who loves power—is in love with Craig as Malkovich, and they embark on a new life together, as Malkovich in a new career (a puppeteer)

and his wife and manager. Maxine is pregnant, and Malkovich has reached new fame, his body and mind occupied by Craig the puppeteer.

What happens to Lotte in the cage? Elisha the chimp, who is supposed to have no consciousness and no memory, vividly remembers being captured in the jungle and being tied up and separated from his family (and also remembers his mother's and father's final words to him), so he understands Lotte's predicament, and he unties her and sets her free.

Another change is about to happen: What does the portal have to do with the 7½ floor? Craig's and Maxine's boss, an elderly man who is far older than he looks, has a scheme: body-snatching. He is long-lived because he has been able to use the portal to travel from body to body. Now it is time to take over another body, and this is the reason for the portal: He has "groomed" John Malkovich's identity for his purposes ever since the actor was a child. And it is not only he himself—a party of elderly friends is also waiting to join him in Malkovich's mind. In order for them to get there, Craig the puppeteer has to be kicked out. Will the boss succeed? Will Malkovich finally get his own body and mind back? Will Lotte and Maxine get together again? And what will be the destiny of the daughter Maxine carries? I won't reveal the ending—you have to see it for yourself.

Study Questions

1. Do visitors to John Malkovich's mind really experience another self or "merely" another body? Explain.

2. What is the significance of Craig's being a puppeteer?

3. What significance does the chimp have for the story? In terms of the general discussion in this chapter, what statement does the film make concerning animal consciousness?

4. Apply Merleau-Ponty's theory of body consciousness to the experience of being in Malkovich's body.

 *Narrative*

Memento

CHRISTOPHER NOLAN (DIRECTOR AND SCREENWRITER)

Film, 2000. Summary.

While *Being John Malkovich* can be said to delve into a problem inherent in Descartes's philosophy, the film *Memento* indirectly reflects the theory of self suggested by John Locke—that our self is, in essence, the same as our memories, our consciousness *in the present and of* the past. What I offer here is really not a summary so much as a commentary, inasmuch as the film runs *backward* chronologically; in order to understand what is really going on—applying Ricoeur's theory of the three levels of understanding, which you'll remember from Chapter 1, and looking for the plot to make sense—you have to journey backward into Leonard's life to understand what brought him to the violent conclusion with which the movie begins. If I summarize the plot in its chronological order, the surprise element of the film is lost.

Leonard (or Lenny) has lost his short-term memory after an accident. He remembers everything up to the moment of the terrible event, but he can only retain the memory of things that happened afterward for ten to fifteen minutes at a time and never past a night's sleep or even a nap. We know the event had to do with the murder of his wife and that he must have been hurt while trying to save her. How long ago was it? Leonard doesn't know, but judging from his body decorations it could have been some time: He has notes to himself tattooed on his body, so he doesn't forget important things—such as the first name and initial of his wife's killer: John G. And he has a large collection of Polaroids, with notes written on them—some are scratched out, and others added. When he encounters someone, he takes a picture and scribbles a note to himself so he will know who the person is when the memory fades. We understand that he is hunting John G. and getting closer. It appears that his wife was attacked by two men; Leonard killed one, but the other, John G., is at large. The police never believed there was a second assailant, but Leonard is sure.

We meet Leonard as he is in the process of identifying a man who shows up at his motel and acts like a friend—a Teddy. But the Polaroid of Teddy says not to trust his lies, and even: "He is the one—kill him." So Leonard drives him—in a Jaguar he thinks is his, though he can't remember—out to an abandoned building that he has a Polaroid of, and shoots him in the head. From here on, we are let in on the secret of Leonard's life and condition, one step backward at a time; and we come to realize that Teddy was right in one of his first (and final) remarks: Does Leonard know who he is now, without recent memories? And perhaps Teddy was also right in another remark, which we hear during our backward journey: that even if Leonard succeeds in finding and killing John G. (and perhaps he already has! How would he know?)—then what good would it do him, since he won't be able to remember it and savor the revenge? Leonard answers that it is a matter of justice, not revenge—but we sense that there is more to it than that. And in the end—the beginning, where we learn of Leonard's wife, how she really died, and who Teddy is—we realize what kind of a quest Leonard was really on, although Leonard will never know himself, because he won't remember.

The plot is almost incidental to the problem: Can you retain your identity and your sense of self if your memories stop at a point in the past? And how can you be sure that you are still the same person you were then? Can you even rely on the notes you have written to yourself and the tattoos on your body—or might they be part of a plan you cooked up in order to shape your future and forget your past?

In Leonard's words, "We all have nightmares to remind ourselves who we really are. . . . Memory can change the shape of a room; it can change the color of a car. And memories can be distorted. They're just an interpretation, they're not a record, and they're irrelevant if you have the facts." But does Leonard have the facts, or is he manipulating his own interpretation?

Study Questions

1. Based on Leonard's experience, would you say *Memento* supports or refutes Locke's theory that our self is the same as our consciousness and that our consciousness rests on our memories? Explain.

2. Does Leonard have a sense of self? Is it a *memory* self, a *transcendental* self, a *narrative* self—or all or none of the above? Explain.

3. You have read about the update of Locke's theory called *reductive identity theory*. Would you agree that Leonard's self now consists only of his long-term memory and that he has no short-term self; or has he really, in Teddy's words, become somebody else even if he doesn't know it?

4. Leonard has the name "Sammy Jarvis" tattooed on his arm. If you have seen the film, what is the significance of that name, and what does it have to do with Leonard's life and his condition?

 *Narrative*

The Metamorphosis

FRANZ KAFKA

Short story, 1915. Summary.

Kafka's short story is perhaps the most well-known of his works in this country, with the exception of *The Trial,* and it may be familiar to you from previous studies. If this is your first encounter with it, I strongly suggest that you read the original—as I would suggest you familiarize yourself with the original of every story summary in this book. "The Metamorphosis" may be one of the most disturbing stories ever written—but Kafka wrote disturbing stories overall. Kafka's fictional protagonists are victims of circumstances over which they have absolutely no control and which baffle them, much more than they seem to baffle everyone else in their surroundings. In *The Trial,* the main character, K, is on trial without ever understanding exactly what he is accused of. Many readers see the story of K as a metaphor for modern life or even for the human condition as such: We are always made to feel guilty, we must take responsibility for circumstances that we don't understand, and we are in a perennial state of confusion and dread over what may come next. There are many parallels between Kafka's view of human life and the worldview of existentialism (see Chapter 4).

The opening paragraph of "The Metamorphosis" is chilling:

As Gregor Samsa woke one morning from uneasy dreams he found himself transformed in his bed to a giant insect. He was lying on his hard, as it were armorplated, back and when he lifted his head a little he could see his dome-like brown belly divided into stiff arched segments on top of which the bed quilt could hardly keep in position and was about to slide off completely. His numerous legs, which were pitifully thin compared to the rest of his bulk, waved helplessly before his eyes.

Gregor, a young traveling salesman, tries to take a nap and forget about the strange situation, but since he can't turn over comfortably, he can't fall asleep, so he gives up and starts worrying: How is he going to get to work? And how is he going to be able to keep his job if he can't get a proper night's rest? On the other hand, Gregor tries to look at the bright side: He hates his job, and this will give him a good reason to quit. After all, he's only stayed in the job for his parents' sake. Gregor lives with his parents and his younger sister, and they are all depending on his income.

Since he is now late, his mother calls through the door, trying to wake him up. His sister chimes in, and then his father. He answers, but it isn't his own voice that comes out; it has a "horrible twittering squeak" to it. He tries to enunciate very carefully so they can understand him and reassures them that he is fine, but those are some of the last words he will be able to utter in his human voice. Gregor is now obsessed with trying to get out of bed, but he is on his back and can't roll over. The little legs are of no use at all. He envisions that two people would be able to turn him over and get him down on the floor so he can be out of bed when they come from the office to inquire about him, as they surely must. And they do: The chief clerk from the office shows up to find out why he is late; Gregor's father tries to defend his son by insisting that he must be ill, but since Gregor won't (can't) open the door, the chief clerk gets abusive, tells him his work has been going downhill, and he'd better shape up. Gregor, in the meantime, is trying to explain himself as eloquently as he can, but it is apparent that the chief clerk doesn't understand a word he is saying—and even comments that it is not a human voice speaking. Now desperate, Gregor succeeds in tumbling down from the bed, crawling over to the door, and propping himself up so he can turn the key with his mouth. The door opens—and his family and the chief clerk get a look at him for the first time. Utter panic ensues; his mother screams and falls down, and the clerk beats a hasty retreat down the stairs. Gregor tries to call out and persuade him that he is quite willing to go to work, but the clerk hears nothing—he is gone. And what does his father do? Tries to chase him back into his room with a stick. Injuring Gregor, he manages to shove him back into his room.

From here on, what remains of Gregor's humanity slowly fades away. His sister puts a bowl of milk with bread, and other leftovers, in his room, but he is only interested in eating the moldy parts of the bread and cheese and the rotten fruit; the fresh food items hold no attraction for him. His sister becomes the only person to remain in contact with him, but even here, Gregor senses confusion and resentment. She tries to accommodate him by removing all the furniture so he can move about, and indeed it makes him more comfortable, but all of a sudden the loss of the furniture represents the loss of his own humanity: He tries to hold on to at least a picture on the wall, but in the process he falls and is injured badly.

Having lost Gregor's income, his father must now come out of retirement—but that has an unexpected side effect. His father feels rejuvenated by having new responsibilities and seems to have forgotten that the roachlike creature in the room is his son. Gregor's mother still loves him and wants to help him, but the mere sight of him frightens her too much. Gregor realizes that if it weren't for him, the family could have moved to another apartment and wouldn't have to take in lodgers—for three strangers are now living in the apartment with them, without having a clue that a strange creature is living in the locked bedroom. Occasionally, Gregor still thinks about getting better and going back to work, but at other times he lets himself just be a bug, drawing long streaks of slime along the wall in his foul-smelling room. He hardly ever eats anymore, even though his sister still throws him scraps from time to time. His injuries aren't healing, and he is getting weaker.

Will Gregor regain his humanity, or will he die like the utmost, complete stranger not only to his family, but also to himself? Please read the story for yourself, and perhaps you will ask yourself, sometimes when you wake up in the morning: Am I still me, or have I been transformed into—something else?

Study Questions

1. Does Gregor react rationally, as you would assume a person would react who has just discovered that he has become a giant insect? What do you think may be Kafka's point by having Gregor focus on the little everyday human things such as going to work?

2. What may Kafka have intended by having Gregor be transformed into an *insect*? Would the story have been different if he had been transformed into a dog or a cat? Explain.

3. What is Gregor's sense of self, as a human and an insect? Does Gregor have self-identity? Why or why not?

4. If we read the story as a metaphor for a human transformation from one life stage to the next, what kind of identity crisis is Gregor undergoing?

 *Narrative*

Peer Gynt

HENRIK IBSEN

Dramatic poem, 1875. Summary and Excerpts.

Henrik Ibsen is probably best known today for his play, *A Doll's House,* a critical exposure of late-nineteenth-century sexism. The Norwegian playwright was a student of human nature and explored the nooks and crannies of human feelings and behavior in his many plays; while he understood human weaknesses, the story of Peer Gynt reveals that out of the many character failings a human being can have, being noncommittal and lukewarm was for Ibsen one of the worst. The Norwegian composer Edvard Grieg put music to the story, and the *Peer Gynt Suite* is one of the most popular pieces of classical music.

Peer is an adventurer who considers himself quite a man of the world. He neglects his old mother and throws away the loyal love of the girl Solveig for more dramatic experiences abroad. He is not without insight into himself, however; at a certain point in time he takes a deep look within himself and finds himself lacking. Looking for a core "self," an identity, he finds nothing. Holding an onion in his hand, he talks to himself:

PEER: Now then, little Peer, I'm going to peel you,
And you won't escape by weeping or praying.
Takes an onion and peels it layer by layer.
The outermost layer is withered and torn;
That's the shipwrecked man on the upturned keel.
Here, mean and thin, is the passenger;
But it still tastes a little of old Peer Gynt.
And inside that is the digger of gold;
Its juice is all gone, if it ever had any.
[Who's this coarse fellow with calloused skin?
Ah, he's the trapper from Hudson Bay.]
This next one's shaped like a crown. No, thank you!
We'll throw that away, and ask no questions.
Here's the student of history, short and tough;
Peels off several at once.
What a terrible lot of layers there are!
Surely I'll soon get down to the heart?

Pulls the whole onion to pieces.
No—there isn't one! Just a series of shells
All the way through, getting smaller and smaller!
Nature is witty!
Throws the pieces away.

But even so, Peer continues to consider himself a whole person. Toward the end, he encounters the Grim Reaper dressed up as a button-moulder (button-maker). The question of who Peer really is comes up again, and Peer, to his dismay, finds that everything good he thought about himself turns out to be of no value at all. The button-moulder intends to melt him down with other no-good average souls just as you'd melt down flawed or used silver buttons. If he can show the button-moulder that he actually stood for something in his life, he gets to preserve his identity.

BUTTON MOULDER: Well met, old man.

PEER: Good evening, friend.

BUTTON MOULDER: You're in a hurry. Where are you going?

PEER: To a funeral feast.

BUTTON MOULDER: Indeed? My eyes aren't too good, but—forgive me—
Your name isn't by any chance Peer?

PEER: Peer Gynt, they call me.

BUTTON MOULDER: Well that's lucky!
You're the man I have to collect tonight.

PEER: Have to collect—? What business have you with me?

BUTTON MOULDER: As you can see, I'm a button moulder. You must go into my casting-ladle.

PEER: What for?

BUTTON MOULDER: To be melted down.

PEER: Melted?

BUTTON MOULDER: Yes. Look! It's clean and empty.
   Your grave is dug and your coffin is ready.
   Tonight the worms will feast in your body.
   But I have orders from my Master
   To collect your soul without delay.

PEER: But you can't! Without warning—!

BUTTON MOULDER: It's an ancient custom at funerals.
   As at christenings, one chooses the day,
   And the guest of honour receives no warning.

PEER: Yes, of course. My brain's in a whirl.
   Then you are—?

BUTTON MOULDER: I told you. A button-moulder.

PEER: Of course.
   [One calls a favourite child by many names.]
   I see. So this is the end of my journey.
   But, my good man, this is most unfair.
   [I deserve more considerate handling than this.
   I'm not so bad as you seem to suppose.
   I've done quite a few good deeds in my life.
   At the worst I may possibly have been
   A bit of a fool.] I've never been a real sinner.

BUTTON MOULDER: [But, my dear sir!] That is just
    the point.
   [By the highest standards you aren't a sinner.
   So] you escape the horrors of torment
   And must go with others into the casting-ladle.

PEER: What does it matter what you call it,
   Casting-ladle or pool of fire?
   [They're the same vintage, just different bins.
   Get behind me, Satan!

BUTTON MOULDER: You're not so rude
   As to suggest that my feet are shaped like hoofs?

PEER: Whether you've hoofs or pads or claws]
   Be off with you, and take care what you do!

BUTTON MOULDER: My friend, you're labouring
    under a delusion.
   [We're both in a hurry, so to save time
   I'll explain the gist of the matter to you.]
   As you have told me with your own lips,
   You aren't what one could call a whole-hearted
   Sinner. You're scarcely even a minor one—

PEER: That's better. [Now you're beginning to talk
   sensibly—]

BUTTON MOULDER: Wait a moment! You are not
   virtuous either—

PEER: I'm not claiming that—

BUTTON MOULDER: You're [halfway between;] neither
   one nor the other.
   [Nowadays one hardly ever meets a sinner
   On the really grand scale.
   There's more to that than just scrabbling around in
    the mud.]
   A man needs strength and purpose to be a sinner.

PEER: Yes, one has to be ruthless and think of nothing else.

BUTTON MOULDER: But you weren't like that. You
   took your sinning lightly.

PEER: I just splashed about on the surface.

BUTTON MOULDER: Ah, we shall soon agree. The
   pool of fire
   Is not for those who splash about on the surface.

PEER: And therefore, my friend, I can go as I came?

BUTTON MOULDER: No. Therefore, my friend, I must
   melt you down.

[PEER: You've learned some new tricks while I've
   been abroad.

BUTTON MOULDER: The custom's as old as sin. It's
   merely designed
   To prevent waste.] You've done it yourself.
   You know that one occasionally moulds a button
   That's useless. For example, without a loop.
   What did you do in such a case?

PEER: Throw it away.

BUTTON MOULDER: Ah, yes. I had forgotten.
   John Gynt was famous for his improvidence
   [As long as he had anything in his purse].
   But the Master, you see, is a thrifty man.
   [That's why He's remained so prosperous.]
   He never rejects as worthless anything
   Which He can use again as raw material.
   Now you were meant to be a shining button
   On the waistcoat of the world. But your loop broke.
   So you must be thrown [into the rubbish bin,
   And go from there] back into the great pool.

PEER: You don't intend to melt me down with other
   dead men?

Frank and Ernest

FRANK AND ERNEST. © 2000 Thaves. Reprinted with permission. Newspaper dist. by NEA, Inc.

The famous mirror self-recognition test is one that a two-year-old child can pass, as can great apes, such as chimpanzees and gorillas. But what is it we recognize? Even if we know the mirror image reflects ourselves, we often have another self-image that we compare it to, especially if we aren't as young or as slim as we once were. As the old joke goes, "Mirrors aren't what they used to be."

BUTTON MOULDER: That is precisely what I intend.
[We've done it, you know, with quite a number
of people.
At the Royal Mint they do the same with coins
That have got so worn you can't see the face on
them.

PEER: But this is the most sordid parsimony!
Oh, come on, be a sport and let me go!
A button without a loop, a worn-out shilling—
What are they to a man in your Master's
position?

BUTTON MOULDER: Oh, as long as a man has some
soul left
He's always worth a little as scrap.]

PEER: No! I'll fight with all the strength I have!
Anything but this!

BUTTON MOULDER: But what else is there? Be reasonable, now.
You're hardly qualified to go to Heaven—

PEER: [Oh, I'm not aiming as high as that.] I'm easy
to please.
[But I'm not going to give up a jot of myself.]
Give me the old-fashioned punishment.
Send me down [for a while] to serve [a sentence]
With Him with the Hoof—for a hundred years,
If need be—that's something a man can bear.

For they say the suffering's only spiritual.
And I think that ought to be fairly tolerable.
[It'll only be a transitional stage,
As the fox said when they started to skin him.]
One will wait; then the hour of liberation
Will come, and I'll start another life,
And hope things will turn out somewhat better.
But this other business—to end one's days
As a speck of dirt in a stranger's body.
To be melted, and to be Peer Gynt no more—
It fills my soul with revulsion.

BUTTON MOULDER: But, my dear Peer, there's really
no need
To get so upset. You have never been yourself.
What does it matter if you disappear?

PEER: I have never been—? I could almost laugh!
Have I ever been anything but myself?
No, button moulder, you're guessing blindly.
If you could look into my heart
You'd find Peer Gynt and only him;
Nobody else, nothing less nor more.

So Peer would rather spend some time in hell (since he isn't good enough to go to heaven) than lose his soul because he wasn't good enough or bad enough. He now embarks on a journey to seek out those who would remember him as having taken a stand, having "been himself," but everyone tells stories of Peer having a weak character.

Now he goes to seek out the devil himself, to persuade him that he led a worse life in the button-moulder's judgment so he can get to keep his self, but all the devil can say is that his little sins don't amount to a hill of beans; he isn't bad enough to join him in hell. So it looks as if Peer is going to be recast with the other souls—but he still has one person who might save his self: Solveig, whom he treated so shabbily.

PEER: Tell me, then!
　　Where was my self, my whole self, my true self?
　　The self that bore God's stamp upon its brow?

SOLVEIG: In my faith, in my hope, and in my love.

In her love, Peer became a whole man—she may have seen something others didn't see, or she may have dreamed that he was better than he was, but in the eyes of the button-moulder, this gives Peer another chance in life, because somebody is willing to speak up for him:

BUTTON MOULDER'S VOICE (*behind the house*): We shall meet at the last crossroads, Peer.
　　[And then we'll see if—! I'll say no more.]

SOLVEIG (*sings louder as the daylight grows*): I will cradle you, I will guard you.
　　Sleep, sleep and dream.

Study Questions

1. The image of the self as an onion without a core is famous in literature as well as in popular culture. Is Ibsen assessing Peer fairly? Do we have to have a core of "self" in order to have an identity? Do we have to have a core of "self" in order to be a good person? Are the two questions synonymous, or are they different?

2. Why would Peer rather go to hell than lose his identity in the melting pot? Would you agree? Why or why not?

3. Peer is redeemed through the love of a woman he treated badly. What do you think of this ending?

4. What do you think of the idea that lukewarm souls who haven't developed a true self get melted down and lose their identity, while truly good and truly bad selves retain their identity? What does this say about Ibsen's view of life and of human nature?

REVIEW

Key Issues in Chapter 7

Having a Mind, a Body, and a Self

- There are three theories of metaphysics: materialism (only matter is real), dualism (mind and body are real), and idealism (only mind is real).

Consciousness Developing: Rival Theories

- *Consciousness: Sentience or Sapience?* Consciousness can be defined as (1) a general awareness of one's surroundings and (2) self-awareness.
- *Cognitive Evolution.* Ian Tattersall says that consciousness developed in *Homo sapiens;* the evidence is language and symbolic behavior. He believes Neandertals couldn't have been conscious the way humans are. Bennett Galeff's theory is that only humans can

teach humans new things. Merlin Donald says that nonhuman primates have "episodic" consciousness. Steven Mithen believes there are several kinds of intelligence: general, technical, social, and cultural (natural history, art, and language)—the Swiss Army knife model of intelligence. Maxine Sheets-Johnstone believes the roots of consciousness lie in an awareness and experience of one's own movement. For her, undoubtedly, the Neandertals were conscious.

- *Husserl: Consciousness Is Intentionality.* Husserl theorizes that our mind is not a container for consciousness; our mind is its content. In our conscious experience there is a subject-pole and an object-pole; our mind can't separate itself from its experience.

What Is a Mind?

- *The Cartesian Mind-Body Distinction.* Descartes's quest for certainty took place against a background of

Christian theology, which taught that there are two substances—mind and matter. Skepticism was a philosophy that doubted that anything could be known. Descartes's method of doubt was to doubt everything methodically in order to find something that couldn't be doubted. He offered the dream conjecture—What if we are dreaming?—and the evil demon conjecture—What if we're being constantly tricked? He found certainty only in *cogito ergo sum*—I think, therefore I am. Descartes was a dualist who believed in two reality substances—the mind (thinking thing) and matter (extended thing). For Descartes, mind is more important than matter: We understand mind immediately, clearly and distinctly; for example, the identity of a piece of wax remains through a series of changes, because our reason tells us it is so.

- *The Mind-Body Problem.* The problem for dualism is that if mind and body are two separate and different substances, how can one affect the other? *Interactionism* says that mind and body interact in the brain, but it is criticized by Ryle, who says a category-mistake has been made, and there is no ghost in the machine. *Parallelism* theorizes that minds and bodies are created simultaneously and are in sync, but don't interact. *Epiphenomenalism* holds that mind is a by-product of brain activity. *Double-aspect theory/ neutralism* holds that mind and body are just two ways of describing the same reality. *Reductive materialism/ identity theory* says that everything about the mind will in the future be explained sufficiently as brain activity. *Eliminative materialism* seeks to eliminate all references to mental states. Critics say that mind experiences don't feel like brain activity. If we can duplicate experiences with drugs or electronically, will they be just as powerful or meaningful?

A Sense of Body

- Western technology is a logical consequence of Descartes's dualism.

- *Damasio: Descartes Was Wrong.* Our minds are not separate from our bodies; the mind is a mind with a body experience.

- *Merleau-Ponty: We Are Our Bodies.* Our bodies are not something we observe outside ourselves, but the tool by which we observe the world and interact with it. My body extends to my clothes and my tools. Examples are the lady with the hat and other body extensions.

- *Feminism: Who's Afraid of the Body?* Women have been considered less cerebral and more physical than men. Men have represented "mind," while women have represented "body." Classical feminism holds that women must be taught to avoid the stereotype of physicality and motherhood. Difference feminism holds that classical feminism has adopted the Cartesian mind-body distinction and has fallen into the trap of somatophobia (fear of the body). Elizabeth Spelman says that the mind-body distinction has become politicized to include gender relations as well as race relations.

A Sense of Self

- Socrates' interpretation of the Greek inscription "Know thyself" was something new. Selfhood has metaphysical, moral, and political meanings.

- *The Western Sense of Self Evolving.* Charles Taylor theorizes that the West has divided the world into "inside" and "outside," and the "self" is supposed to be on the inside. On a basic level we know about ourselves and our own experience of the world. The Western sense of self includes a separation from other selves.

- *Locke: Our Self Is Our Memory.* The theories of Continental rationalism and British empiricism. Rationalism holds that some knowledge is innate, while empiricism holds that all knowledge comes from experience. Locke is an empiricist; he said that our self is the same as our memories. Critics have pointed out that we don't remember everything, and so if we lose our memory, do we then lose our self? New developments, like the Dale Akiki case, have shown that memories can be false.

- *Hume: We Have No Permanent Self.* We are conscious of our impressions and ideas, but not of an underlying self behind those ideas. Every time we look for our self, we find a perception instead.

- *Kant: We Have a Transcendental Self.* We can't look for a self among our perceptions, because our transcendental ego is the condition or foundation for all experience. It structures our experience, but isn't part of it.

- *Ricouer: We Have a Narrative Self.* Ricouer's theory solves Locke's problem of incomplete memories: We tell stories about who we are in order to cope. For Ricouer, narrative identity is something we ought to develop to increase our understanding, but it is not a condition for having identity. In contrast, Daniel Dennett claims that our narrative capacity is a condition for selfhood.

- *Non-Western Philosophies of the Self.* Among tribal philosophies, studies of Aboriginal cultures and American Indian cultures show that some tribal cultures see everything living as having selves, interacting. Buddhism teaches that the belief in a permanent self is an illusion that leads to suffering. We must awaken to the fact that everything is impermanent, that there is constant suffering, and that we have no permanent self.

- *What's in a Name? Names, Selves, and Power.* How much are we affected by the name given to us, or the name we call ourselves? Our personal and professional identities are often greatly affected by the choice of a name. The fairy tale "Rumplestiltskin" tells us that if we know someone's name, we have power over that person. Tribal traditions often have many names for each individual, including a secret power name.

Primary Readings

- René Descartes, *Meditations* 1–2. Descartes embarks on his method of doubt, doubting his sensory experiences as well as his reason in order to find something that he cannot doubt. He finds that he cannot doubt that he exists while he is doubting: I think, therefore I am. He identifies the mind as a thinking thing.

- Maurice Merleau-Ponty, *Phenomenology of Perception.* Our body understands our interaction with the world, as do a woman with a hat, a blind man with a cane, and a typist who understands her keyboard.

- Maxine Sheets-Johnstone, *Primacy of Movement.* Neandertals are described in biased terms, as if humans are the only ones who have been able to plan ahead and form social networks. However, one can cast doubt on these human talents, whereas it appears the Neandertals had a remarkable talent for survival.

Narratives

- *Being John Malkovich,* film. Out-of-work artists find a way to enter into the mind of actor John Malkovich and eventually take over his body.

- *Memento,* film. Leonard has lost his short-term memory and is trying to find his wife's killer by writing notes to himself on Polaroid snapshots. But does Leonard really know who he is?

- Franz Kafka, "The Metamorphosis," short story. Gregor Samsa wakes up one morning in his bed as a giant insect.

- Henrik Ibsen, *Peer Gynt,* dramatic poem. Peer is a shallow, fickle, selfish person who, confronted by Death, tries to redeem himself by pointing out that he has always been himself. Death, in the shape of a button-moulder, says he has to be melted down and recast because he was too shallow.

Notes

1. It is interesting that behaviorists working with wolves have recently concluded that the form of hunting employed by wolf packs often does involve guile: the luring of a prey animal, such as a caribou, into dead-end traps with some members of the pack chasing the prey, other members hidden off to the sides waiting to move in with a "pinch" maneuver, and yet others placed ahead in the direction of the prey's flight, ready to spring the trap.

2. Ian Tattersall, *Becoming Human* (San Diego: Harcourt Brace, 1998), p. 166.

3. A word of warning: Mithen's book is wrought with small and large errors and misconceptions, but even so his theory of multiple intelligences is worth reading. One example of a misconception: He has numerous references to how children have a lower form of intelligence. His evidence is that they can't seem to understand that a stuffed toy is not a real animal, because they treat it like one; what he fails to see is that the children (and possibly early hominids, and primates) *play and pretend* that one thing belongs to the category of another. There is evidence of the gorilla Koko doing such playacting (see Chapter 10). Such a fundamental misconception leads one to doubt many of Mithen's other conclusions.

4. As you'll remember from Chapter 2, the perception that Neandertals had merely rudimentary tools has shifted within the past decade: European Neandertals are still perceived as having had mainly crudely cut stone knives and spearheads, but the Middle Eastern groups are now known to have had more sophisticated tools, as well as jewelry.

5. Maxine Sheets-Johnstone, *The Primacy of Movement* (Philadelphia: John Benjamins, 1999), pp. 31, 33.

6. A conspiracy theory claims that Descartes may not have died from pneumonia but rather was poisoned. Conspiracy theorists cite notes from Descartes's doctor and the fact that the Swedish bishops at the time were worried that Descartes might persuade the queen to reinstate Catholicism in newly reformed Protestant Sweden. The theory is that the bishops may have poisoned the thinker. No firm evidence has been presented, but the scenario is not completely unthinkable.

7. René Descartes, *"Second Meditation,"* in *Discourse on Method and Meditations on First Philosophy,* trans. Donald A. Cress (Indianapolis: Hackett, 1980).

8. Ibid.

9. Ibid.

10. Thomas Huxley, "On the Hypothesis That Animals Are Automata and Its History," in *Reason and Responsibility,* 4th ed., ed. Joel Feinberg (Encino, Calif.: Dickenson, 1978), p. 271.

11. Antonio R. Damasio, *Descartes' Error: Emotion, Reason, and the Human Brain* (New York, Avon Books, 1994), p. 252.

12. Aristotle, *On the Soul,* trans. J. A. Smith (Chicago: Encyclopedia Britannica, 1952), Book I, chapter 3.

13. Maurice Merleau-Ponty, *Phenomenology of Perception,* trans. Colin Smith (New York: Routledge & Kegan Paul, 1962), p. 91*f.*

14. Charles Taylor, *Sources of the Self* (Cambridge, Mass.: Harvard University Press, 1989), p. 112.

15. John Locke, *An Essay Concerning Human Understanding,* ed. A. C. Fraser (Oxford: Clarendon Press, 1894,) Book 2, chapter 27.

16. David Hume, *A Treatise of Human Nature,* ed. L. A. Selby-Bigge (Oxford: Oxford University Press, 1888), Book 1, part 4, section 6.

17. Immanuel Kant, *Prolegomena to Any Future Metaphysics.* 1783. (Indianapolis: Bobbs-Merrill, 1950), p. 82.

18. Hoyt Edge, "Individuality in a Relational Culture," in *Tribal Epistemologies,* ed. Helmut Wautischer (Aldershot: Ashgate, 1998), p. 38.

19. Robert Rÿser, "Observations on 'Self' and 'Knowing,'" in *Tribal Epistemologies,* pp. 17ff.

20. "Questions of Melinda," from *The World of the Buddha,* ed. Lucien Stryk (New York: Anchor Books, 1969), pp. 90ff.

Part 3

Mostly Normative Approaches

Chapter Eight

Stuck Between Good and Evil?

From Descriptive to Normative Theories

While Part 1 of this book (Chapters 1 and 2) dealt with stories of human nature in a broad sense and Part 2 (Chapters 3–7) examined scientific and philosophical attempts at defining human nature, based primarily on a descriptive approach (although we saw that in numerous cases, the step from descriptive to normative was a short one), Chapters 8–10, Part 3, examine predominantly normative theories of human nature. This means that we look at a variety of theories of what a human being has to live up to in order to be considered truly human—or, as many scholars say today, a true person. This chapter examines the conception of a *soul* and of morality in Western and non-Western contexts. Chapter 9 looks at the social and political sides of human nature—in other words, what Western thinkers have considered to be the ideal person in the ideal society. Finally, Chapter 10 explores the very concept of personhood and its possible expansion from the human realm to other species.

Angels and Devils on Our Shoulders

In Chapter 7 we looked at a variety of theories about the human mind; overall, we encountered the approach that the mind, or the self, is a unified phenomenon. In the Western scientific and popular mind-set, one's *mind* (one's consciousness, or one's self) is atomistic, unique, and a singular entity; it doesn't blend with other minds or selves. (Psychoanalysis is one of the modern exceptions to this scientific approach; it claims that we have realms of the mind that are inaccessible to the conscious self.) However, these views are primarily *descriptive,* attempts at scientifically describing the phenomenon of mind. If we look at the Western conception of *spirit,* however, we see another pattern as far back as we can trace Western thinking, a pattern that is alive and well today: The mind as spirit, or *soul,* is a *normative* concept, and the spirit can be unified or singular, but can also be conceived of as having aspects. In most contexts where humans have talked about how the spirit or soul *ought to* behave, there is a clear conception of at least two soul aspects battling each other: the aspect that seeks to "be good" and the aspect that wants to "be bad."

First of all: Do we have a soul? Scientifically, there is no such indication—which is why the question wasn't asked in the previous chapter. In the 1980s a tabloid pursued a story that the body loses weight at the moment of death, and some "doctors" were quoted as saying that would have to be the weight of the soul leaving the body. But you can tell, on the basis of Chapter 7, that such an answer just won't wash: If indeed dualism is true, and we have a mind/soul and a body, then the body is the one with the weight; the soul, being immaterial, can have no weight at all. A more likely explanation for the weight loss is the plain fact that the bladder voids at death. So scientists are generally staying away from any notion of soul. But that doesn't preclude the possibility that the soul might exist; after all, scientists have traditionally stayed away from a number of ideas that have turned out to have merit. But if we have a soul, how might it differ from "mind" or "spirit" or "psyche"? The vocabulary becomes very fluid once we get into such areas; personal interpretations tend to take over, and there really is no philosophical consensus about terminology. I will here use the term *soul* very loosely for any manifestation or experience of mind that goes beyond the everyday variety of being self-aware—a spiritual aspect of mind, one that many of us are sure that we are endowed with, but for which there is no scientific evidence, just a cultural, moral, and religious sense of knowing.

You may remember seeing movies or cartoons featuring someone who has to make a major decision but who is tempted by personal desires, while his or her conscience does its best to turn that person toward better thoughts. Sometimes we see this process symbolized by a little angel on one shoulder and a little devil on the other, each whispering advice to the tormented soul. Sometimes these roles are taken over by friends of the person trying to make the decision, and sometimes we even have galactic involvement, as in the *Star Wars* universe where the Jedi Knights battle the seductive power of the Dark Side. These depictions all suggest that our moral conflicts can be symbolized by two powers within us, one speaking for good and the other for evil. In addition, they usually assume that we have a soul which not only responds to this internal debate, but whose destiny beyond this life is also inextricably tied to whatever decision we make. Additionally, with all the possibilities that today's society presents to us, the theme of the dual soul has been expanded in popular culture from movies to cartoons beyond the good-evil pattern to conflicting goals and desires within one person—a "sensible" self versus a "wild and crazy" self, a career self versus a family self, a rational self versus an emotional self. Later in this chapter we look at fictional stories of twins as illustrations of the idea of two sides to one person; and the Narrative section contains two stories of "dual souls": the classic *Dr. Jekyll and Mr. Hyde* and Hans Christian Andersen's fairy tale for adults, "The Shadow."

Does Life Have a Meaning?

Often, when teaching introductory philosophy classes, I encounter a certain expectation from students: that somehow, the course—often their first

in philosophy—will deal in detail with the question of the Meaning of Life. After all, the question is generally recognized as a very philosophical one, and on the philosophy shelves in bookstores we often find books exploring the subject of life and its meaning. So it is very frustrating for beginners in philosophy (as it was for me) to find that most philosophy instructors skirt the subject, because few of them find themselves actually trained, or willing, to enter into such discussions. However, it is part of human nature to wonder about the meaning of life, so the topic is absolutely relevant for this context—and the most influential philosophers have usually not shied away from expressing their theories of the meaning of life. The problem is that the subject is huge and vague. What do we mean: The reason for the existence of humanity on the planet? God's purpose for us as a species? God's purpose for us as individuals? Each individual destiny?

The mythologist Joseph Campbell, whom you'll remember from Chapter 2, was intrigued by people asking the question of the meaning of life. He remarked that people really only ask this question when they are discouraged about events in their lives, never when things are going well. When we are having fun, he says, we don't ask ourselves, Why are we here? It's something we wonder about only when things aren't going right. Campbell found concern with the question to be very Western, since in most other cultures the meaning of life is considered a given within one's religion and one's moral system. Even in the film *Lawrence of Arabia* (1962), Arab fatalists comment about the British Lawrence that contrary to Muslim belief he doesn't think anything is "written" beforehand: He believes he can change his destiny at will. Here we take a look at some views of the meaning of life. Which one comes closest to the way you feel about life? Feel free to add your own view to the list: The reason we are on this earth is to _____ (fill in the blank).

There Is a Meaning   For many people who believe in the existence of God and an immortal soul, the question of the meaning of life is hardly a question at all, but rather a reminder and a summons: The story of meaning is told by our religious tradition, and we are expected to rise to the occasion. For some, this involves a belief in fate. Fatalism (see Chapter 4) is the belief that everything happens according to a plan already laid out, usually by a divine mastermind, and the realization of meaning consists in seeing God's hand in seemingly random events. For many, the meaning of life involves a realization of ultimate *responsibility* for your life as well as your afterlife: Do the right thing, and your soul will be saved; choose the wrong thing, and you will be lost. Preparation for the afterlife is of major importance in the life of a Christian person. For the Danish Protestant philosopher Søren Kierkegaard the ultimate meaning consists in a true, personal relationship with God: We humans must go beyond the comfortable conviction that God is primarily a guardian of moral values and make a *leap of faith* into the unknown, into believing that we are not to *know* God's purpose, but to have faith in it. In the Jewish tradition one of the deepest expressions of faith may be found in the story of Job, a successful, happy man who is put to the test of faith by God. Everything is taken away from him: his family, his wealth, and eventually also his health. Job protests at this onslaught of unfairness: Has he not been a good man? Has he ever turned away a needy stranger? Has he ever rejoiced at the misfortune of his enemy? And now he can't understand why all these evils befall him. So God asks him in return: Where was Job when God created the earth? Does Job know how to command night and day? Has he "fitted a curb to the Pleiades, or loosened the bonds of Orion"? In other words, who is he to criticize God? And Job admits that life is so complex that he can never know God's purpose, and he repents his rebellious questions.

However, one need not be religious in order to believe in an overall master plan. Aristotle's teleology (discussed later in this chapter) is an example of faith in a built-in purpose for everything without the superstructure of a religious belief in an afterlife. Within each thing, including humans, there is a potential that must be actualized in order for that being or thing to have succeeded in fulfilling its purpose. The purpose is linked to whatever the species seems best capable of, but also has an individual aspect: For Aristotle, in order to be a successful individual, a human must learn to think rationally, because that is part of the general human purpose. But the specific human purpose involves developing one's personal talent—and reaching a level of mental equilibrium and personal contentment, what Aristotle called happiness, or *eudaimonia.*

There Is a Meaning But We Don't Know It   In our modern lives, most of what we do can seem disjointed and haphazard: We change jobs, schools, majors, homes, and partners seemingly at random—and when events seem to follow a path that finally makes sense, then some accident sideswipes us and we find ourselves in a totally new situation with new challenges and worries. The person who believes in a meaning may look for the message in the new situation: The change (loss of a job, an illness, a partner's leaving, the death of a loved one) happens for a reason. We are being tested, or moved in the direction of a new future—or we are placed in our new situation so we can help someone else deal with *their* situation. A friend of mine who survived an accident and a near-death experience brought back with him the clear impression that he was "sent back" because there was something he had yet to accomplish. In narrative therapy (which makes patients tell their own story about things in their lives), it is often assumed that through telling a story of who we were and who we are now, our true nature and our purpose on this earth will reveal itself.

We Make Our Own Meaning   One step removed from the complete denial of any meaning is the existentialist view you will recall from reading about Sartre (Chapter 4), but you will also encounter it again in the philosophy of Nietzsche: There may not be any given plan or meaning, but as we make conscious choices and take responsibility for them, we create our own meaningful ex-

What Dreams May Come, PolyGram, 1998. Chris (Robin Williams) has died in an auto accident and gone to the afterlife. Here he learns that his wife, Annie, despondent after his death, has committed suicide. Thinking that they will now meet, he is soon disappointed: People who commit suicide are, by their own self-absorbed action, isolated in a special hell of their own making. Despite the pleas of the spirits of his dead son and daughter, Chris sets out to find his wife, with the help of a special person, the Tracker (Max Von Sydow). Here they arrive at the ultimate depths of Annie's personal hell, an inverted cathedral, where Chris will try to reach Annie and save her from an eternity of pain and confusion. (This film is featured in the Narratives section.)

istence. And from the theories of storytelling as an important element of who we are comes the added viewpoint that as we tell the story of our life, or recount episodes from our life, we infuse it with a meaning that was not apparent or even present before. Someone who doesn't believe in an overall meaning may agree that, descriptively, there is no meaning to life, but normatively, we have to make one up if we are to become morally mature individuals. There may not be any objective meaning out there, but we are morally remiss if we don't make an effort to create a meaning and a purpose for our individual life, as parents, citizens, friends, spouses, colleagues, or in whatever role we choose to focus our life's energy.

For those of us who strive to find or create a meaning in our chaotic lives, the sharp dichotomy (either-or) between meaning and no meaning has often receded into the background with a realization that the human condition may lie somewhere in between total faith in meaning and complete rejection of meaning. Suppose we can find contentment in the idea of *partial meaning?* Perhaps with a bit of effort we can see some elements of our lives as coming together in a picture that makes sense, even if we don't get a panoramic view of life. This is slightly different from the storytelling approach described earlier in which you *uncover* the underlying meaning by telling your story; here you *create* a meaning by telling your story.

There Is No Meaning   A view shared by many contemporary scientists and philosophers is that there is no overall meaning to life at all, assuming that "meaning" has something to do with a superhuman master plan. What happens to us happens at random. There is no purpose to the life of the species or each individual—we are just thrown into the mix by chance. The materialistic, atheist existentialist will add that there is no immortal soul, either, and when the brain is dead, the person is gone forever. (See the quotation from Bertrand Russell's "A Free Man's Worship" in the next section.) Life is not fair, no one watches over us, life is absurd (as Sartre and Nietzsche would say)—or, as our bumper-sticker wisdom has it, "Life's a bitch and then you die." A rather cynical view that I sometimes profess, playing the devil's advocate, is that the meaning of life is to have fresh meat without refrigeration (in other words, meat on the hoof—we are all food for each other). For some people, this denial of meaning comes as a natural result of a down-to-earth attitude toward life, a materialistic view that life is simply nothing but organisms coming into the world and going out of it; from this viewpoint, any belief in higher powers and meaning is comparable to believing in Santa Claus. However, for some people the denial of meaning comes out of a long series of disappointments or shake-ups in life, perhaps even culminating in a personal crisis.

The Crisis of Meaning   For a good many people, the most fundamental crisis occurs when one finds oneself questioning the meaning that has sustained one for most of one's life and feeling forced to face the possibility that there is no meaning at all. For most people such an event is a religious crisis: The foundations of belief no longer provide support, for one reason or another, and one is faced with the dizzying prospect that there is no one who looks after us, no master plan, no chance of ever seeing the ones we love on the other side of this life, no chance of any life for ourselves beyond this one. For the British philosopher Bertrand Russell (1872–1970), this realization was the final test of moral courage: Can we face the prospect of no higher meaning and certain annihilation at the end of our life? Can we find meaning in our everyday dealings with other people, trying to make life on earth as fair as possible; and can we find contentment in that alone? In Russell's words,

> Amid such a world, if anywhere, our ideals henceforward must find a home. That Man is the product of causes which had no prevision of the end they were achieving; that his origin, his growth, his hopes and fears, his loves and his beliefs, are but the outcome of accidental collocations of atoms; that no fire, no heroism, no intensity of thought and feeling, can preserve an individual life beyond the grave; that all the labours of the ages, all the devotion, all the inspiration, all the noonday brightness of human genius, are destined to extinction in the vast death of the solar system, and that the whole temple of Man's achievement must inevitably be buried beneath the debris of a universe in ruins—all these things, if not quite beyond dispute, are yet so nearly certain, that no philosophy which rejects them can hope to stand. Only within the scaffolding of these truths, only on the firm foundation of unyielding despair, can the soul's habitation henceforth be safely built.
>
> How, in such an alien and inhuman world, can so powerless a creature as Man preserve his aspirations untarnished? A strange mystery it is that Nature, omnipotent but blind, in the revolutions of her secular hurryings through the abysses of space, has brought forth at last a child, subject still to her power, but gifted with sight, with knowledge of good and evil, with the capacity of judging all the works of his unthinking Mother. In spite of Death, the mark and seal of the parental control, Man is yet free, during his brief years, to examine, to criticise, to know, and in imagination to create. To him alone, in the world with which he is acquainted, this freedom belongs; and in this lies his superiority to the restless forces that control his outward life.[1]

For Russell, the meaning we must wrestle from a universe with no meaning is the human freedom to think—to engage in philosophical wondering above and beyond what our everyday life demands of us. Russell himself was deeply engaged in the practical applications of this freedom until the very end of his life; in his late nineties he was taking part in conferences, trying to bring an end to the Vietnam War.

Jean-Paul Sartre reached a somewhat similar conclusion about the meaning of life from quite another angle. Sartre had to overcome the dread of losing his Catholic faith and with it the foundation for values he had been taught to believe in: If God provides the ultimate moral foundation for human life, then without God there just aren't any values, no good and no evil. As you will remember from Chapter 4, Sartre decided that indeed there is no God, and there is also no human nature. All we have as mortal humans is a responsibility to ourselves and our fellow human beings to create a meaning by engaging ourselves in life and making decisions in a state of despair about the absurdity of existence.

The French existentialist author Albert Camus agreed with Sartre and Russell that life has no meaning, and like the other two philosophers he devised a way out of despair: Camus suggests that we become *defiant,* rather than give in to the meaninglessness, and he defines the ultimate giving in as suicide. Instead of giving in, we must take on the absurdity and revolt against it, like Sisyphus in the Greek legend. In Hades Sisyphus was given the task of rolling a huge boulder up a hill, only to watch it roll back down again; he was then forced to roll it back up, for all eternity. Camus suggests that Sisyphus learns to take on the task willingly, instead of being crushed by its absurdity. (In the Narratives section we return to the *Myth of Sisyphus.*)

But the crisis may not stop there: Any human spirit who finds himself or herself on a quest for certainty may discover that ultimately there may not be any such thing. Sartre lost his faith in God, but kept his faith in human values—and eventually in the idea of social equality. Russell, too, kept his faith in humans, because for Russell as well as for most philosophers there is still the fundamental value of exercising one's powers of reasoning—for Russell, the one thing that makes human

beings free. From Aristotle to Kant to Rawls (see Chapter 9) there is a thread of hope strung out across the millennia that human beings can rise above their self-centeredness and *be rational.* So for many thinkers who find themselves incapable of believing in a higher power, there is still the *faith in reason,* the belief that reasonable persons can agree on some core values such as mutual respect for each other's body and mind. Every single court case that goes to the jury relies on the concept of a reasonable person, the assumption that reasonable people can come to a rational agreement about an issue if they make an effort to look objectively at evidence and testimony and travel beyond their personal feelings and assumptions. But can we be certain that humans can make this effort? Increasingly, people seem to lose that faith. We can't even be sure that we ourselves will always rise to the rational occasion. Sometimes our judgment is clouded by personal issues, and sometimes it is influenced so strongly by our cultural background that our "rational approach" may be dramatically different from what another "reasonable person" may think is rational.

And this may be the ultimate crisis for the thinker: that her or his last hope and foundation, the belief that the human condition is fundamentally rational, may also fall by the wayside. For in that case, how can we ever hope to reach any rational consensus? How can we hope to solve conflicts? As the philosopher Dwight Furrow puts it, the human condition is to live on the edge of anxiety.[2] We may have to give up our staunch belief that deep down, everyone can agree on a reasonable answer—but *we can keep trying.* Perhaps that is one of the deepest mysteries of human nature and can only be "unriddled" (as Franz Kafka said) to a certain extent: that we persist, even when odds are against us, even in the face of absurdity. And then, sometimes, against all odds, we succeed and create a new kind of human paradigm, a new kind of story. The credit for such breakthroughs rightfully goes not only to philosophers, but also to *artists:* Unencumbered by traditional ways of viewing the world and expressing themselves, artists will sometimes shock us into facing a new vision of ourselves as humans—in poetry, novels, paintings, music, and other art forms— yes, even in movies! All of a sudden a new image of who we are is created and will become part of our cultural understanding of ourselves as human beings. Being uniformly rational was part of the story of Who We Were to eighteenth-century scholars. Being driven by our selfish Unconscious was part of the story in the twentieth century. We may speculate that the story of Who We Are is already being written for the twenty-first century—perhaps it will be that we are creatures of emotional intelligence? Not 100 percent rational, but not in the grip of selfish emotions, either?

The Question of Life After Death   For many, the question of the meaning of life is inexorably tied to the ultimate question: Is there life after death? You have already seen that Bertrand Russell couldn't believe in any such thing, any more than he could believe in a children's tale. For those who believe life has no ultimate meaning, the idea of "life after death" can only be answered in the negative, unless you interpret it as meaning that all of a living being's molecules are recycled and will appear again in some other form of earth matter. But that is hardly a comforting answer for those of us who would like to somehow be around, even after our body is gone. First of all, is there any scientific indication that some part of our conscious self may survive the death of our body? Interestingly, that depends on what one accepts as "scientific." Numerous anecdotes exist, from all cultures, attesting to near-death experiences, regardless of religious traditions. As you read earlier, a good friend of mine came away from just such an experience, fundamentally changed, and persuaded, for one thing, that his existence on earth had a meaning and, for another, that there was no longer any need to fear death, because it was different from what he had feared all his life.

Furthermore, these stories have striking similarities: The person—usually undergoing some sort of physical trauma such as surgery or a cardiac arrest—has an experience of floating above his or her body, watching it from a distance, and

hearing what goes on in the room—with a strange feeling of detachment. Then there is the journey through a tunnel toward a bright light, where images of departed loved ones welcome the dying person and guide him or her along the way. And then—the person feels yanked or sucked back into life. We don't have any reports of what "happens" if the person actually goes into the light— because, presumably, that is the point of no return. But if there are such astounding similarities in all these personal accounts, couldn't we say that, scientifically, this counts as evidence that something is happening to our psyche or soul? Yes, we might, but not in the sense that we can rely on the accuracy of the reported experience. Scientists have suggested that when the brain is traumatized to the point of shutting down, we experience the limited brain function as a form of tunnel experience; anxiety causes us to populate the dark with images of loved ones that come to comfort us. Or, as some have suggested, it may be a distant memory of the first thing we ever experienced: the journey through the birth canal, out into the light of the delivery room, with guiding spirits (doctor and nurses and family) standing by. Then again, it just might be an accurate reporting of a real event: Our psyche goes on a journey into the unknown when the body shuts down; but it seems that in order to truly find out where the journey leads, we will have to go there ourselves.

A famous philosopher actually had a near-death experience himself and went public with it: He choked on a piece of fish and was unconscious for four minutes. During this experience he felt himself being drawn to a dreadful, pounding red light. He was resuscitated and tried to come to terms with the experience. The interesting twist to the story is that the philosopher was A. J. Ayer, well-known twentieth-century materialistic philosopher and atheist—a man who had repeatedly denied the possibility that the mind survives the body. Ayer's thoughtful response was that true to his life's work, he still didn't think there was a God or any life after death—but he was now willing to keep an open mind. According to reports, he did keep his mind open and displayed a friendlier side to his personality until his death the following year. Incidentally, while the pulsating red light doesn't sound like the classic tunnel experience, it is a well-known image for those familiar with Tibetan Buddhism. The *Tibetan Book of the Dead* (extremely popular during the 1960s and 1970s), which contains admonishments for the entire afterlife trip, the *Bardo,* from one's death until one's next incarnation, specifically warns the dead soul against going toward the pulsating red light—a reincarnation that one should stay away from. The book says to go toward the white light and turn away from the red light. Believers would say that Ayer was given a glimpse into another reality, as an early warning; skeptics would say that perhaps he had once read or heard about that red light and had forgotten about it until it popped up in his subconscious during his minutes of being unconscious. After all, the *Tibetan Book of the Dead* was popular among philosophy students for decades.

So, since science doesn't seem to be able to help us come to an understanding of the existence or nonexistence of spiritual immortality (as yet, anyway), personal conviction and the tradition of one's faith may take over. The great religious traditions are in no way in agreement. Even within the Christian tradition, there is confusion between the official dogma and the popular conception: Do the dead go straight to heaven or hell, or do they have to spend some time in purgatory first? Catholics believe in purgatory, but Protestants don't. Also, when is the *body* supposed to be resurrected? According to the Christian tradition, on Judgment Day—but what does the soul do until then? In the Jewish tradition there isn't even any deep interest in the issue of the fate of the soul after death, because it is one's adherence to God's Law in this life that counts; in the Muslim tradition the good and pious soul will be assigned a place in heaven and the evil soul a place in hell, and on Judgment Day all souls will be evaluated. In the Hindu tradition, as we have seen previously, the soul will be reincarnated depending on the karma accumulated in this life, as well as in past lives. In the Greek classical tradition of Homer, the dead soul spends eternity in the land of Hades, where there is nothing to do but stand around in the eternal twilight, grieving for one's lost life. In the Viking Aesir religion—known popularly as the Odin cult—the dead warriors would go to Valhalla, the gods' abode, where they would fight glorious battles every day; but their homebound families faced a dreary world of the dead, quite similar to that of classical Greek religion: a cold dark place ruled by the Queen of the Dead, Hel, sister of Odin—hence the word *hell.* The world's religions seem to hold only one thing in common in their view of life after death: the assumption that *something* happens to the soul.

Some people develop individual interpretations of what they think will happen to their loved ones and themselves after death—a vision of meeting again "in the sweet by-and-by"; an assignment for the soul as a guardian angel for young relatives; or perhaps a future in a new reincarnation (a notion that is astonishingly popular today, given that the Judeo-Christian tradition doesn't include a belief in reincarnation). Thoughts of purgatory and hell seem to be far less frequent than in previous generations, but even so, many people include in their ideas of the afterlife some concept of justice: a just reward for good people and punishment for those who have escaped human justice in their lifetime. Later in the chapter, we take a look at Thomas Aquinas's theory of divine law extending beyond the human variety. But first we'll examine three thinkers who, each in his own way, have influenced our Western view of the nature and destiny of the soul: Plato, Aristotle, and Augustine.

Plato: The Troubled Soul

You have already encountered Plato on several occasions in this book; now it is time to take a closer look at his theory of the structure of the human soul. While Plato followed the lead of his teacher, mentor, and father-figure Socrates in a great many ways, scholars tend to believe that Plato's theory of the soul and the state is an example of a mature scholar developing his own

Box 8.1   PLATO'S THEORY OF FORMS

Plato's view of reality—his metaphysics—is known as his theory of Forms. It is a dualistic theory, with emphasis on the reality of the mind rather than the reality of matter. It remains one of the toughest challenges to our commonsense perception of what reality is like. In his dialogue the *Republic,* as well as in many other dialogues, Plato outlines his view of the nature of reality: The world we experience through our senses is not the true reality, but merely a faint, shadowy copy of a higher, more perfect, and more permanent reality. That reality is a realm of the mind, not of our physical existence, and it is only through our reasoning mind that we can access it. Plato asks, How do we know the nature of a perfect circle—or a perfect tree or perfect justice—if every circle, tree, and instance of justice on this earth is filled with imperfections? We can do so not just because we can imagine them to be perfect, but also because our mind can access their perfect, ideal nature. This Plato takes to mean that they must actually exist, as Forms (or ideal entities) in a higher, cerebral realm, the World of Forms. These Forms—ideal essences of everything we know and will ever know on this earthly plane—cast their light into our world and create reflections of them, so we think the circles, trees, instances of justice, and everything else that we experience is real and not just a copy of the Forms. The world that we experience can thus not teach us anything about truth, because we are seeing the truth once removed. Only our intellectual search for truth, going directly to the source, the Forms, will yield true knowledge, and any preoccupation with the world of the senses will detract from a deeper understanding of true reality. Plato's own theory of Forms may have been taken literally by many of his students and followers, but the greatest influence it has had in Western history is its impact on Christianity through the teachings of St. Augustine (see chapter text), himself a student of Plato's theories, some 800 years after Plato's death. Augustine was inspired by the theory of Forms in his view of the Christian concept of heaven: The earthly existence is only a prelude to the afterlife, and the life of the soul in heaven is far more real and desirable than any life we may experience in the flesh.

ideas independently of the thoughts of his teacher. (Box 8.1 introduces Plato's famous theory of metaphysics: the theory of Forms.)

The Nature of Reality: Changing or Unchanging?

In Plato's philosophy of Forms, true reality has the characteristic of being unchanging; the more elusive and effervescent something is, the less real it is. So the human being, always a victim of the physical and mental changes wrought by time, ought to focus on the human characteristic that is closest by its very nature to those unchangeable realities, namely, *reason.* It is our reason that directly accesses the Forms by paying less attention to the external world and the life of the body, and so it is through reason that we acquire knowledge of everlasting truths about justice, beauty, and goodness. This means that we can never obtain certain knowledge about the world of the senses, but we can acquire certain knowledge about the Forms. The world is thus divided into two kinds of reality: a tangible but fleeting, shadowy material world where everything is in flux, but which most people believe to be real, and an intangible, but far more permanent and truer reality beyond the world of the senses, the spiritual world of the Forms (see Box 8.1).

Where did Plato get the idea of measuring reality by its permanence? In all likelihood from two sources: Pythagoras (570?–495? B.C.E.) who settled in Croton, Italy, and Parmenides of Elea, Italy (early fifth century B.C.E.).[3] Pythagoras, whom you'll probably remember from your math classes, held that what is truly real is unchanging and eternal—and for Pythagoras, numbers and numerical ratios have such unchanging qualities. For Parmenides true reality, or "being," cannot change, because if it changes, it would change into nonbeing. It has always existed, because otherwise it would once have been nonbeing. And since Parmenides believed that something cannot come out of nothing, then being is timeless and permanent. But because we *human* beings seem to change with the physical world around us—seasons change, and humans grow older and die—then true reality must lie beyond what our senses tell us about ourselves and our world, somewhere in the realm of the intellect. Parmenides' thoughts on the nature of reality are available to us only in the fragment of a poem he wrote, but he was well-known to Socrates' and Plato's generations. In one of his last dialogues, Plato even experiments with the "prequel" format and has the very young Socrates meet old philosopher Parmenides, who sets him straight as to the nature of reality. There is no evidence at all that the two ever met, but the story provides a very nice bridge between the metaphysics of Parmenides and Plato's Forms—and we might say that Plato invented both the sequel (with all his dialogues about Socrates) and the prequel.

As to rivaling theories of reality, Plato actually had a choice; he could have gone with Heraclitus's (c. 500 B.C.E.) theory that reality is change. Heraclitus was famous for having said that you can't step into the same river twice. You may think that you are still the same person who first stepped into the water and that the river is still the same, but in the meantime the river has changed, and so have you. These two views of reality have each played a significant role in the Western metaphysical tradition, but Parmenides' legacy is the one we know best, because that is the one Plato elected to support. Through him, it has become part of the Christian tradition, where the permanence of the afterlife is considered to have a higher reality than life on this planet. The view held by Heraclitus became less common but has occasionally surfaced as an inspiration for Western philosophers such as Nietzsche (German), Bergson (French), and Whitehead (American).

The Tripartite Soul

Our main sources for Plato's theory of human nature are the dialogues *Republic* and *Phaedrus*. Both were written during the mature years of Plato's life, and while they have Socrates as their main character, as all but one of Plato's dialogues do, some scholars now believe that the theory of the soul may be more Plato's own than Socrates'. So why would Plato keep the character of Socrates in his books, if we can no longer assume that Socrates actually held the theories expressed? For one simple reason: In "sequel" after "sequel"—even in a "prequel" such as the dialogue *Parmenides,* taking place when Socrates was a young man—Plato had his hero Socrates express ideas about truth, justice, and goodness. The very fact that Socrates is the character who helps his dialogue partner achieve a higher understanding lends clout and credibility to the dialogue; so in effect, Plato had a reputable spokesman ready-made to express the theories that he himself was developing as a mature and independent scholar. (In addition, we can't discount the possibility that Plato was aware of the danger of standing by one's own views: Socrates was killed for it. By presenting his own views indirectly, Plato may have minimized that danger whether or not it was a deliberate move.)

In addition to being a writer and thinker with a great talent for reasoning, Plato also was gifted with common sense. He realized that our rational understanding is only part of who we are psychologically. Our psyche (or soul) consists of two additional elements: a spiritual willpower (also known as passion, or spirit) and physical desires (also known as appetites). In the harmonious person, these three elements of *reason, spirit,* and *appetites* work together, providing that person with a formidable balance in his or her life, but they also always present a potential conflict that needs to be kept under control. In his dialogue *Phaedrus,* Plato illustrates how hard it is for a person to achieve spiritual balance and harmony: Human nature is like a charioteer with two horses. One horse is well trained and beautifully behaved, while the other is wild and unruly. The charioteer is stuck with these two horses; he can't choose another one. So what must he do? He needs to make the "good" horse help him control the "bad" horse; ultimately, the charioteer controls both horses. The symbolism is clear to Plato: The charioteer is our reason; the good horse represents our spiritual willpower, while the bad horse symbolizes our appetites. A person in balance is not one whose three elements rule with equal strength—it is a person whose reason rules at all times and whose willpower assists in controlling the desires at all times. Plato's theory of human nature thus sees humans as a battleground between our desire for quick gratification and our loftier aspirations. (Box 8.2 explores the cross-cultural tradition of assigning many souls to each person.)

Socrates explains to his friend (and Plato's brother) Glaucon that "Anger is sometimes in conflict with appetites, as if they were two distinct principles. Do we not often find a man whose desires will force him to go against his reason, reviling himself and indignant with this part of his nature which is trying to put constraints on him? It is like a struggle between two factions, in which indignation takes the side of reason." And Socrates illustrates this conflict with a story: A man called Leontius walked up to Athens from the port of Piraeus and came across an execution scene. The bodies of some criminals were lying on the ground, and the executioner was standing close by. "He wanted to go and look at them, but at the same time he was disgusted and tried to turn away. He struggled for some time and covered his eyes, but at last the desire was too much for him. Opening his eyes wide, he ran up to the bodies and cried, 'There you are, curse you; feast yourselves on this lovely sight!'"[4]

Few of us have conversations with our body parts as Leontius does, but Socrates' story is nevertheless a timeless one: In ancient Athens, one may have felt tempted to view executed bodies; today we have to control ourselves and avert our eyes to avoid the temptation to "rubberneck" at the sight of an accident on the freeway. At all times, Socrates advises, we should let our passionate spirit, or willpower, help our reason against our desires. Leontius's willpower and reason lost to his desires, but that is no excuse for the rest of us. This normative, moral view of human nature sees humans as fundamentally weak and easily tempted, but also as having the capacity for greatness and self-control, provided that our reason and willpower team up against our desires. (Box 8.3 explores the concept of the body as a prison for the soul.)

Plato's theory of the three aspects of the soul has inspired several influential theories: The opposition we encounter in the writings of St. Augustine (discussed later in the chapter) between the world of the flesh and the world of spirit is said to have its foundation not in the words of the Old or the New Testament, but in Plato's theory of Forms (see Boxes 8.1 and 8.3). Augustine was introduced to this theory primarily through the teachings of Neoplatonism, a school of thought linking Plato's concept of Forms with a religious mysticism. However, in previous chapters you've encountered a thinker who acknowledged his indebtedness to Plato's theory of the three aspects: Sigmund Freud. Freud's interest was the human mind and its problems, not the "soul" in a religious sense. His theory of the *id,* the *ego* and the *superego* (see Chapter 3 and Box 7.9) was developed mostly on the basis of clinical studies, but was also inspired by Plato's notion that a person's psyche has an aspect where reason resides (the aspect that gives advice), an aspect where our emotions and willpower rule, and an aspect that contains the unruly raw desires.

With Plato's interest in the soul and his subsequent influence on Christianity, you may want to know what Plato thought happened to the soul after death. In several dialogues he broaches the subject, but never in exactly the same way. In the dialogue *Phaedo,* a heartbreaking but also inspirational story of Socrates' last hours before his execution, we hear Socrates say to his friends that his soul will leave his body as we leave a piece of garment behind and that his soul will go to the

Box 8.2 ONE PERSON, MANY SOULS?

Plato's theory of the *tripartite* soul is by no means the only ancient theory stating that the soul, even though not a composite of parts, consists of aspects—nor is it unfamiliar to a modern person. It is in fact a common notion. The ancient Egyptians believed that the soul consists of several parts that can act independently of one another. One part is closely attached to the body and stays with it after death; another part is able to travel in dreams and may haunt the living after death. The most important part of the soul is the *Ka,* which is of divine origin. After death and after a heavenly court process in which the deeds of the spirit's past life are judged, the Ka returns to the gods.

Shamanism also incorporates theories of soul parts. Shamans (men and women who are believed to cure diseases with the help of supernatural powers) are found in pretechnological societies throughout most of the world. There are shamans (once referred to as "medicine men") among the indigenous populations of North, Central, and South America, as well as among the Inuit (Eskimos) and the people of Siberia, Tibet, China, Japan, and India. There is evidence that shamanism was also widespread in Europe of the Stone Age, Bronze Age, and Iron Age—even into medieval times in rural areas.

The shaman, in a trance, may send his or her power soul on quests to seek information or affect events, while the body stays alive and immobile. In some American Northwest Coast tribes, illness was considered to be caused by soul loss, and shamans often were called to recover the souls of sick people. In other words, tribal members believed that some mental or spiritual part kept the body alive, but the important part of the soul was missing from the sick person.

While the Western Judeo-Christian tradition officially uses the concept of a unitary soul that comes in at conception, at quickening, or at birth, and goes to a higher realm after death, folklore and poetry often refer to humans as if we have several souls: In Goethe's epic drama *Faust*, the old scientist Faust exclaims, "Alas, two souls live in my breast." The meaning is clear from the context: He has a moral conflict between what he wants to do and what he feels he ought to do. In a work that acquired its own brand of fame in the twentieth century, Herman Hesse's *Steppenwolf,* the main character Harry quotes Faust and dismisses it: Not one, or two, but many souls live inside us, tearing at us this way and that. This doesn't mean we have multiple personality disorders, but that we are many persons inside one; we wear different psychological masks in different situations; and we are a host of different memories, desires, and voices from our conscience.

From the realm of science there even comes some form of support for the idea that our "soul" consists of parts or at least that our psyche feels divided; not only did Freud suggest that the human mind is divided into three parts: the superego (our conscience), the ego (our ordinary sense of self), and the id (our Unconscious), but he also developed his theory partly as a modern response to Plato's theory of the tripartite soul, because Freud was an avid reader of Plato. In addition, biologists have for years been working with a theory of three evolutionary stages of the brain. Although it is being constantly revised, the theory claims that there is a primitive part of the brain, usually referred to as the *reptilian* part; you encountered it in Chapter 7: the amygdala, the center responsible for the "fight or flight" decision. Next comes the advanced *mammalian* part, shared by other mammals and testifying to our past as prehominids. Lastly comes the *neocortex,* which is the location of the thought processes that most scientists identify as typically human. We might speculate how Plato would relate his theory to this scientific view of the human brain—and from Chapter 7 you'll know that "brain," "mind," and "soul" need not be synonymous at all.

place it came from before he was born. But it is in the dialogue *Republic* where we get the most elaborate explanation, in the Myth of Er, a story told by Socrates about the Land of the Dead: The soul will arrive in Er, confused at first, but then realizing that it has been through this before. It is

Box 8.3   THE BODY IS A PRISON

The principle of the soul being tainted by physical desires is known not only in the Greek and Christian traditions but also in the more ancient Hindu philosophy of India: The idea that the body is a prison for the soul is known as *soma sema* ("the body is a prison"), and it assumes that at death the soul will fly free like a bird out of its cage. This type of view of the soul usually implies that the material world is considered evil and corrupting in its nature. Might Plato possibly have been influenced by Asian ideas regarding the relationship between the soul and the body? It is possible, but not likely. Trade routes did run through the entire Persian realm (which reached from Greece to India at its height). But the Hindu teachings of reincarnation were not widespread yet, and on the whole there was very little cultural exchange between the two continents of Europe and Asia. But Plato was also inspired by the mathematician and philosopher Pythagoras, who held that the body was unimportant compared to the life of the soul and who also believed in reincarnation—as far as we know the only other Greek thinker with a belief in the transmigration of souls. The common Greek belief in the afterlife is the one we know from Homer's epic poems: When a person dies, his or her soul travels to the dark and dank realm of Hades across the river Styx, ferried to its destination by the ferryman Charon. Once you disembark in Hades, nothing more happens—no reward or punishment, just an eternity of being a shadow, remembering life on earth. Sometimes the souls of particularly evil people will be punished, but that is not part of the ordinary Hades experience;

the punishment is mainly to keep them occupied or give them a taste of their own medicine. Mostly the dead just hang out, doing nothing, bemoaning their lost bodies for ever and ever. Thus it is interesting that Pythagoras would have a theory of reincarnation. In the dialogues *Phaedrus* and *Phaedo,* as well as in the *Republic*'s final section, Plato himself professes a belief in reincarnation: Before we are born, our souls exist in the realm of the Forms, where we have full knowledge of eternal truths. Then we are born and promptly forget what we knew—but a good teacher can help us remember. When we die, we go back to the Forms for a "debriefing session," and if we still need to learn more about how to be a good person, we will be born again into another body until we "get it right" (a scenario that has been used in the 1998 film, *What Dreams May Come,* about a soul's journey in the afterlife; see the Narratives). It seems that Plato believed the purpose of one's intellectual quest was to remember the Forms as one would have known them prior to one's current lifetime; when this re-remembering happened, one would not have to be reborn again.

In different dialogues Plato gives slightly different accounts of the fate of the soul and its general structure. In his dialogue *Timaeus* he even states that reason resides in the head, passion in the stomach, and appetites in the genitals—but this should probably be taken as a metaphor and not as a physical description. Later in this chapter we look at how Plato's view of the soul being held prisoner by the body has influenced later Western philosophy and theology.

the land in between lifetimes, and when we are ready for another incarnation and have learned what we needed to learn from our previous incarnation, we will be reborn. Box 8.3 goes into further detail about Plato's theory of life after death.

Aristotle: The Purpose of Human Life

In a sense, Aristotle's theory of the soul belongs in Chapter 7 rather than here, because what Aristotle is interested in is the nature of the soul, its *essence;* in other words, Aristotle's thoughts on the human soul, or rather the human mind, are far more scientific, and thus descriptive, than Plato's theory of the soul, which involves a moral vision. This doesn't mean that Aristotle didn't have a normative theory of human nature, however. We will first take a brief look at his theory of the soul and then proceed to his moral theory, his view of what it means to develop a good character.

The Soul Is Part of Nature

Modern scholars often find it intriguing that many of Aristotle's discussions seem to anticipate modern philosophical and scientific debates, with not much of a connection to the debates that took place in the hundreds of years intervening. Aristotle's *theory of drama,* which views dramatic plays as an outlet whereby the audience overcomes personal tensions, for example, anticipates the view of some contemporary psychologists that violent films and TV shows in moderation can actually be beneficial to the responsible viewer, rather than harmful. His *moral theory* of finding the proper balance between excess and deficiency in our feelings and actions seems timeless to many contemporary readers. (However, there certainly are plenty of Aristotelian ideas that are steeped in an ancient worldview, such as his views on women and slavery!) Aristotle's *analysis of the soul,* especially when contrasted with Plato's, is one example of a viewpoint that seems surprisingly detached from his own day and age, and strangely modern. This may be a twenty-first-century misconception, though: We may have a tendency to read into Aristotle's theory something that is actually more scientific in a modern sense than he had intended and to overlook the elements of his own day and age that mattered to him. I will let you be the judge of that.

What is the soul to Aristotle? A subject for scientific analysis, just like any other phenomenon. While Plato's theory of the soul properly can be classified as a moral theory, we would have to categorize Aristotle's writings about the soul as a study in psychology and even biology. You have already seen in Chapter 7 that Aristotle insisted that any study of the mind or the soul must involve a study of the body to which the soul is connected. With complete assurance, he states that,

> If there is any way of acting or being acted upon to soul, soul will be capable of separate existence; if there is none, separate existence is impossible. . . . [the soul] cannot be so divorced at all, since it is always found in a body. It therefore seems that all the affections of soul involve a body—passion,

gentleness, fear, pity, courage, joy, loving, and hating; in all these there is a concurrent affection of the body.[5]

Aristotle was as interested in the phenomenon of *change* as any other Greek thinker (you will remember from the section on Plato that Pythagoras and Parmenides, and Plato himself, believed that change is less real than a reality that doesn't change, and Heraclitus believed that change is an inherent characteristic of reality). Aristotle has his own explanation of how and why things change, which is much closer to Heraclitus's view than to that of any other previous thinker, and yet it holds a hint of Plato's philosophy: Things change because of the *potential* destiny or purpose built into them, and once that change is accomplished, what was potential becomes *actuality.* This means that inside any seed or fertilized egg lies the potential, or the essence (or form), of what it may become. Change is for Aristotle an absolute fact of reality, but it isn't a random change: It happens according to the essence of a thing, which resides in it as its potentiality.

Aristotle uses these concepts of potentiality and actuality to analyze the relationship between the soul and the body. The soul is to be regarded as the essence, or actuality, of a body (which of course also means that once the body is gone, then it makes no sense to talk about a surviving soul). In Aristotle's own words, "That is why we can wholly dismiss as unnecessary the question whether the soul and the body are one: it is as meaningless as to ask whether the wax and the shape given to it by the stamp are one."[6]

So the soul is the very essence or nature of a live body, much as sight is the essence or nature of an eye—and without the eye there is no sight. Aristotle uses the term *Form* for the essence or nature of a thing shaping its material substance, its matter; and the soul certainly functions as such an essence, but he doesn't mean it in the same sense that Plato used the term *Form:* For Aristotle there was no separate realm, or world, of Forms—he considered that idea a superstition of Plato's. The Form, in Aristotle's view, is within the material world itself, as part of the thing, not in any realm beyond this reality. For Aristotle, there is only one reality: this one where our souls live in our bodies. The soul is thus the source, or the "cause" of the living body in three ways: as (1) the origin of movement, (2) the purpose of the body, and (3) the essence, or actuality, of the body. This means it is in a broad sense a function of the body, rather than just a part of it. It also means that humans are not the only bodies with souls—anything that lives and grows is endowed with a soul, from plants to insects to higher animals and humans. Indeed, it is the nature or essence of soul in each group that provides the classification of the organic world for Aristotle, from a nutritive soul (plants) to appetitive and sensory souls (feeling animals) to locomotive souls (feeling and moving animals) to thinking souls (humans, who grow, feel, move, and think). If you'll recall from Chapter 7, nineteenth-century and early-twentieth-century theories of a life-force in nature within a hierarchy of levels (plants, animals, and humans) bear much resemblance to Aristotle's theory, but later you will find a theory that was directly inspired by Aristotle: Thomas Aquinas's theory of the rational soul. In the Primary Readings section you will find an excerpt from Aristotle's work *On the Soul*.

For Aristotle the thinking mind is exclusively human. The mind, he says, is an "independent substance implanted within the soul" and is indestructible. When a person's mind falters because of old age, it isn't because the mind is being destroyed, but because the physical equipment is running down. Our memories fail us, our emotions fade, because the brain deteriorates; but the mind, being indivisible and rational, presumably lives forever. However, since it will be devoid of content without a functioning body, this theory of mind does not lead to any personal, spiritual survival after death. What indeed happens to the mind at the death of body and soul is something that Aristotle doesn't seem interested in speculating about. While both Socrates and Plato professed a firm belief in an afterlife, and Plato made this belief an important part of his moral theory, Aris-

totle's philosophy is exclusively focused on the world of the living. He refers to a god, but doesn't name him (or her or it). The expression he uses is the *Unmoved Mover,* meaning the principle or spirit that made movement and change possible in a universe that, for Aristotle, was eternal, with no beginning; but we have no evidence that he saw this principle as an object of worship. When he died a year after fleeing Athens at the age of sixty-six, having been accused of corrupting the youth and offending the gods—a charge that Socrates had been found guilty of and executed for two generations earlier—he may have had his private thoughts about the survival of his personal mind, but he didn't share them with posterity.

Aristotle's Teleology

You have just read that Aristotle believed the soul to be a purpose of the body as well as its essence, or Form. But what exactly does it mean that the soul is the "purpose" of the body? Here we must take a closer look at Aristotle's theory of purpose, or *teleology* (from the Greek *telos,* "purpose," or "goal").

You might say the common perception among Greek philosophers was that everything has a purpose, but it is Aristotle who pulls this perception together into a comprehensive theory: For him, everything that has a nature also has a purpose. Who determined that purpose? You might say it was the Unmoved Mover, but you can also just say it lies within the nature of a thing. A humanmade object has the purpose that the human designer or craftsperson put into it, so Aristotle's notion of purpose fits well within our comprehension of utensils, inventions, structures, vehicles, works of art, and the like: Their nature is the purpose for which they were created, and it usually predates their actual creation, unless something is created by accident. But for Aristotle, nature-made objects also have a purpose, and for such objects their nature resides in them as *potentiality*. The inner nature or purpose of a tree was inherent in the tree when it was a sapling; the essence of an adult squirrel is present in the squirrel fetus; and of course the potentialities of a human being are present in the child and in the embryo. Nature's purpose for everything that exists is for that thing or being to *flourish* and unfold its potentiality into *actuality*. (In Chapter 6 you saw a contemporary feminist use of Aristotle's old idea of flourishing, in Louise Antony's view of the good life for human beings. In addition, you read Jane Goodall's view that the nature of humans consists of potentialities, in Chapter 3.) When we understand the purpose of a thing, then we understand the nature of that thing.

How do we discern the purpose of a thing created by nature? First we have to understand that Aristotle looked at the concept of purpose in a slightly different way than we do today. The idea of purpose worked for him as an explanation of the inner nature of a thing. But purpose was only one aspect of reality, although Aristotle would deem it the most important one. Altogether, Aristotle saw four aspects of reality that he gave the name *causes:* The *material cause* of a thing is the "stuff" that the thing consists of; the *efficient cause* is the force that brings it into being; the *formal cause* makes it be the way it is, look the way it looks, and become what its potential has set it up to become—in other words, it contains the *form* of a thing; and the *final cause* is the purpose. The formal cause is the last remaining element of inspiration in Aristotle's philosophy from his teacher Plato's theory of Forms. As for the idea of a Form as a concept that can be applied to all things of the same kind—for example, the Form "circle" applies to all circles—Aristotle moved the debate closer to the modern idea of "concepts" by saying that such ideas were *universals:* They don't have a separate existence of their own, but the "universal" concept of a bed or a dog is shared by other beds and dogs. In the Middle Ages philosophers ran into the problem of whether universals had a separate existence of their own aside from the things they represented, so Aristotle's concept of universals is not completely clear.

Determining the four causes for humanmade objects is generally not difficult, because we know what goes into making such objects. Let's take a burger. The *material cause* of a burger is chopped meat, preferably sirloin. The *efficient cause* is the cook—Mom, Dad, or whoever is the burger-flipper. The *formal cause* is what we all (as efficient causes) try to make our burgers look like: juicy and steaming, with charbroiled stripes and half-melted cheese. And the *final cause?* To be eaten. If you're looking at a burger commercial on TV, however, the burger may look more perfect than anything you can make, but it's inedible, sprayed with polymer spray, its charbroiled stripes painted on. That is because its final cause is different: not "to be eaten," but "to make you want to buy a burger." So for each kind of thing we have to make certain that we understand the purpose before we can claim to understand the nature of the thing.

What about natural objects, like a squirrel? The material cause of a squirrel is its flesh, blood, bones, nervous system, and the rest of the elements that make up the physical squirrel. The efficient cause would be Mom and Dad squirrel (all the way back to what Aristotle calls the First Cause: where squirrels originated); the formal cause would be the idea of a healthy squirrel; and the final cause? What does a squirrel do best? Hide nuts? We have to examine what distinguishes it from all other things; what it excels in doing or being. A cheetah's essence or purpose surely must have something to do with being a very fast runner; a kangaroo's purpose may be to raise babies in her pouch—and hop. But what about the purpose of a chicken? A good friend of mine who teaches critical thinking has observed that when she asks her students to give her examples of typical birds, for example, they mention such birds as robins and eagles, but nobody mentions a chicken! Surely chickens are birds, too, no less than cute robins or majestic eagles. The purpose of an eagle may be to soar among the mountain peaks, but a chicken's purpose? Chicken nuggets and chicken chop suey?

Here we have exactly the mental obstacle that Aristotle himself seemed to have a hard time getting over. Aristotle had some difficulty imagining the purposes of animals and natural phenomena apart from what humans need them for: A fruit tree's purpose would be to provide humans with fruits, and the purpose of rain is to provide human crops with moisture. This *anthropocentric* view is not unusual, but isn't quite objective enough for someone who is trying to make a science out of a theory of purpose. Before there were humans, what was the purpose of an olive tree, a chicken, or rain? To create more olives, chickens, and rainy days, perhaps. But I think we inherently feel that olive trees and chickens, if they do have purposes, are on a completely different level from rain and other natural phenomena. It also reveals the general problem with a *teleological* theory: How do we know what the purpose of something really is? And couldn't something have more than one purpose—perhaps a purpose that is hidden to human eyes? These are deep problems within any teleological theory, including scientific theories that were in vogue all the way up until the end of the nineteenth century, because, until then, theories of natural science had a clear connection to Aristotle's concept of science: understanding the purpose of things. It wasn't until Darwin suggested that animals and plants don't have a built-in purpose or essence that propels them toward further evolution, but evolution takes place as a grand trial-and-error experiment (see Chapters 2 and 3) that Western science slowly began to give up on the notion of a built-in purpose in the natural world.

However, granted that Aristotle believed everything does have a purpose, and the human mind is capable of understanding such purposes, we have to ask: What is the purpose of a human being, according to Aristotle? It must involve some characteristic that humans have or something they do better than any other being on earth: They use their *reason*. But, interestingly, Aristotle sees the human purpose as more far-reaching than that: For what is the use of one's reason, if it doesn't make life better? So we have to ask, What is the final end purpose of all the human activities added up? The ultimate purpose of human existence is simply happiness, or *eudaimonia* (being of a good spirit). In *Nicomachean Ethics* (named for his son,

who compiled the bits of manuscript into a book), Aristotle leads us into his idea of human purpose. To understand it, we must find the function of human beings, their final cause. Humans have life in common with plants and animals and perception in common with animals, but what Aristotle called a thinking mind is peculiar to humans:

> Now if the function of man is an activity of soul which follows or implies a rational principle . . . if this is the case, [and we state the function of man to be a certain kind of life, and this to be an activity or actions of the soul implying a rational principle, and the function of a good man to be the good and noble performance of these, and if any action is well performed when it is performed in accordance with the appropriate excellence: if this is the case,] human good turns out to be activity of soul in accordance with virtue.[7]

So the soul substance that humans share with other living beings becomes the expressly human purpose when it acts as a thinking mind according to principles of reason—but it is also understood that the underlying fundamental purpose of this is to make humans happy, just as every specific activity of soul that makes animals do whatever they do best will result in well-adjusted animals.

The specific life of virtue that Aristotle envisions for humans is not quite the life of virtue commonly invoked by the later Christian tradition: For Aristotle, a virtuous person is not one who shuns a life of pleasure or focuses exclusively on the life of the soul, but one who manages his or her talents well and *excels* in them. In addition, such a good person will be able to discern what action to take at any given point in time, so his or her response will be in accordance with the *golden mean:* the exact right response required at the time, not too much and not too little. Far from being just an average life, this is the life of *excellence,* knowing "when to hold it and when to fold it," when to be a hero and when to be prudently cautious, when to tell a joke and when to be serious, when to spend money and when to hold on to your money. Aristotle sees this excellence as a *moral and practical choice* one must continually make between doing and feeling something *too much, in the right amount, and too little.* A hero is not someone who gets herself or himself killed in the attempt—except when the situation calls for the ultimate sacrifice, not just being a daredevil. Nor are those people heroes who stand by and tell themselves that they could have been heroic if they'd tried: A hero is someone who acts, and succeeds, and lives to act again another day. A virtuous person is capable of discerning when an action is excessive, when it is not enough, and when it is exactly right.

So for Aristotle, there is a human essence that precedes our existence as individuals: Our specific talents as individuals and our general purpose as human beings are present as potentials before we are even born. This is the ultimate definition of the theory that *essence precedes existence,* which you'll remember from Chapter 4 as the theory Jean-Paul Sartre rejected in the mid–twentieth century. Sartre insists that while other animals and things have an essence (or a purpose) that comes before their individual existence, humans do not: We can always make up our minds to be different, because for humans, *existence precedes essence,* and there is no human nature. As you can now see, Sartre was arguing against a very long tradition in philosophy that began with Aristotle's teleology.

We shall shortly get back to Aristotle as an inspiration for later theories; first we go ahead in time some 800 years to the Christian theologian St. Augustine.

St. Augustine: The Human Soul Is Weak

The view of human nature changed drastically from the classical Greek philosophers to the Christian church fathers, and yet there are unmistakable connections between the two realms of thought. In general, the Greeks thought of human beings as living under the fickle influence of the gods and of fate; but even so, humans had it in their power to review their own situations and mold their characters so that they could become per-

sons of virtue—with or without the grace or approval of the gods. And if a person succeeded, a feeling of pride was in order; "proper pride" is on Aristotle's list of virtues. It is hard to imagine a stronger contrast to early Christianity: A human being lives under the influence of God's will, which is by no means fickle. By themselves, individuals can decide to sin and stray from the true path of God, but it is only through the grace of God that a person can become someone of a good character; and if that happens, one certainly may not take credit for it, because to do so would be to display pride—one of the seven deadly sins. But even with certain fundamental ideological differences, the Greek philosophical influence on Christianity can be traced: Plato's influence through St. Augustine and Aristotle's through St. Thomas Aquinas.

Original Sin

The classical Christian view of the human soul is that humans are bad by nature—not necessarily evil, but weak in their character. The story in Genesis about the *Fall of Man* (and woman) is taken to illustrate not only that humans have an inherent tendency to be disobedient to God, but also that the original act of disobedience (when Adam and Eve ate the forbidden fruit from the tree of knowledge and thus acquired a sense of right and wrong similar to God's) is inherited by every single human being ever born. This is what is known as *original sin.* The meaning of original sin has been discussed among theologians and philosophers for a long time: Some see it as the act of disobedience in itself, but for others the sin was really that Adam and Eve had sex, or at least felt desire for each other. This idea is attributed to Augustine by some thinkers, while others believe that he saw original sin as a result of pride, with sexual attraction being the way the sin is passed on through successive generations. However, there is no dispute that for Augustine, Adam and Eve were free to choose not to sin, and yet they chose to sin; therefore, human beings are not free any longer: We are destined to sin. And because it was Eve who tempted Adam, according to the ancient

Box 8.4   LOSS OF IMMORTALITY: POINTING THE FINGER OF BLAME

Part of being human is knowing that life is a temporary thing. Many cultures believe that immortality used to be part of the human legacy, but was lost through the evil plotting or simple carelessness of one or two persons. The Christian tradition talks about the original sin of Adam and Eve and puts the blame on Eve for listening to the serpent's words of temptation and being the direct cause of the Fall from the Garden of Eden into the hard work and painful, short days of human life; however, the Christian tradition also sees Adam as a sinful character, because he let himself be tempted. But around the world humans have thought up stories that blame women for the loss of immortality: A myth from the Trobriand culture of Melanesia tells us that once upon a time, people used to live forever. When they grew old, they would shed their skin and rejuvenate themselves. A grandmother and her granddaughter took a walk while the grandmother was preparing to shed her skin. She stepped aside without telling her granddaughter what was about to happen and returned as a young girl. Her granddaughter refused to believe she was her grandmother and chased her away as an impostor; the grandmother now went back and put on her old skin and returned to her granddaughter, telling her that because of her disbelief, humanity would have to grow old and die from then on. An American Indian myth from the Blackfoot tribe blames mortality on First Woman who disagreed with First Man about whether humans should be dead for four days and then come back to life (four being a sacred number for American Indians) or remain dead forever. First Man wanted to decide the matter with a buffalo chip: If it floated when thrown into the water, then humans would come to life again. But First Woman didn't like the idea of a buffalo chip; she wanted to throw a rock in the water. If it floated, then humans would live again. She thought it was better for people to die and stay dead, because in the face of mortality they would develop kindness and sympathy for each other. So they threw a rock, and of course it sank. Later, when her own daughter died, First Woman changed her mind; but then it was too late—First Man didn't want to change the rules. So in this story both man and woman share responsibility for death, and the story even argues that death is meaningful.

An African myth puts a twist on the theme of immortality. The mischievous trickster-god Hare, a prankster, is asked by the moon goddess to bring humans a message from her, but he tricks them and tells them the wrong message. What he tells humankind is that they shall all die and never come to life again. But the original message from the Moon Goddess was, "As I die, and dying live, so you shall also die, and dying live."

story of Genesis, tradition has been quick to put the blame on her and her gender. (See Box 8.4 for an exploration of myths where women are blamed for losing immortality.)

This is the main source in the Western worldview of the idea that sexuality is evil, devilish, and must be controlled by all means available—an idea that has occupied people through the centuries and that is still very much with us. But scholars disagree about whether Augustine thought sexuality itself was bad or whether he had a broader vision: that the inappropriate use of any human power is bad. The idea of equating "sex" with "evil" doesn't match the Catholic view that God created nature, and because God invented genitals (and God doesn't create anything evil), then sex cannot possibly be considered bad or unnatural in itself. Indeed, early Christianity, before Augustine, between the first and fourth centuries, seems to agree with Judaism that all of God's creations are good, including the physical nature of humans.

But for Augustine all the suffering inherent in the human condition—indeed, all the suffering anywhere, for any reason—is the result of two humans who chose to sin. Elaine Pagels says in her book *Adam, Eve, and the Serpent*, "Both the cause and the meaning of suffering, as he sees it, lie in the sphere of *moral* choice, not *nature*."[8] Augus-

...SO WE FIGURED, HUMAN NATURE BEING WHAT IT IS, THIS SHOULD COVER EVERYONE TODAY

WE KNOW WHAT YOU'RE THINKING, SO JUST KNOCK IT OFF!

WILEY@NON-SEQUITUR.COM

WWW.NON-SEQUITUR.COM

Are we evil by nature? Are we morally frail and untrustworthy? In cynical moments, most of us seem to agree, as does this *Non Sequitur* cartoon.

tine's view of original sin became dogma for the church. The punishment for original sin has, according to the Church, been for all people to suffer the human condition of living, aging, and dying on this earth, experiencing sexual desire, giving birth to children (a painful experience and Eve's punishment for her sin), and scratching out a living under harsh conditions (Adam's punishment for his sin). So even if an individual has never done anything grievously wrong in his or her life (and babies have done absolutely nothing in their lives, good or bad), all humans are considered guilty of that first sin and are thus tainted. According to Augustine, if humans are in the grip of sin and evil from birth, it is their own fault—they could have behaved when they had the chance. If we view this belief in a greater mythological context, we see that many mythologies have had the same idea that some immense advantage, like immortality, is lost through the stupidity, carelessness, frailties, or willful disobedience of one person—most often a woman (see Box 8.4).

The Problem of Evil and the Platonic Connection

In a *literal,* fundamentalist reading of the Bible, original sin is interpreted to mean that since we are all physically descendants of Adam and Eve,

we are all born into their sin. In a *symbolic* Christian reading of the Bible (which views Scripture as using poetic imagery to get a point across, not to convey actual fact), the idea of original sin means that all humans share a common weakness of character. (Box 8.5 discusses the concept of the fall as a moral metaphor.) For Augustine this weakness of character, original sin, pulls at every person and distracts him or her from the true path to God, but God's grace is necessary to put the direction back into the life of the believer. The presence of Jesus in the history of the world rescues human beings from original sin, provided that they believe in him.

Augustine has thus stated that humans are *morally frail* by nature, but does it mean that humans also are *evil* by nature? That depends on how you define *evil*. If we consider popular expressions of the concept of evil throughout Western history, from the church paintings of the Middle Ages all the way to Hollywood horror flicks, we get an impression of evil as a force that preys on human souls—a cunning and devilish superhuman power that uses humans of weak character in its service—or (in a more secular interpretation) as a strictly human phenomenon, such as the sociopath's extreme insensitivity to others' pain and pleasure at causing such pain. However, neither vision of evil was Augustine's. For him, an evil person was a

Box 8.5   FALL AND REDEMPTION

Whether the Christian chooses to view the Genesis story as something that truly happened or as a good story that should be viewed as an *ethical metaphor* for how one should live one's life, the lesson is clear in terms of human nature: Humans are weak and untrustworthy, constantly tempted to do what we are not supposed to do. We are tainted by evil, and our only hope is to be receptive to God's grace. Once humans were immortal—in Eden before the Fall—but that immortality was lost through a human act of disobedience, and death was brought into the world. Salvation of the soul can be regained only through faith and grace. Another example of the Fall as metaphor relates to the view that original sin is tied in with the sexual activity of each individual, but this is not an Augustinian view; rather, it is an interpretation popularized by modern storytellers such as novelists and filmmakers. There is a time in every human being's life where we are asexual, or at least not sexually active: the time of "innocence" known as childhood. The Fall represents the period of adolescence, when the sexual drives awaken and childhood becomes "paradise lost." It is not a classical Christian view, precisely because it is at odds with the dogma that even babies are tainted with original sin and are thus not "innocent."

Must Christians then reconcile themselves to the idea that life is hard and all is lost from the start, because Adam and Eve's sin has condemned us? No, because the presence of Christ in world history makes all the difference: Adam and Eve's sin has been redeemed, as have the sins of all of their descendants (and in a fundamentalist reading of the Bible, we are of course all descendants of Adam and Eve). Christianity—Catholicism as well as Protestantism—generally believes that faith, which must come from God (because we can't *decide* to believe, only to open our hearts to God) is the "saving grace" in itself. Therefore, original sin does not condemn the believer (or the person who wants to believe) to an eternity in hell, according to mainstream Christianity. But what about nonbelievers who are decent people? And all the generations who lived after Adam but prior to Jesus? And babies dying before they are baptized? Are they condemned? Theoretically, yes. The traditional Catholic view of the afterlife reserves certain not-so-bad sections of hell for such unfortunates. A recent policy change by the Vatican has softened the view on babies dying before being baptized as well as its view on the nonbaptized, so the Church no longer teaches that their souls have to suffer eternal damnation.

person in whom goodness is absent; evil is thus not a power, but a *privation* of goodness. If you read Genesis and track down the stories of the influence of evil, you probably won't find this viewpoint: Evil, there, is a force that tries to counteract the goodness of God, that speaks through the serpent tempting Eve and through Eve tempting Adam—and through both Adam and Eve when they disobey God. In the Bible you actually don't find many references to Satan. However, Augustine's image of evil is rather different: When a person does evil, he or she *chooses* not to do good; this means it is a conscious choice, but in a sense it is not a choice to do evil, for according to Augustine, nobody would choose that. *It is a choice to love the world and oneself more than one loves*

God. And when one chooses the world and oneself over God, then one is lacking in goodness, and thus is evil. So, Augustine would remind us, we should focus on a world of greater importance—the world of God's love and the afterlife—and not allow ourselves to be distracted by the joys and sorrows of this world.

If Augustine didn't receive all the inspiration from Genesis, from where did he acquire his view of the human condition and the nature of evil? He was partly inspired by the Apostle St. Paul, but aside from that, the answer lies in his intellectual training. Augustine didn't start out in life as a Christian. He was a Roman citizen, born into a wealthy family in North Africa. From his book, *Confessions,* which is considered the first example of an autobiographical work in Western literature, we know that he was a rather wild character as a young man, hanging out with gangs and being promiscuous. His mother Monica was a Christian, but her influence didn't make itself felt in his life until he was thirty-four years old and converted, after having left his common-law wife of ten years and their son. Before he became a Christian, he was deeply interested in two philosophical schools: *Manichaeism* and *Neoplatonism*. Both theories held contempt for the material world and believed that the soul ought to shun it, and both theories were, at the time, considered both philosophies and religions, as Christianity itself was. Manichaeism taught that good (the soul) and evil (the body) are locked in battle throughout creation and that the soul has to assist the powers of light so the powers of darkness won't win the ultimate battle; Neoplatonism—the school of Plotinus (205–270 C.E.)—revived Plato's idea that the physical world is less valuable and even less real than the spiritual realm. In addition, Plotinus saw Plato's world of Forms as the realm of the deity: Goodness and reality flow from this godhead, "the One," and the world we know acquires its reality from this primary source. But the further you are from the One, the less perfect you are. There is a part of the divine in all human souls, but once we get down to the material level, we just have a shadowy copy of reality (as in Plato's worldview). The material world is lacking in God's presence, and so, in a sense, the material world is evil. Evil is for Plotinus not a power or a force, but just a lack of something, a *privation*. This is the direct inspiration for Augustine's view that a person who does evil is lacking the will to do what God wants; evil is not a force that compels people to do bad things, but a lack of willpower to do the right thing. This also means that since God is the source of everything good (for Plotinus as well as for Augustine), the credit of being the source of evil falls to the being who has a free will to decide not to follow God's rules: the individual human being.

The Platonic training that Augustine received is still in evidence in the traditions of Christianity:

The emphasis on the life of the soul as being more important than the life of the body and the focus on the afterlife as being the life that our earthly existence is supposed to prepare us for are some of the legacies of Plato's theory of Forms. The consequence for Christianity, as many scholars see it, is that Augustine introduced the notion of the body being removed from God and the soul being closer to God by its nature—as some have called it, *somatophobia* (fear of the body). You met the concept in Chapter 7.

Two elements of irony should be mentioned here. For one thing, Augustine may have channeled an important part of the Greek tradition into Christianity, but the legacy of Judaism is also an integral part of the Christian tradition; of course, Jesus himself was Jewish, but so were supposedly three of the Gospel writers (St. Mark, St. Matthew, and St. John; St. Luke was a Roman), as was St. Paul, prior to his conversion to Christianity. The Gospels and the letters of St. Paul were Augustine's primary sources of Christian teaching, and within the Jewish tradition there is very little somatophobia: One is supposed to rejoice at having a body given to one by God. In addition, within the Jewish tradition there is very little emphasis on an afterlife. The idea of life after death is not rejected, but it is not something one dwells on, nor does one do good deeds in order to go to heaven or to avoid going to hell. One behaves well because of respect for God and one's fellow human beings, not out of fear of the devil or hope of a heavenly reward. We have no clear picture of how much early Christianity was influenced by this Jewish attitude aside from what the Gospels and the letters of Paul indicate; but with the advent of Augustine in the Christian tradition, the picture changes forever. It is not the Jewish joy at being a physical person that prevails, but the Platonic sadness at being a soul trapped in a body, with a longing for another world. Later in this chapter we encounter a sharp criticism of this tradition from the German philosopher Friedrich Nietzsche.

Another element of irony is that it was around the time of Augustine that Plato's original school in Athens, the Academy, was closed by Christian bishops after 900 years of teaching philosophy, because it was assumed to be a breeding ground for subversive heretics. At the time the school was teaching skepticism rather than Plato's own thoughts, but nevertheless tradition associated it with Plato's philosophy. When Augustine wrote about Christianity in the light of Plato's philosophy, Plato's ideas nevertheless acquired immeasurable influence with one of the greatest Catholic theologians in history.

Humans May Be Sinful, But We Are Very Important!

In Chapter 7 you read about Elizabeth Spelman's accusation that Cartesian philosophy and some feminists suffer from somatophobia. Many scholars believe somatophobia entered Western thinking with the writings and teachings of St. Augustine and his interpretation of the Fall from the Garden of Eden as a fall into sexuality. However, as you have already seen, other scholars put the original somatophobia at Plato's feet and say that he is the one who teaches us to disregard and control our physical nature so our soul can eventually be free of its prison; in between Plato and Augustine we have the complete hostility toward the body expressed by the Greek school of the Gnostics as well as by Plotinus. Augustine picks up where Plotinus left off and associates the fear or disdain of the body with a broader view of the purpose of life as a preparation for a heavenly afterlife. (We will continue to discuss the connection between Plato and Augustine later in this chapter. In addition, Box 8.6 explores Augustine's view of gender and human nature.)

From the Augustinian view of human nature we should expect a certain type of political fallout, a policy that reflects his viewpoint. At best, such a policy would support the idea that people must be guided, trained, and educated to understand their own weakness of character so they don't transgress. At worst, such a policy would dictate that because people are weak and evil by nature, they must be controlled in the strictest manner by a force that receives its authority from a higher source, from God. Historically, both policies have been in effect in the Christian realm, from times where the Church played the part of parent and educator, to times where the Church was in effect police, judge, and legislator at the same time, as during the Spanish Inquisition (although the Church was officially not the executioner because executions at the stake were the duty of secular law enforcement). Elaine Pagels has this to say concerning certain policies imposed by a religious power structure:

> The "social control" explanations assume a manipulative religious elite that *invents* guilt in order to dupe a gullible majority into accepting an otherwise abhorrent discipline. But the human tendency to accept blame for misfortunes is as observable among today's agnostics as among the Hopi or the ancient Jews and Christians, independent of—even prior to—religious belief. For quite apart from political circumstances, many people need to find reasons for their sufferings.[9]

When asked in an interview why she thought Christians have embraced the notion that they are guilty, Pagels answered that seeing ourselves as guilty and sinful allows us also to conclude that we in fact *have a tremendous power.* We have lost Paradise all by ourselves—not a bad feat for such "weak" creatures. So Pagels sees the immense guilt of the Christian sinner in direct proportion to his or her "illusion of power." There is a "human need to imagine ourselves in control, even at the cost of guilt." In other words, Pagels sees the story of the Fall and Redemption as an example of anthropocentrism (putting humans at the center of things): We may be sinful, but we are very, very important!

St. Thomas Aquinas: The Natural Law

For almost a millennium the theology of Augustine determined the direction of Christianity in western Europe; but with Aquinas (1225–1274) Christian thinking moved in a new direction, and the Catholic Church of today is still fundamentally in-

Box 8.6   AUGUSTINE ON MALE AND FEMALE HUMAN NATURE

You will remember from Chapters 6 and 7 that feminists have pointed out the strong connection in history between the idea of woman and the idea of physicality, and Augustine's theology is most certainly one of those sources. However, Augustine himself does not take the extremist view that women are the source of evil—but he doesn't say that men and women are equal by nature, either. In *The Trinity,* Book XII, he answers the question raised by other Christians, puzzled by the words of Genesis that God created both man and woman in his own image: "Human nature itself, which is complete in both sexes, has been made to the image of God . . . the woman together with her husband is the image of God, so that the whole substance is one image. But when she is assigned as a help-mate, a function that pertains to her alone, then she is not the image of God, but as far as the man is concerned, he is by himself alone the image of God, just as fully and completely as when he and the woman are joined together into one."*

The helpmate issue comes from Genesis, where Eve is, supposedly, created as a helpmate for Adam. Catholic scholars have had some problems explaining why Adam needed a helpmate, and since Thomas Aquinas the official explanation has been that it is in the task of *procreation* that Adam needed help, not in any other way, because he was quite capable of doing everything else himself. So woman is in the image of God when she is married, but man is the image of God even when he is single. When the human mind thinks of God and "contemplates the truth," then the nature of the human mind is the image of God. When the mind is distracted, and part of it contemplates God and another part thinks of worldly things, then it is to be considered partly the image of God and partly not. And when woman performs her "helpmate" functions, she is not in the image of God, and it is because of her physical, sexual function that she is to be considered farther removed from God than man; but even so, says Augustine, women are of course included in the fellowship of Christ, because "they are with us co-heirs of grace." Women have minds as equally reasonable and intelligent as men's; it is just that their sexual nature places them below the level of males in relationship to God.

_____

* Augustine, *The Trinity*, Book XII, in *Philosophy of Woman,* 3rd ed., ed. Mary Briody Mahowald (Indianapolis: Hackett, 1994), pp. 46–47.

fluenced by the philosophy of Thomism (Thomas Aquinas's philosophy). The focus changed with a rediscovery of Aristotle's theories of nature and law and with a shift in the view of the importance of the intellect.

The Aristotelian Connection

After centuries of what we might call *epistemophobia,* fear of knowledge, Aquinas introduced a new openness and respect for the human intellect as a God-given gift with its own purpose. Prior to Aquinas many Christian theologians viewed the powers of the intellect as dangerous, heretical, and in extreme cases devilish; a famous saying from pre-Thomist times was *Credo quia absurdum* ("I believe because it makes no sense"). A good

Christian was supposed to regard his or her critical sense as an obstacle to or a test of the true faith: When in doubt, go with your faith rather than with your reason. Aquinas, however, viewed the intellect as a tool given by God and, used properly, a tool that could aid in understanding God.

Aquinas himself lived only until the age of fifty. A person in the European Middle Ages was lucky to reach fifty, however, being continually exposed to sweeping epidemics of plague and cholera and a general low level of health care. But for us today fifty is considered mid-career, and it is almost unfathomable that Aquinas managed to read and write as much as he did in his professional life. For his time period, Aquinas received an extremely extensive and broad education in liberal arts, theology, and philosophy. He was born in Italy, went to school in Naples, Paris, and Cologne, and received his doctorate ("Magistrate") in theology at the University of Paris. For twenty years until his death he taught at the universities of Paris and Naples, as well as at various Dominican monasteries, and wrote commentaries on the Bible, Aristotle, and a variety of other philosophical topics. Always controversial in his lifetime, he engaged himself in several heated debates over the years. His legacy is considered the most important contribution to Catholic philosophy since St. Augustine, partly because of his favorable attitude toward intellectual pursuits and partly because of his interest in Aristotle.

A scholar today who expresses an interest in Aristotle is hardly extraordinary, but for Aquinas it was a different matter: In spite of the fact that Aristotle's teachings had been in existence for 1,500 years, Aristotle himself was for all intents and purposes a brand new influence on European thinking. Since the Roman Empire converted to Christianity in the fourth century C.E., Aristotle's writings had been by and large forgotten in Western Europe. Plato's influence continued, largely because early Christian thinkers like Augustine had had a broad education prior to their conversion to Christianity. However, there was a part of the world where Aristotle's works had never been suppressed or forgotten: the Arab-speaking Islamic world. Arab philosophers had taken an interest in Aristotle for centuries, long before the rise of Islam. When Islam became the dominant faith in the Middle East, Islamic scholars incorporated much of Aristotle's philosophy into their own thinking, and one might say that Aristotle became as important an influence on Islamic philosophy as Plato became for Augustine's Christian theology; since Islam—unlike early Christianity—was not hostile to science and the development of the intellect, Islam never underwent a scientific "dark age," and the sciences flourished in Islamic countries at the same time as scientists were being persecuted for heresy in Christian countries.

Cultural contact between the Islamic world and Europe—aside from occasional skirmishes—was infrequent until the Middle Ages, when some contact was established in places such as Morocco, the cosmopolitan city of Venice in Italy, and Spain, which at the time was ruled by Muslims. Spain had been conquered by Muslim armies in the Middle Ages, and until 1492 parts of southern Spain were governed by Muslims; scholarship was highly valued, and Aristotle's writings were well known, in Arabic translations from the Greek. Contact between Christians and Muslims may have been sporadic, but in the Mediterranean region from Spain to Morocco to Venice, such contacts, during what we call the High Middle Ages (the first centuries of the second millennium) resulted in a rediscovery of Aristotle.

In addition, we have the phenomenon of the *Crusades:* Hordes of Christian soldiers left Europe to liberate the Holy Land (Palestine) and the presumed tomb of Jesus from Muslim rule, in three major attempts to conquer Jerusalem (if you remember your popular history, Richard the Lionheart from the story of Robin Hood went on one of the crusades to Jerusalem). The Christian armies did succeed in taking and sacking Jerusalem, but never quite succeeded in conquering the Muslim armies. Eventually, after a series of Crusades over almost a century, they were repelled by the Muslim forces and their superior technology, but in the meantime much cultural contact had taken place between East and West, and some of the treasures brought back to Europe from the wars were the works of Aristotle. Translated from Arabic into Latin, these works became a rapidly spreading influence in the European intellectual world, and Aquinas—who had access to translations in Latin directly from the original Greek—read and commented on twelve of Aristotle's available works. We will look at the way Aristotle's writings and in particular his teleology influenced Aquinas's thinking.

The Nature of the Soul and the Problem of Evil

Aquinas sees the human soul as the psychic principle that makes humans humans: the soul is our substantial Form. So far Aristotle would have agreed; however, Aquinas takes this one step further and declares that the soul is immaterial and indivisible. It has no parts, can't be corrupted like the body, and will not perish when the body dies. So Aquinas believes in an immortal soul, in contrast to Aristotle who, at best, is ambiguous about the issue; this also means that the fate of the soul after death plays an important part in Thomistic philosophy, as it does for Augustine and other Christian thinkers. While Aristotle was interested in humans reaching their ultimate actuality in becoming happy persons of good character in this life, Aquinas views the ultimate goal as the human potential actualized in the afterlife, determined by the choices we have made while alive. (Box 8.7 explores the concept of evil.)

Aspects of the soul include our *reasoning capacity* and our *decision-making capacity,* or free choice (Aquinas used "free choice" instead of "free will"). In many ways Aquinas echoes Aristotle's view of when our decisions are free and when they are forced (see Chapter 4): When we decide things without any external compulsion, we act freely, and God has given us that freedom so we ourselves can choose between what is right and what is wrong and be held accountable by God. However, God is all-knowing (*omniscient*), so he has known from the beginning of time what your choice is going to be long before you knew it or were even born. Thus if you choose to do something morally wrong, it is your free choice—but God has foretold, or rather "foreknown," it even before your decision was made. In other words, God is not "in time" with us mortal beings, but outside of time—so he understands and observes all events *sub specie aeternitatis,* from the point of view of eternity. St. Augustine himself had expressed an even more radical theory of divine predetermination, and critics have focused on three problems in particular:

1. If our actions can in any way be predicted with complete accuracy, even if God is the only power capable of doing so, doesn't that mean we are *determined* to commit those actions—that we have no freedom of choice in the matter? You'll recognize the debate from Chapter 4 and the collision between free will and determinism, except here we are not talking about mechanistic determinism of cause and effect, but God's having foreknowledge of everything.

2. But since God is also supposed to be all-powerful (*omnipotent*), then surely God must be controlling those decisions we think we make freely? And then how can we be held responsible for evil acts when God could have made us do good acts instead, but didn't? Aquinas replies that God may know what we intend to do, and he could step in, but he won't, so we can be held accountable. That leads to the next problem.

3. God is also supposed to be good (*benevolent*), so how can he allow evil things to take place? This is the ancient problem called the *theodicy:* How can a good god allow terrible things to happen? How can a god who is supposed to be all-powerful and all-good allow serial killers to molest and murder children? How can he (or she) allow natural disasters and diseases to decimate human populations? How can a parent be allowed to die and leave behind small children? Why does God allow parents to harm their own children, vulnerable and placed in their care? Why do good people suffer, and evil people thrive?

These are the questions every culture that has ever believed in good and powerful gods has always asked, and there are no good answers. In his letters, St. Paul tries to explain these heartbreaking questions by saying that "Now we see through a glass, darkly; but then face to face: now I know in part; by then shall I know even as also I am known" (1 Cor. 13:12). In the afterlife we will understand God's purpose which is now obscure to us. One answer—which Aquinas himself suggested—is that without allowing for evil, there would be no understanding of, or appreciation for, the good. This answer is probably not going to seem sufficient for parents who have lost a child: They might say that it is rather harsh if we are

Box 8.7   WHAT IS EVIL?

The question of the nature of evil is something that some people believe belongs in medieval times—an ancient, outdated concept that should be replaced by ideas drawn from psychology and sociology. However, for others the question of evil is timeless and as much a challenge to us today as it has been at any given time in history. Let us take a brief overview.

For Socrates and Plato, there is no such thing as evil; people displaying what some would call evil behavior are simply ignorant of what they are doing; had they understood the situation better they wouldn't have done it. However, for Plato, the realm of the body is a lesser reality than that of the soul. For Plotinus, evil means the absence of God in nature; wherever there is matter but not soul, there is a lack of God, but evil is not a force in itself. In the Jewish tradition, evil lives in the human heart: It is the urge to disobey God for personal, selfish reasons (in Jewish folklore, there are also evil spirits preying on human souls). For Augustine, evil is *privation,* a lack of goodness in the human soul. But in the Christian tradition that developed, evil has taken on both features: It means deliberate disobedience of God in the human heart, but it also means that evil exists outside of humans, as a constant temptation to disobedience and a distraction toward the world of physical life—personified by the devil.

A modern Western person is likely to dismiss the question of evil as a merely religious concept and deny the existence of evil forces outside of the human mind itself. Inside the human mind, evil is viewed—much as Socrates thought—as an incapacity to fully understand the consequences of one's actions. A person acting "evilly" is interpreted as being a victim of circumstances: a childhood of abuse or genetic predispositions over which the person has no control (you will recognize the theory of determinism here; see Chapter 4); such a person could, in time, learn to understand the forces working inside him or her and so become a different, better human being. However, there is a growing tendency in our modern twenty-first-century world to view the question of evil as real and relevant even if it doesn't have a religious component. A person whom the court has declared sane and competent and who has been proven to be a serial criminal, such as a serial rapist or killer, is often viewed as an embodiment of evil. He or she knew better and yet persisted in preying on other human beings, often getting pleasure out of the pain and suffering of the victims.

Confessed mass murderer Timothy McVeigh and prolific serial killers such as Ted Bundy and the Spokane serial killer Robert Yates are for many people today evil incarnate. They represent not a vessel for any evil force outside of humans—such as demons or other evil spirits—but the worst human nature has to offer: Humans who rejoice in causing pain, using others for their own ulterior motives, and who have no remorse for the pain they have caused—human beings beyond redemption. Whereas, in the past, many people would have suggested that an image of evil would be the devil with horns and goat legs or a ferocious predator animal—a wolf, a mad dog, a tiger—today it seems that evil has acquired a human face and a quite ordinary-looking face at that. While most people would bring up the face of Charles Manson, the instigator of the Tate-LaBianca murders in the 1970s, as the face of human evil, Manson is an exception. For one thing, he revels in his own celebrity status as evil and does his best to play it to the hilt. For another, Manson actually never killed anybody but just sent others out to do the work. We tend to think of the great evildoers of modern life, the serial killers and rapists, as somehow having their evil nature pasted on their face, like Manson, but the chilling reality is that most serial killers and rapists look quite ordinary. Ted Bundy even appeared

made to suffer just so we can be grateful for when we are not suffering, that we can understand evil just fine in theory, and that we are quite capable of appreciating good without having to suffer evil first. But some parents have a different attitude: In the spring of 2001 the Peruvian air force shot down a plane carrying an American missionary husband and wife and their two children, assum-

From 1996 to 1998 a serial killer preyed on women in Spokane, Washington. Speculations were that since he had eluded capture, he must be a particularly intelligent, evil monster. When Robert Lee Yates, Jr., was finally captured in April 2000, the community as well as his victims' families were astonished to find that he appeared to be an extremely ordinary man, both in looks and in lifestyle: The mother of one victim exclaimed in court that "He looks just like a little mouse." Married with five children and living in an upper-middle-class neighborhood, Yates didn't fit the profile of a serial killer—but therein lies perhaps a secret of human nature: One of evil's many faces is when it masquerades as normalcy. Having confessed to 13 murders, Yates now serves a sentence of 408 years and is scheduled to stand trial for two more murders in Tacoma in 2002.

handsome to most people. The philosopher Hannah Arendt, in her analysis of the Nazi leader Karl Adolf Eichmann, coined a phrase that has become famous: *the banality of evil.* Arendt saw most evil acts as having been committed by ordinary people who mainly just go with the flow and follow orders. She may be right that this represents a form of evil, but what most people today identify as evil is the *deliberate* choice to harm others, for self-gratification, gain, or to make some political point. And it seems that people who make such choices don't wear their evil heart on their sleeve; perhaps one of the hallmarks of the deliberately evil per-

son is that he or she is capable of blending in—of *looking* and *acting banal.* You will recall that Chapter 1 listed the body as a moral symbol, as one of the expressions of human nature: It used to be common for people to equate evil with some form of physical disability or deformity (as you will see at the end of this chapter, in the story of *Dr. Jekyll and Mr. Hyde*); however, reality has taught us that we can't judge a book by its cover or a serial killer by his looks. Kind people can have unusual, disturbing physical features (which the story of *Beauty and the Beast* teaches us) and evil people may look like we do.

ing that it was a drug-running aircraft. The wife and the adopted baby daughter died, but the husband and their son survived. When asked on *Good Morning America* by Diane Sawyer what kind of

god would allow for such a thing to happen, the missionary replied that, in his view, the real life is the next life. In other words, this life is just a preparation for what comes next.

For many people dealing with the theodicy problem there seem to be two answers: Either God is *not all-powerful* and can't prevent evil from happening—or he is *not perfectly good* and does not have the happiness of individuals at heart. However, for the Christian tradition and for Aquinas in particular it is vital to believe that God is both good and powerful, so some Christians have chosen to give the problem a different answer: that the human conception of "goodness" need not be what God sees as good. This answer is completely within the tradition of St. Paul, but even so, to many people—Christians as well as non-Christians—the theodicy problem hasn't been solved satisfactorily, either emotionally or intellectually, especially since many believe there is a difference between the "evil" that happens to people in the form of accidents and "evil" that happens as a deliberate act by a human perpetrator. A parent who has lost a child to an illness or in an accident may find peace in the thought that God works in mysterious ways—but a parent who has lost a child to a murderer may find it harder to find peace in that same thought.

Natural Law

The most important Thomistic legacy may have been the development of the ancient Stoic concept of *natural law*: For St. Thomas we are born with certain God-given qualities, and (as Aristotle would say) these qualities have a *purpose*; fulfilling the purpose of the nature that God has given us with the help of our reason becomes one of the goals of human life. Thomistic ethics is thus *teleological,* believing that human life has a divine purpose; and since the purpose exists, it becomes a moral requirement to fulfill it: If one does not strive to fulfill one's God-given purpose, then one is committing a sin. (If you remember the section in Chapter 3 about the *naturalistic fallacy,* you may recognize the topic here: making a mental jump from what *is* the case to what *ought* to be done. Thomistic philosophy does not believe one cannot make that jump, while much of

modern philosophy frowns on moving from an "is" to an "ought.")

For Aquinas, the law is a dictate coming from the ruler of a community. Since (in his view) the community of the universe is governed by God, making it the most perfect community, then the law of the universe is eternal. All things in the universe partake in this *eternal law* insofar as God has determined their nature. And since humans are rational beings, designed by God to have and to use their reason, then humans participate in the eternal law in a very special way: Our reason can help us understand what God's purpose for humanity is, and we can pursue that purpose rationally. This is what Aquinas calls *natural law.* (In Chapter 9 you'll see the British philosopher John Locke refer to the concept of natural law about 500 years later.) On the level of human existence, we of course also have *human laws,* which ideally reflect our understanding of God's purpose—the natural law. But in addition to these three kinds of laws there is also *divine law.* Divine laws take over where human laws are insufficient, for four major reasons: (1) The ultimate purpose for humans is being happy—not in this life, but in the afterlife, in eternal bliss. And since this goal is far beyond what human reason can fathom, we need a divine law to guide us in the right direction. (2) Because human judgments vary, even among rational people of good will, we need a divine law to settle such disagreements. (3) Humans may be able to discern the actions of others, but not what is in their hearts; however, humans must be judged on what is within their hearts, too, so we need a divine law that can take secret thoughts and feelings into account. (4) Within the human legal and moral systems we just can't catch and punish all criminals; some evil acts remain secret forever, but not to God. So we need God's divine law to punish those who have gone undetected by human justice.

But what exactly is natural law? It consists of rules that should be obvious to the human rational mind, because they outline *what is good for humans,* given that human nature is created by God.

As Aristotle would say, everything has an end or a purpose, and when a human, an animal, or a thing fulfills its purpose, then it has actualized its potential and—in contemporary language—is a success. Aquinas relies completely on Aristotle's concept of teleology here: Humans have a potential given by God that we must strive to make actual in order to be morally good persons. What promotes this goal is what Aquinas calls good, and what deflects from the goal is evil. Natural law dictates that we follow the natural inclinations which our reason points out to us. This law is the same for everyone, for our purpose is the same: to eventually reach happiness in the beyond. And what are those natural inclinations? Aquinas focuses on three primary inclinations: (1) The inclination to self-preservation, (2) the inclination to procreate, and (3) the inclination to seek knowledge, in particular about God, and to live in society. In *Summa Theologica* he writes,

> Since, however, good has the nature of an end, and evil, the nature of a contrary, hence it is that all those things to which man has a natural inclination are naturally apprehended by reason as being good, and consequently as objects of pursuit, and their contraries as evil, and objects of avoidance. Therefore, the order of the precepts of the natural law is according to the order of natural inclination. For there is in man, first of all, an inclination to good in accordance with the nature which he has in common with all substances, inasmuch, namely, as every substance seeks the preservation of its own being, according to its nature; and by reason of this inclination, whatever is a means of preserving human life, and of warding off its obstacles, belongs to the natural law. Secondly, there is in man an inclination to things that pertain to him more specially, according to the nature which he has in common with other animals, and in virtue of this inclination, those things are said to belong to the natural law which nature has taught to all animals, such as sexual intercourse, the education of offspring, and so forth. Thirdly, there is in man an inclination to good according to the nature of

his reason, which nature is proper to him. Thus man has a natural inclination to know the truth about God, and to live in society; and in this respect, whatever pertains to this inclination belongs to the natural law: e.g., to shun ignorance, to avoid offending those among whom one has to live, and other such things regarding the above inclination.[10]

So the human good consists of following these inclinations properly, in the right way and at the right time and avoiding anything that might hinder these inclinations in being fulfilled. This means that Aquinas bases a theory of ethics on a theory of human nature.

Consequences and Criticism

The immediate consequence of Aquinas's natural law theory is that humans are given the capacity and the right to choose what is good for them on the basis of their own intellect, not because of moral or religious dictates from above. As such, this theory is equal in magnitude to the moral theory presented by Immanuel Kant some 600 years later (see Chapter 10), which proclaims that the human rational mind can determine the difference between right and wrong by simply asking if it is possible to imagine one's actions becoming a universal moral law, without having to resort to any moral, legal, or religious authority. Aquinas, too, had faith in humanity's rational capacity to understand the purpose of human life, and thus he encouraged the use of the mind—although he saw the third natural inclination to be not just the quest for knowledge in general, but specifically the quest for knowledge about God's will.

However, Aquinas's focus on natural inclinations also begs the question, because who defines what a natural inclination is? Not everything we feel like doing is acceptable as a "natural inclination" within the Thomistic philosophy, but *what makes one inclination more natural than another?* Aquinas says that our intellect can understand God's purpose for us, and that will identify the truly good natural inclinations; but does that mean that other inclinations are evil? Or that things we do that aren't "natural" are evil—such as using fire or heavy machinery? We may have a natural inclination to scratch ourselves in public, but that is surely not one of God's purposes for us. Many people claim that they have a natural inclination to be promiscuous—they just can't help it! But that is not the kind of inclination Aquinas is talking about, either. In both cases it may be clear that the examples aren't relevant, for we have other natural outlets for both our need to scratch (in private) and having sex (such as in marriage), and presumably all it takes is strength of character.

But there are inclinations that feel deeply natural, as part of an individual's purpose, such as sexual orientation: Since Aquinas accepts the natural inclination to propagate as one of God's purposes for us, how does he view the inclination toward same-sex relationships? By definition, it is an obstacle to the inclination to procreate and becomes evil—even though the homosexual/lesbian inclination feels utterly natural to many individuals (and did so even in Aquinas's day). The demand of natural law that humans procreate has met criticism from both outside and inside the Catholic Church, since Aquinas's viewpoint is the basis for the Catholic policy against contraception, abortion, premarital sex, extramarital sex, in vitro fertilization, homosexuality, divorce, and—lately—human cloning. Any action that hinders the natural creation of new humans is a sin if it doesn't happen within the proper frame, which for Aquinas is marriage (because for Aquinas it is natural and good for husband and wife to be partners in the raising of children). But it is also a sin to create new humans in any way other than through intercourse between husband and wife; hence the ban on in vitro fertilization and human cloning.

Aquinas's influence on Catholic theology, which looms so large today, was actually not a major factor in Catholic thinking until the late nineteenth century. In 1879 a revival of his philosophy was initiated by Pope Leo XIII, and in 1914 a group of Catholic teachers created a document of twenty-four propositions containing what they saw as Aquinas's essential philosophy. Today those propositions form the backbone of much of official Catholic philosophy. Critics of this endeavor point out that these propositions appear to be rigid dogmas, while Aquinas himself was far more flexible and open-minded and interested in a much broader spectrum of subjects.

Kant: Evil Equals Deliberate Selfishness

Now we jump to the eighteenth century: You have encountered Immanuel Kant several times in this book, most recently in Chapter 7, where we discussed his theory of the transcendental self. However great Kant's influence has been in the field of epistemology (theory of knowledge), many philosophers regard his most important contributions as being within moral theory (and we return to Kant as a moral philosopher in Chapter 10). Kant agrees with Aquinas that God has endowed humans with reason and that we can, and should, approach moral issues through our reason instead of emotionally. However, Kant goes farther than that: Our reason was given to us not just to seek knowledge about God, but also to explore the moral realm as *autonomous lawgivers,* because we have the tools we need to understand it in the form of our own rationality, even if we don't seek the answers in God's teachings.

As religious as Kant was, he pointed out that morality does not need religion because the human rational mind is completely capable of appreciating the concept of an unconditional moral law. We are *autonomous* because we just need to consult our own reason to find the answers to moral problems; we are *lawgivers* because we can set up rational moral laws for ourselves. And if everyone focuses on being rational instead of being selfish and emotional about moral issues, we will be in full agreement about the laws we set for ourselves. Kant's most famous contribution to solving moral problems is what he calls the *categorical imperative,* an absolute, unconditional command: Ask yourself, when you have a situation in which you are torn between something you want to do and something you know you ought to do, "Could I want the principle of what I am about to do to become a universal law for everyone to follow?" Because if you could only allow yourself to do it, but no one else, then it is an irrational rule that must be discarded: It doesn't meet the requirements of a moral, universal law.

Kant believes that this is not an easy thing to do, because we have different levels in our human nature: We have an *animality* disposition which is purely focused on self-preservation; we have a disposition of *humanity,* which prompts us to compare our own situation with that of others and achieve happiness if we are as well or better off than others; and we have a *personality* disposition, which entails respect for the moral law. In addition, we have three degrees of propensity toward evil, ranging from mild to severe: We can suffer from *frailty* (what people usually call a weak character), from *impurity* (meaning that we may do the right thing but for selfish reasons), and from *corruption* (deliberately disregarding the moral law).

Now what makes someone more evil than someone else? That depends on the moral capacity of his or her willpower: The stronger the willpower to shun evil, the more of a moral character that person has, but it all boils down to a conscious decision, not to some kind of weak character that we can't help. Kant says that "nothing is morally evil . . . but that which is our own *act.*" Someone whose moral willpower is frail makes mistakes from time to time, but someone whose willpower is corrupt has chosen to not even try to fight temptation. This means that Kant thinks that there is indeed a radical evil inherent in our human nature. People are cruel, selfish, and tend to call someone "good" who is just doing what everyone else is doing. But why is this? Could it be what the tradition since Augustine has claimed, a result of humanity's *sensuous and sexual nature?* Kant says no, because we are sexual beings by nature, and since it isn't our doing, we can't be held accountable for that. It would make even less sense to say that humans are evil because their *reason* is evil—because for Kant (being a solid member of the Age of Enlightenment, or the Age of Reason)

reason just can't be evil when applied correctly. What makes people evil is *deliberately choosing self-love,* or selfishness, over the moral law that their reason tells them to follow.

This also means that Kant, being a Protestant, does not believe in original sin—because if sin originated in the beginning of time due to somebody else's morally flawed decision, then how can each new individual be held accountable for that? Instead, Kant sees the origin of evil in each single individual, because we are responsible for what we do: We can choose to respect the moral law and fight the temptations presented to us through our dispositions of frailty and impurity. Or we can choose to discard it and give in to "the perversity of the heart." Make the morally wrong choice *deliberately,* and you're choosing evil.

As you can tell, Kant is a proponent of the concept of free will and sides with other voices in philosophy (see Chapter 4) who argue that without freedom of the will we lose the concept of moral responsibility. He is not without understanding for the difficulties this presents to the ordinary human being: We are frail, and we tend to lie to ourselves about our true motivations. But he is also unwilling to accept any excuses, because we are free agents, and at any given time any one of us can decide to do the right thing.

So can we ever lie, even to save our life or someone else's life? No, because then we elevate practical concerns over respect for the moral law. May we ever choose to do something that runs against the moral law, if it has great social consequences? No, because it shows disrespect for the moral law. Kant's refusal to accept exceptions to his moral rule has elevated him to the status of a moral beacon for many readers, but for others his ethics is too rigid and unforgiving to serve us in real life. (Box 8.8 looks at what it has meant to be "a good person" throughout history.)

Nietzsche: Beyond Good and Evil

In this chapter on the nature of the soul and the issue of good and evil, we have until now looked at major Western influences in antiquity and the

Box 8.8   WHAT IS IT TO BE GOOD?

Plato believed that the highest level in the world of Forms was the Form of the Good, radiating its reality to all lower levels. Most, but not all, religions see their god or gods as being "good"—usually meaning that they have human interests at heart (in the chapter text you'll find a discussion of the paradox that God is supposed to be good and yet allows terrible things to happen: the *theodicy* problem). But what is it for a *human being* to be good? Ethicists and moralists have given us definitions and rules for good behavior, and introductory classes in ethics or value theory usually do their best to cover the most influential of them. In no way can I do justice to all such theories in this context, so a brief overview will have to suffice.

In most traditional cultures moral goodness is closely tied with the notion of *obedience:* Obey your god, your clergy, your officials, and your parents, and you will be officially counted among the good. We find this in the Genesis story of the Fall to Confucius in China to the European Middle Ages and beyond. (As you will see in the chapter text, this is what Nietzsche calls a herd morality.) A close relative is the concept of *respect:* Respect for elders (and "betters," in societies that create social hierarchies) is another traditional hallmark of goodness. For the ancient Greeks, being good usually meant *being good at something,* ultimately at being human; the word *areté,* or "excellence," is the traditional Greek concept of virtue. In the hands of Socrates the concept of goodness acquires a new meaning: a good life is *a life examined* morally and intellectually; going through life with blinders on and without questioning authority is a bad life. With Christianity the notions of *compassion* and *forgiveness* enter the stage of Western culture—although in Asia, from Buddha to

Mencius, the idea of compassion also plays a pivotal role. In Western moral philosophy the concept of moral goodness has branched out in two major directions in the past few hundred years: One is *increasing happiness* and *decreasing misery* for others and oneself, as taught by utilitarianism (see Chapter 10); and the other is *doing one's duty* because it is the right thing to do—the core moral teaching of Kant (see chapter text and Chapter 10).

If you ask a person outside of the philosophical tradition today how he or she would define a good person, you will most often get an example, or an *exemplar*—a role model: Jesus Christ, the Buddha, Mother Teresa, Dr. Martin Luther King, Jr., John F. Kennedy, Nelson Mandela, Jane Goodall, Ronald Reagan, Rosa Parks, Hillary Rodham Clinton (I have seen all these names and more in student papers), or perhaps celebrities who have chosen to make the news media a vehicle for their personal causes. Less often do I hear people mention persons close to them as examples of moral goodness: Mom, Dad, Grandma, Grandpa. But how to define goodness itself? Obedience is not high on the list anymore and neither is respect for elders, but *compassion* and the *desire not to do harm* are; however, some ethicists say that *a sense of justice* should be added to these virtues as essential for a person to be good, lest one's compassion go astray and one feels sorry for people who haven't deserved it. Forgiveness may be a strong element in the Christian tradition, but some believe it should have its earthly limits: Some modern voices say the only person with a right to forgive a perpetrator is his or her victim. The rest of us will just have to find a balance between compassion and justice.

Middle Ages, with one representative from the eighteenth century. But of course thinkers, poets, theologians, novelists, and just about everyone else has weighed in on the subject ever since. A philosopher who made a point of going against the grain in his evaluation of the traditional concepts was Friedrich Nietzsche (1844–1900).

The Masters of Suspicion

The French philosopher Paul Ricoeur, whom you met in Chapter 1, says there are three thinkers who have developed the art of suspicion to the point of mastery: Friedrich Nietzsche, Karl Marx, and Sigmund Freud. You have already encountered Freud in Chapters 3, 6, and 7, and you will meet Marx in Chapter 9. The art of suspicion is important to Ricoeur. It means being able to think critically and with an open mind: We question the logic, the evidence, and the motives of the author of whatever text we are studying. But in a more specific sense it means to question our basic cultural assumptions. Freud questioned our assumption that the human consciousness controls human life; Marx questioned the assumption that culture is independent of economics; and Nietzsche questions the underlying assumptions of Western moral values. Ricoeur says these three thinkers have given Western thinking a jolt that has forced us out of complacency forever: We can't think in terms of the mind, economics, culture, or ethics without taking these men's theories into account. But for Ricoeur it isn't enough for a philosopher to "suspect." Pointing out the hidden assumptions in a text is only half the task. The other half consists in being able to truly listen to what the text wants to say. A complete understanding of something—a text we read, a cultural phenomenon we investigate, a person we talk with—involves two activities: an "unfriendly" one, the suspicion, and a "friendly" one, the listening. These two activities, says Ricoeur, combine to form the proper approach to understanding. For those who spurn Nietzsche (and there are many), Ricoeur would suggest a bit of listening, and for those who adore Nietzsche (quite a few), Ricoeur would serve up a bit of suspicion.

Nietzsche's Background

Friedrich Nietzsche is an extraordinary character in Western philosophy; some would call him an *enfant terrible,* a "terrible child," roguish and unruly. In the second half of the twentieth century he was often called far worse things than that, because of an association with a part of history that to most of us stands out as the worst that the century, and humanity, could present: the Third Reich, Hitler's regime. However, Nietzsche had been dead more than thirty years when his theories became popular among the Nazis, and it is still debatable

how much of a philosophical kinship there is between them, if any.

Nietzsche was born in Leipzig, Germany, and several of the male members of his family were Lutheran ministers. His father was a minister too, but he died when Nietzsche was young, and the boy and his sister Elisabeth were raised by their mother and other women in the family. He was brought up in that Christian tradition which holds that the pleasures of this life are considered sinful and life after death is the true goal of this life. You'll recognize the influence of Plato and St. Augustine; many Protestant theologians based their thinking on the same general idea of this life and the next. As a young man, Nietzsche studied theology for a while; he then switched to classical philosophy and philology, for which he proved to have a true talent. He was made a professor in Switzerland when he was just twenty-five. He served as a medic during the Franco-Prussian war of 1870, but during that time he became ill. He had presumably contracted syphilis a few years earlier, and bad health followed him for the rest of his life. He was forced to retire from his professorship, and in a sense he retired from life, too, living in seclusion with his mother, who took care of him. It was during his retirement, while he was still a young man, that he wrote the works that were to shake up the Western intellectual world and in a roundabout way inspire the ideology of the Nazi movement some fifty years later. When he was forty-five his mental health deteriorated to such an extent that he had to be institutionalized: On the last day of his presence of mind, he witnessed an old horse being beaten to death in the street (a common enough event in those days, and a scenario that even appears in a book he may have read, Dostoyevsky's *Crime and Punishment;* see the Narratives section). He came to the horse's rescue, throwing his arms around the horse's neck, weeping hopelessly; then he slipped into a coma. He lived in the depths of insanity until his death eleven years later, tended by his mother and sister.

It has sometimes been said that the theories of a person whose mind was deteriorating shouldn't be taken for anything more than the ravings of a madman. But the fact is that Nietzsche's mind was quite healthy and vigorous when he wrote most of the works that were to become so influential after his death. (Only a few European intellectuals outside of Germany, such as the Danish thinker Georg Brandes, were aware of his philosophy during his lifetime. Brandes tried to introduce Nietzsche to Scandinavian readers, without much success.) Besides, a theory must be able to stand on its own, and if it seems to make sense, or at least make interesting observations, it can't be dismissed because of the condition of its author. Nietzsche's works have stood the test of time with eerie brilliance.

Nietzsche's Suspicion: Beyond Good and Evil

What is Nietzsche's view of human nature? Are we, from the start, good or evil? He would probably choose to answer that question with a counter-question: What do you mean by "good" and "evil"? This is an important question, because our viewpoint is determined by our cultural and historical background. If you are a nineteenth-century person, if you belong to the Judeo-Christian tradition, or if you are otherwise inspired by Plato, you might say that a good person shuns physical pleasures, because they are sinful, and concentrates on the afterlife, because that is when life really begins. If you are a socialist (see Chapter 9), you might say that a good person is not offensive, willful, or selfish, but subordinates his or her will to that of the community. A good person is meek, helpful, kind, and turns the other cheek. An evil person is selfish, gives orders, thinks he or she is better than others, looks to this life and disregards the afterlife, and wallows in physical pleasures. If this is your view of good and evil, says Nietzsche, then clearly you are a child of your times, and you must reevaluate your values, for now their nature is becoming apparent. Their true nature is *repressive,* and this realization calls for a *transvaluation of values.* What should be the focus of such a transvaluation? The one that was common in ancient times, before people began to value weakness: the

moral value of strength, of *power.* This means that we must go beyond the common definitions of good and evil toward a new definition.

In Nietzsche's view, the way we value human characteristics depends on who we are, and there is no "ultimate truth." It all depends on our perspective, which is why Nietzsche gives this view the name *perspectivism.* (Box 8.9 explores the concept of perspectivism and its connection to postmodernism.) What Nietzsche intends is neither a descriptive nor a normative approach, but rather what we call a *metaethical* approach: an analysis of the meaning embedded within the words we use to discuss moral issues. From his own perspective, Nietzsche gives us an analysis of how Western values have arisen in people's minds—the Platonic and the Christian traditions merging into a worldview, and (in Nietzsche's own day) being joined by socialism and Marxism. As hostile as Marxism is to Christianity—Marx calls religion "opium for the masses"—Nietzsche sees that they have a common denominator: Both cater to the meek for the sake of meekness and have a disrespect for life itself. So in the midst of this metaethical analysis there is actually a normative value hiding: There is, to Nietzsche, a value that stands higher than all others, and that is the attitude that *affirms life.*

We can't look to Nietzsche's writings for a systematic account or a point-to-point criticism of the Western value system: His viewpoints are scattered around in his writings, and one must play detective to get the whole picture. Some material is in his speculative work of fiction *Thus Spoke Zarathustra* and some in his *Genealogy of Morals,* but it is the title and topic of his book *Beyond Good and Evil* that gives us the clue to the clearest version of his cultural critique.

Who is beyond good and evil? In the past, the *masters.* In the future, the *Overman* (or *Superman*).

Master and Slave

For Nietzsche, humanity falls into two categories: those who let themselves be led by others and

Box 8.9   PERSPECTIVISM, POSTMODERNISM, AND MORAL VALUES

Earlier in this book (Chapter 1) you read about the theory of postmodernism and its claim that all cultural perspectives are equally valuable. You may also remember the criticism of this concept: If we abandon the idea that Western science has some objective foundation in facts and isn't just a cultural perspective, then there may be no recourse if science is rejected on the basis of its being a biased Western viewpoint. A jury may reject DNA evidence as having a Western bias, and an accusation of witchcraft may be taken as seriously in the court as evidence of blackmail or rape. That is the downside of postmodernism. The upside is that the postmodernist view has forced a realization that there are other cultural perspectives at play in addition to the traditional Western viewpoints—a realization that broadens the horizon of a Western thinker rather than challenges it, because it doesn't have to mean that all cultural viewpoints are equally appropriate or valid in all situations. The origin of the debate about postmodernism is often forgotten in the controversial drama of the debates, but the credit goes to Nietzsche and his theory of perspectivism. To Nietzsche there is no absolute moral truth, only a matter of perspectives.

You may want to think further here: Is a postmodern view of right and wrong tenable? That is, should morals be regarded as culture-relative? Are all moral viewpoints of equal value? This would mean that we have to accept that there is no reason beyond our cultural preference to argue in favor of respect for other human beings; we can't argue in favor of a global ethic or that the concept of human rights ought to be adopted by all cultures, because the idea of human rights is just a Western preference. Moral views from other cultures allowing practices such as female circumcision, child prostitution, and serfdom must then be regarded as moral viewpoints having equal value to the Western ideals of equality and democracy. For many people, this is a profoundly disturbing notion. Scientific rejection of postmodernism may have a solid basis in the concept of *scientific evidence*—but what is the evidence that a *moral* viewpoint is right or wrong? Some philosophers have tried to answer this question by pointing to a bottom line: A viewpoint that creates suffering for a majority is wrong. Others have tried another approach: A moral view that contradicts itself is wrong. In the next chapter we look more closely at the concept of rights, and in the final chapter we look at the issue of suffering as a moral criterion.

those who are qualified to lead and forge their own path. In our American culture we often use terms such as "leadership material" and "born leaders," whereas such terms are much rarer in the European cultures of today. There seems to be a moral reluctance in Europe to pronounce someone to be "better" or more capable than others and a downright moral repugnance at such ideas in some Asian cultures, where the saying originated that the nail that sticks up gets hammered down; however, the United States has cherished the idea of the capable individual who carves his or her own destiny out of life ever since the beginning of the country's existence—and we say that the squeaky wheel gets greased! To some this focus on the individual is one of the sad things about this country, but for others it is one of the truly great things.

In Nietzsche's view restrictions on the gifted individual signal the downfall of a culture by creating a *herd mentality* that stifles and kills the capacity for individual expression. And for him, that was precisely what Germany and the rest of Europe had become in the late nineteenth century: a population of herd animals who would pick on anyone who dared to be different. Other Europeans have in fact commented on this phenomenon and continue to do so to this day; the

Danish-Norwegian author Aksel Sandemos even invented a concept for it: the *Jante Laws* (from an imaginary town called Jante, pronounced "Yahn-tay"), imposed by a provicial mentality on anyone who tries to rise above (or leave) the community. One of the rules of the Jante Laws is *Don't think you're better than we are.* Sandemose was influenced by Freud and Strindberg, but Nietzsche would have recognized his criticism of the resentment of the extraordinary individual.

How does Nietzsche think this mentality got started? Way back in time, in Greek antiquity and other ancient societies, the social structure was based on two major population groups: the *masters* (or slave owners) and the *slaves*. He didn't see it as his task to comment on the atrocities of slavery; what interested him was the attitude the slaves would have toward the master and each other and the master's attitude toward other masters and the slaves. He saw it as his task to analyze the two moral systems that grew out of the two strictly separated and yet in some ways intertwined communities of the masters (the warlords) and the slaves (their serfs). In the mind of the feudal warlord, a good person is someone who can be trusted and who will stand by you in a blood feud. He is a strong ally, a good friend, someone who has pride in himself and who has a noble and generous character—someone who is able to arouse fear in the enemy. If the warlord wants to help the weaker ones through his own generosity, he can choose to do so, but he doesn't have to: he creates his own values. The warlord respects his enemy if he is strong—then he becomes a worthy opponent—and values honor in his friends as well as in his enemies. Those who are weak don't deserve respect, for their function is to be preyed upon. (The resemblance to Darwin's concept of natural selection and survival of the fittest is no accident: Nietzsche had read, and admired, Darwin's *Origin of Species.*) Someone who is not willing to stand up for himself, who is weak and afraid of you, is a "bad person."

The slave, on the other hand, hates the master and everything he stands for. The master represents *evil*, having strength—the will and the power to rule—and inspiring fear. *Good* is the fellow slave who helps out—the nonthreatening person, the one who shows sympathy and altruism, who acts to create general happiness for as many as possible. The slaves feel tremendous resentment toward the masters, and this resentment ends in revolt. Historically, says Nietzsche, the slaves gained the upper hand and deposed the masters. The "master morality" was reversed to the status of evil, while the "slave morality" became a common ideal. So for Nietzsche the slave morality and the herd morality are the same phenomenon. The meek have indeed inherited the earth already—but the "herd" has retained its feelings of resentment toward the idea of a master, and everything the master stood for is still considered evil, even though there are no more masters:

> The noble type of man experiences *itself* as determining values; it does not need approval; it judges "what is harmful to me is harmful in itself"; it knows itself to be that which first accords honor to things; it is *value-creating*. . . . A morality of the ruling group . . . is most alien and embarrassing to the present taste in the severity of its principle that one has duties only to one's peers; that against being of a lower rank, against everything alien, one may behave as one pleases or "as the heart desires," and in any case "beyond good and evil"— here pity and like feelings may find their place. . . . It is different with the second type of morality, *slave morality.* Suppose the violated, oppressed, suffering, unfree, who are uncertain of themselves and weary, moralize: what will their moral valuations have in common? Probably, a pessimistic suspicion about the whole condition of man will find expression, perhaps a condemnation of man along with his condition. . . . Here is the place for the origin of that famous opposition of "good" and "evil": into evil one's feelings project power and dangerousness, a certain terribleness, subtlety, and strength that does not permit contempt to develop. According to slave morality, those who are "evil" thus inspire fear; according to master morality it

is precisely those who are "good" that inspire, and wish to inspire, fear, while the "bad" are felt to be contemptible.[11]

So as the herd mentality sees it, human nature is wrought with dangerous tendencies that must be controlled so that the benign fellow feeling of the slave mentality can thrive. For Nietzsche, this dichotomy (either-or) between slave and master attitude can be found in every culture, sometimes within the same individual. (In Chapter 9, Box 9.5, we'll look at the relationship between master and slave in the philosophy of another German thinker, Hegel.) The situation initially developed in early European cultures as well as in the Judeo-Christian tradition, which, in Nietzsche's eyes clearly displays the herd mentality with its requirement that you must turn the other cheek and refrain from doing harm if you want to partake of "pie in the sky when you die." This mentality has been carried by Christianity (described by Nietzsche as the "mass egoism of the weak"), by Plato's philosophy, by the moral philosophy of utilitarianism (see Chapter 10), and by socialism; and it has had the effect of reducing everything to averages and mediocrity, because it advocates general happiness and equality. For Nietzsche that is the same as a herd mentality that fears anything that's different, even if what is different is grander and more magnificent.

The Overman

If a pessimistic view of human nature is the outcome of a slave morality, Nietzsche must conclude that his own view is a positive one—and he does. For him, the slave morality *says nay to life;* it looks toward a higher reality (Heaven) in the same way that Western philosophy inspired by Plato has looked toward a world of ideas far removed from the tangible mess of sensory experience. This *Hinterwelt* (world beyond) is for Nietzsche a dangerous illusion, because it gives people the notion that there is something besides this life, and thus they squander their life here on earth in order to realize their shadowy dreams of a world to come, or a higher reality.

Living in such a way, for Nietzsche, is to live wrongly. A proper existence consists of realizing that there is nothing beyond this life and that one must pursue life with vigor, like a "master" who sets his own value. If one realizes this and has the courage to discard the traditional values of Christianity, one has become an Overman (*Übermensch*), or "Superman." The Overman is the human of the future—but not in the sense of a biological, Darwinian evolution, because not everyone in the future will be Overmen, far from it. The Overman is the result not of an automatic, natural selection, but of an aggressive seizing of power. What the Overman realizes is that there is one feature of human life that is overriding: not reason and not fellow feeling, but *will to power.* The slave morality will do its best to control or kill this urge, but the man who is capable of being a creator of values will recognize it as his birthright and will use it any way he sees fit. His right lies in his capacity to use the power, because that power is in itself the force of life. In effect, the right of the Overman is in Nietzsche's philosophy a right created by might, a practical description more than any political statement: You have the right if you can hold on to it and use it.[12]

The use of *man* instead of *human* or *person* is intentional here; Nietzsche, for whatever reasons, mistrusted female characters and female capabilities and did not count women among his future Overmen. Although many thinkers have omitted women from their theories of human nature either because it didn't occur to them to include women or because they adopted the convention that the terms *man* and *he* cover both genders, Nietzsche is a true misogynist who deliberately excludes women from any significant moral existence. One might wonder how his sister Elisabeth felt about that.

Many reactions to the Overman theory have seen the light of day. One has been an intellectual rekindling of the joy of life, even in the face of hard times. This reaction brought with it a critical evaluation of the double standard that existed in Western culture in the past: the condemnation of physical pleasures, combined with tacit acceptance of those pleasures when experienced on the sly. The Victorian Era (the reign of Queen Victoria in England) was particularly infested with this type of hypocrisy, and Nietzsche fought against it whenever he saw it. (You might say that the story of Dr. Jekyll and Mr. Hyde illustrates this double standard, perhaps even inadvertently. See the Narratives section of this chapter.) Many consider this reaction against hypocrisy a *positive* legacy of Nietzsche.

But even so, there is no denying that Nietzsche's most apparent legacy was until recently considered extremely negative, because his idea of the Overman was adopted by Hitler's Third Reich as the ideal of the new German culture. Picking up on Nietzsche's idea that power belongs by right to he who is capable of grabbing and holding on to it (an idea that was taken out of context), the Nazis saw themselves as a new race of Overmen, destined to rule the world. The weak would have no rights, and their sole purpose in life would be to provide fuel for the power of their masters. Here Hitler completely overlooked the fact that Nietzsche's Overman could arise only as an individual, not as a "race" or even a class of people.

Would Nietzsche have approved of Hitler? Absolutely and emphatically not. Nietzsche would have seen in Hitler something he despised: a man driven by the herd mentality's resentment against others in power. Nietzsche's writings may be full of ascerbic remarks about the English, about Christians, and about Platonists, but he didn't spare the German people either. He had little respect for his own Germanic heritage, which is why he moved to Switzerland. Furthermore, he was a sworn enemy of totalitarianism, because he viewed it as just another way to enslave capable people and prevent them from using their own willpower. In addition, Nietzsche had no patience or sympathy for anti-Semitism and had a profound dislike for his brother-in-law, a known anti-Semite (see the next section). And if anyone should still harbor suspicions that Nietzsche would have approved of the Hitler regime's ideology, Nietzsche himself had already gone on record to the contrary long before Hitler. These are the words he wrote to the anti-Semite Theodor Fritsch, who kep sending him pamphlets: "These constant, absurd falsifications and rationalizations of vague concepts 'germanic,' 'semitic,' 'aryan,' 'christian,' 'German'—all of that could in the long run cause me to lose my temper and bring me out of the ironic benevolence with which I have hitherto observed the virtuous velleities and pharisaisms of modern Germans."[13]

The fact remains, however, that Nietzsche's writings include elements that seem to lead to the abuse, or at least the neglect, of the weak by the strong. Because of Hitler's use of his writings, Nietzsche was a closed subject in philosophy for almost thirty years after World War II—he was too controversial to touch. Today we can view his ideas with more detachment, but it is still difficult to reconcile his enthusiasm for life with the disdain for weaker human beings—a disturbing mixture of free thought and contempt. But how did it happen that Nietzsche's ideas became the house philosophy of Hitler and his associates? In order to understand the strange workings of history, we have to take a side trip to the life and times of Nietzsche's sister, Elisabeth.

Elisabeth Nietzsche and the Nazis

Elisabeth Nietzsche's role in her brother's life has long been recognized as an extremely powerful one, and toward the end of his life rather peculiar: She used to invite scholars to "view" her deeply insane brother who was by then unable to communicate. However, her influence on him and in particular his philosophical legacy has been far deeper than previously suspected. As children Friedrich and Elisabeth were close, but for a number of years they were not on the best of terms. Elisabeth married a man whom Friedrich despised; he was a well-known racist agitator, espousing violently anti-Semitic views, and in general rubbed Friedrich the wrong way. Elisabeth's husband, Bernhard Förster, was fired from his position as a teacher because of his racist politics, and soon afterward he started recruiting Germans of "pure blood" for an emigration plan. He viewed Germany as having betrayed its citizens of Germanic descent by allowing people of "non-Aryan descent" to flourish. You'll remember from Chapter 5 that the Aryan race theory was a groundless concoction, based on a theory of language, and here you see it in a broader historic perspective: The grounds for Hitler's racism and anti-Semitic politics had been in place as an ideology in Germany for more than sixty years before Hitler's rise to power.

Elisabeth Nietzsche Förster agreed with her husband in his anti-Semitic views and helped him distribute racist pamphlets. When Förster heard about land being available in Paraguay, he set about to create a "new Germany" where only pure Aryans were allowed and where the Germanic race would flourish without the encroaching influence of non-Aryans such as the German Jews. In 1886 Elisabeth traveled with her husband to Paraguay with a small group of hopeful colonists: fourteen families and their life savings. Three years into the social experiment of restarting the Aryan race, the colony was falling apart: Elisabeth and Förster had mismanaged the colonists' money, and Förster killed himself. Elisabeth got word that her brother was ill in Germany and needed her help, so she abandoned the colonists to their own devices and traveled home to Germany.

Forgotten Fatherland, a book published by reporter Ben MacIntyre in 1992, sheds light on the fate of the colony: Abandoned and forgotten by the world, the colonists struggled to stay alive and racially pure in the Paraguayan jungle. Over the decades and into the twentieth century, it persisted with dwindling, new generations of pure "Aryan" blood, because the colonists had transferred their racial hatred from Jews to the local Paraguayan Indians, and intermarriage was considered an impossibility. The result: massive genetic inbreeding. MacIntyre set out to find the colony in the late 1980s and found a small German village frozen in time, with inhabitants so plagued by genetic diseases and mental problems that a healthy child was a rarity. However, this is not the end of the

story of the Förster colony. A newspaper article in 1998 told the latest news of the colony—a story of change: The problems of inbreeding were dissipating, and the economy was doing much better. A stronger community seems to be emerging—the manifestation of the Master Race? That depends how you look at it: The colonist children have decided to merge with and marry into the local Indian tribes and speak their language. With a larger gene pool, the inbreeding problem has vanished; social ties are expanding, and so is commerce. The older members of the community still speak German and have nice things to say about Elisabeth, but young biracial descendants of the colony feel no connection to the racist philosophy of the colony's founders.

While the colony was struggling, Elisabeth was back in Germany tending to her brother. During his final years she proclaimed herself curator of his works, and after his death she took on the task of editing his unpublished works. It now appears that her editing was quite creative: Some of the material she wrote herself and passed it off as her brother's, giving it an edge of bigotry that would have made Förster proud. Toward the end of her life, in the early years of German Nazism, she managed to get the attention of Adolf Hitler and other prominent Nazis. She inspired them to use Nietzsche's philosophy (with her own edits) as a blueprint for Nazi ideology. Thus the connection was forged between Nietzsche and the anti-Semitic, totalitarian views of the Nazi regime. Hitler regarded her very highly, and when she died, he gave her the funeral of a "mother of the fatherland." Because of the presumed connection between Nietzsche's philosophy and Hitler, it wasn't until the 1980s that philosophers felt comfortable researching Nietzsche's philosophy and writing about him; it then became clear that much of the supposed pre-Nazi leanings of Nietzsche were in fact infused into his works by his sister. This doesn't mean that Nietzsche was beyond bigotry or that everything that Hitler used from his writings was invented by Elisabeth; Nietzsche had strong feelings against many thinkers, individuals, and population groups, and he did advocate the theory of the Overman, but Nazism would have been entirely contrary to his philosophy of the strong individual.

The Eternal Return and the Value of Life

Nietzsche is famous for having said that "God is dead." (A student joker inscribed this line in some wet concrete at the University of California, San Diego, and added another famous line: "Nietzsche is dead, signed: God.") But what did Nietzsche mean by claiming that God is dead? The opinion of an atheist (which Nietzsche called himself) is usually that God is an illusion, not that he is *dead.* This tells us something about Nietzsche's view of reality: In earlier times people believed in God, and that made him alive, as an idea. Now so many people don't believe any longer, so God is dead. For many people that would mean that morality has lost its sanction, so they lose faith in everything and become *nihilists.* Indeed, the word *nihilism* is often mentioned in connection with Nietzsche. It comes from the Latin word *nihil* (nothing) and usually means that there is no foundation for believing in anything and that existence is senseless and absurd. (Some of Sartre's fellow existentialists have been called nihilists, although the term does not fit Sartre, since he believes in the human ability to shape one's own existence.) On occasion Nietzsche himself has been called a nihilist by critics, but is that correct?

There seem to be two differing views of what Nietzsche really meant by the concept: (1) If God is dead, then everything is permitted, and you soon despair because there are no absolute values, so you become a nihilist. (2) Even if you realize that there are no objective values or truth because there is no God, then you make your own values. By doing so you affirm life and your own strength as a human being, and so you are *not* a nihilist. To many contemporary Nietzsche scholars it seems that this is exactly what he is saying, not that there is nothing to believe in. For Nietzsche a nihilist is someone who has misunderstood the message that God is dead and has become a naysayer. Above all, Nietzsche himself believed in some-

thing: in the value of life and of affirming life, *saying yea to life.*

Interestingly, precursors to Nietzsche's transvaluation of values already existed in Western literature: The Russian author Fyodor Dostoyevsky had already asked the questions (1) May the exceptionally gifted individual set his own values? (*Crime and Punishment,* 1866) and (2) If there is no God, is then everything permitted? (*The Brothers Karamazov,* 1881), but Nietzsche seems not to have discovered Dostoyevsky until 1886, the year *Beyond Good and Evil* came out and the year before his *Genealogy of Morals* was published. *Crime and Punishment* follows the young bright student Raskolnikov in nineteenth-century St. Petersburg as he moves inexorably from philosophical thoughts of the brilliant mind being elevated above the morals of the masses to deciding that he himself, a brilliant mind, is not bound by the morals of society—after which he proceeds to commit murder. (You will find excerpts from *Crime and Punishment* in the Narratives section.) In effect, Raskolnikov is a harbinger of Nietzsche's Overman: He sees himself as having special permission to go beyond good and evil, until the magnitude of what he has done brings him back to an appreciation of the common moral law. In a peculiar parallel from the late twentieth century, the serial killer Jeffry Dahmer was interviewed at length after his conviction, while he was serving a life sentence, before being murdered by an inmate. Dahmer spoke from a state of—presumably—deep contrition, explaining that he had gotten the impression from his teachers that there is no God, so everything is permitted, and so he didn't have to heed the common moral (or even criminal) laws, because he would not be held accountable in an afterlife. So he proceeded to do what he wanted: murder young men and dismember them. Later, after he was caught, he returned to a religious point of view and felt remorse.

Among philosophers of the second half of the twentieth century, Jean-Paul Sartre has probably been the most influenced by Nietzsche. You'll remember from Chapter 4 that Sartre was interested in the existential demand of making authentic choices and avoiding bad faith; but, fundamentally, his existentialism is inspired by Nietzsche's view that there is no God, so there are no absolute God-given moral standards, and we have to rise to the occasion and create our own standards. Sartre's standards are envisioned as a guideline for everyone, though, and not for an elite of Overmen.

How did Nietzsche propose to say yes to life? It is easy enough to "love one's fate" when things are going well. Anyone can say yes to life when you're having a good time. The difficulty is to say yes to life when it is at its worst. Nietzsche wants us to love life even at its worst. And what is the worst that Nietzsche can imagine? That everything that has happened to you will happen again, and again, the very same way. This is the theory of *the eternal return of the same*. One anecdote has Nietzsche taking a walk one day and being struck by the awful truth: History repeats itself, and all our fears and joys will be repeated. We have experienced them before, and we will experience them again, endlessly. The idea horrified him, and he was forced to consider the question, Even if you know that you will have to go through the same tedious, painful stuff over and over again, would you choose to, willingly?

As with the theory of nihilism, there are two interpretations of this problem: The first holds that Nietzsche actually believed that everything repeats itself. We're doomed to live the same life over and over again; life is absurd, and our existence is pointless. This interpretation also holds that Nietzsche was himself a nihilist. And, to be sure, such theories surface from time to time. A Hindu philosophy claims that the universe repeats itself endlessly down to the smallest detail, and some astrophysicists believe that the universe will end in a Big Crunch, after which we will have another Big Bang, and so forth. The second interpretation holds that Nietzsche had simply come up with the ultimate test of a person's life affirmation: *What if* everything repeats itself endlessly? In that case, could you say that you would want to live life over again? If you can answer, "Let's have it one more time!" then you truly love life, and you have passed the test.

Which interpretation is correct? Is the "eternal return" real, or is it a *thought experiment* so Nietzsche can make a moral point?[14] Nietzsche experts disagree, but either way, the idea of the eternal return serves as a good test for our love of life. To be sure, Nietzsche's own life wasn't exactly the kind of life one might want repeated: having endless illnesses, endless quarrels with people who didn't see things the way he saw them, and fallings-out with friends; experiencing war; having to give up his job; getting little public recognition or understanding for his writings; being turned down by publisher after publisher; having no personal life to speak of; living with disturbing thoughts and anxieties the further he got into his mental illness; and finally sinking into a mental darkness that we can barely imagine. And yet he himself believed he passed the test of the eternal return and became a yea-sayer.

How would you do on the test? The same exams, the same driving tests, the same falling in and out of love; being stood up, having wisdom teeth pulled, being sick, submitting tax returns; the same vacations, the same marriages and children, the same hopes and fears—would you do it over again, the bad with the good? If yes, Nietzsche congratulates you. You have won the battle against doubt, weakness, lukewarm existence, and nihilism, and you will experience the ultimate joy of life in the face of meaninglessness.

The Question of Souls and the Capacity for Good and Evil

In Chapter 7 we explored the concept of mind and touched on the possibility of nonhuman animals having minds. That is an issue which science and philosophy will probably be able to resolve, perhaps sooner rather than later. However, the issue of whether nonhuman animals have *souls* is something that science can never tell us, because it is a matter of faith. As you saw in the beginning of this chapter, science can't even begin to tell us whether we *humans* have souls and, if we do, how a soul should be defined. In most cases today, the issue of the soul is approached as a normative topic, with a moral aspect to it: If we assume that we have souls, how do we attempt to create *good* souls, and what makes a soul bad or evil? We have seen some of the most influential answers in the Western tradition in this chapter, and now it is time to look beyond humans.

Do Nonhuman Animals Have Souls?

Are humans considered the only carriers of souls and are humans the only ones to whom we can attribute good and evil behavior?

The Judeo-Christian Tradition   The Judeo-Christian tradition offers us a view of the soul based on Genesis: God *breathes* life into Adam and later into his rib, which becomes Eve, so humans are by definition connected to the breath of God. Similarly, the ancient Vedic word for the all-soul in Indian mythology is *Atman,* the same as for "breath." In Scandinavian languages the word for breathing is "andas/ånde," while the word for spirit is "anda/ånd." We don't hear in Genesis that God made clay figures of animals and breathed on *them* (although we of course don't hear that He *didn't* do it, either). In the Jewish tradition, the soul of a newborn enters its body with the first breath, and before that happens, the baby/fetus is not considered a person. In the American Indian tradition as well as the Egyptian tradition, the soul may leave on side trips from the nose, and it is imperative that the passage isn't blocked when the soul returns. The connection to the idea of breath is ancient and cross-cultural.

However, humans aren't the only creatures who breathe, so why is the phenomenon of the soul supposed to be exclusively human? In the Judeo-Christian tradition, there is a sharp line dividing all humans from nonhumans, because based on the biblical tradition, humans alone, among all other creatures, are endowed with souls. However, Christianity was also inspired by the Greek tradition, and Aristotle believed everything living had some form of soul-substance. But what exactly did he mean by "soul"? As you saw earlier, Aristotle has little to say about the destiny of souls

after the death of the body; rather, the idea of soul for him seems to resemble the concept of life-force that you encountered in the philosophies of Max Scheler and Henri Bergson in Chapter 7. Aristotle's view of some kind of spiritual presence in the world inspired not just Scheler and Bergson, but most of all Aquinas, who agrees with Aristotle that all living things have a kind of spiritual element in that they strive to stay alive; in addition, animals strive to perpetuate their species, but only humans have a thinking, *rational* soul. You also read in Chapter 7 how the question of nonhuman souls came up in later discussions among Catholic thinkers and how Descartes's rejection of the possibility that animals have minds reportedly put a stop to that discussion.

Among Christians today there is a movement to rewrite the policy of the Church that animals have no moral standing and can be treated according to any human whim short of cruelty; the argument is that the Church managed to reverse itself on the issue of the humanity of slaves, so might not the same be possible with the moral standing of animals? Few Christians argue that nonhuman animals have souls in the traditional sense, but many agree that animals have minds that, at least occasionally, seem to work along rational lines, and these people want to grant animals some form of moral standing. In addition, in our culture there seems to be an increasing number of people living with pets who feel comfortable with the idea that we will meet our dead pets in the afterlife; a famous story, the "Rainbow Country," is often told to people who have lost a beloved pet. The story is about a place of green fields and rushing streams where the spirits of our dead pets wait for us until our time on earth is up, and that is where we will meet them again. Mark Twain is said to have believed that the pets we have loved and lost are all waiting for us at the gates of heaven—and will presumably follow us when we go inside. An ancient Indian story tells of a king who decided to walk to heaven; it took years, and a dog began to accompany him on the way. In the end, when they reached heaven, the gods wouldn't let the dog in, but the king wouldn't enter without his dog; he wouldn't want to spend eternity in a place where compassion for an animal was not allowed. But it turns out that the dog was the gods' way of testing the king's own compassion: The dog turned out to be a god in disguise, and both entered heaven. Now if one is to believe any story of an afterlife, it seems a given that one has to believe there is a part of oneself that will survive—a spirit, a soul, a form of energy perhaps. If human souls can go to heaven, and we will meet our pets there, then surely we believe they too have souls. This example shows how a belief system can "drift" toward a new frame of mind, and a new kind of story, based on a shift in people's behavioral patterns.

Hinduism For many other cultural traditions the concept of nonhuman souls is not nearly as hard to accept. In the Asian religious philosophy of Hinduism, everything living is endowed with a spirit; these spirits swirl in a near-eternal dance of transmigration. You'll remember the section on karma in Chapter 4; according to the principle of karma, the cumulative effects of one's actions will determine one's next life, and souls are reincarnated ("made flesh again") into the type of creature that best matches those karmic effects. In order to be born a human, you will have had to travel far through lifetime after lifetime as lower forms of animals—for in traditional Hinduism it is definitely more prestigious and advantageous to be born a human, but that doesn't mean other creatures don't have souls or that we should be certain that we have escaped being reincarnated into animal form in the future.

Hinduism, in addition, is an ancient religion with several schools of thought under a large tent: For some Hindus the soul, *atman,* is an individual soul that travels through incarnations, and animals and humans all have such individual souls. For other Hindus, the *atman* is one, and all living participate in it, so we can't talk about separate souls. Given that Hinduism does include the concept of soul or souls expanding beyond the human realm, it is interesting that this expansion doesn't extend to a concept of animal equality or animal moral standing. Since Hinduism reflects an ancient and rigid caste system, we might also say that the fact that humans have souls and are all subject to reincarnation does not lead to any moral or political philosophy of *human* equality, either: Human or animal, we reap what we have sown in the previous life as well as in this one, and if an animal or human occupies a nonenviable station in life, it is because he, she, or it is individually responsible for being in that condition.

Buddhism You'll remember from Chapter 7 that the concept of nonself is an essential part of Buddhist teachings; indeed, the concept of soul is rejected by many teachers and interpreters of Buddhism. The sage Nagasena, whom you met in Chapter 7, teaches King Milinda that "Because of the mind and because of objects of thought arises mental consciousness; simultaneously are produced contact, sensation, perception, thought, focusing of thoughts, vitality, attention. Thus do these physical and mental states originate from a cause, for there is no soul involved in any of them."[15]

Some popular versions of Buddhism have a concept of the soul that resembles the Hindu concept: an individual soul traveling through many incarnations in order to become a better individual. However, as you saw in the previous chapter, Buddhism's idea of the no-self is in part conceived in opposition to the Hindu philosophy of the individual soul traveling through a number of incarnations; and according to Buddhist scholars, the proper way of interpreting Buddhist philosophy is to view the concept of the soul as nonexistent too. But within a theology that teaches about karma and rebirth, the unavoidable question becomes, If there is no permanent self and no individual soul, then *what is it that is reincarnated?* King Milinda asked that of the Reverend Nagasena, too, and Nagasena answered, *Name-and-Form.* Not the same Name-and-Form as in the previous life, but another, governed by the rules of karma (Kamma): ". . . with one Name-and-Form Kamma is wrought, and man does good or evil deeds, and by the power of this Kamma another Name-and-Form is reborn." Milinda then asks, "If, Reverend Sir, it is not the same Name-and-Form that is reborn, surely the man must be released from his evil deeds." Nagasena replies, "If he was *not* reborn, he *would* be released from his evil deeds; but since, great king, he *is* reborn, therefore he is *not* released from his evil deeds."[16] Nagasena illustrates this with an example: If a man lights a fire in a field on a cold day, and then goes away without putting it out, and the field catches fire, and the man is caught, can he then claim that the fire he set was a different one from the fire that consumed the field? No, because one was a direct result of the other. This means that the accumulated good and bad deeds of a lifetime associated with one Name-and-Form create a new Name-and-Form in another life which is directly related to the first, through the karma of his or her actions—but it can't be described as a new incarnation of the same soul, or the same self. The continual rebirth of Name-and-Form will cease only when individuals reach the understanding that they must free themselves from the "Three Poisons": the attachment to life that brings suffering, the illusion that anything has permanence, and the notion that there is a permanent self.

Tribal Views   Most tribal worldviews hold that both humans and animals have souls. While not necessarily believing that the souls migrate into new bodies, tribal views around the world reflect the notion that humans and animals occupy the same world as neighbors; we have fundamentally the same kinds of joys and worries, and occasionally animals are considered better at handling their existence than we are. We find this view all over the world, from Neolithic and Bronze Age Scandinavia to Africa, from Australia to ancient Greece, from Siberia to India, and from Alaska to South America and Oceania. In the American Indian traditions, animals have spirits that live in their bodies, can leave their bodies under special circumstances, and live on after death, the same as human spirits. But in the American Indian mythology, souls aren't reserved for humans and animals: There are spirits in the land itself, in trees, rivers, lakes, mountains, the air. The earth is considered to have a soul or spirit—Mother Earth—and the sky is the home of her consort, Father Sky. Gods mingle with humans when they see the need for it. Human and animal spirits were similar from the beginning of time, and that is why the American Indian views animals as other peoples or nations. This also means that we humans are still related by ancient blood to our fellow animal cousins, and American Indians have often traced such ancestry by way of their *totem* animals. This doesn't mean that humans and animals are morally or politically equal; human spirits don't migrate into animal form in the American Indian tradition, so there is no ban against killing animals. Humans can still kill animals for their needs, but the animal spirit must be shown respect—not just because animals are ancient, wise spirits, but also because they are dangerous spirits that can ruin the life of a hunter who has shown them disrespect.

In "Observations On 'Self' and 'Knowing,'" Rudolph Rÿser tells of the American Indian attitude toward human and animal spirits:

> Other peoples, like the fish, the eagle, and the mountain, have great knowledge that permits them to comprehend the nature of other peoples. They achieve balance in relation to other peoples because of this greater knowledge. Human beings are "little brothers and sisters," and so they must take special measures to learn to live in proper respect and relation to all things. The ultimate goal appears to be that humans will live as a part of the universe as do all living things."[17]

Are Nonhuman Animals Beyond Good and Evil?

Often, Nietzsche mentions animals or "Beasts" with a hint of admiration: They are not caught up in the human moral systems, but act on instinct, and that is what Nietzsche finds attractive and admirable. The Overman himself has to recapture some of the beastly spontaneity in order to create his own values. Here Nietzsche follows the common Western pattern of thought, for a change.

PICKLES. © 2000 The Washington Post Writers Group. Reprinted with permission.

As one of my students remarked, all theories of human nature are invariably expressed from the human perspective, so how can we expect objectivity? Here is an imaginative viewpoint from a nonhuman perspective.

Most thinkers in the Western tradition do agree that nonhuman animals have no conception of right and wrong; sometimes this lack of understanding of morals is considered one of the signs that animals have no souls or even no minds—and are thus below humans in terms of spiritual standing. But are they really considered morally neutral, in the human mind? The very symbolism of saying that a man or a woman is "like an animal," has "animal magnetism," or even feels "animal lust" indicates that animal nature is dangerous and tied in with the physical nature which Plato and Augustine spent so much energy warning us against (and which made Nietzsche angry): Our "inner beast" must be controlled and conquered. In other words, in the long Christian tradition, the nonhuman animal itself has become a symbol of evil, or at least the predatory animal has (prey animals such as the lamb and the deer generally count as the good guys among animals). An interesting illustration is one of the official rationales for establishment of the United States National Parks system in the early twentieth century: Not only would the parks be to the benefit of humans, but they would also serve as *sanctuaries* for deer, elk, and other animals who would never again fall prey to the evil predatory animals in the wild. (This noble idea led to overpopulation of deer and elk in the parks, with subsequent erosion of hillsides and other environmental problems!) This conception of prey animals being "good" and predators being "evil" persists to this day, even in cartoons. Some speculate that the predators are still, as in times of folklore, considered evil because they are the only competitors humans have in the food chain.

Sometimes the lack of animal morals is considered a plus for the animal: They are considered to be innocent, because they don't have any concept of morals—like Adam and Eve before the Fall. However, this notion of innocence has not usually been translated into a respect for those "innocent" animals. Humans are quite capable of admiring, loving, hunting, killing, and eating the same individual. Be that as it may, animals in the West have almost without exception been considered in a category that truly is beyond good and evil, morally and even legally: Mostly, animals have been considered as being unaware of causing pain, incapable of being compassionate, and not responsible for causing harm to humans and other animals, because they don't know any better. The cat playing with the mouse is one of the situations challenging this view, because it looks as if the cat is enjoying the pain of the mouse—but animal behaviorists have told us so many times now that the play serves other functions: teaching kittens to hunt or engaging the play behavior of the adult cat (for whatever reason), but generally the cat isn't assumed to be aware of the anxiety and pain of the mouse. Legally, this means that animals in general have not been held accountable for what humans would call unlawful activity; this doesn't mean that such animals are always forgiven if they transgress our human rules. A tiger who takes a child in India, a dog who mauls a child in the United States, sharks and alligators who prey on humans, are perhaps considered innocent "children of nature" in an abstract sense; but in a very concrete way they are hunted down and destroyed—not punished, mind you, but destroyed, like a piece of property. The great exception to this form of thinking in the West is a time period that stretched from the heart of the Middle Ages up until the eighteenth century, where in some jurisdictions animals were considered morally and legally responsible for the harm they caused and were put on trial and executed, as if evil intentions—*malice aforethought*—could be proved.

In all cultures attributing souls to animals, it is assumed that animals can act within a moral behavioral scheme: They can be vengeful, helpful, compassionate, selfish, and so on, just like humans—not just as a matter of being emotionally engaged in life, but also in terms of having a concept of moral values. Even in a society such as ours with a long tradition of assuming that only humans have souls and animals can't think, there is a body of folklore about good and evil animals. Sometimes in the past it has been an entire animal species that was considered evil, such as wolves and other predators, and at other times stories are told of individual animals and their good or evil behavior. Today most scientifically oriented people have abandoned such ideas in favor of the concept of the nonhuman animal as being beyond good and evil, living in a world of instinctual needs where human concepts of right and wrong are completely irrelevant. Such a view has been considered the more sane and realistic view by many scientists and laypeople in the twentieth century—so it is all the more surprising to find

out that the idea of animals having good or evil intentions is resurfacing, but this time based on intensive animal research, not folklore.

Ape researchers such as Jane Goodall and Frans de Waal have within the past decades published accounts of chimpanzees helping and nurturing other chimps, seemingly going out of their way to help one another—with those same chimpanzees going on the warpath or deliberately misleading and cheating other members of the group. It seems evident to those researchers that the primates don't act at random—the actions are deliberate. The old concept that only humans can lie is being eroded with every new ape study—but so is the concept that only humans can understand how another being feels and only humans are capable of acting on it: Can other primates understand the "inner states" of others, and does it matter to them? Sue Savage-Rumbaugh has demonstrated that this may be the case: Two chimpanzees, Sherman and Austin, who both have a limited knowledge of signs in English, are placed in a lab situation, in two rooms separated by a window with a lock in it. They can see each other; Sherman can also see bananas locked in a box on his side, but the tool kit with the key is on Austin's side. So Sherman signals "key" to Austin, and Austin puts the key through the lock to Sherman. Now Sherman unlocks the box and gets the bananas out while Austin is watching—and then Sherman brings half the food to the lock and passes it through to Austin.[18]

This example is certainly suitable for the discussion about animal minds in Chapter 7—but it is also highly appropriate here. Does Sherman share the bananas with Austin because he wants to or because he has been taught to? Does he do it because Austin is watching? Or does he do it because he thinks Austin has deserved it? All of these may apply, but we can't just say that if Sherman has been taught to share or is afraid of getting caught eating all the bananas and punished, then he has merely instinct and no morals—because most humans act in a morally decent way for a variety of reasons, as well.

Some years ago, in the Brookfield Zoo in Chicago, a small boy fell into the deep gorilla pit and lost consciousness. A female gorilla, Binti Jua, came to his rescue, cradled his head and protected him from the other apes, and then carried him over to the door where the keepers enter the pit and waited until a human showed up. When the news hit the media, people were astonished, because it seemed as if Binti Jua was acting out of compassion—a virtue that is generally considered exclusively human. Many animal behaviorists tried to explain Binti's actions as instinctual, but ape researchers chimed in and said that this kind of compassion is quite ordinary for gorillas and chimpanzees—what was unusual was that Binti directed her compassion toward someone outside of her own species. One must imagine that such an opportunity doesn't present itself very often. So does it mean that Binti thought the boy was a gorilla? Hardly, because she delivered him safely to the human keeper. Ape researchers are generally willing to accept the possibility that she was indeed showing compassion toward someone not co-specific (someone from another species)—which is more than most *humans* get a chance to do in their lifetime and more than some humans would choose to do voluntarily.

So perhaps we have to concede that at least the great apes have the capacity to act in a way we would call morally good, making free choices, based on an understanding of options and consequences. For all of us who love and admire animals, not just because they are cute and furry, but also because they are capable fellow travelers on this planet, there is something formidable in that notion: *Morals may be older than humanity,* as old as social conscious life itself perhaps? But we should beware of making saints out of animals, because in that case we also have to consider the downside: If primates, and possibly other social animals, are no longer beyond good and evil, *innocents,* then does it mean they can conceive of moral *wrongdoing* as well? And if so, who is to hold them accountable? We humans? To what extent? Do we put them on trial for doing harm, as was

done in the Middle Ages? Just as their moral "goodness" must be seen in the context of their own lives, not ours, so too should their moral wrongdoing, if any.

A chimpanzee may not know if she breaks some human rule, but if she breaks a chimpanzee rule, she will know, and the other chimpanzees will take care of identifying the crime and meting out the punishment—for according to Frans de Waal, that is quite common in the ape communities. It would probably not be up to us humans to impose our moral standards on our primate cousins—it would not be practical, and it would not be reasonable. (Chapter 10 deals with the practical problems of such an idea, in a discussion of the Great Ape Project.) So we may have to give up thinking of animals as dumb beasts without souls or minds as well as thinking of them as innocent noble creatures who are totally instinct-driven. Perhaps the answer lies in recognizing, as Jane Goodall suggests, that the human moral categories of compassion and deceit lie as tendencies and potentials in the nonhuman primate, no more and no less. As Maxine Sheets-Johnstone tells us, many elements in our biology and psyche arose in a primitive form before we were *Homo sapiens;* perhaps the sense of right and wrong will turn out to be one of them.

We're Only Human: Good and Evil in Films and Literature

In concluding this chapter we look at a favorite theme in the narrative tradition: stories of good and evil human nature. Then we look at stories of twins and triplets.

Stories of Good and Evil

Stories of good and evil are as ancient as storytelling itself, and we may think that there has always been a fictional line in the sand between the good guys and the bad guys and that the "antihero" with lots of moral flaws is a fairly new invention (anti-hero stories flourished in the 1950s and 1960s in literature and at the movies; think of Camus's *The Stranger* and Steve McQueen and Ali McGraw in *The Getaway*). But in fact lots of very ancient myths have stories about characters that are both good and evil; usually we call them "trickster" stories. In American Indian mythology it is usually the coyote who plays tricks on people and animals, sometimes to the point of disaster for them as well as for himself. But Coyote is also a benign spirit, helping to create good things for humans and animals. In Africa, the hare plays the same dual role as the bringer of good and bad things (see Box 8.4 where Hare gives the wrong message from the Moon Goddess to humans), and Brer Rabbit is a direct descendant of those ancient tales, told by African slaves in the Old South to preserve their narrative heritage. Eventually, we all became familiar with the trickster hare in the shape of Bugs Bunny—in effect derived in spirit from one of the original African American literary contributions! Above all, the trickster is fond of lying simply out of mischief. In Scandinavian mythology the character of Loki (who himself is of mixed heritage, being a child of older, more sinister powers—the Jätte people—as well as of the chief God Odin) helps his buddies among the gods get out of a jam time and time again, but he is also to blame for the permanent death of the young god Balder, everyone's favorite—an event that starts off the end of the world, the *Ragnarok*. It seems that even in ancient times, we were puzzled by the fact that the same person (wife, husband, child) could be so good in some situations and so bad in others—and that the gods could smile on us one year and strike us down the next.

By far the most classic stories are those where good and evil are somehow split out into different spirits or people: The ancient Persian religion of Manichaeism (an influence on Augustine, as you've seen) saw the destiny of life on earth as contingent upon the outcome of the battle between the powers of light and darkness. In Christianity the devil is always at the ready to lure people into temptation; in most of Western literature and film good characters struggle with "bad guys." Mystery novels and films are a prime example of this,

because criminals are usually depicted as evil characters, hunted by the good guys: cops, police detectives, and private investigators. This has carried over into science fiction where a popular sub-genre deals with evil aliens; films such as *Alien* and its sequels, *The Invasion of the Body Snatchers*, and *Starship Troopers* (*Mars Attacks* too, but that was a spoof) don't even speculate that communication with the aliens might be possible—that we might find some common ground. Aliens are simply viewed as evil vermin to be exterminated. While most of us don't believe that good and evil come in neat packages as depicted in the movies, we still enjoy watching and reading about such classic battles between good and evil—not because they are realistic, but because they are symbolic: There may be forces of light and darkness surrounding us, in the form of other people; but those forces can also be imagined as cohabiting inside the human spirit, and many feel their good side needs every bit of help it can get, such as a rallying cry from a stirring novel or film.

Twins, Triplets, and Alter Egos

The exploration of good and evil as part of human nature is particularly effective in tales of twins and alter egos. In both cases, we are talking about a symbolic representation of a dual character: two sides to the same person. The paradigm for alter-ego stories in Western literature is Robert Louis Stevenson's 1886 story, *Dr. Jekyll and Mr. Hyde*. Stevenson's story was loosely based on a real person, a nineteenth-century scientist. The kindly Dr. Jekyll becomes the evil Mr. Hyde by drinking his own invention, a personality-altering drug intended, as the story goes, to distill goodness from evil in the human character. Jekyll, who is not so kindly after all—given that he throws away his life and *respectability* (a notion that nineteenth-century readers found particularly problematic) for the sake of finding knowledge—parallels the ancient story of Dr. Faustus in this respect, but no further. Faustus is tempted to make a deal with the devil, but Jekyll is solely responsible for his decision; no devil character is tempting him, except

Dr. Jekyll and Mr. Hyde, MGM, 1941. Kindly, reliable Dr. Jekyll (Spencer Tracy) has a beast hiding in him, urging him to do whatever his heart desires: pursue pleasures and commit acts of violence. With the help of a drug, the beast emerges and transforms Jekyll to Mr. Hyde—what Freudians would call the uncontrollable id of the doctor. In this promotional still, Mr. Hyde is hovering over the scholar in the illustration to Hans Christian Andersen's "The Shadow." Jekyll himself is beginning to turn from his fiancée on the right (Lana Turner) to the waitress (Ingrid Bergman).

the one in his heart. The symbolism is easy to read: We all have a beast "hyding" in us, an alter ego, and we must not let it loose no matter how much we would like to. The reason why Jekyll keeps returning to his Hyde persona is because it feels good; it amuses him. In other words, he is hooked on the drug that allows a more primitive side of him to emerge, and he gets to do things that Victorian England frowned upon, like going out on the town. Of course he exceeds even modern readers' tolerance when he tortures and kills; he isn't just "letting the badger loose." The moral lesson is broad and completely in tune with Vic-

torian mores, as well as with most of the Christian tradition and Sigmund Freud's theories to boot: Keep your "inner beast" in check, and don't give in to your physical desires. Nietzsche, who, as you know, saw this attitude as sheer repression of life might have rooted for Mr. Hyde and rewritten the end of the story.

While Stevenson's story has now become the classic tale of the alter ego, Hans Christian Andersen experimented with the subject several decades before Stevenson did. Two of the most moving Andersen stories of the dual character are "The Marsh King's Daughter," about a young woman who is a devilish soul inhabiting the body of a beautiful girl at day, but a huge, hideous toad with a sweet, compassionate spirit at night (some would say, a typical male view of women, but there is much more to the story than that) and the chilling story of "The Shadow," in which a man's shadow liberates itself from him, grows to become a powerful political figure, and eventually causes the death of his old master. In the Narratives section we take a closer look at Jekyll and Hyde as well as "The Shadow."

The dual-character theme is used commonly in novels and films. The good-bad twins may be sisters, as in the old Hollywood film *Sisters,* brothers as in *Dead Ringers* and *Twins,* or androids (*Star Trek: The Next Generation*'s Data and Lor), but the theme is essentially the same: Symbolically, the dual characters represent one person with conflicting personalities. Usually, the bad-tempered character is the more interesting one and the one we are warned against. A story that depicts a person split down the middle into a good and evil part is Calvino's short story, "The Cloven Viscount."

On the whole, good twin–bad twin stories tend toward moralizing, with the bad twin as a titillation that carries its own punishment in the end. The twin motif is one of the oldest and most-used themes in myths, legends, and fairy tales. The Romans believed that Rome was founded by the twins Romulus and Remus, who were raised by a she-wolf. American Indian myths tell of the Sacred Twins, one good and the other evil, who nevertheless rule the world as gods; their different personalities complement each other and keep the world in balance. Maya religion teaches of the heavenly warrior twins. A favorite African folklore theme is twin spirits, reflected in traditional twin sculptures. Grimm's fairy tales tell of twins who part and meet again, experiencing parallel adventures in the meantime; one story even tells of an entourage of twin bears, lions, foxes, and hares as faithful companions. A classic American tale of twins is John Steinbeck's *East of Eden,* in which Cal (the bad but misunderstood twin) and Aron (the good twin) take on the roles of the ancient biblical drama of Cain and Abel—a story

come to life as an icon of American culture through James Dean's powerful movie debut performance as Cal. And the film *Dead Ringers* stars Jeremy Irons as identical twin gynecologists who gradually switch roles, socially and psychologically, with eventual tragic results both professionally and personally.

Mark Twain presents another version of the dual-character theme in *The Prince and the Pauper.* The main characters are not twins, but rather identical-looking boys, one the Prince of Wales and the other a poor boy from the lower end of society. The boys switch places, and each learns about the goodness and evil outside of them, in the inegalitarian society of Old England. The story exists in a multitude of versions, from Alexandre Dumas's *The Man in the Iron Mask* to Anthony Hope's *Prisoner of Zenda* to Disney's *The Parent Trap.*

Golding's novel *Lord of the Flies* is a vision of inherently evil human nature. But it can also be seen as a type of "twin" story, or rather a "triplet" story: The good and evil powers battle it out within a person's spirit. Three boys, Ralph, Jack, and Piggy, are the main characters. Ralph tries to maintain the Rule of Law and decency, while Jack leads the "tribal" boys who have reverted to primitive warfare; Piggy, Ralph's friend, tries very hard to keep him focused on the ideals of civilization. But aren't Piggy and Jack really two sides at war within Ralph's own soul? We looked at *Lord of the Flies* closely in Chapter 3. In the classic *Star Trek* episodes a similar situation was explored elegantly: Captain Kirk, a man of both logic and emotion, making decisions with his two "alter egos" at his side, the emotional Bones and the logical Spock. We know the idea well from cartoons, as you will remember from the beginning of this chapter, and that means we have come full circle: A character split between conscience and temptation, with the little angel of conscience on one shoulder and the devil of temptation on the other.

Study Questions

1. In your view, is there a meaning to life? Explain your viewpoint and, if possible, relate it to the

four types of theories: (1) life has meaning, (2) life has an obscure meaning, (3) life has the meaning we give it, (4) life has no meaning.

2. In your view, is there a continuation of human life after death, in some form or other? Explain. You may want to revisit the metaphysical theories of materialism, dualism, and idealism.

3. Give an account of Plato's theory of the tripartite soul, and give an example of how it may illustrate the process of decision making.

4. Give an account of Aristotle's theory of the four causes, focusing on the concept of teleology.

5. Give an account of Augustine's theory of original sin and of the concept of evil.

6. Explain Aquinas's concept of natural law, drawing on his theory of the three natural inclinations.

7. What, to Kant, is the radical evil in human nature? Explain.

8. What did Nietzsche mean by saying that the Overman was "beyond good and evil"? Explain the Overman theory.

9. Which theories in this chapter regard animal souls as a possibility? In your view, do humans have souls? And if yes, can nonhuman animals also have souls? Explain.

Primary Readings and Narratives

The first Primary Reading is an excerpt from Plato's *Republic,* Book IV, in which Plato speculates that the soul has three elements. The second reading is an excerpt from Aristotle's *On the Soul,* Book II, where he outlines his theory of soul as the form of the body. The third reading comes from Thomas Aquinas's *Summa Theologica,* where we hear about the concept of natural law. A fourth reading selection consists of an excerpt from Nietzsche's *Thus Spoke Zarathustra,* where the theory of the eternal return is expressed.

The Narratives section also has a more extensive selection than in most chapters, for the simple reason that so many writers and filmmakers have been attracted to the subject of good and evil, and I wanted to be able to include some of my favorites! In addition, this chapter has several other themes, and some of the stories serve as illustrations of such themes. The first Narrative is a summary of the film *What Dreams May Come;* the second is a summary of Stevenson's famous novel, *Strange Case of Dr. Jekyll and Mr. Hyde;* for comparison, there is a summary of Hans Christian Andersen's "The Shadow." Next you have two short excerpts from Dostoyevsky's *Crime and Punishment,* a summary of Grimwood's novel *Replay,* and finally a summary and analysis of Camus's *The Myth of Sisyphus.*

Primary Reading

Republic

PLATO

Excerpt from Book IV. Translated by Benjamin Jowett. Fourth century B.C.E.

Would you not say that thirst is one of these essentially relative terms, having clearly a relation—

Yes, thirst is relative to drink.

And a certain kind of thirst is relative to a certain kind of drink; but thirst taken alone is neither of much nor little, nor of good nor bad, nor of any particular kind of drink, but of drink only?

Certainly.

Then the soul of the thirsty one, in so far as he is thirsty, desires only drink; for this he yearns and tires to obtain it?

That is plain.

And if you suppose something which pulls a thirsty soul away from drink, that must be different from the thirsty principle which draws him like a beast to drink; for, as we were saying, the same thing cannot at the same time with the same part of itself act in contrary ways about the same.

Impossible.

No more than you can say that the hands of the archer push and pull the bow at the same time, but what you say is that one hand pushes and the other pulls.

Exactly so, he replied.

And might a man be thirsty, and yet unwilling to drink?

Yes, he said, it constantly happens.

And in such a case what is one to say? Would you not say that there was something in the soul bidding a man to drink, and something else forbidding him, which is other and stronger than the principle which bids him?

I should say so.

And the forbidding principle is derived from reason, and that which bids and attracts proceeds from passion and disease?

Clearly.

Then we may fairly assume that they are two, and that they differ from one another; the one with which a man reasons, we may call the rational principle of the soul, the other with which he loves and hungers and thirsts and feels the flutterings of any other desire may be termed the irrational or appetitive, the ally of sundry pleasures and satisfactions? [2]

Yes, he said, we may fairly assume them to be different.

Then let us finally determine that there are two principles existing in the soul. And what of passion, or spirit? Is it a third, or akin to one of the preceding?

I should be inclined to say—akin to desire.

Well, I said, there is a story which I remember to have heard, and in which I put faith. The story is, that Leontius, the son of Aglaion coming up one day from the Piraeus, under the north wall on the outside, observed some dead bodies lying on the ground at the place of execution. He felt a desire to see them, and also a dread and abhorrence of them; for a time he struggled and covered his eyes, but at length the desire got the better of him; and forcing them open, he ran up to the dead bodies, saying, Look, ye wretches, take your fill of the fair sight.

I have heard the story myself, he said.

The moral of the tale is, that anger at times goes to war with desire, as though they were two distinct things.

Yes, that is the meaning, he said.

And are there not many other cases in which we observe that when a man's desires violently prevail over his reason, he reviles himself, and is angry at the violence within him, and that in this struggle, which is like the struggle of factions in a State, his spirit is on the side of his reason—but for the passionate or spirited element to take part with the desires when reason decides that she should not be opposed, is a sort of thing which I believe that you never observed occurring in yourself, nor, as I should imagine, in any one else?

Certainly not.

Suppose that a man thinks he has done a wrong to another, the nobler he is the less able is he to feel indignant at any suffering, such as hunger, or cold, or any other pain which the injured person may inflict upon him—these he deems to be just, and, as I say, his anger refuses to be excited by them.

True, he said.

But when he thinks that he is the sufferer of the wrong, then he boils and chafes, and is on the side of what he believes to be justice; and because he suffers hunger or cold or other pain he is only the more determined to persevere and conquer. His noble spirit will not be quelled until he either slays or is slain; or until he hears the voice of the shepherd, that is, reason, bidding his dog bark no more.

The illustration is perfect, he replied; and in our State, as we were saying, the auxiliaries were to be dogs, and to hear the voice of the rulers, who are their shepherds.

I perceive, I said, that you quite understand me; there is, however, a further point which I wish you to consider.

What point?

You remember that passion or spirit appeared at first sight to be a kind of desire, but now we should say quite the contrary; for in the conflict of the soul spirit is arrayed on the side of the rational principle.

Most assuredly.

But a further question arises: Is passion different from reason also, or only a kind of reason; in which latter case, instead of three principles in the soul, there will only be two, the rational and the concupiscent; or rather, as the State was composed of three classes, traders, auxiliaries, counselors, so may there not be in the individual soul a third element which is passion or spirit, and when not corrupted by bad education is the natural auxiliary of reason?

Yes, he said, there must be a third.

Yes, I replied, if passion, which has already been shown to be different from desire, turn out also to be different from reason.

But that is easily proved:—We may observe even in young children that they are full of spirit almost as soon as they are born, whereas some of them never seem to attain to the use of reason, and most of them late enough.

Excellent, I said, and you may see passion equally in brute animals, which is a further proof of the truth of what you are saying. And we may once more appeal to the words of Homer, which have been already quoted by us,

He smote his breast, and thus rebuked his heart;

for in this verse Homer has clearly supposed the power which reasons about the better and worse to be different from the unreasoning anger which is rebuked by it.

Very true, he said.

And so, after much tossing, we have reached land, and are fairly agreed that the same principles which exist in the State exist also in the individual, and that they are three in number.

Exactly.

Must we not then infer that the individual is wise in the same way, and in virtue of the same quality which makes the State wise?

Certainly.

Also that the same quality which constitutes courage in the State constitutes courage in the individual, and that both the State and the individual bear the same relation to all the other virtues?

Assuredly.

And the individual will be acknowledged by us to be just in the same way in which the State is just?

That follows of course.

We cannot but remember that the justice of the State consisted in each of the three classes doing the work of its own class?

We are not very likely to have forgotten, he said.

We must recollect that the individual in whom the several qualities of his nature do their own work will be just, and will do his own work?

Yes, he said, we must remember that too.

And ought not the rational principle, which is wise, and has the care of the whole soul, to rule, and the passionate or spirited principle to be the subject and ally?

Certainly.

And, as we were saying, the united influence of music and gymnastic will bring them into accord, nerving and sustaining the reason with noble words and lessons, and moderating and soothing and civilizing the wildness of passion by harmony and rhythm?

Quite true, he said.

And these two, thus nurtured and educated, and having learned truly to know their own functions, will rule over the concupiscent, which in each of us is the largest part of the soul and by nature most insatiable of gain; over this they will keep guard, lest, waxing great and strong with the fulness of bodily pleasures, as they are termed, the concupiscent soul, no longer confined to her own sphere, should attempt to enslave and rule those who are not her natural-born subjects, and overturn the whole life of man?

Very true, he said.

Both together will they not be the best defenders of the whole soul and the whole body against attacks from without; the one counseling, and the other fighting under his leader, and courageously executing his commands and counsels?

True.

And he is to be deemed courageous whose spirit retains in pleasure and in pain the commands of reason about what he ought or ought not to fear?

Right, he replied.

And him we call wise who has in him that little part which rules, and which proclaims these commands; that part too being supposed to have a knowledge of what is for the interest of each of the three parts and of the whole?

Assuredly.

And would you not say that he is temperate who has these same elements in friendly harmony, in whom the one ruling principle of reason, and the two subject ones of spirit and desire are equally agreed that reason ought to rule, and do not rebel?

Certainly, he said, that is the true account of temperance whether in the State or individual.

And surely, I said, we have explained again and again how and by virtue of what quality a man will be just.

That is very certain.

And is justice dimmer in the individual, and is her form different, or is she the same which we found her to be in the State?

There is no difference in my opinion, he said.

Study Questions

1. Why does Plato tell the story of Leontius, who couldn't help looking at the executed bodies?

2. What are the three elements of principles of the soul, according to Plato, and how are they supposed to interact?

3. Provide an example from our contemporary reality to illustrate how the three elements of the soul are supposed to work together, and what might happen if they don't.

Primary Reading

On the Soul

ARISTOTLE

Excerpt from Book II. Translated by W. D. Ross. Fourth century B.C.E.

We are in the habit of recognizing, as one determinate kind of what is, substance, and that in several senses, (*a*) in the sense of matter or that which in itself is not "a this," and (*b*) in the sense of form or essence, which is that precisely in virtue of which a thing is called "a this," and thirdly (*c*) in the sense of that which is compounded of both (*a*) and (*b*). Now matter is potentiality, form actuality; of the latter there are two grades related to one another as e.g. knowledge to the exercise of knowledge.

Among substances are by general consent reckoned bodies and especially natural bodies; for they are the principles of all other bodies. Of natural bodies some have life in them, others not; by life we mean self-nutrition and growth (with its correlative decay). It follows that every natural body which has life in it is a substance in the sense of a composite.

But since it is also a *body* of such and such a kind, viz. having life, the *body* cannot be soul; the body is the subject or matter, not what is attributed to it. Hence the soul must be substance in the sense of the form of a natural body having life potentially within it. But substance is actuality, and thus soul is the actuality of a body as above characterized. Now the word actuality has two senses corresponding respectively to

the possession of knowledge and the actual exercise of knowledge. It is obvious that the soul is actuality in the first sense, viz. that of knowledge as possessed, for both sleeping and waking presuppose the existence of soul, and of these waking corresponds to actual knowing, sleeping to knowledge possessed but not employed, and, in the history of the individual, knowledge comes before its employment or exercise.

That is why the soul is the first grade of actuality of a natural body having life potentially in it. The body so described is a body which is organized. The parts of plants in spite of their extreme simplicity are "organs"; e.g. the leaf serves to shelter the pericarp, the pericarp to shelter the fruit, while the roots of plants are analogous to the mouth of animals, both serving for the absorption of food. If, then, we have to give a general formula applicable to all kinds of soul, we must describe it as the first grade of actuality of a natural organized body. That is why we can wholly dismiss as unnecessary the question whether the soul and the body are one: it is as meaningless to ask whether the wax and the shape given to it by the stamp are one, or generally the matter of a thing and that of which it is the matter. Unity has many senses (as many as "is" has), but the most proper and funda-

Is evil a force outside the human soul or part and parcel of who we are as a species? Obviously, Hobbes the stuffed tiger has his own opinion.

mental sense of both is the relation of an actuality to that of which it is the actuality. We have now given an answer to the question, What is soul?—an answer which applies to it in its full extent. It is substance in the sense which corresponds to the definitive formula of a thing's essence. That means that it is "the essential whatness" of a body of the character just assigned. Suppose that what is literally an "organ," like an axe, were a *natural* body, its "essential whatness," would have been its essence, and so its soul; if this disappeared from it, it would have ceased to be an axe, except in name. As it is, it is just an axe; it wants the character which is required to make its whatness or formulable essence a soul; for that, it would have had to be a *natural* body of a particular kind, viz. one having *in itself* the power of setting itself in movement and arresting itself. Next, apply this doctrine in the case of the "parts" of the living body. Suppose that the eye were an animal—sight would have been its soul, for sight is the substance or essence of the eye which corresponds to the formula, the eye being merely the matter of seeing; when seeing is removed the eye is no longer an eye, except in name—it is no more a real eye than the eye of a statue or of a painted figure. We must now extend our consideration from the "parts" to the whole living body; for what the departmental sense is to the bodily part which is its organ, that the whole faculty of sense is to the whole sensitive body as such.

We must not understand by that which is "potentially capable of living" what has lost the soul it had,

but only what still retains it; but seeds and fruits are bodies which possess the qualification. Consequently, while waking is actuality in a sense corresponding to the cutting and the seeing, the soul is actuality in the sense corresponding to the power of sight and the power in the tool; the body corresponds to what exists in potentiality; as the pupil *plus* the power of sight constitutes the eye, so the soul *plus* the body constitutes the animal.

From this it indubitably follows that the soul is inseparable from its body, or at any rate that certain parts of it are (if it has parts)—for the actuality of some of them is nothing but the actualities of their bodily parts. Yet some may be separable because they are not the actualities of any body at all. Further, we have no light on the problem whether the soul may not be the actuality of its body in the sense in which the sailor is the actuality of the ship.

This must suffice as our sketch or outline determination of the nature of soul. . . .

3

Of the psychic powers above enumerated some kinds of living things, as we have said, possess all, some less than all, others one only. Those we have mentioned are the nutritive, the appetitive, the sensory, the locomotive, and the power of thinking. Plants have none but the first, the nutritive, while another order of living things has this *plus* the sensory. If any order of living things has the sensory, it must also have the appetitive; for appetite is the genus of which desire, passion, and wish are the species; now all animals have one sense at least, viz. touch, and whatever has a sense has the capacity for pleasure and pain and therefore has pleasant and painful objects present to it, and wherever these are present, there is desire, for desire is just appetition of what is pleasant. Further, all animals have the sense for food (for touch is the sense for food); the food of all living things consists of what is dry, moist, hot, cold, and these are the qualities apprehended by touch; all other sensible qualities are apprehended by touch only indirectly. Sounds, colours, and odours contribute nothing to nutriment; flavours fall within the field of tangible qualities. Hunger and thirst are forms of desire, hunger a desire for what is dry and hot, thirst a desire for what is cold and moist; flavour is a sort of seasoning added to both. We must later clear up these points, but at present it may be enough to say that all animals that possess the sense of touch have also appetition. The case of imagination is obscure; we must examine it later. Certain kinds of animals possess in addition the power of locomotion, and still another order of animate beings, i.e. man and possibly another order like man or superior to him, the power of thinking, i.e. mind.

Study Questions

1. What, according to Aristotle, is a soul, and where are souls to be found?

2. Where in this text might one find evidence for the assumption that Aristotle doesn't believe in an immortal soul?

3. List what Aristotle calls the psychic powers of all living things. Do you agree with his assessment? Why or why not?

Primary Reading

Summa Theologica: Natural Law

ST. THOMAS AQUINAS

Extract. Translated by Fathers of the English Dominican Province. Thirteenth Century C.E.

WHETHER THERE IS IN US A NATURAL LAW?

Objection 1. It would seem that there is no natural law in us. Because man is governed sufficiently by the eternal law: for Augustine says that "the eternal law is that by which it is right that all things should be most orderly." But nature does not abound in superfluities as neither does she fail in necessaries. Therefore no law is natural to man.

Objection 2. Further, by the law man is directed, in his acts, to the end. . . . But the directing of human acts to their end is not a function of nature, as is the case in irrational creatures, which act for an end solely by their natural appetite; whereas man acts for an end by his reason and will. Therefore no law is natural to man.

Objection 3. Further, the more a man is free, the less is he under the law. But man is freer than all the animals, on account of his free-will, with which he is endowed above all other animals. Since therefore other animals are not subject to a natural law, neither is man subject to a natural law.

On the contrary, A gloss on Rm. 2:14: "When the Gentiles, who have not the law, do by nature those things that are of the law," comments as follows: "Although they have no written law, yet they have the natural law, whereby each one knows, and is conscious of, what is good and what is evil."

I answer that . . . law, being a rule and measure, can be in a person in two ways: in one way, as in him that rules and measures; in another way, as in that which is ruled and measured, since a thing is ruled and measured, in so far as it partakes of the rule or measure. Wherefore, since all things subject to Divine providence are ruled and measured by the eternal law, as was stated above; it is evident that all things partake somewhat of the eternal law, in so far as, namely, from its being imprinted on them, they derive their respective inclinations to their proper acts and ends. Now among all others, the rational creature is subject to Divine providence in the most excellent way, in so far as it partakes of a share of providence, by being provident both for itself and for others. Wherefore it has a share of the Eternal Reason, whereby it has a natural inclination to its proper act and end: and this participation of the eternal law in the rational creature is called the natural law. Hence the Psalmist after saying (Ps. 4:6): "Offer up the sacrifice of justice," as though someone asked what the works of justice are, adds: "Many say, Who showeth us good things?" in answer to which question he says: "The light of Thy countenance, O Lord, is signed upon us": thus implying that the light of natural reason, whereby we discern what is good and what is evil, which is the function of the natural law, is nothing else than an imprint on us of the Divine light. It is therefore evident that the natural law is nothing else than the rational creature's participation of the eternal law.

Reply to Objection 1. This argument would hold, if the natural law were something different from the eternal law: whereas it is nothing but a participation thereof, as stated above.

Reply to Objection 2. Every act of reason and will in us is based on that which is according to nature, as stated above: for every act of reasoning is based on principles that are known naturally, and every act of appetite in respect of the means is derived from the natural appetite in respect of the last end. Accordingly the first direction of our acts to their end must needs be in virtue of the natural law.

Reply to Objection 3. Even irrational animals partake in their own way of the Eternal Reason, just as the rational creature does. But because the rational creature partakes thereof in an intellectual and rational manner, therefore the participation of the eternal law in the rational creature is properly called a law,

since a law is something pertaining to reason, as stated above. Irrational creatures, however, do not partake thereof in a rational manner, wherefore there is no participation of the eternal law in them, except by way of similitude. . . .

Whether the Natural Law Contains Several Precepts, or Only One?

Now a certain order is to be found in those things that are apprehended universally. For that which, before aught else, falls under apprehension, is "being," the notion of which is included in all things whatsoever a man apprehends. Wherefore the first indemonstrable principle is that "the same thing cannot be affirmed and denied at the same time," which is based on the notion of "being" and "not-being": and on this principle all others are based. . . . Now as "being" is the first thing that falls under the apprehension simply, so "good" is the first thing that falls under the apprehension of the practical reason, which is directed to action: since every agent acts for an end under the aspect of good. Consequently the first principle of practical reason is one founded on the notion of good, viz. that "good is that which all things seek after." Hence this is the first precept of law, that "good is to be done and pursued, and evil is to be avoided." All other precepts of the natural law are based upon this: so that whatever the practical reason naturally apprehends as man's good (or evil) belongs to the precepts of the natural law as something to be done or avoided.

Since, however, good has the nature of an end, and evil, the nature of a contrary, hence it is that all those things to which man has a natural inclination, are naturally apprehended by reason as being good, and consequently as objects of pursuit, and their contraries as evil, and objects of avoidance. Wherefore according to the order of natural inclinations, is the order of the precepts of the natural law. Because in man there is first of all an inclination to good in accordance with the nature which he has in common with all substances: inasmuch as every substance seeks the preservation of its own being, according to its nature: and by reason of this inclination, whatever is a means of preserving human life, and of warding off its obstacles, belongs to the natural law. Secondly, there is in man an inclination to things that pertain to him more specially, according to that nature which he has in common with other animals: and in virtue of this inclination, those things are said to belong to the natural law, "which nature has taught to all animals," such as sexual intercourse, education of offspring and so forth. Thirdly, there is in man an inclination to good, according to the nature of his reason, which nature is proper to him: thus man has a natural inclination to know the truth about God, and to live in society: and in this respect, whatever pertains to this inclination belongs to the natural law; for instance, to shun ignorance, to avoid offending those among whom one has to live, and other such things regarding the above inclination.

WHETHER ALL ACTS OF VIRTUE ARE PRESCRIBED BY THE NATURAL LAW?

Objection 1. It would seem that not all acts of virtue are prescribed by the natural law. Because, as stated above it is essential to a law that it be ordained to the common good. But some acts of virtue are ordained to the private good of the individual, as is evident especially in regards to acts of temperance. Therefore not all acts of virtue are the subject of natural law.

Objection 2. Further, every sin is opposed to some virtuous act. If therefore all acts of virtue are prescribed by the natural law, it seems to follow that all sins are against nature: whereas this applies to certain special sins. . . .

On the contrary, Damascene says that "virtues are natural." Therefore virtuous acts also are a subject of the natural law.

I answer that, We may speak of virtuous acts in two ways: first, under the aspect of virtuous; secondly, as such and such acts considered in their proper species. If then we speak of acts of virtue, considered as virtuous, thus all virtuous acts belong to the natural law. For it has been stated (2) that to the natural law belongs everything to which a man is inclined according to his nature. Now each thing is inclined naturally to an operation that is suitable to it according to its form: thus fire is inclined to give heat. Wherefore

since the rational soul is the proper form of man, there is in every man a natural inclination to act according to reason: and this is to act according to virtue. Consequently, considered thus, all acts of virtue are prescribed by the natural law: since each one's reason naturally dictates to him to act virtuously. But if we speak of virtuous acts, considered in themselves, i.e. in their proper species, thus not all virtuous acts are prescribed by the natural law: for many things are done virtuously, to which nature does not incline at first; but which, through the inquiry of reason, have been found by men to be conducive to well-living.

Reply to Objection 1. Temperance is about the natural concupiscences of food, drink, and sexual matters, which are indeed ordained to the natural common good, just as other matters of law are ordained to the moral common good.

Reply to Objection 2. By human nature we may mean either that which is proper to man—and in this sense all sins, as being against reason, are also against nature, as Damascene states: or we may mean that nature which is common to man and other animals; and in this sense, certain special sins are said to be against nature; thus contrary to sexual intercourse, which is natural to all animals, is unisexual lust, which has received the special name of the unnatural crime.

Study Questions

1. How does Aquinas answer the objection that since there is eternal law, we don't need natural law?

2. How does Aquinas define "good" according to natural law?

3. What are the three primary natural inclinations, according to Aquinas?

4. What does Aquinas mean by defining human nature in two ways: (1) what is "proper to man" and (2) what is "common to man and other animals"? Explain what Aquinas means by *sin* within these two definitions. Would you agree with his assessment? Why or why not?

Primary Reading

Thus Spoke Zarathustra

FRIEDRICH NIETZSCHE

Extract. Translated by Walter Kaufmann. 1883–1884, 1892.

ON THE VISION AND THE RIDDLE

1

When it got abroad among the sailors that Zarathustra was on board—for another man from the blessed isles had embarked with him—there was much curiosity and anticipation. But Zarathustra remained silent for two days and was cold and deaf from sadness and answered neither glances nor questions. But on the evening of the second day he opened his ears again, although he still remained silent, for there was much that was strange and dangerous to be heard on this ship, which came from far away and wanted to sail even farther. But Zarathustra was a friend of all who travel far and do not like to live without danger. And behold, eventually his own tongue was loosened as he listened, and the ice of his heart broke. Then he began to speak thus:

To you, the bold searchers, researchers, and whoever embarks with cunning sails on terrible seas—to you, drunk with riddles, glad of the twilight, whose soul flutes lure astray to every whirlpool, because you do not want to grope along a thread with cowardly hand; and where you can *guess,* you hate to *deduce*—to you alone I tell the riddle that I *saw,* the vision of the loneliest.

Not long ago I walked gloomily through the deadly pallor of dusk—gloomy and hard, with lips pressed together. Not only one sun had set for me. A path that ascended defiantly through stones, malicious, lonely, not cheered by herb or shrub—a mountain path crunched under the defiance of my foot. Striding silently over the mocking clatter of pebbles, crushing the rock that made it slip, my foot forced its way upward. Upward—defying the spirit that drew it downward toward the abyss, the spirit of gravity, my devil and archenemy. Upward—although

he sat on me, half dwarf, half mole, lame, making lame, dripping lead into my ear, leaden thoughts into my brain.

"O Zarathustra," he whispered mockingly, syllable by syllable; "you philosopher's stone! You threw yourself up high, but every stone that is thrown must fall. O Zarathustra, you philosopher's stone, you slingstone, you star-crusher! You threw yourself up so high; but every stone that is thrown must fall. Sentenced to yourself and to your own stoning—O Zarathustra, far indeed have you thrown the stone, but it will fall back on yourself."

Then the dwarf fell silent, and that lasted a long time. His silence, however, oppressed me; and such twosomeness is surely more lonesome than being alone. I climbed, I climbed, I dreamed, I thought; but everything oppressed me. I was like one sick whom his wicked torture makes weary, and who as he falls asleep is awakened by a still more wicked dream. But there is something in me that I call courage; that has so far slain my every discouragement. This courage finally bade me stand still and speak: "Dwarf! It is you or I!"

For courage is the best slayer, courage which *attacks*; for in every attack there is playing and brass.

Man, however, is the most courageous animal: hence he overcame every animal. With playing and brass he has so far overcome every pain; but human pain is the deepest pain.

Courage also slays dizziness at the edge of abysses: and where does man not stand at the edge of abysses? Is not seeing always—seeing abysses?

Courage is the best slayer: courage slays even pity. But pity is the deepest abyss: as deeply as man sees into life, he also sees into suffering.

Courage, however, is the best slayer—courage which attacks: which slays even death itself, for it says, "Was *that* life? Well then! Once more!"

In such words, however, there is much playing and brass. He that has ears to hear, let him hear!

2

"Stop, dwarf!" I said. "It is I or you! But I am the stronger of us two: you do not know my abysmal thought. *That* you could not bear!"

Then something happened that made me lighter, for the dwarf jumped from my shoulder, being curious; and he crouched on a stone before me. But there was a gateway just where we had stopped.

"Behold this gateway, dwarf!" I continued. "It has two faces. Two paths meet here; no one has yet followed either to its end. This long lane stretches back for an eternity. And the long lane out there, that is another eternity. They contradict each other, these paths; they offend each other face to face; and it is here at this gateway that they come together. The name of the gateway is inscribed above: 'Moment.' But whoever would follow one of them, on and on, farther and farther—do you believe, dwarf, that these paths contradict each other eternally?"

"All that is straight lies," the dwarf murmured contemptuously. "All truth is crooked; time itself is a circle."

"You spirit of gravity," I said angrily, "do not make things too easy for yourself! Or I shall let you crouch where you are crouching, lamefoot; and it was I that carried you to this *height*.

"Behold," I continued, "this moment! From this gateway, Moment, a long, eternal lane leads *backward:* behind us lies an eternity. Must not whatever *can* happen have happened, have been done, have passed by before? And if everything has been there before— what do you think, dwarf, of this moment? Must not this gateway too have been there before? And are not all things knotted together so firmly that this moment draws after it *all* that is to come? Therefore—itself too? For whatever *can* walk—in this long lane out *there,* too, it *must* walk one more.

"And this slow spider, which crawls in the moonlight, and this moonlight itself, and I and you in the gateway, whispering together, whispering of eternal things—must not all of us have been there before? And return and walk in that other lane, out there, before us, in this long dreadful lane—must we not eternally return?"

Thus I spoke, more and more softly; for I was afraid of my own thoughts and the thoughts behind my thoughts. Then suddenly I heard a dog howl nearby. Had I ever heard a dog howl like this? My thoughts raced back. Yes, when I was a child, in the most distant childhood: then I heard a dog howl like this. And I saw him too, bristling, his head up, trembling, in the stillest midnight when even dogs believe in ghosts—and I took pity: for just then the full moon, silent as death, passed over the house; just then it stood still, a round glow—still on the flat roof, as if on another's property—that was why the dog was terrified, for dogs believe in thieves and ghosts. And when I heard such howling again I took pity again.

Where was the dwarf gone now? And the gateway? And the spider? And all the whispering? Was I dreaming, then? Was I waking up? Among wild cliffs I stood suddenly along, bleak, in the bleakest moonlight. *But there lay a man.* And there—the dog, jumping, bristling, whining—now he saw me coming; then he howled again, he *cried.* Had I ever heard a dog cry like this for help? And verily, what I saw—I had never seen the like. A young shepherd I saw, writhing, gagging, in spasms, his face distorted, and a heavy black snake hung out of his mouth. Had I ever seen so much nausea and pale dread on one face? He seemed to have been asleep when the snake crawled into his throat, and there bit itself fast. My hand tore at the snake and tore in vain; it did not tear the snake out of his throat. Then it cried out of me: "Bite! Bite its head off! Bite!" Thus it cried out of me—my dread, my hatred, my nausea, my pity, all that is good and wicked in me cried out of me with a single cry.

You bold ones who surround me! You searchers, researchers, and whoever among you has embarked with cunning sails on unexplored seas. You who are glad of riddles! Guess me this riddle that I saw then, interpret me the vision of the loneliest. For it was a vision and a foreseeing. *What* did I see then in a parable? And *who* is it who must yet come one day? *Who* is the shepherd into whose throat the snake crawled thus? *Who* is the man into whose throat all that is heaviest and blackest will crawl thus?

The shepherd, however, bit as my cry counseled him; he bit with a good bite. Far away he spewed the head of the snake—and he jumped up. No longer shepherd, no longer human—one changed, radiant, *laughing!* Never yet on earth has a human being laughed as he laughed! O my brothers, I heard a laughter that was no human laughter; and now a thirst gnaws at me, a longing that never grows still. My longing for this laughter gnaws at me; oh, how do I bear to go on living! And how could I bear to die now!

Thus spoke Zarathustra.

Study Questions

1. What is the basis for Nietzsche's argument that everything must happen again? Do you agree?

2. Who is the shepherd into whose throat everything terrible has crawled? And what does it mean that he bites its head off? (A hint: some scholars think Nietzsche himself is gagging on the most terrible thought of all: that everything will return in the same way. In that case, what would be the significance of biting the snake's head off?)

3. One interpretation of Nietzsche's theory of the eternal return is that he intended it as a test of how much we love life. If we love it so much that we would say, "Well then, Once more!" then we have passed the test. How would *you* do on that test?

The Destiny of the Soul

 *Narrative*

What Dreams May Come

VINCENT WARD (DIRECTOR) AND RONALD BASS (SCREENWRITER) FROM THE NOVEL BY RICHARD MATHESON

Film, 1998.

This film had a significant impact on many moviegoers; it deals with life after death—in a positive, but also a didactic (teaching) manner. You'll recognize elements from the discussion of mind and body in Chapter 7, as well as the discussion of what constitutes a self. However, most of the impact comes from its vision of what happens to the soul, and especially to the soul of a soul mate in the darkest despair, which is why you find this film in this chapter. The obscure title, often quoted erroneously as "When Dreams May Come," is taken from one of the most famous stageplay monologues in Western history: Hamlet's "To be or not to be" monologue by Shakespeare:

To be, or not to be,—that is the question:—
Whether 'tis nobler in the mind to suffer
the slings and arrows of outrageous fortune,
or to take arms against a sea of troubles,
And by opposing end them?—To die,—to sleep,—
No more; and by a sleep to say we end

The heart-ache and the thousand natural shocks
That flesh is heir to,—'tis a consummation
Devoutly to be wished. To die,—to sleep;—
To sleep! Perchance to dream:—ay, there's the rub;
For in that sleep of death what dreams may come,
When we have shuffled off this mortal coil,
Must give us pause; there's the respect
That makes calamity of so long life. . . .

Chris Nielsen and his wife, Annie, have always felt that their relationship is especially meaningful; they met on a lake in Switzerland, and in their dream world, captured by Annie in her paintings, they have a home on a lake like the place where they met. It seems that they have an ideal life: They love each other, they have meaningful jobs—he is a pediatrician, she is an artist—and they have two teenage children, a boy and a girl. But one night their happiness is taken from them: Their children die in an auto accident. The blow is terrible to Annie—but somehow, Chris seems to get beyond his grief faster. Flash forward to four years into the future: On a rainy night while Annie is working late at the art gallery, Chris himself is killed in an accident; to his surprise, he is still "there" in spirit, can see and hear everything, is present at his own funeral, and tries to console Annie, who has only the slightest inkling that he is near. Chris is by now accompanied by another spirit—one he can't seem to see clearly at first, but slowly the spirit takes on a shape: a younger version of his old mentor and friend, the black doctor Albert. When Chris finally realizes that his inability to let go is not helping Annie move on, he allows Albert to take him to the next step: the place beyond.

Chris finds himself in a most astonishing place, with beautiful lakeside scenery that seems very familiar to him, because it is Annie's painting of the lake come to life—and like a real oil painting in progress, the paint isn't dry, and comes off on Chris's hands and clothes. But he is in for even bigger surprises: Through the paint-dripping scenery comes a young version of his beloved dog Katie, years dead, and he remembers how Annie explained to his daughter, when they had to euthanize Katie, where Katie would go: "She'll go where we all go—now how can that be bad?" A house shimmers in the wet paint across the lake—their dream house. Not being used to being dead, Chris needs a lesson in who he is from Albert: "If you lost all your limbs, would you still be you? Your brain is a body part—it's gone." Chris tries to understand the nature of his self: "I am a voice in my head—the part of me that thinks and feels, that is aware that I exist at all." Like a good Cartesian (see Chapter 7), Albert responds, "So if you're aware that you exist—then you do! That's why you're still here. When you're in your house, it doesn't mean you *are* your house." In other words, Albert tells Chris that his soul used to inhabit his body, and now the soul is free to create its own world—and the world he has chosen is from Annie's painting. So Chris asks, "Where is God in all this?" Albert: "Up there somewhere, shouting down that he loves us, wondering why we can't hear him."

Being dead, Chris now realizes that he might be in the same realm as his dead children (you get the sense that Albert thinks he should have thought of that sooner). Albert has to take care of business elsewhere, but an Asian female spirit guide shows up and takes Chris to yet another level: a community of spirits, help-ing each other come to terms with life and death, and some even preparing to go back and be born again—for in the afterlife there is optional reincarnation. Through little hints it dawns on Chris that the friendly Asian woman is actually his daughter, who has taken on the shape of a woman she thinks her father admires, and father and daughter are reunited.

But now Albert returns, with dreadful news: Annie, having lost everything in life that she cared for, has committed suicide; we see her, sitting in front of a giant print of Hieronymus Bosch's famous painting, *Garden of Delights*—in other words, a painting of hell—right before deciding to take her own life. At first Chris is happy, because he thinks it means Annie will show up any minute—but Albert tells him that suicides are different: They have "violated the order of their life" and have to go elsewhere—to hell, for an eternity. Not as punishment, says Albert; it just happens automatically. People who commit suicide are so absorbed by their own situation that they don't know they're dead, and nobody can help them—on the contrary, others would become infected with the same hopelessness. But Chris insists: He will go find Annie and help her ascend from hell. Albert realizes that Chris and Annie had a very rare relationship and truly were soul mates; and in that case, perhaps Chris should try, although no one has ever succeeded. So Albert enlists the help of a very special person, the Tracker, to help Chris locate Annie in hell. However, Chris is terribly distracted now, because he has put two and two together and realized that his dead son is indeed near, too—in the shape of Albert! His son, who felt intimidated by his father's high expectations of him in real life, has chosen the face of Chris's mentor as his guiding spirit—because Albert was a kind of father figure to Chris himself. But this bothers the Tracker, who realizes that Chris will never reach his goal of finding Annie while worrying about his son, so at the gates of hell the Tracker sends Albert back to the heavenly community. (And the Tracker knows what he is doing—throughout the ordeal he tells Chris that he won't succeed, but he should try, anyway, for his own sake. He speaks like a father figure to Chris, and eventually Chris realizes that the Tracker, too, is someone from his past life: the doctor, Albert himself, who has chosen the look of an elderly white scholar to be Chris's tracker.)

Through the levels of hell, lit by fires like another Bosch painting, the tracker and Chris now proceed to look for Annie's lost soul. Through dreadful images of fields paved with live human heads, ocean depths full of bodies, and burning ships, they descend to the deepest level, in effect an upside-down cathedral ceiling. At the apex of the ceiling—here, the floor of hell—Annie sits in a ramshackle dark version of the ideal house—terrified, depressed, not knowing that she is dead. The Tracker cautions Chris that he won't succeed and should get out after just a few minutes. Knowing that Annie won't recognize him, Chris approaches the house. And here we find out, in one of many flashbacks, that it isn't the first time Annie has tried to kill herself: She was institutionalized after the children's death because of a suicide attempt, and Annie and Chris's relationship almost came to an end, but they weathered the crisis—only to face this, the worst crisis imaginable. Chris enters the house, and Annie doesn't know him.

Will Chris's love overcome the hopelessness of hell? Will he be able to bring Annie with him to their dream home in heaven? Will the whole family and their dog be reunited in the land of the dead? Not everything should be told about the moving ending of this film, but suffice it to say that even if we think we are the ones who can help someone else, sometimes we are also in need of help ourselves.

Study Questions:

1. If you have read Chapter 7, look for the Cartesian elements in the film.

2. Why do you think Matheson chose this title for his story? Compare the section of Hamlet's monologue with the storyline: Is there a relation?

3. Is this film fair to people who take their own lives? Why or why not? (Suicide is prohibited by the Catholic Church and other Christian churches, but has been considered an honorable solution in many cultures throughout history such as the ancient Roman culture and contemporary Japan.)

4. Evaluate the vision of the soul's journey from life to death and to life again, as it is depicted in this film. Is this an overall positive or a negative image for you? Which philosophical vision does it come closest to—Plato's or St. Augustine's?

5. What might Nietzsche say to this film?

The Alter Ego

Narrative

Strange Case of Dr. Jekyll and Mr. Hyde

ROBERT LOUIS STEVENSON

Novel, 1886.

You may have seen a movie version of this story. The special effects of the movie versions are usually at the cutting edge of whatever decade the movie was produced in, and the transformation of Jekyll into Hyde is generally a grisly process involving lots of contortions. Hyde usually ends up looking like a hairy monster. Only one version so far, a British TV film, portrays an old Dr. Jekyll who is transformed into a young, dapper, attractive Hyde—mirroring his innermost dreams. And that is actually not too far from the original story, which we will look at here.

An unpleasant and dangerous person, Edward Hyde is roaming the streets of London. He seems to have a protector in the well-known philanthropist Dr. Jekyll, who has even written out a will leaving everything to Hyde in the case of his own death or disappearance. Hyde gives everyone who sees him the sense that he is disabled (or "deformed," as the story says), although he is physically normal. Dr. Jekyll's old friend Utterson suspects foul play and imagines that Hyde is somehow blackmailing the doctor, but Jekyll reassures him that everything is fine. Incidents surrounding Hyde become more ominous, and an elderly gentleman is bludgeoned to death in the street. Hyde's quarters are searched, but it appears that he has left in a panic, after burning his papers. Utterson, who knows that Jekyll is somehow mixed up with Hyde, goes to Jekyll's house, but the voice that warns him to go away is not Jekyll's, but Hyde's. Utterson suspects that Hyde has murdered Jekyll and proceeds to break down the door. In the house they find Hyde on the floor, dying from having swallowed poison. There is no sign of Jekyll, but Hyde is dressed in street clothes that are much to large for him.

With Hyde dead and Jekyll missing, Utterson is now at liberty to read two documents that have been left to him, one from his old friend Dr. Layton and the other from Jekyll. Layton tells the first part of the astonishing story: He has personally witnessed the transformation, through the help of a chemical potion, of young, small, nasty Mr. Hyde into elderly, portly, kind Dr. Jekyll. The incident disturbed Layton so profoundly that he died shortly after. The next document, from Jekyll himself, tells the whole story, of how he has always seemed to be the good and kind person, but has really always felt he had a *dual nature*—one that loved knowledge, science, and his career, and another that sought only pleasure and cared nothing for the feelings of others. Over the years his career self won out, but he has always felt the tug of his "lower self":

> With every day, and from both sides of my intelligence, the moral and the intellectual, I thus drew steadily nearer to that truth, by whose partial discovery I have been doomed to such a dreadful shipwreck: that man is not one, but truly two. . . . It was on the moral side, and in my own person, that I learned to recognize the thorough and primitive duality of man: I saw that, of the two natures that contended in the field of my consciousness, even if I could rightly be said to be either, it was only because I was radically both. . . . If each, I told myself, could but be housed in separate identities, life would be relieved of all that was unbearable.[19]

So originally Jekyll wanted to suppress his wicked side—but after taking the brew that is to accomplish this, he finds himself instead transformed into a "younger, lighter, happier" person (younger and lighter because his Hyde personality has not had as much time to develop as Jekyll, so he is a smaller image). But in time, Hyde grows and becomes closer in size to Jekyll. In the beginning Jekyll is merely enjoying himself and feels he can get rid of Hyde at any time (like all addicts in the beginning stages of addiction). But by and by he realizes that Hyde is not just seeking pleasures, but *monstrous* pleasures, because he is completely evil. He doesn't have a mediating element of goodness, which Jekyll himself possesses, as a whole person. This also means that Jekyll is split not into one person of good and one of evil, but into one of evil and one of the normal mix of good and evil. So the Jekyll persona, which is only partly good, is not forceful enough to restrain Hyde, who is all evil. And now the drug begins to have erratic effects: One morning he wakes up as Hyde, having gone to bed as Jekyll. The process now happens at random, and he switches from Jekyll to Hyde when he least wants to. During one of these transformations he seeks help from Dr. Layton, which is why Layton witnessed the disturbing event.

In the end, Jekyll hides in his lab and writes a letter to Utterson. While he is there he is changed back to Hyde for the last time: As Utterson tries to break down the door, Hyde swallows the poison that will end his torments, and Utterson finds him dead on the floor of the laboratory.

Study Questions

1. Is Stevenson right? Do we all have two natures, one good and one evil, fighting for dominance of our soul?

2. Is Jekyll right in classifying the need for pleasure as "evil"? What does this attitude say about Stevenson's own time period? What might Nietzsche say to this story?

3. How might a Freudian (see Chapters 3, 6, and 7) interpret this story? (Remember Freud's distinction between the superego, the ego, and the id.)

4. Would a modern version of the story be likely to draw a parallel between being evil and being "deformed"? Why or why not? (Remember the discussion in Chapter 1 about one of the traditional criteria for being human: having a normal human physique.)

5. There is a genre of stories that are "Jekyll and Hyde" in reverse, so to speak: An ordinary character has an alter ego who is good and strong. Can you think of some examples?

 *Narrative*

The Shadow

HANS CHRISTIAN ANDERSEN

Short story, 1847.

Hans Christian Andersen is one of the world's most beloved and prolific writers of fairy tales, and you have already read about his Ugly Duckling story in Chapter 4. You probably also know the stories of "The Little Mermaid" and "Thumbelina." But Andersen wrote other types of stories, too—stories that, for today's audience, are more like horror and science fiction stories and not well suited for children. All of Andersen's stories have in common the fact that they function on several levels at the same time: They are entertainment, but they are also excursions into the depths of the human mind. "The Shadow" is one of the stories I would rec-

ommend for an adult reader looking into the heart of human nature, but not for a small child. It is a spooky story about losing your soul to the dark side of your-self—kind of a Jekyll and Hyde plot, although it was written and published almost forty years before the Stevenson story. Andersen traveled extensively in Italy, and one day he was particularly bothered by the heat and had to stay in his hotel room. Here he thought up the story of the shadow.

A scholar traveling in southern Europe is confined to his hotel room by the intense heat. He discovers that during the heat of the day his shadow shrinks, but in

Hans Christian Andersen's "The Shadow" (illustration by Vilhelm Petersen). The shadow side of the scholar is growing and will soon claim its independence. Eventually it will cause the downfall of the scholar. (Courtesy of the H. C. Andersen Museum, Odense, Denmark.)

the cool of the night, by candlelight, his shadow grows long and stretches. Every evening someone in the house opposite his hotel is playing beautiful music, but he never sees anyone there. Then late one evening he sees, ever so briefly, a beautiful woman on the balcony, surrounded by a glowing light. After the woman has disappeared, he notices that since he is backlit by the light in his room, his own shadow is now cast on the house across the street—and the balcony door is ajar. Jokingly the scholar tells his shadow to go in and find out what's going on. He turns out his light so he can go to sleep and thinks nothing more of it, until the next day in the street, when he realizes that he no longer has a shadow. "That's too bad," he thinks, "my shadow took me seriously, and now he is gone." But everything grows rapidly in a Southern climate, and in another few days a new shadow is growing out from his feet. Soon he leaves for his home in the North and continues his life, but one day there is a knock on his door.

A thin wisp of a man, very elegant, is standing outside. He introduces himself as the scholar's former shadow. Yes, he says, he went inside the house across the street, and there lived Lady Poetry herself. He didn't go all the way in, for the light was too blinding but he stayed in her antechamber, and that was enough: The exposure to Poetry transformed him and made a human out of him. But because he had no clothes and still had the appearance of a shadow on a wall, he fled and hid. For a long time he hid in wealthy people's homes and discovered all their secrets; it became easy then to make a fortune. Slowly he acquired flesh and bones, and now he would like to ask if his old master would like to become *his* shadow, for he can't seem to grow one. The scholar is appalled at the very idea and sends him away, but the damage is done: he now worries so much that friends say he is "just a shadow of himself." The Shadow returns, repeats his offer, and

makes the scholar promise that he will never mention that their roles have been reversed. The scholar complies, and they both go off on a journey.

After a while they arrive in a foreign land, where there lives a princess whose penetrating eyesight allows her to perceive things others can't see. She promptly sees that the Shadow can't cast a shadow. But the Shadow tells her she's wrong, for he has a very fancy shadow, a flesh-and-bone one. The princess likes the Shadow and even talks to his "shadow," finding the scholar a shadow of much learning and goodness. If a man's shadow is so wise, the man himself must be a truly remarkable person, she tells herself.

The Shadow calls the scholar to him and informs him that he is about to marry the princess. The scholar will be secure for life, provided that he will promise never to let on that he used to be human and the Shadow used to be a shadow. But the scholar balks and threatens to reveal everything to the princess—he can't stand by and watch the princess being deceived. So the Shadow goes to the princess and tells her the sad story of how his shadow is beginning to think that he is the human and his master is the shadow. The princess suggests a quick solution, and she and the Shadow have a magnificent wedding. But the scholar has no awareness of this, for he has been quietly put to death.

Study Questions

1. Compare the Shadow to Mr. Hyde: How are they similar, and how do they differ?

2. What is the implication that the Shadow becomes real and human from exposure to poetry? Discuss in the light of the fact that the Shadow develops into a deceitful, evil person—and that Andersen himself was a poet.

3. Do we all have a Shadow waiting to take over?

Beyond Good and Evil?

Narrative

Crime and Punishment

FYODOR DOSTOYEVSKY

Novel, 1866; film, 1935, 1958, 1959, 1999.

In a sense, *Crime and Punishment* contains elements of an alter ego story; here we witness the struggle between good and evil the way it ordinarily takes place: inside one person. Dostoyevsky's story is not merely about the struggle between good and evil but is also about evil done in the name of good, by a person who believes himself to be superior to most other people—a person who, by virtue of his personal powers and intellect, can act according to his own set of values. Raskolnikov, a handsome young student in the town of St. Petersburg who is down on his luck, is thinking about murdering an old, nasty pawnbroker; he knows that is it a terrible thing to do, and yet he feels justified in his plan and mysteriously drawn to see it through. Dostoyevsky's novel was the first to offer the idea, which was to provide indirect (or even direct) inspiration to philosophers from Nietzsche to Sartre, that if there is no God, then perhaps everything is allowed.

We will look at two scenes that provide clues to Raskolnikov's personality and his struggle with himself. The first illustrates the struggle between good and evil in Raskolnikov himself; the other might serve as a case study of Nietzsche's concept of the Overman, the human who has gone beyond good and evil.

In the first scene Raskolnikov is having a nightmare, the result of psychological pressures relating to his murder plans. In the dream he is a small boy walking with his father past a tavern where a peasant is trying to get an old, sick horse to pull a heavy load. The cart won't move, even though the little mare does her best, and people come out of the tavern to cheer the peasant on. Soon he is beating the horse, and the others shout suggestions for how best to torture the exhausted animal. The boy is frantic, because he loves the horses and often stops to "talk" with them; his father says there is nothing they can do and tries to drag him away. The boy breaks loose and runs to the horse to protect her, but he can't help her—the peasant is now beating the horse to death with a crowbar. The crowd gets in on it; and, grabbing whatever weapon they can, they pound on the mare until she dies.

Raskolnikov wakes up in terror: "Can it be, can it be, that I shall really take an ax, that I shall strike her on the head, split her skull open . . . that I shall tread in the sticky warm blood, break the lock, steal and tremble; hide, all spattered in blood . . . with the ax. . . . Good God, can it be?"

The second scene takes place much later, after the murder has been committed—a bloody, horrible affair where Raskolnikov finds himself forced to kill not just the old pawnbroker, but also a mentally disabled woman who happens to be in the wrong place at the wrong time and who would be able to identify him.

Raskolnikov is talking to friends Razumihin and Porfiry about an article that Raskolnikov wrote some time before the murder. In his article, Raskolnikov suggests that there are some people who are beyond the law, because they are extraordinary individuals. Ordinary people have to live by the law, but "extraordinary men have a right to commit any crime and to transgress the law in any way, just because they are extraordinary." Raskolnikov tries to clarify what he meant; he says that these extraordinary people don't *have* to commit crimes against morality, but they have a *right,* within themselves, to break rules in order to carry out their ideas in practice. So if Newton's theories had required him to kill off a certain number of people to prove his point, he would have had the right to do so—for his theories' sake, not just for personal gain. All great men of history, says Raskolnikov, are criminals: They make a new law by transgressing an old one. Everybody else is just ordinary, inferior, conservative, and law-abiding.

When a great man embarks on setting an idea in motion, ordinary people won't let him do it—they catch him and hang him. But in the next generation that great man will have become their hero.

How many of these extraordinary persons are there? Very few:

> The vast mass of mankind is mere material, and only exists in order by some great effort, by some mysterious process, by means of some crossing of race and stock, to bring into the world perhaps one man out of a thousand with a spark of independence . . . the man of genius is one of millions, and the great geniuses, the crown of humanity, appear on earth perhaps one in many thousand millions.

So how does Raskolnikov deal with having committed this crime, asserting his right as an extraordinary individual? And will he get away with these murders?

I would like you to explore that for yourself by reading this classic tale of murder, conscience, and thoughts of good and evil; but in all fairness to Dostoyevsky I want to mention that as certain as Raskolnikov is of the rights of the special individual in the beginning of the story, it is just as clear to him later, after having faced himself, his actions, and his convictions, that he was wrong.

Study Questions

1. Is Raskolnikov an evil person? Can anyone have a right to go "beyond good and evil"?

2. What function might his dream of the horse have within his murder plot?

3. Would Nietzsche have approved of Raskolnikov's theory of the extraordinary person? Would he have seen Raskolnikov himself as an Overman?

The Eternal Return of the Same

Narrative

Replay

KEN GRIMWOOD

Novel, 1987.

Nietzsche speculates that life may be repeating itself endlessly. For some, this means Nietzsche actually believed in an *eternal return of the same*. Other believe Nietzsche was trying to express something quite different: What if everything repeats itself in the smallest detail? Could you still want to experience life over again? In some ways, Grimwood's novel *Replay* ponders the same question; I will leave it up to you to decide what the moral of this story is, if any.

Jeff Winston is on the phone with his wife Linda when he has a heart attack. He is in his early forties, and their marriage isn't succeeding. They have not been able to have children, and lately communications between them have not been good. Jeff has let a lot of things slide, always thinking that there would be time to correct them. And now he is dying.

The next thing Jeff knows he is lying in a bed in a familiar room. But it isn't his bedroom at home—it is his bedroom from college. Music from the early 1960s is playing, and his old roommate Martin (who died in 1981) is trying to get him to respond. He is back in time, reliving his life as a college student, but he doesn't understand why. He discovers that he has the memories and the mind of his adult self, and as he moves through the events he has already lived through—such as going out with girlfriends—he discovers that he is not bound to repeat his previous actions; he has free will. Because he remembers who won the Kentucky Derby in 1963, he bets on the race—and wins big. This time around he will have money! He starts living the wild life, increases his fortune by betting on the World Series, and invests in IBM, Xerox, Boeing, Polaroid—corporations that were in their infancy in the 1960s. He realizes that there might be something else he can do: prevent the murder of John F. Kennedy. He sends threatening letters to the White House in the name of Lee Harvey Oswald, with the result that Oswald is arrested before the fateful date of November 22. But on that date, President Kennedy is murdered by someone else. So now Jeff begins to understand that he can only change certain circumstances, but perhaps not the entire picture.

On the day Jeff is due to meet Linda for the first time, he is very excited. He sees her from a distance and can't wait to repeat their romance. But this time around Linda doesn't like him at all—he is too cocky and self-assured. So he marries someone else, and they have a little girl who becomes everything to Jeff. He is rich, he has a daughter he loves, and everything is working out. He is even in fine health. But on the day of his first death, he has a heart attack—and dies again. And wakes up in 1963.

This time around he realizes what he has lost, and proceeds with much caution. His daughter, the light of his life, is not even "real" anymore, because she won't exist in this life. So he bets on the horses again and wins and promptly marries a different girl, his college sweetheart. She doesn't understand why he doesn't want children, but he is determined never again to bring another child into the world and then see every trace of her existence wiped out with his own death—for the past which he keeps returning to is his own original past, and the variations created by his previous life are nullified when he comes back. So he and his wife adopt two children, and they lead a good life. On the date of his previous two deaths he goes to the hospital and gets himself hooked up to a life-support system, just as a precaution—but to no avail: he dies just as he did the other two times.

Now life follows upon life. In one life he experiments with drugs and the European jet set; in another he marries Linda again. He notices that every time he comes back, he is a little further along in his original life, and he anticipates that the next lives are going to be progressively shorter. The breakthrough comes when he meets a fellow time traveler, Pamela, who is undergoing a similar experience. They form a deep friendship, and arrange to meet in all future lifetimes. In one life they decide to go public with their special story, but their disclosure leads to a world war (so major changes can happen). In another they try to contact others with the same kind of experience; they find most of them locked away in asylums. Meanwhile their new lives are getting shorter, quicker. It is becoming harder for them to hook up, because Jeff wakes up into his original life years before Pamela does and, inexorably, their wake-up times approach the time of their deaths. When their wake-up moments finally coincide with their moment of death, they experience a rapid, agonizing waking-and-dying succession, still without understanding the meaning of it all.

And then Jeff wakes up—on the phone with Linda. The cycle has been broken, there are no more rebirths. Was it all a dream? No, for on the other phone line is Pamela, who has experienced the same revival. Now Jeff realizes that his multiple lives have had a purpose: to make him understand the importance of making conscientious choices and realize the importance of time itself. Now he sees that nothing is predetermined for the rest of his life, and everything he does will have consequences. From now on, Jeff will approach his life as a responsible person. He and Pamela will link up again, but she has responsibilities in her original life, too, and Jeff has a lot of talking to do with Linda.

Study Questions

1. If you knew that you would be living your life over and over again, how would you feel about it? What is the lesson Nietzsche tries to teach?

2. In what sense does Jeff have free will while he is repeating his life? And in what sense does he have free will after the cycles are over?

3. Is the author right that such an experience as Jeff's and Pamela's will enhance one's sense of responsibility? If you have seen *Groundhog Day,* compare its message with that of *Replay.*

4. What in Jeff's experience can be compared to Nietzsche's theory of the eternal return? Which elements are different? Is there a moral to this story?

5. You will remember from Chapter 4 that in Sartre's existentialism—inspired by Nietzsche—there is no such thing as a predetermined future, but we have to take responsibility for all our choices even not knowing their consequences. How might that relate to Jeff's situation?

Narrative

The Myth of Sisyphus

ALBERT CAMUS

Retelling of a traditional Greek myth, 1955.

You may have seen the film *Groundhog Day,* a comedy with a plot that is quite similar to that of *Replay:* For a reporter, February 2 (Groundhog Day) keeps repeating itself endlessly; nothing he does changes the fact that the next morning he wakes up on February 2. Covering the same mindless story about Punxsutawney Phil, the groundhog who is supposed to see his shadow (or not), every detail of the day repeats itself next day; he can change the events during the day, but it has no effect on the repetition of the next day. Even numerous attempts at killing himself have no lasting results: He wakes up next day, February 2, to the same 1960s tune on the radio. But finally a change occurs: He accepts his situation; realizes that he has been a crabby, unpleasant person; and resolves to enjoy himself and make a difference in people's lives even if it makes no difference in the end. And this is where time, finally, is allowed to proceed beyond February 2 for him. So is this a "Nietzsche story"? Perhaps not nearly as much as it is a "Camus story": Nietzsche has no philosophy that we are actually supposed to learn anything from life's repeating itself, because we won't know about the eternal return of the same, and we can't change what we do, other than our attitude: We can learn to love life. But Camus, in his analysis of the Myth of Sisyphus, teaches a slightly different lesson: That we, in defiance of the absurdity of life, can *choose* to love our destiny.

Greek mythology tells the story of Sisyphus, who, in the realm of Hades, is condemned to roll a big rock up a hill. Every time Sisyphus reaches the top, the rock rolls back downhill, and he has to start all over again. Why was Sisyphus condemned to struggle with the rock for all eternity, and who was he? The story tells us that he was a very clever man who, through guile and theft, was able to get away with just about anything, from seducing princesses to cheating Death and putting him in chains. Once, Sisyphus was sent to Hades

(ruler of the Netherworld) by the gods, but he cheated his way out of being dead by claiming that proper death rites hadn't been performed over him, so he would have to go back to the living to check up on the situation. Once he was back on earth, he evaded Death until he was a very old man. When he finally died of natural causes, Hades put him in charge of rolling the rock, apparently as an occupational device to keep him from disrupting things further in the Netherworld. According to other Greek myths it was customary for offenders in Hades' realm to be condemned to repeat a certain action endlessly, as a form of punishment.

Albert Camus, the existential writer of both fiction and nonfiction, uses the original myth to illustrate the absurdity of life. For Camus there comes a day in each person's life when the absurdity of it all becomes apparent—the daily routine, the nonsense that we must put up with—and one day that person will ask, Why? From that moment on, there are only two possibilities: suicide or recovery. If you recover, it is because you have accepted your destiny fully, even in its absurdity. Indeed, you may even try to keep the absurdity alive by challenging it at every moment. Suicide is no solution, because it is merely giving in to the absurd. So why is Sisyphus condemned to roll the rock up the hill? Because he loved life too much and defied the gods in the process. In other words, he was too passionate about life, and the worst thing the gods could do to him was to assign him a meaningless task. So now he has to toil for eternity, and he has all the time in the world to think about how meaningless everything is, every time he walks downhill. But, says Camus, if Sisyphus approaches this in the right way, he need not be miserable—in fact, he can be happy, because he has the chance to triumph in the face of absurdity. He can *choose his destiny,* and if he does, he will feel in control: He will roll that rock because it is what he wants to do.

All Sisyphus' silent joy is contained therein. His fate belongs to him. His rock is his thing. Likewise, the absurd man, when he contemplates his torment, silences all the idols. In the universe suddenly restored to silence, the myriad wondering little voices of the earth rise up. Unconscious, secret calls, invitations from all the faces, they are the necessary reverse and price of victory. There is no sun without shadow, and it is essential to know the night. The absurd man says yes and his effort will henceforth be unceasing. If there is a personal fate, there is no higher destiny, or at least there is but one which he concludes is inevitable and despicable. For the rest, he knows himself to be the master of his days. At that subtle moment when man glances backward over his life, Sisyphus returning toward his rock, in that silent pivoting he contemplates that series of unrelated actions which becomes his fate, created by him, combined under his memory's eye and soon sealed by his death. Thus, convinced of the wholly human origin of all that is human, a blind man eager to see who knows that the night has no end, he is still on the go. The rock is still rolling.

I leave Sisyphus at the foot of the mountain! One always finds one's burden again. But Sisyphus teaches the higher fidelity that negates the gods and raises rocks. He too concludes that all is well. This universe henceforth without a master seems to him neither sterile nor futile. Each atom of that stone, each mineral flake of that night-filled mountain, in itself forms a world. The struggle itself toward the heights is enough to fill a man's heart. One must imagine Sisyphus happy.[20]

Study Questions:

1. Is there a difference between the original Greek myth and Camus's version? Explain.

2. What might Nietzsche say to this illustration of the absurdity of life? Does the rock of Sisyphus compare with Nietzsche's theory of the eternal return of the same? Why or why not?

3. In what way might the reporter in *Groundhog Day* be a Sisyphus? If we apply Camus's interpretation to *Groundhog Day,* what is the lesson he is supposed to learn from his numerous failed suicides? Is there a lesson to the film that goes beyond Camus?

Review

Key Issues in Chapter 8

From Descriptive to Normative Theories

- *Angels and Devils on Our Shoulders.* Theories of mind are generally descriptive, while theories of the soul or the spirit involve a normative assessment, focusing on "good" and "evil" aspects. Theories of the soul often involve dual characters representing good and evil.

- *Does Life Have a Meaning?* Joseph Campbell pointed out that we tend to ask about the meaning of life only when things are going wrong.
  - *There Is a Meaning.* Various theories assert that life has a meaning. Kierkegaard says that understanding the meaning of life requires a leap of faith. The Jewish tradition is represented by the story of Job: Put to a test of faith by God, Job loses everything and has to admit that only God sees the greater picture. Aristotle's teleology (theory of purpose) sees a meaning to life without a religious superstructure.
  - *There Is a Meaning But We Don't Know It.* The struggle to find meaning in a modern, chaotic world. Narrative therapy asks patients to tell stories about themselves so that a meaning will reveal itself.
  - *We Make Our Own Meaning.* There may not be an objective meaning, but we can create a purpose for our individual lives. There may be partial meanings instead of an overall meaning. Narrative philosophy suggests to create a meaning by telling one's own story.
  - *There Is No Meaning.* Everything happens at random, and there is no meaning or afterlife.
  - *The Crisis of Meaning.* The loss of meaning can result in a crisis. Bertrand Russell thought that we must create a meaningful existence by examining the world and being creative, because there is no meaning to the randomness of nature. Sartre thought we must take responsibility and avoid

bad faith. Camus believed we must become defiant in the fact of absurdity. The ultimate crisis of meaning is philosophical: What if we can't even count on the rationality of human beings? Then we can't ever hope to solve conflicts. Dwight Furrow holds that even though humans live on the edge of anxiety, we must keep trying to communicate by rational means.

- *The Question of Life After Death.* Many people, including the atheist philosopher A. J. Ayer, have experienced a near-death phenomenon. Various religious traditions have a concept of the afterlife.

Plato: The Troubled Soul

- *The Nature of Reality: Changing or Unchanging?* Plato's theory of Forms sees an unchanging reality of Forms and a shadowy material world. Plato was inspired by Pythagoras and Parmenides; Heraclitus provided an alternative view of reality.
- *The Tripartite Soul.* Plato believed three elements of the soul worked together: reason, spirit, and appetites. This is represented by the example of the charioteer. Plato's theory of reincarnation is expressed in the myth of Er, in the *Republic*.

Aristotle: The Purpose of Human Life

- *The Soul Is Part of Nature.* For Aristotle, the soul is a subject for scientific analysis; it can't exist without the body. It is the source and essence of the living body. Aristotle's theory of change is a matter of potentiality becoming actuality. Souls in nature extend from plants to humans; there are nutritive souls, appetitive and sensory souls, locomotive souls, and thinking souls.
- *Aristotle's Teleology.* The four kinds of causes are material, efficient, formal, and final. The theory of the golden mean indicates that a life of excellence falls between the extremes of too much and too little.

St. Augustine: The Human Soul Is Weak

- *Original Sin.* Adam and Eve's disobedience is inherited by every child born.
- *The Problem of Evil and the Platonic Connection.* Evil is privation—the absence of goodness, based on a human's free choice. Augustine's intellectual heritage came from Manichaeism and Neoplatonism.

Some say Augustine introduced somatophobia to Christianity.

- *Humans May Be Sinful, But We Are Very Important.* Elaine Pagels says that Augustine's teachings of guilt and sin allow us to conclude that we are very powerful to have caused a calamity such as the Fall.

St. Thomas Aquinas: The Natural Law

- *The Aristotelian Connection.* Aristotle's writings survived, thanks to the Islamic world, and influenced Aquinas.
- *The Nature of the Soul, and the Problem of Evil.* The theodicy problem asks the question, How can God allow evil to happen?
- *Natural Law.* Aquinas defines four kinds of law: eternal, natural, human, and divine. Humans have three natural inclinations: self-preservation, procreation, and seeking knowledge about God.
- *Consequences and Criticism.* Aquinas's natural law theory gives humans the capacity to choose what is good for them on the basis of their own intellect. But the focus on natural inclinations begs the question, What makes one inclination more natural than another?

Nietzsche: Beyond Good and Evil

- *The Masters of Suspicion.* Paul Ricoeur names Nietzsche, Marx, and Freud as thinkers who made us question our assumptions.
- *Nietzsche's Background.* Nietzsche studied theology, philosophy, and philology; poor health influenced his life and forced him to retire early; his mental health deteriorated, and he had to be institutionalized.
- *Nietzsche's Suspicion: Beyond Good and Evil.* Nietzsche calls upon us to examine our ideas of good and evil and recognize the repressive nature of traditional definitions; this calls for a transvaluation of values.
- *Master and Slave.* European history led to a slave morality and a master morality; as "slaves" deposed the masters, the herd mentality took over.
- *The Overman.* Nietzsche criticizes the idea of the Hinterwelt, the idea that there is a world beyond this one, which causes us to undervalue this life. The Overman is capable of being a creator of values. Nietzsche's sister Elisabeth edited his books and brought them to Hitler; she was anti-Semitic, but Nietzsche was not.

- *Elisabeth Nietzsche and the Nazis.* Nietzsche's sister and her husband tried to establish a colony of "pure Aryans" in Paraguay.
- *The Eternal Return and the Value of Life.* Dostoyevsky's *Crime and Punishment* anticipates Nietzsche's Overman theory. Nietzsche's yea to life: What if everything repeats itself? Would you still want to relive it?

The Question of Souls and the Capacity for Good and Evil

- *Do Nonhuman Animals Have Souls?* In the Judeo-Christian tradition, nonhuman animals have not been considered to have souls, but there is a movement to change that. Other cultural traditions—Hinduism, Buddhism, and tribal groups—have found it easier to accept the concept of nonhuman souls.
- *Are Nonhuman Animals Beyond Good and Evil?* In medieval times, there was a custom of putting animals on trial; today, some people are beginning to argue that great apes have a sense of right and wrong.

We're Only Human: Good and Evil in Films and Literature

- *Stories of Good and Evil.* The trickster is one way good and evil is examined in literature. Good and evil are often split into different characters, the good guys versus the bad guys. Aliens are a modern way to treat the idea of evil.
- *Twins, Triplets, and Alter Egos.* Good and evil are also examined as sides of the same person.

Primary Readings

- Plato, *Republic.* Plato outlines the three elements of the soul.
- Aristotle, *On the Soul.* The soul is the actuality and form; the body is potentiality and matter.
- Aquinas, *Natural Law.* Aquinas explains the necessity of having a natural law and the meaning of natural inclinations.
- Nietzsche, *Thus Spoke Zarathustra.* Zarathustra develops the idea that everything happens again and sees a shepherd with a snake caught in his throat.

Narratives

- *What Dreams May Come,* film. A man, dead in an accident, looks for his wife, a suicide, in the afterlife.

- Robert Louis Stevenson, *Strange Case of Dr. Jekyll and Mr. Hyde,* novel. Dr. Jekyll is both good and bad; Hyde has all his bad qualities.
- Hans Christian Andersen, "The Shadow," short story. A scholar's shadow separates himself from his owner and becomes powerful; the scholar ends up as the shadow of the Shadow.
- Fyodor Dostoyevsky, *Crime and Punishment,* novel. The student Raskolnikov contemplates the murder of an old pawnbroker, considering that he has the right since he is an outstanding individual.
- Ken Grimwood, *Replay,* novel. Jeff Winston dies and comes back to life as a teen, in his own life. This pattern repeats itself, presumably for a reason.
- Albert Camus, *The Myth of Sisyphus,* retelling of myth. Sisyphus is forced to repeat the act of rolling a big rock up a hill; Camus believes that Sisyphus can triumph over the absurdity of his situation by choosing to control his life, to want to roll the rock up the hill.

Notes

1. Bertrand Russell, "A Free Man's Worship" in *The Collected Papers of Bertrand Russell,* vol. 12, *Contemplation and Action, 1902–14* (London: Routledge, 1985). Retrieved from the World Wide Web: http://www.users.drew.edu/~jlenz/fmw.html
2. Dwight Furrow, *Against Theory: Continental and Analytical Challenges in Moral Philosophy* (New York: Routledge, 1995), p. 192.
3. Pythagoras and Parmenides are both considered Greek philosophers although they lived in today's Italy. The classical Greek cultural realm in its heyday stretched from Southern Italy to the Western Coast of Turkey, and philosophers born or living in that general geographical area and speaking Greek are referred to as Greek philosophers, although some of them never set foot in today's Greece.
4. Plato, *Republic,* trans. F. M. Cornford (New York: Oxford University Press, 1945), p. 137 (IV, 439).
5. Aristotle, *On the Soul (De Anima),* trans. J. A. Smith (Chicago: Encyclopedia Britannica, 1952), book I, chapter 1.
6. Ibid., book II, chapter 1.
7. Aristotle, *Nicomachean Ethics,* trans. W. D. Ross (Chicago: Encyclopedia Britannica, 1952), book I, chapter 7. The section in brackets testifies to Aristotle's son's editorial talents; part of the book is pieced together from Aristotle's own lecture notes and notes collected from Aristotle's students.
8. Elaine Pagels, *Adam, Eve, and the Serpent* (New York: Random House, 1988), p. 147.
9. Ibid., p. 146.
10. Thomas Aquinas, *Summa Theologica,* question 94, article 2. Retrieved from the World Wide Web: www.newadvent.org/summa

11. Friedrich Nietzsche, *Beyond Good and Evil,* trans. Walter Kaufmann (New York: Vintage, 1989), pp. 205–207.

12. Nietzsche is not the original author of the idea that "might makes right." We find it for the first time in Western philosophy in Plato's *Republic,* where Socrates argues against Thrasymachus, who insists that whoever has the power has the right to do whatever he wants. We also find it in Machiavelli's *The Prince,* with its principle that the end justifies the means. And as you are going to see in the next chapter, Thomas Hobbes also argued that the original right to self-preservation depends on whether a person has the power to enforce it. Against this type of view Socrates argued that a right that depends on one's practical capacity to carry it out is no right at all.

13. The Nietzsche Chronicle. Retrieved from the World Wide Web: http://www.Dartmouth.edu/~fnchron/1887.html

14. A thought experiment is often used by scientists and philosophers and science fiction writers: You imagine a set of premises, and then you use your reason to calculate their consequences, thus performing an experiment in your mind.

15. "Questions of Milinda," in *World of the Buddha,* ed. Lucien Stryk (New York: Anchor, 1969), p. 107.

16. Ibid. p. 96.

17. Rudolph Rÿser, "Observations On 'Self' and 'Knowing,'" in *Tribal Epistemologies,* ed. Helmut Wautischler (Aldershot, England: Ashgate, 1998), p. 28.

18. Sue Savage-Rumbaugh and Roger Lewin, *Kanzi: The Ape at the Brink of the Human Mind* (New York: Wiley, 1994), Chapter 3.

19. Robert Louis Stevenson, *Strange Case of Dr. Jekyll and Mr. Hyde and Other Stories* (London: MacDonald, 1950), p. 385.

20. Albert Camus, *The Myth of Sisyphus.* Retrieved from the World Wide Web: http://stripe.colorado.edu/~morristo/sisyphus.html

Chapter Nine

The Political Animal

This chapter explores a series of classical political views of the relationship between human nature and society; although these views differ, in common for most—but not all—of them is the view that humans don't know their own minds or are downright too selfish to be allowed to construct their own society and so must be guided or governed by those with a better understanding of community interests. We find this view shared by Plato, Aristotle, Hobbes, Rousseau, and Marx, each with his own different rationale to back it up. The lone dissenter in this company is John Locke, who sees the individual as the sole authority on what is in one's best interest. What is particularly interesting is that Locke has provided more inspiration for the traditional American view of political life than any of the other thinkers mentioned. Here, as in the previous chapters, you will see the strong connection between a thinker's theory of human nature and his or her view of what the necessary consequences of the knowledge of human nature ought to be—in other words, the drift from a descriptive theory to a normative theory of social and political consequences. The chapter concludes with a return to the concept of storytelling, this time within a historical and political context, in the theory of Hayden White.

Plato's Ideal State

In Chapter 6 you encountered one of the most controversial theories from the *Republic:* Plato's view that women should be free to occupy any position in his ideal society that their individual talents made possible: ruler, soldier, or any of the occupations within the lower levels of society. Here we take a closer look at that ideal society, in connection with Plato's theory of the human soul. You will remember from Chapter 8 that Plato views the human soul as consisting of three elements: reason, willpower (passion, spirit), and desires (appetites). In order to become a good, well-balanced person, you have to train yourself to let your reason remain in control at all times; your reason should recruit your willpower in the constant battle to control your desires. And when a person has accomplished this battle for control of his or her own mind, that person then embodies the virtue of *justice.*

Interestingly, Plato's theory of the tripartite soul is closely related to his theory of the ideal state; his analogy is that as an ideal state can be well-balanced, so can an individual. In the *Republic,* Socrates accepts the challenge from his friends to describe the perfect state, and what ensues is one of the most enduring political fantasies ever created.

The same three aspects that make up the psyche also make up the ideal state. At the bottom, analogous to human desires, is the *entire working population:* merchants, artisans, professionals. In the middle, representing human willpower, are the *auxiliaries:* soldiers, law enforcement, and civil servants. At the top we find a group of people representing reason: the *rulers,* or *philosopher-kings* (and *philosopher-queens;* see Chapter 6). Justice in the city-state means the same as justice in the well-balanced individual: harmony among the three parts, governed by reason and a contentment at doing one's share. Translated into politics, this means that if you belong to the working population, you must be content to let others (the philosopher-kings) think for you and make all major political decisions, and also let others (the military) control your everyday lives. Plato uses a mythic image to illustrate this social structure: the philosopher-kings are the people of "gold"; the auxiliaries are people of "silver"; and the working population? Brass and iron. While not to be taken literally, this poetic image is presented by Plato as a "noble lie" to be told to children in order to prepare them for the society of their adult years and for the idea that all is well within the republic as long as individuals fulfill their job according to their place in the hierarchy. In other words, Plato uses political storytelling to create a sense of meaningfulness—which makes Plato the first narrative political scientist.

This image of a static society of strictly separated classes seems to most modern people to be closely related to a class hierarchy and even a caste system. However, one feature distinguishes Plato's ideal state from the familiar systems of class and caste that we have seen develop over the two millennia since Plato and Socrates were alive. Class systems such as the nineteenth-century British hierarchy and caste systems such as the religiously defined social hierarchy of Hindu India rarely allow for upward or downward mobility—if anything, downward mobility is generally possible, caused by loss of fortune or some kind of spiritual or sexual "contamination," but upward mobility is usually an impossibility. Not so in Plato's ideal state. Your status in life, within the hierarchy, is determined by your talent and nothing else. This is the rationale for including women in his ruling classes: What matters is not their family connections, but their intelligence alone. While we must assume that Plato's state might in actual fact be rather static because trades would, as in all traditional societies, be inherited by the next generation, then the occasional spark of unusual talent (or a surprising lack of a particular talent within a talented family) warrants a replacement of the young person within the group his or her talent qualifies for. Suppose you are a soldier's son, but your true talent is in music; or you are a farmer's daughter, but you show a clear talent for abstract thinking; or you are the daughter of a ruler, but you show a talent for the use of weapons. In such cases, your status is determined by that talent.

Plato thus shows a considerable amount of faith in the power of reason, the strength of harmony in the psyche as well as in the state, and the importance of individual talent. But as to faith in the ordinary person's character, we have seen in Chapter 8 that Plato has very little faith that individuals will stay in harmony without a perennial struggle with their own desires. It is inevitable that such a view of human nature leads to a political vision of control and regulations. Thus the "people" can't be trusted to govern themselves, but must be governed by others who know what's best for them. In Plato's own view, the rulers qualify only if they have the best interest of the community at heart and have no personal interests at stake. The best way to choose a ruler is to find someone who is capable but who doesn't want the job; this should ensure that he or she will do the job efficiently, without allowing personal ambitions to influence the task. You have already seen in the Primary Readings of Chapter 6 how the principle of what we today call *eugenics* was to be enforced in Plato's ideal state: Male and female rulers would be paired off in order to create the best offspring, but they would not be allowed to raise their own offspring so as to avoid distractions from the duties of government. As a philosopher commented: "Those who rule can't have; those who have can't rule."

Today this blueprint for the ideal state seems less than ideal. We have a word for the *organic theory* of the state: *totalitarianism*. This is the belief that everyone has his or her given place and that the limbs of society exist basically to keep the ruling head going. Still, we might consider that Plato's ideal state is not the same as the organic state devised by Mussolini, the Italian fascist despot of World War II, because Plato assumes that the organic structure of his state is in the best interests of everyone; the state may take precedence over the individuals, but it is the *community* that is more important than its parts, not merely the head of state, as seems to have been the case with Mussolini's fascism. Even so, critics of totalitarianism in its many forms see Plato as having written the original blueprint for the totalitarian state in his *Republic:* The final goal may be the best interest of the citizen, but the interest is defined, patronizingly, by the political philosopher.

Many philosophers have sent their imagination soaring, speculating about what an ideal place the world would be if only it were run by philosopher-kings. Few philosophers have actually seen their ideal society being made a reality, but many have helped inspire future forms of social and political life.

Did Socrates speculate about the nature of an ideal society, the way Plato describes it in the *Republic?* Perhaps, but some Plato scholars tend to believe that the theory of the ideal state is more a fantasy from Plato's own mind than a political blueprint coming from Socrates. In Plato's case, he actually attempted to create the ideal society he had dreamed of, with disastrous results. Years after authoring the *Republic,* Plato saw a chance to bring his ideal society to life: Dionysus II, the young ruler of Syracuse in Sicily—then considered part of the Greek realm—was in acute need of political guidance, according to his uncle, who had been a student of Plato's. Plato rose to the occasion and traveled to Syracuse, where he had been once before, and attempted to set up an "ideal state" and make a philosopher-king out of Dionysus. The attempt failed miserably, and Plato left for Athens, only to come back a few years later and give it one more try. By then Dionysus had developed into a real despot: Plato barely escaped back to Athens, where he wrote another book about politics, the *Laws,* in which he toned down his political visions considerably.

Aristotle: The Political Animal

As you may remember from Chapter 1, Aristotle, Plato's most illustrious student, is famous for having said that "man is a political animal." You may also remember that his intention was not to invoke images of ferocious, ruthless politicians, but to make a simple connection between human beings and social life. In *Politics,* Book I, Aristotle says,

> If the earlier forms of society are natural, so is the state, for it is the end of them, and the nature of a thing is its end. For what each thing is when fully developed, we call its nature, whether we are speaking of a man, a horse, or a family. Besides, the final cause and end of a thing is the best, and to be self-sufficient is the end and the best.
>
> Hence it is evident that the state is a creation of nature, and that man is by nature a political animal. And he who by nature and not by mere accident is without a state, is either a bad man or above humanity.[1]

Before getting into further detail with Aristotle's political theory, I want to remind you of his theory of *teleology,* which you read about in Chapter 8, because it gives insight into what Aristotle means by the two expressions from this excerpt, "the nature of a thing is its end" and "final cause." For Aristotle, knowing the purpose of a thing is knowing the nature of that thing. A thing's purpose, its "end," is its final cause, the last of four causes Aristotle's system of knowledge operates within: If we know the material cause, the efficient cause, the formal cause, and the final cause, we will have exact knowledge of the nature of that thing—and that is the case for animate as well as inanimate objects and, in some cases, for what we would call cultural phenomena, such as a state. And the *political animal* expression? We have to go back to the Greek origin of the word *political* to understand Aristotle's intention. Humans are, for Aristotle, beings of the *polis,* the city-state: We are by nature "civilized," with a built-in social instinct. A more accurate, but less catchy expression would be that humans are *social* animals, destined by nature to live a social existence in close proximity to others and to be organized into a hierarchical society for the sake of the common good. The true basis for being civilized—a decent city-dweller—is the natural love between family members and between friends.

Box 9.1   RECAPPING ARISTOTLE'S THEORY OF THE GOLDEN MEAN

For Aristotle the virtue of a state as well as an individual lies in the capacity to judge the proper action and response to each situation, finding the happy medium between too much and too little. As you'll remember from the previous chapter, this is what is referred to as "the golden mean." It shouldn't be confused with finding an "average" result, because sometimes what is required is much effort, and at other times very little. For Aristotle, the proper response depends on the needs of the moment and one's individual capacity for virtue. Your ability to correctly assess what the situation requires reflects your moral character. Knowing when you have "hit the bull's eye" in terms of finding the right present for your father's birthday or putting the best possible children's party together for your six-year-old or writing the exact right report for work reflects the fact that you have developed a good character and so can discern between too much effort and too little. For the state to make proper decisions based on the golden mean is a measure of that state's capacity to create a flourishing environment for its citizens.

In his *Nicomachean Ethics,* Aristotle spends much time discussing friendship as a virtue. On the political level, this virtue is what keeps the state together. And we can draw a further inference: The state's highest purpose is to facilitate the happiness of its members. For Aristotle as well as for Plato, social well-being is of the utmost importance in the ideal society. For Plato, it involves allowing people's individual talents and in particular their talent for reasoning to be channeled into the most harmonious, socially balanced structure possible. For Aristotle, it involves a focus on the *telos,* or purpose, of humanity as such and of humans as individuals, allowing citizens to *flourish* as members of the human race as well as in their individual identity: Humans have a nature as a species; it involves a careful, consistent development of what makes us unique as human beings, our capacity for reasoning, but it also involves developing our individual talents. (Box 9.1 recaps Aristotle's theory of developing one's virtues according to the golden mean.) Aristotle shares with Plato the communitarian ideal that the state is more than the sum of its parts; he summarizes his image of the ideal state in this way:

> For a state is not a mere aggregate of persons, but is a union of them suffing for the purposes of life; and if any of these things be wanting, it is as we maintain impossible that the community can be absolutely self-suffing. A state then should be framed with a view to the fulfillment of these functions. There must be husbandmen to produce food, and artisans, and a warlike and a wealthy class, and priests, and judges to decide what is necessary and expedient. And since the whole city has one end, it is manifest that education should be one and the same for all, and that it should be public, not private—not as at present, when every one looks after his own children separately. Neither must we suppose that any one of the citizens belongs to himself, for they all belong to the state, and are each of them a part of the state, and the care of each part is inseparable from the care of the whole.[2]

What does this political theory mean? Society is a natural phenomenon, and humans have never lived outside of it. For Aristotle, it is impossible to live a life outside of the community: If you do, you are either a beast or a god. (In the next section, you will see this theory contrasted with a political theory that has had enormous success since the eighteenth century and even to this day: the *social contract* theory.) The human community is made possible by the human capacities for speech and for reason, and with the ability to conceptualize comes a sense of justice and injustice, of right and wrong, good and evil. Speech makes us both social and moral beings, so ethics and politics are closely related historically as well as in each individual for Aristotle.

The state is thus a given, and so is its structure. As a natural phenomenon, it has a purpose, and that purpose must be fulfilled. (You might say that Aristotle shows us one of the first examples in philosophy of the *naturalistic fallacy*—see Chapter 3—by moving from *what is* to *what ought to be*.) People must find their place in society, and Aristotle had very specific thoughts about people's proper places:

> For that some should rule and others be ruled is a thing not only necessary, but expedient; from the hour of their birth, some are marked out for subjection, others for rule. . . . Again, the male is by nature superior, and the female inferior; and the one rules, and the other is ruled; this principle, by necessity, extends to all mankind. . . . Where then there is such a difference as that between soul and body (as in the case of those whose business is to use their body, and who can do nothing better), the lower sort are by nature slaves, and it is better for them as for all inferiors that they should be under the rule of a master. For he who can be, and therefore is, another's, and he who participates in a rational principle enough to apprehend, but not to have, such a principle, is a slave by nature.[3]

For generations of readers—usually representing the educated dominant classes in Western and Middle Eastern societies—this has sounded like simple common sense: Some are born to rule, others to be ruled; and especially those who are less intelligent than others ought to live their lives as the slaves of the more intelligent members of society. However, for readers today it is a different matter. Most of us see these paragraphs as unacceptably undemocratic—sexist as well as supremacist. We might of course simply discard Aristotle altogether for not being PC (politically correct), but then we would deprive ourselves of an otherwise marvelous body of interesting writing, of a sense of history, and perhaps most importantly, of a chance to brush up on our arguments about why sexism and supremacism are unacceptable. We might instead choose to say that Aristotle didn't

know any better, for these were the thoughts of his day and age. That is not quite sufficient, though, because as we've seen, Aristotle's own teacher, Plato, didn't share his views about women's roles in the ideal state, and he certainly didn't teach Aristotle that there should be rigid class structures without the possibility of internal mobility in that state.

But Aristotle may not be as hardened in his views of political hierarchy as it seems, because while classic Athens had a slave-based economy, and Aristotle approved of the general idea, he was critical of the way it was administered in Athens. Who were the slaves of ancient Greece? Prisoners of war and any offspring they might have in captivity. Many of the prisoners, of course, weren't "born to be ruled" and were capable of many things other than physical labor. These individuals Aristotle believed should never have been enslaved, particularly if the war in which they had fought was unjust. So there are slaves *by law* (and a great many of them ought not to be slaves), there are slaves *by nature* (people who are good at following orders and doing physical labor), and there are *free men by nature* (people who are good at giving orders and using their minds). Ultimately, it is supposed to be good for the natural slaves to be slaves. All humans have a telos, a purpose in life, even slaves. That purpose is to be happy, although male and female slaves (and free women) can never be as happy as a free Greek male landowner who thinks rationally! If the master has abused his slaves to the point where they have no contentment and feel their lives have been misspent and misdirected, then the master is to blame. In the end, the social structure that Aristotle envisions is supposed to be to the advantage of all people involved, based on their individual talents and telos.

Even so, it is difficult for a modern reader to view Aristotle's position on slavery with much sympathy. We should realize, though, that Aristotle is talking not so much about the ideal state (as Plato was), but about the state as he saw it with his own eyes. The society he describes is only a perfected version of what he believed already existed. Furthermore, he was fairly convinced that he was, by and large, expressing the opinion of the majority of educated men, except perhaps on the issue of slavery. This he acknowledged to be a touchy subject. There were those who, despite the fact that the entire Athenian economy was based on the work of slaves (or perhaps because of it), argued that slavery is a crime against nature.

Social and political philosophers have wrestled with these various ideas ever since. We may all agree that "man is a political animal," with its far-reaching conclusion that humans have always lived in a society. Aristotle's theory reaches into the most cutting-edge theories of human prehistory, which speculate that even before we were physically fully *Homo sapiens* (see Chapter 2), we were living in groups, in all likelihood with some form of rules and hierarchies. On the other hand, this does not necessarily mean Aristotle is right in his statement that some are born to rule and others to be ruled. In a more moderate version, this might read, *Some are born leaders, and others are born followers.* In a competitive society such as ours, that hardly raises any eyebrows. If this were all Aristotle had intended to say, many people today would agree with him (although such a theory also would suffer from the problems of the naturalistic fallacy). The trouble is that Aristotle actually talks about people *owning* other people, and this is a fundamental affront to our modern sense of democracy and justice.

The Social Contract Thinkers

Aristotle believed that the human community is a natural phenomenon; there has never been a time where we have lived outside of society, in what has become known as a *state of nature,* a presocial condition. Aristotle was in fact reacting to a challenging view expressed in Plato's *Republic.* Plato's brother Glaucon tells the story of the Ring of Gyges, which you know from Chapter 3; in addition, he speculates that once upon a time, humans lived without a society, rules, or values. For the strong, this was a wonderful state of being, because

they could get away with doing whatever they wanted, including preying on the weak. However, knowing that the predator can also be preyed upon, people decided to give up taking advantage of others, for the security of the rules of society, knowing that from then on, nobody would be able to take advantage of anyone else with impunity—and this is known as justice. While Glaucon was playing the devil's advocate in order to provoke Socrates into praising justice as something more than a matter of personal convenience, his speculation has become the first example of a *social contract theory:* a theory that society developed, with its laws and regulations, as a conscious decision by human beings, coming out of a presocial *state of nature.* What for Glaucon appears to have been a mere thought experiment and a clever way to goad Socrates into talking became for other philosophers a deeply serious vision of the origin of society, of sovereignty, of the rule of law, and even of the concepts of right and wrong.

Thomas Hobbes

You'll remember Thomas Hobbes (1588–1679) from Chapter 3, as a seventeenth-century thinker committed to the view that humans are by nature selfish. In addition, you know from the same chapter that Hobbes would have seen eye to eye with Sigmund Freud, Robert Ardrey, and Konrad Lorenz that humans are by nature aggressive—that we are "killer apes," "children of Cain," the offspring of murderers. You have encountered Hobbes as an early materialistic psychologist believing that reality consists of what we can see and measure in some way; thus there is no room for the concept of "soul" or "spirit." In this section you will see how this theory of human nature plays out as one of the most powerful political theories in the past 400 years.

If we wish to consider different thinkers in the light of the historical period in which they lived—the older Freud's gloomy view of human nature reflected his experiences during World War I; Jean-Paul Sartre's view of life's absurdity was developed against the background of World War II;

and Robert Ardrey's view of human aggression belongs to the time following the Korean War in the 1950s—then Hobbes makes an excellent subject. At the time he was born, the Spanish Armada attacked the British fleet, and Elizabeth I executed her cousin, Mary, Queen of Scots. In his lifetime, piracy and buccaneering were rampant on the high seas; in 1640 England witnessed a civil war that ended with the execution of Charles I. Hobbes fled to France because he was a royalist, but returned after the execution. London was hit repeatedly by fire and plague; women and men were accused of witchcraft and burned at the stake; and there was a state of perpetual strife between England and France. Men of property carried fencing swords at their sides, and duels were common—this was the time of the Three Musketeers! So if one wants to speculate that Hobbes may have had personal reasons for considering life precarious, there are plenty to choose from.

Hobbes's State of Nature and the Social Contract

Hobbes translated his personal life experiences and the world situation (including the budding phenomenon of modern science) into the view that humans always will do what is to their advantage—the view you met in Chapter 3: psychological egoism. Thus, if there are no restrictions to put a damper on human selfishness, humans will be aggressive toward each other to the point of murder, in order to gain an advantage or simply acquire "stuff"—also a theory that you encountered in Chapter 3. How does that translate into a political theory for Hobbes? Since you are by now familiar with Hobbes's theories of egoism and aggression, we can take that further step: It translates into a theory of *power.* According to Hobbes, power is being able to acquire something in the future based on one's present means; power comes in many shapes and forms, such as reputation, riches, success, and eloquence as well as being loved or feared and having friends. Says Hobbes, "I put for a general inclination of all mankind, a perpetual and restless desire of power after power, that ceaseth only in death."[4] But the greatest power is that of human beings "united

by consent, in one person, natural or civil, that has the use of all the powers dependent on his will; such as is the power of the commonwealth."[5] Before we can even achieve such a concentration of power, however, we have to show that it is legitimate and even desirable, and to this end Hobbes spins a tale.

Once upon a time, he says, humans probably lived without any social rules and regulations. This presocial condition Hobbes calls the *state of nature*—a "natural" condition in which morality has not yet come into being, where there are no families or social bonding, and where there are no rules except those inherent in human nature: selfishness and aggression. Because morality arises with the advent of social rules, Hobbes emphasizes that the natural egoism of human beings only becomes morally problematic *within* a society; in the state of nature it is neither morally good nor bad, but just *is,* a fact of life. So what is life like in this state of nature? Hobbes sees it as a "war of every man against every man" and describes it vividly in his book *Leviathan:*

> In such condition, there is no place for industry, because the fruit thereof is uncertain, and consequently no culture of the earth; no navigation, nor use of the commodities that may be imported by sea; no commodious building; no instruments of moving and removing such things as require much force; no knowledge of the face of the earth; no account of time; no arts; no letters; no society; and, which is worst of all, continual fear and danger of violent death; and the life of man, solitary, poor, nasty, brutish, and short.[6]

So for Hobbes this life without rules is not something to pine for. Interestingly, he argues that in the state of nature humans are "created equal," but what Hobbes means is a far cry from the normative, political sense of having equal rights that we know from the Declaration of Independence. To Hobbes, humans are equal in their physical and mental capabilities: The strong may be able to prey on and kill the weak, but the weak can band together and kill the strong, so we are all in danger of each other. And mental equality? The individual similarities are greater than the differences, according to Hobbes, and the greatest mental equalizer is that we are all ready to believe we are very, very smart. That just shows that we are, indeed, very, very similar. The greatest common denominator is our fear of death. So in the state of nature we each have the right to protect ourselves and try to grab whatever we can; in effect, our "right" to hold on to something lasts as long as we are capable of holding on to it. If someone else grabs what you thought of as yours, then you have lost your "right" to it. (Incidentally, Socrates told a friend 2,000 years before Hobbes that such a right is no right at all.)

But the state of nature is not wholly without laws: It is governed by the *law of nature,* or a *natural law.* You'll remember this concept from Chapter 8, and a further clarification might be useful here: In the philosophical and theological traditions, "natural law" has nothing to do with scientific laws of nature such as the law of gravity. Such laws of nature are descriptive statements of constants of nature. But when social philosophers talk of laws of nature, they mean something else, a normative concept: a code of behavior built into human beings by virtue of our rationality. According to Hobbes, "A 'law of nature,' *lex naturalis,* is a precept or general rule, found out by reason, by which a man is forbidden to do that which is destructive of his life, or taketh away the means of preserving the same; and to omit that, by which he thinketh it may be best preserved."[7] This is the foundation for Hobbes's theory of self-preservation, which you saw in Chapter 3: We are, in a sense, programmed to protect our own life by our reason. Our reason tells us to save ourselves, even before we think of saving anyone else.

The first law of Nature, for Hobbes, is *to seek peace.* It is our *natural right* to defend our life and do whatever it takes to preserve it; indeed, we have a natural right to try for anything that might be to our advantage, as long as we can get away with it (in the Primary Readings, you will see a text by Hobbes arguing this point and then a text by Rousseau arguing that this kind of right is not

a true right, echoing Socrates' argument). The second law says that it would be best for us to give up our right to grab whatever we can and prey on others in the name of self-preservation and instead make a *covenant* with others, because it is safer. This is Hobbes's theory of the *social contract:* Life in the state of nature may be enjoyable for the strong, but never for the weak; even so, everyone can be preyed upon, even the strong, and everyone fears for his or her life; and so in everyone's best interests we leave the state of nature and enter into a social agreement where we promise not to prey on one another. We lay down our weapons and hand them over to someone whom we elect to preserve the peace and punish transgressors: the *sovereign.* And this is the most powerful of all human powers: the concentrated power of the sovereign, the monarch, the king or queen. The sovereign must continually strive to keep the selfish human nature of the citizens in check through laws and the enforcement of laws; Hobbes expects the sovereign to protect the citizens against each other; if that does not happen, society will revert to a state of nature. In Chapter 3 you read a summary of Golding's story of *The Lord of the Flies,* one of the most famous examples of Hobbes's theory of human nature worked into fiction.

Incidentally, Hobbes was not the first thinker to view the birth of society as a grim necessity forced upon selfish people by their own aggression. You will remember Plato's brother Glaucon from Chapter 3 (Box 3.6), telling the story of the Ring of Gyges. Glaucon expresses this very similar theory a good 2,000 years before Hobbes, in Plato's *Republic:*

> They say that to do wrong is naturally good, to be wronged is bad, but the suffering of injury so far exceeds in badness the good of inflicting it that when men have done wrong to each other and suffered it, and have had a taste of both, those who are unable to avoid the latter and practice the former decide that it is profitable to come to an agreement with each other neither to inflict injury nor suffer it. As a result they begin to make laws and

covenants, and the law's command they call lawful and just.[8]

Glaucon, we know, was just playing the devil's advocate to provoke Socrates into speaking in defense of justice, but what about Hobbes? Did he believe in his own theory that human society started out with everyone preying on each other, in the dawn of time? It is hard to say. Sometimes he claims that this never really happened. But at other times he treats it as a historical fact and insists that at least the situation between nations reflects a state of nature with no rules and perpetual war (a state that indeed did exist during Hobbes's own time, before the era of international laws); he also points to American Indians of the seventeenth century as a people living close to the state of nature, presumably without any social rules (although we now know that to be very far from the truth). At any rate, there is no evidence that any society prior to the one in which Hobbes lived was ever founded in this manner—however, since Hobbes's day a form of social contract has indeed become part of historic reality with the adoption of the Constitution of the United States (although we can't claim that all citizens were signatories or even that all people living in the thirteen original states were considered citizens).

For Hobbes, the social contract delivered all power into the hands of the sovereign—obviously a type of social contract different from the American Constitution. However, the sovereign does not receive absolute power, for there is a right one can never give up: the right to defend one's own life. If the sovereign fails to protect you, you are entitled to protect yourself. No one can legitimately give themselves up to a condition of slavery, says Hobbes, because one simply can't give away one's ultimate right to self-determination. But all other power rests with the king—as long as he keeps his end of the contract, to defend the people's lives and establish a general condition of peace. If he fails in this respect, the country reverts to a state of nature, and the sovereign can be replaced by the people.

Hobbes's State of Nature as Political Theory   One might wonder if Hobbes spent much time trying to research whether the state of nature was ever a historical fact. The answer is no, but in terms of the historical approach of Hobbes's society, this is no wonder. History had not yet emerged as a science; archaeology would not be invented for yet another 200 years (it is a nineteenth-century phenomenon), and the European cultures had very little understanding of their own historical past, let alone any understanding of human prehistory. When a scholar referred to the historical past, it was generally to make a point about the present or the future, and Hobbes was no exception. Even as far up in time as the end of the eighteenth century, we find that same approach in most social thinkers, such as Rousseau (see the discussion later in the chapter). Hobbes's speculation about the state of nature was thus not really historical, but *political:* Why are we the way we are, and how should we be? State-of-nature theories, as we shall see, usually have a normative rather than a descriptive purpose, supplying an argument in favor of a certain present or future political structure—in Hobbes's case, an argument in favor of *absolute monarchy*. True historical interest in human events of the recent as well as of the dim past was only just awakening in the centuries of Hobbes, Locke, and Rousseau. Karl Marx had a much better factual understanding of human history, based on the advances of the science of history in the early nineteenth century—and, perhaps typically, Marx did not have a social contract theory.

Today we know that humans have lived in groups as long as we have been humans and long before that—for at least 4 million years—and if animal studies are any indication, we may have been social beings for as long as we have been primates; baboons, chimps, and gorillas all live in social groups, as you will remember E. O. Wilson saying in Chapter 3. Another old acquaintance in this book, Don Johanson, and his crew, discovered what has become known as the "first family" in the 1980s: A number of fossilized individuals from *Australopithecus afarensis* (Lucy's people; see

Chapters 2 and 3) turned up in the same spot, which indicates that the group probably all perished together in some disaster. In the group were young people, old people, and mature individuals. Scientists take that as evidence that we have always lived in groups, never in the loneliness of Hobbes's state of nature. But of course we don't know if such groups may in fact have been living in a "state of nature" vis-à-vis other groups, in a perpetual war of group against group.

John Locke

John Locke (1632–1704) was born when Hobbes was a middle-aged man. You will remember Locke as one of the few thinkers in the history of philosophy who argued in favor of some rights for women (Chapter 6), specifically the right to share and retain parental authority. (This was a view that Hobbes actually shared and exceeded, in that he believed the mother is the original holder of parental rights.) You also know him from Chapter 7 for saying that our sense of self resides in our memories. In many ways Locke's thinking was radical for his time, although today he is often seen as the ideological parent of some politically conservative views. A fiscal conservative today (someone who believes the only role of government is to protect our negative rights, but not interfere in the lives of private citizens or businesses) would focus on Locke's views of the right to life, liberty, and property. However, in his own day and for centuries Locke was regarded as a liberal voice arguing for rights of individuals, the abolition of monarchy, and an expansion of women's rights. However one views Locke's historical role, it is an indisputable fact that he is the European thinker who has had the most philosophical influence on the founding of the United States.

There are some similarities between his and Hobbes's life: Locke, too, found that his political connections made it expedient for him to live outside of England for a while; they were both interested in the findings of modern science, especially theories of human nature and, in Locke's case, human perception. Locke's concern for his personal safety, reflected in his request that his two political works, *Two Treatises of Government,* would not be published until after his death, mirrors Hobbes's concern for his life half a century earlier. However, there are also significant differences, the most important one being Hobbes's lack of faith in human nature and Locke's staunch belief that reason would prevail, even under pre-social circumstances.

Locke's Natural Law and the State of Nature   In some respects, Locke builds on an older tradition—one you met in Chapter 8: the tradition of *natural law.* Thomas Aquinas's view of natural law, which has meant so much for the philosophy of the Catholic Church and its view of human nature, acquired a fundamentally political tone in the philosophy of Hobbes and also of Locke. For Locke, as well as for Aquinas, God created humans as rational beings, with the intellectual capacity for understanding God's creation as a work of reason and a moral obligation to comply with the laws of reason. But while Aquinas focused on the moral obligations of the law of nature as he saw it, Locke focuses on the political implications: God has created us as free and equal, and we can infer that from (1) the fact that we are all born randomly "to all the same advantages of nature, and the use of the same faculties,"[9] and (2) the fact that the Bible doesn't teach that the first human (Adam) had dominion over any other humans or that his children had any royal rights above others. So according to the sources that Locke respects—factual, biological evidence and the Bible—God did not intend for anyone to be an absolute ruler or keep others in any kind of subjugation: This means that the absolute monarchy that Hobbes defended so fiercely is for Locke an unnatural perversion, and so is any other political system that refuses to accept its citizens as free individuals with the right to self-determination.

However, the freedom Locke sees for each individual is vastly different from the freedom Hobbes described in the state of nature. For Hobbes, life in the state of nature means that a person's right to something derives from his (or her) ability to hold on to that something. We're free—to try. In other words, might makes right. Hobbes's *laws of nature* involved the fundamental human fear of danger and the wish for safety and peace; this led Hobbes to his notion of the social contract as a tool to acquire safety at the price of personal freedom. For Locke (as later, for Rousseau), this is no freedom at all, because it is arbitrary—it is not guaranteed. The laws of nature recognized by Locke involve the idea of human freedom and equality: As we have seen, Locke believes he has evidence from nature and the Bible that humans are born equal; this means we are free to live as we please (within certain limits, which we will discuss later), and since we have the capacity to use our reason, we also see that this is what God has intended for us. Furthermore, we are naturally inclined toward self-preservation (a view that Aquinas as well as Hobbes would have agreed with), but thanks to our God-given rationality we also see that others wish to preserve their lives, too; and insofar as it is possible, we should try to help others do this. This goes for every human being, and so the theory may not sound too far from Hobbes's view of the social contract— except that for Locke this is also valid for the state of nature:

> But though this be a state of liberty, yet it is not a state of license: though man in that state have an uncontrollable liberty to dispose of his person or possessions, yet he has not liberty to destroy himself, or so much as any creature in his possession, but where some nobler use than its bare preservation calls for it. The state of nature has a law of nature to govern it, which obliges every one; and reason, which is that law, teaches all mankind, who will but consult it, that being all equal and independent, no one ought to harm another in his life, health, liberty, or possessions; for men being all the workmanship of one omnipotent and infinitely wise Maker; all the servants of one sovereign Master, sent into the world by his order, and about his business; they are his property, whose workmanship they are, made to last during his, not another's pleasure; and being furnished with like

faculties, sharing all in one community of nature, there cannot be supposed any such subordination among us that may authorize us to destroy another, as if we were made for one another's uses, as the inferior ranks of creatures are for ours. Every one, as he is bound to preserve himself, and not quit his station willfully, so by the like reason, when his own preservation comes not in competition, ought he, as much as he can, to preserve the rest of mankind, and not, unless it be to do justice to an offender, take away or impair their life, or what tends to the preservation of life, the liberty, health, limb, or goods of another.[10]

For Locke, the state of nature is by no means the free-for-all that at the same time fascinated and terrified Hobbes: Locke holds that God has created us as rational beings, and this remains a fact in or out of society. And if human nature is fundamentally rational, then the difference between the state of nature and the social-contract stage (the stage of structured social life) is, for all intents and purposes, a matter of administration. It doesn't take the Hobbesian fear, or realization that life is brutal and short, for humans to realize that a life with respect for other human beings is better in the long run. Anyone with a rational mind can realize this, even in the state of nature, and Locke's political philosophy is thus one of the most optimistic in the Western tradition: Left to themselves, most humans are going to be decent people, treating one another with respect, and respecting themselves and their own lives as not entirely their own, but also as God's property (and one doesn't destroy or squander God's property). This also means that the political system born out of this philosophy is a fundamental democracy.

So why enter into a social contract at all, if the state of nature is rational and governed by laws of nature? Because the state of nature has only a *moral* authority, founded on God's law; it has no *legal* authority. This means that if someone transgresses against someone else's life or health or goods, then there is no society that can mete out the proper justice—because, of course, Locke doesn't claim that in the state of nature we were *all* decent, wonderful people. He claims that we are all gifted with rationality, but not everyone has the moral will to follow God's laws of reason. Since we can't trust everyone to act on the law of nature, a government is needed. This also means that the chief duty of the government is to protect the citizens from transgressors; however, if this is done by subjugating the people, then the government is in itself a transgressor and should be removed from office. The only priority of any government should be the public good, and the only way the public good can be maintained is for the citizens to consent to being governed; rule by conquest or tyranny, or even by parental authority, is not legitimate as a form of government.

As Hobbes (and later Rousseau) struggled with the question of the actual historical reality of the state of nature, so did Locke. For all three thinkers (as seems to be the case with every social-contract thinker), their vision of the state of nature provides an argument for why their ideal society looks the way it looks: Hobbes's state of nature is frightening and without any concepts of right and wrong, so he claims we need a strong monarch to keep us safe from each other. As we'll see later, Rousseau's vision of the state of nature as idyllic provides an argument for why people are good and compassionate. Locke sees the state of nature as peopled with rational beings who respect each other and who are capable of telling right from wrong—a strong argument in favor of a society where people are allowed to make their own decisions about their own lives. But were we ever in such a state of nature? You know from the previous section that paleoanthropology has shown the state of nature to be a fable: Humans have always lived in groups. But interestingly, Locke's version of the state of nature doesn't contradict this, in spite of the fact that he was as ignorant of human prehistory as Hobbes was. Locke doesn't claim humans lived separately in the state of nature, as lone hermits (the way both Hobbes and Rousseau claimed). Locke's state of nature may cover anything from early tribal living or small family groups—entirely consistent with the recent fossil finds—to complex societies where individuals just haven't yet entered into a democratic political system. Like Hobbes, Locke points out that kings, princes, and nations in effect live in a state of nature vis-à-vis each other, because there is no common law for them to adhere to; but more important,

> It is not every compact that puts an end to the state of nature between men, but only this one of agreeing together mutually to enter into one community, and make one body politic; other promises and compacts men may make one with another, and still be in the state of nature. . . . I moreover affirm, that all men are naturally in that state, and remain so, till by their own consents they make themselves members of some politic society.[11]

Another question usually asked of social contract thinkers is, The original social contract may have been binding for its "signatories," but what about their descendants who haven't agreed to anything? Hobbes finds that the fear of the state of nature is enough to keep subsequent generations happy to be out of it; Rousseau sees every new generation as constantly re-signing the social contract by their participation in social decisions. Locke acknowledges that there is a problem: The community created by the social contract is supposed to be entered into freely—but how do you maintain that freedom of choice in subsequent generations? For one thing, by constantly monitoring how the government is doing, protecting the citizens against transgressors; if it is not doing its job, the citizens take back their right to mete out justice—a right they had in the state of nature—and elect another government. However, if an individual feels discontent with the conditions of his or her society, and the terms of the society were freely chosen sometime in the past, by the *express consent* of a previous generation, then that individual has two choices: To stay or to have possessions within that community means giving one's *tacit consent* to being governed and accepting the need to obey the laws of the community. In other words, if you are dissatisfied with the laws of your community, but you live there, you travel the highways, you buy or sell things, you accept the protection of law enforcement, then you are giving your tacit consent simply by making use of the social facilities of the community. But this also means that *if* you have only given your *tacit* consent and no longer want to be a part of that community, then you can sell your possessions *and leave*. In Locke's day there were places on the planet where one could go where no society (in the British sense of the word) existed (although there would generally be native populations who weren't thrilled at the influx); for Locke, everyone is free to pack up and leave and join another society or start one up of his or her own. However, once one has given *express* consent to some government (by a pledge of allegiance, for example), then that declaration is binding. And foreigners living in another country and obeying its rules to the letter still don't become citizens unless they explicitly enter into a naturalization agreement with their adopted country.

Natural Rights and Negative Rights   Around the time Hobbes lived a concept arose that has provided much discussion and food for thought ever since: the concept of *natural rights*. It is a political consequence of the natural law discussion: If God has created the world and has created humans as rational beings, then we must come equipped with natural rights as rational beings. (In Chapter 10 you will meet a famous criticism of the concept of natural rights from the British philosopher Jeremy Bentham.) In a sense Hobbes operated with a concept of a natural right, the "right" to try to save one's own life in the state of nature and furthermore to grab and hold on to what one can— but one doesn't have a right to keep it if one can't hold on to it. This is what Rousseau criticized as being no right at all, as did Socrates before him. For Locke, the concept of a natural right is far more absolute: It is part of the natural law that humans are born free and equal. Then it becomes our natural right to stay free and equal, and to exercise that freedom and equality as we see fit—

with one important limitation, which is the *right of others* to stay free and equal.

You have already read Locke's words that a person "may not, unless it be to do justice to an offender, take away or impair their life, or what tends to the preservation of life, the liberty, health, limb, or goods of another." The content of this important sentence has been boiled down to three rights: *the right to life, liberty, and property*. And if you think the final right would sound better as "the pursuit of happiness," there are several reasons: For one thing, Locke served as a direct inspiration for the outline of rights in the Declaration of Independence; and for another, Locke himself also refers to the pursuit of happiness elsewhere in his writings. But it is hard to nail down exactly what "pursuit of happiness" is, especially since it could be identified as part of one's *liberty*; so "life, liberty, and property" have become the legacy of natural rights given to us by Locke.

These three rights are commonly referred to as *negative rights,* in the sense that they are rights of noninterference: You have the right not to have your *life* taken away without proper justification; you have the right not to have your *liberty* curtailed except when it infringes on other people's liberty; and you have the right to acquire and keep *property* (from real estate to inheritance and other gifts to wages) without anyone taking it away from you. Each negative right is limited by the negative rights of others: You have forfeited your right to life if you have taken the life of someone else; you have forfeited your right to liberty to the extent that you have interfered with the liberty of someone else; and you have forfeited your property right if you have taken or otherwise interfered with the property of someone else.

Now who is going to enforce these rights? In other words, who is going to protect your negative rights? And what is going to happen to a person who takes someone else's life or interferes with another person's liberty or steals someone else's property? That depends on which stage of civilization we are at, according to Locke. In the state of nature, where natural law applies, natural rights also apply: You have the right to life, liberty, and property, even if there is no society around you (which is an interesting idea in itself—remember that Hobbes says there is no concept of property until we enter into a society that creates rules of ownership). In the state of nature you have a right to preserve your life, but not just in the Hobbesian sense that you have a right to try, and if you don't succeed, then tough. For Locke, you have a right to stay alive; to exercise your freedom of movement, speech, and so forth; and to own property even in the state of nature. And if someone makes an attempt on your life or keeps you imprisoned or takes your property, then you (or your friends) are entitled to hunt that person down, take your property back, and make the transgressor pay for the crime. This also means that the death penalty exists, even before society and civil laws exist, because natural laws and natural rights are present in the state of nature: You are entitled to kill a murderer.

> In transgressing the law of nature, the offender declares himself to live by another rule than that of common reason and equity, which is that measure God has set to the actions of men, for their mutual security; and so he becomes dangerous to mankind. . . . And thus it is that every man in the state of nature has a power to kill a murderer, but to deter others from doing the like injury, which no reparation can compensate, by the example of the punishment that attends it from everybody, and also to secure men from the attempts of a criminal who has renounced reason, the common rule and measure God hath given to mankind, hath by the unjust violence and slaughter he hath committed upon one, declared war against all mankind, and therefore may be destroyed as a lion or a tiger.[12]

For Locke, the death penalty—as well as any other penalty intended to protect the public, make the criminal repent, and deter others—has its firm foundation in the theory of natural rights; however, one might question the very foundation of the theory of natural rights, the assumption that

God has created us as rational beings. We have already seen that thinkers have questioned (1) that we are created by God and (2) that we are created as rational beings. The implications for any natural rights theory of questioning these ideas (which would also involve questioning the foundation of the American Constitution, by the way) I will leave up to you to consider.

The right to punish offenders is one of the rights we have in the state of nature which we give up when entering into the social contract; once we have entered into a social contract, that right belongs to the state; and those who persist in "taking the law into their own hands," become vigilantes, transgressing against the right of the government. *After the social contract,* the government enforces the negative rights—and that is, in effect, the only function the government ought to have, according to Locke: to protect the rights of citizens to conduct their lives any way they please as long as it doesn't interfere with other people's rights. And if someone transgresses, then the government punishes that person by taking away his or her life, liberty, and/or property (through the death penalty, incarceration or deportation, fines).

Locke's three negative rights have become part of the American political legacy, and we find them in a variety of forms in our Constitution and our laws. The fundamental view that the government exists exclusively to protect the rights of individuals is still viewed as the ideal political vision by many Americans. However, as some political scholars will inform us, these rights are by no means clear: What does it mean that your life should not be interfered with—doesn't that, in essence, preclude the death penalty, even though Locke didn't see it that way? What does it mean that your liberty should be respected? How far do we want the *freedom of speech* to extend? The *liberty of assembly,* during violent demonstrations and riots? The liberty to *own firearms?* The liberty to do with one's body as one deems right, such as have an *abortion?* (And does that interfere with the right to life?) Does the right to keep one's property, including one's wages, imply that we can refuse to pay taxes? Locke's negative rights are by no means a dim and distant legacy of our political system. They are part of our fundamental political and moral debates, even in the twenty-first century.

Jean-Jacques Rousseau

Jean-Jacques Rousseau (1712–1778) is familiar to you from his theories of gender differences (Chapter 6), as well as his less-well-known race speculations about cold climates creating smarter people (Chapter 5), but his greatest contribution to philosophy is his theory of the social contract. As you can tell by now, Rousseau is only one of many thinkers theorizing about the idea of a social contract, but Rousseau gave the concept a different meaning than Hobbes or Locke did, and in retrospect it is hard to say which of the three has had the most influence in Western political thinking. (See Box 9.2 for an exploration of the Age of Reason.)

Rousseau was born in Geneva, Switzerland, and spent much of his youth on the move, first fleeing the profession of engraver, for which he had no taste, and later traveling to France, Italy, and then back to France, occasionally tutoring children in music. Several times in his life he changed his religious affiliation—from Protestant to Catholic and back again—but these changes seem to have been politically motivated more than anything else. He tried his hand at a number of professions, including writing an opera, and didn't do too well in any of his efforts.

Rousseau entered the philosophical scene late in life—in his late thirties—with an award-winning essay on arts and sciences in 1750, but he achieved more fame with his next essay, the "Discourse on the Origin of Inequality." This essay, written in Paris, won no awards but is the one we remember today as the first time a powerful new social thinker spoke up. Next followed the books for which Rousseau was to become famous: the novel *La Nouvelle Héloïse* (1761), the story of a strong-willed woman and her lover, whom she discards

to marry an older man; *The Social Contract* (1762), a philosophical analysis of the relationship between the citizen and society; and *Emile* (1762), a blueprint for a new, natural approach to the education of children (which you have heard about in Chapter 6). With the French publication of *The Social Contract* Rousseau feared being arrested and left for his hometown of Geneva, but could find no rest there. His good friend in England, the Scottish philosopher David Hume, invited him to come and stay with him, but after a while this relationship turned sour too. (Rousseau's life, like that of the other *enfant terrible* in philosophy, Friedrich Nietzsche, was littered with discarded friendships.) Rousseau somehow developed the idea that Hume was not the friend he thought he was, and he began publicly ridiculing Hume's work. Although Hume was an easygoing man, his patience with Rousseau came to an end, and Rousseau had to leave and return to France. Twelve years later he died there, suddenly, at the age of sixty-six; those who knew him described him as "emotionally disturbed." Before his death he married his long-time companion Thérèse Levasseur—from Chapter 6 you'll remember that he had five children with her and promptly took each one to the local orphanage.

What kind of a man emerges from this brief profile—a restless man who mistrusts his friends and takes little responsibility for his actions? There is medical evidence that Rousseau actually had a touch of paranoia, and physically he was never very strong. He seems to have suffered from a chronic bladder problem and had a deep mistrust of doctors (but then again, doctors in the eighteenth century would bleed people as a cure-all, even anemic people and wounded soldiers, so Rousseau's mistrust may have been well-earned). Without having any knowledge of bacteria and viral diseases, Rousseau warned against living too close to others because he believed it to be unhealthy (and one also suspects that he found it unpleasant). This troubled, cranky, intelligent man nevertheless managed to usher in a new era, the Romantic Era.

Box 9.2   ARRIVAL OF THE WESTERN ENLIGHTENMENT

In this book you have heard several times about the Western Enlightenment, or the *Age of Reason* (see Chapters 5 and 6). Because the eighteenth century is especially important for the development of the ideas of the social human being, this box will serve as a reminder of the key intellectual achievements: Europeans of the early eighteenth century emerged from a century of wars that took their toll on the economies as well as generations of young conscripted male peasants; science was also emerging from a millennium of strict control by the Church, and a new spirit was forming in intellectual circles: the concept of the individual as a person of dignity, with rights. You have seen the early stages of such a new attitude in the social philosophy of John Locke. Consequently, the fate of "ordinary" people was becoming a political question. In the self-reliant American colonies the questioning of political and religious authority was already an everyday occurrence in the eighteenth century. Whereas citizens in Western cultures previously had been viewed as little more than tools, without rights or dignity of their own, the question now being posed was, To what extent is the ordinary man capable of deciding his own fate, and how much freedom should be granted? You know from Chapter 6 that the issue here was the self-determination of *male* citizens, not all citizens—and from Chapter 5 you also know that the focus was on males of European ancestry. However, we shouldn't forget that even within the population of male Europeans, oppression had been the order of the day in still-feudal Europe of the seventeenth century: Peasants were considered the legitimate property of the land-owning nobility to be used for farm work, warfare, and general breeding of more peasants. The middle class, barely established in the cities, was struggling with strict rules of trade and guilds, making the free choice of profession an unreachable dream. For a social reformer in early-eighteenth-century Europe, there was plenty of righteous indignation to be directed at the oppression of other Europeans; now we are aware that this indignation often stopped short of our modern goal of equal opportunity for everyone. But for the time period, the work of the reformer was an uphill battle as it was, and we should understand that battle in its proper context.

In the eyes of the Enlightenment, education was key. Given the opportunity to learn, the ordinary man (and woman, for thinkers such as Mary Wollstonecraft) could develop the talents and capabilities necessary for political and personal self-determination. Once it was recognized that individuals had such capabilities, the democratic election of officials became a genuine possibility. The general goal was to break up the feudal patterns that had become established in many parts of Europe and give the right to self-determination to those populations who had been victimized by increasing social inequality. This is why most philosophers of the Enlightenment focus on several aspects of human life simultaneously: (1) The *capacity for reasoning* (and thus for understanding science and the laws of nature), (2) the *need for an education* to properly channel the capacity for reasoning, and (3) the political consequence of the development of this capacity, the *right to self-determination*—in a practical sense the right to move freely, to choose one's spouse and one's livelihood freely, and to have the right to vote.

The world Rousseau knew was different from Locke's and even more different from that of Hobbes; but even so, there are parallels. Hobbes and Locke experienced political unrest to the point where both men—probably justifiably—felt their lives to be in danger; both hid out on the European continent for their political ideas before returning home. Both men were subjects of the British monarchy, one of the most powerful in Europe. Rousseau's Switzerland, on the other hand, was far removed from the tradition of absolute monarchy; the Swiss people lived in a close-knit federation of municipalities, with a high degree of political and militia participation from the male citizens. Self-determination and political responsibility were simply part of the life experience of male Swiss citizens. As you will see, this background may have propelled Rousseau toward his political theory, unique for his day and age, and with extremely far-reaching consequences—including the French Revolution as well as elements of Marxist ideology and (to top it off) modern environmentalism.

The irony of this is that while Rousseau's time period was considerably more peaceful than those of the two British philosophers, he, too, felt the need to go into exile, fearing for his life. While historians speculate that Hobbes and Locke were probably more justified in assuming immediate danger to their lives than Rousseau, and Rousseau was probably more prone to see danger lurking than Hobbes or Locke, still Rousseau was not entirely unjustified in being afraid. The eighteenth century was a dangerous time for an outspoken thinker: The Inquisition was still burning heretics at the stake and continued to do so until 1834, albeit not with the fervor of previous centuries. The Church still banned books that were found to be heretical and made life difficult for thinkers branded as heretics. For that reason, secret societies such as the Freemasons thrived, and many philosophers pursued their political interests as members of such organizations—Thomas Jefferson and Benjamin Franklin, for example.

Humans in the State of Nature   Hobbes is known for his view that human nature is self-serving and fundamentally aggressive and untrustworthy when left to itself. John Locke sees human nature as fundamentally rational—certainly interested in self-protection and pursuit of happiness, but at the same time endowed with an understanding that other humans are equally interested in their own happiness and have an equal right to pursue it as long as it doesn't interfere with others. For Rousseau, human nature is neither aggressive nor selfish nor even rational: Humans are, in their natural state, fundamentally good, compassionate beings. And the untold examples of humans preying on each other, displaying an evil side to their character? To Rousseau, this may be part of human behavior, but it isn't *human nature;* it is *human cul-*

ture or, rather, human civilization. In one of the most astounding cultural "paradigm shifts" in Western history, Rousseau declares that *what is natural is fundamentally good.*[13] No longer is nature (including human nature) considered something that needs to be subdued and civilized, but instead Rousseau finds value in the original condition of biological entities, such as human beings, because this condition hasn't been corrupted yet. Children are thus morally better than adults, tribal cultures are better than city cultures, and the wilderness is better than the cultivated field and the city itself. Hobbes's "war of everyone against everyone" is certainly a true picture of the human experience according to Rousseau, but it is not a picture of the state of nature! This "solitary, poor, nasty, brutish and short" life is typical of humans *in early civilizations,* says Rousseau, when natural compassion was cast aside and the necessary rules of civility hadn't yet been established.

Coining the expression "Back to nature," Rousseau is the first Western intellectual to find both an intellectual and a moral value in the concept of untouched nature; and since reasoning is for Rousseau part of what humans do as civilized beings, it is not the best or even the primary human quality. For Rousseau, we are born emotional, compassionate beings; civilization makes us think twice before we help others, which means that it is, in effect, our reasoning capacity that makes us *less compassionate and more selfish*—a viewpoint that many late-twentieth-century thinkers have sided with, on the basis of modern psychology. (See Box 9.3 for other theories of innate human goodness and compassion.) And while we can't call Rousseau an environmentalist, because he didn't engage himself in any philosophies about how to preserve the wilderness, but merely admonished his readers to enjoy it, we can still credit him with providing inspiration for the modern environmentalist movement. Without Rousseau the notion of preserving nature would surely have arisen anyway, but he has provided a major source of inspiration: Not only is the untouched nature good, but we also become better people for wanting to preserve it! Concepts ranging from "Earth

Box 9.3   ARE WE GOOD BY NATURE?

In Chapter 8 you read about theories of good and evil in human nature, and some lines to the moral tradition may be drawn at this point. As unusual as Rousseau's view of fundamental human compassion is, he is not alone in his view. But here we must make a distinction that is familiar to you by now: It matters greatly whether we talk about compassion as a descriptive or a normative characteristic. In religious traditions all over Planet Earth, from Judaism to Christianity, Hinduism, Buddhism, and African tribal religions, the virtue of compassion is taught and held up as a moral ideal. This doesn't mean that these traditions believe humans really are compassionate, but that we ought to strive to be compassionate and fight against our more self-serving nature. However, thinkers—thousands of miles and years apart—have enriched their philosophical traditions with their theories of compassionate human nature as a descriptive theory. In China, Mencius (Meng-zu, 371–289 B.C.E.), a student of Confucius, didn't merely follow his teacher in claiming that humans ought to be compassionate: he held that we are born compassionate and good, but life tends to corrupt the human spirit. It doesn't mean we shouldn't also strive to become compassionate, because most of us have lost that initial feeling. What we have to do is pay attention to that little inner voice, our conscience. Mencius believes that, intuitively, we are still good, and if we look inward to our deepest nature, we can recapture that goodness. If a child has fallen into a well, our first instinct is to save it, says Mencius—hesitation in the face of other people's misfortune happens because we have been corrupted by selfishness. Not every Confucian scholar agreed: Hsün Tzu (ca. 298–238 B.C.E.) claimed that human nature is evil, selfish, and envious, because it is natural to seek self-preservation and self-gratification. But if we follow our nature, we will have social chaos, so teachers and laws must educate and control the population. The moral ideal is self-control for Mencius, but for Hsün Tzu it appears to have been control by the state. Hsün Tzu was very critical of Mencius and found that his view of human nature was fundamentally flawed: Goodness is a matter of controlling one's original nature rather than rediscovering it. In Greece Socrates (427?–347) taught that only ignorance leads to wrongdoing; there is no such thing as a person who does wrong knowingly. In other words, humans may be weak, emotional beings by nature, but they are not evil. In England, David Hume (1711–1776)—who thought of himself as a friend of Rousseau's for a while, until Rousseau turned on him—agreed with Rousseau that humans are fundamentally decent creatures; we are only selfish when there is something to be gained from a situation: If we are not personally involved in an issue, our natural compassion (or "fellow feeling") rises to the surface. Indeed, our rationality is generally employed to make sense out of our emotional responses. In the twentieth century, the American philosopher Richard Taylor joined the optimistic chorus by claiming that all the rational moral systems in the world can't teach us the right thing to do, if our hearts haven't told us already: What is morally repugnant to us is not that an immoral action doesn't make sense, but that it is devoid of compassion.

Day" all the way to commercials touting "no artificial ingredients" can claim Rousseau as an intellectual parent.

How does Rousseau picture the state of nature? It is a peaceful, plentiful outdoor existence, and early humans are strong and resourceful; they know how to make use of nature's big pantry, and they are not yet softened by the comforts of civilization. Once in a while they meet to mate, and from then on the women are alone in their parenting duties (Rousseau's natural men seemed as little affected by duties of fatherhood as himself was), but since women are also strong and resourceful in the state of nature, it presents no problem. When a human meets an injured fellow human, there is no enmity, nothing but compassion, and the early uncorrupted human feels compassion for everything that suffers. However, ordinarily, humans are loners in the great forests of Rousseau's imagination. Physical inequality certainly exists, but since there are few fights, the stronger ones don't use their strength to subdue the weaker ones (a difference from Hobbes's state of nature, where we are all "equal" because we can all kill each other). Social inequality doesn't exist in the state of nature, says Rousseau, because there simply is no society. So if the state of nature was so idyllic, why are we then caught in the web of civilization? Because humans lost this early Eden by thinking and by grabbing:

> The first person who, having enclosed a plot of land, took it into his head to say *this is mine* and found people simple enough to believe him, was the true founder of civil society. What crimes, wars, murders, what miseries and horrors would the human race have been spared, had someone pulled up the stakes or filled in the ditch and cried out to his fellow men: "Do not listen to this impostor. You are lost if you forget that the fruits of the earth belong to all and the earth to no one!"[14]

This is the beginning of the end of the good times, says Rousseau. Eventually tyrants take over, making life miserable for people forever after.

Is there anything factual in Rousseau's description of the state of nature? We know that early humans weren't solitary; Rousseau seems to think that women, with their infants and children, roamed around by themselves in the forests like foxes and bears; adolescents must have been on their own. Now just as you can draw a line from Hobbes's theory of human aggression to Robert Ardrey's theory of the "territorial imperative" (Chapter 3), so can you draw another line directly from Rousseau to Ardrey's romantic infatuation with the freedom of the early male hominid, roaming the savanna, hunting and mating whenever he feels like it. Ardrey's "state of nature" may be dangerous, but it is also portrayed as intensely enjoyable as well as morally important: The natural skills we had then (such as defending our territory) are skills we ought to maintain. In Ardrey's philosophy of aggressive human nature we find a strange synthesis of Hobbes and Rousseau.

Be that as it may, we now think we know better: Early hominids seem to have been quite socialized, not loners, and probably were far more "gatherers" than "hunters." But even so, Rousseau seems to have had a sounder instinct about our distant ancestors than Hobbes. Anthropologists as well as paleoanthropologists today tell us that life may well have been closer to Rousseau's vision: Pretechnological tribal people's lives are generally not "nasty, brutish and short," unless they are in competition with a neighboring technological culture. Although there is today no tribe living in a complete "state of nature," we have ample evidence of low-technology cultures living in small groups, hunting and gathering. If they haven't been exposed to diseases from the civilized world, they are generally quite healthy, aside from the ubiquitous intestinal worms. Their average life span is short, but that is because of the high infant mortality rate. If they live past the age of five, and don't die in childbirth later on, they may have life spans equaling ours in the world of high technology. Were the first humans happy, and did they have lots of free time, as Rousseau predicted? The evidence now indicates that this could well be the case. Based on knowledge of pretechnological societies in the twentieth century, people would work a couple of hours a day—the women somewhat longer than the men—collecting food. The rest of the time they'd take turns watching the kids, telling stories, repairing tools, and sleeping. As new research has shown, the life of toil came about later, with the invention of agriculture (about 10,000 years ago). Crops demand much more attention than is required for a hunting-gathering existence, and crops can feed more mouths, so a more elaborate social structure is needed to keep the growing population under control and keep track of the division of labor; so among the results of the ensuing social hierarchy are stress and aggression (see Box 9.3 for a discussion of whether humans are good by nature).

The Social Contract and Beyond   A few years after formulating his state-of-nature hypothesis, Rousseau published what was to become his most famous work, *The Social Contract*. This book departs from the *Discourse* in a significant way: It views the fate of civilization in a slightly less hopeless light. Here Rousseau theorizes that at an early point in time, after humans left the state of nature, they formed a social contract. Everyone (all males) got together and created rules for society, for the purpose of creating a better life for all, a life morally superior to that of the state of nature. Unlike Hobbes's version of the beginning of society, though, Rousseau's people never give away their personal freedom to any sovereign. Hobbes saw the only right that can't be given away as the right to self-protection. For Rousseau, individuals cannot be asked to give away their *sovereignty*—it is an *inalienable right*. Sovereignty is the right to self-determination—but this is where it gets tricky. Because what Rousseau is talking about is not the right to do anything you please as long as you can get away with it (Hobbes's "right" in the state of nature). Rousseau specifically addresses the issue and ridicules Hobbes's idea: "For, if force creates right, the effect changes with the cause: every force that is greater than the first succeeds to its right. . . . Clearly, the word 'right' adds nothing to force."[15] But Rousseau's concept of right is not even the same as Locke's three negative rights, which function even in the state of nature: the right to life, liberty, and property. For Rousseau, these are not rights at all, because they imply that an individual has rights above and beyond the needs of society. For Rousseau, our sovereignty is, in effect, our right to determine our own life *within* the defined boundaries of our community; in other words, it is our right to help determine what is best for the community. As we shall see, Rousseau's concept of freedom within a society relates to *freedom for the community* rather than *freedom for the individual.*

So how should we form a society based on Rousseau's ideas? We should make all decisions within the group and govern ourselves. No power will be given to any sovereign, president, monarch, or government, for we are the government. Even more literally than the famous words by Lincoln in the Gettysburg Address—a government of the peo-

ple, by the people and for the people—Rousseau intends for everyone (every male) to actually show up and vote about every major and minor issue: No representational government is allowed in Rousseau's social contract, because true democracy involves everyone; you can't allow anyone else to vote for you or represent you. Because Rousseau views humans as good by nature, they can be trusted to rule themselves, provided that society hasn't corrupted them too much. But we can't vote for or pay people to make the decisions for us—that makes a mockery out of democracy. Accordingly, any country that has representational democracy—as do most democracies in the world, including the United States—is not a true democracy. Rousseau's native Switzerland comes close, though, because it is divided into small groups of people who show up to vote (at least they are supposed to), defend themselves with a militia, and govern themselves. It seems that if Rousseau's democratic ideal is to work, his society must be small enough for every citizen to have a direct influence on political decisions.

We all know that power corrupts, though, so how does Rousseau imagine that democratic citizens can stay focused on the common good? He says they must leave their personal wishes and ambitions at home on voting days, so that upon their arrival they will be filled with civic conscientiousness and all their opinions together will form the *general will,* which can never be wrong, because it always has everyone's welfare in mind. "Each of us puts his person and all his power in common under the supreme direction of the general will, and, in our corporate capacity, we receive each member as an indivisible part of the whole."[16] That whole *is* the Sovereign: the governing body of all citizens.

But what if you have done your best to leave your personal ambitions at home, and you vote in all earnest, thinking only about the common good, but find yourself in the minority? Then, says Rousseau, *you must be wrong,* because the general will, which is the majority, can never be wrong: "It follows from what has gone before that the general will is always right and tends to the public advantage; but it does not follow that the deliberations of the people are always equally correct. Our will is always for our own good, but we do not always see what that is; the people is never corrupted, but it is often deceived, and on such occasions only does it seem to will what is bad."[17] So for Rousseau the "will of all" is not always the same as the "general will." The will of all takes private interests into consideration, and the general will strictly looks to the common good. So how do we know what is the general will? It is the will of the majority. This is one of the truly problematic elements in Rousseau's political theory: It does not allow for valid minority opinions—unless you can show that the majority opinion was actually the "will of all" and not the "general will." If a minority group takes a view that differs from that of the majority, it is because they are somehow thinking about their own advantage.

Rousseau's democracy has no place for legitimate minority dissent or discussion, and if you don't agree with the decision of the majority, you have no right to rebel—the majority is right by definition, and your only course of action is to repent your selfishness, even if you voted in good faith. Hobbes gave his citizens the right to take matters into their own hands if their monarch let them down, and Locke had two political solutions for cases when a sovereign transgresses against his or her people: Hold the sovereign to the minimalist task of protecting people's right to life, liberty, and property—and if that doesn't work, or your idea of rights is different from the views of your society, then pack up and leave. For Rousseau's utopian democracy, there is no legitimate recourse to civil disobedience: Anyone dissenting from the general will has no right to his or her opinion because it is born out of private interests. For Locke, your private interests never become illegitimate, and the well-functioning society is based on respecting those interests. For Rousseau, such interests are suspect and have no place in a government of the people. In effect, if the ideas of a dissident are considered too detrimental for the community, the community is entitled to take his or her life. When we remember that Rousseau

provided a considerable amount of inspiration for the French Revolution, this becomes particularly thought-provoking.

The fundamental social philosophies of Hobbes, Locke, and Rousseau still make themselves felt in Western political theories. In itself, it is a fascinating mental exercise to trace these political philosophies to present-day partisan politics in the Western world. (Box 9.4 briefly presents a famous social-contract theory from the twentieth century.)

Karl Marx: Human Nature Will Change

One of the areas where Rousseau's philosophy has had considerable influence is the political theory of Marxism. Regardless of whether the world has seen the last of Marxism as a social experiment or whether Marxist ideology will once again be on the agenda in places of the world other than Cuba and Eastern Asia, there is no denying that Karl Marx was the greatest political influence of the twentieth century, either in the way societies have been shaped according to the rules of communism or in the way societies have defined themselves in contrast to communism and have taken precautions to prevent its spread. This is not a textbook of political theory, and we will not go into great detail about Marxism as such, but Marx developed a distinct theory of human nature that goes hand in hand with his vision of the communist society of the future. As you may remember from Chapter 8, Ricoeur pronounced Marx one of the "masters of suspicion" (the other two were Nietzsche and Freud). Let's take a look at the Marxist brand of "suspicion."

Marx as a Materialist

It is common knowledge that Marxism requires the end of private property, the end of profit-making businesses—in short, the end of the capitalist economic system. Why is it, then, classified as a philosophical theory and not simply a politico-economic one? The reason is that the foundation

Box 9.4   A TWENTIETH-CENTURY SOCIAL-CONTRACT THEORY: JOHN RAWLS

The notion that once upon a time humans got together and decided on building a society from scratch is no longer in vogue, because we now know that humans have always lived in groups. We may, in various historical contexts, have decided on making a new society with a new set of rules, such as the American Constitution—which still is the only document in the world that comes close to a real "social contract"—but it is historically improbable that humans started living in rule-governed groups as a matter of decision making. (And who said that first? Aristotle.) Nevertheless, we don't have to abandon the idea of the social contract altogether, because it works well as a *thought experiment:* The British philosopher Mary Midgley calls it the *Social Contract Myth,* not just in the sense that it is false, but also in the sense that a myth helps us gather our thoughts and put together a normative ideology or a program: We know the social contract never happened, but even so, it works well for us as a kind of guideline for how we ought to live in a society. The American philosopher John Rawls has perfected the social contract as myth or thought experiment with his theory of social justice in numerous books, the most famous being *A Theory of Justice* (1971). Rawls introduces the concept of the *original position* as a modern version of a social contract. Rejecting any political and economic system that gives to the few and lets the many pay the price, and even any system that gives to the many and lets a few pay the price, Rawls seeks a system that is fair to everyone. Imagine yourself being one of the decision makers who will get to decide what an ideal society is going to be. What principle should you use for a fair sharing of the goods and wealth of society? First come, first serve? Power to the intelligentsia? Welfare for the needy? Military rule? The device Rawls uses to decide this is the mind game of the original position: Pretend that, once the new rules take effect, *you don't know who you will be.* You don't know your gender, your race, your age, or station in life. In that new society you may be rich or poor, young or old, healthy or sick. And since you don't know who you will be, you'd better make rules that are so fair that whatever group you end up in will not be short-changed! Rawls also calls this mind game a lowering of a *veil of ignorance* over your knowledge of the future, so you can imagine us all in a state of total equality. Rawls has been criticized, particularly by feminists, for claiming that we can never pretend to be ignorant about who we are; our gender especially is so intrinsically part of who we are that we shouldn't try to de-gender ourselves. But here one might remark that Rawls isn't saying we should consider ourselves as just human entities without any characteristics; his point is exactly that when the new society arrives, we will definitely be *somebody* with a specific set of interests and needs; we should just pretend we don't know *who,* and that will force us to make rules that are fair for all possible future existences.

for the Marxist social structure is a philosophical, even metaphysical one—a theory of the nature of reality. For Marx, reality is what you can see, touch, and measure. In other words, he is a materialist; he believes that reality is material and not spiritual. But he also believes that *reality is change* and that it changes through a process of development known as *dialectical materialism.*

Karl Marx (1818–1883) was born in Trier, Germany, into a Jewish family that had converted to Protestantism. Marx himself became an agnostic.

He studied philosophy and economics in Bonn, and there he was introduced to the ideas of the German philosopher G. W. F. Hegel, who was then at the height of his influence in European intellectual circles. Hegel believed that reality is *spiritual,* and he developed a kind of *absolute idealism:* He said that as history develops, the World Spirit evolves. Any natural item or cultural movement is a manifestation of the World Spirit, and it becomes more and more rational through a certain pattern of development—through opposition.

Any idea will, like a pressure, create its own opposition or counterpressure. This opposition in turn creates its own counterpressure, which is thus related to the original idea. You can compare it to the swinging pattern of a pendulum; however, it is not merely a swinging between two extremes. Each opposition has absorbed and incorporated some of the previous opposition into itself, and this is what Hegel refers to as a dialectic movement. (It is sometimes referred to as the *thesis-antithesis-synthesis* movement, but Hegel never used that expression; it came from another philosopher, J. G. Fichte.) Hegel sees reality as a dialectical movement of the World Spirit, and at every new phase the World Spirit's rationality increases. As time progresses, the World Spirit will have become completely rational, and the world will have reached its maximum, glorious potential, which is a state of complete human self-realization. Western history moved from historical period to historical period, each with a sense of renewal and criticism of the previous one. Antiquity was followed by the Middle Ages, which in turn were followed by the Renaissance, and so forth. Hegel seems to have believed that reality had in fact reached the peak of reason in his own lifetime with the Prussian state of the early nineteenth century, and thus the Prussians (including himself, as one of their spiritual icons) were the most developed people in the world.

This theory, strange as it may sound, nevertheless swept Europe in the nineteenth century, and Hegelianism became a way of life among intellectuals. Why? It may be because it was one of the most *positive* theories in terms of human progress. The nineteenth century saw a tremendous growth in technology and science in general, and intellectuals and laypeople alike wanted to believe the world was getting better and more manageable—that scientists were becoming more knowledgeable and that people in general were becoming wiser. This positive metaphysical view of life met its defeat in the early twentieth century where the general faith in science and human wisdom came to an abrupt halt, through a series of disillusioning experiences—including the savage slaughter of World War I, which put an end to the faith in human wisdom, and the wreck of the *Titanic,* the marvel of technology that was supposed to have conquered nature.

But at Hegel's time and for the rest of the nineteenth century, it seemed to the Western world that nothing was impossible in terms of creating morally better people (see the section on Darwin in Chapter 3) and better technology. The novels of Jules Verne testify to this optimism: The first examples of science fiction literature, Verne's stories of future technology did incorporate elements of horror and visions of mad scientists, but overall they were intended to be a tribute to the indomitable human spirit. In a way, stories such as *20,000 Leagues Under the Sea* and *The First Men on the Moon* are stories that put Hegel's optimism into a technological context: Yes, there are frail and evil humans threatening our future, but overall we are becoming more rational and better at handling the technological challenges of the future.

The enthusiastic faith in the progress of the future did not become part of the twentieth century; rather, a profound cynicism came to characterize most of the century in the West. But already before the end of the nineteenth century, Marx had supplanted Hegel's dialectic idealism with his own version of reality, dialectic materialism. Marx decided that Hegel was right that historical developments are the result of a pendulum pattern between opposing beliefs, but he wasn't right in assuming that this process marked the evolution of a World Spirit. To Marx, such developments were simply the result of economics; the dialectical movement was a *material* development, not a spiritual one (hence the term dialectical materialism). The cultural developments of the world, the intellectual and moral states of affairs, are for Marx directly dependent on the economic systems in place. His "suspicion" consists of suspecting that society is not what it appears to be on the surface—a collection of independent cultural institutions. Churches; libraries; educational systems; theaters; health care systems; sports events; defense systems; rules for moral behavior, for retirement, for marriage and divorce, for child care; and so forth—all of this is labeled the *superstructure* by Marx. It rests firmly on a foundation of a system of economy, and when the economy changes, the superstructure will change. For Marx, mind does not determine society; rather, society (the economy) determines one's state of mind. Even religion is created and perpetuated by economic forces and is nothing but the "opiate of the people," a pacifying influence designed to make an oppressed populace believe that life has to be miserable and that one must look to the afterlife for comfort and justice instead of trying to do something about oppression and misery in this life. (You will remember that Nietzsche was equally adamant about the pacifying, oppressive powers of Christianity, but believed that socialism was no alternative because of its "herd mentality"; see Chapter 8.)

Believing that culture is independent of economics is a false ideology for Marx, and such faulty notions must be exposed. Thus, in essence, any cultural idea derives from its economical substructure: Social ideas developed during a barter economy are specific for that type of economy. Social ideas developed during feudalism derive from a feudal economy. And social ideals conceived during the capitalist economic system should be subject to critical examination and most likely dismissed, because they derive from an economy of profit making. This is why the arguments that communism neglects *human rights* has never had much effect on hard-line Marxists; for them "human rights" is a concept that emerged from within the capitalist middle-class consciousness and is just another economy-dependent notion that must be critically examined.

Marx believes that society developed according to the pattern reflected in Hegel's dialectics; in Marx's materialist view of history, the economic system of tribal barter was replaced by feudalism, which in turn has been replaced by capitalism. Each system replaces the other because the inner contradictions of the system cause it to break down and make way for its opposite, and thus capitalism is also doomed to fail and eventually be replaced by socialism, a precursor to communism.

And will communism in turn fail too? No, because Marx sees communism as the equivalent of Hegel's end point of the World Spirit: With communism the internal contradictions of the previous economies have been resolved, and the world will have reached its optimal state.

Why Communism?

In 1843, after completing his studies, Marx went to Paris, where he met German socialist Friedrich Engels (1820–1895). This was to be a friendship that lasted for the rest of his life. Engels was the manager of a factory in Manchester, England, and through him Marx became acquainted with the effects of industrialism on society and its individuals. Together they wrote *The Manifesto of the Communist Party* (1848). Marx and Engels took part in both the French and German revolutions of 1848. But after these failed, Marx went to England, where he spent the rest of his life. Here he worked part-time as a journalist and wrote his most famous work, *Das Kapital* (1867).

Today it is a common assumption in the West that the world can be made a better place without resorting to a ban on private property and profits. We think in terms of providing better health care and child care, providing education and food for starving nations, or raising ecological awareness; we may also think in terms of securing the rights of individuals to pursue their own brand of happiness. The difference may not be merely in ideology but could also be in the different nature of the problems we face.

What Marx saw in the cities of nineteenth-century Europe was poverty—not just the problem of making ends meet from paycheck to paycheck, but *extreme* poverty, such as we today still see in the slums of certain cities of what used to be called the Third World. In Marx's time people literally were worked to death. There was no legal protection of the working population and no support for the unemployed—they and their children faced starvation. The children worked in factories themselves, ten to sixteen hours a day, with no

Box 9.5   HEGEL'S THEORY OF THE MASTER-SLAVE DIALECTIC

Years before Marx's theory of the abuse of the worker in the creation of profit—the *labor theory of value*—G. W. F. Hegel had laid the groundwork: In his immensely influential book, *Phenomenology of Mind* (1807), Hegel outlines the inner workings of the dialectical movement of history, a theory that Marx adapted to his own economic theory. Part of Hegel's analysis includes an example of the dynamic relationship between a master and a slave. The slave is, of course, not free. He is dependent on the master for food, clothing, and, above all, the master's goodwill—but the master also is not free. He is dependent on the slave, and not just for the slave's labor. There are things the slave has control over, but the master does not (like keeping house). Moreover, the slave has to be kept under surveillance, because by the nature of the master-slave relationship the slave can't be trusted. So the master is, in effect, also a captive of the slave, since he has to remain constantly aware of the slave, while the slave has free moments in which he can scheme and connive as long as he stays clear of the master. And so the slave, becoming aware of this, in effect becomes the master of the master. Marx interpreted Hegel's master-slave passage and developed it into his labor theory of value: The worker must become aware that the product of his labor has been appropriated (stolen) by the employer, who is, in effect, stealing the time and product of the worker's life. But the employer is dependent on the worker—the exploiter is dependent on the exploitee—and this fact the worker must be made aware of, as a step toward casting off his chains of dependency in a revolution.

health insurance and no minimum wage. Industrialization had created jobs for millions but, as Marx saw it, had also robbed the working class of its spirit and given a life of bare existence in exchange. How had this come about? By taking the time and labor of the worker, making him or her work for wages as low as possible, and then *selling the finished product for more than the worker was paid*. This we call profit. Marx calls it *surplus value* and views it as exploitation of the worker.

The process Marx calls *realization of labor* is one where the worker's own work time is made into a product that is bought and sold (an "object"), and the product itself takes on an existence apart from the worker. He or she has no control over the production process as a whole, only over a small part of it. The workers thus experience a "loss of reality"; they don't control their own time or products anymore. The result? *Alienation.* You can't possess the things you yourself produce, because they cost too much, and you're making them for others who make a profit from them, a profit they don't share with you. You never really know what happens to the finished product of your work, so what you've worked on at the assembly line leaves your hands without your ever feeling that you have anything to do with it. This is damaging to your sense of self. The result is that you, as a worker, don't enjoy working, and you look forward only to the end of the workday. But when you come home, what can you do? You barely have enough time to eat and sleep, and that's all you can afford, anyway. Then it's back to work. The only enjoyment left is procreation, and (in Marx's day, a cheap thrill) booze. You are reduced to an animal existence of food and drink, sex, and sleep.

Why did this happen? Because of capitalism: private property and division of labor. The factories, the farms, the tools (what Marx calls *productive forces*) are in private hands, and workers each have their own separate tasks. They have no sense of the whole and no fellow feeling for others in the same situation. (Box 9.5 gives a brief introduction to a theory that had considerable influence on Marx: Hegel's theory of the master-slave dialectic.)

Human Nature and Capitalism

Work wasn't always exploitative and demeaning, says Marx. At one time, humans enjoyed working—when they were in charge of the entire creative process and got to keep their own product or trade it themselves or give it away—in other words, when they had control over their product. In those days people experienced *self-activity*—pleasure in work. And humans can't be happy unless they experience self-activity. For Marx, humans need food, shelter, clothing, and meaningful work; without it, we are not fully human. Under the capitalist system there is no hope for the working classes to ever become "fully human," because their self-activity has been made impossible. And in a sense, the owners of the productive forces (the employers) are suffering, too, because exploiting their fellow human beings reduces their own humanity. So what happens? Human nature itself becomes warped. Humans begin to think in terms of *ownership*.

Previously I alluded to Rousseau's being a source of inspiration for Marx, and here is an example: Remember this quotation from Rousseau? "The first person who, having enclosed a plot of land, took it into his head to say *this is mine* and found people simple enough to believe him, was the true founder of civil society." For Marx as well as for Rousseau, this signifies the beginning of human exploitation. But Marx sees it in a broader perspective: Humans now view work versus free time as an example of evil versus good, and they develop what many in the Western world would see as typical human traits: a selfish concern for taking care of number one and an overwhelming interest in the accumulation of material goods. And Marx sees these developments as a tendency that has been perfected and taken to an extreme by the capitalist system.

So what must we do? We can't just sit back and interpret the world anymore, as philosophers have done for so long, says Marx. Now it is time to change things. And the way to change them is not by changing the cultural institutions, because that would be merely patchwork. What it takes is altering the base of the superstructure: the economic foundation.

Human Nature and the Socialist System

Marx tells us how to change the economic foundation of society:

> Thus things have now come to such a pass that the individuals must appropriate the existing totality of productive forces, not only to achieve self-activity, but, also, merely to safeguard their very existence. This appropriation is first determined by the object to be appropriated, the productive forces, which have been developed to a totality and which only exist within a universal intercourse. From this aspect alone, therefore, this appropriation must have a universal character corresponding to the productive forces and the intercourse.[18]

These words from *The German Ideology* are the actual call to arms: Now it is time for the *revolution*. The working classes, the proletariat, must rise and take over the factories, the farms, the distribution centers, and so forth (and today any revolutionary would add, "control of the media"). Furthermore, because commerce is complex and multinational, the revolution ought to be universal. A famous slogan of Marxism is "Workers of the world, unite; you have nothing to lose but your chains." In this way nationalism will also become a thing of the past, and it is no accident that the battle song of Marxism carries the title of *Internationale*. It is futile to try to improve capitalism from the inside; it has to be abolished altogether. But this change must be effected by the workers in the big cities, whose misery has reached the extreme proportions that warrant the dialectic change to the opposite kind of system. Farmers, be they ever so miserable and exploited, can't undertake the revolution, because they haven't gone through the experience of alienation; they aren't ready. In the new system, all productive forces will become common property for the workers, and a new era will arise: the era of communism. (Box 9.6 lists the general goals of the Marxist revolution.)

Box 9.6   THE GOALS OF THE REVOLUTION

The general, immediate goals of the Marxist revolution as listed in the *Manifesto* are, in brief,

1. Abolition of private property

2. Imposition of a heavy or graduated income tax

3. Abolition of inheritance rights

4. Confiscation of the property of emigrants and rebels

5. Centralization of all credit and monetary institutions in the hands of the state

6. Centralization of the means of communication and transportation in the hands of the state

7. Creation of a master plan for productive forces and agriculture

8. Establishment of the equal liability of all to work; establishment of industrial armies

9. Combination of agriculture and manufacturing industry; gradual abolition of distinction between town and country by redistributing the population

10. Establishment of free education of children and abolition of child factory labor.

"To each according to need, and from each according to ability." This is Marx's creed for the new society. In the beginning wages must be paid for work, but no profit will be made. This is the socialist phase. The eventual goal is to establish a communist society where money is abolished, because it is not necessary. Each individual receives what he or she needs—food, shelter, clothing—and is given the opportunity to work at whatever he or she enjoys doing. From then on, humans can be trusted not to exploit one another *because human nature will have changed.* As we know, Marx believes human nature is determined by the economic base, and selfishness is a trait in the capitalist superstructure, not a universal characteristic. (Box 9.7 explores the concept of positive rights and compares it to negative rights.)

In Marx's own words, "Does it require deep intuition to comprehend that man's ideas, views and conception, in one word, man's consciousness, changes with every change in the conditions of his material existence, in his social relations and in his social life?"[19] All ruling classes have elevated their ideas of society and human nature to a form of eternal law, says Marx, but it is merely relative to the economy.

In the new communist society people will have no desire to accumulate money and "stuff" because they will receive what they need, so they will not want more. What they want will coincide with what they need. When this condition exists, the communist era will have arrived (and many critics have responded that in that case it will never arrive).

Marx's Critics

Over the years a number of challenging questions have been asked of Marx himself and of his followers. Here are some of the most famous objections:

- *Marx is a millennialist.* Having just passed into a new millennium, most of us know the term quite well. Therefore, it is interesting to know that many of Marx's critics have used that same term in a figurative sense to describe Marx's dream of communism. Since we are the first generation of a Western high-tech mass culture to actually pass from one millennium into another, we tend to forget that the term has been used for centuries to describe a religious phenomenon. The term is common in Christianity where it is assumed that Jesus, after his Second Coming, will reign in peace and prosperity for a thousand years, and then Judgment Day will arrive. The term *millennium* has thus come to

Box 9.7 NEGATIVE AND POSITIVE RIGHTS

Locke's concept of negative rights, rights of noninterference, have acquired an important place in the American political consciousness with their implication that each individual has the right not to be interfered with in terms of his or her life, liberty, and property. However, in the modern political world we also talk of *positive rights:* rights that each individual presumably has to *receive* something, usually from the government. Positive rights are rights of *entitlement.* Such entitlements may include food, shelter, clothing, education, health care, and other needs that are considered basic. Marx's communist philosophy encompasses the broadest of all concepts of positive rights, with its creed that each person should receive according to need and work according to his or her ability; on the other hand, the notion of negative rights has no place within the communist ideology: you have no right to noninterference by the government. A middle ground between the fiscal conservatism of negative rights and the communist and socialist focus on positive rights is suggested by American Liberals such as John Rawls, who see the ideal society as having negative rights supported by positive rights: We need the right to liberty, for example, but if someone is homeless and destitute, then what use is it that she can move about the country, have free speech, and can run for office? The tricky part is to decide *which* positive rights are needed to ensure that indiviudals don't fall through the cracks of modern society. In addition, some political thinkers argue that providing those positive rights collides with other people's negative rights (such as being compelled to contribute to social programs benefiting someone else).

mean some utopia in the far future where the good will be saved and the evil will perish (although it is not quite compatible with the Christian belief). It is in this sense that Marx's communist era has been labeled a millennialist theory. To critics, Marx promises salvation for the workers, and capitalists are promised only perdition, eternal damnation, unless they are "reeducated" and realize the benefits of communism.

- *Communism has failed.* The one obvious objection to communism that would occur to most people who have witnessed the fall of the Eastern Bloc in Europe and the Soviet Empire in Russia is, communism has been tried, and it didn't work, so Marx was wrong. I'll venture a guess at what Marx might have said—and Marxists have been responding in the same way: The Eastern European and Soviet social experiment called communism did not follow the Communist *Manifesto.* First of all, Marx had expected the revolution to arise from urban centers when the inner tensions between workers and employers had reached a peak—he didn't expect

the revolution to begin, or succeed, in a rural, feudal culture. But in Russia the revolution was not begun by workers in the cities alone, but also by the feudal population of farmers (and this goes for the Chinese and the Cuban revolutions too). As such it was doomed, because it could never reach the proper dialectic turning point. In addition, the communism of the Eastern Bloc was never true communism: Wages were paid, and there was social inequality; the system employed what some have called state capitalism, and at best these countries reached an intermediate stage between capitalism and communism.

- *Doesn't dialectical change happen automatically?* Other objections aren't as easy to dismiss: For one thing, if the revolution occurs through a process of dialectical determinism—in other words, if it happens automatically, why have a revolution?

- *How can we criticize our own system?* If people's state of mind is determined by whatever economic system they live in, how can we ever get to a point where we can be critical of our own system? Isn't Marx's critique of capitalism in it-self a product of capitalism, since that was the system of his day?

- *Why should the communist stage be the final one?* If reality is change, and history moves dialecti-cally, why should the communist stage necessar-ily be the final one? Why shouldn't the process continue? (Ironically, some might say that is precisely what did happen in the Eastern Bloc: Inner contradictions made the systems im-plode.) Such paradoxes do exist in Marx's own thinking, and various answers have been sug-gested, but most non-Marxist thinkers find that no truly satisfactory answers have been given.

- *Who will do the dirty work?* Marx did, in his own text, try to anticipate and refute certain other ob-jections: One of these is reflected in the question, If the Marxist society gives everybody meaning-ful work according to their own wishes, then who will do the dirty work? Marx says that we must take turns: You go fishing on Mondays while I empty the hospital bedpans, and then I'll teach school on Tuesdays, and you'll empty the bed-pans. This system was in effect attempted, even more radically than Marx had envisioned, dur-ing the sweeping Cultural Revolution in China by Mao Ze-dong in the late 1960s: Intellectuals were sent out to do farm work, and schools were closed.

- *Why work harder if you don't get more?* If you get only what you need, what is the incentive to get a better education and work harder, if you won't make more money? Marx would reply, You speak from capitalist presuppositions. In the new society people will want to work as hard as they can for the sheer satisfaction of it. Doing what you do well is a reward in itself, so you will not want further rewards, because hu-man nature has changed. But can we be sure of that? A wicked parody of the communist dream has been proposed by the author Ayn Rand, one of communism's fiercest critics, and you'll find a synopsis of it at the end of this chapter. In her book *Atlas Shrugged,* Rand tells of a factory where the owners decided to shift to the system of "to each according to need, and from each accord-ing to ability." The result is a rapid reduction of needy factory workers to whining parasites stripped of their human dignity and total ex-ploitation of those workers who have displayed abilities.

- *Aren't we selfish by nature?* Some critics have ob-jected that Marx failed to take human biology and psychology into consideration. On the basis of sociobiology and evolutionary psychology (see Chapter 3), they argue that a certain ele-ment of self-preservation is present in everyone, even if we may not be 100 percent selfish. But Marx does not consider the biological factor; for him, human nature is culturally (meaning economically) defined. Humans create a certain form of society that, in turn, creates another type of human being. Other than agreeing with Aris-totle that humans are social by nature, Marx does not seem interested in biology or psychol-ogy as an argument.

- *Why would all aspects of human nature change?* Many philosophers have a problem with Marx's insistence that all aspects of human nature will change when the economic base changes. Why, they ask, should reason change? The rules of logic are supposed to be absolute and cultur-ally independent: Logic is always logic, and math is always math, regardless of what kind of economy you have. And if we are capable of dispassionate reason, which most philosophers traditionally assume that we are—Rawls, for example, wants us to draw a veil of ignorance over our knowledge of who we will be in the fu-ture—then why should our findings be tainted by our economy? Interestingly, Marx here finds support among postmodernists who in the late twentieth century claimed that cultural views are based on a diversity of perspectives and that no perspective has more truth value than an-other. But since Marx would not accept his own social view as "just another perspective," post-modernists' support is of little value to Marxists.

- *Times have changed, and we don't need a revo-lution.* A final objection might be that Marx's vision was meaningful and perhaps even necessary for his troubled century. But thanks to the awareness of exploitation that he created, we are doing much better now in terms of working conditions and human rights, and we no longer need a socialist revolution. Many of Marx's goals involved making a better life for the majority (through unions, retirement, decent housing, fair wages, gender equality, better working conditions), and many of these have been accomplished or at least approached without a revolution. Marx would probably not have imagined that the working class of the Western world would become, to a great extent, *the middle class*—property owners with cars and TVs and conservative interests. If Marx could have looked into the future, would he have changed his mind? That is hard to say, but traditional hard-line Marxists say no. For one thing, many feel that deep exploitation is still going on—the Western world is exploiting the less industrialized countries. For another, Marxists argue that a content, property-owning working class is not the answer. The philosopher Herbert Marcuse (1892–1979) warned that the seemingly better conditions for workers (and for everybody else, for that matter) are just a result of *repressive tolerance*. The political powers let you think you have a nice life, but they control you nevertheless with an iron fist by imposing economic restrictions as well as cultural, religious, and moral rules. And when you complain, they pretend to listen to you politely, but your words have no effect on them: Your viewpoint is being tolerated yet repressed at the same time. This covert oppression, Marcuse says, is more dangerous than blatant oppression, because you don't recognize it—you are duped (*indoctrinated*) into thinking that you are free, whereas you are really a pawn in their game. So what is the duty of the Marxists? It is to raise your consciousness and open your eyes to the fact that you are being manipulated, regardless of whether you want to know. It is also to tell you that you don't know yourself well enough;

and once you realize that you have been the victim of a *false ideology,* you will realize that Marx was right.

Marxism thus aligns itself with the majority of social theories in this chapter which claim that you don't know what is good for you and that you can't trust your own judgment about what is good for society—only the enlightened social critic knows. As you will remember, the only dissenting voice among the historically influential theorists in this chapter is John Locke, who defends the right of the individual not to be interfered with by social forces unless he or she transgresses on other people's rights.

Sociopolitical philosophy, and its speculations about human nature, has of course continued into the twentieth century; one example is John Rawls's theory of the original position (see Box 9.4). This chapter has served as an overview of the social theories of human nature leading up to contemporary times, rather than an overall picture of current theories. However, in conclusion, we look at a twentieth-century social theory that ties the concept of our humanity to the notion of storytelling: Hayden White's theory that the way we understand ourselves as social beings with a past is to tell our history as a form of a moral tale.

Hayden White: Cultural History Is Storytelling

In Chapter 1 you heard about the theory that storytelling may be a fundamental human characteristic; most of the chapters in this book have contained some reference to this theory—and of course all the chapters conclude with stories about who we are as human beings. One of the landmark books of the late twentieth century that paved the way for this viewpoint was Hayden White's *Metahistory* (1973).

White (b. 1928) is a professor of History of Consciousness, with equal expertise in literature and history. The common assumption is that there is a world of difference between these two fields.

Stories of literature are made up, but history, as Aristotle said, deals with facts (unlike poetry which, for Aristotle, deals with truth); and if we find that our written account has somehow exaggerated the influence of a historical figure or downplayed the influence of some other factor, we do our best to correct it. Consider Christopher Columbus, for example. Upon the 500-year anniversary (1992) of his landing in the Americas there was a tremendous debate over whether his "discovery" of America was a heroic deed or the act of a greedy person in love with glory and fortune. In addition, debate raged over whether the effects of his discovery were a boon for humankind or the beginning of the end for some of the noblest cultures that ever existed. Laypeople usually assume that historians find out what really happened by studying their sources—*somewhere* there must be sufficient evidence to support one view or another. But most historians know that it is not as easy as that, because much of what we consider "evidence" and "facts" is colored by our viewpoint. It can be said to be a fact that Columbus landed in the Americas in 1492, but to say he "discovered" them is not fact, but interpretation. So history does not automatically rest on any firm foundation of truth: historians tell biased stories, just as eyewitnesses often give biased accounts of what they have seen: not out of ill will, but because they were predisposed to view a certain situation a certain way.

What is, to White, the relationship between history and historiography (the writing of history)? We read a book about Athens during the lifetimes of Socrates and Plato or about the Underground Railroad helping Southern slaves escape to the North during the Civil War, and we think we have read about a piece of history. But strictly speaking, it is only history *writing* we have encountered, and it is usually the only access to actual history that laypeople have. Historians can never have access to all the facts, let alone the thoughts and motivations of the past; and they can probably never do more than approximate what actually happened. And today, with the em-

phasis on rediscovering the histories of groups that have been neglected by most Western male historians until recently (such as women's history, the history of minorities in the United States, and the local histories of suppressed population groups around the world), time periods we thought we knew are acquiring a new face altogether. By the 1980s and 1990s scholars were becoming accustomed to the idea that there may be no such thing as "historical truth," a view expressed by the philosophy of *postmodernism*. According to many scholars today there are a number of truths, all depending on through whose eyes you view history. While postmodernism doesn't seem quite so attractive to many scholars as it did a decade ago—because a side effect of postmodernism is a form of cultural relativism that claims that anybody's view of history is as valid as anyone else's, regardless of tangible, provable facts (see Boxes 1.1, and 8.8)—postmodernism has still provided a shot in the arm for the Western idea of cultural identity: Habit and politics have prevented some of us from seeing all the different cultural perspectives that together make up our culture as well as the cultures of the world, and now these perspectives are becoming part of the mosaic of who we are.

We may think that the postmodern perspectivization of history writing breaks with an early tradition of regarding history writing as the ultimate version of what happened and why. But that has not always been the goal of history writing. Hayden White points out that some early histories, such as medieval *annals,* didn't even bother to list events that we would consider important, and they certainly didn't try to explain why something happened. Often, these accounts chronicle important activities, such as coronations, but fail to mention certain other events altogether, such as an outbreak of plague. And there is no attempt to link events causally. Our contemporary conception of history is a causal *analysis* of events ("the kingdom collapsed because of famine") rather than a plain *listing* of them ("In year X there was famine, The next year the kingdom collapsed"), or as some would say, "one d——d thing after another," but that is a fairly modern way of writing history. White sees history writing emerging as causal explanations some time in the Western Renaissance.

For White, modern history writing works like telling a story (in some languages, like German, the words for *history* and *story* are identical). Something begins, develops, and ends, and it is up to the historian to make sense of it, because we assume that somehow it must make sense. We are driven by the need for the world, and our lives, to make sense, and because of this we apply the structure of a story to our historical research. We look for a beginning, a middle, and an end, and those choices can be quite arbitrary. If we wish to tell the story of Columbus, where do we begin? With him sailing off into the sunset? Or with his first notion of sailing across the sea to Asia, in order to avoid the Muslim trade empire? With Ferdinand and Isabella kicking the Moors out of Spain and then feeling free to indulge themselves in an overseas venture? Or perhaps with the conflict between those who said the earth was round and those who said it was flat? We also could begin with the Aztec prediction of the fall of their empire upon the return of the bearded white god. The Danish Nobel Prize–winning author Johannes V. Jensen even chose to begin the story by assuming that Columbus was of Longobard (Viking) blood, which explained his longing for the sea and blazing new trails. We make a choice as to what the beginning of our story will be, and that choice also determines our middle and our end. But then again, we generally choose the beginning based on what we consider important about the ending! If we think the ending is tragic, we look for signs of the tragedy in the beginning. If we think the ending is triumphant, we look for some heroic beginning (or a mundane beginning that the hero rises above).

To White, the way human beings achieve a self-identity today, understanding themselves as part of a culture, is through storytelling based on selected evidence and undertaken with the assumption that history must be made to make sense,

just like a novel makes sense. In a more religious age one might have assumed that history made sense because "God wrote the story." But historians today rarely make such assumptions: They are concerned mainly with the idea of causality. Everything has a cause, and when we have understood the cause, we will also have understood the event. And the storytelling of history goes even deeper than that, says White, because any narrative, even the narrative of history, makes a *moral statement,* approving or disapproving of the story it tells.

So when we tell the traditional story of Columbus discovering America, we applaud his courage and tenacity and support a vision of the future in which the Old World comes to the New World and is transformed forever. But if we tell the story of Columbus as the beginning of the genocide of indigenous cultures, the beginning of the enslavement of Africans in the New World, and the start of a power imbalance on earth, we show disapproval of Columbus and his time, and we show disapproval of the behavior of Western culture since that time. In all fairness, a third kind of story can be told, of course: The story about what Columbus *intended* to do (find a trade route), what he *thought* he accomplished, and what the results have been for the world *regardless* of Columbus's intentions. This we can do without making a judgment as to whether Columbus setting sail for Asia by going west was morally "good" or "evil." Our moral judgment would not be absent, though, because our judgment would be that in this case it is morally appropriate not to make any judgment. We mustn't assume, according to White's way of thinking, that we can ever make an objective statement about history, but at least we can try to be open-minded. We can make a moral statement of tolerance for the ideals and mistakes of other times and other cultures, and we can include constructive suggestions for how to make the best of our present situation.

White has been accused of being too Eurocentric in his view of history writing. Indeed, the concept of historiography as a story of cause and effect is very Euro-American. Other cultures may see history as something that repeats itself endlessly or something that is determined by divine powers or something that is simply a chronological account of past events (like annals). But White doesn't say that all history writing *should be* storytelling that includes a moral judgment. He just points out that this happens to be the way we have done it in the Western culture for some centuries and that it is about time we became aware of it.

However, a deeper problem has been pointed out by the philosopher Louis Mink, himself a historian who believes that history is told as a story in order to make sense. Mink says that White simply assumes that all stories are moralizing; he doesn't prove it, and he can't, because it isn't true. Some stories are downright anti-moral (such as many of Mark Twain's short stories). Besides, Mink argues forcefully against the idea that humans didn't begin to tell their history as a narrative until recently. For Mink, we have *always* tried to explain our history as story. But even if White were right that this style of doing history started in the Renaissance, then that doesn't mean *individuals* can't have tried to keep their lives under some control by telling cause-and-effect stories since time immemorial; and as a matter of fact, we know that they have done just that through myths and legends. Myths and legends have served as ready-made explanations for why things happen, good as well as bad, and they have even served as an early form of history writing. Humans do indeed understand themselves, their past, and their future, through story telling. In all cultures we encounter stories of how the earth was created, how humans and animals were created (see Chapter 2), how important food items were created, and which gods were involved in the creation process (good gods and sometimes trickster gods). And all cultures tell stories about heroes of the past, men and women who lived up to the highest ideals of the culture; most cultures include in their stories events that actually happened to the people, such as war and famine, and often the story concludes with a happy ending to the war or the famine, usually brought about by the heroes.

Even in our Western cultures where we think we have stopped telling myths and legends, we still have cultural heroes exemplifying what an admirable individual is: We tell about Rosa Parks who refused to abide by racial segregation laws, about Christa McCauliffe, the New Hampshire schoolteacher who was proudly going into space but instead perished in the *Challenger* space shuttle disaster. We tell about Martin Luther King, Jr., and John F. Kennedy, murdered for their convictions. The American Indian heroes Chief Joseph and Crazy Horse are also becoming known outside the American Indian communities. In our Western culture we generally tell stories about people who have broken through a barrier, individuals who have proved that we can strive beyond what we think are our limits; other cultures may not be as inclined to celebrate the rebel and the rogue, but that's just an American "thing," provided that the rebel and the rogue work for some common good. In all fairness, we also tell rags-to-riches stories of celebrities and politicians because we'd really like to imagine that the same thing might happen to us. All in all, we mold our cultural consciousness and identity through stories of people we admire—even though we may seriously distort the truth in the telling. Myths and legends are by no means a phenomenon of the past—something that director George Lucas knew very well when he, with the help of his friend and mentor, the mythologist Joseph Campbell, wrote the *Star Wars* trilogy, a modern myth about righteous rebels fighting against a vast, evil governmental machinery in a galaxy far, far away.

So being a social human being seems to involve seeking and finding one's place in a greater narrative about one's culture: where it has been and where it is going. And this may also involve *rebelling* against the stories of one's culture, trying to redefine them or change them. Writing and rewriting our cultural identity—sometimes with deep regard for facts and sometimes with none at all—is one of the primary social human occupations, from Plato to Rousseau to Marx, and we seem to be as preoccupied with this as ever, here at the beginning of the twenty-first century, expanding what used to be a Euro-American cultural narrative into a story of a multitude of cultures and traditions.

Study Questions

1. Describe the structure of Plato's ideal state, and relate it to his theory of the harmonious person.

2. What does Aristotle mean by saying that man is a political animal? Explain, and place the saying in the context of Aristotle's political philosophy.

3. Outline the major similarities and differences in the theories of the state of nature and the social contract of Hobbes, Locke, and Rousseau.

4. Does Rawls's concept of the original position seem closer to Rousseau's disregard for private interests or Locke's respect for private interests? Explain.

5. Imagine that a new social structure could actually be achieved where everyone has meaningful work and experiences self-activity, at least part of the time. Is Marx right that this condition will seem sufficient for future humans, as long as they receive what they need, or do you think humans need more of an incentive to "work according to ability"? Explain.

6. How does White propose that we understand our past? Is he correct in saying that history writing involves a moral judgment?

Primary Readings and Narratives

The first Primary Reading is an excerpt from Aristotle's *Politics*, Book I, in which he describes the nature of the state and what he sees as the natural hierarchy of its inhabitants. The second text is an excerpt from Thomas Hobbes's *Leviathan* where we hear about the state of nature. The third text is taken from Jean-Jacques Rousseau's *Social Contract*, in which he outlines past human history as he sees it and prescribes how the social contract should be established. The fourth and final Primary Reading is an excerpt from Karl Marx's and Friedrich Engel's *The Manifesto of the Communist Party* explaining how human nature is a product of social conditions. The first Narrative is a summary of the film *Dances with Wolves;* the second is a summary of a section from Ayn Rand's novel *Atlas Shrugged;* and the third is a summary of the film *The Grapes of Wrath,* based on John Steinbeck's novel.

Primary Reading

Politics

ARISTOTLE

Extract from Book I. Translated by Benjamin Jowett. Fourth Century B.C.E.

. . . When several villages are united in a single complete community, large enough to be nearly or quite self-sufficing, the state comes into existence, originating in the bare needs of life, and continuing in existence for the sake of a good life. And therefore, if the earlier forms of society are natural, so is the state, for it is the end of them, and the nature of a thing is its end. For what each thing is when fully developed, we call its nature, whether we are speaking of a man, a horse, or a family. Besides, the final cause and end of a thing is the best, and to be self-sufficing is the end and the best.

Hence it is evident that the state is a creation of nature, and that man is by nature a political animal.

And he who by nature and not by mere accident is without a state, is either a bad man or above humanity; he is like the

> Tribeless, lawless, hearthless one,

whom Homer denounces—the natural outcast is forthwith a lover of war; he may be compared to an isolated piece at draughts.

Now, that man is more of a political animal than bees or any other gregarious animals is evident. Nature, as we often say, makes nothing in vain, and man is the only animal whom she has endowed with the gift of speech. And whereas mere voice is but an indication of pleasure or pain, and is therefore found in other animals (for their nature attains to the perception of pleasure and pain and the intimation of them to one another, and no further), the power of speech is intended to set forth the expedient and inexpedient, and therefore likewise the just and the unjust. And it is a characteristic of man that he alone has any sense of good and evil, of just and unjust, and the like, and the association of living beings who have this sense makes a family and a state.

Further, the state is by nature clearly prior to the family and to the individual, since the whole is of necessity prior to the part; for example, if the whole body be destroyed, there will be no foot or hand, except in an equivocal sense, as we might speak of a stone hand; for when destroyed the hand will be no better than that. But things are defined by their working and power; and we ought not to say that they are the same when they no longer have their proper quality, but only that they have the same name. The proof that the state is a creation of nature and prior to the individual is that the individual, when isolated, is not self-sufficing; and therefore he is like a part in relation to the whole. But he who is unable to live in society, or who has no need because he is sufficient for himself, must be either a beast or a god: he is no part of a state. A social instinct is implanted in all men by nature, and yet he who first founded the state was the greatest of benefactors. For man, when perfected, is the best of animals, but, when separated from law and justice, he is the worst of all; since armed injustice is the more dangerous, and he is equipped at birth with arms, meant to be used by intelligence and virtue, which he may use for the worst ends. Wherefore, if he have not virtue, he is the most unholy and

the most savage of animals, and the most full of lust and gluttony. But justice is the bond of men in states, for the administration of justice, which is the determination of what is just, is the principle of order in political society.

3

Seeing then that the state is made up of households, before speaking of the state we must speak of the management of the household. The parts of household management correspond to the persons who compose the household, and a complete household consists of slaves and freemen. Now we should begin by examining everything in its fewest possible elements; and the first and fewest possible parts of a family are master and slave, husband and wife, father and children. We have therefore to consider what each of these three relations is and ought to be:—I mean the relation of master and servant, the marriage relation (the conjunction of man and wife has no name of its own), and thirdly, the procreative relation (this also has no proper name). And there is another element of a household, the so-called art of getting wealth, which, according to some, is identical with household management, according to others, a principal part of it; the nature of this art will also have to be considered by us.

Let us first speak of master and slave, looking to the needs of practical life and also seeking to attain some better theory of their relation than exists at present. For some are of opinion that the rule of a master is a science, and that the management of a household, and the mastership of slaves, and the political and royal rule, as I was saying at the outset, are all the same. Others affirm that the rule of a master over slaves is contrary to nature, and that the distinction between slave and freeman exists by law only, and not by nature; and being an interference with nature is therefore unjust. . . .

5

But is there any one thus intended by nature to be a slave, and for whom such a condition is expedient and right, or rather is not all slavery a violation of nature?

There is no difficulty in answering this question, on grounds both of reason and of fact. For that some should rule and others be ruled is a thing not only necessary, but expedient; from the hour of their birth, some are marked out for subjection, others for rule.

And there are many kinds both of rulers and subjects (and that rule is the better which is exercised over better subjects—for example, to rule over men is better than to rule over wild beasts; for the work is better which is executed by better workmen, and where one man rules and another is ruled, they may be said to have a work); for in all things which form a composite whole and which are made up of parts, whether continuous or discrete, a distinction between the ruling and the subject element comes to light. Such a duality exists in living creatures, but not in them only; it originates in the constitution of the universe; even in things which have no life there is a ruling principle, as in a musical mode. But we are wandering from the subject. We will therefore restrict ourselves to the living creature, which, in the first place, consists of soul and body: and of these two, the one is by nature the ruler, and the other the subject. But then we must look for the intentions of nature in things which retain their nature, and not in things which are corrupted. And therefore we must study the man who is in the most perfect state both of body and soul, for in him we shall see the true relation of the two; although in bad or corrupted natures the body will often appear to rule over the soul, because they are in an evil and unnatural condition. At all events we may firstly observe in living creatures both a despotical and a constitutional rule; for the soul rules the body with a despotical rule, whereas the intellect rules the appetites with a constitutional and royal rule. And it is clear that the rule of the soul over the body, and of the mind and the rational element over the passionate, is natural and expedient; whereas the equality of the two or the rule of the inferior is always hurtful. The same holds good of animals in relation to men; for tame animals have a better nature than wild, and all tame animals are better off when they are ruled by man; for then they are preserved.

Again, the male is by nature superior, and the female inferior, and the one rules, and the other is ruled; this principle, of necessity, extends to all mankind. Where then there is such a difference as that between soul and body, or between men and animals (as in the case of those whose business is to use their body, and who can do nothing better), the lower sort are by nature slaves, and it is better for them as for all inferiors that they should be under the rule of a master. For he who can be, and therefore is, another's, and he who participates in rational principle enough to apprehend, but not to have, such a principle, is a slave by nature. Whereas the lower animals cannot even apprehend a principle; they obey their instincts. And indeed the use made of slaves and of tame animals is not very different; for both with their bodies minister to the needs of life. Nature would like to distinguish between the bodies of freemen and slaves, making the one strong for servile labour, the other upright, and although useless for such services, useful for political life in the arts both of war and peace. But the opposite often happens—that some have the souls and others have the bodies of freemen. And doubtless if men differed from one another in the mere forms of their bodies as much as the statues of the Gods do from men, all would acknowledge that the inferior class should be slaves of the superior. And if this is true of the body, how much more just that a similar distinction should exist in the soul? but the beauty of the body is seen, whereas the beauty of the soul is not seen. It is clear, then, that some men are by nature free, and others slaves, and that for these latter slavery is both expedient and right.

Study Questions

1. What, to Aristotle, is the origin of the state?

2. Find evidence in this text to support the view that Aristotle did not have a social contract theory.

3. What was Aristotle's view of slavery?

Primary Reading

Leviathan

THOMAS HOBBES

Excerpt, Chapters 13 and 14. 1651.

OF THE NATURAL CONDITION OF MANKIND AS CONCERNING THEIR FELICITY, AND MISERY

Nature hath made men so equal, in the faculties of the body and mind; as that, though there be found one man sometimes manifestly stronger in body or of quicker mind than another, yet when all is reckoned together, the difference between man and man is not so considerable, as that one man can thereupon claim to himself any benefit, to which another may not pretend as well as he. For as to the strength of body, the weakest has strength enough to kill the strongest, either by secret machination, or by confederacy with others that are in the same danger with himself.

And as to the faculties of the mind—setting aside the arts grounded upon words, and especially that skill of proceeding upon general and infallible rules, called science; which very few have, and but in few things; as being not a native faculty, born with us; nor attained, as prudence, while we look after somewhat else—I find yet a greater equality amongst men than that of strength. For prudence is but experience, which equal time equally bestows on all men, in those things they equally apply themselves unto. That which may perhaps make such equality incredible, is but a vain conceit of one's own wisdom, which almost all men think they have in a greater degree than the vulgar; that is, than all men but themselves, and a few others, whom by fame, or for concurring with themselves, they approve. For such is the nature of men, that howsoever they may acknowledge many others to be more witty, or more eloquent, or more learned, yet they will hardly believe there be many so wise as themselves; for they see their own wit at hand, and other men's at a distance. But this proveth rather that men are in that point equal, than unequal. For there is not ordinarily a greater sign of the equal distribution of anything, than that every man is contented with his share.

From this equality of ability, ariseth equality of hope in the attaining of our ends. And therefore if any two men desire the same thing, which nevertheless they cannot both enjoy, they become enemies; and in the way to their end, which is principally their own conservation, and sometimes their delectation only, endeavor to destroy, or subdue one another. And from hence it comes to pass that where an invader hath no more to fear than another man's single power; if one plant, sow, build, or possess a convenient seat, others may probably be expected to come prepared with forces united, to dispossess and deprive him, not only of the fruit of his labor, but also of his life or liberty. And the invader again is in the like danger of another.

And from this diffidence of one another, there is no way for any man to secure himself so reasonable as anticipation; that is, by force or wiles to master the persons of all men he can, so long, till he see no other power great enough to endanger him: and this is no more than his own conservation requireth, and is generally allowed. Also because there be some, that taking pleasure in contemplating their own power in the acts of conquest, which they pursue farther than their security requires; if others, that otherwise would be glad to be at ease within modest bounds, should not by invasion increase their power, they would not be able long time, by standing only on their defense, to subsist. And by consequence, such augmentation of dominion over men being necessary to a man's conservation, it ought to be allowed him.

Again, men have no pleasure, but on the contrary a great deal of grief, in keeping company, where there is no power able to overawe them all. For every man looketh that his companion should value him at the same rate he sets upon himself; and upon all signs of contempt, or undervaluing, naturally endeavors, as far as he dares (which amongst them that have no common power to keep them in quiet, is far enough to make them destroy each other), to extort a greater value from his contemners by damage, and from others by the example.

So that in the nature of man, we find three principal causes of quarrel. First, competition; second, diffidence; thirdly, glory.

The first maketh man invade for gain; the second, for safety; and the third, for reputation. The first use violence to make themselves masters of other men's persons, wives, children, and cattle; the second, to defend them; the third, for trifles, as a word, a smile, a different opinion, and any other sign of undervalue, either direct in their persons, or by reflection in their kindred, their friends, their nation, their profession, or their name.

Hereby it is manifest that during the time men live without a common power to keep them all in awe, they are in that condition which is called war; and such a war as is of every man against every man. For *war* consisteth not in battle only, or the act of fighting, but in a tract of time wherein the will to contend by battle is sufficiently known, and therefore the notion of *time* is to be considered in the nature of war, as it is in the nature of weather. For as the nature of foul weather lieth not in a shower or two of rain, but in an inclination thereto of many days together; so the nature of war consisteth not in actual fighting, but in the known disposition thereto, during all the time there is no assurance to the contrary. All other time is *peace*.

Whatsoever therefore is consequent to a time of war, where every man is enemy to every man; the same is consequent to the time, wherein men live without other security than what their own strength and their own invention shall furnish them withal. In such condition there is no place for industry, because the fruit thereof is uncertain: and consequently no culture of the earth; no navigation, nor use of the commodities that may be imported by sea; no commodious building; no instruments of moving, and removing, such things as require much force; no knowledge of the face of the earth; no account of time; no arts; no letters; no society; and which is worst of all, continual fear, and danger of violent death; and the life of man, solitary, poor, nasty, brutish, and short.

It may seem strange to some man that has not well weighed these things, that nature should thus dissociate, and render men apt to invade and destroy one another; and he may therefore, not trusting to this inference, made from the passions, desire perhaps to have the same confirmed by experience. Let him therefore consider with himself, when taking a journey, he arms himself and seeks to go well accompanied; when going to sleep, he locks his doors; when even in his house he locks his chests; and this when he knows there be laws, and public officers, armed, to revenge all injuries shall be done him: what opinion he has of his fellow-subjects, when he rides armed; of his fellow-citizens, when he locks his doors; and of his children, and servants, when he locks his chests. Does he not there as much accuse mankind by his actions, as I do by my words? But neither of us accuse man's nature in it. The desires, and other passions of man, are in themselves no sin. No more are the actions that proceed from those passions, till they know a law that forbids them: which till laws be made they cannot know; nor can any law be made, till they have agreed upon the person that shall make it.

It may peradventure be thought, there was never such a time nor condition of war as this; and I believe it was never generally so, over all the world: but there are many places where they live so now. For the savage people in many places of America, except the government of small families, the concord whereof dependeth on natural lust, have no government at all; and live at this day in that brutish manner, as I said before. Howsoever, it may be perceived what manner of life there would be, where there were no common power to fear; by the manner of life which men that have formerly lived under a peaceful government, use to degenerate into in a civil war.

But though there had never been any time wherein particular men were in a condition of war one against another; yet in all times, kings, and persons of sovereign authority, because of their independency, are in continual jealousies, and in the state and posture of gladiators; having their weapons pointing, and their eyes fixed on one another; that is, their forts, garrisons, and guns upon the frontiers of their kingdoms; and continual spies upon their neighbors; which is a posture of war. But because they uphold thereby the industry of their subjects, there does not follow from it that misery which accompanies the liberty of particular men.

To this war of every man against every man, this also is consequent: *that nothing can be unjust.* The notions of right and wrong, justice and injustice, have there no place. Where there is no common power, there is no law; where no law, no injustice. Force and fraud are in war the two cardinal virtues. Justice and injustice are none of the faculties neither of the body nor mind. If they were, they might be in a man that were alone in the world, as well as his senses and passions. They are qualities that relate to men in society, not in solitude. It is consequent also to the same condition, that there be no propriety, no dominion, no *mine* and *thine* distinct; but only that to be every man's, that he can get; and for so long as he can keep it. And thus much for the ill condition which man by mere nature is actually placed in; though with a possibility to come out of it, consisting partly in the passions, partly in his reason.

The passions that incline men to peace are fear of death, desire of such things as are necessary to commodious living, and a hope by their industry to obtain them. And reason suggesteth convenient articles of peace, upon which men may be drawn to agreement. These articles are they which otherwise are called the Laws of Nature. . . .

OF THE FIRST AND SECOND NATURAL LAWS

The right of nature, which writers commonly call *jus naturale,* is the liberty each man hath to use his own power, as he will himself, for the preservation of his own nature; that is to say, of his own life; and consequently, of doing anything, which in his own judgment and reason, he shall conceive to be the aptest means thereunto.

By *liberty,* is understood, according to the proper signification of the word, the absence of external impediments: which impediments, may oft take away part of a man's power to do what he would; but cannot hinder him from using the power left him, according as his judgment and reason shall dictate to him.

A *law of nature, lex naturalis,* is a precept or general rule, found out by reason, by which a man is forbidden to do that which is destructive of his life, or taketh away the means of preserving the same; and to omit that by which he thinketh it may be best preserved. For though they that speak of this subject, use to confound *jus* and *lex, right* and *law;* yet they ought to be distinguished: because *right* consisteth in liberty to do or to forbear, whereas *law* determineth and

bindeth to one of them; so that law, and right differ as much as obligation and liberty; which in one and the same matter are inconsistent.

And because the condition of man, as hath been declared in the precedent chapter, is a condition of war of everyone against everyone; in which case everyone is governed by his own reason, and there is nothing he can make use of that may not be a help unto him in preserving his life against his enemies: it followeth, that in such a condition every man has a right to everything; even to one another's body. And therefore, as long as this natural right of every man to everything endureth, there can be no security to any man, how strong or wise soever he be, of living out the time which nature ordinarily alloweth men to live. And consequently it is a precept, or general rule of reason, *that every man ought to endeavor peace, as far as he has hope of obtaining it; and when he cannot obtain it, that he may seek and use all helps and advantages of war.* The first branch of which rule containeth the first and fundamental law of nature; which is, *to seek peace and follow it.* The second, the sum of the right of nature; which is, *by all means we can, to defend ourselves.*

From this fundamental law of nature, by which men are commanded to endeavor peace, is derived this second law: *that a man be willing, when others are so too, as far forth as for peace and defense of himself he shall think it necessary, to lay down this right to all things; and be contented with so much liberty against other men, as he would allow other men against himself.* For as long as every man holdeth this right, of doing anything he liketh, so long are all men in the condition of war. But if other men will not lay down their right, as well as he, then there is no reason for anyone to divest himself of his: for that were to expose himself to prey, which no man is bound to, rather than to dispose himself to peace. This is that law of the Gospel: *whatsoever you require that others should do to you, that do ye to them.* And that law of all men, *quod tibi fieri non, vis, alteri ne feceris.*

To *lay down* a man's *right* to anything, is to *divest* himself of the *liberty,* of hindering another of the benefit of his own right to the same. For he that renounceth or passeth away his right, giveth not to any other man a right which he had not before; because there is nothing to which every man had not right by nature: but only standeth out of his way, that he may enjoy his own original right, without hindrance from him, not without hindrance from another. So that the effect which redoundeth to one man, by another man's defect of right, is but so much diminution of impediments to the use of his own right original.

Right is laid aside, either by simply renouncing it, or by transferring it to another. . . .

Whensoever a man transferreth his right, or renounceth it; it is either in consideration of some right reciprocally transferred to himself, or for some other good he hopeth for thereby. For it is a voluntary act; and of the voluntary acts of every man, the object is some *good to himself*. And therefore there be some rights which no man can be understood by any words, or other signs, to have abandoned or transferred. As first a man cannot lay down the right of resisting them that assault him by force, to take away his life; because he cannot be understood to aim thereby, at any good to himself. The same may be said of wounds, and chains, and imprisonment: both because there is no benefit consequent to such patience, as there is to the patience of suffering another to be wounded or imprisoned; as also because a man cannot tell, when he seeth men proceed against him by violence, whether they intend his death or not. And lastly the

motive, an end for which this renouncing and transferring of right is introduced, is nothing else but the security of a man's person, in his life, and in the means of so preserving life as not to be weary of it. And therefore if a man by words, or other signs, seem to despoil himself of the end for which those signs were intended, he is not to be understood as if he meant it, or that it was his will, but that he was ignorant of how such words and actions were to be interpreted.

The mutual transferring of right, is that which men call *contract*. . . .

Study Questions

1. What does Hobbes mean by saying that nature has made men equal? How does this statement compare with the American Declaration of Independence?

2. What are the three primary causes of quarrel, according to Hobbes? And what are the consequences?

3. In this excerpt Hobbes mentions two laws of nature. What are they?

4. How can the contract be said to be a transferring of rights?

Primary Reading

On the Social Contract

JEAN-JACQUES ROUSSEAU

Extract from Book I. Translated by Donald A. Cress. 1762.

CHAPTER I: SUBJECT OF THE FIRST BOOK

Man is born free, and everywhere he is in chains. He who believes himself the master of others does not escape being more of a slave than they. How did this change take place? I have no idea. What can render it legitimate? I believe I can answer this question.

Were I to consider only force and the effect that flows from it, I would say that so long as a people is constrained to obey and does obey, it does well. As soon as it can shake off the yoke and does shake it off, it does even better. For by recovering its liberty by means of the same right that stole it, either the

populace is justified in getting it back or else those who took it away were not justified in their actions. But the social order is a sacred right which serves as a foundation for all other rights. Nevertheless, this right does not come from nature. It is therefore founded upon convention. Before coming to that, I ought to substantiate what I just claimed.

CHAPTER II: OF THE FIRST SOCIETIES

The most ancient of all societies and the only natural one, is that of the family. Even so children remain bound to their father only so long as they need him to take care of them. As soon as the need ceases, the natural bond is dissolved. Once the children are freed from the obedience they owed the father and their father is freed from the care he owed his children, all return equally to independence. If they continue to remain united, this no longer takes place naturally but voluntarily, and the family maintains itself only by means of convention.

This common liberty is one consequence of the nature of man. Its first law is to see to his maintenance; its first concerns are those he owes himself; and, as soon as he reaches the age of reason, since he alone is the judge of the proper means of taking care of himself, he thereby becomes his own master.

The family therefore is, so to speak, the prototype of political societies; the leader is the image of the father, the populace is the image of the children, and, since all are born equal and free, none give up their liberty except for their utility. The entire difference consists in the fact that in the family the love of the father for his children repays him for the care he takes for them, while in the state, where the leader does not have love for his peoples, the pleasure of commanding takes the place of this feeling.

Grotius denies that all human power is established for the benefit of the governed, citing slavery as an example. His usual method of reasoning is always to present fact as a proof of right. A more logical method could be used, but not one more favorable to tyrants.

According to Grotius, it is therefore doubtful whether the human race belongs to a hundred men, or whether these hundred men belong to the human race. And throughout his book he appears to lean toward the former view. This is Hobbes' position as well. On this telling, the human race is divided into herds of cattle, each one having its own leader who guards it in order to devour it.

Just as a herdsman possesses a nature superior to that of his herd, the herdsmen of men who are the leaders, also have a nature superior to that of their peoples. According tho Philo, Caligula reasoned thus, concluding quite properly from this analogy that kings were gods, or that the peoples were beasts.

Caligula's reasoning coincides with that of Hobbes and Grotius. Aristotle, before all the others, had also said that men are by no means equal by nature, but that some were born for slavery and others for domination.

Aristotle was right, but he took the effect for the cause. Every man born in slavery is born for slavery; nothing is more certain. In their chains slaves lose everything, even the desire to escape. They love their servitude the way the companions of Ulysses loved their degradation. If there are slaves by nature, it is because there have been slaves against nature. Force has produced the first slaves; their cowardice has perpetuated them. . . .

CHAPTER III: ON THE RIGHT OF THE STRONGEST

The strongest is never strong enough to be master all the time, unless he transforms force into right and obedience into duty. Hence the right of the strongest, a right that seems like something intended ironically and is actually established as a basic principle. But will no one explain this word to me? Force is a physical power; I fail to see what morality can result from its effects. To give in to force is an act of necessity, not of will. At most, it is an act of prudence. In what sense could it be a duty?

Let us suppose for a moment that there is such a thing as this alleged right. I maintain that all that results from it is an inexplicable mish-mash. For once force produces the right, the effect changes places with the cause. Every force that is superior to the first succeeds to its right. As soon as one can disobey with impunity, one can do so legitimately; and since the strongest is always right, the only thing to do is to make oneself the strongest. For what kind of right is it that perishes when the force on which it is based ceases? If one must obey because of force, one need not do so out of duty; and if one is no longer forced to obey one is no longer obliged. Clearly then, this word "right" adds nothing to force. It is utterly meaningless here. . . .

CHAPTER VI: ON THE SOCIAL COMPACT

I suppose that men have reached the point where obstacles that are harmful to their maintenance in the state of nature gain the upper hand by their resistance to the forces that each individual can bring to bear to maintain himself in that state. Such being the case, that original state cannot subsist any longer, and the human race would perish if it did not alter its mode of existence.

For since men cannot engender new forces, but merely unite and direct existing ones, they have no other means of maintaining themselves but to form by aggregation a sum of forces that could gain the upper hand over the resistance, so that their forces are directed by a means of a single moving power and made to act in concert.

This sum of forces cannot come into being without the cooperation of many. But since each man's force and liberty are the primary instruments of his maintenance, how is he going to engage them without hurting himself and without neglecting the care that he owes himself? This difficulty, seen in terms of my subject, can be stated in the following terms:

"Find a form of association which defends and protects with all common forces the person and goods of each associate, and by means of which each one, while uniting with all, nevertheless obeys only himself and remains as free as before?" This is the fundamental problem for which the social contract provides the solution.

The clauses of this contract are so determined by the nature of the act that the least modification renders them vain and ineffectual, that, although perhaps they have never been formally promulgated, they are everywhere the same, everywhere tacitly accepted and acknowledged. Once the social compact is violated, each person then regains his first rights and resumes his natural liberty, while losing the conventional liberty for which he renounced it.

These clauses, properly understood, are all reducible to a single one, namely the total alienation of each associate, together with all of his rights, to the entire community. For first of all, since each person gives himself whole and entire, the condition is equal for everyone; and since the condition is equal for everyone, no one has an interest in making it burdensome for the others.

Moreover, since the alienation is made without reservation, the union is as perfect as possible, and no associate has anything further to demand. For if some rights remained with private individuals, in the absence of any common superior who could decide

between then and the public, each person would eventually claim to be his own judge in all things, since he is on some point his own judge. The state of nature would subsist and the association would necessarily become tyrannical or hollow.

Finally, in giving himself to all, each person gives himself to no one. And since there is no associate over whom he does not acquire the same right that he would grant others over himself, he gains the equivalent of everything he loses, along with a greater amount of force to preserve what he has.

If, therefore, one eliminates from the social compact whatever is not essential to it, one will find that it is reducible to the following terms. *Each of us places his person and all his power in common under the supreme direction of the general will; and as one we receive each member as an indivisible part of the whole.*

At once, in place of the individual person of each contracting party, this act of association produces a moral and collective body composed of as many members as there are voices in the assembly, which receives from this same act its unity, its common *self,* its life and its will. This public person, formed thus by union of all the others formerly took the name *city,* and at present takes the name *republic* or *body politic,* which is called *state* by its members when it is passive, *sovereign* when it is active, *power* when compared to others like itself. As to the associates, they collectively take the name *people;* individually they are called *citizens,* insofar as participants in the sovereign authority, and *subjects,* insofar as they are subjected to the laws of the state. But these terms are often confused and mistaken for one another. It is enough to know how to distinguish them when they are used with absolute precision.

Study Questions

1. What does Rousseau mean by saying that man is born free, but in chains? And how does he criticize Hobbes?

2. How does Rousseau argue against the right of the strongest?

3. What is supposed to happen when the social compact (contract) is established? Explain the concept of the general will.

Primary Reading

Manifesto of the Communist Party

KARL MARX AND FRIEDRICH ENGELS

Extract, 1848.

. . . All previous historical movements were movements of minorities, or in the interest of minorities. The proletarian movement is the self-conscious, independent movement of the immense majority, in the interest of the immense majority. The proletariat, the lowest stratum of our present society, cannot stir, cannot raise itself up, without the whole superincumbent strata of official society being sprung into the air. Though not in substance, yet in form, the struggle of the proletariat with the bourgeoisie is at first a national struggle. The proletariat of each country must, of course, first of all settle matters with its own bourgeoisie.

In depicting the most general phases of the development of the proletariat, we traced the more or less veiled civil war, raging within existing society, up to the point where that war breaks out into open revolution, and where the violent overthrow of the bourgeoisie lays the foundation for the sway of the proletariat.

Hitherto, every form of society has been based, as we have already seen, on the antagonism of oppressing and oppressed classes. But in order to oppress a class, certain conditions must be assured to it under which it can, at least, continue its slavish existence. The serf, in the period of serfdom, raised himself to membership in the commune, just as the petty bourgeois, under the yoke of the feudal absolutism, managed to develop into a bourgeois. The modern laborer, on the contrary, instead of rising with the process of industry, sinks deeper below the conditions of existence of his own class. He becomes a pauper, and pauperism develops more rapidly than population and wealth. And here it becomes evident that the bourgeoisie is unfit any longer to be the ruling class in society, and to impose its condtions of existence upon society as an overriding law. It is unfit to rule because it is incompetent to assure an existence to its slave within his slavery, because it cannot help

letting him sink into such a state, that it has to feed him, instead of being fed by him. Society can no longer live under this bourgeoisie, in other words, its existence is no longer compatible with society.

The essential conditions for the existence and for the sway of the bourgeois class is the formation and augmentation of capital; the condition for capital is wage labor. Wage labor rests exclusively on competition between the laborers. The advance of industry, whose involuntary promoter is the bourgeoisie, replaces the isolation of the laborers, due to competition, by the revolutionary combination, due to association. The development of Modern Industry, therefore, cuts from under its feet the very foundation on which the bourgeoisie produces and appropriates products. What the bourgeoisie therefore produces, above all, are its own grave-diggers. Its fall and the victory of the proletariat are equally inevitable. . . .

Let us now take wage labor.

The average price of wage labor is the minimum wage, i.e., that quantum of the means of subsistence which is absolutely requisite to keep the laborer in bare existence as a laborer. What, therefore, the wage laborer appropriates by means of his labor merely suffices to prolong and reproduce a bare existence. We by no means intend to abolish this personal appropriation of the products of labor, an appropriation that is made for the maintenance and reproduction of human life, and that leaves no surplus wherewith to command the labor of others. All that we want to do away with is the miserable character of this appropriation, under which the laborer lives merely to increase capital, and is allowed to live only in so far as the interest of the ruling class requires it. In bourgeois society, living labor is but a means to increase accumulated labor. In communist society, accumulated labor is but a means to widen, to enrich, to promote the existence of the laborer.

In bourgeois society, therefore, the past dominates the present; in communist society, the present dominates the past. In bourgeois society, capital is independent and has individuality, while the living person is dependent and has no individuality. And the abolition of this state of things is called by the bourgeois, abolition of individuality and freedom! And rightly so. The abolition of bourgeois individuality, bourgeois independence, and bourgeois freedom is undoubtedly aimed at.

By freedom is meant, under the present bourgeois conditions of production, free trade, free selling and buying.

But if selling and buying disappears, free selling and buying disappears also. This talk about free selling and buying, and all the other "brave words" of our bourgeois about freedom in general, have a meaning, if any, only in contrast with restricted selling and buying, with the fettered traders of the Middle Ages, but have no meaning when opposed to the communist abolition of buying and selling, or the bourgeois conditions of production, and of the bourgeoisie itself.

You are horrified at our intending to do away with private property. But in your existing society, private property is already done away with for nine-tenths of the population; its existence for the few is solely due to its non-existence in the hands of those nine-tenths. You reproach us, therefore, with intending to do away with a form of property, the necessary condition for whose existence is the non-existence of any property for the immense majority of society.

In one word, you reproach us with intending to do away with your property. Precisely so; that is just what we intend.

From the moment when labor can no longer be converted into capital, money, or rent, into a social power capable of being monopolized, i.e., from the moment when individual property can no longer be transformed into bourgeois property, into capital, from that moment, you say, individuality vanishes.

You must, therefore, confess that by "individual" you mean no other person than the bourgeois, than the middle-class owner of property. This person must, indeed, be swept out of the way, and made impossible.

Communism deprives no man of the power to appropriate the products of society; all that it does is to deprive him of the power to subjugate the labor of others by means of such appropriations.

It has been objected that upon the abolition of private property, all work will cease, and universal laziness will overtake us.

According to this, bourgeois society ought long ago to have gone to the dogs through sheer idleness; for those who acquire anything, do not work. The whole of this objection is but another expression of the tautology: There can no longer be any wage labor when there is no longer any capital.

All objections urged against the communistic mode of producing and appropriating material products, have, in the same way, been urged against the communistic mode of producing and appropriating intellectual products. Just as to the bourgeois, the disappearance of class property is the disappearance of production itself, so the disappearance of class culture is to him identical with the disappearance of all culture. That culture, the loss of which he laments, is, for the enormous majority, a mere training to act as a machine.

But don't wrangle with us so long as you apply, to our intended abolition of bourgeois property, the standard of your bourgeois notions of freedom, culture, law, etc. Your very ideas are but the outgrowth of the conditions of your bourgeois production and bourgeois property, just as your jurisprudence is but the will of your class made into a law for all, a will whose essential character and direction are determined by the economical conditions of existence of your class. . . .

Does it require deep intuition to comprehend that man's ideas, views, and conception, in one word, man's consciousness, changes with every change in the conditions of his material existence, in his social relations and in his social life?

What else does the history of ideas prove, than that intellectual production changes its character in proportion as material production is changed? The ruling ideas of each age have ever been the ideas of its ruling class.

When people speak of the ideas that revolutionize society, they do but express that fact that within the old society the elements of a new one have been created, and that the dissolution of the old ideas keeps even pace with the dissolution of the old conditions of existence.

When the ancient world was in its last throes, the ancient religions were overcome by Christianity. When Christian ideas succumbed in the eighteenth century to rationalist ideas, feudal society fought its death battle with the then revolutionary bourgeoisie. The ideas of religious liberty and freedom of conscience merely gave expression to the sway of free competition within the domain of knowledge.

"Undoubtedly," it will be said, "religious, moral, philosophical, and juridicial ideas have been modified in the course of historical development. But religion, morality, philosophy, political science, and law, constantly survived this change.

"There are, besides, eternal truths, such as Freedom, Justice, etc., that are common to all states of society. But communism abolishes eternal truths, it abolishes all religion, and all morality, instead of constituting them on a new basis; it therefore acts in contradiction to all past historical experience."

What does this accusation reduce itself to? The history of all past society has consisted in the development of class antagonisms, antagonisms that assumed different forms at different epochs.

But whatever form they may have taken, one fact is common to all past ages, viz., the exploitation of

one part of society by the other. No wonder, then, that the social consciousness of past ages, despite all the multiplicity and variety it displays, moves within certain common forms, or general ideas, which cannot completely vanish except with the total disappearance of class antagonisms.

Study Questions

1. What is the significance, to Marx and Engels, that the proletarian (working-class) movement is the first majority movement?

2. Why is the fall of capitalism inevitable, according to the authors?

3. Why do Marx and Engels want to do away with private property? Explain in detail. Do you agree with their assessment? Why or why not?

4. Do you agree that "man's consciousness changes with every change in the conditions of his material existence"? Explain.

Life in the State of Nature

 *Narrative*

Dances with Wolves

KEVIN COSTNER (DIRECTOR) AND
MICHAEL BLAKE (SCREENWRITER)

Film, 1990, from the novel by Michael Blake. Summary.

Benjamin Franklin once remarked that white people who had been rescued from long-term captivity with American Indians most often grabbed the first chance to escape back to the woods and their former captors, no matter how well they were being treated by white society. Hollywood has explored this idea in films such as *Duel at Diablo, Two Rode Together,* and *A Man Called Horse.* In the film credited with reviving the Western genre in the 1990s, *Dances with Wolves,* we get not only a story about a white captive who doesn't want to go back to white society, but also a full-scale Rousseau-style vision of human nature: Civilization (the white soldiers) represents all that is corrupt, crude, and evil, and the American Indian represents all the best in human nature—a connection with nature, and a sense of community, humor, and compassion.

The film is long, and part of it is in the Lakota language (subtitles are provided). Critics didn't have much hope for the success of this film, but in spite of everything, *Dances with Wolves* became a tremendous success and was the recipient of several *Academy Awards.*

John Dunbar, hero of the Civil War, is posted to a remote cavalry fort on the plains—a post most soldiers would have considered sheer punishment, but this post is a dream come true for Dunbar and, by his own request, a reward for his wartime heroism. On arrival he

Dances with Wolves, Majestic Film, 1990. John Dunbar (Kevin Costner) is here about to embark on his first buffalo hunt with his newfound friends, a band of Lakota Indians. One of the chiefs, Kicking Bird (Graham Green, right) strives to understand Dunbar's world and language, and in turn teaches Dunbar about the ways of the Plains Indians. With imagery reminiscent of Rousseau's vision of nature being good in itself, and people living in close proximity to nature sharing in that original goodness, Dunbar and his Indian friends almost blend into the scenery.

realizes that he is the only soldier present: everyone else is gone, and the fort appears abandoned. He begins to repair the fort and observe his surroundings. His closest neighbor is a wild, scruffy-looking wolf—a shy creature who after a while becomes sufficiently used to him to accept food from him. Nature is beginning to communicate with Dunbar, and he responds. His closest human neighbors, a local Lakota Sioux tribe, appear far more dangerous, at first: Young men try to steal his horse, and warriors turn up at the fort, looking menacing. Dunbar is fully aware of the stories of Indian atrocities, but is genuinely interested in understanding the Indians on their own hunting grounds, so to speak. He dresses up in his army finest and sets off to pay a visit to the tribe—but on the way he encounters one of its members in distress: A woman from the tribe has gone off into the wild to take her own life, a

traditional response to losing her husband in battle. He interferes, ties up her self-inflicted wounds, and takes her to the Lakota village—a different kind of introduction to the community than he had intended. Her life is saved—and he realizes that she is a white woman, a captive who has accepted Indian cultural standards as her own.

Now contact is established between Dunbar and the Lakota tribe: Warriors come to visit him at the fort and are introduced to sugar and coffee; they swap the first words in English and Lakota that will make communication possible. Good will is apparent on both sides, although not equally among all the Indians. But American Indians have a tradition of each individual having a right to his or her own opinion without having to comply with the view of the elders; each voice is heard in council, and consensus is needed for major decisions. Dunbar discovers much about the customs and values of the Indians, takes part in the ritual buffalo hunt, and celebrates afterward with the tribe. The white woman, Stands with a Fist, becomes his friend and language teacher, and once her mourning period for her dead husband is over, she and Dunbar get married; Dunbar now leaves the fort to settle in with the Indians, assuming that the fort has been permanently abandoned. When Dunbar finds himself defending the Indian village against its arch enemy, the Pawnee Indians, whose cruelty and bloodthirstiness is appalling (and who killed Stands with a Fist's family years ago), he realizes that this is the first meaningful battle he has ever participated in: He is fighting for his home and his loved ones and not for other people's principles, as he did in the Civil War. In the meantime, Dunbar has acquired the Indian name *Dances with Wolves:* On one of his visits to the fort he plays a game of tag with his neighbor, the wolf, and is observed by his astonished Indian friends—so here the white soldier is "outnaturing" the people of nature, the Indians.

As the tribe prepares to leave for its winter grounds, in effect moving farther away from the encroaching white civilization—because Dunbar has convinced the elders that the whites will not stop coming—Dunbar feels he must go back to the fort to retrieve his journal, which, if found, would give away the location of the Indians. This proves to be a disastrous decision. As Dunbar approaches the fort, he sees that the cavalry is back; because he is dressed in Indian gear, they mistake him for a hostile, shoot his horse out from under

him, and capture him. When they discover his identity, they accuse him of treason and prepare to take him to the headquarters at Fort Hays to be tried and possibly hanged; making matters worse is the fact that no soldiers are still alive who remember his being posted to the fort. The trader who took him to the fort was killed by the Pawnee, and the officer who sent him off to his post destroyed the orders and killed himself.

But Dunbar never reaches Fort Hays. As the troop prepares to ford a river on the way to the fort, we see that Dunbar's Indian friends have followed him and are preparing to rescue him.

Is Dunbar rescued? What happens to him and his Indian friends? I suggest you rent the movie and see for yourself.

Study Questions

1. While Lakota Indians (and many others) applauded the sensitivity of *Dances with Wolves,* Pawnee descendants found it racist and stereotyping. Are they right? Did Blake and Costner succumb to old stereotypes, or did they tell an authentic story?

2. Dunbar and Stands with a Fist are, by and large, the only sympathetic white people in the film. What is the rationale behind this portrayal? Is this a reasonable portrayal? Why or why not?

3. Is Dunbar a traitor? Explain.

4. Identify the features in this film that make it a statement in the tradition of Rousseau.

Communism and Human Nature

 *Narrative*

Atlas Shrugged

AYN RAND

Novel, 1957. Summary.

Embedded in her mammoth novel *Atlas Shrugged* is Ayn Rand's anti-Marxist narrative about the factory. A bit of background: *Atlas Shrugged* is the story of an American revolution of the future—not by armies or by workers, but by employers and producers of goods. Like the Greek god Atlas, who has the earth perched on his shoulders, if the financial "movers and shakers" of Planet Earth decide to shrug, then the earth shakes.

Rand's vision is a future movement among these peo-ple (led by the character of John Galt) supporting the economy of the earth, a growing realization that they are being taken advantage of by liberals and socialists claiming a right for people to be supported by the state without giving anything in return. To Rand, the employ-ers, factory owners, inventors, and financiers ought to wise up and start laying down the rules: Nobody has a right to anything except not to be interfered with by the government in terms of one's life, liberty, and prop-erty. Aside from that, nobody has a right to expect any support from the state. This philosophy of *negative rights* (see the discussion of John Locke) is comparable to the philosophy of the Libertarian Party and criticizes the concept of extreme *positive rights* embedded in Marxism: rights to receive according to needs. In the story of the factory, Rand satirizes the triumph of petty human nature over the grand Marxist ideals.

The factory used to be a regular automobile com-pany that made a profit, but new owners decided, and announced to the workers, that changes would be made, for the good of everybody. Everyone would now be required to work according to ability and would re-ceive payment according to their individual needs. The workers were never really told in detail how this was going to work out, but each thought that the other knew. Everyone was impressed by the good will and com-munity spirit of the new owners, because it sounded like such a noble idea. However, within four short years the factory community had descended into its own private hell. One of the survivors tells the story to the main character of the novel, Dagny Taggart.

If you are supposed to work according to ability, then you will do so in the beginning, because you find the idea attractive and selfless, and you are able to put in a lot of work. But later you begin to think about ex-actly who you are working for—because you don't get anything out of it yourself: You're working for your neighbor's dinner, his wife's operation, his mother's wheelchair, the medical bills for his child's measles, be-cause those are their needs. Of course you get your needs taken care of, too, but if your needs are simple, then you just get the basics: food, shelter, clothing. And if you're an honest man or woman, then you don't cre-ate or invent additional needs that must be paid for by

the others, but not everyone is like you: Soon cousins begin to arrive from the country who must be taken care of, a child needs braces, and some of the families just keep having babies so they have to receive more and more of what you make with your ability. So you can't apply for a car until everyone else has one, too. You have to prove you need a new pair of shoes, because you have no right to your own earnings, and so you end up claiming that you need things you don't really need just to get a little extra, because so many are mooching off of you. So what happens? Instead of turning into noble creatures of a new era, everybody turns into beg-gars and moochers.

There was one young man who was really bright, and he worked out an improvement for the work sys-tem so they would all save money. He was put on extra duty and worked to the bone, because his ability was so great. Next year he had wised up and made sure he didn't come up with any new ideas. The capitalist sys-tem was supposed to show the evil side of human na-ture, but the opposite happened: Receiving according to need and working according to ability made every-one slow down, trying not to work according to their ability, because then they would just be worked all the harder. Faking unfitness destroyed everybody's spirit in a system that was supposed to do just the opposite.

Soon people began to hate those who had extra needs, even if those people couldn't help it. If people had more children, they were frozen out. People would pick quarrels with others just to get them thrown out of the community, and they would spy on each other to see if they could catch others committing antisocial offenses. An old lady broke her hip on the cellar stairs, and everyone knew how expensive her surgery would be for the community. She was found dead the day she was supposed to leave for the hospital, and the cause of death was never established. So what was supposed to bring out the best in everybody actually brought out the worst: The escaped factory worker concludes that if people are made to live by the Marxist rule, they turn into liars, moochers, and resentful beggars.

Study Questions

1. To your knowledge, is this a fair assessment of a communist society? Why or why not?

2. How would Marx respond to the factory story? Remember that he thinks human nature will change with a change in the economic base.

3. Would you say this is a realistic assessment of human nature? Why or why not? If no, explain why

not. If yes, what kind of political system and social policies must be in place in order to make a community work? Draw on what you have read about Plato, Aristotle, Hobbes, Locke, Rousseau, and Marx.

Narrative

The Grapes of Wrath

JOHN FORD (DIRECTOR) AND
NUNALLY JOHNSON (SCREENWRITER)

Film, 1940. From the novel by John Steinbeck, 1939. Summary.

When a famous book is made into a film, scholars of literature usually choose to refer to the story line of the original novel rather than to the film, unless the film becomes more famous than the book. In the case of *The Grapes of Wrath* it is probably a toss-up as to which version has become more famous, and in terms of artistic quality most people who enjoy movies as well as books would say that they are different, but equally great masterpieces. I have chosen to refer to the film rather than the book because it is a fascinating example of a director creating one of the most eloquent works about socialism without being himself a socialist or (probably) even suspecting that he was about to leave a socialistic legacy to movie audiences. Ford, who was a master at depicting human relationships and human emotions on screen, but who never bothered to intellectualize about what he was doing, succeeded in telling a story of human hardship that has universal appeal on a purely compassionate level; in addition, he presents a story of the sufferings of people exploited by Big Money—a vision that a socialist could probably agree with.

It is the Great Depression of the 1930s. The Joads have been living on their land as sharecroppers in the Oklahoma "dust bowl" for more than fifty years. But now the bank is kicking them off the land and everybody else, too. Tom Joad comes home from prison (he has been paroled) just in time to help his family load up the Ford and head for California. They have heard

there is work to be had there picking fruit. And so they join the migration of other "Okies" who are fleeing the dust bowl: Tom's ma and pa, his grandma and grandpa, his pregnant sister and her husband, his grown brother, his uncle, and his little brother and sister. Keeping them all company is the ex-preacher Casey; he used to preach up a storm, but he has lost the call and doesn't know what to tell people any more, so he figures he may as well come along.

As they approach California they have the distinct feeling that they aren't welcome anywhere. People mistake them for beggars, and the Joads' family pride is deeply wounded. At one checkpoint a guard remarks to the other, "Okies ain't human, no human could stand living the way they do." At a truck stop Pa Joad asks if he can buy a loaf of bread for ten cents for Grandma, for she can't chew, and they can't afford a sandwich. The waitress has no understanding of their plight, but the truck stop owner tells her to give them the bread for ten cents. When Pa Joad asks about the price of candy sticks for the two kids, she looks at the children and suddenly understands what it is all about—she gives him two for a penny. After he leaves, two truck drivers remind her that the candy sticks are five cents apiece. When she wants to give the truckers their change, they generously refuse to accept it.

En route to California both Grandma and Grandpa die and are buried by the roadside. The rest of the family arrive in California only to learn that the fruit they

The Grapes of Wrath, 20th Century Fox, 1940. Tom Joad (Henry Fonda) learns a lesson about civil injustice and the strength of working people fighting together in a common cause. The Joads have joined the swelling ranks of migrant workers fleeing the Oklahoma dust bowl of the 1930s to the fields of California, but work is scarce and the migrant workers are treated mostly like third-class citizens. In the process of recapturing the dignity and self-reliance of the family, Tom reaches the conclusion that "People are living like pigs . . . while rich men let good land lie fallow."

expected to pick already has been picked, and the cotton isn't ready yet. Besides, thousands of fliers were printed, telling how workers were needed, but in fact only a few hundred jobs are available. The employers wanted to create competition for the jobs so that wages could be kept low. All of the employers seem crooked; they pay less than what they initially promised. The contractors are dishonest, and anyone who complains is called a Red and an agitator. Tom doesn't know what a Red is, or an agitator, but he soon finds out. A guard fires at a man who complains about lowered wages; the shot hits a woman instead. Tom and Casey attack the

guard. Casey decides to "take the rap" so that Tom can get away; Tom can't risk violating his parole.

The Joads find work on a farm surprisingly soon. Outside the fence around the property are a lot of what look like other Okies; police officers seem to be keeping them at bay. But the Joads' pay is good, and they settle into a shack and go to work immediately, picking peaches. When Tom tries to find out about the trouble, he is stopped by a guard. Later he manages to sneak out of the compound and finds, to his surprise, Casey, who is now one of the workers being kept off the farm. Tom learns the whole story: The workers are on strike because the owners won't pay them what they promised, but only half the amount. Tom and his family are getting the higher amount, but, says Casey, this is a trick. Once the strikers leave, the Joads' wages will be reduced. One of Casey's friends tries to tell Tom that they can win if they would just unite, but Tom sees the situation only from his own perspective: For once, his family has meat for dinner, and why should he give that up for some strangers? Casey, however, has found a new call: he tries to tell Tom that something new is happening—he doesn't quite know what it is yet, but he is learning. Their conversation is cut short when they hear sounds of men approaching. Soon there is a raid on the strikers' camp. Casey is killed, and Tom strikes out at Casey's killer, dealing him a lethal blow.

Now Tom is in big trouble, because he got hit in the face, and he can be identified. In the night he and his family sneak out, with Tom hiding in the car. They finally arrive at a place where they are treated like human beings—a government camp for migrant workers.[20] There are no camp police, and the camp elects its own officers. There is a ladies' committee setting up child care. For a while things are good, but soon the police show up looking for Tom. He has to leave his family, perhaps for the last time. He and his mother have their last talk at night, before he leaves, and Tom tries to tell her how he feels now. People are living like pigs, he says, while rich men let good land lie fallow, and farmers are starving. But if we all got together . . . Tom still doesn't quite know what to do, but since he is a fugitive anyway, he will try to find out.

Ma Joad, the matriarch of the family and its emotional center, is worried about the family splitting up.

She asks Tom how she ever will know what has happened to him. And Tom says that maybe Casey was right: "A fellow ain't got a soul of his own, just a little piece of a big soul, the soul that belongs to everybody." He tells Ma that she can think of him as being everywhere—"Wherever there's a fight so hungry people can eat, I'll be there; whenever a cop is beatin' up a guy, I'll be there . . . when people are eatin' the stuff they raised and living in the houses they built I'll be there, too."

Tom leaves, but the story isn't over; in fact, it goes on and on. Ma and Pa and the remaining children (the sister's husband has run off in the meantime) head for the cotton fields. Pa Joad feels lost and abandoned, but Ma Joad is in much better spirits: "Rich fellers come up, and they die, and their kids are no good and they

die out, but we keep a-comin'. We're the people that live—they can't wipe us out, they can't lick us, we'll go on forever, Pa, 'cause we're the People."

Study Questions

1. What is the meaning of the episode at the truck stop?

2. What might it mean that the only decent place they find is a government-run place?

3. Why might this be interpreted as a socialistic story? Is that a reasonable assessment?

4. Given that the director John Ford considered himself a political conservative, what do you think he would say to an assessment that the film is a socialistic story?

Review

Key Issues in Chapter 9

- Plato, Aristotle, Hobbes, Rousseau, and Marx all argue that people don't know what is in their best interest, and must be guided. Locke argues that the individual knows what is in one's best interest.

Plato's Ideal State

- Plato's theory of the tripartite soul has an analogy in his theory of the ideal state: The ideal state is made up of philosopher-kings, auxiliaries, and the working population. The "noble lie": The story of the people of gold, silver, and brass and iron is told to prepare people for their roles in society. In Plato's ideal state, eugenics play a role in pairing off guardians to produce children with the best qualities. Plato's ideas have been equated with totalitarianism: The philosopher decides the best interests of the citizens and community; the community is more important than its parts.

Aristotle: The Political Animal

- Humans living in cities are political creatures. Society is a natural phenomenon. Aristotle's views on slavery held that some are slaves by law and some by nature; others are free by nature. Aristotle envi-

sions a social structure that is best for all involved, based on their individual talents and telos.

The Social Contract Thinkers

- *Thomas Hobbes.* Hobbes lived during a time of war and political upheaval, and his theories reflect that situation.
  - *Hobbes's State of Nature and the Social Contract.* Hobbes sees the state of nature as a presocial condition, where human life is solitary, poor, nasty, brutish, and short. Everyone is equal, because everyone can kill everyone else. The law of nature forbids a person from doing what is destructive to his or her life. We have a natural right, however, to defend our life and do whatever we can get away with. The social contract is a compact in the interest of self-preservation and peace in which we give away our right to self-determination to the sovereign—but not our right to self-defense. Hobbes's ideas are prefigured by Glaucon, in Plato's *Republic.*
  - *Hobbes's State of Nature as Political Theory.* Hobbes's speculations about a state of nature are not historical, but political: an argument in favor of absolute monarchy. Hominids have indeed lived in groups, not in isolation, for at least four million years.
- *John Locke.* Like Hobbes, Locke feared that his opinions could endanger his life; his writings had

great influence on Jefferson and the Declaration of Independence.

- *Locke's Natural Law and the State of Nature.* Locke builds on Aquinas's tradition of natural law, viewing humans as rational creatures, but focuses on the political implications, not the moral ones. Locke's view of the state of nature involves human freedom and equality, not a struggle. He finds evidence for human equality in the Bible. Even in the state of nature, humans are rational, governed by a natural law of reason. The state of nature has a moral authority only, not a legal one; that is why we need the social contract. Communities can exist prior to the social contract; it takes a conscious commitment to the laws of the community to make it into a contract. If you haven't agreed to the contract yourself but benefit from it, you show tacit consent. If you disagree, you can leave.

- *Natural Rights and Negative Rights.* Locke says our natural right is to stay free and equal, the way we were born, recognizing others' right to the same. The three negative rights are life, liberty, and property.

- *Jean-Jacques Rousseau.* Rousseau lived an unsettled life, moving frequently; he didn't begin writing until relatively late in life. He also feared that his opinions endangered his life.

  - *Humans in the State of Nature.* What is natural is good. Rousseau's description of life in early human communities is generally in agreement with modern anthropological views.

  - *The Social Contract and Beyond.* Rousseau's social contract theory: Males get together and create the sovereign out of their assembly; they don't give away their sovereignty. Freedom means freedom for the community rather than for the individual. If the general will prevails, power can't corrupt. In you disagree with the general will, you are by definition in the wrong.

Karl Marx: Human Nature Will Change

- *Marx as a Materialist.* Marx studied the ideas of G. W. F. Hegel, who developed the theory of the dialectical movement of the spirit. Marx's theory of dialectical materialism holds that all cultural developments are grounded in the economic structure of the society. The world will have reached its optimal state when the dialectical movement reaches the point where communism is the economic system.

- *Why Communism?* Marx theorizes that the realization of labor and the exploitation of the worker result in alienation.

- *Human Nature and Capitalism.* Before capitalism, humans enjoyed self-activity; the joy was lost under capitalism, but will be reinstated with the communist revolution. "To each according to need, and from each according to ability" is the principle of the communist society.

- *Marx's Critics.* Criticisms include charges that Marx is a millennialist, that communism has failed, that dialectical change happens automatically and doesn't need a revolution, that Marx's criticisms come themselves out of a capitalist viewpoint, and that the communist stage will not be the final one. Questions are raised: Who will do the dirty work? Why work harder if you don't get more? Aren't we selfish by nature? Why would all aspects of human nature change? Times have changed, and we don't need a revolution.

Hayden White: Cultural History Is Storytelling

- Early history writing didn't try to tell a story, but modern historiography does. It focuses on cause and effect, based on selected evidence. We seek understanding of the past and our own culture by telling our history as story. All history writing makes a moral statement of approval or disapproval.

Primary Readings

- Aristotle, *Politics.* The state is described as a natural phenomenon.

- Hobbes, *Leviathan.* Life in the state of nature is described as solitary, poor, nasty, brutish, and short.

- Rousseau, *The Social Contract.* The general will characterizes the establishing of the social compact.

- Marx and Engels, *Manifesto of the Communist Party.* The capitalist society will fall to the proletarian movement.

Narratives

- *Dances with Wolves,* film. A U.S. cavalry soldier in the nineteenth century learns to appreciate the ways of the American Indian.

- Ayn Rand: *Atlas Shrugged,* novel. The story of the factory that was run according to communist principles.
- *The Grapes of Wrath,* film and novel. A family of migrant workers from Oklahoma in the 1930s travels to California to find work.

Notes

1. Aristotle, *Politics,* trans. Benjamin Jowett (Chicago: Encyclopedia Britannica, 1952), Book I, 1.
2. Ibid., Book VII, chapter 8; Book VIII, chapter 1.
3. Ibid., Book I, chapter 5.
4. Thomas Hobbes, *Leviathan* (New York: Prometheus Books, 1988), chapter X.
5. Ibid., chapter XI.
6. Ibid., chapter XIII.
7. Ibid., chapter XIV.
8. Plato, *The Republic,* trans. F. M. Cornford (London: Oxford University Press, 1970), Book II, 358–359.
9. John Locke, *Second Treatise on Government,* Chapter II, sec. 4. Retrieved from the World Wide Web: www.swan.ac.uk/poli/texts/locke/locke01.html
10. Ibid. chapter II, sec. 6.
11. Ibid. chapter II, sec. 14, 15.
12. Ibid. chapter II, sec. 8, 11.
13. "Paradigm shift" is an expression borrowed from Thomas Kuhn, a philosopher of science: A paradigm shift occurs when a model of explanation is no longer sufficient to explain a natural or cultural phenomenon. A new model may then be suggested, usually leaving the innovative thinker open to ridicule. Slowly, the new model may gain acceptance, sometimes supplementing the old explanation (as in the case of nuclear physics supplementing Newtonian physics) and sometimes supplanting the old explanation (such as Copernicus's heliocentric model supplanting the ancient geocentric model).
14. Jean-Jacques Rousseau, "Discourse on Inequality," trans. Donald A. Cress (Indianapolis: Hackett, 1983), p. 140.
15. Jean-Jacques Rousseau, *The Social Contract,* trans. Donald A. Cress (Indianapolis: Hackett, 1983), Book I, chapter III.
16. Ibid., Book I, chapter VI.
17. Ibid., Book II, chapter III.
18. Karl Marx, *The German Ideology,* Part I, D, The Necessity, Preconditions, and Consequences of the Abolition of Private Property. Retrieved from the World Wide Web: http://www.Marxists.org/archive/marx/works/1845.gi/part_d.html
19. Karl Marx and Friedrich Engels, *The Manifesto of the Communist Party.* Retrieved from the World Wide Web: http://csf.Colorado.edu/psn/Marx/Archive/1848-CM/cm.html
20. "Migrant worker" used to mean a seasonal worker who travels as the work season changes. Today it often refers to immigrant workers who are sometimes undocumented. In this context you have the original meaning.

Chapter Ten

Personhood: The Community of Equals

Theories of Human Nature as Political Statements

Throughout this book you have seen examples of the ways in which theories of human nature may be used in a political context. You have seen how theories of human evolution, and of race and gender—even though they appear to be descriptive—can be used normatively, to differentiate between humans—to create systems of hierarchies. In addition, you have seen theories of human rights built on more fundamental theories of human goodness or on human selfishness. In this final chapter we look at the concept of personhood as the ticket to political equality, perhaps the ultimate normative issue in the discussion of human nature, and we ask two questions: (1) Are we now at a stage where personhood has become inclusive for all humans, so we are no longer left with a residue of humanity classified as somehow "less than human?" and (2) Given that a normative definition of personhood depends on certain values brought to the table by the philosopher or politician, are we staying true to our definition of personhood and including everyone who meets our criteria, regardless of *species?* In other words, are there beings who should be granted personhood, although they are not genetically human?

We touched on this topic in Chapter 1; recall the *Star Trek* story about the trial for Data's life as a person. Now we bring the debate full circle and ask, What are our criteria for personhood, and are we applying them fairly? If we are to have a community of equals on Planet Earth, who should be members of that community, and how are they to be chosen?

Who Counts, and Who Doesn't?

You have been introduced to a variety of viewpoints about human nature, from strictly deterministic views to the existential view that there is no human nature. Interspersed with these views you have found speculations about race, gender, minds and bodies, the soul, and the political aspect of human life. Throughout the text the term *person* has appeared, usually synonymous with *human* (as a gender-neutral alternative to the term *man,* which is now deemed too gender-specific to be used as a generic term for the human race). But there is more to the choice of the word *person* than being "politically correct." The term *human being* is itself problematic, as you already know from Chapter 1, because it implies so many things, from biology and genetics to politics. Using the term *person* implies for most scholars today that we are not discussing the biological side of a human as much as the cultural expectations of that human's participation in the community. A "person," as opposed to a "human being," is a social entity rather than a biological one. The question of personhood is at once narrower and broader than questioning someone's status as a human being: narrower, because it leaves aside the biological issue; broader, because it takes an individual's relationship to the community into account. Is a fetus a human being from conception? Absolutely, because its DNA is human. But is the fetus a person? In other words, does a fetus participate in her or his community? No—but neither does a newborn. Is Data (from *Star Trek*) a human being? No, he isn't; he is an android, a machine. But is he a person? According to the fictional universe of

Star Trek, yes he is, because he interacts, presumably as an autonomous individual, with his community. In this chapter we take a look at these political and moral implications. At the end of the chapter you will find a companion story to the *Star Trek* episode, but one where the issue is humanity rather than personhood: *The Bicentennial Man.*

We are at a point in history where we assume that all living (postnatal; that is, already born) human beings are also persons, meaning that *they ought to have moral standing.* No person in any community, or outside it, should be treated like prey or like property—even criminals who have preyed on society don't lose all their rights. Everyone deserves fair and equal treatment in the courts, in the workplace, in school, and in any other public arena one might imagine. In addition, we would like to think that individuals are taught, as a part of their education, to treat each other fairly and without discrimination, on a global level. And I think at this point the dream begins to break down, because we know that reality hasn't yet conformed to our fantasy of global equality.

But before we involve ourselves in depressing thoughts of how far we are from actually treating each other as persons with dignity, we should remind ourselves of how far we have come in a few hundred years. You know from Chapters 5 and 6 that race and gender relations have made enormous strides toward nondiscrimination, although there is still work to be done. For all of Socrates', Plato's, and Aristotle's wisdom, and in spite of the fact that democracy as a concept was developed in ancient Greece, we should remember that what we consider political equality was not even a fantasy among the most radical of thinkers in antiquity. Ancient Greece was a collection of independent city-states, with free adult male citizens—but no one else—having a political voice. Greece was built on the enslavement of prisoners of war, and so was Rome. And so, indeed, were the Germanic cultures making the Roman borders to the north unsafe, and the later Viking culture farther north,

and African tribal cultures to the south. Within each culture there has been a hierarchy of who counts and who doesn't—and another hierarchy has existed between "us" and "them," between each culture: All over the world, tribal cultures have preferred to name themselves "The People," as opposed to those other guys across the river who surely must be less human. As we saw in Chapter 5, there seems to be a human tendency to set up pecking orders and hierarchies, so you may feel resentful at not being at the top, but as long as there is some group lower than you, then you have someone to pick on. So if this is a global phenomenon, isn't it part of human nature, and how can we ever hope to change it?

For one thing, we have been changing it, for several hundred years, with legislation as well as with education. And for another thing, here we should remember Sartre's existentialism: Believing that something is embedded in human nature is just a bad excuse for not doing anything about it. There are many tendencies, or potentials (as Jane Goodall calls them) embedded in our nature, but that is all they are; we may have a biological tendency toward males being slightly less monogamous than females, but it doesn't mean we can't decide to adhere to monogamy as a rule. We may have a tendency to love one of our children more than the others, but that doesn't mean we can't try to treat them with equal love and affection. We may have deeply embedded tendencies toward causing hurt to other people, but, as John Douglas would say, we can control ourselves if we have a "policeman at the elbow." No need to rehash the entire issue of determinism: We may have such tendencies, individually or as a species, but we also have a moral choice, as Aquinas, Kant, and every other moral philosopher will insist. What matters is that we, as a species, decide what our future community of equals will permit and what it will exclude.

So let us assume that we, a united humanity or at least part of humanity wishing all of humanity well, decide on a declaration of Human Rights;

that has of course been accomplished already by the United Nations, issuing its *Declaration of Human Rights,* stating that nobody should be enslaved by anyone else, everyone should be entitled to be a citizen of a country, everyone should have a right to marry freely and move about freely within the borders of his or her country, and so forth. The bottom line is that every human individual should be respected and considered valuable in himself or herself. But United Nations declarations have no judicial value, and they don't imply universal agreement, either. At best they can be used as a guideline for a World Court, as they were after the war in Bosnia with the war crimes tribunal. There are nations on the planet that are not members of the UN, and there are UN nations—as Amnesty International will tell us—who disregard their own guidelines. Slavery exists to this day in many places all over the globe; parents sell their young girls into prostitution; indentured servitude and sweatshops are common not only overseas, but also within immigrant groups right here in the United States, where individuals—from inside or outside the immigrant community—prey on people within the community. Feudalism is alive and well in parts of India and Pakistan, with land barons literally owning "their" villagers. We are accustomed to thinking that although the idea of universal equality may not be universally accepted, still the idea itself surely must be as old as time. However, you already know from Chapters 5, 6, and 9 that universal political freedom and equality is a concept dating back not much further than the eighteenth century.

Throwaway People?

But even with all this goodwill, how are we in the United States doing on an everyday basis? Are we being treated as persons by others, and are we treating everyone else with the dignity they deserve as persons? Hardly. From small incidents of selfishness and thoughtlessness—cutting people off in traffic, telling white lies to avoid an uncomfortable situation—to genuine instances of bigotry and discrimination, all the way to complete disregard for other humans as people, it all thrives within our modern world. Here are a few recent examples from our own backyards:

- From 1932 to 1972 a government-controlled experiment was conducted in Tuskeegee, Alabama, on 300 African American males. Today it is known as the Tuskeegee Syphilis Experiment. Male patients with syphilis were told they were being treated, but in reality given placebos so the effects of the disease among blacks could be studied (in spite of the fact that the effects of syphilis had been known in detail for centuries by the medical community). Unknown to most people until the 1980s, the Tuskeegee study now rates as one of the most infamous examples in the United States of human beings reduced to medical guinea pigs without concern for their humanity.

- In the 1960s and 1970s, Navajo (Dineh) workers were hired to mine uranium out of the Utah desert mountains. More than 400 of these miners have died so far, succumbing to various forms of cancer caused by an intense, prolonged exposure to radiation. They were not issued any form of protective gear or informed that their work might entail any health hazards. While some compensation has been issued to the families, there is still a sense among the Navajos that they were used by the government without any regard for their personal safety or indeed their dignity as human beings. This strikes some Navajos and others as particularly odd since Navajos were considered eminently useful by the government during World War II, when the Navajo language was used as the code to transmit military secrets—a code never deciphered by the enemy and a deciding factor in winning the war.

- Along the U.S.-Mexico border large numbers of illegal immigrants from Mexico and elsewhere die trying to cross over into *El Norte.* In the spring of 2001 fourteen Mexicans coming from south of the border were found dead and desiccated by the desert heat in the border region of southwest Arizona. The U.S. Bureau of Land Management estimates that about 1,000 people cross the wilderness each year to get into the United States. Regardless of how we might feel about illegal immigration (and being a legal immigrant I myself don't have much sympathy for people breaking the law to achieve an immigration advantage) we shouldn't be oblivious to the fact that these desperate people suffer and die trying to achieve their goal. In winter, they perish in the cold of the mountains; in spring, the swollen rivers carry them off; and in summer, the desert takes its toll; and it doesn't help matters that they are often taken advantage of by human smugglers, *coyotes,* and abandoned to die or downright murdered for their few possessions. But rarely is their plight mentioned prominently in the news, partly because it is considered a result of their own choice and partly because they are "just illegals." Nevertheless, they are persons; they may be breaking the law, but death is surely not an appropriate punishment. (In the Narratives section we take a look at the award-winning film *El Norte.*)

- Similarly, rape and murder victims in the big cities often get media and law enforcement attention to the extent that they are members of the middle class and the education or business community; serial killers preying on prostitutes and drug addicts on the downtown "strip" often have years to work their hunting grounds before the community realizes that people are dying, because transients, prostitutes and drug addicts are often not considered persons worth spending community resources on.

- Murder and violence on gang turf are sometimes not pursued as vigorously as these crimes are in affluent neighborhoods because residents of those latter neighborhoods don't feel threatened.

- The phenomenon of homelessness seems to have become a permanent aspect of life in big cities, and we have to be reminded periodically that homeless people could do with some help

from the community, beyond the Thanksgiving and Christmas food drives. (This doesn't mean there aren't social forces at play that explain many of these phenomena or that every person on the street is an innocent victim of circumstances, but it means that if we can avoid facing these issues in our everyday life, then many of us will turn our heads the other way, because it's easier and because the victims are "only" transients, migrant workers, gang members, or prostitutes.)

- Another side of the coin is taking a closer look at the court system: We like to think that everyone gets a fair shake, but statistics, as well as the cumulative personal experiences of individuals, tell a different story. Someone once said that if you are planning to commit a crime, make sure you have a hefty bank account—meaning that the courts are skewed in favor of the wealthy, not necessarily because judges can be bribed, but because money buys lawyers who will put up a fight for their client. Regardless of how you feel about the death penalty as a form of punishment, it is an undeniable fact that more people who can't afford top legal representation are on death row according to some statistics than are wealthy defendants—and since in our society many black defendants can't afford top lawyers, a disproportionate number of black convicts are on death row. It may be a matter of discrimination (and has certainly been in the past), but it is definitely also a testimony to the power of money.

Please feel free to add to this list according to your personal experience or your familiarity with recent news items: Stories of people being treated with less than human dignity are abundant, here and abroad. As we have seen in previous chapters, sometimes it may be a matter of discrimination, sometimes of economics; from Chapter 5 you'll remember *environmental racism,* an example of both phenomena rolled into one: Toxic dump sites placed close to minority communities are perhaps not a conscious act of discrimination, but most definitely reflect the lack of political and economic clout within the community (and the plight of the Navajo miners recounted here may be said to be an extreme form of this phenomenon).

What can be done? The late philosopher Philip Hallie suggested that we stop thinking in abstract terms about other humans and instead think in terms of "names and verbs," because then we begin to see others as individuals, not as faceless groups. If we belong to such a group ourselves, wouldn't we want to be considered an individual? Furthermore, we may belong to a group of people experiencing discrimination and lack of consideration from the rest of the community, but that is no excuse for reducing anyone else from any other group to a faceless group identity, even if it may be tempting—the old "us" versus "them" is apt to rear its head whenever it is convenient. One method tried by concerned members of the media and law enforcement is to repeatedly show the pictures of crime victims, with their names and individual history, so they become more personal to the community. In the city of Spokane prior to the April 2000 capture of Robert Yates, the suspected serial killer who had been preying on women since 1997 and perhaps even longer than that, a billboard was erected showing the faces of each murder victim and pleading, "Help Us Find Our Killer." Making these anonymous victims familiar to everyone passing by may have helped the community realize that these were not throwaway people, but individuals with lives of their own and relatives and friends who loved them.

So it is sadly apparent that we, as human beings, may have come far but not far enough in respecting one another as persons, regardless of the religious and moral ideals supposedly held high by our tradition. For that reason some human rights advocates believe we ought to put all our effort into ensuring that all humans are treated with respect, and our focus ought to remain on our fellow human beings until conditions have changed globally. For those who hold such a conviction this is simply not the time to concern ourselves about whether other inhabitants of Planet Earth should be evaluated for possible personhood, because

the struggle for human rights is hard enough as it is. However, for others the time has come to expand the range of personhood to beings who, in so many ways, are like us, genetically, emotionally, and intellectually: the great apes. Later in this chapter we look at the arguments for and against considering apes as persons.

What Does It Take to Qualify for Personhood?

If personhood is used as a criterion for political inclusion in the community of equals—the only community on earth where members are guaranteed a minimum of respect and consideration by the ruling species (or at least those who perceive of themselves as running the show)—then the stakes are high. Many see it as a clear *dichotomy,* an either-or situation: Either you are in and can't be used by others as a piece of property, or you are out and are fair game for anyone who wants your land, your pelt, your babies, your ability to work, or your flesh. That this may be a *false dichotomy,* a neat trick of *bifurcation* (the logical fallacy of making you think that there is no third alternative), is something we will get into later. Here we look at some suggestions about where we should draw the line between persons and nonpersons. Some of them you have encountered before but now are placed in a new context; others have not previously been introduced. Here we look at three famous criteria for personhood: rationality, self-awareness, and language.

Rationality as a Criterion for Personhood: Immanuel Kant

In the long tradition of philosophy, human beings (or at least *male* human beings!) have been repeatedly defined as rational beings. You have seen it in the sections on Plato, Aristotle, Descartes, and just about any other thinker attempting to define a human being up until the twentieth century; David Hume, Jean-Jacques Rousseau, and Karl Marx make for interesting exceptions. Until the late twentieth century, female philosophers

Bicentennial Man, Columbia TriStar/Touchstone Pictures, 1999. The robot Andrew (Robin Williams) has just arrived at the home of the Martins, who have purchased him, and gives a holographic display of the regulations he has been programmed with, such as not harming a human being. In the course of a life span of 200 years, Andrew will come to know many generations of the Martin family and will eventually petition to be considered a human being with human rights.

would usually focus on getting women included under the rationality tent, rather than look for alternative criteria. Descartes's dualistic vision, seeing humans as two-substance beings, having body and mind, has had an enormous influence on the philosophical tradition (see Chapter 7). However, as a political and moral influence, the German philosopher Immanuel Kant (1724–1804) far surpasses Descartes. You will remember Kant from Chapters 5, 6, and particularly 7, with his theory of the transcendental self, and from Chapter 8, with his theory of evil. However, his theory of personhood reaches much farther into the world of political decision making: In his famous little book, *Grounding for the Metaphysics of Morals* (1785)—also referred to as *Groundwork* or *Foundations,* depending on the translation—Kant launches his theory of the moral and practical criterion for personhood. At a time when part of Europe was slowly emerging from feudalism, but other parts were still deeply immersed in the economics of land barons "owning" entire villages, with the villagers performing mandatory work for the land baron as serfs, Kant declares that whoever is capable of rational thinking possesses moral dignity and should be treated accordingly. The determining factors ought not to be wealth, birth status, or geography, but strictly the human capacity for rationality.

As a product of the Western Enlightenment and a gigantic influence on the development of human rights, Kant is to be credited with being the author of a major expansion of the idea of "who counts":

> Now I say that man, and in general every rational being, exists as an end in himself and not merely as a means to be arbitrarily used by this or that

will. He must in all his actions, whether directed to himself or to other rational beings, always be regarded at the same time as an end. . . . The practical imperative will therefore be the following: Act in such a way that you treat humanity, whether in your own person or in the person of another, always at the same time as an end and never simply as a means.[1]

What exactly does it mean to treat others as *ends in themselves?* For Kant it means that you, as a rational being, are your own goal and purpose in life, and nobody has the right to use your life (or have you surrender or force you to surrender your will) for his or her own purpose, even if that purpose has beneficial consequences overall, because in that case you would be used as *simply a means to an end.* Treating someone—yourself included—as an end in oneself means acknowledging that a being with a rational nature is its own goal and should not be reduced to a stepping-stone—simply a means to an end—for others' purposes.

This principle is extremely far-reaching as a normative rule, because we transgress against the rule so often, and people transgress against us: Do you remember being treated like a stepping-stone by someone who just wanted some advantage out of you—a ride to the airport, an introduction to your boss, a date with your sister or brother? Do you remember doing such a thing to someone else? That is only a mild form of what Kant is talking about, but it counts. Further, any time we lie to others to gain an advantage or get out of a nasty situation, we treat them like tools, instruments, mere means to an end, without giving them the respect their rationality has earned them. Every time people—burglars, drug dealers, sexual predators, or con artists, for that matter—prey on others, they reduce their victims to a mere means to their own gain or gratification. Any time some cultural institution treats a part of the population as instruments to be used as the power structure sees fit—slaves, conscripted soldiers (under certain circumstances), women reduced to birth factories for the next generation of workers and soldiers—then these people are being treated simply as a means to an end, with mere *instrumental value.* This is the grand warning and vision of Kant's social philosophy: Humans must recognize each other as having *intrinsic value* (value in themselves)—in other words, as ends in themselves.

You may have noticed that Kant emphasizes "*simply* a means to an end." That is because we treat others as a means to an end all the time, without thereby doing something awful to them. When you take your car to the shop, you surely treat the mechanics as a means to an end, but they treat you that way, too: You are both tools for each other. The mechanics get paid, and you get your car fixed! No harm done, as long as we treat one another with respect and realize that we all have a life: Mechanics are not chained to the shop, and you are not put on this earth to give them your business. But let us face it—even in those daily give-and-take situations we could do with a little more respect and consideration all around; it is all too easy for busy, thoughtless, selfish people to treat other members of humanity as simply a means to an end, even if we didn't intend to.

So what is it that qualifies someone to be treated with respect? Our capacity for reason. In Kant's words from *Grounding,*

> Beings whose existence depends not on our will but on nature have, nevertheless, if they are not rational beings, only a relative value as means and are therefore called things. On the other hand, rational beings are called persons inasmuch as their nature already marks them out as ends in themselves, i.e., as something which is not to be used merely as a means and hence there is imposed thereby a limit on all arbitrary use of such beings, which are thus objects of respect.[2]

So either you are a *person*—a subject—or you are a *thing,* an object. Either you're *in* and have rights, or you're *out,* and have none. This is one of the strongest dichotomies of rights in Western philosophy, and its influence is making itself felt increasingly in the current debate, as we shall see. A dichotomy as strong as this has spawned strong reactions: (1) For one thing, are all human beings rational? And if not, do they lose their personhood status and get reclassified as things, as property? What about severely mentally disabled humans? What about humans in a coma? What about children and infants? Interestingly, Kant himself realized that he had created a problem, and in one of the last works he was ever to write (for which the *Grounding* was actually supposed to be a preliminary work), *The Metaphysics of Morals* (1797), Kant actually came up with an intermediate category, realizing that he had created a false dichotomy. Unfortunately, not many people read *The Metaphysics of Morals,* and his earlier theory is far better known. But to set the record straight, Kant did invent the category of "being a person akin to a thing," where those humans who are not completely rational (such as children) can have protected status. So the protection of not-quite rational humans is built into Kant's philosophy, even if it happened at a late date. However, the next powerful reaction is different: (2) For another thing, are humans then the only rational animals, and are all other animals to be classified as things? Yes, says Kant, even in his final book. Nonhuman animals are not rational and are to be regarded as things. Not that an animal should be treated cruelly, because the more we get used to disregarding animal pain, the less we think about causing pain to humans, says Kant.

So here Kant becomes an unexpected voice against animal cruelty (also something that he is rarely given credit for), based on two viewpoints: One is that unnecessary suffering should be avoided—because contrary to Descartes, Kant had no problem imagining that animals can feel pain—and the other is that callousness toward (or even enjoyment of) animal pain can lead to callousness or enjoyment of human pain. Kant was not the first to point this out—Thomas Aquinas had said the same thing 500 years earlier—but interestingly, criminal psychology now supports this view. Part of the FBI profile of a serial killer

has become common knowledge: As children, most serial killers display a pattern of bed-wetting, setting fires, and *torturing animals*. However, any consideration for nonhuman animals based on respect for their mental capacity finds no support in Kant's philosophy, because he excludes them on principle: Rationality is what qualifies one for personhood, and according to his view, animals are not rational.

What did Kant mean by rational? That is of course the next question. Unfortunately, the answer is not simple. To cut a long debate short, Kant believed that rationality is not just a matter of identifying a goal and reaching it in the quickest way possible—a common definition of rationality today and one that does not exclude animals as having a form of rationality. For Kant, rationality implied being able to view yourself and others impartially: *Could you imagine what you are about to do becoming a rule of behavior for everybody?* If yes, then the rule is acceptable. If no, then you shouldn't do it. This is the short version of Kant's moral philosophy, the famous principle of the *categorical imperative.* If you can't put yourself in a frame of mind where you can ask that question, then you are not a rational being. But suppose an animal could ask herself that question? Then Kant, as a good philosopher, would have to change his criterion. In the world of fiction we know of someone who could and did ask himself that question, although his status as a person was being disputed: Data, in the *Star Trek* episode, "The Measure of a Man." Would Data qualify as a person for Kant? In Kant's own words, "Man and in general every rational being, exists as an end in himself"; might that mean that you don't have to be genetically human in order to be considered a person? Absolutely, although this is hardly what Kant had envisioned. If all it takes is the capacity for reason, then Data qualifies as a person in the Kantian moral universe and so do all future rational beings we might encounter. Intelligent aliens, androids and gyneoids, and any other form of artificial intelligence, as long as they all demonstrate intelligence and a capacity to apply it freely—for

Kant believed in the freedom of the will for human beings.

Twentieth-century Kantians have added to his definition of rationality, in order to make it abundantly clear that animals don't qualify. The American philosopher Carl Cohen has introduced the theory of *contractarianism* based on Kant's concept of rationality: Whoever is capable of *mentally or physically signing a contract* qualifies for rights, says Cohen. This would imply that you understand the terms of an agreement and the repercussions if you break the terms; so you have to understand what a *duty* is in order to enjoy *rights*. And only humans have that capacity, according to Cohen, so animals are precluded from having rights because they can't understand mutual agreements. But what about the numerous human beings who can't understand agreements or sign contracts? Are they then to be kept out of the respect loop? Cohen has an answer, because he knows the problems caused by Kant's theory not supplying an answer soon enough: Since most normal humans understand about contracts, then the courtesy of respect is granted those who can't, because they belong to a species that generally has the capacity. So babies or mentally disabled persons are precluded from being treated like property. Cohen's critics ask, Why is it just the *human* version of contracts that interests Cohen? And why should rationality be limited to a litmus test of contract signing, when there are so many other ways of testing rational mind activity? And if *one* animal should display the capacity of understanding agreements, while others of that species don't, does it mean that we have to disregard that capacity and go with what is normal for the species, thereby excluding that one animal from personhood?

Philosophers are not the only ones making an effort to defend the status of human beings as *the* rational beings: Some animal behaviorists add to the criterion of rationality that it must involve behavior that goes beyond trial-and-error learning. Many animals learn from situations and the environment to improve their response to new situations. All birds and mammals have this capability, and for many laypeople this seems like a fine example of logical, rational thinking. (And perhaps it is! This is a controversial area.) However, some animal behaviorists insist that this learning style is not enough to qualify animals as rational; in order to qualify, they have to demonstrate that they can think *abstractly,* not just respond to a concrete situation. They must show that they can classify situations in their minds as certain types of situations and act on principle, without actually having encountered the particular situation before. For some, we are finally getting to what distinguishes rational behavior from all other animal behavior. For others, this is just scientists moving the goal posts farther and farther back because they are worried about having to welcome nonhuman species as fellow rational beings.

In Chapter 7 you read about the Cartesian tradition and its firm denial that animals have the capacity to reason, feel, or have any mind activity at all; however, several thinkers prior to the twentieth century considered it a given that nonhuman animals engage in some form of practical thinking. You have already heard that Aristotle believed animals to have a practical mind activity (but not rational thinking as such), and so did Max Scheler. You have also read that Darwin in the nineteenth century saw animal mind activity as evolutionarily related to human intelligence and emotion. But nobody prior to the late twentieth century made quite as strong a statement about animal rationality as did David Hume, whom you also know from Chapter 7. In his *Treatise of Human Nature,* Hume writes,

No truth appears to me more evident, than that beasts are endow'd with thought and reason as well as men. The arguments are in this case so obvious, that they never escape the most stupid and ignorant.

We are conscious that we ourselves, in adapting means to ends, are guided by reason and design, and that 'tis not ignorantly nor casually we perform those actions, which tend to self-preservation, to the obtaining pleasure, and avoiding pain. When therefore we see other creatures, in millions of instances, perform like actions, and direct them to like ends, all our principles of reason and probability carry us with an invincible force to believe the existence of a like cause. . . . 'Tis from the resemblance of the external actions of animals to those we ourselves perform, that we judge their internal likewise to resemble ours. . . . The common defect of those systems, which philosophers have employ'd to account for the actions of the mind, is, that they suppose such subtilty and refinement of thought, as not openly exceeds the capacity of mere animals, but even of children and the common people in our own species.[3]

Hume is here applying the principle that a simpler explanation is preferable to a more complex explanation. We know the principle as *Occam's Razor,* from William of Occam, a medieval scholar who taught his students not to add more assumptions to an explanation than the minimum needed; it is also known as the *principle of parsimony.* Hume thus dispenses with the idea that animal and human minds differ from each other in kind, because a far simpler and more appropriate explanation is that they don't: They differ from each other only in degree. His simple principle is, If animals and humans behave in similar ways, and we conclude from the human behavior that humans can think, then it is only logical and consistent to conclude that in that case, animals can think too. You may be more familiar with the principle in this version: If it quacks like a duck and walks like a duck, then it's a duck. Anything else would be illogical. Some critics have responded that what we see in animal behavior may be *instinct,* but when similar actions are done by humans, it is because of reason. And in fact some of Hume's examples lead us to think that he ascribes rational activity to some animal behaviors, like birds' nest building, which probably should be labeled as instinct, since the bird can't help building the same kind of nest as every other bird of its species. But overall, Hume's point is not that all animal behavior is rational—it is that whenever we see similar human and animal behavior, such as learning from past mistakes, it is wrong to assume that for animals it is nonrational, but for

humans it is a rational form of behavior. Today, Hume might have adopted the term *speciesism* to describe the idea that human behavior differs in nature from animal behavior.

The Criterion of Self-Awareness

Lets us return for a moment to the *Star Trek* story from Chapter 1: The android Data had to prove to the court that he was a person in order to avoid the dismal fate of being taken apart by the scientist Maddox so that Maddox could produce any number of new Datas to be used as machines in space exploration. Data's defense attorney, Captain Picard, proved to the court that Data satisfied all three criteria for personhood (or "sentience" as Picard calls it) set down by Maddox himself: *being intelligent, being self-aware, and having consciousness.* We have already seen that Data would qualify for the first criterion according to Kantian standards. How about the second? Picard puts Data on the stand and asks him if he knows who and where he is. Data has a fine grasp of the situation: His personhood is on trial, and his life hangs in the balance.

The screenwriter of the episode, Melissa Snodgrass, may or may not have had some philosophical training; interestingly, her three criteria for personhood echo one of the most famous articles in moral philosophy coming out of the 1970s, Mary Ann Warren's pro-choice article on abortion and personhood, "On the Moral and Legal Status of Abortion." Written in 1972 and published in January 1973 immediately before *Roe v. Wade,* Warren argues that it is illegal to murder a person, and if the fetus qualifies for personhood, then it ought to be illegal (which it was at the time) to abort a fetus. But if the fetus is not a person, abortion ought to be legal. What does personhood entail for Warren? That an individual has (1) capacity for reason and for feeling pain, (2) self-awareness, (3) capacity for communication in a number of ways and about a number of topics, (4) self-propelled activity, and (5) social consciousness. Warren's point is that in order to be considered a person, an individual has to demonstrate that he or she meets at least two or three of these criteria, preferably all of them. Several things are obvious: For one thing, our friend Data qualifies on all counts (except feeling pain, because he is an android and has no feelings or sensations, at least at this stage of his development). We know he is intelligent, because his brain is a supercomputer with immeasurable problem-solving capacity. But is he also self-aware? In other words, does he have an inner life? His keepsakes and cherished memories testify to that—and, besides, he knows the gravity of his situation in court. Snodgrass's three criteria, self-awareness, intelligence, and consciousness, correspond nicely to criteria 1, 2, and 3. But we should also remind ourselves that the story of Data is fiction and serves only to show us a scenario for what we may have to face in the future or what some people have had to face in the past when human populations were denied full personhood because it was assumed that they were lacking in one or several of the criteria listed. Would robots in our future then be assumed also to have an inner life? Of course we can't assume that, but it is not the issue here. The issue is whether we are prone to jump to conclusions about others' personhood based on what we think we know about their background. (Box 10.1 explores the concept of personhood as it specifically relates to the crime of murder.)

What interested Warren in 1972 was that a fetus qualifies for none of the criteria except perhaps for the feeling of pain (which we now know is developed in the sixth month of pregnancy). This meant to her that a fetus does not qualify for personhood, and killing a fetus is thus not murder, but tissue removal. While this is a powerful argument against the personhood of a fetus, its logic also compels us to ask, Who else in the human population can't live up to these criteria? The most obvious answer is *newborn infants*. They have the capacity for pain, but not yet for reason. They are not self-aware (and we shall return to that in a minute); they have no language; their ability to move about in a goal-oriented way is limited; and they have no sense of their own place in the community or even within their own family. The unfortunate consequence? That infanticide is not murder. Warren had to answer this argument, and did it in a rather unique way—you be the judge of whether or not she did a good job. She saw the logic of her own argument and stood firm, claiming that infants aren't persons, either—but since society frowns on killing infants, they should be protected because of public opinion. (So if public opinion changes about fetuses, then should *they* be protected regardless of personhood status?) We don't have the space here for a more detailed discussion, but we will draw on some of her criteria and continue the discussion below (see Box 10.1 for more about the question of murder, fetuses, and personhood). For now, we'll return to the issue of self-awareness.

As we saw in Chapter 7, humans generally feel self-aware and assume that others do too. We may never have privileged access to anybody else's mind but our own, but our sense of self and of our own time and place is clearly an important feature of who we are. But in a practical sense, isn't there any way we can actually determine whether others are self-aware? Yes, there is, given that you accept that we are not being tricked by an evil demon and that the world actually consists of things other than what our mind cooks up for us.

The first step in ascertaining someone else's self-awareness would be to do exactly what Picard did when he asked Data, Who are you and what are you doing? Data was able to answer, and the judge took him at his word that he knew his own situation. However, suppose Data was *programmed* to answer that way? Or suppose Data's speech program all of a sudden crashed? Would we then have to assume there is no self-awareness, since he can't communicate it? In that case we are in the same situation as when we try to find out whether small children or nonhuman animals are self-aware: They can't tell us. But there is actually a way to find out: *the mirror recognition test*. You have read about it before. The test amounts to this: Wait until your test subject is asleep (and let us assume we are curious about the self-awareness

Box 10.1 MURDER AND PERSONHOOD

The biblical commandment "Thou shalt not kill" is, as many people are aware, a mistranslation of the original commandment "Thou shalt not murder," a much narrower concept. If there is any universal moral and legal principle around the world, it surely must be that murder is unacceptable. Each society protects itself against killing committed with evil intent and with a variety of ways to punish the transgressor. You read in Chapter 9 that John Locke believed that due to the rational quality of human nature, a murder committed even outside of society, in the state of nature, could morally be punished by death. Whether a society opts for the death penalty, for life imprisonment, or for some other penalty such as fines, confiscation of property, or banishment, depends on its tradition; but most societies take actions against captured and convicted killers. So could we say that a human universal is the recognition of the wrongness of murder? That depends on how we define *murder*.

This is where *personhood* comes into play: If we grant that murder is killing with evil intent, we still haven't defined, killing of whom? Or of what? Today we assume that it implies the killing of a human being, *homicide* (although not all forms of homicide are murder, and many vegetarians would call *killing anything with a face* murder). The common view today in our Western culture is that any killing of any human being, with evil intent, ought to be called murder, but history has not seen it that way: Killing a slave in any slave-based culture will generally be punished based on the slave's monetary value to the owner (and fines will be payable to the owner), not on his or her value as a human being. The killing of a stranger, in a tribal society, may not rate as seriously as killing a tribal member. In India and Bangladesh it was, until recently, not illegal for the groom's parents to kill a young bride who brought in too little dowry, the so-called *dowry deaths*. They'd keep the dowry and free up the young husband for a new marriage, with more dowry. Within the same tradition, the *suttee* suicide (the expected self-immolation of a widow on her husband's funeral pyre) was already the focus of much Western attention in the nineteenth century. Incidentally, both kinds of deaths, even when enforced by the community, would not qualify as murder in the local culture because, presumably, no fully social persons are killed, and society has no evil intent. While the West is no longer so sure that it always has the right to criticize the customs of others, there is a growing feeling among socially aware Westerners that perhaps a line should be drawn between tolerance of other cultures' customs and apathy at customs that violate human rights.

But we also have to look at our Western legal definition of murder: the killing, with evil intent, of a postnatal, *born* person. Legally, as well as morally for most people who are pro-choice, a *fetus* doesn't qualify as a person, and thus it is not considered murder to kill it. However, since the concept of personhood is what is in question, we have to face that it is a matter of choice of definition—some would call it an arbitrary choice. If we choose to be pro-choice, we must take on the task and explain (1) why a fetus is not a person and (2) if we decide the fetus is a person, when the killing of a person who hasn't committed a crime is justifiable (such as in self-defense). If we are not pro-choice, we generally consider the fetus a person, and only in the case of extreme danger to the woman's life might an abortion be considered acceptable. For St. Augustine a fetus becomes a person when it develops the capacity to feel pain (and our science today tells us that happens between the fifth and sixth months). For St. Thomas Aquinas it happens between forty and eighty days after conception, depending on whether it is a male (forty days) or a female (eighty days) fetus, because this is when Aristotle said the soul enters the body. In the Jewish tradition the soul enters the body at birth with the first breath, so the fetus has no personhood before birth. In countless pretechnological societies the newborn child was not considered a person until after it had shown itself to be viable, usually after three months to one year, because of the high infant mortality rate; and infanticide was thus not considered murder.

of a four-year old child). Then put a dot of (non toxic!) red paint on her forehead. When she wakes up, observe her behavior when she looks in the mirror: Does she reach toward the red dot on the face of the child in the mirror? A one-year-old might do that. But a one-and-a-half-year-old will *rub her own forehead* to see what the dot is. So she knows she is looking at an image of herself: the simplest form, and the simplest proof, of self-awareness. It doesn't have to be fancier than that. It appears that we humans acquire this fundamental form of self-awareness somewhere between the ages of one-and-a-half and two.

The question of animal rationality is very slippery, but the question of animal self-awareness is not: It is quite easy to test. Do dogs know they are looking at themselves in the mirror, or do they think it is another animal? As far as we can tell at the present, they do not know it is themselves. They can get used to the fact that the "other dog" is harmless, and they'll stop being curious about it, but it doesn't seem to shift to an understanding that they are looking at themselves. Put dots on their heads, dress them up in funny hats, they still don't appear to know (or else they just don't give a hoot). Neither do monkeys. *But apes do.* Do the red-dot experiment with a chimpanzee, a gorilla, or an orangutan past early childhood, and they will look at their face in the mirror with much curiosity and *rub their forehead* to find out what the dot is. Apes looking in the mirror *know they are looking at themselves*, not at another ape. In addition, researchers recently announced that the phenomenon of self-awareness seems to be shared by *dolphins,* too—the first time such a claim has been made about a nonprimate species based on observations of behavior under controlled circumstances: Stripes were painted on the sides of unconscious dolphins, and an underwater mirror surface was made available. When they awoke, they tried to twist themselves to, apparently, get a good look at their side in the mirror. According to the researcher, they undoubtedly knew they were observing themselves. If self-awareness is supposed to be a criterion for per-

sonhood—perhaps one of many—then it seems that some creatures other than humans should be allowed a chance to try out for membership in the personhood club. Indeed, if we go to Warren's fifth criterion, social consciousness, both apes and dolphins seem to have that in abundance, clearly being aware of the hierarchy of their group and their place in it. From ape research we know that apes play their friends and relatives against each other in the hierarchy; they pass on "cultural inventions" such as mat weaving and medicinal plants discovered by apes generations ago, and keep the knowledge of such inventions alive; and apes reared under controlled conditions recognize each other and themselves in photos. The gorilla Koko even chose her prospective mate, the gorilla David, from a photo lineup.

Is there then nothing more to self-awareness than recognizing ourselves in the mirror? Of course there is, but it is the foundation and the beginning: Without the basic recognition of ourselves, we can't proceed to be aware of our role in our family, in our community, and our culture. Without the self-recognition we can't become the storytelling animal that we are. Although some social large-brained species may share the basic understanding of "self" with humans and even an understanding of their role within their community, they don't necessarily have as sophisticated a sense of self as humans.

Language as a Personhood Criterion

Being able to communicate in a variety of ways was one of Warren's personhood criteria. She did not call it language, to avoid the underlying assumption that it necessarily has something to do with speech, and I, too, am relying on our being able to use the term *language* in a broad sense: use of words or other symbols and gestures to convey a meaning about an external thing or event.

We know that humans have language to an extreme degree: We think in words most of the time, we sometime dream in words, and babies babble words before they are even a year old. Indeed, hearing-impaired babies retain the babble-urge and are said to "babble" with their hands, being incapable of associating language with sounds, and, reportedly, some deaf people sometimes dream of signed words, so sign language can be said to be as natural a response as spoken language, if not nearly as common. It has taken a long time for philosophy as well as linguistics to recognize that language comprehension and language production can take on many forms, and the spoken form is only one of many. Aristotle firmly believed that a deaf person was also dumb, both in the sense of mute and in the sense of being less intelligent (the term used to be "deaf-and-dumb," meaning deaf and mute, but certainly to a modern person there would be a false association to some lack of intellect). Descartes, having graduated to a slightly more advanced viewpoint, points out that even the deaf are "in the habit of inventing for themselves various signs through which they make themselves understood to those who are usually with them and have leisure to learn their language."[4] Descartes's observations reflect a time when there was no understanding of or interest in educating hearing-impaired children.

The American linguist Noam Chomsky focuses almost exclusively on the structure of *written* language as the prototypical human language. Throughout the course of philosophy there has been a prejudicial leaning toward identifying the spoken or written use of words as the true language format, but scholars now have a broader conception of language. This wasn't achieved until the 1960s when American Sign Language (ASL) was officially accepted as a true language, largely thanks to the research of the linguist William Stokoe, even though Rousseau had already speculated in the eighteenth century that the spoken word was preceded by a combination of gestures and singsong words. A modern-day Cartesian (a follower of Descartes), the anthropologist Ian Tattersall still leans toward equating language capacity with speech capacity. In his book *Becoming Human* (1998) he argues that apes have no language capacity because the ape larynx is incapable

of uttering human sounds (see discussion later in chapter); and on the basis of an interpretation of Neandertal physiology (now disputed), he argues that even Neandertals didn't have language, "at least in the form in which we are familiar with it."[5] (See Chapter 7 for a discussion of the cognitive development of Neandertals.)

Philosophers have claimed that anything that can be thought of can be expressed in language and that the entire perceived world around us is categorized by our brain in terms of concepts; this was something Kant taught us in the eighteenth century. We use the term *conceptualization* for the process of making an idea or a feeling more concrete and structured, implying that we do our thinking through words or concepts.

But words may not be everything to the thinking mind; in the early to mid-twentieth century, British-American philosophers developed a theory that thinking in words is the only true form of thinking. Many great advances in thinking—philosophy, science, and other conceptual fields—have of course been advanced by the invention of new concepts to carry new ideas, so naturally there is a connection between thinking and language. The question is, Is this connection necessary—*must* there be language in order for there to be thinking? If yes, this of course precludes any creature from thinking who isn't thinking in words; but *ask yourself if you have ever engaged in a form of rational thinking that doesn't involve words?*

I am really asking two questions here: (1) Can we engage in a form of thinking that doesn't rely just on words (but that we could put it into words if we had to) and (2) Can we engage in a form of rational mind activity that precludes words? Let us look at the first possibility, which you first saw suggested in Chapter 1: Have you ever engaged in some rational activity where your mind doesn't fill up with words, but you get the job done, anyway? If you say yes, you have probably engaged in a considerable amount of technical activity, which certainly qualifies as rational behavior. Are you a good cook? Do you enjoy building models or working on your car or repairing electronics?

How about sewing, hunting, or driving a car in a strange town? All these activities require an alert mind, but they also require the accumulation of technical know-how. Sometimes the technical know-how can take over, and we "cruise" through the cooking, the model making, and the driving; but at any point in time something unexpected may happen, or special skills may be required, and we have to stay alert. Do you "think in words" as you move through the activity? "Now add salt!" "Go left!" "Add the wing to the plane before the glue dries!" Probably not. Now imagine that you have to *teach someone* to cook, hunt, sew, or drive a car. If all thought activity is word-based, it should be a breeze to put your activity into words—but it isn't! You probably can, but it takes some time for you to find the words, and sometimes you may not even know the appropriate concepts; you just know how to turn out a great lasagna or make that clock run again, and you resort to saying "a pinch of this and a pinch of that" and attaching "doodads" to "thingamajigs." This talent is no less rational than many cerebral activities; it is just based on a practical experience and hasn't rated highly among philosophers of language— but nevertheless it is a rational activity that is not primarily word-based: "Knowing how" to do something and plan ahead using that knowledge is certainly a rational activity, but it is not the same as "knowing that" something is the case, to the extent that you can communicate it easily.

The second possibility, Can we think in a way that *precludes* the use of words? is a tougher question because it is harder to draw on common sense here; if such an experience exists, then talking and writing about it actually diminishes it or even falsifies it, if it can only be undertaken in the mind somewhere beyond language. Putting it into words will be a kind of betrayal of the experience, if indeed it can be expressed and shared at all. But as a matter of fact, many of the world's great religions draw on exactly such experiences. Perhaps you would rather call what happens experience than thinking, but it is presumed that your mind is somehow active and cognizant while it is happening. Some religions call it a *mystical experience,* or a union with God, and within the context of such religions it is indeed considered a betrayal, or at best a watered-down experience, to try to express what happens in words and/or in writing. While some philosophers would question the validity of such an experience and call it a fantasy or an illusion, we can't just deny that some of the most cherished human experiences are important to those who have undergone them, and those who would like to experience them. Some believers spend their entire lives trying to achieve such an experience, and within such traditions this mystical union is generally considered the highest form of *knowledge,* precisely because it is wordless. The prejudices of a Western concept-oriented tradition shouldn't prevent us from taking such experiences into consideration when we try to understand the nature and power—and limits—of language.

But even within the Western tradition—as in most other traditions—there is a phenomenon that is familiar to a great many people: the difficulty of expressing strong *emotions* in language. Lovers invent words to say how much they love each other, because "love" doesn't seem to be enough. A grieving person may not be able to find words for her or his feelings at all. Great joy—observing your child at play, watching your team win, having a perfect vacation day—as well as great anxiety may leave us "speechless," or "at a loss for words." But within our human language we have invented an outlet for such experiences: *poetry.* A poet may succeed in expressing the inexpressible, but not in any direct, descriptive language—the experience is captured in *metaphors,* in language that is emotionally poignant but descriptively inaccurate. The mind takes a leap, going from the poetic expression to its meaning: Is that a leap within or outside of language? Much religious language borders on the poetic for the same reason. And how about the painter, the sculptor, and the composer, creating works of art out of an intense, goal-oriented mind activity that often involves no inner dialogue—are we to judge that they are not "thinking" while they work? Surely that would be the utmost hubris on the part of an intellectual profession (like that of the philosopher or the linguist) whose tools are words, words, and words. With such ordinary and extraordinary experiences of the *inadequacy of language* to express our thoughts and feelings, how can we claim that intelligence, or thinking, is exclusively language-dependent?

So it seems that there may be some forms of human experience where the mind is conscious and self-aware, but there is no direct or even indirect connection to language. Some yoga meditation techniques strive to achieve just that state of mind. If this is the case, why deny that it is possible for nonhuman animals to experience a form of alert, clear mind function without language?

What I am getting at is a more tolerant view of what intelligence is; as we saw in Chapter 7, there may be many forms of intelligence in the human mind, if indeed the mind is like a Swiss Army knife: conceptual thinking, technical knowledge, social intelligence, and so forth. Some of these forms may be language-based, others may not. So we should remain equally open-minded when it comes to nonhuman animal intelligence: Some animals may be highly "smart" even if their intelligence is not language-based.

But just suppose language comprehension—while not a sole requirement for intelligence—is far more widespread than philosophers used to think? Suppose it is actually built into advanced nonhuman animal brains that they can comprehend language—human language or any language—if taught early enough?

Evaluating Animal Language Capacity

In the late summer of 2000 twenty-seven of the top scientists in the field of animal intelligence research got together at a symposium in Chicago, for the first time discussing the subjects of animal intelligence, language, and socialization with minds open to the possibility that humans are not the only thinking, talking, and emotionally bonding beings on the planet. The *Chicago Tribune* predicted that the symposium might prove to be historic in its scope. The scientists came from a large number of disciplines, each one focused on the behavior of a certain species, such as primates, elephants, dolphins, killer whales, seals, lions, hyenas, and birds. While the serious study of animal cognition has been going on for a couple of decades, this was the first time ever that scientists from a variety of fields assembled to hear about each other's findings. Not only was it unprecedented that all these researchers got together, but also the entire scope of the symposium—accepting the possibility that animals might be intelligent, have a form of language, as well as a complex emotional life—reflects a kind of thinking that is so revolutionary among animal behaviorists that—one can only say—this is a sign that a new century (and millennium) has arrived, for this direction of thinking is reversing a hundred-year-old scientific trend toward skepticism concerning animal minds. Since the conference, scientists and philosophers have begun to weigh in on the subject in the media as well as in scholarly publications in greater numbers than before: Evidence of animal use of arithmetic, mental maps, message systems within their species, tools, and human language (with limited comprehension) is now appearing so frequently that it is getting increasingly harder to refute. Books such as Marc Hauser's *Wild Minds,* Daisie and Michael Radner's *Animal Consciousness,* and Lesley Rogers *Minds of Their Own* are, indeed, beginning to change minds.

But why is the thought of animal intelligence so outlandish? Most laypeople who have had pets at some point in their lives find the thought quite unspectacular. Most pet people and farmers have "smart animal" stories. I myself can bore you for hours about my dog opening cabinets and doors and understanding over 200 words in English (and a few in Danish). As you have just read, David Hume said that if animal behavior is similar to human behavior, it must be because we have somewhat similar minds; Charles Darwin was convinced that humans and nonhuman animals were on a *continuum* in terms of their developed intelligence as well as their sense of right and wrong—a natural thought for someone who believes that evolution accounts for the diversity of species. So

PICKLES. © 2000 The Washington Post Writers Group. Reprinted with permission.

What is language? Is it the meaningful production of words and signs? Is it comprehension of words and signs? Or does it have to involve production of sentences with a syntax? Here the *Pickles* cartoon seems to be doing a spoof of the Noam Chomsky approach to language: Only words put together according to the rules of grammar qualify as language. Or is this cartoon perhaps a spoof of the whole animal language issue?

why did it become so controversial to suggest that animals have some form of rational thought processes and capacity for understanding language that scholars who did so stood a good chance of losing their bid for tenure and risking lifelong ridicule during most of the twentieth century?

It may be a combination of several factors. For one thing, the assumption that there is a connection between *intelligence, language,* and *having a soul* is ancient in the Western tradition; if beings other than humans also have intelligence and language, chances are we'll have to talk about whether they have souls too (or contemplate the possibility that humans have no souls either), and that is tremendously disturbing to many people. The biologists Alan and Beatrix Gardner (see "Can Animals Understand Human Speech?") suggest that many scientists are reluctant to consider that apes might have intelligence and language capacity because that removes some important realm of our human uniqueness. So there may be strong psychological barriers in our culture for wanting to consider the possibility of animal cognition. However, there have also been some powerful arguments presented by scientists in the twentieth century against the notion of animal intelligence—

powerful not so much in the sense of being "good" arguments, but powerful in a political sense. We'll look at some of them in the discussion that follows.

The Grammar Question   Right now, the debate over whether animals can be taught to understand and even use language is heating up. To a great extent it appears that a generational abyss has opened in the behavioral sciences (which doesn't mean that either group has a monopoly on the truth): Some older scientists continue to argue that humans are unique in the use of language, while some younger scientists lean toward a more inclusive definition. One might wonder what makes it so hard for them to agree, when on the one hand we have a globally speaking humanity and on the other an animal world where human language is nonexistent—but in the middle a few animals who have learned to recognize words and use them quite proficiently. Doesn't that look as if some animals can learn to use human language under certain conditions—which would mean that language is not a uniquely human phenomenon? But what it boils down to is a *definition of language:* Those who consider language an exclusive human property generally identify language not only as the use of words and other gestures but also as the combining of them into a *grammar*.

The linguist Noam Chomsky put the question of language capacity in the framework of grammar proficiency and claimed that only the human brain has a built-in syntax-processing capacity, a "language acquisition device" or language organ. Otherwise, said Chomsky, children would never be able to pick up on the immense complexity of human language or understand what their parents were saying to them. But as the chimpanzee researcher Roger Fouts explains, there is no medical evidence for such a brain center. Chomsky, says Fouts, approached the phenomenon of language logically, from studying written texts, and concluded that it was so complex that it could not be learned without a ready-made grammar-reading brain structure. Chomsky didn't consider that language is not originally written English, but a form of social communication, and is accompanied by facial communication, gestures, and other body language (as Rousseau said over 200 years ago). The facial expressions, the gestures, and the body language are all part of human communication—and ape communication. So language is something broader than Chomsky had envisioned, and the break with Chomsky in language research came in the early 1970s with the study of "motherese." Motherese is the simplified singsong language mothers (and fathers) use when talking with their babies—and it is universal. Even deaf mothers use a simplified form of ASL when signing to their infants. Since then there has been a tendency among linguists to approach the issue of language differently, as a form of child development and communication theory.

The new approach to language is to view it in a broad sense, including gestures, facial expressions, and body language. When language-as-words is the focus, researchers such as Sue Savage Rumbaugh look at the use of combinations of words (or signs) to convey a meaning, both as language *comprehension* and as language use. In her work with the bonobo chimpanzees Kanzi, Panbanisha, and others, Rumbaugh has found that they pick up human language comprehension almost as easily as a human child if exposed to it from infancy. Kanzi and Panbanisha were never "taught" human language but were immersed in a speaking environment from the time they were babies, and both picked up language comprehension as well as language use (by using a "talking board" with symbols, a lexigram) without being taught how. Their intellectual development has progressed past most predictions, to the point where both Panbanisha and Kanzi can now write words in chalk; Panbanisha seems to have picked up spelling from the computer screen.[6] In addition, she is now teaching her young son to use the lexigram and translates her mother's wishes to the humans, because the older ape doesn't know how to use the board. Rumbaugh theorizes that primates have a capacity for language comprehension that precedes and predates the human larynx evolution—for without the larynx deeper in the throat than the apes we wouldn't be able to speak. Since human babies are born with a higher larynx, they can't speak, either, until the larynx starts dropping within the first year of life, but they can *comprehend* what is being said to them far earlier than that. So for anyone who thinks ape research is only interesting if it has some human relevance, here are two aspects of relevance: Rumbaugh's research has enhanced our knowledge of *human* language acquisition. In addition, both Rumbaugh's and Fouts's work with apes has yielded insight into human children with *autism:* These children usually have problems with the spoken language, but ape research has shown that they have a much higher language comprehension than previously thought; ape language training applied to these children gives them an outlet for communication that their vocal cords and general condition did not previously allow. So for ape language researchers the issue is far more than syntax, although syntax is still somewhat important for such scientists because it allows for the construction of basic sentences; however, many linguists now view the main issue as being the evolution of language comprehension, and many of them now see it as something that preceded the evolution of the human brain.

Can Animals Speak? When you were a child, you probably read a book or saw a movie about talking animals, or perhaps you have read such a story to a child or watched movies such as *The Jungle Book, Lady and the Tramp,* or *Babe* with a young person. The ancient Greeks, and about eighty generations since them, have told the fables of Aesop, where the mouse assures the lion that even a little creature can be of help, and the fox who can't reach the grapes claims they're sour and not worth having. Regardless of Descartes's seventeenth-century insistence that animals have no minds, Western folklore is full of talking-animal stories, and so is every body of oral (folklore) literature around the world. What can we conclude from that? Not that animals used to talk, but that (1) at the folklore level it doesn't seem like an impossibility, and (2) animals are great narrative vehicles for telling about human quirks and problems. In some cultures, such as the American Indian tradition, the idea of talking animals is anything but a children's tale; the animal capacity for speech is generally understood to be a *spirit-language,* not used like human speech, and only the select few can hope to communicate with animal spirits. An ordinary person doesn't go out on the plains, expecting to swap yarns with the nearest coyote. In adult stories of talking animals the speech is usually some form of metaphor for a higher truth, a communication with gods, or a parody of human life, such as George Orwell's *Animal Farm.* So on the one hand we are used to stories of talking animals from Aesop to Disney and beyond, but on the other hand they are not realistic stories, but symbolic.

However, it is a general, ancient assumption that animals have *their own language* (the cow says Moo, the cat says Meow, and so forth) and understand each other. Is that possible, or is it a children's story too? Yes and no: As far as we can tell, they don't have words, and they don't have syntax, but every animal who breathes seems to have a *sound capacity*—and even fish apparently make

noise with air bubbles! Furthermore, it now appears that the sounds they make are not random: Recent research into monkey sounds, especially those of vervets and baboons, indicate that some sounds may carry meanings. Under research conditions the warning call a vervet makes when a predatory bird appeared was taped and played back to other monkeys (with no bird in the sky), and they all looked up. The "leopard" warning was played, and the troupe began to scan the horizon. Research into whale songs and dolphin "clicks" has revealed that whale songs are shared, in minute detail, by the entire pod of whales within a season, and dolphins may understand the concept of a *name,* since they always utter the same specific sounds when greeting individual dolphins. In the 2000 Chicago symposium researchers shared their knowledge of dolphin "language": whistle signals among bottlenose dolphins show that dolphins often respond to each other with matching signals, and they learn and repeat signals from their friends—an ability linguists had previously identified as one of the early steps toward language. No consensus exists yet as to whether this may be a true form of language communication or just one of many forms of instinctual communication among social animals; however, some linguists today argue that human language must have started out as just that, one of many forms of communication within a social species.

Can Animals Understand Human Speech? But what about animals understanding *human* language? We all know that dogs, horses, and dolphins can be trained to obey commands (it's harder with cats, but not impossible), but do they respond to the tone of voice or the meaning of the word? That depends on your viewpoint, and to a great extent your experience raising dogs and horses. (My own experience tells me it is probably a combination of both.) We might actually have been much closer to answering that question if research into animal language hadn't come to a dead halt in 1900 because of a certain famous case of fraud, or at least of scientific bungling: the case of *Clever Hans,* the horse who could do math.

Hans's owner would travel to carnivals with Hans as a sideshow act, because he believed Hans could count. Ask him a math question, said the owner, and Hans will tap the right number with his front leg! And Hans did, to the astonishment of the German crowds and to the astonishment of German scientists who in turn asked him questions that he answered correctly. The illusion of Clever Hans was shattered with the advent of the experimental psychologist Oscar Pfungst: Hans knew the answers when the questioner did—otherwise he was lost. What happened was that Hans carefully watched the questioner's reactions; when Hans had reached the right number of taps with his leg, the questioner would subconsciously give him a *cue* by straightening up, taking his hands out of his pockets, smiling, nodding, or doing something else. (Your instructors may do the same thing when you answer their questions correctly! Just watch them.) So when Pfungst blindfolded Hans, he couldn't be cued and went on tapping. So was Hans clever? Yes, he was very clever at reading humans. But he was never credited for that.

Since that day, and all the way until the 1960s, any attempt at demonstrating animal language comprehension was dismissed as a Clever Hans story. Even in the 1980s scholars like Thomas Sebeok were saying that dolphins and lab chimpanzees involved in animal intelligence research were just a bunch of Clever Hanses. In order to avoid this accusation, those involved in today's animal language research go through rigorous training themselves and wear masks that hide their eyes and facial features in order to avoid the Clever Hans syndrome. This means that research into how much a dog actually understand when she obeys your command and fetches the paper is at this time still in its infancy and still as controversial as a hundred years ago.

In 1966 a scientist couple, Allen and Beatrix Gardner, decided to rear—to "cross-foster"—a baby chimpanzee, Washoe, as a member of their human family. They talked to Washoe and at the same time signed ASL to her; and Washoe became the first "talking ape." Over the years she learned a vocabulary of several hundred words and was able to use sentences with more than two words in them as well as to use prepositions and other language features. She was observed teaching her adopted chimpanzee son sign language as part of his upbringing. Even though funding ran out, and Washoe was relegated to a prison-like existence in a university lab for years, she never forgot her ASL and, now living in more natural surroundings with other chimpanzees, she still has not forgotten the humans who raised her and those she developed friendships with, such as Roger Fouts (see Primary Readings). Chimpanzees can live for about sixty years "in captivity," and Washoe is at the time of this writing an older mature adult, but not yet a senior. (This also means that if you as a scientist want to take on a language research project with baby apes, be aware that they stop being cute babies, but they remain dependent on those who have taught them language communication—and rely on that added stimulus as a cultural and emotional need for the rest of their lives, usually more than half a century. It is quite a responsibility to initiate such a relationship.)

In the 1970s another language researcher, Herbert Terrace, who was a student of B. F. Skinner's (see Chapter 4) undertook his own ape language project, by acquiring a chimpanzee baby he named Nim Chimpsky (a little pun on Noam Chomsky's name). But unlike Washoe, Nim was not raised together with a human family. He was raised under controlled lab conditions with no social interaction with humans or apes and drilled in language training six hours a day, except for weekends, by a total of sixty teachers. In Fouts's words, "Project Nim was an experiment in social deprivation."[7] The attempt was to use Skinner's method to condition Nim to ask for food and toys. After three years of training—without taking any precautions against the Clever Hans syndrome of cueing—Terrace evaluated videos of Nim's use of language and concluded that Nim was not using language spontaneously; he was merely "aping" what the language trainer was saying. So Terrace concluded that Nim hadn't learned to use language; and furthermore, that *all other apes are also just imitating their trainers.* Apparently Terrace didn't see that this was what he had been teaching Nim for three years: to imitate his teachers in order to get food and toys. Terrace's conclusion—that he had been "fooled by Nim"—was published and touted as proof that no ape can ever learn human language, and another obstacle was placed in the path of genuine animal language research. According to Roger Fouts,

> the most compelling rebuttal of Terrace came from Nim himself. After he returned to Oklahoma in 1977, a new study showed that his spontaneous signing increased dramatically when he was allowed to socialize naturally under relaxed conditions. Nim's "language deficit" had nothing to do with his intelligence and everything to do with Terrace's rigid training procedures. Terrace had deprived Nim of social conversation, then accused him of not having spontaneity and other elements of social linguistic behavior.[8]

In the 1970s other ape language experiments were undertaken, some of which go on to this day with expanded participation of new apes. The ASL-signing gorilla Koko may be the most famous of them all: Koko's human companion Francine Patterson, coauthor of *The Case for the Personhood of Gorillas,* also wrote a popular children's book featuring Koko and her kitten, and Koko herself went on the Internet some years ago, with her trainers conducting a question-and-answer chat. Once Koko asked for a cat for her birthday, and after a while she was allowed to choose a kitten, which she named "All Ball" because he had no tail. In spite of the kitten's being very aggressive, Koko loved him and was very gentle with him, treating him like a gorilla baby; so when the kitten was run over by a car and killed, Patterson didn't quite know how to break the bad news to Koko. According to her children's book,

> I went to Koko at once. I told her that Ball had been hit by a car; she would not see him again. Koko did not respond. I thought she didn't understand, so I left the trailer. Ten minutes later, I heard Koko cry. It was her distress call—a loud, long series of high-pitched hoots. I cried, too. Three days

later, Koko and I had a conversation about Ball. "Do you want to talk about your kitty?" I asked. "Cry," Koko signed. "Can you tell me more about it?" I asked. "Blind," she signed. "We don't see him anymore, do we? What happened to your kitty?" I asked. "Sleep cat," Koko signed.[9]

Do we know now that Koko is capable of putting words together? Yes. Does it qualify as human language? That depends on one's definition and conception of language. Some scholars say no, others say yes. But let us take it one step further: Does this conversation reveal something about Koko's intelligence and capacity to express it? Again, this depends on how generous we are with our definition of intelligence. Had Koko heard someone else describe death as "sleep"? We don't know. Was she merely doing a "Nim Chimpsky" on Patterson? Possibly. But consider this: If this conversation happened as spontaneously as Patterson suggests, then we have two things occurring, not just one: Koko clearly understands the situation and is capable of conveying it in words, *and* (perhaps equally important for a discussion on the philosophy of human nature) it appears that Koko has a *conception of death.* If you remember from Chapter 1, only humans are supposed to be able to realize that life is finite and living beings die. So here Koko may have broken yet another human-animal barrier. (See Primary Readings for an excerpt from *The Case for the Personhood of Gorillas.*) An objection may be that "sleep" is how we describe to children that a loved one or a pet has died (been "put to sleep"), and small children usually don't know what it means, so Koko is perhaps just displaying a childlike misunderstanding of death. Let us say that is the case—but then we also have to admit that Koko is capable of as much comprehension of language and life as a small child! And we don't refer to small children as dumb animals.

Incidentally, how does Koko fare on the mirror test? She likes to dress up in funny hats and will sit in her compound in front of the mirror, unaware that she is being observed, with a red hat on her head, and sign to herself, "Pretty Koko!"

The gorilla Koko with her first kitten. When the kitten was run over and killed, Koko exhibited what her human companions identified as grief and expressed an understanding of the concept of death. Koko now masters about 1,000 signs in the American Sign Language; she recognizes herself in the mirror and in photos and has taken part in an Internet chatroom event. Koko's ability to communicate has led the way for many researchers to conclude that animal intelligence may not be different in kind from human intelligence, merely different in degree.

As mentioned earlier, she chose her mate from a series of photos of male gorillas, knowing full well that she is not a human being. And how about Mary Ann Warren's criterion of "communicating in a number of ways about a number of subjects"? Some time ago a young man and woman among the personnel decided to have a quiet smooching session, because nobody could see them, except for that old ape. . . . Well, the next day the whole compound knew about their romance, because Koko likes gossiping and had delighted in telling everyone!

Can Animals Feel?   As you'll remember from Chapter 7, Descartes affected the debate about

animal minds hundreds of years into the future by claiming that animals have no minds and thus can neither think nor feel pain. Earlier we looked at the claim that animals can't think—but what about feeling? Descartes was talking primarily about physical sensation: the feeling of pain and pleasure, and we get back to that question later in the philosophy of Jeremy Bentham. But what about emotional feelings? Of course, the existence of such would be denied by Descartes, too, and the notion that animals lack emotion was adopted by the scientific community over the centuries. Even folklore joined in the consensus: Since the cat appears not to feel sorry for the mouse she is playing with and wolves will deliberately hunt down baby animals regardless of their vulnerability (actually because of it), it was concluded that animals (especially predators) are cold-hearted, selfish beasts. We know expressions such as a "dog eat dog world" and "catty" women, and even the ancient Romans chimed in with the expression, *Homo homini lupus,* "man is a wolf to man." But here is where folklore speaks with a forked tongue, because we also have proverbs and stories of animals being excellent mothers and nurturers; anecdotes abound of animals helping each other and grieving when a companion dies. And finally, in the last ten to fifteen years, science has followed suit: Jane Goodall opened up the field by reporting from Gombe that chimpanzees can be so emotionally attached to each other than when one dies, the other may lose the zest for life and grieve to death. Dog owners among philosophers and animal behaviorists tell of similar occurrences. Elephant and dolphin researchers have supplied similar accounts. A popular book by Jeffrey Moussaieff Masson and Susan McCarthy, *When Elephants Weep* (1995), was received with much skepticism by scientists, but its thesis that animals have rich and complex emotional lives has since been supported by several animal studies. And, perhaps most important, biological evolution is on the side of the theory of animal emotion: As you read in Chapter 7, the most ancient part of the human brain, the *amygdala,* is something we share with other mammals as well as with reptiles. It is the seat of the fundamental fight-or-flight decision; in other words, it is the ancient seat of the emotion of *fear.* Other emotions may be far more sophisticated, requiring very complex social intelligence, but it is thought-provoking that, fundamentally, a great many of the creatures we share the planet with also share our capacity for fear.

Apes on the Verge of Personhood?

To some of us, the issue of language is all-important; for some, it is the key difference between humans with a soul and animals without one; it was for Descartes, and the feeling persists to this day, which is probably why many ape language researchers feel that their research is what will earn the great apes membership in the personhood society. But not all philosophers have attached the same importance to language and reason.

In the late eighteenth century, the British philosopher and jurist Jeremy Bentham questioned the treatment animals were receiving and said, "The question is not, Can they *reason?* Nor Can they *talk,* but Can they *suffer?*" Bentham was not an early advocate of personhood for apes, and he wasn't much concerned about rights for animals, or human rights either, for that matter: Bentham was a *utilitarian,* and the utilitarian moral philosophy believes in striving *to maximize happiness and minimize misery for as many as possible.* This is known as the principle of utility. Bentham found the discussion of natural rights (see Chapter 9) abysmally flawed: For him, there was no such thing as "natural" rights. Humans are born with talents and potentials, but they are not born with "rights." Bentham ridicules the French Revolutionary Declaration of the Rights of Man and the Citizen for declaring that people have innate rights (and he could just as well have mentioned the U.S. Declaration of Independence, because it claims the same thing). For Bentham, we shouldn't talk fantasies about something that doesn't exist, but instead try to create a world where people lead happy lives if at all possible. It appears that Bentham actually misunderstood the very concept of rights that he was criticizing, because when we say that "All men are created equal," we are not really saying that everyone is equally strong or smart or tall, but that we should treat everyone in a political sense *as if* we are created equal; in other words, Bentham seems to think the concept of rights is descriptive, while it actually is normative.

Be that as it may, what Bentham wanted was to make people use a principle to increase happiness in the world by looking at the end result, the consequences of each action taken or considered: Which path will yield the most happiness for all involved or the least unhappiness? This utilitarian moral principle has become one of the most successful in Western history over the last 200 years, in spite of its built-in difficulties, which have become notorious: What if the only way you can create happiness for the many is to make a few miserable or even cause their death through suffering? In Bentham's philosophy that would be worth it, so that is what we must do, provided that the happiness of the many truly quantitatively outweighs the suffering of the few—a process known as the *hedonistic* or *hedonic calculus*. This philosophy appeals greatly to some because of its overall good will and practicality, and to others it is a travesty of potential human abuse. What concerns us here is that Bentham refused to limit his moral universe to "those who can reason or talk": He wants to include in the moral universe *anyone who can suffer.* And for Bentham this of course meant nonhuman animals; as you know, by the eighteenth century Descartes's view that animals feel no pain had very few proponents. Even Kant, who saw humans as the only rational creatures, had no problem assuming that nonhuman animals are capable of feeling pain, and Kant and Bentham were approximate contemporaries.

As you can probably tell, the focus has shifted here slightly from rights and personhood to the issue of preventing suffering. However, the idea of personhood and Bentham's idea of pain prevention come together in the philosophy of Peter Singer, a modern-day utilitarian and about as controversial as they come. Singer, a longtime animal activist, argues on the basis of Bentham's utilitarianism that since we know animals can feel pain, there is no excuse for not taking them into consideration as morally relevant beings. This means the end of painful animal lab experiments, of animals used for medical research, and of household products and cosmetics tested on animals.[10] Interestingly, one reason why Singer's name has become not only controversial, but even notorious in some circles, has to do with his view on human pain, not animal suffering: An Australian holding a position as professor at Princeton, Singer has publicly argued for legalization of euthanasia, on the basis of the utilitarian opinion that if you can't increase happiness for someone, the

least you can do is be allowed to decrease their misery. This viewpoint is shared by many other people and is not in itself terribly controversial today; however, Singer has also chosen to speak for brain-damaged newborns, advocating access to euthanasia for them. What is so problematic is that the infant, as opposed to the adult, can't *request* euthanasia, and it is up to parents and doctors to judge if the child can hope to live a quality life or not.

Here Singer is completely in accordance with his general theory of utilitarianism: Those who have a capacity for enjoying life should have it enhanced if possible; and those whose pain will outweigh their possibility of pleasure should have access to an easy death. He applies the principle to humans as well as to animals, and that means he would argue in favor of saving some animal who has a pronounced capacity for enjoying and experiencing life (such as a chimpanzee or a dog), over saving a human who has little or no capacity for such enjoyment, such as someone in an irreversible coma or someone with severe brain damage. This, to some people, is eminently sensible and compassionate, while to others it is nothing short of perverse, bordering on the Nazi philosophy of exterminating the "unwanted" in society, a comparison that Singer himself vehemently rejects.

Some years ago, this controversial scholar got together with Paola Cavalieri and other philosophers and scientists to create the *Great Ape Project,* which in essence combines Singer's interest in animal welfare with the idea of personhood. In *The Expanding Circle* (1981), Singer argued that as we have expanded our sense of who counts among humans from early tribal days to the twentieth century, it is now time to expand our moral concept of who counts into the other great apes (because of course humans are a biological subspecies of great apes; we are all primates, and the group of great apes includes gorillas, chimpanzees, bonobos—and humans).

The Great Ape Project (GAP) suggests three rights for all great apes: *The right not to be killed, the right not to be kept in captivity, and the right not to be tortured.* I myself was an advance reader on the Web site for the GAP Frequently Asked Questions (FAQ), and the questions surrounding these proposed rights are by no means easily answered. Even among the scientific ape research community, feelings are mixed; the ape linguist Sue Savage Rumbaugh is in favor of the project because she believes it will create protection for apes in the wild as well as further understanding of the close similarities between us and the apes; on the other hand, the primatologist Frans de Waal is against it, because he sees his ape behavioral research endangered by zealous animal activists ready to close all research facilities down regardless of how much these facilities respect the freedom of individual apes. Further, de Waal also sees inherent problems in the way the three rights are formulated. However, in the last few years of the twentieth century, Australia, New Zealand, and Great Britain all issued decrees that medical research using apes as test subjects would no longer be allowed; New Zealand went furthest in its declaration that apes are to be considered *fellow hominids.*

The right to life involves the right not to be killed frivolously (for sport, for research, or for entertainment) or for food. The right not to be held captive means closing ape compounds in zoos and (possibly) closing all facilities using apes as research subjects, including language research projects. The reason why that is controversial among GAP supporters is that language research helps us understand apes better, and the apes seem to thrive with the intellectual challenges. The right not to be tortured involves a ban on apes used in any kind of research involving medicine or household products. Now if the GAP succeeds in shifting public opinion toward personhood for apes, and apes can no longer be displayed in zoos or used in research, what are we supposed to do with all the surplus apes? We can't send them back to the wild, because they will perish; they have been acculturated within a human culture and wouldn't have a clue how to survive in the jungle. "Ape nations" will have to be created, great sanctuaries where the apes can create communities free of human involvement. That is the dream. In reality

(and the GAP advocates know this) such sanctuaries are already being created; but it is with heavy human involvement, because these apes have depended on humans since they were born, and this dependency doesn't stop just because they get more room to move about. As a way for us human primates to recognize the personhood of individual other great apes, GAP undertook a *Census 2001* for nonhuman great apes, as a way of accounting for and recognizing each ape living in the United States as an individual with a personal history. At the time of this writing, life stories of chimpanzees, bonobos, gorillas, and orangutans living in the United States are being compiled.

At this point it is necessary to look at some objections: For one thing, in its Declaration (see Primary Readings), GAP calls for an "expansion of the community of equals" to include apes. You will notice that I have used the expression "community of equals" in the title of this chapter. But what exactly is this community, and how are apes to be considered equals with humans? The Declaration states that "The community of equals is the moral community within which we accept certain basic moral principles or rights as governing our relations with each other." The term "equal" is thus a moral concept, signifying that our relationship to other "equals" should be governed by moral principles, but this leads to further questions. Equal in what way? Since we know that apes are not as intelligent as humans and don't function socially in exactly the same ways, GAP can't imply that they should have the *same rights* as people, such as to vote, run for office, marry whomever they want, receive an education, get a passport for overseas travel, and so forth. But there are many humans who can't make use of such rights, either, such as small children, mentally disabled individuals, or individuals with Alzheimer's. Then on the other hand, apes have abilities that humans don't have, such as enormous physical strength—so again, the concept of equality is a normative term, not a descriptive term: We are not physically or intellectually equals, but being morally equal means we have to consider other great apes as morally relevant persons and take their specific needs and interests into consideration, even if they are not capable of seeing us the same way.

But even so, declaring that a nonhuman animal species is from now on to be regarded as an "equal" to humans raises a red flag among many humans and not just because they think humans are unique in creation: The term "equality" is, in our part of the world, so laden with historical baggage that the issue tends to become very emotional. As I mentioned in the beginning of this chapter, we still have a way to go before all humans are considered members of the community of equals of Planet Earth. And for some humans who have themselves had an uphill battle being recognized as full members of that community (or whose ancestors did), the proposed inclusion of apes is nothing short of an affront, a mockery of their own battle. Advocates for an expansion of the community of equals will have to explain why an inclusion of apes is a credit to our humanity and not a diminishing of the human fight for equality. As similar as apes may be to humans, there is still a 2 percent genetic difference between us, and that 2 percent accounts for all of human culture; so of course we are not "the same," but we are similar enough that the similarity should be an argument in favor of protecting the apes as our cousins.

The second objection comes from concerned animal activists, claiming that the GAP focuses primarily on the similarities among *apes* and not among other social animals, or even other animals in general. They believe this to be an attitude of discrimination, a speciesist attitude. They would prefer that the GAP be considered a first step on a long journey ending in complete liberation of all nonhuman animals: no animals used for food, clothing, tools, or anything else. Within the GAP, this is the great watershed: Some supporters advocate giving tentative personhood to the great apes because of the undeniable genetic and behavioral similarities to humans, but for now withholding personhood from other species (this of course doesn't imply that other species are considered fair game; it only means that the

political issue of personhood is to be reserved for primates). Other supporters see this as a first step toward a ban on animal use altogether, arguing that essentially there is no difference between animal *use* and animal *abuse*.

A very relevant comment comes from professor of physiology and writer Jared Diamond, in *The Third Chimpanzee* (1992):

> If our ethical code makes a purely arbitrary distinction between humans and all other species, then we have a code based on naked selfishness devoid of any higher principle. If our code instead makes distinctions based on our superior intelligence, social relationships, and capacity for feeling pain, then it becomes difficult to defend an all-or-nothing code that draws a line between all humans and all animals. Instead, different ethical constraints should apply to research on different species. Perhaps it's just our naked selfishness, reemerging in a new disguise, that would advocate granting special rights to those animal species genetically closest to us. But an objective case, based on the considerations I just mentioned (intelligence, social relationships, etc.), can be made that chimps and gorillas qualify for preferred ethical consideration over insects and bacteria. If there's any animal species currently used in medical research for which a total ban on medical experimentation can be justified, that species surely is the chimpanzee.[11]

Is it possible to give personhood rights to a nonhuman species without undermining human rights? What happens when the rights of a human being collide with an ape's rights? If the concept of rights in any way involves the concept of duties (as Carl Cohen argues), then does an ape have to understand negative rights in order to have his or her own rights respected—meaning, does the ape have to be made to understand that you don't trespass on other apes' rights? And how do we punish an ape who has transgressed against other apes or humans? Should the apes have a right to mate in the sanctuaries, or should they be neutered/spayed so that there will be no more new generations of apes in captivity? The list of questions is endless, but that doesn't mean it isn't worthwhile to attempt some answers. We wouldn't approve of legal torture of our four-year-old children, and if indeed the emotional and rational intelligence of an ape reaches the level of a four-year-old human child, then these are issues we have to deal with before there are no more surviving apes in the wild—a day that will come a lot sooner than the day when we have to legislate whether the androids of the future are to be considered persons or machines.

A Personal Perspective

Writing a book about human nature has been on my list of "Things I'd like to do" since I was fourteen years old, and regardless of all the other things I have written until now—books, articles, papers, and more—writing these final pages is quite special for me. Initially I never thought of becoming a philosopher—I wanted to be a paleontologist. But because that education wasn't available in Denmark, and I had no intention of leaving my home country (rather ironic to think about at this time, now that I've been a U.S. resident for over twenty years), I decided to become an anthropologist instead. But taking mandatory classes in philosophy while studying about other cultures sealed my intellectual fate, and I switched to philosophy, something I have never regretted—in part because it allows you to examine in depth the philosophical issues underlying any subject you might ever become interested in. And Descartes himself said so, albeit with tongue in cheek: *Philosophy provides the means of speaking with probability about all things!* I realized that studying human nature from a philosophical viewpoint had become infinitely more faceted and, to me, more interesting, than if I had channeled my professional energy into paleoanthropology or anthropology. So my interest in human nature never went away—it just underwent a disciplinary adjustment. As part of this adjustment I realized that you can't study human nature without investigating what is *not* human nature: You have to set boundaries. And that, to me, became the true challenge: evaluating the criteria for these bound-

aries. I think I have probably made that apparent throughout this book.

So have we now covered all relevant subjects within philosophy of human nature? Hardly. We have focused on some of the issues that thinkers have been engaged in over the years in the Western tradition and some issues occupying thinkers in other traditions. But there are "human universals," characteristics that all or most humans share, that we haven't even approached, and I would like to think that you might find inspiration to pursue such subjects on your own. Examples include the human propensity to decorate our skin with paints or tattoos, the custom of wearing clothes, the custom of cooking or otherwise treating our food before eating it, the entire tradition of expressing ourselves through pictorial art and music, and the traditions we resort to during trying times when we experience the loss of loved ones: how to treat the dead and how to properly grieve over them. In common for all these examples is that they are part of the human condition—but in this book we have focused primarily on the underlying layers that make us into beings who cook, grieve, create art, and so forth and the ways in which we have developed into people who set up rules for how to be a proper human being. I have selected the chapter topics based partly on what the Western tradition has focused on as essential questions about human nature and partly on my own interests, as someone who has her professional training in philosophy, an educational acquaintance with anthropology and human evolution, and a lifelong passion for stories.

Some philosophical subjects can be presented in an objective form regardless of one's personal viewpoint; philosophy instructors are skilled at presenting all kinds of theories without necessarily putting their own stamp of approval or disapproval on anything—partly because we are used to being adversarial and criticizing all theories for their weaknesses, including our own. But some subjects call for a personal engagement more than others, because they deal with abstract viewpoints that have enormous practical consequences for living individuals. You'll have noticed that throughout this book I have pointed out the possible moral and political consequences of abstract, descriptive theories, and some of those consequences are of particular significance; to me, Chapters 5 (race) and 6 (gender) examine subjects with significant practical impact. As you have probably already noticed, I also consider the subject of this final chapter to have such an impact. This means that I find myself personally engaged in the issue of personhood and its political and moral consequences. So while I've tried to present several opposing viewpoints fairly, I don't pretend to be neutral on the issue of personhood any more than I am neutral on the issue of race or gender. For the human race I find myself emotionally and intellectually engaged in the quest for global equality and mutual respect, echoing Kant's philosophy of never treating anyone merely as a means to an end. But lately I have also found myself engaged in the question of personhood being expanded beyond the human realm: Apes have demonstrated consciousness, self-awareness, "self-motivated activity," and a form of technical and social intelligence that needs to be taken into consideration, if we use the same kind of criteria to let *humans* qualify for personhood. However, as we have seen in this chapter, this proposed expansion creates a new set of issues that shouldn't be minimized. In essence, it boils down to whether we consider the fundamental criterion for personhood to be *similarity to humans*—in other words, using a norm of human nature as our measure—or whether we are (or should be) willing to conceive of "equals" who are not "like us"? Wherever the debate will take us, we should keep in mind that we now tend to judge history on how humans have treated members of their own species in the past. Now is a good time to begin clarifying our criteria for personhood and evaluate whether we are being arbitrary in the way we judge some beings to be persons and others nonpersons.

An argument worth considering comes from a rather unlikely source, a professor specializing in human neurology, Antonio R. Damasio. You encountered him in Chapter 7 as a critic of Descartes. While humans can think deeper thoughts and express more with our language that any other creature, Damasio says, we shouldn't consider ourselves so far removed in our nature from other beings on the planet:

> Yet long before the dawn of humanity, beings were beings. At some point in evolution, an elementary consciousness began. With that elementary consciousness came a simple mind; with greater complexity of mind came the possibility of thinking, and, even later, of using language to communicate and organize thinking better. For us then, in the beginning it was being, and only later it was thinking. And for us now, as we come into the world and develop, we still begin with being, and only later do we think. We are, and then we think, and we think only inasmuch as we are, since thinking is indeed caused by the structures and operations of being.[12]

So for some scholars of the twenty-first century, as well as for Darwin, the life of the mind is a *continuum:* We are certainly the creature who excels in using its mind, and there is nothing wrong with extolling the virtues of the human mind, because it is a magnificent evolutionary achievement. But it doesn't mean we are alone on this planet: Other beings have some capacity for language and some understanding of self. Many more beings think in some rudimentary way, and even more have an elementary form of consciousness; and all living creatures share what some philosophers call *being.* And this existential foundation links us to all other living beings on the planet: The life of the mind is directly related to the way we live in this world as physical beings or, as Maxine Sheets-Johnstone says, to the way we move deliberately. Some of us are viewed as persons, and others are not; where do we draw the line? Given that we may be the only beings on earth who tell stories about ourselves to make sense of life, it will be interesting to see what stories will be told about personhood in the near future. Will Western authors and screenwriters continue the cultural trend of telling stories about humans with the underlying moral of fundamental equality—and will we begin to see stories appear more frequently about persons who are not human? In this book you have already seen a few of those, and the final Narrative, *Bicentennial Man,* is just such a tale. Clearly, such stories have a dimension in addition to their entertainment value: They serve as thought experiments, ethical explorations of the future—whether we're talking about giving apes the status of persons or opening up the theoretical possibility of treating future robots and aliens as equals—or whether we are just pondering what makes us human in order to ensure that all humans are regarded as ends in themselves.

Since we humans are the ones who are capable of raising the issue of personhood, it is up to us to define it in a way that will not come back to haunt us, as so many divisions between "us" and "them" have done in the course of human history, Western as well as non-Western. The future may well judge us on where we decided to draw the line between persons and nonpersons.

Study Questions

1. Identify examples of human beings who, in the course of history as well as today, have been deprived of full personhood recognition.

2. Discuss Kant's personhood criterion of rationality: What are the advantages, and what are the problems?

3. How do we demonstrate self-awareness? Explain the mirror recognition test, and discuss its implications. Would you agree that dogs and cats have no self-awareness, based on the test?

4. Can we think without using words? Explain why or why not.

5. Should Bentham's criterion of capacity for suffering guide us in determining who counts, morally? Does capacity for suffering equal personhood? Why or why not?

6. How may the future judge the way we draw the line between persons and nonpersons?

Primary Readings and Narratives

The first Primary Reading is an excerpt from Descartes's *Discourse on Method* in which he argues that animals have no rational capacity. The second is taken from Kant's *Grounding for the Metaphysics of Morals,* where Kant argues that all humanity should be treated as ends in themselves. The third is an excerpt from Roger Fouts's *Next of Kin* in which he argues that gestures are the fundamental form of language for humans and apes. The fourth is the *Declaration on Great Apes* in its entirety; and the final Primary Reading is a report issued by Francine Patterson about the ape Koko. The Narratives are a summary of the film *El Norte* and a summary of the film *Bicentennial Man.*

✍ *Primary Reading*

Discourse on Method

RENÉ DESCARTES

Excerpt from Part 5. Translated by Donald A. Cress. 1637.

I have given a sufficient explanation for everything in the treatise that I had intended earlier to publish. And I went on to show of what sort the fabric of the nerves and muscles of the human body must be, so that the animal spirits within might have the force to move its

members; thus one observes that heads, shortly after being severed, still move about, and bite the earth, even though they are no longer alive. I also showed what changes ought to take place in the brain to cause wakefulness, sleep, and dreams; how light, sounds, odors, tastes, heat, and all the other qualities of external objects can imprint various ideas through the medium of the senses; how hunger, thirst, and the other internal passions can also send their own ideas; what needs to be taken for the common sense, where these ideas are received, for the memory which conserves them, and for the imagination which can change them in various ways and make new ones out of them, and by the same means, distributing the animal spirits in the muscles, make the members of this body move in as many different ways, each appropriate to the objects presented to the senses and to the internal passions that are in the body, as our own bodies can move, without being led to do so through the intervention of our will. This ought not seem strange to those who, cognizant of how many different automata or moving machines the ingenuity of men can devise, using only a very small number of parts, in comparison to the great multitude of bones, muscles, nerves, arteries, veins, and all the other parts which are in the body of each animal, will consider this body like a machine that, having been made by the hand of God, is incomparably better ordered and has within itself movements far more admirable than any of those machines that can be invented by men.

And I paused here particularly to show that, if there were such machines having the organs and the shape of a monkey or of some other nonrational animal, we would have no way of telling whether or not they were of the same nature as these animals; if instead they resembled our bodies and imitated so many of our actions as far as this is morally possible, we would always have two very certain means of telling that they were not, for all that, true men. The first means is that they would never use words or other signs, putting them together as we do in order to tell our thoughts to others. For one can well conceive of a machine being so made as to pour forth words, and even words appropriate to the corporeal actions that cause a change in its organs—as, when one touches it in a certain place, it asks what one wants to say to it, or it cries out that it has been injured, and the like—but it could never arrange its words differently so as to answer to the sense of all that is said in its presence, which is something even the most backward men do. The second means is that, although they perform many tasks very well or perhaps can do them better than any of us, they in-

evitably fail in other tasks; by this means one would discover that they do not act through knowledge, but only through the disposition of their organs. For while reason is a universal instrument that can be of help in all sorts of circumstances, these organs require a particular disposition for each particular action; consequently, it is morally impossible for there to be enough different devices in a machine to make it act in all of life's situations in the same way as our reason makes us act.

For by these two means one can know the difference between men and beasts. For it is very remarkable that there are no men so backward and so stupid, excluding not even fools, who are unable to arrange various words and to put together discourse through which they make their thoughts understood; but, on the other hand, there is no other animal, perfect and well bred as it may be, than can do likewise. This is not due to the fact that they lack the organs for it, for magpies and parrots can utter words just as we can, and still they cannot speak as we can, that is, by giving evidence of the fact that they are thinking about what they are saying; although the deaf and dumb are deprived just as much as—or more than—animals of the organs which aid others in speaking, they are in the habit of inventing for themselves various signs through which they make themselves understood to those who are usually with them and have the leisure to learn their language. And this attests not merely to the fact that animals have less reason than men but that they have none at all. For one sees that not much of it is needed so as to be able to speak; given that one notices an inequality among animals of the same species, just as is the case among men, and that some are easier to train than others, one could not believe that a monkey or a parrot which is the most perfect of its species would not equal in this one of the most stupid of children, or at least a child with a disturbed brain, unless their soul were of an utterly different nature from our own. And one should not confuse words with natural movements that display the passions and can be imitated by machines as well as by animals; nor should we think, as did some ancients, that animals speak, although we do not understand their language; for if that were true, since they have many organs similar to our own, they could also make themselves understood by us just as they are by their peers. It is also remarkable that, although there are many animals that show more inventiveness than we do in some of their actions, one nevertheless sees that they show none at all in many other actions; consequently, the fact that they do something better than we do does not prove that they have a mind; for were this the case, they would be more rational than any of us and would excel us in everything; but rather it proves that they do not have a mind, and that it is nature that acts in them, according to the disposition of their organs—just as one sees that a clock made only of wheels and springs can count the hours and measure time more accurately than we can with all our powers of reflective deliberation.

After this, I described that rational soul and showed that it can in no way be drawn from the potentiality of matter, as can the other things I have spoken of, but that it ought expressly to be created; and how it is not enough for it to be lodged in the human body, like a pilot in his ship, unless perhaps to move its members, but it must be joined and united more closely to the body so as to have, in addition, feelings and appetites similar to our own, and thus to make up a true man. As to the rest, I elaborated here a little about the subject of the soul because it is of the greatest importance; for, after the error of those who deny the existence of God (which I believe I have sufficiently refuted), there is nothing that puts weak

minds at a greater distance from the straight road of virtue than imagining that the soul of animals is of the same nature as ours and that, as a consequence, we have no more to fear nor to hope for after this life than have flies or ants; whereas, while one understands how much they differ, one understands much better the reasons that prove that our soul is of a nature entirely independent of the body and, consequently, that it is not subject to die with it. Now, since one cannot see any other causes that might destroy it, one is naturally led to judge from this that the soul is immortal.

Study Questions

1. How can we tell the difference between humans and animals, according to Descartes?

2. How do we know that animals can't speak, according to Descartes? Would you agree? Explain.

3. How does Descartes link this theory of intelligence and speech to his theory of the two substances (thinking and extended substance), which you know from Chapter 7?

4. According to Descartes, can a nonhuman animal ever reach the conclusion "I think; therefore, I am"? Why or why not? Is he correct?

Primary Reading

Grounding for the Metaphysics of Morals

IMMANUEL KANT

Excerpt. Translated by James W. Ellington. 1993.

Now I say that man, and in general every rational being, exists as an end in himself and not merely as a means to be arbitrarily used by this or that will. He must in all his actions, whether directed to himself or to other rational beings, always be regarded at the same time as an end. All the objects of inclinations have only a conditioned value; for if there were not these inclinations and the needs founded on them, then their object would be without value. But the inclinations themselves, being sources of needs, are

so far from having an absolute value such as to render them desirable for their own sake that the universal wish of every rational being must be, rather, to be wholly free from them. Accordingly, the value of any object obtainable by our action is always conditioned. Beings whose existence depends not on our will but on nature have, nevertheless, if they are not rational beings, only a relative value as means and are therefore called things. On the other hand, rational beings are called persons inasmuch as their nature already marks them out as ends in themselves, i.e., as something which is not to be used merely as means and hence there is imposed thereby a limit on all arbitrary use of such beings, which are thus objects of respect. Persons are, therefore, not merely subjective ends, whose existence as an effect of our actions has a value for us; but such beings are objective ends, i.e., exist as ends in themselves. Such an end is one for which there can be substituted no other end to which such beings should serve merely as means, for otherwise nothing at all of absolute value would be found anywhere. But if all value were conditioned and hence contingent, then no supreme practical principle could be found for reason at all.

If then there is to be a supreme practical principle and, as far as the human will is concerned, a categorical imperative, then it must be such that from the conception of what is necessarily an end for everyone because this end is an end in itself it constitutes an objective principle of the will and can hence serve as a practical law. The ground of such a principle is this: rational nature exists as an end in itself. In this way

man necessarily thinks of his own existence; thus far is it a subjective principle of human actions. But in this way also does every other rational being think of his existence on the same rational ground that holds also for me; hence it is at the same time an objective principle, from which, as a supreme practical ground, all laws of the will must be able to be derived. The practical imperative will therefore be the following: Act in such a way that you treat humanity, whether in your own person or in the parson of another, always at the same time as an end and never simply as a means.

Study Questions

1. Explain what Kant means by saying that every rational being should never be treated merely as a means, but should always be treated as an end.

2. What are the implications for human beings? How would Kant evaluate today's world situation in terms of treating humanity as an end in itself?

3. What are the implications for nonhuman animals?

Primary Reading

Next of Kin

ROGER FOUTS

Excerpt, 1997.

For thousands of years, people have noticed two curious facts about human communication. First, infants begin gesturing—showing, pointing, glancing—before they begin speaking, and second, gesture is a kind of universal language that all of us fall back on when we can't communicate through a common spoken language. Both of these observations led to the very old idea that language may have originated in gesture.

Modern linguists, however, dismissed the gestures of early hominids as unrelated to the spoken language that followed. And they also dismissed the first gestures of modern-day infants as unrelated to the words those children later form. This discounting of gesture was partly due to an inherent bias of speakers—

whether they are linguists, child psychologists, or anthropologists—who tend to equate language with speech. The power of words is vested with a great deal of magic and mystique in every human culture. Speech, after all, is the distinguishing trait of humankind in creation myths around the world. It seems difficult for most people to imagine Adam in the Bible naming the animals with signs instead of words. In addition to this bias, gesture looked like an evolutionary dead end to linguistics until they discovered, in the 1960s, that sign languages are every bit as complex and grammatical as spoken languages. (Darwin himself did not believe that spoken language evolved from gesture, probably because sign languages were so poorly understood during his time.)

Considering how unpopular and misunderstood gesture has always been, it's not surprising that the two main schools of thought about language origins both focus on speech. The "early origins" school says that language first appeared more than one million years ago, along with stone tools and the enlarging brain of *Homo habilis* or early *Homo erectus*. The "recent origins" school argues that language arose only in the past hundred thousand years among fully modern, big-brained humans who had fully descended vocal tracts that enabled them to produce speech.

Both of these theories of a vocal origin for language run into several major evolutionary obstacles. Pick up almost any book on the origins of language and you will find the author grappling with the first problem for the vocal approach: *How did the grunts of apes evolve into the words of hominids?* This doesn't seem too difficult—perhaps "ugh ugh" became "ma ma"—until you realize that an ape's involuntary grunts, like human screams, are controlled by the limbic system, the most primitive part of the brain. If our power of speech evolved directly out of the limbic system we'd never be able to convey a simple message like "There's a lion standing behind you" without bursting into uncontrollable alarm calls or screams. And in fact, in the human brain, voluntary speech is not controlled by the limbic system.

Fortunately for us, language didn't have to evolve out of the grunts of apes, or we might still be grunting. Washoe's ability to sign showed us that even though our common ape ancestors may not have been able to control their food barks or alarm calls, they could communicate with voluntary and visible gestures. We know that evolution always follows the path of least resistance, so our earliest quadrupedal, hominid ancestors must have communicated with their hands, just like their quadrupedal ape cousins did. Once these early hominids began walking upright, their hands were freed to make even more elaborate gestures, eventually stringing together sequences of gestures to convey more specific information.

Here, in the expansion of the language system, is where the vocal schools run into a second, and even more formidable, evolutionary roadblock. Even if words somehow emerged from ape grunts, and even if humans built up a large vocabulary for naming different objects, this naming ability is still a far cry from a rule-governed language. How did early humans get

from "I" and "bear" to "I caught the bear" or "The bear caught me"? How did they make the great leap from individual symbols to a logical system that can create millions of meanings?

This leap is so vast that most linguists say random chance must have been involved. The linguist Derek Bickerton has said that "syntax must have emerged in one piece, at one time—the most likely cause being some kind of mutation that affected the organization of the brain." In other words, we hit the jackpot, biologically speaking, and a universal grammar was the result. Other linguists have suggested an even more unlikely scenario: a *series* of fortuitous mutations that hardwired a universal grammar into the hominid brain over time.

But experts in sign language, who assume a gestural origin for language, can explain the emergence of syntax in a much simpler, more commonsense way. You can test it yourself right now by following this suggestion of David Armstrong, William Stokoe, and Sherman Wilcox from their book, *Gesture and the Nature of Language*:

> *"If you will, swing your right hand across in front of your body and catch the upraised forefinger of your left hand."*

By enacting this gesture, say the authors, you have just illustrated the most primitive form of syntax. "The dominant hand is the agent (it acts), its swinging grasp is the action (verb), and the stationary finger is the patient or object. The grammarians' symbolic notation for this is familiar: SVO [subject-verb-object]."

It is easy to imagine our earliest ancestors using this gesture to communicate, HAWK CAUGHT GOPHER. And they might have modified this sentence with adjectives (two fingers for two gophers) and adverbs (raised eyebrows for expressing disbelief: HAWK SOMEHOW CAUGHT GOPHER). These variations on a relationship are the beginnings of language as we know it.

The above example illustrates the essential difference between a primitive vocal system and a primitive gestural system: words symbolize objects; gestures symbolize relationships. Getting from spoken words to spoken grammar involves a huge leap, which is why linguists assume that one or more major brain mutations were necessary. But getting from *gestures* to grammar is no leap at all. Gesture *is* grammar. Early humans didn't need to have the grammatical rule for subject-object-verb encoded in their brains if they could already perceive that relationship in the world and mirror it in a gesture.

Over time, this gestural grammar would naturally become more complex, and the gestures themselves would evolve from gross motor movements to more precise motor movements. Driven by this, the human brain would get better and better at producing long sequences of fine motor movements. And that sequential cognition would produce, as Gordon Hewes theorized, a dividend: the ability to make and use more complex tools.

This is the point where the theory of a gestural origin for language traditionally ran into its own roadblock. It was fairly easy to see that as the gestural system became increasingly precise it would eventually produce today's modern sign languages. But how did a gestural system lead to *spoken* languages? This mystery was solved by my autistic students, Mark and David. Just as their signing triggered their first meaningful vocal sounds, our ancestors' precise gestures and toolmaking triggered precise movements in their tongues. My own guess is that our species began shifting to speech about two hundred thousand years ago. That date coincides with the appearance of markedly improved toolmaking among early *Homo sapiens*. These specialized stone tools were made by a process that required a precision grip, exacting pressure, and the kind of eye-finger-thumb coordination that Doreen Kimura found to be associated with vocal speech. In other words, the early humans who produced these tools possessed the kind of neural mechanisms that would have also let them produce words.

At this point, vocal words became a part of our ancestors' gestural communication. And there were immediate advantages even to primitive speech. Those who spoke could communicate words when their hands were full or when the listener's back was turned. Eventually, evolutionary pressures would bring about the innovations in our anatomy that were necessary for full-blown speech: we would develop a fully descended vocal tract and the ability to speak and comprehend words at increasing rates of speed. Over tens of thousands of years, spoken words would slowly crowd out gestures and become the dominant mode of human communication. In the meantime, humans would blend precise gestures and spoken words into a unified language system.

This prolonged overlap of gesture and speech overcomes the third and final hurdle that arises for any vocal origins theory. Before a spoken language could function on its own, it would require a low enough vocal tract, a minimal number of phonemes, and the ability to transmit those sounds quickly. In the meantime, our ancestors would have been speaking with a limited number of confusing sounds at a very slow rate and with lots of errors in comprehension—much like a modern two-year-old child. These inefficient and arbitrary sounds would probably not have conferred any adaptive advantage on our ancestors—*unless they were able to make their meanings clear by using gestures.* Without a gestural system to supplement speech in its first millennia of use, it probably would not have survived. As Gordon Hewes once wrote, "If all adults were stuck with the kinds of speech deficiencies normal enough in early childhood, we would probably still be using a well-developed sign language."

This gestural scenario explains how language might have evolved along an unbroken continuum over millions of years, without resorting to unlikely mutations or impossible leaps. It's also consistent with Charles Darwin's radical thesis that human language emerged from other forms of animal communication. Language is firmly rooted in the anatomy, cognition, and neuromuscular behavior of our common ape ancestors. Without this evolutionary continuity it is impossible to explain why modern-day chimpanzees are able to manipulate linguistic signs.

The continuity between gesture and speech also explains our own modern-day use of gesture whenever spoken language proves useless. As our species' oldest form of communication, gesture still functions as every culture's "second language." For example, when we are in a foreign country where we don't speak the language, standing near a noisy jet airplane, scuba diving beneath the ocean, or sending signals on the baseball diamond, we automatically revert to gesturing. And when the mechanisms for vocal language break down in any one individual—the deaf, the autistic, the mute, or any number of others—that person naturally adopts an entire *system* of gestural communication: sign language.

Human infants also illustrate the continuity between gesture and speech through that famous dictum of biology: *ontogeny recapitulates phylogeny.* The history of the individual retraces the evolutionary history of the species. Through the development of his body and behavior, each human infant roughly reenacts the multimillion-year journey of our ancestors from gesture of the hands to gesture of the tongue.

The human infant is born with a vocal tract like a chimpanzee's and is incapable of speech. He first communicates by facial expression and simple hand gestures. At five or six months of age, an infant exposed to sign language begins forming his first signs. At this same age, the larynx begins its long descent into the child's throat (it will not achieve the adult position until fourteen years of age), but he will not control his tongue sufficiently to form his first word until he is about one year old. Once he beings speaking he does not suddenly stop gesturing with his hands. Just as our hominid ancestors did, the child strings together words and gestures to make himself understood. Then, sometime between the ages of two and three, the vocal apparatus fully kicks in and there is an explosion of words that add to the gestural signals that we never stop using. Gesture of the hands and gesture of the tongue are forever inseparable.

It is important to point out that human language, whether signed or spoken, is not in any sense "better" than the communication system of wild chimpanzees.

Evolution is not a ladder of "improvement" culminating in the human species; it is an ongoing process of adaptation for millions of related species, each on its own evolutionary pathway. Modern human communication and modern chimpanzee communication—like our different ways of walking, eating, and reproducing—are each an ideal product of six million years of adaptation. And both of these specialized products can be traced back to the gestures of our common ape ancestor. As a result, every time we speak or sign, we are displaying our evolutionary kinship with Washoe and other chimpanzees.

Study Questions

1. Which form of language came first, according to Fouts, speech or gestures? Explain why.

2. Why does a complex gesture illustrate a primitive form of syntax, according to Fouts? Explain.

3. Some scientists have determined that since *Homo erectus* wasn't as evolved in neural control of their breathing as humans are, then they had no language, in spite of the fact that the area in their brain that controls language (Broca's area) was developed. What might Fouts say to that conclusion?

Primary Reading

A Declaration on Great Apes

THE GREAT APE PROJECT

Reprint of Web document, 2001. (http://www.greatapeproject.org/gapdeconline.html)

We demand the extension of the community of equals to include all great apes: human beings, chimpanzees, gorillas and orang-utans. The "community of equals" is the moral community within which we accept certain basic moral principles or rights as governing our relations with each other and enforceable at law. Among these principles or rights are the following:

1. *The Right to Life.* The lives of members of the community of equals are to be protected. Members of

the community of equals may not be killed except in very strictly defined circumstances, for example, self-defense.

2. *The Protection of Individual Liberty.* Members of the community of equals are not to be arbitrarily deprived of their liberty; if they should be imprisoned without due legal process, they have the right to immediate release. The detention of those who have not been convicted of any crime, or of

those who are not criminally liable, should be allowed only where it can be shown to be for their own good, or necessary to protect the public from a member of the community who would clearly be a danger to others if at liberty. In such cases, members of the community of equals must have the right to appeal, either directly or, if they lack the relevant capacity, through an advocate, to a judicial tribunal.

3. *The Prohibition of Torture.* The deliberate infliction of severe pain on a member of the community of equals, either wantonly or for an alleged benefit to others, is regarded as torture, and is wrong.

Study Questions

1. What are three rights suggested for all great apes, and what are some of the implications of these rights?

2. What does GAP mean by the "community of equals"? Can someone be a member of a community without being able to understand his or her role as a member? Explore the question, taking the theory of *contractarianism* by Carl Cohen into consideration (see chapter text).

3. Would you consider granting these rights to great apes? Why or why not? Can you think of alternative approaches?

Primary Reading

The Case for the Personhood of Gorillas

FRANCINE PATTERSON AND WENDY GORDON

Excerpt from Web site, http://www.koko.org. June 3, 2000.

We present this individual for your consideration: She communicates in sign language, using a vocabulary of over 1,000 words. She also understands spoken English, and often carries on "bilingual" conversations, responding in sign to questions asked in English. She is learning the letters of the alphabet, and can read some printed words, including her own name. She has achieved scores between 85 and 95 on the Stanford-Binet Intelligence Test. She demonstrates a clear self-awareness by engaging in self-directed behaviors in front of a mirror, such as making faces or examining her teeth, and by her appropriate use of self-descriptive language. She lies to avoid the consequences of her own misbehavior, and anticipates others' responses to her actions. She engages in imaginary play, both alone and with others. She has produced paintings and drawings which are representational. She remembers and can talk about past events in her life. She understands and has used appropriately time-related words like *before, after, later,* and *yesterday.*

She laughs at her own jokes and those of others. She cries when hurt or left alone, screams when frightened or angered. She talks about her feelings, using words like happy, sad, afraid, enjoy, eager, frustrate, mad, and, quite frequently, love. She grieves for those she has lost—a favorite cat who has died, a friend who has gone away. She can talk about what happens when one dies, but she becomes fidgety and uncomfortable when asked to discuss her own death or the death of her companions. She displays a wonderful gentleness with kittens and other small animals. She has even expressed empathy for others seen only in pictures.

Does this individual have a claim to basic moral rights? It is hard to imagine any reasonable argument that would deny her these rights based on the description above. She is self-aware, intelligent, emotional, communicative, has memories and purposes of her own, and is certainly able to suffer deeply. There is no reason to change our assessment of her moral status if I add one more piece of information, namely that she is not a member of the human species. The person I have described—and she is nothing less than a person to those who are acquainted with her—is Koko, a 26-year-old lowland gorilla.

Study Questions

1. Did it affect your attitude toward this report when you realized that the "she" referred to is a gorilla? Should it? Why or why not?

2. Comment on the following two aspects of the report: Koko laughs at her own jokes, and she is uncomfortable talking about death. What does that imply about these so-called typical human characteristics?

3. Go back to Chapter 1, and look at the list of characteristics that have been considered typically human. Which ones does Koko share, and which ones does she seem not to share? Can you think of essential human characteristics that Koko doesn't possess?

Narrative

El Norte

GREGORY NAVA (DIRECTOR), GREGORY NAVA AND ANNA THOMAS (SCREENWRITERS)

Film, 1983 (re-release announced for 2001).

El Norte has been celebrated as one of the ground-breaking films about the plight of Central American political refugees and called a modern *Grapes of Wrath* by film critic Roger Ebert. On the Internet an enthusiast praises it as "the best movie ever made." It has been planned for re-release for years, but at the time of this writing it is a rare find in video rental stores. Even so, I prefer not to let you know the ending of the film, hoping that it will be made available on video/DVD soon and that you will choose to watch it yourself.

Enrique and Rosa, young adults, live with their mother and father in a small Indian village in Guatemala; the fabric of their lives seems solid and in harmony with the rest of the village. But we also know from the start that their father, Arturo, is not happy with the political situation. One evening he is preparing for a secret meeting while they are having a good time with visitors: Rosa's godmother Josefita and her husband. Josefita, as always, can't stop talking about *El Norte,* the United States, which she knows well—from hand-me-down issues of *Good Housekeeping.* Everyone has a flushing toilet! Everyone has electricity! And everyone has a car, even if they're poor! Rosa loves the stories, but everyone else is getting tired of them.

Arturo leaves for his meeting, and the mother is obviously disturbed. Enrique runs after him, and they have a talk on the path toward the old hacienda where the meeting is to take place. Arturo tells his son what is going on: Their land is being stolen by rich people from elsewhere. Arturo has worked in Mexico, and he knows: "For the rich, the peasant is just a pair of arms—that's all they think we are, arms for work. They treat their animals better than they do us. For many years we've been trying to make the rich understand that poor people have hearts and souls . . . that they feel. . . . We are human, all of us." Enrique kisses his father's hand, and we feel the portent: Something dreadful is about to happen. Arturo goes off to the meeting after sending Enrique home. At the meeting he and other male villagers make plans for a revolution, without knowing that they have been betrayed by one of their own: The army descends on their meeting, hunting down all the participants and killing them, including Arturo. Enrique, sick with worry, finds his father's head hanging from a tree, as a warning to other rebellious peasants. While trying to retrieve the head, he is attacked by a soldier and fights back. The soldier dies, and Enrique now knows he can't stay in the village. When their mother is kidnapped with other wives (and presumably killed), Rosa and Enrique decide to flee the village, for El Norte. Enrique tells Rosa that then they will escape abuse—and they will make a lot of

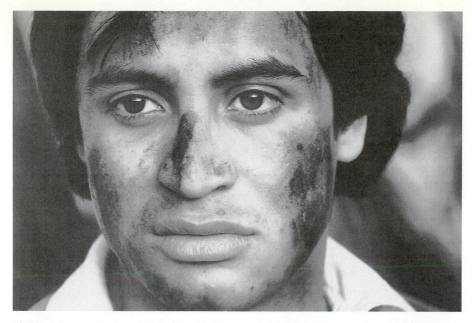

El Norte, Cinecom International Films, 1983/2001. Mayan Indians Enrique (David Villalpando) and his sister Rosa barely escape a massacre by the military in their homeland Guatemala. Together they make the journey to what they think of as the Promised Land, *El Norte:* The United States.

money. Rosa goes to Josefita and tells her about their plans and begs for help: Josefita takes all the money she had hidden away for her own future in El Norte and gives it to Rosa. Meanwhile, Enrique is also being enriched—by the advice of old Ramón who used to work in the United States. Ramón tells him to pretend they come from Mexico, so they won't be deported to Guatemala, and the way to sound like a Mexican is to use a certain sexual expletive in every sentence!

The next part of the film has the two traveling through Mexico. They are treated like country bumpkins by the truck driver who takes them north, but he is indeed using that certain sexual expletive in every sentence. On the bus to Tijuana a Mexican man calls them "bloody Indians." In Tijuana they fall for the friendly charm of a *coyote,* a human smuggler, and tell him they have lots of money. When he takes them across the border that night and robs them, he finds that all they have is the equivalent of $20—but to them that's a lot of money. The U.S. immigration officers (*La Migra*) send them back to Mexico after ascertaining that they are indeed Mexican (because Enrique uses

that expletive all the time), but soon after they cross with the help of an old friend of Ramón's, undergoing a grueling ordeal of sneaking through the old sewer pipes to San Diego.

Moving on to Los Angeles, Rosa finds work in a clothing factory, and Enrique starts working in a restaurant. They rent a small apartment, dirty, with bare lightbulbs, and a filthy toilet—but they are overjoyed: Josefita was right that everyone has a flushing toilet and electricity in El Norte! The dream is coming true.

At the restaurant, Enrique finds that inner tensions abound: the Mexicans and the Chicanos (Mexican Americans) hate each other. Rosa barely escapes a raid on the factory by La Migra, but with a newfound friend, Nacha, she now hires out as a cleaning lady in wealthy American homes. Nacha suggests that she stop dressing and looking like an Indian, so Rosa buys new clothes and changes her hairdo. Both Enrique and Rosa take state-sponsored night classes to learn English. And when Enrique gets a promotion, it looks as if their troubles are over—now nothing can stop them, and they will be treated like human beings, "with heart and soul," as his father wanted. But it seems that fate strikes down those who are cocky: Enrique is turned in as an illegal by the Chicano who was passed over for promotion and must hide out—and in the meantime, Rosa comes down with a fever, and Nacha takes her to the hospital. Does this mean that the dream is coming to an end? Have Rosa and Enrique found the respect they were looking for? I hope you will have a chance to see this film and judge for yourself. I will give you the barest of hints: Enrique tells Rosa that you have to keep hoping—but for the migrant worker there seems to be no resolution, just more work, haunted by the memories of home.

Study Questions

1. Enrique and Rosa go north because they hope to be treated as human beings—and make money. Do they find what they are looking for? What will it take for someone to feel that he or she is being treated as a human being?

2. *El Norte* has been called a modern *Grapes of Wrath*. What are the similarities, and what are the differences?

3. In the entire film there is no mention of the fact that Enrique and Rosa are breaking the law, trying to get into the United States illegally. Should this have been emphasized? Why or why not?

4. As you can tell, characters in the film are stereotyping each other: Guatemalans are stereotyping Mexicans, Mexicans are stereotyping Guatemalans and Chicanos, Americans are stereotyping everyone south of the border, and they in turn are stereotyping Americans. A visiting Mexican professor in literature, Alex Ramirez, recently talked about the widespread discrimination against Mexican Americans among Mexicans. Does the film actually exploit these stereotypes, or does it try to bridge the gap of differences?

 *Narrative*

Bicentennial Man

CHRIS COLUMBUS (DIRECTOR) AND
NICHOLAS KAZAN (SCREENWRITER)

Film, 1999, based on short story by Isaac Asimov and novel by Isaac Asimov and Robert Silverberg. Summary.

We began with a story of a robot needing the protection of personhood to save his life: Data from *Star Trek*. We end with a similar story, but with a different twist: A story of how much an artificial human is willing to give up in order to be considered a true human being. There are many ways to approach the issue of wishing to be considered a human being and receive recognition as an equal, and I find the story of Andrew, who wishes to obtain what is a natural heritage for the rest of us, to be a moving story of what it means to be human—emotionally, intellectually, and politically. For the sake of the point made about Andrew and his quest for humanity, I have chosen to tell the entire story, without omitting the ending.

In the not-too-distant future, a delivery van brings a big coffinlike box to the Martin family home. Mr. Martin calls his wife and two daughters to the front door and reveals the content of the box: an android, all shiny and metallic, to help with the housework and to be a nanny for the kids. The smallest girl is frightened but fascinated; the older girl is less than impressed; several of her friends' families already have one. The little girl misunderstands the word "android" and thinks it is an "andrew," and the name sticks: He is Andrew from now on. In a display worthy of a large audience, with much pomp and circumstance, scaring the family half to death, Andrew's built-in holographic projector introduces him with the three laws of robotics:

A robot may not injure a human being or through inaction cause a human being to come to harm; a robot must obey all human orders except when those orders come in conflict with the first law; a robot must protect itself so long as doing so does not conflict with the first two laws.

But that same evening, the big girl, "Miss," resenting being looked after by a robot, tricks Andrew into harming *himself:* She orders him to jump out the second-story window, which he does; he is capable of self-repair, but the incident leaves him with a fear of heights for years to come. As a lesson, Dad tells the girls that Andrew is not a person, but property; however, property is important, so in this household he will be treated as a person.

The little girl, "Little Miss," and Andrew also seem to be off to a bad start: On the beach she shows him her prized possession, a miniature glass horse. His big mechanical hands lose their grip, and it falls and shatters on the rocks. Seeing her distress and anger, Andrew is himself distressed and gets an idea: From a piece of driftwood he fashions a little horse (while studying up on wood carving at a furious robot pace). That evening he gives the horse to Little Miss, and from then on they are each other's best friend; she gives him one of her favorite stuffed toys, the dog Woofie, and he understands the gesture. When Martin sees Andrew's talent at woodcarving and finds him listening to opera at night on an old phonograph he has repaired himself, he realizes that Andrew has begun to develop and think for himself. Martin takes Andrew to the Robotics company to find out why he has developed a social awareness and artistic skills; the manager is clearly disturbed, offers to replace Andrew, displays a fear of a lawsuit, and in the end is eager to get his hands on the robot to undo his uniqueness. To the manager, he is merely a "household appliance," but we also sense that he is interested in whatever fortune he can make out of Andrew's uniqueness—either way, Andrew is to him merely a tool, a means to an end. Martin, "Sir" to Andrew, warns him never to touch Andrew, or he will have a lawsuit on his hands.

Now Sir begins to see it as a responsibility of his to educate Andrew. There is much the robot doesn't understand: Why do humans use imprecise language?

What is humor? What is sex? What is life? To the best of his ability, Sir tries to teach Andrew, with varying success. He explains to Andrew that illness and death are not things he has to worry about—he is immortal.

Fifteen years have passed. The robot has built wood-carved clocks so that the house is full of them. As always, Andrew refers to himself as "one," not I. "One is pleased to be of service" is a standard comment of his—even when we understand that he is disappointed, or facetious, over the lack of human comprehension. When the family wants to sell his clocks, Little Miss points out that he should get to keep the money himself, even if he is a machine. After some soul-searching, Sir talks to the family lawyer, and an account is set up for Andrew. In no time he has made a fortune.

When Little Miss wants Andrew to be an usher for her wedding (and Andrew loves Little Miss and doesn't think much of her future husband), Andrew realizes a few things: For one thing, he wants a physical upgrade, so he will look more human according to the newest technology, and his bank account will take care of the expenses. For another, he likes wearing the tux, and wants Sir's permission to wear clothes from now on. Little Miss gets married, and Andrew and Sir sit alone after the wedding, each a comfort to the other.

Now twelve more years pass, and Andrew has reached a new turning point: He wants to obtain his freedom. Sir, getting on in years, doesn't understand the problem: Andrew can do whatever he wants, so why does he want to be free? But it is Sir himself who has put Andrew on this road: He has given Andrew history books to study, and Andrew has learned that humans have fought and died for freedom, so "One wants to purchase one's freedom." But Sir wants no money. He gives Andrew his freedom, and then sends him away, his feelings hurt. Andrew tells him that any time Sir might need him, "I'll be there." Andrew has started calling himself "I." He builds himself a little house by the beach, but it will be another sixteen years before Sir calls for him, on his deathbed. Holding Andrew's hand, Sir tells him that he was right in wanting his freedom.

Now Andrew is haunted by the thought that he is unique and sets out on a long journey to find others of his kind. But every robot with his serial number has been terminated, and no one seems to have developed consciousness. A perky female robot, Galatea, turns out to have only a personality chip, not a real awareness. But her owner is a different matter: Rupert Burns is the son of the original designer of Andrew's series, and he is able to give Andrew a new makeover, this time making him look exactly like a human being, with latex-type skin. (During the makeover process Andrew gets a shock: He looks at himself in the mirror without a face on his head and screams in terror, "I saw the inner me!")

Many years have passed, and Andrew returns home, to a changed household: Little Miss is old, and her granddaughter Portia, who looks just like her when she was young, isn't charmed by Andrew at all, even if he looks human. Little by little Portia and Andrew become friends after all. But now it is Little Miss's turn to say goodbye to life, and the tragedy of Andrew's immortality is beginning to gnaw at him: Everyone he loves dies, and he can't cry over them. Portia is getting engaged, even if she is emotionally attracted to Andrew, because she "can't invest her emotions in a machine." So it's back to Rupert: Andrew wants to be biologically human, and with his superb intelligence, he designs biological, artificial organs which in themselves will help humanity live longer—and Galatea entertains them to distraction by singing "If I only had a heart" from *The Wizard of Oz* while Andrew is being made over, again. He is given a nervous system and then a digestive system and functioning genitals. He now pursues Portia and convinces her that she loves him. They make love—and his stomach growls, he breaks wind, and he has a huge breakfast: He finally feels human. But he also heeds Portia's sad comment that nobody will accept them as a couple, so he embarks on his final quest: to become legally recognized as a human being.

Andrew takes his case to the World Congress. The Congress points out that he is not genetically human; he responds by pointing out that many members of the Congress have artificial organs that he himself has developed and are thus not fully human, either. The World Congress responds: Perhaps his heart is part human, but not his magnificent artificial brain. Andrew is immortal; and while immortal robots can be accepted, an immortal human being can't—that is too alien. So his petition is denied.

Years later: Portia is getting old and tells Andrew that death is normal for humans—that there is an order to things. So now Andrew goes to Rupert for the last time: Rupert says that every human being sooner or later does something monumentally stupid, but he complies, and makes Andrew's mechanical organism susceptible to aging, exclaiming, "Welcome to the human condition!"

Next time we see Andrew, he has grown old. There is another hearing in the World Congress. He could have lived forever, but he explains that "I'd rather die a man than live forever as a machine; to be acknowledged for who and what I am, no more, no less." With that recognition, he will live or die with dignity. The Congress promises to reconsider; and as Andrew's two-hundredth birthday approaches and he lies dying, with Portia herself on life support, Congress pronounces him the oldest living *human being*. This validates their marriage and acknowledges his humanity—but the ruling comes too late: Andrew is dead, without having heard the news. But as Portia says while preparing to shut off her life support, he didn't need to hear it—he already knew who and what he was.

Study Questions

1. Why is it a turning point when Andrew, having achieved his freedom, begins to call himself "I" instead of "one"? (You might refer to Chapter 7: "A Sense of Self.")

2. A favorite choice of artists in film and literature is to explore human nature by telling a story about someone who wants to be human but isn't. Do you think this is an interesting way to explore the subject, or do you think it distracts from the real issue? Explain. Can you think of more stories of the same kind?

3. Andrew spends his entire long life trying to become human, but, genetically, that is something he will never be. Had Andrew at his hearing had a Captain Picard (*Star Trek,* "The Measure of a Man"), who could have argued on his behalf that he should be considered a *person*, do you think the World Congress would have agreed sooner? What is the difference between requesting to be considered a *human*

being and requesting to be considered a *person?* How might Andrew respond? Can you be a *person* without human DNA? Can you be a *human being* without human DNA? Explain. (Remember the distinction between descriptive and normative!)

4. What do you think of the ruling of the World Congress that an immortal robot can be tolerated, but not an immortal human being? Is there "an order to things"? Is death inevitably part of the human condition? Why or why not?

5. If you recall, Data in *Star Trek* was compared to Pinocchio. There is a parallel to Andrew that is even closer: the Tin Man from *The Wizard of Oz*. If we haven't picked up on it before, we get a clue when Galatea sings the Tin Man's song. The Tin Man seeks the Wizard, because he would like to get a heart (and the Lion would like to get courage, and Scarecrow wants a brain). At the end, it is clear that the Tin Man has had a heart all along and needs no magic to acquire one. Is Andrew a Tin Man?

Review

Key Issues in Chapter 10

Theories of Human Nature as Political Statements

- The political question of personhood: Is it now inclusive for all humans? And are there persons who are not human?

- *Who Counts and Who Doesn't?* Personhood is a normative concept; we have been using education and legislation to attempt to change human nature so that we treat others with respect and as equals. We have free will to make a moral choice, despite any predetermined tendencies. So far, the world has failed to live up to standards of equality.

- *Throwaway People?* Examples of human beings who have been treated as less than persons in recent history include victims of the Tuskegee Syphilis Experiment, Navajo uranium miners, illegal immigrants, crime victims in poor neighborhoods, the homeless, and others. A suggested remedy is to personalize victims by focusing on their names and life stories.

What Does It Take to Qualify for Personhood?

- Where do we draw the line between persons and nonpersons? Is it an either-or?

- *Rationality as a Criterion for Personhood: Immanuel Kant.* Kant's criterion is rationality: A rational being should never be treated simply as a means to an end, but always as an end in himself or herself. Beings who aren't rational should be regarded as things, not persons. Twentieth-century Kantians introduced *contractarianism*: If you can agree to a contract and take on the responsibility, you are a person, so animals aren't persons. Counterargument by David Hume: If animals and humans behave in similar ways, and humans are considered rational, then animals can think too.

- *The Criterion of Self-Awareness.* Does Data from *Star Trek* have self-awareness, intelligence, and consciousness? The criteria established for Data are similar to the five criteria for personhood suggested by Mary Ann Warren: capacity for reason and for feeling pain; self-awareness; capacity for communication about a variety of issues; self-propelled activity; social consciousness. So Data qualifies as a person, but fetuses don't, and neither do newborn infants.

- The test of self-awareness is the mirror recognition test. Children at the age of two recognize themselves, and so do apes.

- *Language as a Personhood Criterion.* Language is broadly defined, including gestures and ASL. Can we think rationally without using words? We do so in technical thinking, the mystical experience, and emotional experiences. So if humans can think without using language, so perhaps can some other animals.

- *Evaluating Animal Language Capacity.* The 2000 symposium on animal intelligence reversed a hundred-year-old trend toward skepticism. The issue of language definition includes whether grammar is a defining element of language (Chomsky's theory is challenged by ape language researchers). In fairy tales, religion, and new scientific research, we hear stories of animals speaking. Study of animals understanding human speech and communicating were undermined by the case of Clever Hans. Washoe the chimpanzee, Nim Chimpsky (when allowed to socialize), and Koko the gorilla have offered examples of true communication.

- *Apes on the Verge of Personhood.* Jeremy Bentham's criterion for moral inclusion is capacity for suffering. Peter Singer's argument for inclusion of apes into personhood is based on Bentham's ideas and has expanded into the Great Ape Project, which aims to protect apes' rights to life, liberty, and freedom from torture. Two objections to the goals of the Great Ape Project are that giving apes personhood undermines human uniqueness and that giving apes personhood merely expands human speciesism.

- *A Personal Perspective.* Humans are at the far end of the continuum that is the life of the mind, but all creatures share the condition of being. We as humans may be judged by the future on how we draw the line between persons and nonpersons.

Primary Readings

- Descartes, *Discourse on Method.* Descartes argues that animals have no rational capacity and no capacity for speech.

- Kant, *Grounding for the Metaphysics of Morals.* All rational beings should be treated as persons, but nonrational beings should be regarded as things.

- Fouts, *Next of Kin.* The language of gestures predates the language of speech.

- *Declaration on Great Apes.* The community of equals should include all great apes: human beings, chimpanzees, gorillas, and orang-utans. All should have the right to life, to liberty, and to protection from torture.

- Francine Patterson and Wendy Gordon, "The Case for the Personhood of Gorillas." Koko the gorilla has many traits we consider essentially human, so she should be considered a person.

Narratives

- *El Norte,* film. Immigrants to the United States from Guatemala struggle to get across the border and make a life for themselves in Los Angeles.

- *Bicentennial Man,* film. The robot Andrew tries to educate himself as a human being over the course of his long life and eventually petitions for recognition as a human.

Notes

1. Immanuel Kant, *Grounding for the Metaphysics of Morals,* trans. James W. Ellington (Indianapolis: Hackett 1981), pp. 35–36.
2. Ibid.
3. David Hume, *A Treatise of Human Nature* (Oxford: Clarendon Press, 1960), part 1, section 16.
4. René Descartes, *Discourse on Method,* trans. Donald A. Cress (Indianapolis: Hackett, 1980), part 5, 57–58.
5. Ian Tattersall, *Becoming Human* (San Diego: Harcourt Brace, 1998), p. 172.
6. Even if apes don't have opposable thumbs like humans do, apes have shown themselves to be quite capable of handling and making tools of many kinds.
7. Roger Fouts, *Next of Kin* (New York: William Morrow, 1997), p. 274.
8. Ibid., p. 277.
9. Francine Patterson, *Koko's Kitten* (New York: Scholastic, 1985).
10. Peter Singer has himself added an element to the debate about animal suffering that—to some people—is a relevant and logical outcome of his utilitarian philosophy; for others, it just shows that Singer is primarily intent on being controversial (not that the two are incompatible). Singer argues, in a 2001 review of Michael Dekker's book, *Dearest Pet,* that sexual relations between humans and animals should be judged by utilitarian standards: If it causes harm to the individual animal, it should be avoided; but if it causes no harm or causes pleasure, we should reevaluate our instinctual aversion toward the phenomenon, as we have reevaluated so many other sexual practices that used to be considered offensive—since it implies no offense to our status and dignity as human beings. Critics have pointed out that because there can be no question of a mutual sexual relationship between a human and an animal given the emotional complexity of adult human sexuality, sex with animals is as abusive as sex with children, regardless of whether or not harm is caused.
11. Jared Diamond, *The Third Chimpanzee* (New York: HarperCollins, 1992), p. 30.
12. Damasio, *Descartes' Error* (New York: Avon, 1994), p. 248.

Selected Bibliography

Allen, Roger McBride. *Orphan of Creation*. New York: Simon & Schuster, 1988.

Anderson, Hans Christian. *Eventyr og Historier*. 16 vols. Odense, Denmark: Skandinavisk Bogforlag, Flensteds Forlag, n.d.

Antony, Louise M. "'Human Nature' and Its Role in Feminist Theory." In *Philosophy in a Feminist Voice*, edited by Janet Kourany. Princeton: Princeton University Press, 1998.

Aquinas, Thomas. *Summa Theologica*. Second & revised edition, 1920. Online edition. Copyright 2000 by Kevin Knight. Retrieved from the World Wide Web: http://www.newadvent.org/summa

"Archaeology News: Hybrid Humans?" *Archaeology*, July–August 1999.

Ardrey, Robert. *African Genesis*. New York: Dell, 1967.

Arendt, Hannah. *The Human Condition*. Chicago: University of Chicago Press, 1998.

Aristotle. *Nicomachean Ethics*. Translated by W. D. Ross. In *The Works of Aristotle*. Vol. 2. Chicago: Encyclopedia Britannica, 1952.

———. *On the Generation of Animals*. Translated by Arthur Platt. In *The Works of Aristotle*. Vol. 2. Chicago: Encyclopedia Britannica, 1952.

———. *On the Soul*. Translated by J. A. Smith. In *The Works of Aristotle*. Vol. 1. Chicago: Encyclopedia Britannica, 1952.

Bæksted, Anders. *Guder og Helte I Norden*. Poltikens Forlag, 1978.

Beauvoir, Simone de. *The Second Sex*. Translated by H. M. Parshleyy. New York: Knopf, 1952.

Begley, Sharon. "The Parent Trap." *Newsweek*, 7 September 1998.

Bekoff, Marc, and Jamieson, Dale, editors. *Readings in Animal Cognition*. Cambridge, England: Bradford, 1996.

Belenky, Mary Field, et al. *Women's Ways of Knowing: The Development of Self, Voice, and Mind*. New York: Basic Books, 1986.

Belluck, Pam. "Kansas Will Delete Mention of Evolution in Class Curricula." The *San Diego Union-Tribune*, 12 August 1999.

Berofsky, Bernard, editor. *Free Will and Determinism*. New York: Harper & Row, 1966.

Berteaux, John, and Doppelt, Gerald, editors. *Dimensions of Culture I*. La Jolla: University of California, San Diego, College Custom Series, 1995.

Birch, Christopher. "Memory and Punishment." *Criminal Justice Ethics* 19, no. 2, Summer/Fall 2000.

Blakeslee, Sandra. "Experts Learn More on Why Memory Changes, and How." New York Times News Service, *San Diego Union-Tribune*, 22 September 2000.

Blum, Lawrence. "Antiracism, Multiculturalism, and Interracial Community: Three Educational Values for a Multicultural Society." Lecture given November 1991. Distinguished Lecture Series, 1991–92. Office of Graduate Studies and Research, University of Massachusetts at Boston.

Bly, Robert. *Iron John: A Book About Men*. Reading, Mass: Addison-Wesley, 1990.

Boyd, Robert S. "Animal Intelligence Getting More Credit." *San Diego Union-Tribune*, 9 February 2001.

Braine, David. *The Human Person: Animal and Spirit*. Notre Dame: University of Notre Dame Press, 1992.

Campbell, Joseph. *The Masks of God*, Vols. I–IV. New York: Penguin Books, 1959–1969.

Camus, Albert. *The Myth of Sisyphus*. Translated by Justin O'Brien. New York: Knopf, 1955.

Colapinto, John. *As Nature Made Him: The Boy Who Was Raised as a Girl*. New York: HarperCollins, 2000.

Collins, Patricia Hill. *Black Feminist Thought: Knowledge, Consciousness, and the Politics of Empowerment*. London: HarperCollins, 1990.

Cook, Gareth. "Chimps May Have a Clue of Each Other's Thoughts." *San Diego Union-Tribune*, 15 November 2000.

Cornell, Steven, and Hartmann, Douglas. *Ethnicity and Race*. Thousand Oaks, Calif.: Pine Forge Press, 1998.

Crimshaw, Jean. *Philosophy and Feminist Thinking*. Minneapolis: University of Minneapolis Press, 1986.

D'Souza, Dinesh. *The End of Racism*. New York: The Free Press, 1995.

Dahl, A. P. *Fra Homer til Orpehus—en linje i gammel græsk religiøsitet*. Copenhagen: Gyldendalske Bogforlag: Nordisk Forlag, 1940.

Damasio, Antonio R. *Descartes' Error: Emotion, Reason, and the Human Brain*. New York: Avon, 1994.

Darwin, Charles. *The Descent of Man*. 1871. New York: Prometheus Books, 1998.

Delamotte, Eugenia, Meeker, Natalie, and O'Barr, Jean, editors. *Women Imagine Change*. New York: Routledge, 1997.

Descartes, René. *Discourse on Method.* 1637. Translated by Donald A. Cress. Indianapolis: Hackett, 1985.

———. *Meditations on First Philosophy.* 1641. Translated by Donald A. Cress. Indianapolis: Hackett, 1985.

Diamond, Jared. "Race Without Color." *Discover,* November 1994.

———. *The Third Chimpanzee.* New York: HarperCollins, 1992.

Dostoyevsky, Fyodor. *Crime and Punishment.* New York: Bantam, 1959.

Douglas, John, and Olshaker, Mark. *The Anatomy of Motive.* New York: Scribner, 1999.

———. *The Cases That Haunt Us.* New York: Scribner, 2000.

Edge, Hoyt. "Individuality in a Relational Culture." In *Tribal Epistemologies,* edited by Helmut Wautischer. Aldershot, England: Ashgate, 1998.

Eisler, Riane. *The Chalice and the Blade.* New York: Harper-Collins, 1987.

Eliade, Mircea. *A History of Religious Ideas.* Vols. 1–3. Translated by Willard R. Trask, Alf Hiltebeitel, and Diane Apostolos-Cappadona. Chicago: University of Chicago Press, 1978–1985.

Encyclopedia of Philosophy. Vols. 1–8. New York: Macmillan, 1972.

Erdoes, Richard, and Ortiz, Alfonso, editors. *American Indian Myths and Legends.* New York: Pantheon Books, 1984.

Eze, Emmanuel Chukwudi, editor. *Race and the Enlightenment, A Reader.* Cambridge, Mass.: Blackwell, 1997.

Faludi, Susan. *Stiffed: The Betrayal of the American Man.* New York: Perennial, 2000.

Foucault, Michel. *Madness and Civilization.* Translated by Richard Howard. New York: Random House, 1965.

Fouts, Roger. *Next of Kin: What Chimpanzees Have Taught Me About Who We Are.* New York: William Morrow, 1997.

Frankenberg, Ruth. *White Women, Race Matters: The Social Construction of Whiteness.* Minneapolis: University of Minnesota Press, 1993.

Furrow, Dwight. *Against Theory: Continental and Analytical Challenges in Moral Philosophy.* New York: Routledge, 1995.

Gilligan, Carol. *In a Different Voice.* Cambridge: Harvard University Press, 1982.

Golding, William. *Lord of the Flies.* New York: Wideview/Perigee Books, 1954.

Gorner, Peter. "Talking the Talk." *Chicago Tribune,* 25 August 2000.

Gould, Stephen Jay. "The Geometer of Race." *Discover,* November 1994.

Great Mysteries of the Past. Edited by Gardner Associates. New York: Readers Digest, 1991.

Grimwood, Ken. *Replay.* New York: Berkley Books, 1988.

Hanley, Richard. *The Metaphysics of Star Trek.* New York: Basic Books, 1997.

Hannaford, Ivan. *Race: The History of an Idea in the West.* Baltimore: Johns Hopkins University Press, 1996.

Hauser, Larry. "Why Isn't My Pocket Calculator a Thinking Thing?" *Minds and Machines* 3, no. 1, February 1993.

Hinman, Lawrence M. *Contemporary Moral Issues: Diversity and Consensus.* Upper Saddle River, N.J.: Prentice-Hall, 1996.

Hobbes, Thomas. *Leviathan.* New York: Prometheus Books, 1988.

Hoffmann, Ole, editor. "Perspektiv." *Illustreret Videnskab* 1 (1996): 89.

Hublin, Jean-Jacques. "The Quest for Adam." *Archaeology,* July–August 1999.

Huxley, Aldous. *Brave New World.* New York: Bantam, 1953.

Ibsen, Henrik. *Peer Gynt.* In *The Plays of Ibsen,* Vol. IV. Translated by Michael Meyer. New York: Washington Square Press, 1986.

Jersild, P. C. *Darwins ofullbordade.* Stockholm: Bonnier Alba, 1997.

Johanson, Donald, and Johanson, Lenora. *Ancestors: In Search of Human Origins.* New York: Villard Books, 1994.

Kafka, Franz. *The Basic Kafka.* New York: Washington Square Press, 1979.

Kant, Immanuel. *Grounding for the Metaphysics of Morals.* Translated by James W. Ellington. Indianapolis: Hackett, 1993.

———. *Prolegomena to Any Future Metaphysics.* A revision of the Carus translation with introduction by Lewis White Beck. Indianapolis: Bobbs-Merrill, 1950.

———. *Religion Within the Limits of Reason Alone.* Translated by Theodore M. Greene & Hoyt H. Hudson. New York: Harper Torchbooks, 1934.

Kipling, Rudyard. *The Jungle Books.* Vols. 1 & 2. New York: Doubleday, 1948.

Kramer, Samuel Noah. *Mythologies of the Ancient World.* New York: Anchor, 1961.

Krippner, Stanley. "Waking Life, Dream Life, and the Construction of Reality." *Anthropology of Consciousness* 5, no. 3 (1994).

Lai, Tracy. "Asian American Women Not for Sale." In *Changing Our Power: An Introduction to Women's Studies,* edited by Jo Whitehorse Cochran, Donna Langston, and Carolyn Woodward. Dubuque: Kendall/Hunt, 1988.

LeGuin, Ursula. *The Telling.* New York: Harcourt, 2000.

Leake, Jonathan. "Scientists Teach Chimpanzee to Speak English." *The Sunday Times* (London), 25 July 1999.

Leake, Jonathan, and Cohen, Julie. "So Pleased to Meet You: The Talking Chimp." *The Sunday Times* (London), 25 July 1999.

Leakey, Meave. "Perspectives on the Past." *Archaeology,* July–August 1999.

Leakey, Richard. *The Origin of Humankind.* New York: Basic Books, 1994.

Leakey, Richard, and Lewin, Roger. *People of the Lake.* New York: Avon, 1978.

Leeming, David. *Mythology.* New York: Newsweek Books, 1976.

———. *The World of Myth.* New York: Oxford University Press, 1990.

Lerner, Gerda. *The Creation of Feminist Consciousness.* Oxford: Oxford University Press, 1993.

———. *The Creation of Patriarchy.* Oxford: Oxford University Press, 1986.

Lewin, Roger. *Bones of Contention.* New York: Touchstone Books, 1987.

Lloyd, Genevieve. *The Man of Reason.* Minneapolis: University of Minnesota Press, 1984.

Lopez, Donald S., Jr. *Buddhism in Practice.* Princeton: Princeton University Press, 1995.

Lorenz, Konrad. *On Aggression.* New York: Bantam, 1967.

MacIntyre, Alasdair. *After Virtue,* 2nd ed. Notre Dame: University of Notre Dame Press, 1984.

———. *Whose Justice? Whose Rationality?* Notre Dame: University of Indiana Press, 1988.

MacIntyre, Ben. "An Interview With Panbanisha." *The Times* (London), 28 July 1999.

———. *Forgotten Fatherland: The Search for Elisabeth Nietzsche.* New York: HarperCollins, 1992.

Maddaloni, Arnold. "Is Human Nature Really Improving?" *San Diego Union-Tribune,* 19 March 1998.

Mahowald, Mary Briody, editor. *Philosophy of Woman,* 3rd ed. Indianapolis: Hackett, 1994.

Malcomson, Scott. "The Color of Bones: How a 9,000-Year-Old Skeleton Called Kennewick Man Sparked the Strangest Case of Racial Profiling Yet." *New York Times Magazine,* 2 April 2000.

Malinowski, Bronislaw. "Myth in Primitive Psychology." In *Magic, Science, and Religion.* Garden City, N.Y.: Doubleday Anchor, 1954.

Malraux, André. *Man's Fate (La Condition Humaine).* Paris, 1933.

Marger, Martin N. *Social Inequality: Patterns and Processes.* Mountain View, Calif.: Mayfield, 1999.

Masson, Jeffrey Moussaieff, and Susan McCarthy. *When Elephants Weep: The Emotional Lives of Animals.* New York: Delta, 1995.

McDonald, Rob. "Stereotypes on Both Sides of Border, Professor Says." *The Spokesman-Review,* 2 May 2001.

McKernan, Maureen. *The Amazing Crime Trial of Leopold and Loeb.* New York: Signet Books, 1957.

Merleau-Ponty, Maurice. *Phenomenology of Perception.* Translated by Colin Smith. New York: Routledge & Kegan Paul, 1962.

Midgley, Mary. *Beast and Man: The Roots of Human Nature.* London: Routledge, 1995.

———. *The Ethical Primate.* New York: Routledge, 1994.

Mink, Louis. "Everyman His or Her Own Annalist." In *On Narrative,* edited by W. J. T. Mitchell. Chicago: University of Chicago Press, 1981.

Mitchell, W. J. T., editor. *On Narrative.* Chicago: University of Chicago Press, 1981.

Mithen, Steven. *The Prehistory of Mind: The Cognitive Origin of Art and Science.* London: Thames & Hudson, 1996.

Morgan, Elaine. *The Aquatic Ape.* New York: Stein & Day, 1984.

———. *The Descent of Woman.* New York: Stein & Day, 1972.

Nietzsche, Friedrich. *Beyond Good and Evil.* Translated by Walter Kaufmann. New York: Vintage, 1989.

———. *Thus Spoke Zarathustra.* Translated by Walter Kaufmann. New York: Penguin, 1966.

Nye, Andrea. *Feminist Theory and the Philosophies of Man.* New York: Routledge, 1989.

Olshansky, S. Jay, Carnes, Bruce A., and Butler, Robert N. "If Humans Were Built to Last." *Scientific American,* March 2001.

Ore, Tracy, editor. *The Social Construction of Difference and Inequality: Race, Class, Gender, and Sexuality.* Mountain View, Calif.: Mayfield, 2000.

Pagels, Elaine. *Adam, Eve, and the Serpent.* New York: Vintage, 1988.

Patterson, Francine. *Koko's Kitten.* New York: Scholastic, 1985.

Patterson, Francine, and Gordon, Wendy. "The Case for Personhood of Gorillas." Koko.org report, 3 June 2000.

Pinker, Steven. *Words and Rules.* New York: Basic Books, 1999.

Plato. *Republic.* Translated by Benjamin Jowett. Chicago: Encyclopedia Britannica, 1952.

———. *The Republic of Plato.* Translated by Francis MacDonald Cornford. London: Oxford University Press, 1970.

Pontoppidan, Henrik. "Ørneflugt." In *Håndbog i dansk litteratur.* Edited by Falkenstjerne and Borup Jensen. Copenhagen: G. E. C. Gad, 1961.

Popper, Karl. *The Poverty of Historicism.* London: Routledge & Kegan Paul, 1972.

Poulsen, Frederik. *Den delfiske gud og hans helligdom.* Copenhagen: Gyldendal, 1924.

"Racial Profiling: Disturbing Issues Need More Study by SDPD." Editorial, *San Diego Union-Tribune,* 18 May 2001.

Radner, Daisie and Michael. *Animal Consciousness.* New York: Prometheus Books, 1996.

Rand, Ayn. *Atlas Shrugged.* New York: Signet, 1957.

Rawls, John, "Justice as Fairness." *Philosophy and Public Affairs* 14, no. 3, 1985.

———. *A Theory of Justice.* Cambridge: Harvard University Press, 1971.

Ricoeur, Paul. *Oneself as Another.* Translated by Kathleen Blamey. Chicago: University of Chicago Press, 1992.

Rosen, Claire Mead. "The Eerie World of Reunited Twins." *Discover,* September 1987.

Rosenstand, Nina. *The Moral of the Story: An Introduction to Ethics,* 3rd ed. Mountain View, Calif.: Mayfield, 2000.

———. *Mytebegrebet.* Copenhagen: GADs Forlag, 1981.

Rousseau, Jean-Jacques. *Discourse on the Origin of Inequality.* Translated by Donald A. Cress. Indianapolis: Hackett, 1983.

———. *On the Social Contract.* Translated by Donald A. Cress. Indianapolis: Hackett, 1983.

Rydell, Robert W. *All the World's a Fair: Visions of Empire at American International Expositions 1876–1916.* Chicago: University of Chicago Press, 1984.

Rÿser, Rudolph C. "Observations on 'Self' and 'Knowing.'" In *Tribal Epistemologies,* edited by Helmut Wautischer. Aldershot, England: Ashgate, 1998.

Sartre, Jean-Paul. *Existentialism Is a Humanism.* Translated by P. Mairet. New York: The Philosophical Library, 1949.

Savage-Rumbaugh, Sue, and Lewin, Roger. *Kanzi: The Ape at the Brink of the Human Mind.* New York: Wiley, 1994.

Scheler, Max. *Man's Place in Nature.* New York: Farrar, Straus, & Giroux, 1961.

Schneider, Bart, editor. *Race: An Anthology in the First Person.* New York: Crown, 1997.

Sheets-Johnstone, Maxine. *The Primacy of Movement.* Philadelphia: John Benjamins, 1999.

———. *The Roots of Power.* Chicago: Open Court, 1994.

———. *The Roots of Thinking.* Philadelphia: Temple University Press, 1990.

Shephardson, Mary. "The Gender Status of Navajo Women." In *Women and Power in Native North America,* edited by Laura F. Klein and Lillian A. Ackerman. Norman: University of Oklahoma Press, 1995.

Shreeve, James. "Terms of Engagement." *Discover,* November 1994.

Skinner, B. F. *Science and Human Behavior.* New York: Macmillan, 1953.

Smedley, Audrey. *Race in North America: Origin and Evolution of a World View.* Boulder: Westview Press, 1993.

Solomon, Robert. *Introducing Philosophy.* Fort Worth: Harcourt Brace Jovanovich, 1993.

Spinoza, Benedict de (Baruch). *Ethics, Including the Improvement of the Understanding.* Translated by R. H. M. Elwes. New York: Prometheus Books, 1989.

Steinberg, Stephen. *The Ethnic Myth: Race, Ethnicity, and Class in America.* Boston: Beacon Press, 1989.

Stern, Andrew. "Talk Like the Animals." *Reuters,* 24 August 2000.

Stevenson, Leslie, editor. *The Study of Human Nature: A Reader.* New York: Oxford University Press, 1981.

Stevenson, Robert Louis. *Strange Case of Dr. Jekyll and Mr. Hyde and Other Stories.* 1886. London: MacDonald, 1950.

Stone, Irving. *Clarence Darrow for the Defense.* New York: Bantam, 1958.

Stone, Merlin. *Ancient Mirrors of Womanhood.* Boston: Beacon Press, 1979.

Strong, J. S. *Experience of Buddhism.* Belmont, Calif.: Wadsworth, 1995.

Stryk, Lucien, editor. *World of the Buddha.* New York: Anchor Books, 1969.

"Study of Monkeys Hints at a Thinking Ability Without Language." *San Diego Union-Tribune,* 24 October 1998.

Tannen, Deborah. *The Argument Culture.* New York: Random House, 1998.

———. *I Only Say This Because I Love You.* New York: Random House, 2001.

———. *You Just Don't Understand.* New York: Morrow, 1990.

Tattersall, Ian. *Becoming Human: Evolution and Human Uniqueness.* San Diego: Harcourt Brace, 1998.

———. "Rethinking Human Evolution." *Archaeology,* July–August 1999.

Taylor, Charles. *Sources of the Self.* Cambridge: Harvard University Press, 1989.

Taylor, Paul W. *Principles of Ethics.* Belmont, Calif.: Wadsworth, 1975.

Titus, Harold, Smith, Marilyn, and Nolan, Richard. *Living Issues in Philosophy,* 9th ed. Belmont, Calif.: Wadsworth, 1995.

Tobar, Hector. "A Battle Over Who Is Indian." *Los Angeles Times,* 4 January 2001.

Waal, Frans de. *Good Natured: The Origins of Right and Wrong in Humans and Other Animals.* Cambridge: Harvard University Press, 1996.

Walker, Alice. *The Temple of My Familiar.* New York: Pocket Books, 1990.

Wasserstrom, Richard A. *Philosophy and Social Issues.* Indianapolis: University of Notre Dame Press, 1980.

Waters, Mary C. "Optional Ethnicities: For Whites Only?" In *Origins and Destinies,* edited by Sylvia Pedraza and Ruben G. Rumbaut. Belmont, Calif.: Wadsworth, 1996.

Watson, J. B. *Behaviorism.* New York: Norton, 1925.

Wautischer, Helmut, editor. *Tribal Epistemologies.* Aldershot, England: Ashgate, 1998.

Will, George F. "Racial Profiling or Crime Fighting?" *San Diego Union-Tribune,* 19 April 2001.

Wilson, Edward O. *On Human Nature.* Cambridge: Harvard University Press, 1978.

Zack, Naomi. *Thinking About Race.* Belmont, Calif.: Wadsworth, 1998.

Web Sites

ABC News: Latest Evolution Battlefield: http://abcnewsgo.com/sections/science/DailyNews/evolutiondebate990812.html

Behaviorism Links: http://www.chapman.edu/wilkinson/psych/faculty/ac/rellswor/Behav.htm

Bertrand Russell: "A Free Man's Worship": http://www.users.drew.edu/~jlenz/fmw.html

A Clockwork Orange: http://www.filmsite.org/cloc.html

David Hume: *A Treatise of Human Nature:* http://panoramix.univ-paris1.fr/CHPE/Textes/Hume/treat0.html

Dictionary of Philosophy of Mind: Materialism: http://www.artsci.wustl.edu/~philos/MindDict/materialism.html

Equality Beyond Humanity: The Great Ape Project International: http://greatapeproject.org

Injured Migrant Survives Desert: http://news.excite.com/news/ap/010610/12/waiting-for-rescue

Internet Encyclopedia of Philosophy: Jean-Jacques Rousseau: http://www.utm.edu/research.iep/r/rousseau.htm

Internet Encyclopedia of Philosophy: Thomas Aquinas: http://www.utm.edu/research/iep/a/Aquinas.htm

Jean-Paul Sartre: Philosophy and Existentialism: http://members.aol.com/DonJohnR/Philosophy/Sartre.html

John B. Watson: http://userwww.sfsu.edu/~rsauzier/WatsonB.html

John Locke: *An Essay Concerning Human Understanding:* http://humanum.arts.cuhk.edu.hk/Philosophy/Locke/echu

John Locke: *An Essay Concerning Human Understanding:* http://www.orst.edu/instruct/phl302/texts/locke/locke1/contents2.html

John Locke: *Second Treatise on Government:* http://www.swan.ac.uk/poli/texts/locke/lockcont.htm

Karl Marx: *The German Ideology:* http://www.Marxists.org/archive/marx/works/1845-gi/part_d.htm

Light as Ayer (A. J. Ayer): http://www.weeklystandard.com/magazine/mag_5_19_00/Epstein_bkar_5_18_00.html

Manifesto of the Communist Party: http://csf.Colorado.edu/psn/marx/Archive/1848-CM/cm.html

Martin Luther King: I Have a Dream: http://web66.coled.umn.edu/new/MLK/MLK.html

Masculinism: http://isource.net/~flash/

Memento (film): http://us.imdb.com/Title?0209144

Metaphysical Materialism, by Richard C. Vitzthum: http://www.infidels.org/library/modern/richard_vitzthum/materialism.html

Myth of Sisyphus: http://www.nyu.edu/classes/keefer/hell/camus.html

Napoleon Chagnon: http://kroeber.anthro.mankao.msus.edu/information/biography/abcde/chagnon_napoleon.html

Nietzsche Chronology, 1887: http://www.Dartmouth.edu/~fnchron/1887.html

Occam's Razor: http://pespmc1.vub.ac.be/OCCAMRAZ.html

Patty Hearst Shaw: http://www.courttv.com/trials/soliah/hearst_ctv.html

Rudyard Kipling: http://rudyardkipling.cjb.net

Ryle's Concept of Mind: http://www.artsci-ccwin.Concordia.ca/philosophy/GNOSIS/ryle.html

Socrates: The Mind-Body Problem: http://www.uab.edu/philosophy/faculty/Arnold/4-Mind-body.htm

Summa Theologica: http://www.newadvent.org/summa/

Thomas Aquinas: http://nd.edu/Departments/Maritain/etext/stthomas.htm

UniSci: Selfish Gene Theory of Evolution Called Fatally Flawed: http://www.unisci.com/stories/20002/0425001.htm

Credits

Index

Page numbers in *italics* refer to illustrations. Page numbers in **bold** refer to primary readings or narratives.